GILBERT MURRAY OM

Gilbert Murray on his 90th birthday

GILBERT MURRAY OM
1866–1957

Duncan Wilson

CLARENDON PRESS · OXFORD
1987

Oxford University Press, Walton Street, Oxford OX2 6DP
Oxford New York Toronto
Delhi Bombay Calcutta Madras Karachi
Petaling Jaya Singapore Hong Kong Tokyo
Nairobi Dar es Salaam Cape Town
Melbourne Auckland
and associated companies in
Beirut Berlin Ibadan Nicosia

Oxford is a trade mark of Oxford University Press

Published in the United States
by Oxford University Press (USA)

British Library Cataloguing in Publication Data
Wilson, Duncan
Gilbert Murray OM.
1. Murray, Gilbert   2. Philologists — Great Britain — Biography
I. Title
880.9   PA85.M8
ISBN 0-19-211781-5

Library of Congress Cataloging in Publication Data
Wilson, Duncan, Sir.
Gilbert Murray, OM.
Bibliography: p.   Includes index.
1. Murray, Gilbert, 1866–1957.   2. Classicists — Great Britain — Biography.
3. Translators — Great Britain — Biography.   4. League of Nations — Biography.
I. Title.
PA85.M8W55 1987   880'.9 [B]   86-23917
ISBN 0-19-211781-5

Set by Dobbie Typesetting Service
Printed in Great Britain
at the University Printing House, Oxford
by David Stanford
Printer to the University

For
Mary and Geoffrey Warnock

FOREWORD

I WAS twenty-two when my grandfather died, and like all my brothers and Murray cousins I knew him well. Our grandparents' house on Boar's Hill was always open to us, for holidays, 'baby-sitting' in wartime (us being the babies), convalescences, flying visits on bicycles, Oxford exams, Sunday Lunch—that meal at Yatscombe being a noted Oxford institution then—and a dozen other excuses. So when he died in 1957, a year after our grandmother, it was not just two much-loved people, but a whole world that vanished: a world with its own variegated population, British and foreign, young and old, great and small, and including even the spirits of the dead—their own children on one side, and Rupert Brooke and his like on the other—framed in photographs on a shelf we called 'The Morgue'.

Sir Duncan Wilson's biography has taken me back into that world, encouraging an orgy of boyhood memories, and temporarily eclipsing all that has happened since. It has eclipsed among other things those shifts of opinion which perpetually erect a sort of apartheid between each generation and the idealists of its recent past; and which today make those meetings for Temperance or the League of Nations, Greek plays at Somerville, and speeches for Basque refugees, all seem a bit old-fashioned. Perhaps it has been easier for me to forget this particular apartheid, than for those who never knew my grandfather or anyone like him. But with Sir Duncan Wilson's biography to help, I am confident anyone can now do it.

In taking me back to that boyhood world Sir Duncan has also, let it be said, taken me to corners my generation of Murrays knew nothing about. To learn that our grandfather could ever attract suspicion as a hypochondriac was a surprise. At 90 he would still, on a walk, suggest formidable 'short-cuts', and his general resilience to mishap was almost a national proverb (one newspaper published a barely disguised obituary when he fell downstairs at 80, and had pneumonia and pernicious anaemia at the same time: they had clearly been taken aback at his survival). It was the same with the early strains of marriage mentioned in chapter XI. By the time people like me came on the scene—I just recall their Golden Wedding—my grandparents were the incarnation of kindly harmony, whose most moving phase, in retrospect, came when my grandmother had lost her memory. When she finally slipped away it was he who lost a world, and the few who were present remember the blow.

So there are things in this biography that we never knew about, and probably things we recall that cannot have a place in this biography. But then a biography has to be made from the ensemble of documents, private and public; and so, by an ironic necessity, to present a picture never seen by any one human being at the time, however intimate; nor indeed by the subject himself (for we all forget a lot of our own past).

But that is the metaphysics of biography. It is not the basis of my own assessment of this one, which is that its picture of Gilbert Murray and of the circles he moved in is eminently and delightfully recognizable. 'Delightfully' I should qualify, 'to me'; but I hope to others too. I once protested to Sir Duncan about some sentence which I thought made my grandfather too 'human'. He resisted, gave his reasons, and replied with his own protest: that he would not have chosen to devote his declining years to someone he did not—not from personal acquaintance but from reading thousands of letters—deeply like and admire. That comes over, as it must do, surely, in any biography which is not to leave the reader less edified than he began.

Sir Duncan's mention of declining years, sad at the time, returned with new sadness when he unexpectedly died, in 1983, just before finishing this book. The event renders this biography a memorial not just to one, but in different ways to two humane and distinguished men. Its publication is a witness to the devotion also of a third person, Sir Duncan's widow, who prepared the text for publication. Anyone who has tackled work of that sort will know what it involves, and what it means when I record, as an observer, that Lady Wilson has been fully a match for it.

ALEXANDER MURRAY

PREFACE

IN 1980 Duncan Wilson was invited to write the biography of Professor Gilbert Murray OM for the Oxford University Press. Three years later he died, leaving a fully annotated manuscript of Murray's life until 1935 (when Murray was rising 70). I have completed the text as best I could until Murray's death in 1957, and done what I could over editing and checking—a task which I could never have tackled without the support and help of many friends whom I shall name below. However I take full responsibility for errors of fact or judgement.

First I must acknowledge with gratitude the help Duncan had from the Murray family: especially from Stephen Murray and his son Alexander (Gilbert's literary executor); from Lawrence Toynbee and from Barbara Calvocoressi. Professor Hugh Lloyd-Jones kindly read all the classical chapters and Duncan greatly valued his comments. He had help also from Kathleen Haynes and Jan Nasmyth. Four (at least) of Murray's one-time secretaries contributed their memories, Jacqueline, Lady Fulton, the late Miss Audrey Richards, Mrs Mary Fletcher and the late Professor Lucy Mair. Duncan talked and corresponded with many others; with Frank Pakenham (Lord Longford), Sir Archibald Ross, Dr Henry Adam, Dr R. H. Thouless, and the late Sir George Schuster, to name only a few. Barbara Strachey kindly showed him relevant papers. Lilian Bainbridge typed all his manuscript. He was allowed to see the Castle Howard Archives by kind permission of the late Lord Howard of Henderskelfe; and Somerville College, Oxford kindly gave him access to their papers. The list is long, but I am sure it is not comprehensive and I apologize to those whom I have inadvertently omitted.

Now to my thanks: first again to the Murray family; many of whom have contributed photographs. Alexander Murray collected these and prepared them for the Press. Ann Paludan and her husband had me to stay in Cumbria and showed me the Howard country and took me to Boothby to meet Wilfred Roberts and his daughter Joanna Matthews. Plate 4 was her gift. Stephen Murray, Alexander Murray, Ann Paludan, Pamela Henderson, and Kathleen Haynes all contributed photographs, and Venetia Murray sent letters. Peter Calvocoressi read all the text from 1918 onwards and I have greatly benefited from his wise comments and strong support. I am also much indebted to Professor Michael Balfour, for his researches and advice. Pamela Neville kindly read the whole text and checked on many points of detail. I thank also Roger Raphael for his comments on the later chapters. Dr Malcolm Davies and Dr David Whittaker corresponded with me. I thank also Sir Owen Chadwick for checking detail, and Sir Richard and Lady Southern for their interest and encouragement. A special thanks to Anne Clark for her typing and for the warm welcome she and her family gave me by their peat fire when I appeared with MS on stormy winter evenings.

There remains some very special joint thanks: to Mrs Mary Clapinson of the Bodleian Library who catalogued the Murray papers so well, and greatly helped us both.

But above all I thank on behalf of us both Mary and Geoffrey Warnock whose hospitality made compilation of the book not only possible but wholly enjoyable. We have both stayed for weeks on end at Hertford College. Especially I want to thank them for their support when I took over: Mary has been my principal adviser and the book owes much to her judgement and sound sense. Geoffrey also gave wise advice and read proofs for me.

Duncan has given the appropriate bibliography chapter by chapter, so a general bibliography seemed unnecessary.

Lastly, I must thank our two daughters Cathy and Elizabeth — both of them have often stepped in with some shrewd criticism or apposite suggestion and have been equally concerned that, as far as in us lay, this book should do justice to Duncan, as well as to its hero, Gilbert Murray.

ELIZABETH WILSON

Cala na Ruadh,
Port Charlotte,
Islay, Argyll

CONTENTS

LIST OF PLATES

ABBREVIATIONS

CEWC   Council for Education in World Citizenship
CIC   Committee for Intellectual Co-operation
CO   Conscientious Objector
FO   Foreign Office
HUL   Home University Library
IIIC   International Institute of Intellectual Co-operation
ILP   Independent' Labour Party
IPC   International Peace Campaign
LEP   (American) League to Enforce Peace
LFNA   League of Free Nations Association
LN   League of Nations
LNS   League of Nations Society
LNU   League of Nations Union
OUP   Oxford University Press
SPR   Society for Psychical Research
UDC   Union of Democratic Control
UN   United Nations
UNA   United Nations Association
Unesco   United Nations Educational, Scientific, and Cultural Organization
UNO   United Nations Organization
WEA   Workers Educational Association

CHAPTER I
Australian Childhood

1. Earliest years — father dies 1873 — to England with his mother 1877.
2. Religious background.
3. Australian schooling.
4. Influence of Australia.

1

GEORGE GILBERT AIMÉ MURRAY was born on 2 January 1866, in Sydney, New South Wales, the second child of Sir Terence Aubrey Murray by his second wife Agnes (née Edwards), and the youngest child of his father's total family of five. Leila, Evelyn, and Aubrey were his half-sisters and half-brother; his full brother, Hubert, four-and-a-half years older than himself, was born in 1861.

In his old age, Gilbert Murray would speculate about the genetic mixture on which his character was built.[1] His mother, of Welsh ancestry, had once been a pupil at a French convent school; she came to Australia as governess in the family of Mr Justice Stephen, moved to a similar post in the Murray family, and married Sir Terence in 1860 after the death of his first wife. On her side, Murray reckoned that he was descended from 'generations of school teachers from whom I learned the habit of being good and tidy and reasonable and learning lessons'.[2] However, he was also the offspring on his father's side of a Scottish family which had settled in Ireland and produced generations of Irish rebels. An ancestor, Denis Murray, had been the only one of seven brothers who escaped alive from the Battle of the Boyne in 1689. Gilbert's great-grandfather was out in the Irish rebellion of 1798, and lost his leg in the fighting. For these men and their descendants England was the great tyrant and oppressor, and Government was in the wrong, unless the contrary could be clearly proved. This side of his inheritance caused Murray much pride and provided him with many favourite anecdotes.

His grandfather, another Terence, had served with Wellington's army in the Peninsular campaigns and, according to family tradition, at Waterloo.[3] The sword which he was said to have carried there hung on the wall of the family house in Australia; it was once seized and brandished by the young Gilbert in a desperate attempt to frighten off some older boys who were bullying him. Long afterwards he wrote to a friend: 'They simply turned and fled, and I chased them with an extraordinary feeling of triumph and of freedom.'[4] In 1817 Murray's grandfather was posted to Australia as Paymaster to the British forces in Sydney, returning to Britain in 1825. He sold his commission two years later in order to take up a considerable grant of land in Australia, and went back there in 1827, bringing with him this time his son, Terence the younger (Murray's father), who at the age of 17 had just completed school in Ireland and was a keen and competent classical scholar. However, he was allowed no time to go to the University. Instead he was appointed in 1831 to a frontier Magistracy. It was a heavy and responsible job for a young man of under 21, but these were heroic days in the 'colony'.

Terence the younger went off to his post in the bush, taking with him as servants a number of ticket-of-leave convicts, mainly Irish and many of them guilty of no greater crime than being on the wrong spot at the wrong time during the Irish rising in 1798. Later he inherited his father's estates at Yarralumla, on the present site of Canberra, and at Winderadeane, on Lake George. Here and elsewhere Terence built up a considerable fortune from stock-raising. He exercised an almost feudal influence as local magistrate and general adviser over his tenants and neighbours, largely Catholic and Irish. Life on Australian country estates at this time was lonely, rough, and dangerous. Terence Murray had to be handy with his fists and with his gun. Many stories of his early experiences were told in the family, and some were later recorded in the vivid *Unfinished Autobiography*, which Gilbert wrote at the end of his long life. He probably 'improved certain stories in his mind';[5] his memory may have betrayed him at points and it was certainly selective; but the book remains an invaluable source.

Australia in the mid-nineteenth century was still a land of pioneers. However, Terence Murray took great pains to acquire an up-to-date library, read very widely, and with a deliberate and continuous effort maintained the high cultural standards which he later imparted to his family. By the time of his second marriage in 1860, he had become a notable figure among the New South Wales aristocracy; he was a rich stock-farmer, a member and then Speaker of the New South Wales Lower House, and later President of the Upper House, or Legislative Council. He was knighted in 1869. However, money came and went quickly in Australia at that time, and by 1865 his fortune had been dissipated by successive droughts and floods, and also by his habits of lordly hospitality and generosity, of which he could not break himself in changing circumstances.[6] Of his estates, Yarralumla went first; Goulburn was sold in 1865, along with its precious library, and Winderadeane shortly afterwards. Even so Terence Murray's friends had to pay debts and liabilities of over £25,000 to keep his head above water.[7]

Gilbert's earliest memories relate to a succession of 'large houses and grounds in the suburbs of Sydney . . . but the houses grew smaller and smaller as my father grew poorer'. When in his old age Gilbert talked of himself as a 'little boy from the Australian bush',[8] he was exaggerating, and fusing memories of his own schooldays with stories of his father's young days. A succession of ever-smaller suburban houses in Sydney was the hard reality. They witnessed growing moodiness and depression on the part of Sir Terence, and growing unhappiness for the family as a whole. Gilbert's elder brother, Hubert, was seriously affected. In a letter to Gilbert of 1894, he referred to 'that living death in Macquarie Street' [Sydney][9] after his father's financial crash. Gilbert himself, it seems, was too young to be aware of the strain put upon his mother by Sir Terence's melancholy and extravagance, and by his heavy drinking, which probably hastened his death in 1873.[10]

Sir Terence Murray cuts a great figure in his youngest son's memoirs. It was he who taught Gilbert swimming, cricket, and, in the last year of his life, when Gilbert was only 7, the use of firearms. His love of justice and hatred of cruelty were conspicuous and took practical forms. The family strongly supported the Society for the Protection of Aborigines; Sir Terence mixed with them freely and genuinely liked them. He was also President of the Society for the Abolition of Capital Punishment. In these fields his influence on Gilbert and Hubert was strong and lasting.

Of Gilbert's mother very little is said in his writings. Such of her letters as have been preserved date from 1889 and 1890 — the last years of her life — and throw curiously little light on her character. Yet she must have been a very courageous, competent and cultured woman. She was clearly a good mother to her stepchildren, adored her own two sons, and worked very hard for them in the difficult years following her husband's death. In 1873 she began to run a girls' school at Springfield, Sydney, with great success. However, three years later she was suffering severely from asthma; she sold the school at a good price in 1876, and then was able to leave Australia for England with her younger son in 1877. It had probably always been her ambition to return, if only to offer wider opportunities for her two sons, Hubert and Gilbert. She joined the Edwards's family home in London, where her mother and two sisters were living. Here too she soon set up a school, together with her sisters, and Gilbert, her younger son, was, in her own words, her 'especial care and comfort during 16 years of struggling widowhood'.[11] Hubert stayed on in Australia, to complete his schooling in Sydney, and followed to England in 1879. After a year at Brighton College and another year in Germany he went to Magdalen College, Oxford, to read Classics overlapping in his last year (1885) with Gilbert. After a further three years' study at the English Bar, he returned to Australia in 1888.

Gilbert's relations with his mother must have been very close at this time, but he wrote little of her and few of his letters to her are preserved. 'I scarcely shed a tear at my mother's death', he wrote later to his wife. 'I think it is very easy for grief to be too deep for tears.'[12]

2

Until 1869 Murray had no Christian name. A passage in the *Unfinished Autobiography* explains this.

A note in my mother's hand (after the opening entry of her husband's diary for 1869) gives some picture of the general life of the family:

'I am sorry to say that we have distinguished New Year's Day, as we do most memorable days, by omitting our customary family prayers. Baby, who is strict in these matters, did not allow us to do more than taste our respective cups of tea before he appeared, book in hand, and we acknowledged at once the superiority of his conduct . . . '

As for the baby who came, prayer-book in hand, to set his elders a good example, a certain technical difficulty deters me from mentioning his name. He had no complete name at the age of three. His christening had been postponed till it had been settled whether the ceremony should be Catholic or Protestant, my father being the first and my mother the second. It was settled by a graceful but rather confusing compromise. I was registered at birth in one name and christened afterwards in another — registered as 'George Forster Wise' after old friends of my father, but baptised later in a Catholic Church — as George Gilbert Aimé, the Gilbert coming from my mother's uncle, the father of W. S. Gilbert, and the Aimé from her sister Amy. It was rather a shock to George Gilbert Aimé in later life, when required to produce a birth certificate, to find that apparently he had never been born at all.[13]

G. G. A. Murray, duly christened as a Catholic in 1869, was throughout life 'George' to his family elders and contemporaries. For a schoolboy or undergraduate in the 1880s there was virtually no need of a Christian name—Murray was sufficient. The name Gilbert was not generally adopted until his marriage in 1889. Nevertheless his biographer will henceforth call him Gilbert.

The christening involved admission to the Roman Catholic Church. Sir Terence was a Catholic, but of an easy-going kind. One of Gilbert's stories was of him ordering steak at an inn. The waiter said 'It's Friday, Sir Terence.' He replied, 'Oh, then bring me some fried fish too.'[14] Agnes Murray was a Protestant but shared her husband's tolerance. A codicil was attached to Sir Terence's will in 1871, drafted in consequence of a widely reported legal decision of April 1871 (*Hawkesworth* v. *Hawkesworth*), under which the children of a Catholic father and a Protestant mother were taken away from the latter, after the death of the former, in order to receive a Catholic education. With this in mind, Sir Terence provided as follows:

I hereby entrust and commit the religious education and spiritual guidance of all my children who may be under twenty-one years at the time of my death, wholly and absolutely, to my wife, Agnes Murray, free from any control and interference whatsoever on the part of my relatives or of the Roman Catholic Church . . . still from boyhood I have but very partially accepted its doctrines . . . It has been throughout my object to impress the broad principles of Christianity on the minds of my children, and to keep them free from the narrow sectarian prejudices which in all ages have done so much mischief in society.[15]

Murray later recorded that within the family they were all greatly interested in religion and yet all sceptical.[16] There were family prayers in the Murray household, and also in the Edwards's home in London. Throughout his schooldays in Australia and England Murray had to attend divine service. As a result he knew his Bible much better than would the sceptic of today—a knowledge reflected in the language of his public lectures and his writings. Hubert later became a Catholic but Murray remained a sceptic. He later gave two explanations of his scepticism

It began entirely as a moral rebellion in early childhood. Oddly enough, it was the miracle of the Gadarene Swine that first shocked me . . . so monstrously cruel to drive a lot of unoffending pigs over a precipice.[17]

and:

My father was a Catholic and my mother Protestant, and both perfectly tolerant. But we knew by hearing that all strict Catholics were taught that

Protestants were doomed to eternal punishment, while strict Protestants were mostly taught the same about Catholics . . . To us, being deeply attached to both our parents, this whole attitude seemed quite obviously absurd, as well as wicked and cruel.[18]

The development of Murray's anti-religious feelings will be a continuing theme of this book.

3

Formal schooling began for Murray at the age of 8, when he was sent for a short time as a day-boy to a Mr Stephen's school at Sydney. His main memory was of the gymnastics, which he much enjoyed. In 1875 he was sent to a boarding-school, Southey's, some 80 miles from Sydney, near Nattai in the Blue Mountains. This provided him with some traumatic experiences and lasting memories.

He was miserable at being banished from home. At his request, his mother armed him with a half-sovereign over and above his pocket-money, in case he felt the absolute need to run away. His fears were well grounded. Bullying was rife at Southey's, which in this respect was at much the same stage as English schools about half a century earlier. Murray soon learned that the only alternative to being bullied was fighting: he had to be ready to fight anyone of his own size or a little bigger. The next essential was 'to be good at games, if I could manage it, and as far as possible to be like everyone else'.[19]

It took him some time to realize or forget this last eternal schoolboy ambition. Bad language was a particular shock, so much worse than he had expected. Murray had to make 'a bargain with the powers above. I had a strong objection to obscene language, but . . . though I might satisfy popular feeling by swearing, I did it entirely as a matter of calculation. I got little or no pleasure from it but in order to be less unpopular, I deliberately swore at every second sentence.'[20] A wise elder of 13 broke him of the habit by saying that there was no sense in swearing if one wasn't angry.

Worse for Murray than bullying and bad language was the extreme cruelty habitually shown to animals. He was deeply humiliated by being made occasionally to join in. Once he was bullied into throwing a stone 'in the general direction' of a wounded bird. The impression made on the small boy by the acts of cruelty which he witnessed was profound. Here was a trauma which remained with him for life. 'I hate blood sports,' he said in a broadcast decades later, 'I can't help it; killing animals for fun somehow makes me sick'.[21]

Murray found his second 'quarter' [term] even worse than his first, and thought seriously of using that half-sovereign and running away; but he confided his plan to other boys, who pointed out the difficulties and laughed him out of it. With typical courage, he tried to tell the headmaster about the cruelties that went on, but his halting efforts earned him no more than some good-humoured chaff. Next, he recounts, he half-resolved to end his miseries by suicide, and got so far as to find a suitable rope and tree; he even jumped from a branch, with the loosened rope round his neck, 'partly rehearsing, partly play-acting to deceive myself'. Eventually he began to appear more normal to other boys, to make friends, and to find himself reasonably content. But the misery of his first impressions would be hard to exaggerate. During a voyage round the world in 1892–3 (undertaken on doctor's orders) he kept a fragmentary diary in which he declared himself 'almost determined to write an account of my life at Southey's—seems interesting to me: my self-examination very keen then.' He then jotted down notes, most of which were developed sixty years later in his *Unfinished Autobiography*.[22]

After his first two 'quarters', the school moved to Mittagong, and Murray found that he was actually enjoying himself. His athletic ability does not seem to have been affected by nearly losing his thumb in an accident with fireworks. He loved cricket and 'used to have vivid dreams of cricket in heaven and the different styles of bowling used by the various sublime persons'.[23] There were also free Saturdays in the bush, 'generally with a loaf of bread, and a tin of sardines between two, with a bathe under the waterfall, a fearful exploration of the long shafts of a deserted coal mine, and the occasional discovery of wild honey . . .' One of these expeditions nearly ended in disaster when the young Murray became separated from his companions, and found himself thoroughly lost. He spent a long day of adventure; he endured hunger and thirst, the proximity of snakes and wild cattle, and the distant terror of a pack of dingoes, before running into a member of the search party which had been sent out to find him.

It was after the move to Mittagong that Murray took up Greek: 'My first word [was] Μοῦσα a Muse (of course they pronounced it as if it was a term of praise for a cat).'[24] There is no word about further progress at the time, though in 1936 Murray described the 'ragged little boy' that was himself as having fallen in love then with Greek and Euclid.[25] But Australian schooldays were nearly over.

He left for England with his mother early in 1877, shortly after his eleventh birthday.

4

What did the Australian experience of his first eleven years mean to Murray in later life, and how did it affect him in his second homeland? Murray enjoyed in his old age romanticizing his childhood, presenting a picture of the uncouth little boy from the bush. Perhaps he deliberately heightened the effect by a distinctive quality of voice—whether a slight Australian accent or a slightly conscious avoidance of it on certain vowels. The evidence on this point is curiously inconclusive. Sybil Thorndike found in his speech remnants of the 'warm intonation that characterizes the best Australian speech'.[26] Maurice Bowra found that a 'slight Australian twang . . . mitigated what might otherwise have been too mellifluous an utterance'.[27] A former secretary, Lucy Mair, detected a 'faint echo of Australia—or of consciously avoiding Australia—in his way of pronouncing such words as "day" with a wider open vowel than most English people would.'[28] From my own memories of his Oxford lectures in 1931–2, refreshed by listening to recordings, I can say no more than that Murray had a most unusual and beautiful voice.

Having been brought up for eleven years in an attitude of greater social equality than prevailed in England, equality with older members of his family as well as with people of different social position, was an advantage for him when confronted by some of the oddities of the English public school system. In particular the narrowness of classical education as then practised, the concentration on the letter rather than the message of Greek and Latin literature, was for Murray from an early age an aspect of the English intellectual scene not simply to be endured as a given fact, but remediable and to be remedied. His attitude probably derived more from membership of an exceptional family than from a specifically Australian background; but in any case his early upbringing enabled him both to get the best out of an English upper-class education, and to look upon it with a certain objectivity.

The lasting power of his childhood impressions of Australia also made him throughout life a comparatively detached observer in England and Scotland, however British he had become in many ways, and however 'expatriate' he may have seemed to full Australians. In 1892 he stopped in Australia on his voyage round the world. He described to his wife the strong renewal of his childhood impressions after nearly sixteen years of absence:

As soon as I started off, I was seized with a feeling that this was really my home, my native surroundings. It was unexpected and full of thrill. I felt as if I loved the place. Everything came back upon me vividly, as a remembrance of childhood does . . . the hot tingling bracing air, scented with eucalyptus . . . the strong healthy undergrowth, the masses of wild flowers . . .[29]

and about a month later:

The extraordinary scent of Australia was in the air. The deep burning crimson of the passion-flowers made me almost dizzy, and I felt that this is the country I love. There may be places as beautiful, but I love this place in the same way as I love you. No other place can be to me what this is . . .[30]

The deep sincerity of these words cannot be doubted. Murray never returned to Australia again but he always carried something of Australia within him.

CHAPTER II
Education in England

1. Arrival in England 1877.
2. Merchant Taylors' 1878–1884.
3. St John's College, Oxford 1884–1888.

1

OF the next twelve years of Murray's life, from 1877 to 1889, relatively little is known. His own account of his later school and university days is sketchier than his account of his Australian childhood, but a few facts and impressions emerge from his other occasional reminiscences. School and college records provide further bare details about his scholastic achievements. But the record remains scanty for most of this formative period of his life.

On 22 January 1877, one of the few days which remained firm in his memory, Murray left Australia for England with his mother on board the P. & O. liner *Bangalore* (4,000 tons), changing to the *China* (6,000 tons) at Point de Galle. The voyage on what seemed to him huge ships was an exciting experience. He later recorded his interest in the Lascar crew, and his instinctive sympathy with them as 'underdogs'. One memorable incident occurred while the ship was anchored at Suez. Murray was standing on the bulwark, umpiring some games, when he was pushed overboard by a little girl, indignant at one of his decisions. He had only a few yards to swim in his clothes, but was cold and wet when he returned to the boat. He

remembered having heard that a proper medicine was hot port wine and water. So I went to bed and ordered some. My mother was talking to some friends when she heard someone speak of 'the poor little boy who had fallen overboard' and asked about the tragedy. 'Why, didn't you know? It was your little boy.' So she rushed to the cabin and found me enjoying my hot wine and water.[1]

At least the independent little boy did not take to alcohol in consequence. Murray late in his life told a granddaughter of another incident on the voyage which had made a deep impression on him. A lady passenger told him she had psychic powers and would demonstrate them if he could give her something belonging to his dead father which she could hold. Murray gave her his father's ring which she held and then told him many things about his father which Murray was sure she could not possibly have known in the normal course of events. The incident lay buried beneath the surface of his mind for many years but, as will be seen, the world of psychic phenomena was to recur in his life.[2]

His mother and he left the ship at Brindisi, visiting Rome and Florence before completing their journey to England overland. Rome thrilled the young Murray because of Horatius and Lars Porsena of Clusium. The two travellers also had an interview with Pope Pius IX, 'when, like the ill-mannered young cub that I was, I freely interrupted his Holiness, or so they told me afterwards, and was rewarded with some special attention and a blessing.'[3] Like the port wine, the blessing gave rise to no addiction.

The first months in England were depressing. They were spent with his mother's mother and sisters, in a small house with no garden, under cold and sunless London skies. Manners as well as space seemed to the 'young Australian cub' to be unduly restrictive. His new-found aunts had to be addressed as 'Aunt Fanny' and 'Aunt Harriet', whereas in Sydney his mother's brother had simply been 'Bill' to him. There seemed to be nothing to do (familiar complaint of childhood) and Murray remembered relieving his youthful spirits with a certain amount of 'colonial blow'.

He started his new school career with a year (presumably September 1877 to July 1878) at a small Dame-school at Brighton, with an assistant master who 'dropped his aitches and bullied the boys'. The next summer he went with his mother to Malvern to try for an entrance scholarship at the school there, but it was soon apparent to his mother, who had not started to earn any money in England, that it would be much cheaper to send him as a day-boy to Merchant Taylors'. There he went in autumn 1878, on the Clode entrance scholarship, the only one which was open to competition rather than being awarded by nomination. The examination had evidently not been formidable; the only incident recorded by Murray was his fear of being thought to show off by admitting that he knew the full Greek derivation of the geometrical term 'isosceles'.

2

The boy who entered Merchant Taylors' School, at its old and restricted site in Charterhouse Square, was clearly talented and good at his books. There is no talk in his own or other people's reminiscences of an infant prodigy; but his love affair with the Greek language continued. He liked working, worked hard, and was probably conscious from his first years in England of the need to lessen the financial burden on his mother. He certainly rose up the school as fast as was possible, getting into the top form in 1881 when he was just 15 (less than two-and-a-half years after entering the school). He did not as a result slacken his efforts to master the Latin and Greek languages, which were by far the greatest part of the curriculum:

I remember once being asked by a master how long I had taken in writing some Greek verses; he expected one-and-a-half to two hours, but I had really taken ten. The fact was that I had fallen in love with the verses and thought about them all day till they were finished. It was, I suppose, the one form of art that the traditional education of that day provided. One read a piece of English poetry very carefully, trying to appreciate the meaning and the force of every line, and then came the excitement of trying to get the same effect into Greek or Latin. I generally enjoyed the Greek most . . .[4]

Murray's first appearance in the Merchant Taylors' School *Exercise Register*, which contained outstanding compositions in Latin and Greek, is dated 23 March 1881; it takes the form of a fluent and idiomatic Greek iambic translation of some Tennyson blank verse. The record of the school Speech Day proceedings in December 1881 states that 'Mr. G. G. Murray read a translation from Shelley's *Prometheus Unbound* into Greek verse which was marked by unusual ability';[5] and the *Exercise Register* for 5 May 1882 contains some Greek anacreontic verses ('O swallow, swallow, flying south') of remarkable virtuosity. The list of his classical prizes at school is astonishing. In his last year, 1883–4, Murray was Head Monitor, a post for which qualities of character as well as of scholarship were required, and carried off no less than eight of the school's chief prizes. His examination for the St John's scholarship was remarkable; in 'prepared books' he obtained 245 marks out of 250, gaining full marks for a searching paper on the Agamemnon [of Aeschylus], as well as for the Cicero papers.[6] Moreover in 1884 he shared the school prize for History and Literature, and won the French prize as well. He had also developed a strong dramatic talent. He twice won the Tyler Elocution Prize (1882 and 1884), and was long remembered for his acting as well as his classics. A junior contemporary remembered him over thirty years later as 'a wonderful head monitor and a brilliant actor'.[7]

The political interests, so much a feature of Murray's family life in Australia, were revived by the school Debating Society, in which he took an active part. He did not intervene in the first debate of the autumn term, 1881, on the motion 'that classics occupy too exclusive a place in education', but a week later he spoke in support of the motion 'that war is out of date'—a motion that was heavily defeated. On 10 November he was one of the principal proponents of the motion 'that it is the duty of England to grant Ireland a separate existence'. The *Taylorian* reported:

Murray started with asserting that every nation desiring freedom should obtain it. The Saxons had always oppressed Ireland; their injustice condemned the wretched peasant to poverty and misery; no class thrived under their dominion; the union was a ridiculous swindle; and not till released from this yoke would Ireland recover prosperity.[8]

Thus the young Radical of 15. Later in the same academic year he had a brief interlude of frivolity, contending for the existence of the sea serpent, and recounting 'a personal adventure with a real one'. However he generally pursued an implacably serious line. He spoke for the 'higher education of the lower classes', attacking the proposition that men should stay in the position in which they were born; and he opposed the introduction of the *clôture* [guillotine] in the House of Commons on the simple ground that it was a Tory measure.[9]

These schoolboy debates illustrate the general climate of political opinion and the degree of political awareness among intelligent English public schoolboys of the 1880s (this compares favourably, I would say, with political awareness at Winchester 1924–30).

He also exercised some moral influence at Merchant Taylors', even before his last year there when he was Head Monitor. In 1887 he wrote to Mrs Howard, afterwards Lady Carlisle, justifying his own moral character: 'at Merchant Taylors', when I was 15, I joined the Head of the School in two crusades against some serious evils—principally dishonesty in Exams. He and I could never walk in the playground for 2 terms without being hissed by a hundred boys or more.'[10]

Murray's schoolboy life was not lived entirely at this level. He was always a devotee of physical exercise, and a skilful games player. He played rugger for his school in his last year and is described surprisingly as 'A heavy forward (11 st. 3½ lbs.) greatly improved, does a deal of work in the scrimmage, should learn to dribble.'[11] The *Taylorian* makes no mention of Murray's cricket. He was always very keen on the game and helped his brother Hubert to entertain the Australian team visiting England in 1882, when the great bowler Spofforth revealed to him something of his craft.[12] Probably, as a day-boy at Merchant Taylors' with a long journey to make, he had not the time to play at school, and kept his hand in with some club cricket at Kensington.

In Murray's brief recorded impressions of his public school life, it is the masters who bulk much larger than the boys. This can be explained easily enough. Murray, like most of his schoolmates, was a day-boy, and he had less time than boarders to make close friendships with his contemporaries. His 'colonial' background, scholarly tastes, and high moral tone also removed him somewhat from the ideal pattern of uniformity which even older boys like to achieve. Again while Murray was a competent athlete, his primary interests at this stage were intellectual. His father's death, moreover, had left an intensely felt gap in his life; 'a psychologist would say that as a young man I was always unconsciously seeking for a father', he once said.[13] It was older boys or young men whose company he seemed to prefer.

Of his contemporaries in Merchant Taylors' only two, and those both older than himself, were close to him from the first and remained so — his predecessors as Head Monitor, F. S. Marvin and H. J. Maynard (later Sir John). Both preceded Murray to St John's College, Oxford,[14] and were good classical scholars. Marvin was for long an Inspector of Schools; he finally became Professor of Modern History at the University of Egypt. Maynard rose high in the Indian Civil Service, becoming Vice-chancellor of the University of the Punjab, and also the foremost British expert on the Russian peasant economy.

The one who exercised most influence on Murray in his school-days was Francis Storr, a Cambridge classical scholar; he headed the modern side of the school, and took the top form for English literature. Murray remained in touch with him as a friend; and the links between them were strengthened by the marriage of Storr's daughter, Erica, to Sandy Lindsay, a pupil of Murray's at Glasgow University, and later a famous Master of Balliol College, Oxford.

Shortly after the return to England, the Edwards family moved to Observatory Avenue, Campden Hill, where his mother with the help of her sisters opened a school. The household consisted of Murray's grandmother, her three daughters, Fanny and Harriet Edwards and Agnes Murray, as well as Gilbert, and (for a time) his brother Hubert. The three sisters were attractive company and their 'At Homes' were crowded. Throughout his life Murray professed himself exceedingly shy of strangers and he and Hubert were 'much reproved for stealing away to avoid the company'. Not that the company was necessarily dull. A frequent visitor was Murray's uncle, Henry Sutherland Edwards, a noted music critic and writer on Russian affairs, who had introduced Bakunin to the household during his stay in London (1861–3).[15] The most famous *habitués* of the Edwards's salon were their relations the Gilberts, the playwright W. S., and his mother and father, who was brother of Grandmother Edwards. Murray, a bookish and highbrow child, found Mr Gilbert a delightful companion, who was ready to talk to him about 'Egypt, the sins of Bismarck, and peculiar forms of insanity'. W. S. ('Schwenck' to the family) was probably more alarming to the young. As Murray delicately put it, 'his literary sensitiveness was apt to spill over . . . into ordinary life, and make him unduly irritable'. His decision to leave the Bar and to write operas was a matter of much concern in the Edwards family, and his success caused great joy. Murray and his elder brother Hubert knew most of the lyrics from the Savoy Operas by heart, and Gilbert fully appreciated his cousin's metrical ingenuity and taste for punning.[16] Much later, talking of politics, he said that he had felt for 'Schwenck' the same sort of veneration which he felt for Asquith.

Another and apparently incongruous acquaintance was the young Rudyard Kipling, an exact contemporary of Murray, with whom he kept up a periodic and rather uneasy acquaintance:

I thought him extraordinarily clever and exciting, though there was something in him that repelled me. He threw his stick at a cat and he thought 'Do not be ashamed to marry the housemaid' was a correct Sapphic and a fine translation of *Ne sit ancillae tibi amor pudori*.[17]

Murray was no doubt even more shocked by Ruddy's assault on the cat than by his ignorance of Roman metres and customs, and he probably did not tell Kipling that the verse hardly covered the possibility of marriage. He was also invited to collaborate on an epic poem ranging over this world and the next, but the young Kipling soon went off to join his father in India, and when Murray met him again twenty years later the epic was forgotten.

Of his daily routine and diversions outside the home very little is known. He evidently visited his brother Hubert at Oxford and impressed Herbert Warren, then a tutor at Magdalen, who much prized social graces. He wrote to Lady Murray 'Your younger son is a most interesting fellow . . . I am delighted with the mixture of modesty and intelligence, imagination, wit and sense.'[18]

The three years and more which he spent in the top form at Merchant Taylors' left him ample time to pursue his own intellectual bent. He wrote later to William Archer, the dramatic critic: 'What happened to me was that at school I read philosophy in my spare time, and then got kindled again towards Greek when I went to Oxford.'[19] Murray seems to have explored deeply, even for a precocious schoolboy. As a fifteen-year-old, he visited Paris in 1881, tramping the streets and parks alone. There he discovered Rousseau, and thirty-five years later, he recalled the 'revelatory' effect which the *Contrat Social* had had on him. The essays of W. K. Clifford, another source of schoolboy enthusiasm, were introducing him to Swinburne. A more wholesome object of devotion was John Stuart Mill, a lasting influence throughout Murray's life. Mill guided him forward to Herbert Spencer, who inspired Murray with a guilty sense of his own innumeracy, and also backwards to Godwin and Shelley. This proved for Murray a more fruitful direction. Shelley's poetry in particular gave him 'just what he was longing for' and was a source of lasting inspiration. It survived triumphantly the difficult test of being translated into Greek verse, and stimulated him to write his first published poem in English, a blank verse fragment describing the vain efforts of a romantic pilgrim to banish all traces of cruelty to living things.[20]

Murray's interest in religious questions, dating from his Australian boyhood, was also deepened at this time. F. S. Marvin introduced him to Comte and Positivism.

I sometimes went with my Aunt Fanny . . . to attend Congreve's Positivist service in Lamb's Conduit Street. I never became a Positivist, as Marvin did, but I seemed to find under those guides an escape from cruel superstition and at the same time a fairly clear explanation and justification of the moral law and the ultimate duty of man.[21]

It must have been at this time he first heard and met the Positivist philosopher, Frederic Harrison, who became a good friend.

The Murrays and Edwards were in fact a thoroughly serious family in their search for moral laws and ultimate truths. In time 'Aunt Fanny' was converted to Catholicism, as were Murray's elder brother Hubert and long afterwards his elder daughter Rosalind. Murray himself by the age of 18 seemed likely to take a very different course. In a 'generally conservative milieu he began to be a radical.'[22] This development may not have been welcomed within his home. In 1889

Lady Murray wrote that she had been made a Conservative by the 'rabid Socialism' of her sister Fanny.[23] Much later Murray remarked that youth is always at the mercy of abstract principles, and anxious to find the secret of life. It is obvious to the young, he continued, that their parents and uncles have not done so. 'This tendency had some effect on me; not enough to make me really disagreeable at home, but enough to keep me always hoping for a new light.'[24]

3

In autumn 1884, Murray went up to St John's College, Oxford, with which Merchant Taylors' School had a special connection. He was the recipient of a closed Merchant Taylors' scholarship, and also of a special scholarship for Latin and Greek composition, and a special exhibition, worth £30 and £40 respectively. With this help he did not depend on his mother for an allowance which she could have ill afforded. It is plain from his termly 'battels' at St John's that he lived very frugally; but he himself wrote that several of his friends were in the same position.

The most striking feature of his Oxford career was that he became a notable figure within less than a year of coming up. The Headmaster at Merchant Taylors' had recognized the extraordinary quality of his Latin and Greek compositions, and had sent him for special coaching, before he arrived at St John's, to a famous Latin teacher, J. Y. Sargent, with whom he spent a happy month in Cumberland. Murray duly won the Hertford Scholarship for Latin composition in 1885, in a field open to second-year as well as to first-year undergraduates; later in the same year he proceeded as a freshman to win the Ireland Scholarship for Latin and Greek, open to all undergraduates of whatever year. This was an astonishing achievement, rivalled only twice before.[25] It pointed strongly to his future profession, and immediately opened to him the world of mature scholars of Oxford. This must have been a heady experience for the young man, and First Class Honours in the two parts of the Oxford classical course seemed a minor achievement in comparison.

By the end of his time as an undergraduate, Murray had received offers of Fellowships at a number of colleges. New College, which normally elected by examination, offered to waive the requirement for Murray.[26] He chose to sit the examination, and it was no surprise when he was elected in 1888, along with his friend H. A. L. Fisher. Things appeared to come easy to Murray, but his successes were based on unremitting application, particularly to the Greek language. Sir Maurice Bowra wrote of him: 'He must have worked incredibly hard in his youth and what he then learned he remembered for the rest of his life. He knew large tracts of Greek poetry by heart and had so absorbed them that he was entirely at home with them and understood them from the inside.'[27] Mrs Mary Fletcher, who was Murray's secretary for over two years from February 1938, once asked him whether he knew all the plays of the Greek tragedians by heart. He thought a bit and said, 'If you gave me any quotation, I could identify it, and go on from there.'[28]

The whole-hearted application to his work, which was the foundation of Murray's career, had one incidental result: it led to the deterioration of his eyesight—a failing which plagued him for many years (in 1887 he seems to have been ordered to stop reading completely for a year—an injunction which he certainly did not obey).[29] This set him rather apart from his contemporaries. Nevertheless Murray was not a bad 'college' man. He loved cricket, though he had little time for it; he claimed in his autobiography to have made 40 runs in the Oxford Freshmen's Match but the records suggest that his exploit must have been in a college game.[30] He played rugger as required and rowed in the Torpids (Lent term races), but his activities in his last four terms as an undergraduate must have been severely curtailed by an injury to his arm, which necessitated first an operation and then some violent traction.[31] He was a prominent member of the college Debating Society, and a founder-member of the college Essay Society. On the occasion of its 50 year jubilee in 1937, he recalled: 'The essays which I read to the Society as an undergraduate were on Suicide (warmly recommended for the right people), Pure Malignity (denying its existence against F. H. Bradley), and on Longus.'[32]

Outside St John's, Murray had close links with Magdalen where in 1884 his elder brother Hubert was in his last year. Hubert was not only a classical scholar, but also a notable boxer, who taught Gilbert something of the art. Gilbert may have looked to Hubert as a potential father-figure, and certainly admired him greatly, but there was little intimacy between them during their single year together at Oxford.

Murray's deepest friendships in Oxford were formed with men who were already Fellows. These included his own tutor at St John's, T. C. Snow, a fine example of the Oxford eccentric, with collar occasionally fastened by string, a strange stammer, unheralded excursions into the world of saga and comparative philology, and a scientific theory of ancient Greek pronunciation—a man 'really learned, really interested himself, and therefore interesting to us; really imaginative and unworldly, and kind.'[33]

Another vintage eccentric was Robinson Ellis, a Fellow of Trinity, and famous Latinist. He would take Murray with him on holiday at seaside resorts for continuous discussion of classical subjects. 'A singular figure: very tall, rather shabby, with long overcoat and with one boot . . .or sometimes both . . . slashed open to give his toes more room . . . He was genuinely rather indifferent to the material amenities of life.' This was a high compliment from Murray, himself indifferent to these. Ellis was worried, for instance, by the trouble of having to order lunch. ' "What did we have yesterday?" "Mutton and rhubarb tart, sir." "Well, we'll have that every day." And so we did.'[34] Ellis was also the author of a devastatingly negative reply, much cherished by Murray, to a dinner invitation: 'It's not so much the food I mind, it's the company.'[35]

Another Oxford character, D. S. Margoliouth, Fellow of New College, was only a little older than Murray and became a great friend. Son of a Jewish rabbi who became a Christian clergyman, Margoliouth was primarily an Arabist, but also an accomplished Hebraist and Greek scholar. Margoliouth invited Murray to the Lebanon in the summer of 1888, and took him, duly armed with a revolver, on a memorable ride to Baalbek, Damascus, and Jerusalem.

His Arabic apparently was more classical than colloquial, and sometimes the Syrians found him hard to understand, but apparently they admired him all the more for that, and sometimes addressed him as 'Ya Abu-Suleiman'—'O Father of Solomon'—partly because his name was David, partly as a tribute to his wisdom.[36]

Even Margoliouth's dog partook of his academic dignity, responding only to commands such as 'Assume a recumbent position', rather than 'Lie down'. It was Margoliouth who set the Fellowship examination at New College in 1888, and was said to have devised papers 'calculated to extend Murray of St John's'.[37] It was he too who at New College stimulated Murray's interest in the metre, text, and dialect of Pindar.

From his schooldays onwards, Murray's warmest feelings were reserved for those who could sympathize with his political ideas and aspirations. He could never talk freely with the conservative clergymen who in the late nineteenth century formed so large a proportion of the teaching profession. He had been disappointed in his first experience of Oxford: 'I had expected so much; new lights

in life, new learning, enlightenment and philosophy. I found on the
contrary, much the same influence as I had felt at school.'[38] However, his two main teachers from 1884 were men of a different stamp.
Of T. C. Snow something has already been said. Arthur Sidgwick
of Corpus Christi was an outstanding teacher of ancient Greek. He
also had a sparkling wit which Murray could appreciate and rival;
above all he was a Liberal with whom Murray could talk over a large
range of subjects.

Murray was becoming increasingly concerned with political causes,
partly for private reasons to be discussed in the next chapter. That
nearest to his heart during his Oxford days was Irish Home Rule,
perhaps the most hotly debated issue of the time. It was not a popular
cause in Oxford. Of 288 Fellows who voted Liberal in the General
Election of 1878, only 17 could be securely reckoned as 'Home
Rulers' after the great split in the Liberal Party on the subject in
1886.[39] In this year Murray with the support of Walter Ashburner
(a St John's friend of American origin) founded an Oxford Home
Rule League, which John Dillon consented to address; Arthur
Sidgwick took an active interest and presided at a 'Great Home Rule
Meeting' in December 1887. The *Oxford Magazine* described it in
a feeble mock-Irish poem, which celebrated Murray's speech:

> Then came Murray, John's College, the darlin'!
> An Australian from over the say.
> May the Saints shower blissings upon him,
> And help him to get his degray! . . .[40]

In February 1888 Murray was one of the principal speakers in a
formal debate on Home Rule at the Oxford Union in opposition to
Lord Randolph Churchill. The motion (22 February) was that 'in
order to satisfy the just aspirations of the Irish people, it is necessary
that a Statutory Parliament be forthwith established at Dublin.' The
debate was adjourned for a week, and then defeated by a large
majority (159–359). Lord Randolph himself disappointed the *Oxford
Magazine*'s reporter, who described the debate as a 'meeting to
condemn Home Rule, but Mr Murray of St John's got in.' His speech
they found 'quite excellent, but his voice affected a susceptible gallery
to tears.'[41] Murray later joined the local branch of the Irish
National League, which thanked him, when he left Oxford, for 'many
good offices received.'[42]

By Michaelmas term 1887, at the beginning of his final year as
an undergraduate, he had come into contact with some of the Radical
'Establishment' outside Oxford, and was ready to speak at the Union

on some of their favourite themes. He supported motions in favour of total abstinence among all classes, and of the total closure of Public Houses on Sundays; both were defeated only by the President's casting vote.[43] He was also concerned with foreign policy and defence. The only motion which he himself proposed at the Union was 'that this House views with intense suspicion the rise of the Capitalist Classes in Political Power.' Murray used this motion as an occasion to warn the House of the danger threatening Europe from the militarist powers, Germany and Russia, and to appeal for unity of the free nations in their common defence. The motion was defeated in a small House.[44] Murray showed a more practical concern for defence by joining the Oxford Volunteers, in which 'I rose like Napoleon and Hitler to the rank of Corporal, and had hopes of being a Sergeant when I was called away to Glasgow. My helmet and red coat and striped trousers lived to a useful old age in private theatricals.'[45] His letters to Mrs Howard of 1887–8 show him taking riding lessons with the Life Guards in London, and in camp with the volunteers just after taking his Finals.[46]

Meanwhile Murray continued to meditate deeply about religion and the meaning of life. He was disgusted to find that his most revered secular saint, J. S. Mill, was treated by Oxford philosophers primarily as an inaccurate and inconsistent thinker. When writing later on this theme, Murray may have had in mind particularly the dissection of Mill's utilitarianism by the idealist philosopher F. H. Bradley—an exercise which Murray would surely have regarded as missing Mill's whole point.[47] It took Murray some time to digest such attacks and to formulate his own answer— that Mill had indeed like every other philosopher, 'failed to make a complete and consistent explanation of the universe, but had at least thought out a fairly coherent system which enabled him in practice to judge rightly on every moral and political question of his time.'[48]

It was perhaps to this period of Murray's spiritual development that an episode belongs of which he wrote later to his elder daughter, Rosalind:

Yes, I used to be a Buddhist once. I dropped it because Frank Russell and others were superior Buddhists and went in for miracles and Mme Blavatsky. (I think that I was only involved for part of one term, but I do think that it is the best of religions.) I am not sure that Westerners ought to have a religion; it is a way of looking at things which does not go with science and politics.[49]

A man who exercised a great and permanent influence on Murray's outlook from his undergraduate days, however, was Charles Gore, Head of Pusey House in the 1880s, and later Bishop of Oxford. In the summer of 1886 Gore took Murray and others on a walking party in the Dolomites. Long afterwards Murray wrote: 'I loved him partly because he was a delightful humorous companion and very kind to me, partly because . . . quite simply . . . he was a saint . . . he seemed to live continually, even in the midst of his delightful gaiety and laughter, in close relation with something higher than the material world.'[50] Gore was unsuccessful in his attempts to convert Murray to Christianity; but his letter on the subject is worth quoting fully for the light which it throws on Murray's character and beliefs at the time. The letter was written, it must be remembered, to a young man of 20, and is a strong indication of the attractive power of Murray's personality:

My dear Amate, if people are conceited and self-willed and priggish one can even tolerate their alienation from a Faith meant, one believes, to make all lives happy . . . I do find it hard to tolerate it in a being like GGAM who doesn't seem possessed of those elevating attributes which lift men out of the common wants and happiness of mankind. All of which means that I do so long to see you more of a Christian than you are . . . it cheers me . . . when you say that as a *Life* Christianity attracts you and you feel its spirit has an appeal to you . . .

One other thing. You seem to me to assign too strong a negative weight to suffering . . . It is a great mystery but in the case of the highest nature . . . suffering appears not at all as a mere evil . . . the deepest and highest beauty of character only comes through suffering . . .

Dear Murray, your affectionate friend,
Charles Gore.[51]

At least Gore's example, if not his eloquence, taught Murray that all saints were not secular and inspired in him over the years a greater tolerance towards formal religion.

In his student days, as subsequently, Murray had his intellectual relaxations. One of these was writing his only novel, *Gobi or Shamo*. He said long afterwards that this was the work of a month only, in 1888–9, but his correspondence shows that by the summer of 1887 he had been at work on it for some time.[52] The book was no doubt designed to take advantage of the vogue for romantic adventure novels started by Stevenson with *Treasure Island* (1883) and *Kidnapped* (1885), and by Rider Haggard with *King Solomon's Mines* (1885). Murray's story has its own peculiar twist; the travellers discover on the far side of Tibet a lost Greek tribe, descendants of

Greeks deported by Darius from Ionia in the early fifth century BC, who are considerably more civilized than the barbarians of Central Asia or than the British themselves. The surprise effect resembles that so brilliantly achieved by C. S. Lewis in his first novel *Out of the Silent Planet* (1941), in which, contrary to the established conventions of space travel, the strangers from another world prove to be morally better than the human explorers.

Gobi is no neglected masterpiece, but a curious mixture of adventure story and comedy of manners with Utopian moral lessons. The mixture of styles is equally marked, with straight narrative and use of the 'historic present'. There were Oxford in-jokes, incidental poems (on which, as appears from Murray's correspondence with Mrs Howard, he lavished much pure scholarly apparatus including untranslated sentences of ancient Greek), and much buttonholing of the gentle reader.

By far the most interesting element in it today is the Utopianism. In Murray's Hellenic state the reader can see not only his passionate devotion to ancient Greece and his criticism of many aspects of contemporary England, but also traces of the traumas suffered in his Australian schooldays, and elements of self-portraiture. Murray's Mongolian Hellenes were direct and charmingly polite in speech. They did not bother with too many books, because they knew so much good literature by heart. Their exquisite public buildings included temples for the Olympian gods, but these had been humanized into symbolic figures. They had at one time made great progress in the applied sciences. They could still defend themselves by charging the surrounding mountain approaches with electricity, or directing against their enemies enormously powerful shells, detonated by exposure to particular rays; but they had deliberately rejected many scientific inventions, in order to preserve the simple and deep virtues of their own way of life. Their Western visitors were not allowed to stay, in case they should corrupt Utopia. Their description of Western customs had aroused incredulous horror. An armaments race, private medicine rather than a state service, vivisection—all anathema to a good Hellene.

Gobi was refused by various publishers, Kegan Paul, Bentley and Macmillan. It was published in autumn 1889 by Longman, following the intervention of Andrew Lang. Murray had doubts about publishing under his own name, having just been appointed to a position of academic dignity, but a leak in the *Pall Mall Gazette* determined both author and (fortuitously) the name by which he later became known; *Gobi* was the first published work of

'Gilbert Murray'. The novel made little stir at the time, though such notices as appeared were favourable.

By his attainments and by his high moral scruples Murray was inevitably set a little apart from his contemporaries. He was, he wrote, a good deal isolated from his fellows by his unpopular tastes: 'Few people like teetotallers, still fewer can tolerate vegetarians; in the ancient universities which I frequent, they don't much like Liberals . . . and I am all those objectionable things. Furthermore, I hate blood sports.'[53] Murray's account of himself fifty years on may not be entirely accurate. However, his portrait of himself as a young man suggests an inhuman innocence and priggishness:

I think I must have been rather a nice boy, but my greenness was unbeliev-able. I believed passionately in the progress of man. It was perhaps not quite inevitable, but it only needed the removal of a few stupid superstitions, the dying out of a few selfish and reactionary old people, to make the world a new garden of Eden, with more scientific gardening . . . Lots of young men were like that in the 1880s.[54]

There were two aspects of himself which Murray did not mention in this reminiscence. During his last year as an undergraduate he was deeply, and it appeared to him hopelessly in love. He concealed this from his friends, and saw himself in a tragic light. The other and contrasting aspect of his character was that from his student days onwards those who knew him best always found his gaiety and wit enchanting. An Oxford contemporary could say of and to him, 'I always think of you as a very mirthful person, full of laughter . . .'[55] Arthur Sidgwick, who knew him as well as anyone, found him full of jests and implored him for more letters: 'Please write me another letter; you always make me laugh.'[56]

The dry, serene, and detached humour of Murray's old age has been illustrated already in the extracts quoted from his autobio-graphical writings. He also possessed from boyhood the gift of telling hilarious and fantastic stories, without calling in aid either profanity or obscenity; and perhaps the majority of his letters are illumined by some glancing shaft of unmalicious and imaginative wit. Innocent he certainly was, but from the first anything but a colourless prig.

CHAPTER III
Courtship, Professorship, and Marriage

1. Courtship — correspondence with Lady Carlisle.
2. Elected Professor of Greek at Glasgow.
3. Acceptance.
4. The wedding — Murray and his mother-in-law.

1

MURRAY'S last year as an undergraduate at Oxford was deeply coloured by his first love affair. It had all started with a river picnic organized by the Sidgwicks at Oxford in the summer of 1887. He recalled later how he was talking with one of the Sidgwick daughters, who was engaged in 'colouring the Cherwell blue from a small paint-box', when suddenly an impressive lady whom he did not know said to him in a severe voice, 'Mr Murray, are you a teetotaller?' 'I'm afraid I am', he replied. She followed with questions on Home Rule and Woman Suffrage which he answered to her satisfaction.[1] The impressive lady was Mrs Rosalind Howard, whose husband in April 1889 became the 9th Earl of Carlisle (she is best known as Lady Carlisle, and will be so described here, even before 1889). Murray had given the right answers. She was to become President of the British Women's Temperance Association, and of the Women's National Liberal foundation, and was deeply committed to Home Rule, at the cost of marital harmony. Later that summer she invited Murray to join some other promising young men at the family home in Yorkshire, Castle Howard, set among the eponymous 'Howardian hills', and familiar to television viewers as 'Brideshead' of Evelyn Waugh's *Brideshead Revisited*. The party included Walter Ashburner, Leonard Hobhouse, then a Fellow of Merton College, Oxford, and afterwards a noted prophet of Liberalism, Hubert Llewellyn-Smith, who as a civil servant later had much to do with implementing the social legislation of the early twentieth century, and Charles Roberts, later a Liberal politician of some distinction and a Howard son-in-law. They were carefully picked for Liberal principles or prowess at cricket, a sport which Lady Carlisle patronized with no expert interest:

We had great times at Castle Howard. There was cricket with villages around and lawn tennis and bathing and walks; but above all there was an extraordinary atmosphere of lively discussion. It was sometimes based on the news or parliamentary debates, of which Lady Carlisle was a diligent reader; sometimes it was ideas and the purposes of life. She was impetuous and formidable, but we all felt free to say what we thought. We were, after all, a keen and clever set of undergraduates, and we mostly felt that we had never had such lively talks, nor such a wide sphere of interest.[2]

Fun at Castle Howard was combined with an ascetic discipline. Breakfast at eight, no alcohol, smoking permitted, but nevertheless rare. It was a strange mixture of Whig aristocratic splendour and radical good causes; a great collection of paintings (Lord Carlisle was himself a painter, personally familiar with Burne-Jones, Watts, and William Morris) and a passionate devotion to good causes and the championship of oppressed nations against the worst forms of Imperialism. Fifteen years later Murray wrote to Bertrand Russell about life at the other Howard castle, Naworth, near Brampton, in terms which convey the earlier atmosphere of Castle Howard:

There is a combination of beauty and discomfort that would appeal to you. (Me they make comfortable . . . for the weakness of my flesh; but the discomfort is in the essence of the place . . .)
   Conversation (deficient in subtlety, but magnificent in force and directness!) ranges over all the field of politics and ethics.[3]

Murray had been mentally prepared for the intellectual atmosphere by his early readings in J. S. Mill and Shelley. What the scene needed was *das ewig Weibliche* embodied in a form younger and less overwhelming than that of Lady Carlisle. The appropriate form was to hand—Mary Howard, the eldest daughter of the family, who was a few months older than Murray:

she had not only the appearance; she had all the idealism, the saintliness, the inward fire, and also, as it happened, like Shelley's heroines, a remarkable gift of eloquence. She had not been to a university, but spoke French, German, and Italian, was deeply grounded in Mazzini's *Duty of Man* and in religion was at least free from any cramping conventionality.[4]

Lady Mary was a very beautiful girl at the time. Murray fell in love immediately and whole-heartedly. However, the course of true love did not run smooth. There was what Lady Mary later called a 'bad dream'[5] from 1887 to 1889 when she was unwilling to allow Murray to pay his addresses, or (he thought) to take him seriously as a character. The story of Murray's two-year courtship is a very strange one, with comic as well as tragic elements. He never alluded to it himself in any of his autobiographical writings, or in letters to his intimate friends. It emerges (and this is one of the strangest facts about it) from an extraordinarily copious (though not quite complete) correspondence between him and his future mother-in-law, Lady Carlisle, preserved among the Castle Howard archives. He himself was only 21, the object of his affections just 22, Lady Carlisle herself 42.

Murray's first visit to Castle Howard lasted some three weeks from 20 July to about 10 August 1887. He wrote to his hostess shortly afterwards, alluding indirectly but unmistakably to his feelings for her daughter: 'One thought — you can imagine what — is continually before my mind and preventing my reading or talking or thinking like a rational creature. I can not help saying so much, but will not revert to the subject again.'[6]

By the end of August Murray had written again in answer to a letter telling him that Lady Mary felt little interest in him:

Your interpretation of my letter is quite right. What you tell me is of course painful, but I am very glad to have learnt it now and not later. I am so accustomed to disappointment in all the major things of life. But . . . now that my way is definitely closed, I shall find no difficulty, though a certain amount of suffering, in reconciling myself to the situation.

All this from a man of only 21. Later in the same letter he explained how he had come to speak to Lady Carlisle in a way which had not surprisingly told against him with mother and daughter alike. He had been attracted a few days before meeting Miss Howard by someone else, and despised his own inconstancy:

in this state of mind, and with the deliberate intention of spiting myself . . . I told you what I did [tell] you upon our walk . . . in a somewhat exaggerated way which I afterwards tried to correct . . . I did not in any sense of the word make love or speak sentimentally to the girl of whom I spoke to you.

This was not a good start, and Murray probably did not improve his chances by explaining further that he had been 'instantly struck by [Miss Howard's] likeness to a purely ideal character who has been prominent in my mind for about a year, and whom I intend to make the heroine of my second novel.'[7]

However one benefit accrued from his correspondence. As he wrote a little later, 'I had no expectation whatever that you would consent to think of me as a son-in-law . . . I expected that as soon as any one supposed I was falling in love I should be got rid of.'[8]

Lady Carlisle's reception of his statement of intentions had in fact been kind in tone. She had behaved to him all along as a friend and his revelation 'left their friendship unimpaired'.[9] However, by mid-September all Murray's philosophy had deserted him. He was back at Castle Howard

in constant misery . . . I utterly overrated my strength when I spoke confidently of getting over this . . . I believe now I am suffering as much almost as a nervous system can suffer. I never conceived any misery like it before . . . I have lost . . . for the time—every vestige of hope or interest in my life. I only wish to God that I was dead.[10]

Two days later he was allowed to have a tête-à-tête with Lady Mary. It went badly. 'I knew from the beginning that I was condemned . . . and all my words and thoughts failed me . . . She has been very, very kind to me, though for a time, at first, she chastised me with scorpions . . . ' At least she had agreed that he might have some dim hope of her ultimately caring more for him. Lady Carlisle evidently thought that a more confident approach by Murray would have been more appropriate. 'You call me weak. I *know* that I am not that. What I want is not strength but faith. Till the last few years, my life was full of hardships and temptations and I had very few friends.' He was inclined to go off to Tenerife or Australia for six months and return in time for his finals at Oxford, but Lady Mary had told him not to, and he had 'ceased even to wish it'. All he asked of Lady Carlisle was to give him an equal chance with others (Charles Roberts was at the time a rival suitor, and even had in his rooms a photograph of Lady Carlisle): 'I am in your hands and trust you perfectly, as I have cause to do . . . I shall think of her always as she was on the lake, or reading Dante with the voice of an angel.'[11]

Lady Carlisle in a letter not precisely dated reported her daughter's reaction to the idea of marrying him:

I should have a miserable life . . . he will be a brilliant genius, I dare say, but I feel no mission to be a sort of Mrs. Carlyle to him. His despondency is natural to him . . . he gives me no feeling of certainty that his love will last . . . When he was most passionate he seemed to me still selfish . . . he has no settled aim . . .

Above all there had been that cynical and foolish style of talk during the early days when 'he was being petted'. It was useless to explain that he had at first been indulging in a sense of humour perhaps peculiar to the Murray and Gilbert families. Lady Carlisle's advice to him was to dedicate himself, 'not to her, but to a great cause with her'.[12] Murray felt that he had been accused of ineptness in his love-making, and admitted in reply that he had grovelled: 'I saying "I love you more than all the world: all my life and strength are yours." She answering: "You have, I admit, a superficially agreeable manner and a certain amount of brains, but you are entirely selfish and also cynical, aimless and untrustworthy." '[13] These surprising charges rankled. He enclosed with his letter to Lady Carlisle a letter to Lady Mary, the first to be preserved, out of a long series covering nearly seventy years, from him to her.

I can only disprove them [your charges] in one way . . . by letting you know me better. If, as I believe, you have completely mistaken me, and under-rated my sober qualities as much as you have overrated my brains, I shall succeed in justifying myself. If you are right in your estimate, we are both in the same position as before.

I never have for anybody, not even for you, tried to seem other than I am, and I never will try. I only ask you seriously whether you think it just, on the strength of a three weeks' impression, to condemn me finally without even a remote opportunity of clearing myself.

I have other ideals besides the winning of your love. I was a soldier in the service of man before I entered yours. But the others are ideals of duty only, this is of happiness too. Deny it me, and I shall do my life's work much the same as before; that will engross me again as it did before I met you; only half the force will be gone and all the brightness.

Think before you condemn me.

> I remain,
> Yours sincerely,
> G. G. A. Murray[14]

Murray saw Lady Mary at least twice more in autumn 1887, once in London where she made him feel that 'any small attentions on my part were disagreeable to her, and even that she preferred any casual person's conversation to mine.' She appeared to think one of his letters to her mother (which he thought should not have been shown to her) was written deliberately to hurt her feelings. It was all too much.

My heart is all but breaking with pain . . . never for one instant [have I had] a single angry thought or feeling of bitterness towards her . . . If you too [Lady Carlisle] are going to quarrel with me, do so now. Let me lose my love and my warmest friendship at the same time . . . P.S. You know I mean don't ever quarrel with me.[15]

He enclosed another letter to Lady Mary, accusing her of cruel misjudgement, and reminding her of that day on the lake (at Castle Howard):

when we lay still behind the island, and I told you of my novel and you told me of your Italian history . . . Were we born only to wound each other? . . . Take back your last decision and tell me again, as you have told me twice before, that you will give me a fair trial, and that, if I bear the test, I may have some glimpse of hope.[16]

Lady Carlisle had after three months already become his 'warmest friend', but she now wrote to him quite sharply, telling him that he was 'only 22' (in fact only 21) and must learn to be more humble and to take criticism better. However, she also invited him to Naworth, the Carlisle castle near Brampton, for a day or two in mid-term, at the end of October. Here, she wrote, 'she grew personally fond of him',[17] but his criticisms of Lady Mary made her doubt whether he was really in love. This drew another anguished and reproachful cry from Murray: 'The love which you doubt is eating my heart away.' He knew he was unworthy, that there was something spiritual and lovely about her moral nature which filled him with awe. He himself saw things at an ordinary human level, but

I love her all the more for the theories I don't believe . . . She says to me, as you do 'Are you devoted heart and soul to the service of humanity?' . . . I can only answer 'No: I am very selfish; when I do an unselfish act it is chiefly from personal sympathy, not from high principle . . .

I have told her of my love four times: each time I have asked for less, and each time she has refused what I asked: I have in front of me now her refusal of my last request, a decision as absolute as it can be made . . .

You have told me she was once slightly interested. When she saw me again interest gave place to indifference. Since my unfortunate letter, the indifference has become contempt . . .

You told me face to face that you could not wish me to win her love. 'My rival was a much better man than I and more suited to her in character . . .' You tell me I am self-satisfied, vain, full of intellectual pride . . . a thing I detest.

I love her: I have no hope: my love is misery to me, and makes my life useless. I am trying to get rid of it—that is, of all the passionate element . . .

Henceforth I write to you again simply as one who wants your friendship and sympathy in a rather hard struggle, not as a suitor trying to propitiate you, and certainly not scheming to work upon her feelings indirectly through you.[18]

This was the low point of Murray's romance. Two days later he wrote, apologizing for his last letter, 'written under the influence of a paroxysm',[19] and stating that he had already changed a good deal in the direction desired by Lady Carlisle. He thought that he had detected a ray of hope in her letter: 'I give myself over to you altogether . . . ' If she thought he might have a better chance if he changed in some way, he would change.

As regards necessary changes, Murray had from the start of his connection with the Howard family devoted himself actively to the cause of total abstention from alcohol. He had signed the pledge to abstain in July,[20] and from mid-August had been evangelizing for temperance. He had, however, to record his failure to convert the butler in the house where he was staying; but shortly afterwards, again at Castle Howard, he was 'in the thick of Temperance meetings'.[21] Two months later he had begun social work for Oxford House. Evidently he was defending himself actively against the charges of aimlessness and frivolity.

In Lady Carlisle he had found not only a counsellor in his affair of the heart but also an intellectual companion and counsellor in the great world of politics. He discussed at length with her various passages in *Gobi*, not least the occasional poems. Her main criticism was of his neo-Hellenic Utopia—'so dull and terribly didactic'.[22] He also sent her occasionally other poems, including one of which the subject was Lady Mary:

> She walked in the morning air
> When the sun was happy and high.
> A white rose fell from her hair.
> She saw, and she passed it by . . .[23]

By the beginning of 1888 Murray, though 'terribly hurt for a time' by a long silence from Lady Carlisle,[24] was writing to her about the most various problems. Ill health, for example. He had to undergo traction to recover the use of his arm, and was made to lie on a sofa for five days, drinking brandy—medicine of which he could hardly have approved.[25] There were University affairs. St John's College was almost bankrupt, and cutting down on scholarship money, as well as on dons' salaries (Murray was strongly against any collective protest by the scholars). This meant that the College could not afford a Fellowship for him.[26] There was activity at the Union and difficulties concerning the annual dinner of the Palmerston (Liberal) Club at Oxford in May 1888. Should the reply to the principal guest (Lord Hartington) be given by a Liberal Unionist, or by a Home

Ruler? Murray was eventually chosen to reply, presumably, he wrote, as being 'more likely to disown principles than any other Home Ruler'.[27]

In fact practically all that is known about Murray's doings during his last year as an undergraduate comes from this series of letters. In the anguished autumn of 1887, he had despaired of getting a First Class in Greats, but by 1888 he was hard at work again. There was a pre-Greats reading party at Ruta, near Camogli in Liguria, with Ashburner, Mildmay, and later Fisher. On his way back in Paris, Murray found riots in progress after the attempted coup by General Boulanger, and was himself attacked and briefly arrested—an episode which further strengthened his Liberal convictions.[28]

Meanwhile he had made considerable progress in the good graces of Lady Carlisle. In April 1888 she told him that she was no longer neutral: 'My mind is gradually installing you on a conquering throne', she wrote. 'I believe you will some day have her love'.[29]

At the end of June 1888, after Murray's Finals were over, he was allowed to see Lady Mary again at Castle Howard. He must have had high hopes, but she received him no more warmly than before, and he had a short fit of the tragics. He wrote to Lady Carlisle, before he left her house: 'I was suffering greatly and dared not speak [to you]. My only chance was to affect coldness and indifference. Very soon I shall leave you never to come back.'[30]

A week later he wrote again, telling her with a shade of pique that his mother had taken the news with perfect self-possession and advised him to accept Margoliouth's invitation to Mount Lebanon.[31]

Very few of Murray's letters to his mother survive, and he spoke and wrote little of their relationship. It is certain that she was fully in his confidence with regard to *Gobi*. Probably she knew from the start about his love affair. What remains uncertain is how much she knew about his special relationship with Lady Carlisle, and how far she approved of or resented it. In late summer 1888 she set out for Australia to attend Hubert's wedding and did not return until early 1890.

Murray himself duly set out for the Middle East, and wrote from Cairo to Lady Carlisle about his hopes of a career at Oxford. When Jowett died, Bywater would become Professor. Who would succeed him as Reader? Margoliouth would not be available, and the choice might be between W. R. Hardie and Murray himself.[32] After joining Margoliouth and making a strenuous tour with him, he wrote from Jerusalem, partly about the charms of the country—'red, black, and green, like the Dolomites', partly about the city itself—'vile, desolate and crumbling', the Chapel of the Holy Sepulchre distinguished by its particular tawdriness: Oriental Christianity was 'repulsive': the only true memory left for him in Jerusalem was that of the Crusades.[33]

He was soon back in Oxford as a Fellow of New College, and kept Lady Carlisle posted on events. The Home Rule League was in better shape than he had expected and the temperance campaign in the college had also had some success. He himself had the 'regular task of reading all Greek literature up to Christ—a thing which will take some years', and had begun to cherish a plan for a *History of Greek Literature from Callimachus to the present day*'. Early in 1889 *Gobi* started its round of the publishers and Murray was busy canvassing for County Council Elections in Limehouse.[34]

In the spring of 1889 Murray visited Ireland. He attended the elections at Falcarragh, but addressed no meetings, and kept well within the bounds of the law; in spite of which he was 'followed by spies day and night'. He was much impressed by the organization of the Home Rule League and by the extent of the boycotting (or 'begridging'—a half-way stage towards it) of landlords, their agents, and police.

He reported his experiences to Lady Carlisle—by this time her husband had in fact succeeded to his title—from Dublin. At the same time he wrote of the possibility of standing for Parliament at the next general election (which was not due until 1893). John Morley had asked him to do so and had offered to pay for his election expenses. He had decided to accept, thinking that during the intervening years he should be able to find means of livelihood in London.[35] Seven weeks later Murray had begun to waver. He had indeed been pressed by Bryce as well as Morley. He then turned down an offer of standing for East Wiltshire, but thought that perhaps he might stand for Woodstock. Another week and his love of Greek prevailed. He had definitely refused to stand for mid-Oxfordshire: 'there is exciting work ahead in settling the language of the Sicilian Greeks.'[36]

Murray's decision was welcomed both by Lady Carlisle[37] and by his own mother, in letters from Australia. But his mother confided to him a little later, and probably not entirely in jest, that her ambition was to see him in due course as Prime Minister. She also advised him from Australia to qualify for the Bar as a stepping-stone to politics, but urged him to concentrate on academic pursuits, if only to spare his voice, which was easily tired by public speaking.[38] Lady Carlisle regarded the idea of going to the Bar with misgivings.[39]

2

Murray's academic career was taking an unexpected turn. He had been less than a year teaching at New College, Oxford, when he put in for the Professorship of Greek at Glasgow University. The post was becoming vacant on the move of Sir Richard Jebb, perhaps the most famous Grecian of the day in Britain, to the corresponding chair at Cambridge. Jebb himself had drawn attention to the young Murray as the most accomplished Greek scholar of his time on the basis of his Oxford reputation alone. Application for the post involved in the first place soliciting testimonials, and these constitute a remarkable collection. Benjamin Jowett's verdict was monumental: 'I consider him to be the most distinguished undergraduate of his time.' Arthur Sidgwick wrote: 'I have never seen a man of whom I should more confidently prophesy that his success in such a post would certainly be great and might very probably be remarkable.' Henry Nettleship was the fullest and most prophetic. He noted Murray's 'ardour, simplicity and tenderness of character which, more than anything else, give a man influence and authority with the young . . . Classical education in his hands will not be a mere engine of literary culture, but a general training of the character and affections.'[40]

The first indication given to Murray that his candidature was being taken seriously was a summons to London to be interviewed by G. G. Ramsay, the Professor of Latin at Glasgow. He pooh-poohed Murray's testimonials, and said that he was much too young, his politics pernicious, and his views on religion deplorable. Nevertheless Murray was told to call on the Electors of Glasgow University at their Scottish residences.[41] This proved to be a painful and depressing ceremony. The Electors' guardian Beadles seemed to think that Murray was likely to be a dun; and a further difficulty was involved: 'The Baillies are ready to admit knowledge of Greek, but point out that none of my testimonials says that I come of a respectable family. They made a great deal of bother about this and said that it was a "significant omission" . . . ' Murray successfully appealed to the Earl of Carlisle and James Bryce to repair it.[42]

On 22 July, Murray was able to report again to Lady Carlisle. The two academic electors, it seemed, were in favour of him, the four business men were afraid of the outcry which would ensue if so young a man were elected. His politics were against him but the religious test surprisingly was no obstacle; he had only to pledge himself 'not to attempt to undermine in any Professorial lectures

Lady Murray (Agnes)

Sir Terence Aubrey Murray

Gilbert Murray's parents

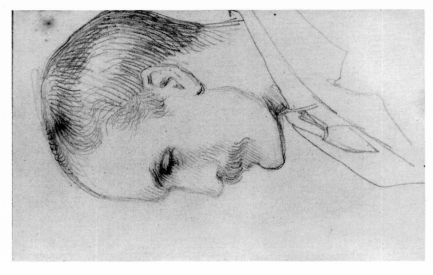

Gilbert and Lady Mary Murray shortly after marriage

Gilbert Murray, Professor of Greek at the University of Glasgow, 1891

Rosalind (née Murray) and Arnold Toynbee's wedding group at Overstrand, 1913

Back row (l. to r.): Two maids, Maggie Baldock (assistant to 'Nursie'), Gilbert Murray, The Lady Cecilia Roberts, Charles Henry Roberts, Denis George Murray, David Davies (friend of Arnold Toynbee, secretary to Asquith), Agnes Elizabeth Murray.

Front row: Miss José Blomfield ('Bombie'), The Lady Dorothy Howard (later Lady Henley), The Lady Mary Murray, Arnold Toynbee, Rosalind Toynbee, Mrs Toynbee (Arnold's mother), Miss Nellie Parker ('Nursie' No. 17), a servant.

Foreground: Basil Andrew Murray holding Stephen Hubert Murray.

the principles of the Confession of Westminster, whatever they may be.'[43]

He was duly elected to the Professorship late in July 1889. The outcry feared by the business men Electors occurred in the *St James's Gazette* and *Truth*, where Labouchere wrote that even the 'outrageous job' of appointing A. C. Bradley to the Chair of English at Glasgow was 'surpassed by the appointment of an utterly unknown young man to the Chair held by Jebb and Lushington.'

Murray was upset and asked Lady Carlisle's advice (probably not very seriously) on whether to refuse the Chair in the face of such criticism. He must have been reassured by the mass of congratulatory letters which followed his acceptance. A surprising number of them came from distinguished political figures, such as Lord Rosebery and Lord Lytton. Even more flattering to Murray was an offer from his own former Oxford tutor, T. C. Snow, to work temporarily as his assistant at Glasgow.[44] A similar offer from John Burnet of St Andrew's, three years his senior, was accompanied by embarrassingly precise proposals for division of work, and Murray had to assure him that he did not require so much or such skilled assistance.[45] A fact of great importance to him was that the professorship carried with it a salary of £1,350 per annum. He was now financially independent.

3

Murray's love story was now drawing towards a happy ending. Early in June 1889 he was invited to visit Castle Howard later in the summer. He replied that he was more glad than he could say to accept the invitation. Lady Murray on her way back from Australia was glad that Lady Carlisle had not forgotten him but 'trembled for his peace of mind', should he pay a further visit to Castle Howard.[46]

Shortly afterwards, Lady Carlisle wrote to him in terms of open encouragement: 'I feel so certain at last that the happy ending is at hand.' She advised him to go slow over furnishing his new house at Glasgow: 'before six months are over you may well be in her hands'. By the end of September Murray was at Castle Howard. He saw Lady Mary again without any rebuff, and was advised to woo her 'slowly but surely'.[47] There was a last ditch stand by 'Madonna', as Murray and Lady Carlisle now called her. She attempted to make conditions, but Lady Carlisle overruled her. On 7 October Lady Carlisle wrote to Murray that 'she had striven all day to make her [Lady Mary] live in an atmosphere of real passion'.[48]

On 8 October Lady Mary made the first and vital concessions and Murray wrote to her: 'I have never been so happy in my life before. It was not that I hoped too much, but it is such delight that you allow me to love you, that you have let me sit by your side and try to tell you all I wanted . . . ' He described his Oxford life, the congratulations which he continued to receive on the Professorship, and the preoccupations of moving:

But what has it all to do with me if you are not here? If you ever do love me, then I shall rejoice in all these things for your sake, but if you do not love me they are worse than poison. Do let me lay all I have at your feet. Do not doubt me any more; do not be afraid. I believe I am the one man in the world who can watch over you and make you happy and give a full .life for your marvellous character to live . . . O my angel, I know that I can help you . . . I can make your life wider and stronger, almost as much as you can make mine deep and sublime by your heavenly purity and infinitely blessed by your love . . . if you only give it me.[49]

The exact stages of progress towards a full engagement cannot be traced from the correspondence, but Lady Mary had formally surrendered by 16 October, when Murray cabled the news to his mother.[50] The bride's first letter to her fiancé is dated 21 October; it is written in the grand style, noble and passionate:

My own Knight Aimé,
You who have braved so many storms for my sake and have subdued my fortress and made me yours at last . . . Believe me, beloved, I shall be yours more and more, 'body, soul and spirit', as the weeks and months pass by . . . so much yours that it will be no more a question of yours and mine, but we shall be one and the same . . . Do not think I shall only say 'good night, Gilbert' . . . 'good morning, dearest', I shall think of you always, your voice will sound for me in the waves, your poor weak eyes full of infinite sad tenderness and appeal will gaze at me from the sky, and you will always be by my side . . .
    As we said the first hour we shall always say to the last—'We lay our passionate love, our two lives in one, our hopes and powers all in absolute surrender on the altar of the 'unknown God'—who yet to us is known as humanity, all the fellow men and women who have never known the love and hope and power which are ours . . . '[51]

At such moments the biographer has an inclination to slip stealthily away.
    The Howard family warmly welcomed the engagement. Lord Carlisle, with whom Lady Mary was a particular favourite, wrote

to Murray from Pisa, indicating incidentally the problem of
nomenclature which was mentioned in Chapter I (his own Christian
name was George), and ending with a postscript: 'I observe that you
have begun your career of son-in-law most successfully by sending
me your letter without a stamp.'[52] Shortly afterwards Murray wrote
to his faithful friend and ally, Lady Carlisle, addressing her as
'Carissima Socrus, I am driven to Latin for refuge, in looking for
a name for you . . . ', and entertaining her with a lively account of
his Glasgow students and how he enrolled them.[53] His Christian
name had by now been determined as Gilbert for general use, though
his own family continued to call him George, and Lady Murray told
Lady Mary that she would use both the names till she had got used
to the new one.[54] Indeed Lady Mary herself seldom used the name
in writing to him;[55] but by the end of October he had finally
become Gilbert Murray to her and to the world.

The Edwards family, apart from Lady Murray, was more surprised
than the Howards—Murray's courting had been done almost exclusively in Yorkshire. Margaret, the wife of Henry Edwards, called him
a 'sly old boots to keep your secret so long to yourself'; Fanny
Edwards referred to 'those two beautiful smiles. I knew they must
have some unusual meaning, and I guessed rightly.'[56] The Edwards
may have thought, naturally enough, that Murray's marriage into
one of the great Whig families of England would remove him finally
from their own circle. Circumstances combined to reinforce this
impression. Lady Carlisle was insistent that the marriage should take
place without delay, and the date of the wedding was fixed for a
time when Lady Murray could not be present. Lady Murray resented
this all the more because she had planned to keep house for him in
Glasgow 'until one nearer and dearer takes my place.'[57] Even more
bitterly and explicitly she resented the absence of any special message
to her at the time of the wedding.[58] Murray did his best to bring
her together with his wife's family; but Agnes Murray died only a
year after her return to England, early in 1891.

Meanwhile, as news of the engagement was published, letters of
congratulations poured in. A young Oxford friend wrote of Murray's
distant manner during his last weeks at Oxford, and 'of the time when
you came back to us . . . so much more human than we had known
you before.'[59] At the other end of the scale, James Bryce wrote a
moving tribute to Lady Mary, and ended: 'Till I heard of this, I felt
disappointed somewhat that even to fill the chair of Young,
Lushington and Sandford, you should have abandoned politics; but
now I have no complaints to make . . . '[60]

Among Murray's Oxford friends, Robinson Ellis, about whose reaction some of Murray's friends had shown lively curiosity, offered some typical observations:

That you should marry a beautiful woman is only fair, as your friends will all agree in a similar admiration for your own personal appearance. . . . By the bye, if there is a thing in the Scotch which is incurable it is their drinking; of which I remind you, as you ought to be careful in your advocacy of temperance principles in a people so greatly addicted to alcohol.[61]

The most delightfully Oxonian tribute was sent by Arthur Sidgwick in the form of some Homeric hexameters, which are proof that Greek composition in the hands of a master can be the vehicle of genuine beauty as well as of cleverness.

4

The wedding took place at Castle Howard, on 2 December 1889, some six weeks after the engagement had been announced. Jowett officiated, a clergyman of suitably liberal views and high prestige to suit the preference of Lady Carlisle. Murray himself would have preferred Charles Gore, but evidently some words had been uttered to Lady Carlisle about his rather High Church principles. Practically every move towards the wedding can be followed in bewildering detail through the exchange of letters between Murray and his bride; one or more daily on each side, all delivered at what now seems more than telegraphic speed.

One main point of difficulty was that Lady Carlisle took almost exclusive charge of the decoration of the new house in Glasgow, 5 The University. Murray found his home full of workmen and wrote that he hadn't quite realized 'how much there would be to do in the house, and how impossible it is to read with painters and plumbers calling every ten minutes and taking one up and downstairs to see all sorts of uninteresting taps and pipes . . . '[62] The decorations were settled completely at Castle Howard, where there was a vast store of papers and chintzes. For the drawing-room there were to be 'Morris-green pommegranite [*sic*] wallpaper . . . Indian chintz curtains—red chintz on the chairs, red serge curtains embroidered for the portière and oil paintings on the walls.'[63] Murray was no doubt happy to be relieved of any burden of choice in these matters, but on the date and festivities of his own wedding he was naturally more sensitive. Lady Carlisle, however, was the complete autocrat and carried through all her plans. Murray had to lecture in Glasgow on 1 December, the eve of his wedding, but 'soon after midnight arrived at the castle, and in a few minutes was dancing down the ballroom with his affianced bride.'[64] The marriage ceremony took place at 10.30 a.m. on 2 December, the bride attended by her six brothers, her bridesmaids, and eighty girls of the Friendly Society, all to be shaken hands with outside. Late the same evening they reached Naworth, to be greeted by a bonfire, the Rifle Band, and a coach drawn by the crowd.

Lady Mary had prepared Murray for this in a letter of 3 November, making it clear that the plans had been drawn up by her mother personally: 'It will not be precisely a "quiet" wedding but at all events all that is done and given will be for pleasure of our poor neighbours to whom it will be a distinct and unique pleasure.'[65]

Lady Carlisle, who had done so much to promote the match, intended to occupy a special and privileged position in the Murrays' family life. No relationship involving her could be an easy one. Lady Mary's younger sister, Dorothy Henley, wrote revealingly of a confrontation round about 1894 between Lady Carlisle and Lady Mary, who in so many ways resembled her:

Mary, always unafraid, always definite, was replying to my mother. 'No, mother, you are selfish . . . ' My mother flushed and breathed angrily and said 'I *never* want to do things for myself: I don't think of *my* pleasure, but of other people's.' 'No', said Mary, 'it's not that kind of selfishness: but you are an Egotist. You *must* do what *you* want to do for other people . . . '[66]

It would be unfair to suggest that this is anything like a final judgement on this extraordinary woman. Dorothy Henley's husband described her in words which Murray himself remarked to be admirably judicious. Good Liberals regarded her, when at her best, as a person 'of greater warmth and force than any other they had known . . . She gave her life, and gave it abundantly to those she met. This feeling of a great warm breath of life woke many sleepers and heartened many people of good will.' Murray added some comments to Lady Henley on this point:

It is just the point that is apt to be forgotten by those who live with your mother and feel how tyrannical she is in the small things of daily life.

In some ways, I, coming as a stranger, felt this great force of inspiration which she had, rather more than the real family did. On the other hand . . . I feel how comparatively superficial my contacts and impressions were, partly, I suppose, as she didn't bully me, and partly because I had a sort of instinct of self-preservation and kept off dangerous places. . . .

In a later letter to Lady Henley, Murray developed the last point:

Your mother was never angry or unjust to me, always kind and considerate. I think (1) I was quite satisfactory on Temperance, Home Rule, Suffrage and general radicalism, and (2) my main interests were in subjects about which she had no views. She was quite prepared to believe that I was a fine Greek scholar and there to leave the matter . . .[67]

He could have added much about what his long courtship owed to Lady Carlisle. She was indeed in many ways his warmest friend, as he had described her in 1887, and it was she above all to whom he continued to confide over the next twenty years his most inward aspirations about political affairs and about spreading the gospel of Hellenism. The exchange of thoughts between Murray and this extraordinarily dynamic woman for long formed an integral part of his marriage and of his life.

CHAPTER IV

Glasgow: The Professor as Teacher

1. Sources for the later life—first encounters with students—inaugural lecture.
2. First year of marriage.
3. The students' professor.

1

THE early life of the young George Murray has had to be pieced together from Murray's own much later autobiographical writings, from the odd records in school and university magazines, and from occasional memories of his contemporaries. From October 1889 there is a plethora of material about his life, thoughts, and daily activities preserved in voluminous correspondence. He and his wife tended to keep and file all incoming letters. Murray himself kept no manuscript copies of his outgoing letters, but a good many copies are extant thanks to the chance that from an early age he was prone to writer's cramp and began to use a typewriter. Many of his outgoing letters have been preserved; some are in the Bodleian and others are available in other collections. In particular the long series of diary letters to his wife—he wrote daily when away—provides valuable private and contemporary comment on his public activities. There are inevitably some large gaps. The practice of keeping letters was a habit of the time. However, Murray can be absolved from any charge of writing with an eye to a future biography. He needed constant urging to work at his own autobiography—a task which he thought too egotistical.[1]

By the date of his marriage, Murray had been in Glasgow for two months and was working extremely hard. He had a good number of psychological as well as material difficulties to contend with. His appointment to a very prestigious chair at the age of 23 had inevitably given rise to public criticism. Local criticism was likely to be more wounding, particularly when it mentioned Murray's 'blue ribbon and red neck-tie principles'.[2] However, his greatest difficulties were caused by his own sense that he had indeed been appointed too early, and by the extraordinary efforts which he made to justify the faith shown in him.

There were certainly some disadvantages, both to the College and to me, in so young an appointment. A professor is a professor, especially a Scotch professor. I became a dignitary and lost something of my youth . . . I had enthusiasms, and no doubt was crude and impulsive about them . . . Of course, being so young, I was rather nervous . . . I felt my ignorance of the world. I was afraid of making mistakes, rather afraid of displeasing my colleagues.[3]

However Murray had little time for deliberate consideration about how he was going to set about the job. He was plunged immediately into a strenuous routine, and the burden of it was considerable. His first impressions were recorded in daily letters to the Carlisle family. Admission of students to the class, which involved collecting his salary in cash, was his first chore and he wrote to Lady Carlisle:

. . . at present [I am] engaged in enrolling students, who don't come . . . the last, who has just left the room, says he is subject to fits, and (two more!) wants me to (another) carry him out of class if need occurs . . . Some of them are (four more — two more — dozens more) so nervous they can hardly speak. They sit on their hats and nearly all of them take away the pencils I give them to write their names with. Then Murdoch [an assistant] pursues them and recaptures the pencils, while they grovel and blush . . .[4]

He wrote later:

One took three guineas from student by student for about three days, put the money each day into a stout leather bag and then, armed with a good walking stick, carried it to the bank. I was once advised to have a companion with a real cudgel, but cannot remember whether I did so.[5]

These difficulties apart, the new Professor had to face the usual war of nerves from the students, no doubt intensified in Murray's case because of his youth. Of his work in the junior class, he wrote to Lady Mary:

It was an awful strain . . . It seems that the whole work is policing. You have, so I'm told, never to look at your book, and never to look at one man for more than a few seconds. You keep your eyes wandering up and down every corner of the room, watching for insubordination. Of course I shall beat them in the end, but it is such degrading work.[6]

However Murray had natural authority. Five days later he could write that

They were very good and quiet except when, after I had described the process of consulting the Delphic Oracle, they were so pleased that they all applauded. I stopped them instantly; it was quite *bona fide*, no idea of sarcasm nor even rowdiness; but it seemed very strange.[7]

The habit of authority grew upon him. It is recorded that on a train to London at about this time he found himself sitting up suddenly in his sleeping-berth and saying in firm tones 'I insist on silence'; whereupon a clergyman quavered from the upper berth 'I beg your pardon, sir, I have been told that I snore.'[8]

The Glasgow audience may have been rowdy, if they thought that they could get away with it, but the best of them had a zeal for knowledge not often known, or at least not often owned, at Oxford. Murray wrote to Lady Mary:

A good many of the men were older than I am. One gave an address seven miles from Glasgow, so Murdoch said 'I suppose ye'll come by train', to which he replied: 'No, mon, I walk.' He had to be with me by 8.0 a.m. Murdoch knew one man who used to walk twelve miles before the senior class; but he died in the first session. I suppose he had not enough to eat.[9]

The bulk of Murray's students were working for a general or pass degree rather than for Honours — Greek was still a compulsory subject for the general degree. Being paid by the head, the large numbers added to his income, but involved him in an enormous quantity of work and variety of teaching, not only in Greek literature, but also in comparative philology and Greek history. It was from the lectures given to large classes, and not from any private teaching, that the students expected to derive their education, and Murray had to make sure that his lectures were good. Years later he told a granddaughter that he had a recurring nightmare throughout his life that he was on the dais of the lecture room facing a sea of earnest young Scottish faces eager to get their money's worth and no words would come. He was then over 80 and the nightmare could still disturb his sleep.[10]

The preparation of the lectures and the routine of the examination system kept him fully stretched from the first. Against this hectic background he delivered his inaugural lecture, *The Place of Greek in Education*,[11] on 6 November. It was his first public credo about the general value of Greek studies and of the Hellenic spirit, and there is little in it which he would have wished to alter at the end of a long life. The argument of Murray's Glasgow inaugural is a pointer to the rest of his career as a teacher of Greek and as a Hellenist.

The serious study of ancient Greek language and thought — the 'laboured quest of that mysterious Hellas' — was begun, he said, by the scholars of the Renaissance. 'In the year 1620 this sort of education (Latin and Greek literature, history and thought) was about as good as it could be. In the year 1820 it was almost as bad as could be', with classical scholars totally immersed in composition, to the neglect of modern literature and science. In 1889, Murray said, the system of classical education was being attacked both from the 'cultivated' and from the 'mercantile' standpoints. The proponents of a wider culture said that the routine study of the classics strangles all natural talent; the 'mercantilists' said that the study of Greek fosters no inventions and furthers no careers. 'My point is that these two criticisms are of exactly opposite aims. The former calls for a fuller and better education: the latter is the secret enemy of any education at all.' Murray distinguished sharply between education and apprenticeship; for him the most recondite educational or humane studies helped forward 'the great purpose of many ages, the invincible expansion of the spirit of man.'

This purpose could no longer be served by any attempt to revive a sort of Encyclopaedist education, as recommended by the French philosophers of the eighteenth century. Specialization was by now too far advanced, though a certain minimal knowledge was essential for everyone in a number of subjects, including science and history. Greek as a language was not for study by everyone. However,

We must remember . . . that Greece, not Greek, is the real subject of our study . . . There is more in Hellenism than a language . . . It is quite possible for a man who cannot read a single page of Plato intelligently to acquire a tolerable proportion of the Greek spirit; to enter more or less into that peculiar way of looking at things, that extraordinary shrewdness and knowledge of the world, that child-like impulsiveness for wild hopes and idealism which seems to leave a certain stamp of genius upon almost any sentence that has fallen from an Athenian pen.

There was an element of disingenuous cunning and irony in Murray's final recommendation of the Greek spirit: ' . . . with the true lowliness and wide-mindedness of philosophers, they (the Greeks) were the one nation that grasped and assimilated the teaching of Christ.' This gave him another reason for maintaining that 'popularisation and "redistribution" of Greek from the more to the less socially privileged was and remained a near-sacred duty.'

2

Murray's message was of course not entirely new. An anonymous correspondent reminded him how much his predecessor, Jebb, had done for the general reader by his translations and introductions to the plays of Sophocles (Jebb himself was not pleased by Murray's failure to mention this and other achievements in the inaugural lecture).[12] However, there was something very personal in Murray's exposition of his ideas and aims. It seemed to represent a true marriage between the scholarship of Oxford and the progressive spirit of Castle Howard. It was Murray's most intimate friend at Glasgow, A. C. (Andrew) Bradley, brother of the idealist philosopher F. H., who had already pointed to the link which existed between radicalism and Hellenism, which included the idea of good citizenship. He spoke prophetically for Murray in 1880: 'With every step in the moralising of politics and the socialising of morals, something of Greek excellence is won back.'[13] Lady Mary responded in heroic tones to the message of the inaugural and prophesied all the good that would be achieved by Murray's and her own joint activities at Glasgow.[14] Indeed the newly-weds at first envisaged the work of spreading the light of Hellenism as a common enterprise. Even the teaching of the Greek language was to be shared. Murray was giving occasional lessons to Lady Mary in the autumn of 1889; and when he found that students did no unseen translations—a wide gap in Jebb's system— he proposed that she should help him in looking over such translations. He reckoned that this would involve five hours extra work weekly of an 'easy mechanical kind.'[15]

For some years Lady Mary's letters to Murray abounded in gratitude for his teaching and recorded her progress when left to herself, with details of the numbers of lines read, or reactions to favourite passages set to her for reading.[16] But it is doubtful whether the project for the joint teaching of students ever came anywhere near fruition. Lady Mary, though she had an excellent command of modern French, German, and Italian, did not make quick progress with ancient Greek, and the special teaching lapsed. She understood enough to make it possible for Murray, when writing postcards to her, to veil discreetly in Greek any thoughts which should be hidden from over-curious eyes, e.g. about Fanny Edwards, 'her nonsense irritated me so'; and the nature of *Mrs Warren's Profession* was revealed by a Greek word which his wife would surely have had to look up in a dictionary.[17]

Lady Mary could not collaborate with Murray on his chosen ground, but in the first years of her marriage with Murray her sense of their joint dedication to humanity remained complete. Even her great physical happiness was devoted to the cause. 'They blaspheme and wrong the beauty and holiness of love who say that in a passion like ours there is aught ugly or wrong . . . It is the flame of passionate loving service, seeking truth and beauty and bearing them to those who do not know them.'[18] She could help or take the lead in working at Glasgow for all the social causes which had occupied her mother and herself at Castle Howard; she could also give individual attention to his students and entertain them in her home— a habit which was to continue for over sixty years.

In the event social and political causes soon had to take a subordinate place—though not before Murray had gained a certain notoriety for his advocacy of temperance and his enthusiasm for radical principles. By autumn 1890 Lady Mary was about to have her first child known as 'Teralind' [a mixture of Terence and Rosalind] until a daughter was born in late October. Murray himself had begun before that time to suffer from the very heavy load of work that he felt bound to undertake. Each warned the other about the dangers of dissipating energy. At the end of July, Murray was on a strenuous walking and climbing holiday in Switzerland; he wrote lovingly and tactfully to Lady Mary, who had evidently been complaining of feeling aimless and unable to apply herself:

You have so much power of a kind which I haven't got. You have such directness and fire . . . I have always been frank, sometimes cruelly frank, with my loved one; I am now perfectly sure that all the misgivings and all the feelings of failure and weakness come from a cause which is bound soon to disappear altogether—the want of definite lasting work, that is specially yours, that you can do specially well, that fills you with a conviction of its own importance. That work is bound to come. Teralind will be in it: Glasgow will be in it. . . . I am certain that if we try to live quiet strenuous lives, gently catholic in sympathy, absolutely honest and free from either selfishness, or malice, or narrowness of view; and if we love and respect each other through and through, we shall be able to do such work in our lives that they shall seem like two good days of hard labour in the service of the world, after which rest is welcome, though all the work has been its own reward . . .[19]

Lady Mary replied in kind:

Your letter makes me wish more than ever to live very, very simply and economically . . . it would be utterly unwise for you to take active part even in social politics and work . . . Our subscriptions this year ought to be 4 times as much as they have been . . . but if we cannot do, we can be . . . it seems the right way for everyone to do his own work (it may not be philanthropic work). To live an entirely strenuous, simple and Republican life. I think that for the present you must stick to your work as closely as an artisan does perforce to his, but that need not prevent the social problems of Glasgow being vital to us nor even prevent us from being able to help indirectly in word and deed . . .[20]

Less than six months after Rosalind's birth Lady (Agnes) Murray died in February 1891. It seems strange that so little is recorded of an event which must have affected Murray deeply. Seven years later he wrote to his wife that it was a grief too deep for tears (Chapter 1 p. 4). We know that Lady Murray had felt bitterly about being excluded from the wedding and it is natural to suppose that Murray was unhappy about this and probably not without some feelings of guilt. He had hurt his mother in a way that later his daughter Rosalind was to hurt him. But if so, he pondered all this in his heart. Here we see the inner aloofness and reserve which caused his son-in-law Arnold Toynbee years later to write of him as 'the remotest of men'.

In her reminiscences written fifty years later, Molly Hamilton, daughter of one of Murray's Glasgow colleagues, gave some glimpses of the young couple at work. The only faults held against them in her father's liberal circle were that Murray was not a good enough hater and that the pair unfortunately 'had no time for mere living'.[21] To some extent (if not in the teaching of Greek) the Murrays could work as a team. When Murray had to cancel a lecture to the Henry George Society because of toothache, Lady Murray replaced him, offering 'Egypt, Mazzini and Women's Rights as her subjects'.[22] Either of them could speak eloquently to a loyal Liberal audience. Some rough notes are preserved for a speech by Murray (but it could equally well have been by Lady Mary) to a meeting of the National Liberal Federation in 1896. They deal with various forms of economic oppression under which the sufferers are too weak to stand up against, e.g., their domestic masters or employers. And 'the weakest of the weak are women'.[23]

Here indeed was a cause which Murray could champion in the normal course of his duties. He had not taught women during his year at New College, Oxford, but at Glasgow University the question of teaching women had become actual by 1890. He wrote proudly to his mother, after giving a public lecture on the 'new Aristotle Papyrus' (the 'Constitution of Athens'): 'I introduced the thin end of the wedge by having Lady Mary and the two Greek students from Queen Margaret's. The men applauded when they came in.'[24] Long afterwards Murray wrote:

Male professors had a right to refuse such teaching (and there was no question yet of degrees for women pupils), but of course to my wife and me it was the fulfilment of a cherished dream. And certainly, as it happened, the few women who dared to take the Greek course class in that first year or two were a chosen band, remarkable both for brains and character.[25]

One of them was Janie Malloch, a romantically glamorous figure,[26] afterwards married to H. N. Brailsford; another was Janet Spens, later English tutor at Lady Margaret Hall, Oxford, and a close friend of the Murrays throughout their lives. Murray did all that he could for these students individually, and incidentally got Lady Carlisle to invite them to Castle Howard.[27] He worked for them with a special and innocent zeal which, as he later said, he did not admit to himself at the time:

We old champions of Women's Rights began like Plato by stoutly denying the existence of any particular difference between men and women, I used to maintain that teaching Greek to a woman was exactly the same process as teaching it to a man. Any other view I repudiated with indignation. Yet of course I was quite wrong. In the woman pupil there was mostly an instinctive wish to please, in the man teacher a wish — how shall I put it? — to protect or help, rather different in quality from the corresponding relations in an ordinary class of men.[28]

3

The Murrays were energetic in entertaining at their home those students who seemed to want or need attention. Many of these afterwards became family friends; many too distinguished themselves in their several walks of life. Murray himself wrote later of the most remarkable among them. There was for example John Buchan, who at a tender age was editing Bacon's essays for publication. He impressed Murray profoundly by approaching him at the end of a lecture to ask for a source from which Bacon could have quoted a Latin translation of the Greek philosopher, Democritus.[29] Buchan left Glasgow for Oxford in 1895, but continued to correspond with Murray over many years on his literary and political plans. His early novel, *Sir Quixote of the Moors*, was dedicated to Murray. Another pupil, H. N. Brailsford, later a famous Radical journalist, had much less definite ideas about a career, and was more subject to Murray's influence. He had come to Glasgow from Oxford, reversing the normal student procedure, and confided to Murray: 'I suffered from a wet soul at Oxford (that doesn't mean that I drank too hard) . . . I have often got more from a single lecture [of yours] in Glasgow than from all the courses I attended at Oxford . . . '[30]

Another young man who knew Murray at Glasgow and continued to correspond with him over the years was Norman Leys, a general student who subsequently turned to medicine and became a devoted medical officer and critic of the British colonial administration in Kenya. It was he who voiced most clearly the appreciation of the non-specialist student for what Murray achieved at Glasgow. Leys never even heard Murray lecture, but got to know him personally.[31] He was a Christian Socialist at the time, not interested in the niceties of the Greek language but in the message of Hellenism. Writing from Glasgow, when Murray's departure had been announced, Leys testified to his moral influence: ' . . . you will be specially missed by the men in College, who like myself feel themselves born into a world too big for them, full of questions and quite empty of answers. You have been a great help to us in fighting our cowardice . . . '[32] Later Leys wrote from Africa:

I know I must be merely one of many to whom you have done service. I am astonished that you can make yourself so little the scholar and so much the friend of the common man . . . Professors feed passmen on the husks of scholarship and keep the interpretation of thought to a few whose minds are supposed to be able to support high ideas . . . Is there a greater need in the country than to give us ordinary men some clear vision of the main issues of life and some instruction on the way to use our minds on them? . . . This explosion is the result of trying to praise you for not being afraid of being popular . . .[33]

These are conspicuous examples of Murray's influence. However he had to cater for a majority of students less brilliant than Brailsford or Buchan. His fame as a general teacher spread abroad early. By mid-May 1892 the Greek students of Paisley Grammar School had written to ask if it was possible for him to give them a correspondence course in Greek prose.[34] Later, when asked by William Blackwood in 1897 to write a new Greek syntax, he refused but sent Blackwood a short synopsis drawn up by himself as a foundation for the lectures which he had to give on this subject.[35]

Murray's papers also show that he was ready to help a wide variety of students in many more general ways and to act as a moral adviser. The witness of Leys has already been quoted. Molly Hamilton describes a debate between Murray and her father, Professor Adamson, about a student destined for the Ministry, who began to have doubts about his calling. Adamson thought that the young man should be left to think out his problem for himself. Murray was for direct advice. No young man who could be saved for free-thinking should be allowed to wed himself to religion.[36]

In a letter to his mother we see more of his sensitive concern for his students:

This morning long interview with a poor student, who has come hopelessly to grief in his Greek. He is in a desperate state of mind and says he can't work and is going to the dogs. He was also rather impertinent at first. I had about an hour's talk with him, giving him all the encouragement I could and cheering him up. He cried a little, but seemed very grateful and somewhat comforted. I shall give him some help privately. He expected to be scolded.[37]

Thus Murray worked towards fusing the Scottish tradition of good public lecturing with the Oxford tutorial tradition; and he interpreted the tutorial tradition in its fullest sense.

But the lectures in class remained the centre of his activity in Glasgow, and they left a lasting impression. One of his women pupils wrote more than fifty years later:

Hippolytus was the theme. You can picture the scene in the Greek Classroom, the youths in the front tiers, and us behind, quite high up . . . It happened now and then [that] after analysing a lyrical passage he would read his own version, which was received by the youths (of course they were really a picked lot) with appreciative stamping on the floor, in the way that Scottish students show their pleasure. It was really quite moving.[38]

Again, when Lord Lindsay of Birker (as Sandy Lindsay, a pupil of Murray at Glasgow) spoke for the first time to the assembled students of the new University of Keele, he looked back to his own student days at Glasgow and to the high standard of teaching there for ordinary degrees:

When I was a student at Glasgow, professors gave their best to their ordinary classes. The wonderful impression which A. C. Bradley and Gilbert Murray made on the students of the University was made through their ordinary classes, not on a mere handful of people who took honours in English or in Greek . . . That tradition . . . produced in me the impression that anyone could teach honours subjects but that it required one's whole imagination and energy to teach the ordinary class.[39]

Murray paid a certain price for his fame among his colleagues. His position as a very young Professor with assistant staff older than himself was bound to be awkward. Even his assiduity and the very heavy burdens which he assumed himself were not always likely to commend him. He wrote to Lady Carlisle of a typical case when in 1894, an assistant, R. M. Burrows, refused to 'do the senior papers' (probably correcting rather than setting): 'By uniting in my

manner the chief traits of a dove and a worm—bar the turning—
I managed to get him started. I wonder if he is as rude to his wife
as he is to his Professor.'[40] Two months later Burrows still refused
to shake hands with Murray or to enter his house.

A further burden for Murray was administration in the University
context (e.g. the determination of fees for students, or of salary for
assistants in his Department, and the provision of sports facilities).
He could not pretend to enjoy such work and was often impatient
of the proceedings of the Arts Faculty or the Glasgow Court (a sort
of Hebdomadal Council or Council of the Senate, in Oxford or
Cambridge terms), with whose other members he had to discuss
general or even departmental problems.

Murray's active liberalism made him an uncomfortable colleague
to many of his seniors. He wrote to Lady Carlisle of his own bitter
feelings when 'Ramsay and Lord Kelvin are doing something illiberal
or reactionary, or injuring the women students, and I am powerless
to resist them.'[41] The bitter feelings were no doubt reciprocated.
Sometimes too the shadow of the Kirk loomed darkly over Murray;
he was shocked to learn of a movement to secure that Edward Caird,
the philosopher who was appointed to succeed Jowett at Balliol,
should be replaced only by a committed Presbyterian.[42] He himself
won a minor victory for Free Thought over traditional piety in the
matter of reciting the Lord's Prayer at the beginning of every class;
he compromised initially by reading it in Greek, and in 1892 dropped
it altogether.[43]

In sum, however brilliant Murray's lecturing and however warm
his relations with his students, he did not fit too easily into the
Glasgow University scene. His highly individual and dramatic style
of lecturing, his aristocratic connections and radical sympathies,
even the width of his interests, all set him apart from older and
less brilliant colleagues. His health problems, discussed later, and
his frequent absence on sick leave could easily be misinterpreted.
Misunderstandings would often be dissipated by personal charm;
but they could also be aggravated, among those who knew him least,
by a deep essential shyness, a trait which persisted throughout his
life. It is for example surprising that the first 'grown-up' party to
be given by the Murrays at Glasgow did not take place till January
1897, over seven years after they had settled at 5 The University.
He wrote of it to William Archer, 'I am told that if you ask enough
people, you can always get off to bed unobserved.'[44]

Murray was in fact very much a student's professor at Glasgow.
His new friendships, often lasting, were formed mainly with his

pupils. The most notable exception was A. C. Bradley, the
Shakespearian scholar. The bond between him and Murray was not
only intellectual—throughout his life Murray yielded to many in his
enthusiasm for Shakespeare. They were linked by a common zeal
for social improvement, and also by a common passion for golf, into
which Murray was initiated in his Glasgow years—'a splendid game,
intensely interesting and exercising every muscle of the body.'

CHAPTER V

Glasgow: Research and Outside Interests

1. Ponders line of research—correspondence with Wilamowitz—settles for Oxford text of Euripides.
2. Seminars—publishes *History of Ancient Greek Literature*.
3. Original drama.
4. Political development—interest in social issues.

1

BY the time of his appointment to Glasgow, Murray had acquired an extraordinary knowledge of Greek, but had had little opportunity for original research. In Glasgow teaching, administration, outside interests, family preoccupations, and weak health, all made it hard for him to settle to work at any major scholarly project. Moreover the climate of classical studies in Britain at this time did not much favour research. At universities as well as at schools there was heavy emphasis on the importance of 'composition' (the translation from English prose or poetry into Latin or Greek), and this was a field in which Murray was incomparably good. Otherwise, the main task of the advanced classical scholar was considered to be the establishment of correct Latin or Greek texts from a meticulous examination and collation of the remaining manuscripts. This was work which had been pursued for centuries and, unless new sources were discovered, it was unlikely to improve substantially the existing texts. It could be regarded as a perfectionist pursuit, suitable mainly for the Germans.

In recommending Murray for the Glasgow Chair, T. C. Snow had stated that 'his brilliance does not at all stand in the way of the most unattractive researches'.[1] Another famous classical scholar, J. U. Powell, in congratulating Murray on his appointment, expressed the hope that he would write books, but said that if they 'showed research', Murray ought to give teaching up and vacate his Chair.[2] All this should be remembered when it comes to an assessment of Murray's contribution to scholarship. And of course the 'redistribution' of Greek could easily stand in the way of scholarly studies for the few.

On the other hand Murray was ambitious and uneasily aware that he had no solid work to his name. He realized the deficiencies of the current Oxford and Cambridge pattern of studies, in respect not only of spreading the Hellenic spirit, but also of deeper scholarship. He had hoped to take time off from New College in order to study for a year at Göttingen, and had told his fiancée that 'Germans are like a superior race to scholars' imaginations'.[3] He had hardly had time, amid his teaching duties at Oxford, to choose a special subject for study. However, he had become much interested in the text, metre, and dialects of the early Greek lyrical poets; he was therefore delighted when an invitation reached him in November 1889 to work on an edition of the Greek lyric poets, for publication in a new Library series by Rivington's. Murray's efforts seem first to have been concentrated on Pindar, then to have sunk under the pressures of more ambitious plans, routine work, and illness.[4]

Meanwhile the scope of classical studies was being greatly enlarged. Papyri, with new Greek texts and new versions of old texts, were being found in Egypt. With the publication of J. G. Frazer's *Golden Bough* in 1891, anthropology had begun to appear in comparatively respectable form over the horizon of classical scholars. And archaeological researches were being energetically pursued in Greece and the Near East. In spring 1894 Murray paid what was in effect his only 'working visit' to Greece—Athens, Delphi, and Boeotia. He was shocked by the slender financial resources of the British School at Athens—a total income of £400 per annum, of which half went on the Director's salary—and contrasted its situation sadly with that of the corresponding French, German, and American institutions, none of which received less than £2,000 annual government support. He was fascinated by the great French excavations at Delphi and saw the newly discovered frieze of the Treasury of the Athenians there. He had a strenuous and adventurous tour, since his visit coincided with a series of heavy earthquakes, the worst of which he experienced when staying at the monastery of Hosios Loukas, near Delphi. He was profoundly shocked by the sufferings of what he regarded as a priest-ridden people, and of their animals.[5]

This was an interlude which led to no important developments in Murray's own classical work. Much more important to him was his discovery of the writings of the famous German scholar, Ulrich von Wilamowitz-Moellendorff. These made a deep impression on Murray and did much to liberate him from British amateurism and the narrower traditions of British classical scholarship.[6] In 1954 he published his *Memories of Wilamowitz*, and related how as a young Professor at Glasgow he felt greatly:

the need of guidance from some older and more advanced scholar . . . when I read Wilamowitz's edition of Euripides' *Herakles* with its celebrated introduction to Greek Tragedy I was overcome with admiration. Never had I seen such wide and exact learning inspired by such a lively and vigorous mind. I read his other books . . . and wished ardently that I could have guidance from such a man.[7]

Indeed it is hard even for an amateur today to read the introduction to *Herakles* without being carried away by Wilamowitz's energy and broad conception of classical scholarship.

The story has long persisted that Murray studied for a time, one professor at the feet of another, in Wilamowitz's seminar in Göttingen and that Wilamowitz's admiration for his talents was mingled with a certain national resentment that it was the British participant who always got the answers right. This was not so, though Murray periodically sent good pupils to work with Wilamowitz — the first was Dorothy Murray (no relation) in 1901.[8] The two scholars did not meet till Wilamowitz came to Oxford in 1908.

In 1894 Murray initiated a correspondence with him, however, and received much advice and active help. Murray's opening letter was in Greek, to prove 'that he was not merely frivolous'.[9] Wilamowitz's reply to him is preserved, for those who can decipher his minuscule and obscure German handwriting. He was not noted for endearing personal manners, but in this case he was friendly; he envied Murray his Greek typewriter, but expressed the view that it would be better for each to write in future in his own language.[10] The two men proved to be very well suited to each other, for while Wilamowitz was the greater master of detailed scholarship, he shared Murray's passion for bringing the classics to life in modern terms. He had translated Euripides' plays into his own language, and had seen them successfully staged in Germany. Like Murray, he thought that Euripides had a message for modern times, and he seemed to view the Greek as a predecessor of Ibsen. In his commentary on the *Hippolytus*, published in 1891, a year after the first performance of *Hedda Gabler*, Phaedra is described as

altogether the high society lady, knows and does her duty; she has a husband and children, relations and a social position . . . Her reputation is blameless, but she has no inner relationship to husband or children; let alone to any other object. Her life lacks the blessing of work, and she is too intelligent to be content with idleness and empty social activity . . . So she is ripe for passion . . .[11]

This may be held to anticipate and outdo Murray's own later exercises in subjective interpretation; it certainly indicates a deep affinity between Murray (an enthusiastic Ibsenite) and Wilamowitz. Murray would not have accepted guidance so readily from anyone whose heart he felt to be in the wrong place.

He consulted Wilamowitz in the first place on two separate projects. The first he had launched in December 1893, when he sent to a selection of the most eminent Greek scholars in England and Scotland a printed circular proposing a new series of Glasgow critical texts, and asked for views on his ideas.[12] The new critical texts should not be cluttered with footnotes about alternative readings. They should contain the main notes of the ancient commentators (*scholia*) and their traditional lives of the poets. Students should be faced with a plain text, and taught to evolve any comments from their own reading. With the circular were enclosed some specimen pages of Aristophanes' *Clouds*, edited on the new principles. Murray himself later described the idea as not very practical,[13] but it was taken seriously by most of those who received the circular. Many eminent scholars, including Bywater, S. H. Butcher, and Robinson Ellis, were strongly for the scheme. Others raised doubts about how far the new series could be expected to commend itself to schools, though Murray's old headmaster, Dr Baker of Merchant Taylors', bravely promised to try any completed text on his own sixth form. Then there were likely to be difficulties with publishers. Macmillans' representative explained to the Glasgow University printer that there would be duplication with other series, and that the great expense involved in printing might well not be justified. The scholar W. R. Hardie said that similar schemes had more than once been urged on the Clarendon Press, and that one of the main difficulties had been to find suitable editors. By the end of 1894 the scheme had lapsed.[14]

Another ambitious project was that Murray himself should produce a Lexicon of the Language of Euripides. He wrote to Wilamowitz about this, as well as about the Glasgow texts. In reply Wilamowitz enclosed some notes of his own on a passage of Euripides and gave full advice on the procedure most useful for a Lexicon, as well as putting questions about its relation to a well-established text.[15] Murray had originally regarded the Lexicon as a preliminary to a definitive edition of Euripides.[16] However, as early as January 1894 he had also been planning a series of texts of Euripides' individual plays.[17] And in Mid-1896 he received a letter from the Oxford University Press which reversed his priorities.

They were beginning to publish their famous series of classical texts, and Murray was cautiously asked by one of their staff if he could 'move the delegates . . . in the direction of asking you to make a text of Euripides', on the model of Ingram Bywater's edition of Aristotle's *Ethics*.[18]

Murray had already visited Florence in March 1896 to study a manuscript of Euripides in the Laurentian Library, and immediately on receipt of the OUP's letter wrote to his wife that he was delighted to undertake the work.

Henceforward this became his principal task in the field of technical scholarship. His 'Oxford text' appeared in three volumes, published in 1901, 1904, and 1909, and served as his credentials for those of his colleagues who did not care for his work of popularization.

2

Detailed work on the Euripides text was begun in Glasgow. Before he left his post there, Murray received various other proposals for editing or translating individual plays of Euripides—proposals which he did not accept at the time, though they may in some degree have stimulated him later to publish the translations which were beginning to take shape as a by-product of his lectures.[19] Meanwhile he was busy enough on other work. With the German model in mind he tried to raise the standard of advanced classical scholarship by organizing seminars, on some general subject and with individual students preparing papers on various aspects of it, all under the guidance of the Professor: 'The class might set itself to collect all the references to Homer in writers before Aristarchus . . . or to collect the names, history and arguments of Greek thinkers who maintained that Homer knew all sciences or wrote in allegory.'[20] Nothing seems to have come of the scheme, and soon Murray was engaged on another task of popularization. This was *A History of Ancient Greek Literature*, the first of his works to come before a comparatively wide public. The original proposition came from Edmund Gosse, who was engaged in editing for Heinemann a series of *Short Histories of Literature* (he conducted his business largely from his office at the Board of Trade). Gosse wrote to Murray on 28 May 1895: 'I desire to make the volumes not text-books but contributions to graceful permanent criticism of a wholly readable class.' Murray agreed to write a book of 90,000 words for a fee of £150, by the end of November 1896, and Gosse reminded him that it was to be addressed to 'ignoramuses like me'.[21]

Here was work which, Murray hoped, would flow directly from
the lectures given at Glasgow, but it is clear from his correspondence
that the composition of the book caused him a lot of trouble. It
consists of a series of essays on high points of Greek literature. The
chapter on the 'Homeric question' (broadly how many authors was
'Homer', and when or over what range of dates did he or they write?),
stands out as an essay on scholarship rather than on literature. Other
chapters, devoted to types or schools of literature, tend to lapse into
bare catalogue work. Those on individual writers—Herodotus,
Thucydides, the tragedians—are often stimulating, but here too it
was hard for Murray to keep the balance between pure description,
background information, and critical judgement. The selection
of main subjects could also be regarded as idiosyncratic. If a chapter
on Plato was included, why not one on Aristotle? And was it
reasonable to bundle all Greek literature after the fourth century BC
into a single chapter at the end? Some of these points were made by
Andrew Lang, both directly to Murray, and also (with considerable
bitterness) to Edmund Gosse, who did not hesitate to pass them on
to Murray.[22]

In a different respect the *History of Ancient Greek Literature*
is a very curious book. A later generation of readers must ask
whether the enterprise as envisaged by Gosse and accepted by Murray
could conceivably succeed. Was it possible, even in 1897, when there
was a wider general knowledge of and about ancient Greek than
exists today, to give the 'general reader' much or any idea of Greek
literature without treating it much more summarily or much more
fully? And does not Murray's treatment fall exactly between two
stools, meaning little except to those who already have a fair
knowledge of Greek literature, and probably not meaning enough
to them? The point was made trenchantly by Frederic Harrison, the
Positivist prophet, who wrote to Murray 'At first glance . . . it is
either (1) too learned and argumentative for a popular resumé . . .
or (2) too short for a history of Greek Literature.'[23] Lang was
(curiously as it now appears) the only classical 'expert' to pick on
the same point.[24]

Copies of the book were sent to a number of more professional
scholars; the acknowledgements preserved among the Murray papers
are polite but not enthusiastic, except that of W. G. Rutherford, who
found much to praise as well as to criticize, and talked of Murray's
genius—'the use of the word is deliberate'. He, like Lang and Jebb,
objected to a 'want of gravity' in Murray's style ('Athens came a good
third' is cited as a horrid example).[25]

Reactions from Murray's less learned friends were more favourable and interesting, and the reviews, if not specifically favourable were surprisingly full, appearing in comparatively popular periodicals. The cultural world of London was firmly based on classical learning of a sort, and a new 'popular' book on Greek literature commanded at least the appearance of wide interest. One of Murray's correspondents noted that the *Bookman* included his book among the six volumes 'for which London of late has been clamouring most importunately, along with Nansen's *Miss Kingsley* and Charles Gore's on the *Sermon on the Mount*.'[26]

The essence of the book was best grasped, naturally enough, by those closest to Murray's family circle. Lady Mary's first reaction was that the book was 'your own dear self through and through'. Two days later she raised a doubt: 'I have read the Literature to the end of the "Song", and think it simply delightful . . . except certain love passages which unreasonably pain me.'[27]

The morals of the Greek elegists were unlikely to commend themselves to Lady Mary and, writing of Theognis of Megara, Murray had quoted one of his 'bitter' maxims: 'Few men can cheat their haters, Kyrnos mine; Only true love is easy to betray'.[28]

He wrote to his wife:

Why need you really mind? There is only the one line that I told you of, 'easy to betray' . . . that has any reference to that time, and that is a self-reproach. Of course I cannot talk to you about the self-reproach. But it absolutely never leaves me.[29]

'That time' probably refers to the period soon after he first met Lady Mary in 1887, when he had publicly advertised some doubts about his own constancy.

Murray's cousin, Albert Edwards, interpreted the *History* as 'a sort of guide to Mary, who I remember used to read Greek with you: it has the tone of one who tries his best to teach clearly a favourite subject to a favourite pupil.'[30] Murray was indeed trying to bring the Greeks to life again for his nearest and dearest, as for his pupils in general; but his work, like that of many philosophers, is best understood by an appreciation of what he was reacting against. Murray wanted to show the ancient Greeks, not as heroes, nor as calmly classical models for statues and pursuers of the golden mean, but as men of like passions to ourselves, faced with philosophic and political problems which were not unlike our own. The falseness of the 'statuesque' conceptions of the Greeks, he felt, arose 'partly from inadequate knowledge of the nuances of the language, partly from

the comparative lack of romantic imagination among persons of my
profession. To bring this out, I have ventured on a good many short
verse translations . . . '[31] Murray's own extraordinary grasp of the
Greek language, his possibly excessive romantic imagination, and
his strong sense that the spirit of the Greeks had been misrepresented
all led him in the same direction, whether he was writing a 'popular'
history, preparing a critical text, or meditating verse translations.

3

Amid all his other preoccupations in Glasgow, Murray still found
time to try his hand at writing his own plays. The drafting of his
first play *Carlyon Sahib* occupied him during his voyage round the
world in the winter of 1892–3. Later he wrote *Andromache* and one
or two minor plays. His plays were not staged until after he left
Glasgow and are better discussed in the context of his theatrical work
in a later chapter. But in assessing Murray's burden of work in
Glasgow and the strain it imposed on him, account must be taken
of the many hours spent in writing his own plays. Time too was
needed for discussion of them with old friends and with new—the
men of the theatre to whom this new interest introduced him.
Notable among them was the dramatic critic William Archer who
became a lifelong friend and the companion of many cycling holidays.

4

In Glasgow Murray had little time to spare for politics but his Liberal
interests were not forgotten. On the two issues which split the party
in the last years of the century, Murray, while still at Oxford,
had come out strongly in favour of Home Rule. The second divisive
issue—about attitudes towards Empire—was a running sore
throughout the nineties. The Boer War brought it to a head, when
Morley and the Radicals were openly pro-Boer as against the 'LIMPS'
(Liberal Imperialists). In 1888 Murray had given an address to the
Russell Club (Liberals) in Oxford on the theme *Liberalism Old and
New*,[32] in which he affirmed his belief that the Empire could be run
on paternalistic principles acceptable to good Liberals. His views
derived partly from his Australian family background: his father (as
later was his brother) had been in the best tradition of colonial
servant: partly from correspondence with John Maynard, his Oxford
friend, who had joined the Indian Civil Service.[33] However, by
1899 Murray was firmly in the Radical and pro-Boer camp.

Though Murray took little part in active politics at Glasgow, he had been trained to support the favourite causes of Lady Carlisle and of his wife — women's suffrage, women's rights in general, and temperance. However, he was also led to think more widely about the need for social legislation. Already in 1889 he had been elected a director of the Glasgow Workers District Co-operative. He was particularly active in 1897–8 on behalf of the strike organized by the Amalgamated Society of Engineers in support of an eight-hour working day, and countered by a lock-out by the Engineering Employers' Federation. Murray consented to join a Committee organized by Vaughan Nash (later Asquith's private secretary) of Toynbee Hall to further conciliation between employers and workers, Nash's general sympathy being with the latter. Murray refused to become Treasurer of the Committee, but was active in trying to secure support for it, particularly from Edward Caird, his Glasgow friend, now Master of Balliol College, Oxford.[34] It was in this context that Murray wrote one of his more important political letters to Frederic Harrison. In the engineers' strike, he thought, the socialists and the employers must not be allowed between them to reduce the Trade Unions to bankruptcy. Murray inclined to the plan of having the eight-hour shifts, with a temporary reduction of wages — leisure being, in his view, more important for the skilled artisan than an increase of wages.

I fully agree with you that the working classes are being badly led, and that the tincture of revolutionary socialism which now infects all working class movements is a mere dead falling away from progress . . . You are doubtless as discontented as I am with the ordinary inert stationary Liberalism, which coquettes with Jingoism on the one hand, and secretly hopes that its own measures will not pass on the other . . . The policy I believe in is that one may roughly call by the old name of Philosophic radicalism, the leader I believe in is Morley.[35]

The mention of John Morley has particular significance.

There was much about Morley which would naturally appeal to Murray. In politics, Morley was a disciple of Mill, and held with him that most causes of human suffering are remediable, that progress is the only alternative to collapse, that political progress means principally the substitution of justice for privilege, and that it could only be achieved gradually through compromise. Morley's foreign policy was largely Gladstonian — Home Rule for Ireland and distrust of Empire. In the summer of 1897 when Murray was on sick leave in a remote Speyside village, Morley and Herbert Fisher were his neighbours. Morley welcomed his new young political allies; Murray, he wrote, was a 'fine fellow' who exhorted him 'by the hour to take down my sword from the wall.'[36] On foreign affairs there was little need for discussion between them; but in the course of their long conversations they talked 'a good deal of socialism and Labour policy',[37] and Murray's letter to Harrison quoted above probably reflects some of Morley's views. Murray's allegiance was shaken over the next years, when Morley failed to commit himself totally either to anti-Imperialism or to active domestic policies along radical lines.[38]

Meanwhile Lord Salisbury's government was offending against Murray's deepest convictions on foreign policy. In February 1897 Greek troops landed in Crete and proclaimed its independence from Turkey. The British fleet was the most powerful force in the neighbourhood but, in the interest of 'preserving the European concert', it refrained from any timely intervention and, to Murray's incredulous fury, seemed ready to fraternize with the Turkish navy.[39] The Cretan incident developed into a Greco–Turkish war in April; Murray's old pupil, H. N. Brailsford, went off to fight on the Greek side, consulting Murray first and borrowing the revolver with which he had armed himself for the Lebanon in 1888.[40] Murray himself, in spite of ill health, thought about the possibility of following his pupil to the scene of action. He wrote about it to William Archer: 'I think of making my janitor, who is an old soldier, come to Greece as a volunteer. It is humiliating to think what an incredibly bad soldier one would make, apart from the possibility or probability of cowardice.'[41] Such thoughts were probably not very much more realistic than Murray's plans for suicide as a schoolboy. In any case they were soon overshadowed by the looming storm-clouds in South Africa, which portended a new crisis both for the Imperialist idea and for the cohesion of the Liberal Party.

CHAPTER VI

Leaves Glasgow: Politics and the Boer War

1. The growing family — strains on Lady Mary.
2. Murray's health leads to resignation from Glasgow.
3. Move to Barford Surrey — political journalism — 'pro-Boer' radicalism.
4. Post-war political affiliations.

1

THE first three children were born in Glasgow, Rosalind in October 1890, Denis in March 1892, and Agnes in June 1894. Lady Mary's own health was none too good. After Rosalind's birth at the Howard's London house in Palace Green, Lady Mary was not considered well enough to return to Glasgow till January 1891. In 1894 after Agnes's birth she wrote that her nerves were all in pieces and she 'couldn't stop crying'.

The Murrays, in accordance with upper-class practice of the time, had in fact little to do with the direct care of their children in their early years. Each child had its own nurse and there was a big staff to support the nurseries. It was an 'event' when Murray took the two-and-a-half-year-old Rosalind for a walk. The children were all sent to boarding schools at a very early age except for Rosalind, whose health was a cause of worry till she was 18. When Murray was in Greece in 1894, Lady Mary was seeing Rosalind through diphtheria (luckily mild). In 1897 Rosalind had pneumonia and afterwards it was considered better for her health that she should live abroad. During the next seven years she spent long periods in Italy or Switzerland in charge of 'Bombie' (Miss José Blomfield), and one or other of her parents visited her regularly. To a modern mind this raises many questions — was it really better for the child to have such long separations from her parents and to be left so much of the time with no doubt devoted attendants but still people of relatively little education?

Apart from worries about her own health and that of her husband and Rosalind, Lady Mary took a large share of the burden of attending on Lady Carlisle. During the nineties the Carlisle marriage was breaking up and Lady Carlisle, not surprisingly, was both difficult and unwell. She was seriously ill in 1892. In 1893 she was well enough to accompany Lady Mary to Italy (when she went to meet Murray on his return from his world voyage), but once there, ill enough to require her daughter's full attention, which must have somewhat blighted the longed-for reunion. In 1896 Lady Carlisle thought she was dying and insisted on having Lady Mary continuously at her side. Murray was left in Glasgow in charge of the children, but Lady Mary wrote to him that he was only expected 'to say "good morning" and then see the children for half an hour in the evening' so as not to interfere with his work.

Apart from nursing her mother, Lady Mary was expected to play a full part in the 'Carlisle Causes', speaking in London and elsewhere at Women's Liberal and Temperance meetings. She pursued these interests also in Glasgow, and served on a hospital committee there. When Murray went on separate holidays with his friends (which his wife encouraged him to do) he was at least 'away from it all', though clearly he spent much of these times working intensively. The equivalent separate holiday for Lady Mary would be spent at Naworth or Castle Howard under the dominance of her mother, and, much as she loved her mother and her old homes, such holidays cannot have been altogether restful and refreshing. The same was true of the joint holidays spent at the Carlisle castles, but in 1895 they managed a six-week family holiday at Sheringham.

Neither of the Murrays spared themselves in their work or their duties and it is understandable that the Glasgow years were years of strain for them both which told upon their health. By the spring of 1898 the Murrays had made up their mind to leave Glasgow the following March, and in September Murray informed the University of his decision.

2

Murray held his Professorship in Glasgow for rather less than ten years. His retirement from the post in March 1899 was undoubtedly due to ill health. His record of illness and absence over his near-decade at Glasgow was indeed deplorable, and only the fact that he was a brilliant teacher would have induced the University authorities to keep him on in spite of it. The high points of Murray's career as an invalid are noted below.

There was always a list of minor ailments. Writing to his mother early in 1891, shortly before her death, Murray says: 'My letters lately would form a manual of Pathology. Scrivener's palsy has made

way for an abscess under a favourite double tooth.'[1] By the autumn
things were more serious. In September 1891 Murray received
treatment at Matlock Spa (waters and massage) for 'exhaustion of
the system' and especially of the liver. The doctors there prescribed
a voyage round the world as essential for Murray, if he was not to
become a permanent invalid.[2] From October 1892 to February
1893 he was absent on this voyage to Australia which involved
him in two terms' absence from Glasgow. The private diary which
he kept for the latter part of this time (a fascinating document in
many other ways) records plenty of sea-sickness, sleeplessness and
a general sense that he was 'not very well'.[3] However the sea-voyage
seems to have set him up for the next eighteen months. Then in
October 1894 Murray consulted Farquhar Buzzard, a rising young
London specialist, who seems to have given some common-sense
advice — less work, routine jobs only, plenty of food, and some wine;
Burgundy might be constipating, so a half-bottle of Montilla sherry
should be taken at dinner. The main trouble, Buzzard thought, was
neurasthenia and had nothing to do with digestion. If Murray were
to resign from Glasgow, which he had thought of doing, he would
regret it for ever after. Lady Mary was very sorry about the sherry,
but 'if it cannot be helped, it must be endured'.[4] But by the end
of the year he was climbing in Switzerland where he first met
A. W. Verrall and his family. Again there was an interval, this time
of over two years, during which Murray suffered from nothing more
serious than sore throats and hay fever.

Then in spring 1897, after much hard work on the *History of
Ancient Greek Literature*, Murray wrote of himself as once more
'almost broken down in health'.[5] At the beginning of May he had
to undergo an operation in London for a cyst on the eye. Later
he decided to abandon the Glasgow summer session, and retired
to a cottage at Kincraig on Speyside. This time he earned only
a short respite from ill health. By mid-March 1898, he had been sent
to London to stay for six weeks at the private nursing home of a
Dr Eccles in Hertford Street. Eccles's cure was designed 'to keep
up oxidisation and combustion and prevent auto-intoxication'.
This reflects the fashionable medical doctrine of the time that the
whole organism could be poisoned by constipation.[6] The treatment
involved rest, massage, and dieting, to put his liver into proper order.
Murray put on some weight (the former 'heavy forward' of the
Merchant Taylors' Rugby team weighed less than ten stone when
he went into the nursing home), but he had no confidence in the
cure. 'If it does me any good, it will be a bona fide cure with no

faith-healing in it; for at present I really have not the faintest anticipation of any result.'[7] Moreover Murray's nerves were not soothed when he found Eccles to be boastful, obscene, and anti-feminist. The irritation was mutual:

I annoyed him last night by expressing the opinion that fornication was bad for the character. I do not generally express opinions to him, but just pray silently for him to go away or say something interesting . . . I do not quite like the idea of sending a woman to be treated by him, though I dare say that his actual conduct is blameless.[8]

A week or so later Eccles caused a relapse by talking politics to his patient, glorifying the Jameson Raid and Rhodes, and

railing angrily at the equalisation of rates, and at his having to contribute to the maintenance of the poor of Whitechapel. I was so angry that I could hardly eat and had a vile night . . . To my astonishment he began again about all the same subjects early this morning . . . singing the praises of what he called 'Brutality'. I had to speak rather curtly, asking him to discontinue the conversation.[9]

It is hard to feel that Dr Eccles's nursing home provided good value for money. The aftercare recommended, and duly undertaken by Murray, was a strenuous bicycle tour in France, during which he gained an idea of the depth of anti-Semitic feeling aroused by the Dreyfus case, and illustrated by the writings of what he called 'the scholiasts of the W.C.s'.[10] However, in this summer his teeth 'were breaking constantly' and he suffered from his usual hay fever. In October he was in bed again with a sore throat, reluctantly taking two tablespoons of 'Pork wine' for it four times a day.[11]

This brief record takes account only of Murray's most conspicuous periods under special medical treatment. His correspondence at such times, especially with his wife, reads like the diary of a confirmed hypochondriac; and she could usually retaliate with an equally detailed record of her own ailments or of those of their children, especially Rosalind. Murray's exchange of letters with his great friend, A. C. Bradley, also illustrates, in Bradley even more than in Murray, a constant preoccupation with ill health and particularly with dyspepsia.[12]

In spite of the wealth of information given about symptoms it is hard indeed without expertise in medical history to divine what was the basic trouble with Murray's health. As regards intellectual activity, Murray plainly had little idea of relaxation. He could indeed have been criticized for reckless dissipation of mental energy.

Moreover his family relations, not least when he had to soothe alternately or simultaneously Lady Mary and her mother, involved a high level of continued tension throughout his Glasgow years. He was also something of a fanatic for physical exercise. His correspondence records not only a concern for improving sports facilities at Glasgow University, but also a growing addiction to golf, occasional games of (squash) 'rackets', strenuous bicycle tours with William Archer and others, and holidays in Switzerland which included some unguided climbing. There was also the rugged travel programme undertaken during his stay in Greece in spring 1894.

Murray did not either build up or undermine his health in these years by a particular diet. He was indeed a teetotaller, so far as doctors would permit him to be so; but any statements by Murray in old age about his constant vegetarianism must be treated with caution. He ate eggs and bacon during his voyage round the world in 1892–3.[13] The sufferings of the paschal lambs in Greece (April 1894) induced in him a 'loathing for flesh and fowl';[14] but he could report to William Archer in 1895 that, although for six weeks at Sheringham he and Lady Mary had practised vegetarianism, on moving on to Castle Howard he had 'taken to carrion again' and was on the whole better.[15] At least it is clear that, whether vegetarian or not, Murray was much preoccupied at this period with his diet.

Murray himself often longed to get away from the routine and hurry of Glasgow. A first attempt was made by New College, Oxford, to lure him back there on grounds of ill health as early as 1890.[16] This he refused without hesitation, but by the time that he was on his voyage to Australia in 1892, he was beginning to have occasional visions of getting back to his own University. He had been reading with admiration Mrs Humphry Ward's then famous novel about an unorthodox Christian clergyman, Robert Elsmere, with its portraits (too recognizable in Murray's view) and he wrote to Lady Mary:

. . . the book awakes in me a great longing for Oxford. I wonder if you and I would do as good work as at Glasgow. On the whole I do not think there is the least reason to wish for a change . . . it is merely a passing mood that I tell you of. The intense quiet intellectual life, and the delight of coaching undergraduates come strongly over me, here out in the noisy wilds of a big ship off Cocos Island.[17]

A year after Murray's return he was again thinking seriously of Oxford. He drafted (but did not send) a letter asking Robinson Ellis to inform him if there was ever a vacancy for a teaching Fellow. At Glasgow, he found that he could not 'turn out scholars'. 'He could raise the standard and keep the teaching efficient, but that was at the expense of all the time and health he would have liked to spend on something a little more congenial.'[18]

It was in September 1898 that Murray officially informed the Glasgow authorities of his intention to resign. He had made up his mind to leave several weeks earlier, for the sake of his family's health as well as of his own, and had been house-hunting in Surrey during the summer.

The formalities of resignation were not without their embarrassing moments, however. He had no private income, and was giving up a job worth £1,350 per annum; even though Lady Mary had quite substantial means and there were frequent and large gifts from Lady Carlisle, he needed a pension, at least temporarily, on retirement; and for this he had to petition the Court of Glasgow University. He explained to the Principal his decision to do so, in a letter of great dignity:

I think it highly improbable that I am really 'laid aside' for the rest of my life, though I may never again be capable of carrying on the arduous, insistent duties of a Chair like that which I resign. I do certainly hope after some 3 or 4 years, to find some similar work and sufficient health to throw myself into it.[19]

He stated further his intentions to forgo any pension from Glasgow, as soon as he found other lucrative employment. Murray then discovered that his medical consultant refused to sign the certificate required by the Court as a basis for its decision—this in spite of full consultation two months before. Two other doctors, who were members of the Court, urged Murray strongly to withdraw his decision to resign, one of them, Dr McVail, writing severely on the subject. Bradley and no doubt other friends were indignant, but Murray was left with the alternatives of getting a new certificate from a London specialist, or withdrawing his request for a pension. He chose the latter course.[20]

Unfortunately the doctors' opinions are not directly recorded, only reported by the Secretary of the Court in a letter to Murray. We do not know therefore whether they found him fully fit. They are unlikely to have regarded him as a malingerer, though possibly they thought he was hypochondriac and that he should be able to pull out of it.

3

Already in June 1898 when Murray returned from his prescribed cycling tour in France he had set about looking for a house in the Farnham-Hindhead district. Murray's guide was the composer, Ralph Vaughan Williams,[21] introduced by his brother-in-law, Herbert Fisher. The Murrays settled temporarily at Whitmead Mill, near Farnham, from where Lady Mary conducted further explorations in person. Late in August they had decided that Barford, in the village of Churt, met their requirements better than any other house they had seen.

Murray did not find Barford very prepossessing. In October 1898 he wrote to Archer that it reminded him of Pope's lines:

> That to be hated needs but to be seen,
> Yet seen too oft, the aspect of his face
> We first endure, then pity, then embrace.

He added, with only moderate accuracy, that Churt was the Russian word for the Devil.[22] However, the Murrays soon set about the formalities of purchase. The purchase price, £4,000, was given to them by Lady Carlisle, who later sent them a further £2,000.[23] In November 1898 the purchase was concluded, and in January 1899 Lady Mary was staying at Barford before taking Rosalind (suspected of tuberculosis) to Alassio.

During the summer of 1899 the Murrays moved their furniture and books into Barford, where a good deal of structural adaptation was required. It was a difficult and exhausting move, and almost the entire brunt of it fell on Lady Mary. Murray himself at the end of the Glasgow term went to join Rosalind at Montreux and then was busy in London, mainly with his political plans. It was not immediately necessary for him to earn his living, even though he had forfeited a large income when he resigned his post at Glasgow. However, economically his situation was not altogether satisfactory. The Murrays had to provide for three children, of whom the eldest, Rosalind, was nearly 9, and there was constant and considerable expense on doctors and sojourns abroad. Psychologically too it was impossible for Murray, even in doubtful health, to resign himself to a period, much less a life, of idleness.

His thoughts first turned to politics and to political journalism, at least as soon as his health would permit. A letter of early March 1899 to Lady Carlisle shows that he contemplated standing for Parliament, and she had arranged by the autumn that he should be offered the Liberal candidature at Leeds, an important seat.[24] Not surprisingly, he hesitated. Health apart, other and more lucrative possibilities had become open to him in 1899. The weekly *Speaker* was involved in a change of control and policy that summer, and there were plans for Murray to become a regular political commentator. He started to correspond with J. L. Hammond, who wrote early in June that the new editorial board planned to start up in October.[25] Murray attended a dinner of the *Speaker* staff in July 1899, and made a speech covering mainly domestic policy. He was not impressed by their attitudes: 'Social Reform-benevolent indifference; Women-hostile indifference; temperance-utter flabbiness.'[26] Temperance was of course a vote loser.

The one thing that they accepted enthusiastically was Murray's line about 'Justice to foreign nations and the duties of Empire'. It was provisionally arranged with Hammond, whose personal views were very close to Murray's, that he should

write an article a week in the middle of the paper on any subject which I like—urging my views, for about the first 8 weeks. Then we can reconsider. My plan is, at present, to do a series of imaginary conversations or interviews with an old Radical who considers himself quite behind the times; he will really represent my own views and be a good deal in advance of the times. I shall take up all manner of questions, literary as well as political, and shall be strong on Women's causes in general.[27]

In the end Murray's health did not allow him to write regularly for the *Speaker*. He made occasional contributions under his own name (literary 'causeries' and scholarly reviews); and it emerges from his correspondence that he also wrote some 'middles', anonymous and not easily identifiable, on social and political subjects.[28]

Meanwhile the South African war had broken out after long negotiations and military manœuvring by both sides. Murray saw Milner's negotiations of the summer in the light of what he had heard from R. B. Haldane in 1898 about the need for war against the Transvaal.[29] The franchise demanded for the Uitlanders was 'a quiet and constitutional way of getting possession of the country without fighting or raiding. As soon as the "outlanders" are in a majority, they will vote for union with the British Empire.'[30] Murray agreed with this view, as put to him by Montague White, Consul-General for the Transvaal in London. Milner's despatches suggested an indefinite series of claims, each to be pressed as its predecessor was granted. Murray wrote to Lady Carlisle:

As I read the cries of 'Rule Britannia' in answer to every appeal to reason and fairness, it seemed to me like the real cry of the nation in its madness;

the people shouting seemed to express the one thing Jingoes care for—to go on conquering, ruling more and more till the crash comes and the world will not tolerate such a nation any more.[31]

Murray did not change his views as the war proceeded on its initially disastrous course, which exposed him to the charge of being 'pro-Boer'. He heard rumours for example that the Liberal Imperial Council (an extreme 'LIMP' body) were pressing to have him expelled from the party.[32] Worst of all for Murray, he found that his elder brother, Hubert, had volunteered, as commander of a New South Wales battery of artillery, to fight in South Africa, and had arrived in the Cape Colony early in 1900. Murray would have been 'less surprised had he been on the other side.'[33] Hubert had not yet embarked on the career which led him to be a famous Governor of Papua, and Murray on his visit to Australia in 1892 had noted with distress signs that he was too much attracted by strong drink and Catholicism; but he remained an object of great respect to his younger brother.[34]

Murray's position on the war, quite apart from his state of health, made it impossible for him to participate in parliamentary activity until some new radical group was formed. He therefore finally refused the offer of the Liberal candidature at South Leeds. The excuse given to Lady Carlisle was suitably ambiguous—he did not think that he could stand the strain of a contested election,[35] at this time not only disagreeable but also physically dangerous.

When Murray had recovered from the first shocks of the Boer War, he came to the conclusion that his primary career must continue to be in the teaching of Greek, or more accurately in the spreading of the message of Hellenism. This conclusion did not involve a total abandonment of politics, or of political journalism. When H. W. Massingham was ousted in November 1899 from the editorship of the *Daily Chronicle*, Murray was actively engaged in canvassing for financial support for a new journal, on which Massingham could work.[36] And he could still find means of expressing publicly his own political views. In summer 1900 a book was published entitled *Liberalism and the Empire*. This consisted of three essays, by F. W. Hirst (the main editor and organizer), J. L. Hammond, and Murray himself. His contribution 'The Exploitation of Inferior Races in Ancient and Modern Times' could be regarded as the most original and substantial of the three. In it he accepted from the start the fact and beneficial possibilities of Empire; he began with a careful statement of the imperial problem 'How is the British Empire to get its work done?', and with a quotation from Tiberius Gracchus which had a clear contemporary reference: 'Our soldiers have no ancestral shrines any more; they only fight to defend the wealth and luxury of strangers.' The main argument as regards 'Modern Times' centred on the use of Indian troops and of African labour. The troops might turn against us, and might lead us to practise more savage methods of warfare. The use of forced labour was a greater danger. Tested by three points, it might be regarded as slavery. Free men refused to do the work involved; those who did it lapsed into a state of degradation; and finally they might despair and die. The argument ended with a question: 'Is this subjection . . . to be absolute and eternal, or is there any prospect of educating them up to the point of freedom and self-government?'

A slightly later political essay was franker in its condemnation of facile patriotism. Its subject was 'National Ideals, Conscious and Unconscious', and it was first printed in the *International Journal of Ethics*, February 1901. This too is a document of its time, instinct with the bitter feelings inspired by the Boer War, which was about to enter its final and most degrading phase. Murray thought it worthwhile to have the article reprinted twenty years later, in his *Essays and Addresses* (1921), as an 'expression of the feelings of the Liberal minority during the Boer War'. Its main argument is that the professed ideals of nations are unimportant compared with the ideas which lie concealed in the instincts and unconscious mind of men, and supply nations with a mass momentum. Murray incidentally applied the same argument to the interests of classes within nations; for example, whatever explicit reasons they advanced, slave-owners resisted emancipation simply from instinct. What really stirred the average Englishman's 'central ego' was the ideal of 'his own prosperity, success and expansion'. Another characteristic feature of the world is the lack of social and moral forces to restrain the highest units of society. Within a nation, a man's private life is largely controlled by such social forces. At national and international level, there is no such control. The conduct of any nation is apt to be subhuman, and Murray implicitly compares it to that of the great tit, which, when hungry, pecks out its brother's brains, pecks at the dead body, and then sits exultant on its branch.[37] Chauvinism and expansionism are persistent and dominant forces among the nations; they are stimulated by capitalist-controlled newspapers, which depend on advertisements for their life, and misinform the public by printing mainly 'those facts which rich English people on the whole would like to be published'. Such counter-force as there is resides in those (like Murray himself) who are now 'stigmatized as Dreamers'; but their dreams may later be transformed into reality.

At the same time, in the *Positivist Review* of February 1901, Murray published an article entitled 'Intransigence',[38] reflecting even more explicitly the bitterness of the radical minority within (or no longer within) the Liberal party. He pointed out the moral dangers and political uselessness of becoming 'irreconcilable' but left his readers with the impression that there was little alternative for the man of principle. He wrote as one of the 'various groups in our own country who are known as pro-Boers'— an accurate description, he conceded, of those critics of the war (there were many others) who harboured the feeling that 'we cannot ask God to defend the right without praying for the success of the enemy'. In reading moderate criticism of British statesmen and their tactics, Murray felt that the real issue had not been touched: 'it was not more cleverness that was needed in our South African policy, but more sympathy and more sense of right and wrong; that in fact "these men are stupid because they are wicked."'

His conclusions were pessimistic:

We are a very small minority . . . the extreme wing of a thoroughly weak and beaten party. An influential section even of this Party would sooner side with our opponents than us . . . We have been living in a Fool's Paradise . . . misled by the enormous prestige which has attached to the word 'Liberal' during nearly the whole of the last century . . . [There has been] no time when the mass of the nation was genuinely and in cold blood Liberal . . . to expect a nation to be Liberal is to expect a very great deal.

Murray was shocked at the leaders rather than by the mass of the people as he found them. In May 1900 he encountered a 'Mafeking' carnival procession in London:

I was . . . prepared to be annoyed. But rather delighted. I had never before seen my fellow-creatures so brotherly and sisterly to one another. All were laughing and dancing and occasionally embracing. I was not kissed by any one . . . but if ever one ceased smiling one was tickled on the lips by a peacock's feather. . . .[39]

The only logical course for Murray at this stage was to retire from any active role in party politics. However, he had a political contribution to make as a private citizen. He was among those academics who, along with the Cadburys and Rowntrees, some prominent Liberal journalists, and some churchmen, sponsored the South African Conciliation Committee, which concentrated (in contrast to the extreme radical Stop the War Committee) on the outlines of a future settlement in South Africa. The Committee incidentally saw clearly the major European/African tension that underlay the Boer/British conflict.[40]

At the end of 1900 another committee was formed to alleviate the distress among Boer women and children caused by the policy of burning farms and concentrating the inhabitants in special camps. This was a cause taken up, after Emily Hobhouse's revelations of conditions in camps, by the Women's Liberal Federation and Lady Carlisle. Murray and his wife gave handsomely to the Boer Women and Children's Clothing Fund and their contribution of £100 was personally acknowledged by General Botha.[41] Such generous initiatives, hard to imagine in any country but Britain, helped to strengthen the foundations for a generous settlement with the Boers.

The Peace of Vereeniging was concluded in May 1902. It was followed by negotiations between the Boer generals and the Conservative Government in London. Murray met the generals in November 1902 and described to Lady Carlisle the scene at a reception for them:

they stood on the landing and we shook hands . . . A woman was gushing at them excitedly . . . I thought to myself 'How silly to say anything! . . . ' Then when I found myself in the same position, a lump came in my throat, and words came out of my mouth! I don't know what I said, but it cannot have been so imbecile as Botha's answer, 'On the contrary, it is I who am proud to meet you!'

Murray wrote to Lady Carlisle: Botha is

. . . an immense man, towering and straight as an arrow, with a face at the top of the great frame like that of a dreamy child. Very large cow-like eyes, dreaming and gentle. An almost chubby face . . . De Wet looked like himself as much as the others looked unlike themselves. Rough, hard, vivid, angular, with flashing, laughing eyes and excitable gestures . . .[42]

The Peace helped to relieve the conscience of the radicals within the Liberal Party and to heal its internal tensions.

4

After the formation of the Balfour Government in July 1902, Murray was ready for fresh political activity in the anti-Conservative cause. He was among the sponsors of a projected review to deal with domestic problems — drunkenness, housing, labour relations, women's education, the rapid increase in public expenditure, and the 'Land Question in all its bearings' — a list that looked backwards to Gladstone and forward to Lloyd George. The review was also intended to treat the 'great problem of relations between the mother country and her colonies and dependencies'. The plans for it came to nothing, but it is significant that Murray the radical allowed his name to appear in a distinguished list of sponsors that included Bryce, John Burns, and Edward Grey.[43]

He was also casting about for fresh political allies. Now that the war was over, Webb could be considered again, in spite of the support which he and many Fabians had given to it.[44] By 1902 Murray had met Bernard Shaw. Their conversation and correspondence covered politics as well as the drama and Murray became better acquainted with Fabian ideas. Some notes are preserved in his papers of an address to the Fabian Society, probably given in the second half of 1902.[45] The political essence of the talk was an attempt to convince the Fabians that on domestic issues they were more radical than Socialist. Radicals and Fabians alike believed in the futility of violent revolutionary policies; they were opposed in common to Tory government, which was in league with the Church, financiers, and the drink trade, and hostile to all but technical education. Liberalism had entirely lost its hold on the rich as a class. Murray professed to think a split more likely between the various kinds of socialists than between Fabians and radicals. They should join together in common political propaganda against 'the cause of Wealth, Force and Inertia . . . Personally I expect that in spite of Mr. Webb your party will in the end prefer the principles of Liberalism and Democracy to considerations of symmetry and convenience.'

At the same time Labour's radical wing, the Independent Labour Party, had begun to adopt Fabian tactics of collaborating with the Liberals against the Conservative Government. The ILP leader, Ramsay MacDonald, had met Murray in 1900 and invited him to 'come and discuss Greece' with a small group that included Herbert Samuel, C. P. Trevelyan, J. A. Hobson, and Graham Wallas.[46] By summer 1902, the MacDonald family were visiting Barford and discussing the position of the ILP.[47] Murray was particularly interested in their attitude to foreign and imperial affairs. He was also in close touch with J. A. Hobson, whose book on South Africa (1901) had evoked appreciative comment from him.

In summer 1902, Hobson sent to Murray the proofs of his famous book on *Imperialism* for correction on points of fact. Murray wrote to Lady Carlisle about it, as 'a strong sane statement of the Radical–Socialist anti-imperialist position . . . it misses being first-rate because he did it too rapidly, and has not collected enough instances to prove his points.'[48]

Murray's comments on the proofs are not preserved, but Hobson described them as 'most valuable, leading me in nearly all cases to some change and modification which will benefit the passage . . . I see you question my view that class government means the antagonism of nations . . .'[49]

Lenin is said to have derived from Hobson some of his doctrine about imperialism as the final stage of capitalism, and it would be ironic to find that Murray had had some indirect influence on the teachings of Vladimir Ilich.

The range of Murray's friendships prevented him from being too much bound to any party or doctrine. In 1902 he was renewing his old acquaintance with Kipling, and wrote to Hobson about the strong moral element in Kipling's conception of Empire. Hobson replied that this well illustrated his own difficulties as a propagandist against Imperialism: ' . . . if moral enthusiasm can blind to facts one who has seen some of the worst pieces of Imperialism at close quarters, how is it possible to convince or deter those for whom all the facts are glossed or falsified?'[50]

The breadth of Murray's sympathies is even more clearly illustrated by his correspondence with John Buchan, by now fully occupied, as a member of Lord Milner's 'Kindergarten' with the task of reconstruction in South Africa. In the preface to his translations from Euripides, published at the end of 1902, Murray had only just refrained from drawing an explicit parallel between the Athenian war-demagogue Cleon and British Conservative leaders. Buchan commended this restraint, emphasizing the poetry and religion so widely evoked by the idea of Empire.

Murray replied (and the words may be regarded as his considered view on the problem of Empire):

The consciousness of belonging to a very great nation with a high and peculiar task (or destiny) before it acts in two ways. First a sort of *Noblesse Oblige* ; an Athenian, or an Englishman, is bound in self-respect to be in various ways better than his neighbours, worthy of his country. This feeling I recognize frankly as existing in numbers of people of the Rhodes or Kipling type, and, though it often seems to me . . . rather blatant and lacking in self-criticism, I respect it and think it a powerful instrument for good. Secondly, there is a perversion of this. 'An Englishman never tells a lie' and 'an Englishman always likes fair play' and such like principles, which are really statements of ideals, are taken as statements of fact. The majority of men easily get to think that their countrymen are really ideal Englishmen

and have all the ideal virtues, and that foreigners are inferior creatures
... Thirdly, I cannot help seeing in modern England what certainly existed
in Athens, a dangerous extension of this: an argument that because
Englishmen are superior creatures . . . therefore they should be allowed a
little extra latitude. This last is very dangerous.[51]

Murray saw the other side of big questions and relied too much
on persuasive reason to have succeeded easily in politics. He remained
also too much of a Puritan, as is well illustrated by his lecture to
the Fabians:

I do not for an instant believe that the happier life which Socialism aims
at will be attained by any slackening of the grip in which civilised man is
accustomed to hold himself, by any loosening of self-control. There is a
reaction against Puritanism at present in this country . . . And in so far as
this reaction is based on a desire for freedom, for understanding and for
enjoyment, it is probably justified . . . But I cannot imagine a life that will
be able to dispense with the Puritan virtues—to get on without courage,
without fortitude, without the power of sacrifice. And I think that
observation shows that those persons who are really capable of attaining
a great joy—poets, artists, discoverers, or what one roughly calls heroes,
are people who can and do renounce a vast quantity of smaller and
commoner things for the sake of their great thing.[52]

A heroic creed, and one by which Murray stood throughout his
long life, but deficient in common sympathy, and certainly no
vote-catcher!

CHAPTER VII

The Literary Man

1. *Carlyon Sahib* staged 1899 — reactions.
2. *Andromache* rejected by big theatres — put on by Stage Society 1901.
3. Murray's own early poetry — starts on verse translations of Greek dramatists.

1

BY 1900 Murray had decided to abandon party politics for the mean time. He wrote to Lady Carlisle telling her of his intention to devote himself now to a large and full history of Greek literature:

Greece has a profound and permanent message to mankind, a message quite untouched by 'supernaturalism' and revealed religions; it is human rational and progressive, and affects not Art only but the whole of life. I think it possible that I may be the most suitable person to interpret Greek poetry as Morley interpreted the French Encyclopaedists. . . . The work as I conceive it might be something really great if carried out by a person with great powers. I think it unlikely *in the extreme* that I could achieve any result of that sort — anything comparable to what Ruskin or Renan might have made of the subject. But I think it also very unlikely that I should completely fail . . . I *have* got faith and a message; they may be mistaken or vulgar or valueless, but they are there, and I want to speak them out.[1]

Morley to whom he had written in the same vein encouraged him to abandon politics for literature in the prevailing political atmosphere.

I won't pretend to say anything about your literary scheme, except that it interests me profoundly. But it deserves most ample consideration and discussion. Be, I pray you, like Milton, 'long in choosing'.

   In the general policy of such a proceeding, I am wholly with you. I mean in the transfer of interest and labour to literature. This is the field that needs working now, even for the advantage of politics and social causes. The *character* of the country is the most important thing now in issue.[2]

Murray also had to meet his commitment to complete the new edition of the Greek text of Euripides for the Oxford University Press, in order to maintain his reputation as a scholar. By the end of summer

1899 he was also quite far committed to George Allen & Unwin to complete his translations of plays by Euripides and Aristophanes, a task which he could reasonably regard as propaganda for the gospel of Hellenism.

However, in 1899 Murray had quite another aspiration—to be an original dramatist. Here was a will-o'-the-wisp which had long danced before his eyes—perhaps since his days as a schoolboy actor at Merchant Taylors'. Molly Hamilton recorded fifty years on how Murray talked her out of a passion to go on the stage, saying (with perhaps more tact than accuracy) that he had had the same dream before deciding that he would be better employed in writing plays.[3] Early in 1899 he may have thought that the dream of becoming a dramatist was not an *ignis fatuus*. He had always been much interested in the theatre. The family connection with W. S. Gilbert had no doubt roused his interest, and he was probably a regular play-goer from an early age. One of his former secretaries, Mrs Fletcher, writes of a set of lectures which he prepared between early 1938 and summer 1940 on nineteenth-century Theatre. 'It was a brilliant set of talks, with great knowledge and a light touch. I remember especially a hilarious description of, and reading from "The Italian Straw Hat".'[4]

In the 1890s Ibsen's plays, championed by Bernard Shaw and William Archer, were being presented in London by the impresario Charles Carrington and his actress wife, Janet Achurch. Ibsen was a hero at Castle Howard,[5] where his portraits of women frustrated by social conventions were enthusiastically received, and Murray did his best to popularize him in Glasgow. 'I think', he wrote to Lady Carlisle 'that Ibsen rather spoils one for appreciating ordinary plays' (he was contrasting the social purpose of Ibsen with the frivolities of Molière's *Fourberies de Scapin*!)[6]

It was certainly Ibsen who provided the inspiration for Murray's first original play, *Carlyon Sahib*. He had worked at the first draft of this on his recuperative voyage to Australia and New Zealand in 1892–3, and wrote much to his wife about the progress of the play. It was a sombre and rather melodramatic study of how the passion for power, even if a man exercises it for noble ends, may come to dominate and destroy his human instincts. The plot starts at the house in England of Sir David Carlyon, the retired Governor of an Indian province. His devoted daughter Vera, a student of ophthalmology, is being courted by Adene, a young philologist with radical convictions. He is planning to go out to India, to Carlyon's old province, partly to further his academic studies, partly to expose any misdeeds of his countrymen of which he may learn. Vera finds out by personal inspection that he is suffering from a disease of the eye, indicative of a cerebral tumour. In Act II, her diagnosis is confirmed by a German specialist, who warns Vera against telling Adene of the nature of his disease. However Carlyon has now learned of Adene's political intentions. He himself had poisoned some wells in order to spread cholera among hostile natives, and is anxious to keep Adene back. He tells Vera some of the truth. She warns Adene of the state of his eye, but without effect.

Act III finds Adene in India. He has found Carlyon's old servant, Selim (thought by his master to be dead), and is hot on Carlyon's trail. Carlyon fears the worst, and has sent out Vera to 'nurse' Adene by methods which will involve killing him. In Act IV Carlyon, back in India, learns that Adene is still alive, and is also being cured. Vera will not raise a finger against him. Selim tries to revenge himself by stabbing Carlyon with a poisoned dagger. Carlyon wrests it from him and kills him, but scratches himself in the process and dies instantaneously on the stage. Tableau.

From this bald summary, the reader (who has been spared at least one sub-plot) may conclude that Murray never had in him the makings of a dramatist. This judgement would be unjust. The complicated and melodramatic plot of *Carlyon* ran true to the dramatic traditions of its time, and it aroused plenty of interest in theatrical circles. In summer 1893 Murray began to correspond with possible producers. Janet Achurch expressed a lively interest and it was submitted to Henry Irving and Frank Benson among other possible producers.

Early in 1895 Carrington showed the text to the influential dramatic critic, William Archer, who was much interested. He described it to his brother Charles as 'a curiously grim and powerful but unskilful piece of work . . . the most original and powerful play I have ever come across in manuscript, to my recollection; and I should very much like to see it brought to perfection.'[7] Murray immediately entered into correspondence with Archer, and asked him for advice. Archer in fact rewrote part of the first act, and Murray with the most generous intentions, but rather naïvely, suggested that the play should be presented as their joint effort. Archer, while free with his advice on stagecraft, was anxious, in his primary capacity as dramatic critic, that his contribution to the finished play should not become publicly known.[8]

This was the beginning of a more general interchange of views, which developed into a close personal friendship between the two men. Archer was able to introduce Murray to producers, actors, actresses, and critics. He himself profited from Murray's knowledge of the Greek drama and of classical literature. Each delighted in the other's company, and they went on strenuous bicycling tours together in France, East Anglia, and Yorkshire.

One of Archer's long-standing plans was to launch a company, the *New Century Theatre*, for the commercial performance of serious plays, new and old, with particular reference to Ibsen and Shaw. Another moving spirit in this scheme was Elizabeth Robins, the actress-novelist, with whom Murray was in correspondence.[9] Archer hoped that the New Century would embark on its first season in autumn 1898, and that *Carlyon* would form part of its programme. At the beginning of 1898, Murray (when still at Glasgow) promised to subscribe £1,000 immediately to the New Century, and £400 annually, if he kept his professorial job (this was shortly before he entered Dr Eccles's London clinic for treatment). Archer told him not to be so 'millionairish', to which Murray replied in his professorial persona 'you forget how much I economise on string, bootlaces and soap'.[10]

By December 1898 the New Century Theatre's season had been indefinitely postponed. However, unexpected success now appeared to be round the corner. Early in 1899 the text of *Carlyon* reached the most famous British actress of the time, Mrs Patrick (Stella) Campbell. She wrote to Murray on 27 March that she was delighted with the play (in which she was to play the part of Vera Carlyon), and would like to hold the entire rights for eighteen months and take five per cent of the gross receipts wherever it was played.[11] By the end of April, rehearsals were due to start, and Murray (in Switzerland with Rosalind) was busy with changes in the text. It was thus left to Lady Mary to mediate between author and principal actress. This was an interesting conjunction of two powerful personalities. Lady Mary thought Mrs Campbell was far too exacting in her demands for changes in the text of *Carlyon*; she saw Mrs Campbell's beauty, and considered that it must be attractive to men, but was not amused when 'Mrs. Pat' said 'rather under her breath that "you were a darling man"' and thought she behaved 'like a foolish child'. Flattery of Lady Mary's schoolgirl complexion did not mollify her.[12]

Murray himself never seems to have been much affected by Mrs Campbell's charm. A little later Lady Mary, after a heart-to-heart talk with 'Mrs. Pat', came away 'her sworn friend'.[13] Murray's own verdict (to Archer) was that he liked her a good deal, and found her 'perfectly frank and kindly, though frantically nervous.'[14]

Carlyon was produced at the Kennington Theatre on 18 June 1899. Murray had returned to England in time to be present at rehearsals, which caused him a good deal of pain, particularly when 'Patricia did not know her lines and refrained from acting most of the time'.[15] In a letter to Rosalind, Murray dwelt on the lighter side:

the chief man who ought to act in it has got ill. He is a sort of bloodthirsty giant in the play, and in real life he has to be laid on a sofa and fed with soup—not a bit like a giant . . .

Another character had to scream at a particular place in the story.

So she stopped me yesterday and said: 'Please, Professor Murray, about my scream, do you think this would do?' Then she leaned back and gave a wild squeal that nearly knocked me down. I said I thought it was a very nice scream, because if I had said that I did not like it, she would have gone on screaming till I said it was right.[16]

Things went better on the first night. However, Murray described the first performance to Archer as 'the most trying nervous ordeal I have ever been through. I feel rather shattered still, and have not mustered courage to go back.'[17]

The play was a failure and was taken off after a fortnight's run. In the explosive summer of 1899, while Milner's negotiations over the Transvaal were in progress, *Carlyon* was predictably regarded as an attack on British imperial policy. John Maynard, who had seen an early draft in 1895, criticized its anti-ICS tone: 'it appears calculated to revive the antiquated notion of the Anglo-Indian official as an unscrupulous Titan wading through seas of blood.'[18] The same thought had helped to frighten off the famous actor-manager, Forbes Robertson, to whom it was later submitted. Inevitably many newspapers and periodicals condemned Murray's play. *The Times* even urged its readers to attend a performance of *Carlyon* in order to demonstrate against its anti-imperial tone.[19] In the preface to the reading edition of it, published by Heinemann early in 1900, Murray put up a spirited but naïve defence of himself:

The play never had the ghost of a glimmer of a conscious political allusion in it; nor did it occur to me . . . that any sane person would suppose that I wished to attack the I.C.S. The plays on my bookshelves teem with villains of the most diverse professions . . . I do not think that I should chafe at the appearance of a villainous Professor of Greek.

Murray had certainly not scored a triumphant success as a dramatist, but there were consolations. Princess Louise, a friend of the Carlisles, attended the first night and spoke kindly to Murray, who afterwards wrote to Archer that she would have been a very nice woman, 'if born into decent society'.[20] More important, there were words of praise from discerning critics. Archer wrote a very full and favourable review in the *Manchester Guardian* though he prophesied privately that Murray would be written off as an Ibsenite. Mrs Campbell did much better than he had expected—'it's the most dramatic piece of work she's ever done'—and by and large he was delighted with how the play had turned out.[21]

Other critics were mixed, but in a personal letter J. M. Barrie, who raised a number of critical objections, also found that 'If it is your first play, as I suppose, it is the best acting play for a first that I ever saw.'[22] Murray wrote to Archer 'I think it is good for me to have had the thing produced, even as a failure.'[23]

He had been introduced to the working world of the theatre; it had taken him seriously and he had been fascinated by it. The failure of the production was certainly not spectacular enough to make him give up original work for the theatre.

2

While negotiations about the staging of *Carlyon Sahib* dragged on, Murray had begun work on other plays. In some cases no more than the title or a leading idea is known (for instance 'The Duke of Africa', or a 'Rousseau-esque comedy').[24] Serious work may never have started on these, but two other complete dramatic texts are preserved. The first, *Leaves of the Sibyl*, is a tragedy, which Archer turned down flatly in 1895, for understandable reasons. It is as melodramatic as *Carlyon*, and the main theme is less clear. There is incidental interest at certain points. A scene about lock-out action at a factory illustrates Murray's social preoccupations. One of the characters uses a planchette for sinister purposes—the first evidence of Murray's interest in psychical research. And there is a portrait of an Australian politician, drawn from memory:

Sir Simon Drage . . . is a genuine attempt at bringing out a type which I remember among old friends of my father at Sydney—many of them Irish: courtly, ceremonious, full of 'Sir' and 'Madam', swearing smoothly—without emotion, and charged with the most outspoken *ancien régime* contempt for people they disliked, or thought beneath them. 'Get along, Sir. Go to the Devil, Sir. You're a Vagabond,' is a sentence I actually heard said, and said with an unruffled smoothness of contempt.[25]

The second unperformed play is *Mithia*, a comedy designed for Mrs Campbell, who finally found the main character too 'shadowy' and the general effect 'a little boneless'.[26] Again there are points of incidental interest about it. The principal figure, by no means heroic, is a British journalist sent to cover the Cretan revolt against the Turks in 1897; Mithia herself is a sort of resistance heroine; and the villain is the proprietor of a newspaper, who for financial reasons calls off its support for the revolt.[27]

A more substantial item in Murray's dramatic career was his tragedy *Andromache*, an attempt to translate Greek saga material into terms suitable for the modern theatre. This was eventually produced and published, with little success. Its importance today is indirect. The genesis of *Andromache* led to some extremely interesting correspondence between Murray and Archer; and its ultimate failure was one of the main factors which turned Murray back to the idea of producing translations of original Greek drama.

The Preface to the printed edition of *Andromache* (1900) took the form of an Open Letter to Archer, which began: 'The germ of this play sprang into existence on a certain April day in 1896 which you and I spent chiefly in dragging our reluctant bicycles up the great hills that surround Rievaulx Abbey.' In November 1896 Archer opened correspondence with Murray on the idea, which they had discussed, of adapting classical themes to the modern stage. The intention was,

as it were, to take the wigs and high-heeled shoes of the people in *Andromache*, make them Greek in costume — *allgemeinlich* in speech, and construct the play according to the more vivid of *mouvementés* methods of modern drama.[28]

Murray replied,

About re-writing Greek plays, it is an idea that has often been in my mind. I think there are two possible ways. One, to take the saga as your basis and treat it in a Sophoclean spirit, with more liveliness and use of the freer conventions and greater resources of the modern stage. It would have to be in verse, I think. The other way would be to go a step beyond Euripides; to take the real facts and characters and situations that are implied in a story like that of the Andromache or the Agamemnon — every bit of which might in a sense have really happened, and treat it realistically . . . in prose. I have often wished to try this.[29]

Some time elapsed before Murray could pursue his ideas. It was September 1897 before he wrote again to Archer about his own neo-classical drama:

Snails, but I will forthwith write an Andromache! The N[ew] C[entury] T[heatre] can act it hereafter for the benefit of my widow . . . Prose, modern though simple methods, no pomp and circumstance, naive and rather severe psychology . . .'[30]

Thereafter things moved briskly. Murray first sent Archer a synopsis of his proposed play, to which Archer replied by sending a copy of Racine's *Andromaque*. Murray stuck to Greek models, mainly Euripides, in his treatment of the story. Andromache, widow of Trojan Hector, is shown as the concubine of Pyrrhus, Achilles' son, at his barbarous court in northern Greece. Bitter experience has taught her a maturity and humanity quite beyond the grasp of Pyrrhus himself, and of Agamemnon's son, Orestes, who arrives to kill Pyrrhus and abduct his wife, Hermione.

Murray's first draft of the complete play followed on 21 September: 'There is not that perfect finish which is observable in work on which great authors spend longer time, some, I believe, as much as a fortnight.'[31] The draft, like the play in its final form, was in prose, and Archer questioned whether verse would not be more appropriate. Murray replied in words which look odd in the light of his future practice:

As to verse, I have thought and thought. I could write blank verse of an 'exquisite' kind, like an imitation of Tennyson or Swinburne (when I say 'I can', I mean that my stomach does not refuse) but I cannot make anything of dialogue in metre. Either it becomes quasi-lyrical, as in Orestes' songs in Act II, or else it is fustian, i.e. it is original prose cut into lengths . . . Again . . . I do not really like verse on the stage.[32]

By mid-October Murray was working on the Preface and was writing to Archer about the limitations of the subject-matter of Greek Tragedy, and the advantages which these limitations entailed for the Greek dramatists.[33] He starts with the advantages of Saga as a source for tragedy. It was rich and interesting and meant to be true. The dramatist could not deviate too far from the given stories, and this meant that audiences did not have to worry about probabilities. Then the Saga characters needed no careful introduction, but were still highly dramatic—simple well-marked personalities; primitive in a way, but with plenty of room for psychological development, and also 'articulate and full of high and delicate sensitivity—with a power of seeing and suffering . . . elsewhere associated with very advanced and complex stages of society.'

Murray admits the objection that such characters will not be familiar to London audiences, and weakens the force of his previous argument by saying, on the authority of Aristotle, that the Athenians themselves had little knowledge of the more obscure myths. For

Londoners and Athenians alike 'a very faint glimmer of something like knowledge in the minds of a tenth part of the audience gives confidence to the rest and makes the thing go.'

Murray admits to one major deviation from the original Greek versions, in that his Pyrrhus was killed in Phthia, not in Delphi:

I feel that the Gallery would be justified if it rose and hissed at such a barefaced falsification of notorious fact. If they do, I hope that Pyrrhus will have the presence of mind to revive unexpectedly and challenge Orestes to meet him again at Delphi.

Finally Murray owns that such archaeological conscience as he has may make him seem pedantic; however, his period is 'not any particular century . . . it is vaguely, and in the Saga sense, the Heroic Age.'

Archer was not too hopeful about the finished product. The style, he thought, read like a translation; the modern audience knew too little of the Greek Saga setting (should there be a narrative prologue?), and it was very hard to combine anthropology with tragedy.[34] Murray went his own way, and the finished piece was read aloud to a family house party at Naworth on New Year's Eve, 1897. Archer and Elizabeth Robins had hoped to include it, along with *Carlyon*, in the repertory of their New Century Theatre. When its season had to be postponed, *Andromache* went the rounds of various managers (including Mrs Tree and Forbes Robertson) without success. By the end of January 1901 Murray reckoned that the 'list of distinguished refusals' was complete.[35] Mrs Campbell expressed interest in the principal role, but made conditions which proved impracticable.[36] The best that could be done was a production by the Stage Society in February, with Edyth Olive in the title part. The preliminaries were as usual troublesome. Murray wrote to Archer:

Do you remember the beautiful words of the song of Deborah? Curse ye the Stage Society, saith the Angel of the Lord, Yea, curse ye bitterly the Dramatic Manager thereof. For he will not read the play, that he produces; he is blowed if he will even read the Dramatis Personae and the directions for Scenery. For he believes that Pylades is the chief part in Andromache, and he believes that an Old Palace front will do for all the scenery. At least, saith the Lord, he did until yesterday, when he was informed otherwise.[37]

The play was produced by the Stage Society on 24 February 1901, and a few performances were given later at the Garrick Theatre. The production was under-rehearsed and inadequate. However, the play (and even more the book of the play), published soon afterwards by Heinemann, had a certain *succès d'estime*. Murray received various letters from friends who saw or read it. A. E. Housman found it 'very interesting, very unlike anything one could have anticipated, and the end of it really moving. The piece of verse on p. 70 [Orestes' improvised ballad] is so good that I wish you would write more.'[38]

More important to Murray as a dramatist were two successive letters from Bernard Shaw; he was scathing about the production, but wrote: 'I really did not believe that the play could have drawn as much blood as it did with Andromache inarticulate and all the other drawbacks.'[39]

There was some balm here: some also in a message received afterwards from Tolstoy (probably via Tchertkoff). Murray wrote in the preface to the third edition of *Andromache* (1931):

He sent me word that he liked it. Thrilling with pride and pleasure I tried to get more details, but only elicited that it . . . 'was the right sort of thing, and so few books now were.' This was of course most gratifying, but has always left me with the uneasy suspicion that it was the doctrine rather than the artistic merits of the play that had won the great Master's approval.

Murray as usual met failure with outward calm. He wrote his verdict to Archer:

As a book, Andromache, in prose, as it stands was worth writing, because it does give a picture of primitive Greece unlike any other that is known of, with a certain poetic and a certain 'interpretative' value. I mean that it will actually help a small number of students and others to understand Homer and the tragedians . . . as a play, I confess, it seems to me to fail. The element of realism is so impossible for the audience, and the poetry evaporates much more from its being written in prose.[40]

The implications of this passage are surely that Archer had been right all along and that, as he had put it, tragedy was not easy to combine with anthropology. Also Murray had deceived himself about the nature of his play, and this he later came to recognize. In the preface to the third edition (1931) he said that in 1901 he thought that he was writing a 'boldly realistic and Ibsenite play', but by 1914 his view had changed, and even after some revision 'in the direction of severity' the play struck him as ultra-romantic.

It is hard to read the play now without seeing in it a tract for the times, against war. Murray himself said much later that *Andromache* was sometimes taken 'by branches of the League of Nations Union, who act it, to be a post-war League of Nations play.'[41] There are some powerful dramatic effects, in particular the reaction of Andromache to the entry of her and Pyrrhus' child, Molossus, exultant at having killed his first man; and the provocative ballad of the disguised Orestes at the same court, with its refrain 'the son is falser, falser than the sire'; but the points made by Archer must operate strongly against the effect of *Andromache* on the stage.

After the failure of *Andromache* and Mrs Campbell's criticisms of *Mithia*, Murray's career as an original dramatist was at an end. There are indeed hints in his correspondence of occasional later dramatic projects.[42] The most intriguing of these is a *jeu d'esprit* typical of his correspondence with Shaw.[43] Murray describes the 'scenario of a play on the murder part of the Oedipus', along the following lines. General Gordon is known to have escaped from Khartoum, and to be wandering somewhere in Central Africa. Winston Churchill ('in love with Gordon's daughter, naturally') volunteers to find him, in face of incredible dangers. Rumours then begin to circulate that Gordon has been killed by a white man. Winston pushes an official inquiry, and it is found that the white killer was Winston himself, firing in a panic at an unidentified figure. Unfortunately there is no sign that these ideas were pursued further.

3

In Autumn 1900 Murray told Archer that he must now abandon *Mithia* and 'finish Euripides'.[44] He was working at the time on his translation of the *Bacchae*, as part of a book for George Allen & Unwin. This was to include also verse translations of Euripides' *Hippolytus* and of Aristophanes' *The Frogs*, as well as a long preface designed to present both dramatists as political thinkers, intensely aware of the dangers threatening Athenian democracy in the late fifth century BC.

Murray's verse translations had evolved naturally and gradually. He probably wrote a good deal of poetry as a young man, as is suggested by his early correspondence with Lady Carlisle. Much later he wrote to Isobel Monro (later Henderson) some revealing sentences:

I incapacitated myself from writing poetry when I was young, partly by being ashamed of it and not wanting anything I wrote to be seen, and partly by feeling too much that my real main duty was Education—which has a lot to answer for. So I would say to you, dear, do 'follow the gleam' . . .[45]

His verse translations had originally been made for practical purposes. In the course of his lectures at Glasgow he had wished to quote particular passages in Greek tragedy, and had found that existing translations would only strengthen the impression among readers or listeners that Greek drama was just part of a dreary routine imposed by an unimaginative educational Establishment on equally unimaginative or at best rebellious students. In one of his letters to Archer, Murray gave a good example of translator's illiteracy:

The situation between Andromache and Hermione is beautifully expressed in Paley's translations of the opening words of the chorus in Euripides' *Andromache*: 'I regret to hear that you are involved in an odious quarrel about a double bed.'[46]

The reaction of Murray's classes to his own original verse translations had been heartening.

Murray's use of rhyme for the translation of the unrhymed but metrically strict iambic verse of Greek tragedy was criticized from the first, and he was at considerable pains to defend it. His arguments against blank verse were various. In 1912 he wrote of his 'many experiments in blank verse', and of his decision to reject it because it normally relied on 'rich and elaborate language' with 'very little metrical ornament.'[47] In 1913 he defended his use of rhymed couplets on broader grounds:

Let us remember that it [tragedy] is at heart a religious ritual. We shall then understand . . . perhaps . . . the formal dignity of language and actions. It is verse and, like all Greek verse, unrhymed; but it is not at all like the loose go-as-you-please Elizabethan verse . . . In Greek tragic dialogue the metrical form is stiff and clear; hardly ever could a tragic line by any mistake be taken for prose; the only normal variation is not towards prose but towards a still more highly wrought musical lyric. Yet inside the stiff metrical form the language is clear, simple and direct. A similar effect can, in my opinion, only be attained in English by the use of rhyme.[48]

From 1900 onwards Murray gave readings from his new versions to friends, whose reaction was often enthusiastic. The volume of translations, containing the *Hippoplytus* and *Bacchae* of Euripides and the *Frogs* of Aristophanes, was published by George Allen & Unwin late in November 1902. For all his zeal to propagate the message of Hellenism, Murray was uneasy about publication. He wrote to Lady Carlisle: 'What shatters me, is not anxiety that Edmund Gosse and Andrew Lang should praise me, but the mere strain and pain of having taken out a bit of my heart and exposed it to shop windows.'[49] Lady Mary had something of the same feeling:

You know how I love the work—so that it seems just a little strange to me to see it all in full dress for the world—but I hope with all my heart that it will serve the propagandist purpose you wish and also let the few capable of judging know what a poet my Gipsland is.[50]

However, Murray was soon reassured. Though the book did not sell particularly well at first,[51] reviews were mostly favourable. Archer wrote in the *Morning Leader*, welcoming the translations, whatever their scholarly value, as 'substantial additions to English Literature'. He praised Murray for abandoning blank verse which

be it never so well written, is, for the English ear, saturated with associations wholly foreign to Greek tragedy . . . Mr. Murray has chosen a measure which has as yet no dramatic associations in English — the flowing rhymed pentameters, carefully emancipated from the bonds of the couplet, which Keats and William Morris borrowed from their great master, Chaucer.[52]

Archer also thought that Murray had been successful in rendering the quick artificial line–by–line dialogue of Greek tragedy (stichomythia), and outstandingly so in translating the lyrics.

There was naturally enough more caution among the learned periodicals about Murray's very unliteral way with his Greek texts; but the *Athenaeum* (14 Feb. 1903) put well the case for his style of translation:

he has produced a charming poem, much more nearly reproducing the effect of the original than a verbally faithful rendering would have done, and it is surprising to see, on a close analysis, how few of his words are really excessive.

The *Speaker*, though it detected 'touches of vague 19th century romanticism' in the choruses, divined Murray's purpose exactly. The Greeks

are to be tried by the tests which apply to modern writers . . . they are not the exclusive property of an initiated class, though they need an initiated class to interpret them. These, one guesses, are Mr. Murray's views. They will make him enemies. But they will make him friends more numerous and more ardent, who will hold that he has . . . made Euripides accessible to the English reader with a success that is astonishing.

The reviews contrast by and large very favourably (and this may have caused Murray some embarrassment) with those devoted to a volume published simultaneously in the same series, the translation of Sophocles (in rhymed couplets, after the manner of Dryden) by John Phillimore, Murray's successor in the Glasgow chair.

Murray's friends were enthusiastic, with a few reservations. Jane Harrison voiced objections, which afterwards became established, against 'that accursed rhyming measure that so easily besets you . . . and . . . lames it all with a sort of explanatory insistence and sometimes lets you down to Wordsworth at his worst.'[53]

However, the general opinion was voiced by H. A. L. Fisher (the choruses 'quite exquisite—such momentum, yet so delicate and beautiful')[54] and John Buchan ('The chorus "Could I fly into some cavern for my hiding" . . . I think easily among the most beautiful verse written for years.')[55] Even more pleasing to Murray must have been the suggestion from some friends that in these translations he had found his true *métier*. The Headmaster of Bedales wrote that Murray had achieved his general purpose: 'To give to those who can never get it for themselves a vision of the beauty and power of Greek literature; and to give encouragement and reward to those still struggling with its difficulties.'[56]

And there was a belated, important, and mixed verdict from John Maynard in India. As an ICS man still committed to the Imperial idea, he objected strongly to Murray's long political introduction, with its implicit comparison between degenerate Athenian imperialism and the British Empire of the twentieth century. However, it was also 'quite clear to me that you have found your true métier in translating Greek poetry.'[57]

CHAPTER VIII
Famous Friends

1. Shaw.
2. Kipling.
3. Russell—philosophic exchanges.
4. Visit to *I Tatti* Feb. 1903.

1

EVEN before the success of his published translations, Murray had gained something in self-confidence during the three years following his departure from Glasgow. The shadow of the Boer War had passed by. His health was gradually beginning to improve. And now that he was settled near London, he was forming friendships with some of the leading spirits of his time, who stayed from time to time within bicycling distance of Barford; Murray, when fit, was a strenuous cyclist (but by spring 1904 he had been driving a friend's car at Cambridge, and was 'strongly inclined to get a £145 Humber motor car').[1] One of Archer's favoured modern dramatists was Bernard Shaw; and the Shaws at Haslemere were quite close neighbours of the Murrays at Churt. Writing after Shaw's death in 1951, Murray said that he knew Shaw first when

I was in my early 20s and he in his thirties. We were both teetotallers, both vegetarians, both great 'world-changers', to use a recent keyword of Shaw's, but, unlike other world-changers, neither of us at all grumbly or unamiable . . .[2]

The suggestion that Murray met Shaw before 1890 is not supported by any other evidence, and is probably due to a mild failure of memory. The first of Shaw's letters to the Murrays to be preserved is addressed to Lady Mary, dated 1 September 1898 (when she had first come to stay near Farnham). In it, he teased her outrageously for her championship of temperance and Liberalism, and argues this to be in effect anti-feminist, since nothing could be worse than the lot of the wife of a man who wants drink and cannot get it.[3] Murray himself was drawn into the argument about the Liberal policy of 'Local Option' for licensing, and this was the start of a regular correspondence and friendship over half a century. He was asked periodically for advice on classical subjects, first in 1900 about *Caesar and Cleopatra*. He wrote to Archer:

I have copied out for Shaw a real receipt for treating baldness written by Cleopatra and cited in Galen, Vol. XII. It begins 'Burn four domestic mice.' I think Caesar and Cleopatra a magnificent thing in its way, but of course desperately guyed, and with its flashes of insight marred by somewhat pedantic detail on the one hand and large historical misconceptions on the other.[4]

The general point was tactfully wrapped up in a letter to Shaw of summer 1900:

If I thought great men were like your Caesar, I should like them better. I do not know if any Great Man has ever been generous or frank, Napoleon, Frederic, Cromwell and Co. seem to me to be essentially mean and untruthful — like Chamberlain, only vastly more so.

As to Cleopatra, do not you think you ought at any rate to represent a highly civilised court and society surrounding her, even if she personally was a savage?[5]

Shaw's depiction of Britannus as the eternal respectable British hypocrite also came in for some criticism. Shaw in reply claimed to have made some modifications to meet Murray's points, but stuck to his general conception both of Cleopatra and of Britannus.

The exchange continued, as between one dramatist and another. Shaw's comments on *Andromache* have already been quoted. Shortly before it was produced, Shaw's *Three Plays for Puritans* had been published. Murray wrote a long review of these for the *Speaker* of 9 February 1901, the essence of which lies in the sentence 'It would make any one angry to see such really great conceptions as those on which Caesar and Cleopatra is built treated with frivolity . . . ' The review concludes:

There is a delightful figure (which ought to be ruthlessly cut out!) in Caesar and Cleopatra, an ancient Briton, with mutton-chop whiskers, and the spirit of a Moderate County Councillor, who on certain occasions observes . . . 'O Caesar, great Caesar, if I could but persuade you to regard life seriously, as men do in my country!' I heartily echo his words, and subscribe myself BRITANNUS.[6]

Charlotte Shaw thought the review excellent, just the things that GBS ought to have said to him![7]

Murray developed his criticisms of Shaw in a later letter, written apropos of *Man and Superman*, which may conveniently be quoted here:

It makes on me, in general, the same kind of impression as *Caesar and Cleopatra*, of an extraordinarily good thing gone somehow wrong. I wonder when you will write the real thing that is in you—the thing that will not go wrong!

My main theory of what is wrong with you—for of course I keep several—is that you suffer from a lack of moral courage. This is borne out by the way you boast of your shamelessness, as a worldly man always boasts of his unworldliness. You express divers original or unpopular or odd opinions (always with a sense of your own courage, I think!), but do you ever stick to one and take the consequences? (In art, I mean; not in politics, which I do not know about). Never. You lead your admirers on and on; and then, in a sudden panic, thinking that you may be laughed at, you laugh yourself and say it was a joke, which it was not.[8]

This is the most serious of Murray's letters to Shaw, and contains much shrewd judgement. More typical, and probably more welcome to Shaw, was the sort of advice on pronunciation of Latin contained in a letter of about the same time:

'Brit. Annus' without doubt, though, if I met him, I should perhaps address him in the vocative, as 'Brit. Anne'. This is the sort of question that makes me feel the real superiority of a classical education over all others—Fancy the humiliating position you would be in, if you did meet him—no position for a creator.[9]

Meanwhile Shaw took Murray's work, whether original drama or verse translations, seriously enough. Early in 1900, Murray had begun to read his translations to select audiences. One of these, incongruously, was the Haslemere Microscope and Natural History Society—attended on this occasion by GBS, his wife, and Frank Storr. In moving a vote of thanks to Murray, Shaw said that 'he had felt, while the reading was in progress, that the Professor was reading one of his own original compositions, and being so generous as to give Euripides the credit for it.'[10]

The same idea was often repeated later, by less kindly critics. Shaw was pressing Murray to have his translations published soon, without straining after perfection. Murray pleaded not guilty to undue delay, and added: 'As to the Lues Professoria [Professor's plague], the mental disease which makes them aim at what they are pleased to call perfection, I entirely agree with you. It is largely due to timidity and partly to laziness.'[11]

Murray's friendship with Shaw survived Shaw's caricature of the Murray family in *Major Barbara* (discussed in Chapter IX), and seemed indeed to be strengthened by it. Murray adapted himself in some degree to the style of his company, and Shaw elicited from him thoughts and even language which he would not communicate or use to anyone else. When the *Oedipus Tyrannus* was produced in London in 1912, the two men exchanged notes on their Oedipodean fantasies. They were of a startling frankness, Shaw's being enclosed in an envelope marked *Private*, in case it should be intercepted by a lady secretary. Lady Mary might not have been amused at Murray's reply: 'I cannot imagine having any sense of horror at discovering that my wife was my mother or my sister.'[12]

About the same time, Murray advanced to Shaw a strange incidental justification for the classical education. In the good old days, he wrote,

When a young man felt lecherous he honestly looked up obscene passages in Latin authors or Aristophanes and revelled in them, knowing what he was doing. The modern young men and women do the same thing with Aubrey Beardsley or Anatole France . . . and say it is art.[13]

And, much later, Murray's one recorded written use of a four-letter word occurs in a letter to Shaw. He is expressing disgust at the 'snivelling obscenity' of a Noël Coward play: 'Do you know the Greek saying "Corcyra is free! Shit wherever you like!"?'[14]

Shaw indeed exercised a liberating effect on Murray, as on many others, and Murray greatly prized his friendship. Shaw on his side found plenty to admire in Murray, apart from the learning, moral earnestness, and wit displayed by 'Professor Cusins' in *Major Barbara*. He wrote in 1909 to Arthur Pinero about Murray as one who combined the 'genuine artistic anarchic character' with great learning and with important attachments in the political and social world.[15]

2

Shaw was not the only famous writer to seek guidance on classical matters from Murray. His boyhood acquaintance with Rudyard Kipling has already been mentioned. The relationship had lapsed for some years, and seemed most unlikely to be revived. The strain of harshness or cruelty in Kipling repelled Murray. He reported with some pain to Lady Mary during his voyage round the world a story which he had heard about some heartless practical jokes played by Kipling on a fellow passenger on a P. & O. ship.[16] Kipling's enthusiasm for Rhodes, the Boer War, and 'dominion over palm and pine' was also bound to repel Murray, even when combined with a high sense of the white man's burden, and the cautions of the

'Recessional'. However, in the summer of 1902, after the Peace of Vereeniging, Murray and Kipling resumed contact. The Kiplings were at Rottingdean; Murray's younger daughter, Agnes, went to stay with them there and Murray and Kipling exchanged visits.

Murray tried some target-shooting at Kipling's private rifle-range and earned a stiff shoulder. He found Kipling

. . . wonderful. Ridiculously like his books, and with a nice, quasi-Irish instinct for exaggeration. He spoke of a man in Sussex who kept buffaloes and kangaroos, and continued 'But in Hindhead, you know, simply *every day* you meet escaped kangaroos going round, frightening the farmers.'[17]

Kipling was beginning to work at this time on the historical stories for his children, afterwards published in *Puck of Pook's Hill* and *Rewards and Fairies*. He consulted Murray about the background for his centurion, Parnesius: 'What I really want, if possible, is details of the Numidian Legion, which I believe was in the South of England for some time, I think it was the 14th, but am not sure.'[18]

Murray evidently responded (his letters to Kipling are unfortunately not preserved). In the event Kipling wrote his Norman and Saxon stories before going back to the Romans; but in a letter of August 1905 he warned Murray that he would consult him shortly about 'Mithras and things'. Three months later he wrote that he had just finished the story of a young centurion on the Roman Wall and that Murray's 'confirmation about Mithras and his rites . . . had been his prop.'[19] It is interesting to know that Murray made some contribution to what must be ranked among Kipling's masterpieces.

Murray in turn sought advice from Kipling, probably on a point in the translation or production of Euripides' *Electra*. What sort of noise would Aegistheus make as he died beneath the unexpected stroke of Orestes' sword? Murray's letter is not preserved, but it made Kipling 'rock with laughter'. He replied in grisly detail about the behaviour likely to be observed in dying men, with particular reference to the 'late Mr. Aegistheus'.[20]

There is no record of subsequent contacts between Murray and Kipling.

3

Another notable figure to play an important part in Murray's life was Bertrand Russell. Russell was a cousin of Lady Mary, six years younger than her and Murray. The first communication from Russell to Murray preserved in the Murray papers is a letter of June 1900 (addressed to 'Dear Gilbert' and subscribed 'Yours ever'), in which Russell discussed Murray's chapter for *Liberalism and Empire*. His main point of substantial criticism was typically heretical—that equality for women involved the dying out of the race.[21]

In 1901 Murray's relations with Russell developed into an intimate friendship. Murray was beginning to give lectures on Greek drama, containing—indeed, mainly consisting of—readings from the translations soon to be published by George Allen & Unwin. A visit to Cambridge was planned for January 1901. This had to be put off, owing to Queen Victoria's death. Murray found that 'the feelings of the University of Cambridge are such that they could not bear to hear me so soon after the demise of the Crown, but they hope to be better by the 9th [February].'[22]

The reading, of the *Hippolytus*, took place early in February. Russell attended it, was profoundly stirred by the beauty of Murray's poetry, and described his translation as a 'new masterpiece'. He had learned by heart immediately, he said, the lyric with which Murray had ended his reading—that famous chorus which begins 'Would I fly me to some cavern for my hiding', entering a minor objection only to the expression 'bird-droves' (one of the more literal of Murray's phrases).[23]

This was enormously encouraging to Murray. In his reply he wrote:

I will not say that I feel pleased or delighted by your great enjoyment of my *Hippolytus* because my feelings are quite different from that. It is rather that your strong praise makes a sort of epoch in my life and in my way of regarding my work.

He had felt great emotion in translating the play, but had reflected that previous translators had probably felt just as strongly and failed entirely to communicate their emotion. 'That is the normal state of the case. But what seems to have happened in our case is that you have somehow or other understood and felt the whole of what I meant to convey.'[24]

This initial exchange led to a good deal of correspondence between Murray and Russell over the next four years, and particularly in 1902. Russell's first marriage was in a very precarious state, and he was in an almost constant emotional and intellectual crisis. During the summers of 1903 and 1904 he was a close neighbour of the Murrays at Churt and Tilford, and by 1905 it seemed possible that he would settle at Churt on a more permanent basis. Murray wrote to Lady Carlisle about an important pre-condition of neighbourhood:

'Bertie and I have tried to think of all the points that we may quarrell [*sic*] upon, and settle them in a definite manner.'[25] Meanwhile both he and Murray enjoyed epistolary discussion. This continued to refer in detail to Murray's translations, but also ranged widely over philosophical and moral problems. It is important as an index to Murray's general thinking in the first decade of the twentieth century. Of politics there is little mention.[26]

Each informed the other as far as possible about the progress of his work. Murray of course was only a partially trained philosopher, and nothing of a mathematician. Yet Russell sent him for comment some of the papers which were afterwards embodied in *The Principles of Mathematics*, and Murray felt bound to exercise his mind on the problems of series and order:

The part that I could best follow was the criticism of Lotze. I have often wrangled with Andrew Bradley and others about relations, and about lamp-posts being only ideas in the mind of God, and the like, and, as far as I can see, your criticism of Lotze's grounds here is quite destructive.[27]

Murray in turn kept Russell *au courant* with the progress of his classical work and with the state of his health as a limiting factor:

I have a special disease which I strongly recommend. It is clean, non-dangerous, exquisitely painful, and incapacitating. Doctors come on bicycles to see it acting, and rub their hands in interest. It is cramp in the throat . . .

[Work on the Euripides text] . . . is dreary . . . but one gets occasional delight from the beauty of the stuff in what one is working upon. It is like laboriously cleaning a very beautiful statue.[28]

In 1902 the two friends settled down to a prolonged discussion by letter of moral and ethical problems. Russell related his beliefs much less than Murray at this time to the obviously political and social aspects of life. In a letter of 3 April, he described Murray as a utilitarian *tout court*.

Towards the end of the year, Murray was much beset by nervous strain, the difficulties of family life, and fundamental doubts about his vocation. Was he to earn the epitaph of having passed his life in 'elegant leisure devoted to translating the classics'? Russell's appreciation of the *Bacchae* comforted, without wholly convincing him: 'Your letters *are* a comfort. — Many people tell me in various degrees that I do the thing well or cleverly or something, but you keep up this belief in the dignity and worth of the thing itself . . . ' Nevertheless Murray felt at this time profoundly

that rending asunder of life between the claim of common duties and that of something that seems intoxicatingly high and beautiful. I understand vividly why, and how, the majority of middle-aged Englishmen find that ideals and Beauty generally are too troublesome to live with, and the best thing is to fix your mind on your business, arm-chair, newspaper, drink and tobacco—and even those only to an un-delirious degree.[29]

The correspondence for 1902 continued at a high contemplative level. Russell aired his fury at J. W. Mackail's 'democratic' insistence that his charwoman was 'more in contact with real things than anybody else he knew'.[30] This drew from Murray one of his best letters (at his best he often resorted to a Dickensian style):

I have a feeling—rather mystical—like this; that there is, really existent, a Glory, a thing like Heaven or God, of which we can get glimpses in many different ways—music, poetry, mathematics, heroic conduct, etc., and that, while I do not insist that all Common beings for any *a priori* reason must be able to have the glimpse somehow—that is mere religion or sentiment—still I should not be surprised to learn (from an angel or Reuter's Agency or the like) that my gardiner [*sic*] or Mackail's charwoman had been having vivid and intimate glimpses of it under my very nose, when I could see nothing . . .

About being unable to think in London, and the stream of light on the river,[31] I have often wondered how that sort of feeling arises. All these people who annoy us and make the world ugly or trivial are really wonderful and beautiful things, and infinite in their way, just as the river is. But owing to the extreme activity of their being, they are always throwing masses of trivialities in our faces . . . It is as though the River kept talking all the time saying 'This barge was built at Rochester; best Norwegian timber; rum curve at the bow; full of coal, much of it wet, owner's name Judkins', and so on . . . in the main I find my human affections increase with age— mixed up certainly with the Love of God. But I am not sure that I do not twist them round to my selfish purposes even more, if possible, than in youth.[32]

4

Murray's belief in the common man, his distrust of the exclusive search for perfect Beauty, were being subjected, when these letters were written, to a severe test. He had long planned a stay in Florence to study manuscripts of Euripides in the Laurentian Library and elsewhere; Bertrand Russell had long wished him to meet Bernard and Mary Berenson (Russell's sister-in-law) at their famous villa *I Tatti* near Florence. Murray's plans were complicated by a commitment to join the Cambridge classical scholar, Jane Harrison, in Italy. However, he was able to stay at *I Tatti* for a time, and Jane Harrison joined him there.

Here is a piquant and happily well-documented episode. It can be seen through the eyes of Murray, writing to his wife, Archer, and Lady Carlisle, and of Mary Berenson writing to her sister Alys (Bertrand Russell's wife). The flavour of this strange encounter can best be conveyed by a chronological treatment alternating the impressions of guest and hosts.[33]

(i) GM to MM, 30 February [*sic*]

In the drawers of the cupboard, instead of newspapers, little silk quilts stuffed with lavender . . . B.B. very nice, but makes me feel an ignoramus . . . I want plainness and fresh air and . . . Oh, Lord, something or other . . .

(ii) Mrs Berenson to Alys Russell, 1 March:

We are all enchanted with GM, only BB, who *always* takes his pleasures sadly, is raging, at not having known him *ever* so long ago. He is the most congenial man, except Bertie, he has ever come across . . . Mrs Walter Sickert . . . brought with her . . . gossip that we felt was not at all à la hauteur of GM, although we enjoyed it well enough . . .

(iii) GM to MM, 2 March:

. . . this over-brilliant, exotic society here . . . How often have I repeated W. Grosvenor's words, 'My address henceforth is 1 High Street, Gath.'

(iv) GM to MM, 3 March:

Mrs B has told B that their conversation shocked me — which in a sense it did . . . a feeling of disgust, the eternal scandals and divorce cases . . .

(v) GM to MM, 4 March:

BB is certainly a wonderful man, and on the whole I like him. He is so clever, so gentle and funny. I don't wonder at people falling in love with him — nor yet at their hating him. Somehow I like and understand him better as a Russian . . .

(vi) Mrs Berenson to Alys Russell, 5 March:

BB and GM had been out walking by moonlight . . .

There seemed quite a *tendresse* in the air — most unusual in BB's presence — and BB said that he had been impelled to open his heart to Murray . . . Emily, Logan and I all feel our 'moral tone' distinctly inferior to his, but his presence inspires one to 'try to be good' like children . . .

(vii) GM to W. Archer, 6 March:

BB . . . knows all pictures and has read all books in all languages and quivers with emotion when he speaks or thinks about anything of any importance. I play the role of a robust genial Philistine in the house, and have never felt so ignorant in my life before. (And indeed too much Art and too much intellectual exclusiveness are very sinful things in life!) I observe that, in avoiding commonplace Philistine topics, there is a tendency to relapse into obscenity.

(viii) **Mrs Berenson to Alys Russell, 6 March:**

Last night . . . a fearful gulf opened, a dark chasm between our spirits. It turned out that Gilbert admired Dickens extremely, put him *very* high as a novelist, and BB and Logan and I all loathe him . . . We spoke of it all evening, not exactly arguing . . . It was very pleasant to sit and discuss for two hours without a trace of 'animus'. I think it was due to Gilbert's sweet spirits.

(ix) **GM to MM, 16 March:**

First signs of weakness on the part of my companion J.H. [Jane Harrison]. The Berensons got out their 'Golden Urn' of selected lines of the quintessence of poetry from the chief English poets — famous passages were read and we sat in judgment rejecting and condemning and occasionally bracketing a line or a word. I joined in, chaffing them and protesting and from time to time saying things were too good for their Urn. Miss Harrison said little, though I felt that like me she disapproved of the whole system. But on coming upstairs she burst out and slightly wept with indignation at the impiety and preposterousness of the whole proceeding.[34] I was rather disconcerted . . . Of course I agree with her; perhaps if I had been alone, I should have felt the same rage, instead of taking it good-humouredly and chaffing them.

(x) **Mrs Berenson to Alys Russell, 16 March:**

Everybody likes him [GM] at once, feels sorry he is so ill, and has a sort of instinct to plan for and take care of so delightful and helpless a being . . . Poor Gilbert — what he clearly needs is what he gets here — hours lying on a chaise-longue in the sun, doing nothing . . . BB says 'He is an angel, I love him with all my heart . . . '

. . . the frightful bomb that Murray threw into our midst. I asked him which, in his secret heart, he preferred — Shakespeare or Milton. He replied that he did not even consider Milton one of the greatest of English poets . . . [His own list was] Chaucer, Shakespeare, Shelley and Tennyson . . . discussion ensued, GM reading 'Come into the garden, Maud.' BB and he fell to, but both with angelic gentleness; for Gilbert's goodness and sweet reasonableness is so infectious that BB also began to sprout wings . . . Gilbert, who reads *divinely*, read a lot more, with always the same results, vulgar commonplace it seems to us, everything *described*, nothing *communicated* . . . Then Logan gave him Keats' 'Ode to a Nightingale' . . . He admitted that, if *that* was one's standard, Tennyson wasn't in it, but complained of our standard being too high . . . At the end of the evening, he was positively surprised to hear he had put Tennyson, as a poet, above Keats and Wordsworth . . . Murray is so candid in argument, so palpably anxious to know what his opponent thinks, so conscientious about admitting any

point against himself, that no one but a beast could have the least desire
to trample on him . . . The truth is, I suppose, that Murray has never
distinguished clearly among his different sets of interests, his aesthetic,
technical, dramatic and benevolent interests. He is very aristocratic, and
exclusive by nature, but forces 'catholicity' upon himself by principle.

(xi) GM to MM, 21 March:

I scarcely realised till I got away what a strain *I Tatti* was.

(xii) GM to RC, 4 May:

The Berensons were very interesting, and just as I was beginning to lose
my temper with them (for their fatuous artisticness and intellectual foppery)
Miss Harrison arrived and lost hers so instantly and violently that I felt
perfectly serene again.

   The biographer need not pay much attention to the substance of
the great debate. The verdict of *I Tatti* was correct on one point.
Murray's strong moral interests made it hard for him to judge
literature by anything except its effect on the character. Murray's
own last word to Lady Mary is also significant, if taken at its face
value, as it probably should be. Mrs Berenson was left with the
impression of an utterly charming, high-minded, unworldly
academic, unable to cope with any intrigue or practical demand. She
did not realize, as Shaw did, what strength of conviction and purpose
was concealed by those delightful manners, and what nervous strain
was involved in the concealment.

CHAPTER IX
Man of the Theatre

1. Staging of translations of Euripides—success of
   Hippolytus 1904.
2. *Trojan Women* 1905—*Electra* 1906—*Medea*
   1907—critical comparisons made with Bradfield
   School's productions of plays in the original Greek.
3. *Major Barbara*—Shaw's caricature of the Murrays.

1

BETWEEN 1902 and 1908 Murray published with great success
many of his verse translations of Greek drama. He also had the
satisfaction of seeing a number of them well produced on the stage,
and received with some critical acclaim. To Murray the propagandist,
deeply convinced of the importance of the Hellenic spirit to the
modern world, the theatre offered new opportunities of making it
more widely known. Murray the scholar thought that his understanding of Greek tragedy could best be deepened by bringing his
dramatic sense to bear upon it; and how could this be done better
than by supervising the production of his own translations in the
fascinating world of the theatre?

The early years of the twentieth century were propitious for a
theatrical revival of the 'Hellenic Spirit'. The fashionable pictures
of Lord Leighton and other Victorian painters might appear to have
little to do with directness or simplicity but they set the tone for a highbrow fashion in Greek effects. This affected (rather absurdly) women's
clothing, and provoked the wit of satirists. Oscar Wilde wrote that
'over a substratum of pure wool, such as is supplied by Dr Jaeger
. . . some modification of Greek costume is perfectly applicable to our
climate, our country and our century.'[1] And W. S. Gilbert, to whom
Murray was likely to pay more attention, satirized in *The Grand
Duke* of 1896 the trendy devotion to Greek costume and dances.

In 1886 and again in 1890 Euripides' *Helena* was staged, in a
translation by Dr James Todhunter, a graduate of Trinity College,
Dublin. The performances enjoyed considerable success and inspired
the enthusiasm of W. B. Yeats.

Murray probably knew little of such productions but admired
Yeats's plays and initiated a correspondence with him early in 1903.

Yeats had read Murray's translations published at the end of 1902, and tried to involve him in a new project for producing plays of merit, unlikely to meet with commercial success. This was to be called the Theatre of Beauty, the directing committee to include, besides Yeats and Murray, Arthur Symons, Sturge Moore, and Edith Craig, together with others who 'preferred beauty and beauty of speech in particular' to problem plays.

Yeats's letter reached Murray at *I Tatti* where he was feeling particularly robust amid so much refinement. To Lady Mary he wrote that he was greatly interested—rather surprisingly, since he valued literature primarily for its moral content; but he found the proposed title for the new organization 'preposterous' and even 'offensive'.[2] The name was changed by Yeats to *The Masquers*, but the organization remained very unprofessional and had an air of remote artiness. Murray soon grew to dislike it. In July 1903 he wrote to Yeats that the Masquers could offer nothing which the Stage Society did not already provide, and that for them 'the charms of suicide . . . seem to me greater every day'.[3] Meanwhile he enjoyed some fun at their expense. Alys Russell wrote at about the same time to her husband: 'Gilbert gave the most killing description of the Masquers, which shocked Mary and sent Miss Blomfield into fits.'[4] Yeats was not totally discouraged, and proposed that Murray should write a play on the Deirdre story, which was being 'overdone and badly done' in Ireland.[5]

This proposal too was turned down, but it shows that Murray was becoming known in 'aesthetic' literary circles. However, it was the Ibsenites who launched Murray as a translator-dramatist. Much has been said already of Murray's friendship with William Archer. A new figure was now to join forces with Archer—one who was to exercise a major influence on London theatrical life. This was Harley Granville Barker, an actor who had played the minor part of Selim in Murray's *Carlyon Sahib* in 1899, and was now to begin his career as actor-manager. The Royal Court Theatre in Sloane Square had been bought in 1900 by a businessman, J. H. Leigh, whose manager was Paul Vedrenne. Barker was introduced to them by Archer, and evolved a plan to run a series of 'uncommon dramas' at the Court Theatre. The season should be mainly on a subscription basis, with fresh productions every fortnight, expenses being reckoned at £250 per week, and maximum prices for seats at five or six shillings. A guarantee of £5,000 was needed, and Murray subscribed towards it. Barker went into partnership with Vedrenne for three years from Autumn

1904[6]—a partnership which proved to be notable in London theatrical history.

Vedrenne had decided to take this step after seing Barker's production of the *Hippolytus* on 26 May 1904 at the Lyric Theatre, which had been set up by Archer. The production was intended to be as far as possible naturalist in style. Naturalism is not the quality which modern readers most readily associate with Murray's verse; but the verdict of Sybil Thorndike, a devoted admirer of Murray and performer of his translations, was that their success on the stage was due above all to the 'beauty and clarity of Murray's verse and its dramatic speakable-ness.'[7] For whatever reason the *Hippolytus*, with Edyth Olive as Phaedra and Ben Webster as Hippolytus, gained an outstanding success in May 1904. Broadcasting over fifty years later, on his 90th birthday, Murray recalled that

the first day there were about fifty people in the house. The second day perhaps a hundred. On the third the house was full. On the fourth I found a crowd stretching down Shaftesbury Avenue and thought I must have come to the wrong theatre.[8]

Murray's translations became a not very lucrative part of the Court Theatre's seasons. *Hippolytus* was included in the opening repertoire. It received enthusiastic reactions from Murray's friends, though there was also criticism. A. E. Housman reserved whole-hearted approval for the statues in the background[9] designed by Jane Harrison.[10] Shaw criticized the cast, including the Aphrodite who had 'the qualifications of a horse for a quiet family—no vices'. But at the same time he wrote: 'those Greek plays of yours . . . are to me so fine that every single stroke in their production ought to be an inspiration.'[11]

2

Murray was now able to embark on a series of new translations of Euripides for performances on the stage, and to prepare the way for the performances by readings at lectures. In November 1904 he recited extracts from his translation of the *Trojan Women* to the Socratic Society of Birmingham.[12] He had a beautiful reading voice, and though Sybil Thorndike found his declamation of his own lines 'rather monotonous and sing-song',[13] most audiences found it hard to resist the mesmeric effect of his readings.

The next of his plays to be staged was the *Trojan Women*, a stark tragedy primarily about what war meant for the defeated. Eight matinées were given at the Royal Court between 11 and 28 April 1905, with Edith Wynne Matthison as Andromache, Edyth Olive as Cassandra, and Marie Brema as Hecuba. The production was poor and resulted in a considerable financial loss.[14] But the *Trojan Women* came later to be considered as one of Murray's most powerful propagandist anti-war pieces. Even in 1905 there was a significant private comment from his old Oxford friend, L. T. Hobhouse, who refused to see the production on the ground that it 'revived troubles that lie too near'—a reference to Emily Hobhouse's agitation in 1900–1 against the British treatment of the Boer civilian population in South Africa.[15]

Murray and Barker were by now becoming intimate friends. Before the next production of Murray/Euripides, they set out early in 1905 for a Mediterranean cruise on a small Greek cargo boat from Liverpool. This was preceded by some leisurely correspondence. Murray explained that his first object was to escape from hay fever; he had the choice of mountains and glaciers, a barren and sandy seashore somewhere near by (to avoid a long railway journey) or a sea voyage. The last seemed preferable; it would be a concentrated holiday, Murray wrote, and restful, though the bad cooking would offset heavenly weather, and Barker's opinion of him would sink very low. 'When you get home again, you will give thanks in a loud voice, and leap like a young lamb just discharged from penal servitude.'[16]

The voyage did not unduly lower Barker's opinion of Murray; one of his memories was of 'a steadily tapping typewriter in the grilling deckhouse of a Mediterranean cargo-boat.'[17] In London active collaboration continued. It was agreed to produce *Electra* early in 1906, if possible with Mrs Campbell in the title role. Murray thought her probably the best they could get, but had doubts whether she would want the part, and whether she could cope with long continuous speeches.[18] She was in fact interested, but negotiations fell through owing to her demand for exclusive rights in the USA. Barker and Vedrenne were strongly against this demand, for interested motives.[19] The play was duly produced in January 1906 for two weeks with Edith Wynne Matthison as Electra, the young Henry Ainley as Orestes, and the young Lewis Casson as Castor. Again Murray received extensive comments from Shaw whose final verdict was that the play was 'immense' and that parts of it went far beyond acting. 'Acting is only possible half-way up the mountain: at the top they [the actors] should efface themselves and utter the lines.'[20] In one respect Murray was pleasantly surprised by the production. The *Electra* is as grimly realistic as anything that Euripides wrote. However, he reported to his daughter Rosalind that it came out 'much more beautiful than I expected—not horrid, but strong and tragic';[21] and even the tragedy brought some incidental light relief. At the first night, Mrs Campbell was in the box next door to Murray's, and the following conversation took place after the play:

At the end Mrs. C. beckoned to me and presently said 'Well, how did you like it all?' And I said 'Well, I heard too much of your conversation, Mrs. Campbell, but otherwise I liked it very much.' 'You didn't, I'm sure you didn't! I hardly spoke! And even the others in my box could scarcely hear me!' 'I missed a sentence or two here and there, but I heard nearly everything', I answered—which was, of course, an extreme exaggeration. She looked very angry, and I was very sorry afterwards that I had done it.[22]

At about this time a critical note began to be heard about the merits of Murray's translations. Bradfield School was now putting on performances of Greek tragedies in some approximation to the original Greek, and these had a considerable *succès d'estime*. Murray wrote to Archer early in 1906:

That phrase about the superiority of Bradfield seems to be running like the measles through cultural circles. Desmond McCarthy went in for it heavily, and the less tactful of my friends say it to me a good deal . . . Of course if this point of view is right, my whole work as scholar and translator is useless. I am trying to understand the plays more closely and thoroughly and to help English readers to do so. But if English readers can get a better result from something they don't understand! . . . Yet I can remember being tremendously moved, as a boy, by the Agamemnon in Greek, which I couldn't really follow.[23]

The vogue for Bradfield and original Greek did not stop Murray from working at further translations, nor Barker from staging them. A letter from Murray to his daughter Rosalind gives a rare glimpse of the poet-translator at work:

I have done a chorus this morning bang through in one go. I began about 7, in bed, and did not get up but just lay working, and had it done by about 11.30. Then I got up, walked to the post; altered the last six lines, and wrote it out. When I looked at my watch and found it was 12.30, I had expected it to be about 10. (It is about the disadvantage of having children; but it is mostly sons that are spoken against.)[24]

The next play to be put on was the *Medea*. Mrs Campbell proved not to have been offended by Murray beyond the point of reconciliation, and expressed interest in 'the title role'; but once again Barker and Vedrenne stood against her over the question of rights in

America.[25] There were difficulties too about an alternative Medea.
Murray (and of course Barker) thought that Barker's wife, Lillah
McCarthy, should undertake the role; but they had to give way to
Vedrenne, who had promised the part to Edyth Olive.[26] *Medea* was
eventually put on at the Savoy Theatre, not the Royal Court, in
October 1907.

This was the end of Murray's partnership with Vedrenne and
Barker, and the results of the last production were much the same
as usual — good criticisms, some prestige, hopeful requests to read
or play the translations in the USA, not very full houses, and scanty
receipts.[27]

The next phase of Murray's activity as a translator-dramatist is
treated in Chapter XIII, which also contains some account of his
problems in dealing with the presentation of the Greek chorus, and
of his uneasy partnership with various musicians.

3

Meanwhile Murray had developed a secondary dramatic life as a
character in one of Bernard Shaw's plays. This was *Major Barbara*,
produced late in 1905. In one of a series of broadcast talks in 1954,
Murray recalled the origins of the play — Shaw, he said, 'never felt
quite at ease with you till he had somehow seen you as an object
to laugh at.' Murray had suggested to Shaw, probably about the
beginning of 1905, that he should write a sequel to *The Taming of
the Shrew*, showing Katharine in complete control of Petruchio:

He said, 'I can't, I'm doing a play called Murray's Mother-in-Law'. That
was of course *Major Barbara*, in which I and still more my wife are pictured
and caricatured.[28]

And still more, as might be gathered from Shaw's proposed title,
Lady Carlisle.

Major Barbara in the play is a young and beautiful aristocrat
intent, as an officer of the Salvation Army, on converting social
misfits. She is the daughter of Lady Britomart, an archetypal bossy
upper-class woman (her first scene, with her son, is extremely funny
and faithful to Lady Carlisle's style); Barbara's father is Andrew
Undershaft, an armaments manufacturer who is effectively separated
from his wife (as the Earl of Carlisle was from his Countess), and
is looking, according to his father's tradition, for an heir outside his
family to take over the 'Undershaft inheritance'. Barbara is betrothed
to Professor Adolphus Cusins, a young Australian Greek scholar,

who quotes Euripides (in Murray's version) and is ready, in order to help Barbara, to beat the Salvation Army drum in a Dionysiac manner, but with a certain scepticism. The second Act shows Major Barbara at work with her down-and-outers; there are some quick successes and much disillusion to follow them. In the third Act, Undershaft tries to persuade Barbara and Cusins that they will do much more good from a utilitarian point of view by taking over the management of his great armament factory, with its magnificent welfare installations, than by chancy individual conversions. Only by serving Mammon can they effectively serve God. Finally they close with Undershaft's offer, in the conviction that they can use his power for good ends—a conviction which he does not share.

Shaw in his pre-prefatory note mentions Murray's translation of the *Bacchae*, which 'came into our dramatic literature with all the impulsive power of an original work,' and says that Major Barbara 'stands indebted to him in more ways than one.' The phrase has more implications than are at first apparent. The play was read by Shaw to Murray at Oxford on 1 October 1905, with Barker and a family friend, Miss Lewis, present. The second Act, depicting Major Barbara at work among her 'cases', Murray from the first found extremely good,

really most moving and finely conceived. Perhaps the best thing he has ever done . . . As funny as his best work, but so true and poignant. It made me cry a little, and—to my relief—I saw that Barker was in the same plight.[29]

The difficulty lay in the contrast between the second and third Acts.

The latter Shaw himself felt to be very unsatisfactory in its original version.[30] On 2 October, Murray wrote to Shaw, suggesting a great change of emphasis in the denouement of Act III, and illustrating his point in the form of some new dialogue which he enclosed. The 'real dénouement', Murray thought, should make 'Cusens' [Murray's normal misspelling] 'come out much stronger' and thus avoid 'a simple defeat of the Barbara principles by the Undershaft principles.' The right and more interesting solution, he wrote, was

that the Barbara principles should, after their first crushing defeat [in Act II], turn upon the U. principles, and embrace them with a view of [*sic*] destroying them or subduing them for the B.P.'s [Barbara principles'] own ends. . . .

I expect that one error—perhaps the only one in the bones of the thing—is that you have made Undershaft too strong and both Barbara and Cusens too weak. You can't get any but an unhappy solution if they are really overpowered.[31]

Murray had drafted some new dialogue for Shaw and wondered how he would take it.[32] In fact, Shaw took it very well,[33] and built on Murray's ideas, though not entirely in the sense that Murray had indicated. In the final version, there is no question of a victory for Barbara's and Cusins's principles over Undershaft's; but the detailed researches of Professor Sidney Albert into the successive versions of Shaw's manuscripts show that the roles of Barbara and Cusins were greatly strengthened and that Undershaft himself, if not unambiguously weakened, emerges more as the representative of unknown social or cosmic forces than as a free agent. Little of Murray's dialogue was used in the end, but his critical ideas played an important part in stimulating Shaw to a new denouement. This may still be far from satisfactory—Murray said of the final version that it had 'the inconsequence of madness in it'[34]—but at least Shaw's rewriting of the third act ('the first time I have ever had to do such a thing', he told Beatrice Webb) considerably strengthened the play as a whole.[35]

Shaw's debt to Murray included also a number of semi-private allusions in the text of *Major Barbara*—probably many more than can be easily identified. One of these had to be expunged. In the original draft, Lady Britomart was made to say at the end of Act I, scene i, to her son, Stephen, 'Never call me Mother again.' Murray insisted on a weaker version, on the ground that Lady Carlisle had actually used those words to one of her sons in one of the many stormy scenes that punctuated her family life.[36] Again Shaw admitted that he never showed Murray the final version of Act III before performance, fearing, he said, a protest over a reference, towards the end of it, to Murray's gift of a revolver to H. N. Brailsford in 1897, and the moral that Cusins is made to draw from this:

My best pupil went out to fight for Hellas. My parting gift to him was not a copy of Plato's Republic, but a revolver and a hundred Undershaft cartridges. The blood of every Turk he shot . . . is on my head as well as on Undershaft's. That act committed me to this place for ever.[37]

Another allusion which only Murray would recognize is Cusins's question in Act III, during his discussion of terms with Undershaft: 'Is three fifths more than half or less?' Murray had himself told Shaw of his difficulty in deciding whether a new royalty rate, expressed in terms of pence per shilling, was or was not an improvement on the former one expressed as a percentage.[38]

One further aspect of *Major Barbara* should be discussed. How far did the Murrays and Lady Carlisle resent Shaw's caricature? Murray told Lady Mary rather disingenuously that Lady Britomart was 'fortunately utterly unlike your mother . . . merely a stage figure. Not a word to hurt sensitive feelings.'[39] One might still have expected Lady Carlisle to take offence; but Murray wrote to Shaw that, on seeing the play, 'she did not mind a bit'.[40] Lady Mary too seems to have been little affected by any element of personal caricature in the title role. Indeed there are no very evident likenesses between Major Barbara and Lady Mary except good looks and good works.[41]

As for Murray, he was not exactly gruntled at the picture of himself. To Shaw he suggested that the 'labelling of Cusens as me' was an artistic flaw. He had hesitated to say this,

lest it should seem that my feelings were hurt. They are not in the least hurt, there is nothing whatever to hurt them; but my judgment remains pretty firm . . . If you get Barker up like me, with spectacles and a moustache and a bald wig . . . it would have a kind of music-hall funniness for the few people who knew about me . . . But I feel now . . . something that leads one on a wrong scent.[42]

To Lady Mary he was more querulous:

The caricature of me is rather tiresome. The man is not like me — more like the poet in *Candida*, unless Shaw adopts some proposals of mine to soften him . . . I don't know whether they will get him up like me or not. But I am clear that, since duelling is not in fashion, there is no possible course except indifference. If I object, the incident will be more piquant. There is no harm in the character.[43]

Shaw made little effort to minimize whatever offence there might be in the stage performance. Any reasonably alert members of the audience could have had no doubt about the original of Cusins. The part was played by Granville Barker himself who, as Shaw wrote to Murray, had 'cultivated the closest possible resemblance to you in his private life' for two weeks before the performance.[44] Nature proceeded to imitate art when a new suit bought by Murray proved to be exactly like the one Cusins wore in the play.[45] Murray wrote to Shaw after the first performance that the 'personal likeness did not add to the value of the play', but also expressed his wonder that Shaw could be so personal without being offensive.

To his daughter Rosalind he went into more detail:

> . . . the caricature of me . . . is outrageously personal, but not a bit offensive or malicious. Mr Barker is got up rather like me, but not quite. (No moustache, and different baldness) . . . there are all kinds of little things that nobody would know about—e.g. that I gave Brailsford a revolver when he went to the Greek war. I felt shy for a minute or two, and even afterwards, between the acts, I sat still, in order not to be noticed, but during most of the play I really forgot all about it. Especially during Act 2, which is splendid . . .[46]

The playwright had serious reasons for making Cusins a Murray-like figure. Cusins, he explained, was designed to be the exact reverse of the conventional strong man of the theatre, without the 'smallest show of physical robustness or brute determination.'[47] Murray should be thankful that Shaw had not portrayed him as a Rhodes Scholar (given Murray's attitude to Rhodes's African policies, this would have been the ultimate insult). Shaw was in fact paying Murray a considerable compliment by casting him for the role of the clear-sighted intellectual who would prove to have at least as much strength as the conventional strong man. There is also something more than outrageous teasing in the description which Shaw gives of Cusins in the printed version of *Major Barbara*. In fact this shows a highly imaginative perception both of Murray's basic strength of character and of the psychosomatic strains to which he was subject:

> Cusins is a spectacled student, slight, thin haired, and sweet voiced . . . His sense of humour is intellectual and subtle, and is complicated by an appalling temper. The lifelong struggle of a benevolent temperament and a high conscience against impulses of inhuman ridicule and fierce impatience has set up a chronic strain which has visibly wrecked his constitution. He is a most implacable, determined, tenacious, intolerant person who by mere force of character presents himself as—and indeed actually is—considerate, gentle, exploratory, even mild and apologetic, capable possibly of murder, but not of cruelty or coarseness. By the operation of some instinct which is not merciful enough to blind him with the illusions of love, he is obstinately bent on marrying Barbara.[48]

Those who have thought of Murray as an over-reasonable and rather woolly Liberal would do well to ponder this description.[49]

CHAPTER X

Return to Classical Studies

1. Work on Oxford texts of Euripides — Wilamowitz on Vol. I — visits Laurentian and Vatican Libraries for Vol. II 1903.

2. Interest extends to archaeology, anthropology, and the evolution of religions.

3. Helps Jane Harrison decipher Orphic Tablets at Naples 1903.

4. Elected Fellow of New College 1905 — move to 131 Banbury Road, Oxford — work on Vol. III of Euripides — lectures at Harvard 1907.

5. Harvard lectures published as *The Rise of the Greek Epic*.

6. The Wilamowitzes visit Oxford — elected Oxford Professor of Greek Oct. 1908.

1

MURRAY'S translations formed an important part of his grand design for transmitting the message of Hellenism to a wider public. However, he had to reckon that further work in the field of 'pure scholarship' was necessary for him. He might not be able, because of physical weakness, to hold a prestigious Chair of Greek again; but he needed some position in the academic world, if only to provide him with the library facilities essential to a serious scholar. And he was firmly committed to completing the new text of Euripides for the Oxford University Press.

The editing of texts was far from being a lucrative task. Murray's total payment for the three volumes of Euripides was only £75.[1] However, it was the sort of hard grind which was recognized as praiseworthy and indeed essential work. If Murray wanted to make his name known among established scholars in Britain and Germany, to earn himself a reputation for soundness, and to work his way back to a new Chair, this was a good way of doing so.

The work involved studying at first hand the surviving manuscripts of Euripides, as well as existing printed editions of them. An editor had to be familiar with the scholia (ancient comments on the manuscripts) and with citations from Euripides in later Greek or

Latin works; also (before Murray's work on Euripides was completed) with the fragments of Greek tragedy preserved in Egyptian papyri which were now coming to light. A new edition traditionally involved a text collated from all these sources, and also footnotes explaining in a sort of Latin shorthand how and why the edition varied from its predecessors. These notes were known as the 'apparatus criticus' — the production of which was a traditional and severe test for the classical scholar. Murray knew that he must undergo the test, but there is a note of irony in an exchange on the subject with William Archer, who had asked him what an *apparatus criticus* was. Murray replied that it was 'a list of MS variations, with occasional remarks thereon. Only men of the highest moral character, religion and social graces can produce one satisfactorily.'[2]

One immediate benefit for Murray from his work on the text of Euripides was that it brought him into close professional contact with the great German scholar Wilamowitz. In June 1901 Wilamowitz consented to read Murray's proofs of Volume I (published in January 1902). He had not really the time to do so, he wrote, but Euripides 'is too near my heart, and your invitation is so flattering that I cannot resist it.'[3] Murray was delighted at the prospect of collaboration with him and wrote to Archer, 'It is very interesting dealing with a man who knows every detail of the whole business — and possesses something like genius as well.'[4]

The preparation of the new text involved close collaboration with many other scholars. However, it was his debt to Wilamowitz which Murray felt to be particularly great; this is acknowledged in the introduction to the first volume of the text (I have translated from Murray's elegant formal Latin):

Finally throughout the book Ulrich Wilamowitz-von Moellendorf [*sic*] has made available to me a mass of material, and helped me most liberally by his advice and hard work. Whether in respect of his great kindness, or of its great usefulness to me, I can hardly thank him adequately.[5]

The introduction also contains a passage which well illustrates the links between Murray's textual criticism and his dramatic interests:

This is not the place in which to explore many important problems concerning interpolations, repetitions, revisions, changes made by the actors (to whose whims the text of Euripides was exposed much longer than that of the other tragedians), the Euripidean style and genius, and the production of the plays. It seems to me that Euripides needs interpretation more than emendation. Nor, I think, can anyone, however learned, interpret him adequately unless he knows something of dramatic art, unless he is constantly conscious of dealing with a great man and a great poet, and unless in each play he is careful to fix his mind's eye continuously, not only on the lines and the sentiments, but also on the characters in action — on their grief, fear, or rage.[6]

Work on the next volume of Euripides made it necessary for Murray to travel abroad. Strangely enough, he never seems to have visited Germany at this time. As already mentioned, he went to Florence in February 1903. His primary object on this occasion was not to discuss literature with the Berensons at *I Tatti*, but to consult an important twelfth-century manuscript of Euripides in the Laurentian Library. Here for the first time he sounded a critical note about Wilamowitz:

. . . I find [the MS in question] interesting, but fear that Wilamowitz has led me into more than one mare's nest! He was too anxious to discover significant minutiae, and in one case he must have misread his own notes.[7]

However, there were poetic compensations for the mare's nests. Three years later, in preparing a lecture course for Harvard, Murray recalled a moment of illumination as he examined in Florence,

a MS. of Euripides, which was very hard to read, blurred with age and sea-water and exposure to the sun. And as I pored over it, there gradually showed through the dusty blur the first words of a lyric in the *Alcestis*. It was as old as the hills, and I had long known it by heart. Yet the freshness of it glowed through that rather stale air like something young and loving. I remember a feeling of flowers and springing water.[8]

Murray went on to work at another Euripidean MS in the Vatican Library at Rome. In a letter to John Buchan he described some of the trials of a travelling scholar.

The Library is organized rather like a preparatory school for boys. Open from 9 to 1; the Papal Prefect sitting all the time at a big desk in the middle, and the readers at long tables in front of him. Windows not opened since the time of the Borgias.[9]

He developed the last point in a letter to his wife: 'the room is so ill-ventilated (or so utterly unventilated) and the crowded priests (I fear) smell so, that it is a trial to work there.'[10]

In England another correspondent on occasional points of detail was A. E. Housman, with whom Murray was on terms of cautious friendship. He much admired Housman's poetry,[11] and was not repelled by Housman's notorious asperities towards other scholars, though he himself set great store on preserving due courtesy in

academic duels.[12] Housman on his side admired Murray's mastery
of Greek and wrote favourably of Volume II of the Euripides text,
which he described in a letter as 'much the pleasantest edition'.[13]
He admired too Murray's poetic gift; but he had no sympathy with
Murray's radical and reforming aspirations, and derived some
sardonic amusement from the puritan and ascetic side of Murray's
character. His endeavours to lure Murray to spend an evening with
him at a music-hall in London were persistent but vain;[14] this is
hardly surprising since Murray was shocked even by the general tone
of Oscar Wilde's *The Importance of Being Earnest*.[15]

A more generally congenial collaborator for Murray was the
Cambridge scholar, A. W. Verrall. They met in Switzerland in
December 1894. They shared many tastes and went on climbing
holidays together in the Alps and had a common interest in telepathy
or extra-sensory perception. Verrall was noted in the world of
classical scholarship for extreme and perverse ingenuity, not only
in his editions of manuscripts, but also in his interpretations of the
thought of the Greek dramatists, Euripides particularly.[16] Murray
never went to such extremes as Verrall, but there was some mental
kinship between them; both were over-anxious, if not for the same
reasons, to read modern messages into ancient texts.

Murray thought that, thanks mainly to Wilamowitz, his Euripides
would be the best edition available (indeed it is only now being
superseded), but he was not over-confident of his ability: 'I make
more mistakes than most people! And I may be disgracing myself
by some uncorrected asininity!'[17]

He was anxious to find scholarly work in some field other than
that of textual criticism.

2

Murray had grown up among English scholars for whom composition
and textual criticism comprised almost their whole duty. However,
he was a traditionalist with a difference. He had a knowledge of
ancient Greek unrivalled in his own time. He was intensely interested
in the technique of lyric poetry and of drama. He was moreover a
political man of his own time. Like many Victorian statesmen and
historians before him, he was inclined to interpret classical Greece
in the light of his own political interests and convictions, and in some
hope that the solution of current British problems, particularly those
of Empire, could be eased by proper attention to Greek examples.

He was above all a moralist, who judged literature and civilizations by their contribution to the progress of the human spirit. For Murray Greek literature was one of the supreme moral peaks of human achievement; he was therefore profoundly interested in the factors which had determined the nature of literary and intellectual life in Athens of the fifth century BC.

Murray was led by his literary studies to consider deeply the religious beliefs, ostensible, half-hidden, or implied, which lay behind so much of the work of the Greek Tragedians. He was an agnostic, ready to mock politely the complacent assumptions and unthinking formulas of any Established Church. However, he was also deeply interested both in the problems involved in man's relations with an unseen world, and also in the practice of generations of men in formulating and ritualizing these relations—in other words in the history of religion. Friends described him as a 'collector of religions'. By the early years of the twentieth century such an approach was bound to lead him away from the purely literary approach to classical studies, and to link him with others who were exploring the world of ancient Greece from very different angles.

By the last decade of the nineteenth century it had become impossible to base any comprehensive view of ancient Greece solely on surviving Greek literature. Charles Newton, responsible for the main collection of Greek ceramics in the British Museum, had long predicted that Greek vases would prove an important new source for the examination of Greek mythology and of social life in ancient Greece.[18] Another important indicator of change was the work of Andrew Lang. He had busied himself during the 1880s in explaining the Greek myths as an inheritance from an uncivilized stage of society and in finding parallels to ancient Greek myths and rituals among other still uncivilized peoples—American Indians, Australian aborigines, or Eskimos.[19] Lang was at best a brilliant amateur, whose greatest successes were his translations of the Iliad and Odyssey, and his collections of fairy-stories. However, some ideas thrown up in his anthropological writings were developed in much greater depth and much more systematically by two outstanding scholars. William Robertson Smith, a 'higher critic' of the Bible, published in 1889 the *Lectures on the Religions of the Semites*, in which he found the essence of Old Testament religion to lie in ritual observances, closely interwoven with social life as a whole, and directed towards preserving and increasing the welfare of the tribe or nation. This was a widely influential book, whose message could be linked with a structuralist approach. The French sociologist

Durkheim in particular viewed literature and religion as expressions and reinforcements of the social pattern of various societies.

Robertson Smith's work was followed by another, which had a more immediate effect on classical specialists. The first instalment of J. G. Frazer's *The Golden Bough* appeared in 1890, the year after Murray took up his Chair at Glasgow. Frazer's work started by a detailed examination of the Roman cult of the priest-king in the sacred grove at Aricia—

> The priest who slays the slayer[20]
> And shall himself be slain.

This was extended into a wide-ranging survey of comparable primitive cults throughout the world, and not least of the ritual associated with the worship of Dionysus in classical Greece. Frazer wrote:

neither the polished manners of a later age, nor the glamour which Greek poetry and art threw over the figure of Dionysus, sufficed to conceal or erase the deep lines of savagery and cruelty imprinted on the features of this barbarous deity.[21]

The god Dionysus demanded sacrifices (originally human), but he was often himself the sacrifice, who was torn to pieces and buried and then rose again. Frazer related this and other myths, after the manner of Durkheim, to tribal needs—the gathering of the harvest, the burial and resurrection of the seed (St Paul and the ballad of John Barleycorn echo the sequence)—and also to tribal rituals.

At this point, about the turn of the century, the new anthropology was linked with classical traditions by a group of Cambridge scholars whose general outlook was later described colourfully by Jane Harrison, then a Fellow of Newnham College. She and other Hellenists of her generation had been 'a people who sat in darkness', but then they saw the 'two great lights'—archaeology and anthropology.

Arthur Evans set sail for Crete, 'and telegraphed news of the Minotaur from his own labyrinth;[22] and at the sound of those magical words "the Golden Bough", the scales fell from the eyes of the "classical deaf-adders".'

The Cambridge group fascinated Murray and he became closely associated with it.

3

When Murray originally met Verrall in Switzerland in December 1894,[23] Verrall had offered to help him over his projected Lexicon of Euripides. In July 1900 he again spent some weeks with the Verrall family in Switzerland, and there they were joined by the most colourful representative of the new school, Jane Harrison. A Tutor in Greek History at Newnham College, she had been a pioneer in the use of visual evidence to interpret ancient history and literature; and in her *Mythology and Monuments of Ancient Athens* (1890), written in collaboration with Verrall's wife, she had deduced much from inscriptions, architectural ruins, and vases about pre-Olympian religion.

For some years before 1900 Jane Harrison had been deeply occupied with the studies embodied in her *Prolegomena to the Study of Greek Religion* (1903). She was a student of Nietzsche and a precursor of D. H. Lawrence. For her the classical serenity of the Olympian religion, established by the fifth century BC, was only a veneer covering, often very thinly, the worship of darker forces, directly concerned with the fertility of the earth and of man. These forces, she felt, corresponded to a deeper level of the human being, more important and effective than the rational mind. She had no use for official religions. In her view, if the Greek advanced towards religious enlightenment from the crude propitiation of earth spirits, it was by means of the Orphic cults, which in their mysteries and ceremonies of initiation provided communion between the individual and divine forces.

It was while Jane Harrison was concerned with these broad themes that she and Murray met. What were the qualities in each that attracted the other? The answer is probably the same in either case— open-mindedness, imagination, and a willingness to look over the barriers which scholars of the traditional type had tended to erect between themselves and the world—even the academic world— around them. Murray wrote to his wife after his first meeting with Jane Harrison: 'I like her very much indeed . . . she strikes me as having a generous mind, which is rare among scholars—she is overflowing with interest in all sorts of subjects.'[24] She, as something of a Bohemian, was fascinated not only by Murray's intellect, but also by a quality she discerned as sheer goodness in him and Lady Mary:

You are both so hypermoralised and superspiritualised that you force me to think of righteousness, temperance and judgement-to-come . . . you have done me good in one way: I will never again set my influence, as I have done in the past, against all good things because I see in you two how beautiful it all is.[25]

Jane Harrison had been present when Murray read his translation of the *Hippolytus* at Cambridge (February 1902). She shared the enthusiasm aroused in Bertrand Russell by the occasion. Here was a scholar from the traditional camp, with all the linguistic equipment which she lacked, who could look at Greek literature with new insight and was something of a poet, not prepared to subordinate all the deeper springs of emotion to reason.

The first two of Murray's translations of Euripides to be published were the *Hippolytus* and the *Bacchae*. Both could be interpreted as poetic sermons on the theme that man can only at great peril ignore his deepest instincts and the gods that represent them. Neither Aphrodite nor the great Dionysus can be mocked, and they may interpret as mockery any attempt at totally rational behaviour by man. Jane Harrison, the new preacher of Dionysus, was enchanted by these themes and by the lyrical gifts which Murray brought to them.

When she received her copy of Murray's book of translated plays in December 1902 she wrote a letter in which she not only argued against Murray's rhyming measure but also analysed his character in shrewd terms:

I shall always believe you were meant to be lyrical not only through Euripides but for yourself—I believe you succeed with him because he releases you from a sort of arduousness and conscientiousness of thought—induced by the moralist within you. You are best when as in the Orestes scene in Murray-Andromache you say what has to be said in prose—then break when you needs must break into song—I feel so strongly, never use verse . . . unless you can't possibly help it—I feel so often that you are a poet caught, tangled and hampered in all manner of mental stages that are you and are not you as a poet—and that only once and again you give the poet his head.[26]

Jane Harrison did not get to know Murray soon enough to derive much benefit from him in the production of her *Prolegomena*, though he read through the whole book in proof.[27] However, she secured Murray's help in the deciphering of some tablets, inscribed with fragments of Orphic ritual and preserved at Naples.[28] It was in March 1903 that she joined Murray at *I Tatti* and travelled on with him to Naples. Her motives in this expedition seemed to Mary Berenson not to be entirely scholarly:

. . . poor Gilbert is to be torn from his haven of repose for an 'amorous adventure' of which he is, and will remain, perfectly unconscious . . . He said yesterday he felt as if it was going straight into the inferno—not on account of her, but on account of the noise and fatigue of travel . . . He even thought of going to bed and feigning illness (I suggested it!) but his Puritan conscience would not allow him to adopt this ruse! J.H. talks about the nervousness and stupidity of Lady Mary (she admits she is 'awfully good').[29]

Jane Harrison admitted in her reminiscences that she had never ceased to be in love with people and things, but Murray's account of the heroine of his 'amorous adventure' would have disappointed the gossips of *I Tatti*. Miss Harrison, he wrote, was

much more like a man, a middle-aged bachelor accustomed to Club life, than a woman. She insisted on a good substantial dinner, good wine and plenty of tobacco (I personally have a tendency to fall back on boiled eggs and cocoa . . .) and, receiving these, she talked at her ease, like a brilliant man of letters.[30]

He also indicated that he was doing the lion's share of the work on the Orphic tablets. Jane Harrison soon got 'stupefied' by it. None the less it was stimulating:

I have been feeling the Greek scholar in me revive very much rather than the dramatist. I wish they would make me Professor of Greek at some nice place. But of course there is no place except Oxford.[31]

In another letter Murray indicates that he was perhaps being influenced by Jane Harrison's view of the importance of the primitive in modern life as well as in Greek religion:

I find amid the horrors of Naples a stimulating quality. Things that are concealed in more decent Northern communities are set forth in the open here. It requires a fearful effort to face them, but you must face them if you are to have a real understanding of life. But, oh, the horrors of it! — yet I don't dislike the people, and I don't think the world is really a Hell.[32]

4

In 1904 Murray was largely preoccupied with the living theatre. However, towards the end of the year he received an invitation which set him once more firmly on the road to the Professorship which he most coveted. He had renewed his working connections with Oxford after he retired from Glasgow, and particularly with Balliol, where the Master, Edward Caird, was an old friend of his from Glasgow days, and much more congenial to Murray than his worldly predecessor Jowett. He examined for the 'Ireland' (the main classical event at Oxford) in 1901, awarding the prize without great enthusiasm to Raymond Asquith.[33] He also examined in the summer of 1903 at Winchester, where the myth was current that in his morning bath he would, by association of ideas, evolve emendations for the Agamemnon.[34]

It was in fact New College which took the initiative in getting Murray back to Oxford. At the end of October, one of the classical Fellows, Percy Matheson, sounded him out. A vacancy was occurring in the Fellowship. Was there any chance of Murray returning to Oxford?[35] Murray must have replied promptly and positively. On 6 and 11 November, the Warden of New College, W. A. Spooner, made concrete proposals to him—a Fellowship from October 1905, lectures to be given three times a week during two terms, a salary of £100 a year ('perhaps more than the College should afford for two terms' work'), tutorial work to be additional and payable at whatever was the normal rate.[36] The subjects of his lectures, Murray confided to Archer, would be left to him.[37] Caird at Balliol encouraged Murray to accept the New College proposals, tutorials and all.[38]

It was indeed a suitable base in Oxford for his long-term scholarly work that Murray most wanted at this time. He had long thought of moving from Barford, partly for the sake of Lady Mary, who found the house too much for her.[39] He had been particularly attracted by Boar's Hill, where he visited Arthur Evans in September 1903, and found the view quite equal to Hindhead.[40] In spring 1905 he was in touch with R. W. Macan, who advised building, and with Robert Bridges who suggested that Murray should join with himself and others to join a sort of syndicate for buying land 'by Hen Wood, adjoining Mr. Evans', thus protecting each other against undesirable neighbours.[41] However the plans fell through; by midsummer 1905 the Murrays had to leave Barford unsold and to establish a new home, 131 Banbury Road, where they stayed for the next four years.[42]

During these years, when he was again a Fellow of New College, Murray came nearer to full participation in the life of an Oxford college than before or afterwards. There were difficulties; it is questionable whether then, or even now, a teetotaller could ever rank as a 'good College man' at either of the ancient English Universities. Nor did Murray, as a radical Liberal, find the political atmosphere of Oxford congenial. There was for example an awkward meeting, or non-meeting, between him and Alfred Milner in 1905.[43] He also had an exacting family life in Oxford and, outside it, he pursued actively his interest in the staging of his translations.

However, within these limits Murray seems to have played a full part in the life of New College, particularly among the younger classical Fellows. The college remained more of a home to him than Christ Church, to which he was attached ex officio from 1908. He could observe at New College the progress of a remarkable generation of undergraduate scholars, notably J. D. Denniston, senior scholar in 1906, 'a bit of a poet' and interested in Ibsen, and a younger 'portent', Arnold Toynbee, who in an examination essay had 'reviewed Latin literature from Augustus to the 6th century in the most comprehensive and almost alarming manner.'[44]

Meanwhile on his return to college lecturing and tutorials, Murray was fully absorbed again in traditional classical work, and also in preliminary discussions within the University about the need for radical reform in the whole system of classical teaching and examinations at Oxford. He had moreover to complete his edition of Euripides. Volume III of his 'Oxford text' did not appear until 1909, and publication was preceded by the usual volume of correspondence with German and English scholars. There was a new dimension to the work. Murray was engaged during 1906 in helping A. S. Hunt to decipher and edit the fragments of Euripides' plays found among the papyri at Oxyrrhynchus in Egypt, one of which he described to Archer as ' a beautiful bit, the best bit that they have ever got from a papyrus, I think. Hypsipyle singing to the baby which she is watching.'[45]

Murray's thoughts had turned by 1905 to the next major classical subject which he should tackle after Euripides. No doubt he felt that he had had enough of textual work.[46] Early in the year he had written to Arthur Evans, suggesting that he might come out to Knossos for a time to assist in the excavations. He received a friendly but discouraging letter.[47] The thought of these two highly imaginative men in collaboration is piquant. It was not to be, but Murray had clearly given some thought to extending his main focus of interest backwards in history. Shortly afterwards he received a letter which did much to determine him in this direction. In March 1905, the Harvard Department of Classics invited him to give six public lectures of a fairly general character 'on some subject connected with Greek literature', in 1905 or 1906.[48] The proposed timing was clearly impossible for Murray, but by the end of 1906 it was settled that he should deliver a course of lectures at the end of April 1907.[49] He was faced with the need to prepare a substantial course of lectures, preferably on a single definable subject; the attraction of the challenge was increased by a suggestion from Humphrey Milford that the OUP should publish in book form the lectures about to be given in America. Murray replied with typical banter:

Now do you consider that a business-like letter? When I get a business letter from a publisher, I expect him to mention his terms—say, 3d in the shilling on the first 1,000 copies, and 13d (thirteen) in the shilling afterwards. He generally adds that he would sooner read thirteen of my books than twelve of anyone else's, and will pay extra accordingly. And he ends by mentioning a number of eventualities in which he would prosecute me, which adds dignity and firmness to the whole proceeding.

However, perhaps this standard is too high. I shall be very glad . . .[50]

He now had every incentive to produce a substantial work, appealing to a wider public than could be reached by a definitive text of Euripides, but also confirming his scholarly credentials to the University world. The result was *The Rise of the Greek Epic*. There are few traces in Murray's correspondence of the work that went into it, mainly in the Long Vacation (July–September) 1906; but clearly he was developing the concept of Homer as a 'traditional book' built up from a number of more primitive sources, and the possible parallel between the evolution of Homeric and Old Testament texts which had been adumbrated from the Hebrew end, so to speak, by Robertson Smith. He wrote to Russell:

I am working rather hard, writing my American lectures, and reading the Bible and the works of divines. They are very good, abler men, I think, than classical scholars now . . . I know an awful lot about High places, Historiography, and Hittites . . . from which you may conclude that I have got the Encyclopaedia Biblica . . .[51]

In mid-April, together with Lady Mary, Murray embarked for the USA on the SS *Ivernia*. Very little can be concluded directly from the records which he kept about his success as a lecturer at Harvard and elsewhere. He noted one or two incidents in letters to Bertrand Russell. From Bryn Mawr in mid-May he wrote:

The worst result that I anticipate is that I shall never again be happy without a private bathroom. And I shall never have one in England until I am made a Liberal Peer for ending the House of Lords.[52]

Years later he also gave Russell some advice about giving lectures in the USA:

You merely have to shout them [the lectures] in a large hot room. Do not complain of the heat, because Sedgwick, the curator, asked me if I knew the cause why the English found the heat of his room oppressive. I began to suggest various reasons, but he interrupted me, 'No, Sir, no, simply alcoholism.'[53]

The Harvard *Crimson* (the students' newspaper) paid Murray the compliment of summarizing each of the last four of his six lectures in leading articles,[54] but in a scholarly way refrained from any comment. However, there is no doubt that Murray enjoyed a resounding success. The lectures, according to Professor J. A. K. Thomson, created a

mild furore. It was told of the famous President Eliot of Harvard (who was known to favour modern subjects) that when he saw the crowds waiting to hear Murray he exclaimed 'What is the meaning of this?' 'Perhaps, Mr. President', said a colleague, 'it means a new Revival of Learning?'[55]

In the USA Murray would not have encountered at this time, even among small audiences, that combination of expertise and traditional conservatism which bred some scepticism in the older British Universities about his wide-ranging surveys of the classical world. At the same time his imaginative approach and the beauty of his voice worked their magic as fully on the Western as on the Eastern side of the Atlantic. The many invitations which he received after spring 1907 to lecture or reside in the USA testified amply to the success of his first stay there.

5

The Rise of the Greek Epic, published late in 1907, was a book in which Murray was able to combine scholarship with an appeal to a large, educated public. It is not a work of profound original research, but rather a synthesis and attempt to reconcile many conflicting views on the 'Homeric Question'. The question assumed its pre-modern form in Friedrich August Wolf's *Prolegomena to Homer*, published in 1795. He dissolved Homer into a succession of fairly primitive editors working on a large collection of primitive heroic lays, orally transmitted for many centuries and finally patched together in the sixth century BC in very much the form that has come down to us. Against Wolf and the 'disintegrators' who succeeded him, the 'unitarians' argued from the artistic unity to be found in the *Iliad* and *Odyssey* in favour of a single author or single final editor. Murray saw clearly the anomaly between the inconsistencies of the received texts of the *Iliad* and *Odyssey*, and what was to him the clear evidence of the essential artistic unity of each book. For him, these traditional books embodied 'not the independent invention of one man, but the ever-moving tradition of many generations of men.'[56] He detected the movement of this tradition in traces of excisions from the present texts; for example, of passages indicating the use of poisoned arrows, homosexual practices (though Murray would never, given his own inhibitions and those of his time, mention these explicitly), and mutilation of Hector's body by Achilles. Such excisions had been made as the result of two influences — 'a general humanising of the imagination which, as it loved beauty, hated cruelty and uncleanness', and the remnants of some race prejudice, 'some far-off idealised image of the Achaean or northern spirit' (as opposed to the lower spirit of aboriginal elements in Greece).[57]

Through the creative work of generations of improvers, the Homeric epics had become 'the embodiment of a force making for the progress of the human race.'[58] In his prefatory chapter, Murray uses this same phrase in a wider context, applying it with great eloquence to Greek literature as a whole.[59]

Certain points may be noted about Murray's general thesis. He had been encouraged by Jane Harrison to look for primitive elements not far beneath a comparatively civilized surface. The idea that the Homeric epic was somehow the common work of the Greek peoples could be traced back to the writings of Vico and Herder in the eighteenth century. And the idea of progressive expurgation could be paralleled — indeed Murray explicitly drew the parallel — in the studies of Old Testament literature by Robertson Smith and G. R. Driver.[60] The findings of these scholars, as they bore most directly on Murray's work, were essentially that the Old Testament books dealing with the earliest periods of Hebrew history represented the composite production of successive writers, who re-created the national past in accordance with the nation's perceived contemporary needs, political and religious. Each major book of the Pentateuch had gone through various editions and successive phases of expurgation, but these had never been complete enough to eliminate all unsuitably primitive material.[61] Murray no doubt took a sly pleasure in reinforcing by a Homeric parallel the case of anti-unitarian Old Testament critics, as well as in using their findings to back his own Homeric thesis.

Where do Murray's general arguments leave the person of Homer, and the establishment of the texts of the *Iliad* and the *Odyssey*? He regards 'Homer' as an imaginary ancestor of a special school of bards, the Homeridae. The epic texts, he thought, were first evolved in the Ionic dialect for recitation at great public occasions in the Aegean. Then in the mid-sixth century, when Pisistratus was tyrant of Athens, the *Iliad* and *Odyssey* were selected exceptionally from the other existing epic poems for recitation at the great Panathenaea—the all-Athenian festival. These are the bare bones of Murray's hypothesis or chain of hypotheses.[62]

His aim was to produce some kind of synthesis between the unitarian and the disintegrationist, or analytic, theories about Homer. The book belongs to a past phase of Homeric scholarship, and its reception even among scholars of Murray's own time was mixed. Jane Harrison was predictably enthusiastic about Murray's use of anthropological and archaeological evidence, and about his poetic insights:

Another reader will say 'Most interesting and delightful, very suggestive and stimulating as a whole, but surely at least half the book is pure work of the imagination'.

It is.[63]

Wilamowitz evidently felt differently about pure works of imagination. There are severe implications in his remark:

I am analytic by nature, and start from the given facts. This tendency increases, as my understanding of what is given improves.[64]

More detailed private criticism came from S. H. Butcher:

to be quite candid, when you explain the actual *process by which the poems came into being*, I am not able to get at your view.

And later

On p. 228 . . . I seemed to see a Homer emerging; too late in the day, as I thought, to do the job . . . Still, he is there in some shape; 'how great or how small a poet' matters much, I cannot but think. However even for that mercy, I breathed a DEO GRATIAS, and now I add a warmer 'gratias' to G.M.[65]

Many reviews accused Murray (unfairly, it seems) of ignoring the artistic evidence for unity. The *Times Literary Supplement* in addition strongly attacked the analogy between Homeric and Old Testament expurgations.[66]

However, favourable verdicts carried the day. J. B. Bury rather unexpectedly expressed full agreement with Murray's doctrine,[67] and the *Spectator* wisely found that

the merits of the book are independent of the argument. It is everywhere delightful reading, for its author is full of wit, brilliancy, and poetic feelings . . . He has a special, almost unique, gift of making dead poetry live again for us moderns.[68]

The book sold well for one on such a subject. In the months preceding 31 March 1908, 1,312 copies were sold in all (over 200 in the USA), and Murray received royalties of £55 4s. 3d.[69] A second edition was published in 1911. Further editions followed in 1924 and 1934, and then it was issued as an Oxford Paperback.[70] In his preface Murray allowed himself a little fun with his unitarian critics, particularly Andrew Lang:

. . . I am anxious to find common ground with my unitarian critics. I only differ irreconcilably from those who reject all analysis *ab initio* : who assume as an unquestioned starting-point that towards the end of the second millenium B.C., when to the best of our knowledge there was no Greek literature, a single miraculously gifted man, of whose life we know nothing, living in the heart of a rich, widespread . . . civilisation, which no history mentions and which all excavation has signally failed to discover, composed for an audience unable to read two poems much too long to be listened to; and then managed by miraculous but unspecified means to secure that his poems should be preserved practically unaltered while flying *viva per ora virum* [live on the lips of men] through some six extraordinarily changeful centuries . . .

When he sent the MS of the second edition to the OUP he suggested a preliminary notice:

RISE OF THE GREEK EPIC
NEW EDITION
NOW READY
DAMN SIGHT LONGER

Full of Piquant Personalities
The Truth about A-dr-w L--g
The Author of the Iliad unmasked
What Zenodotus Suppressed![71]

Such was Murray's controversial style, good-tempered, ironic, and on occasion deadly. And such was the noise of the battle long ago over the mangled corpse of the Homeric question.

6

The summer of 1908 witnessed the first personal meeting between Murray and Wilamowitz. The German scholar came to Oxford in May 1908, to deliver two lectures, on *Greek Historical Writing* and *Apollo*. Murray did not think them entirely worthy of the great man,[72] and had great trouble with the translation of them which he had undertaken personally. He wrote to Lady Mary a mock communication to Wilamowitz which illustrates his amused exasperation with the vagaries of their correspondence:

Struth [probably = 'zwar'] only first for-yesterday is one, and struth the second of the Williamsonian [= Wilamowitz] Forreadings, struth in your name but still nonetheless on that account to my house directed, to me come. The therewith however accompanyingly enclosed letter stated, another Forreading, and struth the by rights first one, namely Apollo, be already begun, will however only first after onetwo weeks be postally offsent. Struth already the history writing one is well good six hours in Delivery to occupy likely, and all whatsoever even only moderately intelligible englishing strongestly resists. The your devotedest G.M.[73]

Wilamowitz's wife stayed by her own special request with the Murray family in Oxford: 'You cannot imagine', he wrote, 'the charm of an English nursery, and particularly of the inhabitants, for a German mother and grandmother.'[74] The visit went well, and was afterwards to be counted among Wilamowitz's 'most smiling memories.'[75]

This, however, was by no means the most important event for Murray of summer 1908. It had been a time of stress, near to crisis, in his family life. It also led to the highest point of his professional career. Early in June it was known in Oxford that Ingram Bywater, the Regius Professor of Greek there, would be retiring after a long tenure of the Chair. Murray was the obvious candidate for the succession, but took no steps to further his own claims. His health had been causing him trouble, and in June he retired to Cornwall for a long holiday. On 21 June, Lady Mary reported to him that L. R. Farnell had called on her to talk about the Professorship. Had they heard that there would be a vacancy and would her husband like it? Lady Mary answered yes without hesitation—they had probably discussed the possibility. Farnell went on to warn her that T. W. Allen of Queen's had asked him for a testimonial, and that the Prime Minister, Asquith (in whose gift the job effectively lay), would probably consult his own College, Balliol; they would probably recommend John Burnet of St Andrew's. Lady Mary said that Murray would probably not want to take any active steps to promote his own candidature; she went on to ask whether his continued stay in Cornwall would be interpreted as a sign of excessive aloofness. Farnell replied that it was just as well for him to be in Cornwall, and Lady Mary suggested to Murray that he should stay on there if possible rather than going on, as he had planned, to Cambridge.[76]

This news aroused Murray's anxieties and fears. He expressed them to Lady Mary in three instalments. His first letter was dated (surely wrongly) 21 June. He expressed worry about any idea of competition, particularly with Burnet, and said that 'if it came to that, I think I'd decline to send in testimonials.'[77] On 22 June he wrote again:

It is a sign of the comparative lack of faith and interest which I have in my work just now that I feel rather worried about the Greek Chair . . . And I think that if some one else is appointed I can, first, see that the appointment may well be right . . . and secondly, I can make him a chariot. At least, I can make Burnet a chariot, though it would be difficult with W. [T. W. Allen] because I don't respect him enough.[78]

Three days later he wrote in even more resigned vein.

In the watches of the night . . . it has become pretty clear to me that I am not fit for the Chair of Greek. I am not learned nor industrious enough to organise the study; I am too diverse in my interests. I do not feel exactly ashamed in reviewing my work, but I see clearly that none of it is of great solid achievement. Nothing which would entitle me to be called a great scholar. I am not ashamed; because I think in a way I have been faithful to something—to some sort of Hellenism, some task of interpretation and keeping alive; and I doubtless get my reward. But the suitable reward is not the Chair of Greek. Of course I should accept it if offered, I don't mean that I could refuse. Only that I no longer feel that I am the man to appoint. I could work very well with Burnet.[79]

The appointment of Murray to the Regius Chair was publicly announced on 17 October 1908. Lady Carlisle wrote that she had long known through political channels that Mr Asquith's mind was made up.[80] By mid-October the appointment was an open secret in Oxford; nor had it escaped the notice of the spirit world. Mrs Verrall reported a message via her table to a company assembled on 16 October:

'Trozene where roll the sad sea waves look in times to-morrow worth a hundred of the best who hath the old in new-born fancy dressed.' Here it stopped, then after a short pause, went on 'the just reward of toil according to the worth'.[81]

CHAPTER XI
Family Affairs

1. Problems of the growing family — Lady Mary's health.
2. The young father — companionship with Rosalind.
3. Strains within the marriage — Murray's preoccupation with the world of the theatre.

1

THE marriage between Gilbert and Lady Mary Murray was one of unimaginably lofty minds, but inevitably the hard realities of married life — even of the privileged life which they continued to enjoy — often drove their generous dreams into the background.

For a young couple with great talents, considerable riches, and no extravagant personal tastes, the Murrays had their share of problems in the first decade of their married life. By the end of the century, when they left Glasgow, they had three children to look after and Murray's own health appeared to be seriously undermined. The uncertainties that arose from this state of affairs threw a heavy burden upon Lady Mary. The least part of this was financial; she had private means and her mother would always give financial support as necessary, even if she also exacted a price for it in terms of psychological pressure. Two more children were born to them, Basil in 1902 at Barford and Stephen in 1908 at Oxford.

It was family administration that told increasingly on Lady Mary. She had to bear the brunt of moving from Glasgow and resettlement in Surrey. The same was true of their subsequent moves to Oxford and within Oxford. In that happy age Murray, illness apart, was not expected to concern himself with domestic affairs; they always had domestic help, as well as nurses and a family companion. But Lady Mary found the administration of Barford, a large and hospitable house, a heavy burden. In addition she had begun to undertake some of the duties of a secretary to her husband — in particular those of filing his correspondence, not without complaints, which a biographer may echo, about the sloppy habits of Mr Archer, Mr Bradley, and Miss Harrison in failing to date their letters.[1] All this was in itself enough to push the great causes further into the background.

How far did she also have to act as nurse? Lady Mary was genuinely concerned about Murray's health and Rosalind's. In later years she liked to have children or grandchildren ill under her care, and even to discover illnesses not obvious to others. Stephen declares he used to threaten his children with a beating on return from visiting the grandparents if they let themselves be put to bed and succumbed to the invalidism Lady Mary was always ready to thrust upon them. Her doctor while at Barford was a homeopath, Dr Christopher Wheeler, and according to Stephen it was under his influence that Lady Mary's medicine cupboard began to be stocked with a plethora of 'natural remedies' which she delighted to deal out on all occasions with a liberal hand and quite unscientifically.[2] This attitude certainly operated in some degree towards her husband. She would press him to limit commitments, for example over examining; prescribe nostrums for him such as 'peptonized cocoa';[3] or urge him to take complete holidays. But she was also concerned with his career as a great man in many fields and does not seem to have sensed any major contradiction between the long list of his ailments and the incessant activities, scholarly, dramatic, and political, which occupied him from summer 1899 onwards.

Both Murrays seem to have been astonishingly naïve or credulous in their attitude to health and doctors. For instance in 1905 Rosalind was again at Alassio for treatment. One doctor thought a month there would set her up, but this was brushed aside by Lady Mary as 'simply foolish' and Rosalind stayed there with 'Bombie' for the better part of three years at great expense. At the end of 1908, when Rosalind was after all 18 — hardly a child — Gilbert could report that:

she does seem, in a slow and doubtful way, to be really conquering her disease, whatever it is. If it were not for this eye trouble, which is a tiresome symptom, I should feel that she was getting near the edge of the wood. (Like all other symptoms, it is ambiguous; Basso and Boon both say that it comes either from rheumatism or tuberculosis or anaemia, and as usual cannot say which.)[4]

Today it seems extraordinary that any parents could leave a child in the hands of doctors, who, over a period of years, were unable to distinguish between three such horrifying diseases. Nor did the Murrays show any awareness that Rosalind's vague illnesses and treatment were such that only the very rich could afford.

Increasingly Lady Mary herself was subject to periods of nervous strain and ill health, particularly after the birth of a fourth child, Basil, in June 1902. Murray now had gradually to become the lesser invalid of the two. He would often be left on his own for quite long periods, while Lady Mary was recovering her health, either in Italy or Switzerland, or at a favourite nursing home, Gorse Mount, Grayshott, in Surrey. Moreover, with suitable assistance from a nurse, he often had to take charge of the older children on such occasions, or to take his turn in accompanying Rosalind for treatment in Italy and Switzerland. In later years he was probably a rather remote father, a final court of appeal, with little time for 'childish things'. This is clearly not true of him in his mid-thirties. He enjoyed his children's company, and recorded faithfully for Lady Mary their sayings and doings, even if he was also too anxiously concerned about their intellectual progress. The eldest, Rosalind, in particular became for him an intellectual companion, such as Lady Mary, for all the interests and causes which she shared with her husband, had never been. She had found Rosalind as a small child 'clever, cold and unloving',[5] and to some extent probably resented the intimacy between her husband and her daughter, which was in a way forced upon them by her own illness. Murray's assumption of new family responsibilities gave him a feeling of virtuous satisfaction, but did not evoke unmixed gratitude from Lady Mary.

2

It is a delightful task to trace Murray's relations with his children in the first two decades of his marriage. He was a young father — Rosalind, his first child, was born when he was 24. He viewed the world afresh through his children's eyes, and had a good ear for their sayings. He also enjoyed teaching them Latin and Greek, and guiding their first poetic efforts. The dangers of such close intellectual attention were not immediately apparent.

Murray's letters to Rosalind from her sixth year onwards show him at his most painstaking and charming. When she was 8, he commented in detail on a poem which she had written:

Try to rewrite the last five lines; I like the sense of them but they do not rhyme.

> T'is the world of Nature and her daughter spring,
> who from her wonderful cupboard
> Many a curious plant doth bring.
> Then look at the sky and the sunny cloud
> That seem so near and are really so high.

Part of my business as a Professor here [at Glasgow] is to make out what
old Greek poets really wrote, when their poems have been wrongly copied.
I should guess here that you meant to write

> T'is the world of Nature and her daughter spring,
> Who from her wonderful cupboard doth bring
> Many a [bright and?] curious thing.
> Then look at the sunny cloud and the sky
> That seem . . .[6]

During Murray's turns of duty with Rosalind in Italy or Switzerland
he and the 'Gosling', as he called her, became close companions. He
encouraged her intellectual precocity and her capacity for imitating
his favourite models. From Montreux in 1899 he wrote to Lady
Mary: 'R and I made a lot of poems this morning: one was a parody
of part of the Ode to a Grecian Urn about her eggs and this place:
"More happy eggs, more happy hoppery eggs / Forever cold, yet
still to be enjoyed . . . " '[7] The tone of their intellectual exchanges
was often more serious, even when she was a schoolgirl. Written
on her eleventh birthday (15 October 1901) Murray's letter contained
a copy of one of his most famous translations, which he had
completed shortly before: 'Will they ever come to me, ever again,
the long, long dances?' The last lines run:

> To stand from Fear set free, to breathe and wait;
> to hold a hand uplifted over Hate;
> And shall not loveliness be loved for ever?

To them Murray added a note for Rosalind's benefit: 'In the last
bit, Euripides is thinking of himself. He had escaped from a lot of
cruel enemies at Athens, and was living in a wild place near Mount
Olympus, protected by the King of Macedon.'[8]

Agnes too was encouraged to write poetry at an early age, or to
utter poetic thoughts. When she was not quite 7, Murray reported
to Archer that reflecting on the meaning of 'hard', she had said:

The hardest thing in the world, I should think, would be to plead and plead,
with a hard, hard mother . . . For *sad* I think of quite different things
. . . a lover and his wife, you know; or a lonely angel ashamed in a wood.
All this in a stentorian drawl . . .[9]

A little later Murray quoted a poem overheard as she played

> I wandered by the lonely shore
> When the moon and stars were low.
> Ah, how distinctly I remembered
> That unhappy marriage, long, long ago.[10]

Unexpected from a 7-year-old child, but perhaps inspired by talk with her nursemaids.

Agnes was an original, but was not entirely occupied with higher things. Murray wrote to his wife of a tea-party at which the 6-year-old child was given bread and cream instead of bread and butter. 'When she finished her bread, she looked round the company with a gravely courteous smile and said "If you will excuse my manners, I will now lick the plate." And so she did, with much grace.'[11]

Murray never developed the same companionship with his sons. Basil, born in 1902, was indeed an original, like Agnes, and Murray had many stories to tell of him in his early years: 'He is certainly clever—I like his poetry. It scans and rhymes even when all the words are nonsense . . . Most people think of the sense and spoil everything.'[12] The poetic sense was expressed in other ways. Once on a drive to Marston, he said: 'Stop, I want to fill the lane.' Murray's quick emendatory sense suggested 'feel'; but no, Basil wanted to 'fill the lane with his joy'. When Murray tickled his feet, he said: 'Stop; it tastes like beer'[13]—a compelling argument to his parents. A little later, Murray overheard a remark which he reported to Archer: ' "I don't suppose Sir Galahad would ever bite his Nurse?" It throws a somewhat lurid light on the speaker's own practice.'[14]

Basil even seems to have enjoyed his first steps in Greek mythology. One evening (aged 4) he said, 'he was going to count a trillion, and would I tell him all about Spikey while he did so. I found it was Cupid and Spikey that he meant.'[15]

Murray wrote to Agnes in October 1905: 'Basil said "Look at these angels on the marmalade glass walking up and down." Nurse— "They are not angels, but they are flies." Basil—"I know they are flies but they are ezzactly like angels so I call them angels." '

The elder son Denis seemed from the first to be more of a problem to his parents. When he was only two-and-a-half, Lady Mary was worried by his backwardness,[16] and his father a little later found him (at the age of 4) something of a puzzle:

He is a charming boy in his way, but I never feel confidence in his discretion or his affection. I feel on stand-off terms with him, just as one does with a school-boy. Whereas with the Gosling, I feel as if she were my long-lost sister come for a chat.[17]

About a year later, Murray quoted innocently what must be regarded in a post-Freudian era as a highly significant remark by Denis: 'When my nurse is nice, I like her, and when she isn't I dislike her; but when I don't love Dad I hate him.'[18]

Consciously or not, both the Murray parents probably set standards which over a wide field were too exacting for the average child, and at heart they could not conceive of their own children being average. On Denis's fourth birthday, for example, one of Murray's Glasgow colleagues gave him tin soldiers—'I have warned him of your displeasure', Murray wrote to his wife, but in consolation 'Denis is very unmilitary,'[19] and 'you can never make a boy peaceful by excluding guns and swords from his ken.'[20]

Steady efforts were made to raise Denis's academic standards. Early in 1900 he gave his father satisfaction, as recorded in a letter to Lady Carlisle:

Denis, who originally thought the 'Wooers' in the Odyssey, the Moors of Richard I, and Boers were all the same persons, has now set himself to grapple with the facts of the South African war, and has settled that he is for the Boers, because the English refuse Arbitration. This was not suggested by me, but puzzled out in private. It pleases me.[21]

Teaching, formal and informal, clearly formed a part of family life. Murray gave private tutorials with varying success, academic and psychological, to Rosalind, Denis, and Agnes. At the end of 1901 he decided to teach Rosalind and Denis regularly for an hour a day. One subject was the works of Dickens and a printed examination paper in *David Copperfield* is preserved, set to Rosalind and other local children in Churt.[22] In summer 1904, Rosalind went to boarding school at Priorsfield, and by this time Denis had embarked on the English male's traditional round of boarding schools— Bedales 1903, Copthorne 1904, in final preparation for Winchester (autumn 1905). To get him on to this conveyor belt was probably a hard grind for both Murray and Denis, but there were occasional rewards. Murray wrote to Lady Mary from Naworth in August 1903, describing how he had broken off a game of ping-pong with Denis, saying

'Oh! I have letters to write. My life is a burden!' Denis was wrestling with me to prevent my going and said 'Is your life a burden? Then I have something to tell you that will make it not a burden . . . I have thought it for four days, but I would not tell you till I was sure . . . I like my Latin!'[23]

Winchester was probably not a good place for Denis. The school as well as his parents expected too much of him, and both Murray and Lady Mary took from the first against his housemaster, the Revd F. P. David. Murray clearly enjoyed writing to Rosalind of their first encounter in September 1905:

We took Denis to Winchester yesterday. The air was thick with rain and with the most crusted Toryism that I have smelt for years. Mother and I lay back in our chairs and gasped for some time, then I lifted up my horn. I managed to be very polite all the time, but I contrived to tell a Bishop that he was immoral, while mother showed him that he was illogical, and also to tell David . . . that if he could not get discipline into his boys without sending them to Aldershot for military training, he must be rather unskilful with boys.[24]

This was not a happy start (although Denis himself liked the housemaster very much indeed) and clearly Denis received bad reports for some time. The Murrays blamed his housemaster, and reacted strongly against some suggestion that Denis should perhaps be removed from the school, as a bad influence from the Church of England standpoint. Murray wrote:

I trust that the tone of your letter to me is due to temporary irritability and lack of self-control. If so I shall be glad to hear from you further before consulting Dr. Burge the Headmaster as to whether the authorities whom you refer to as 'We' share your sectarian objections to Denis' presence at Winchester.[25]

It is not clear whether this letter was ever sent and it would hardly have eased Denis's position. Next spring it seemed that the Murrays themselves might remove Denis when they began to suspect that immoral practices were rife in the house. However Murray was able to reassure Lady Mary:

I have had the talk with Denis. It was less serious than I thought. Nothing of that kind at all. It appears that two elder boys talked obscenely and Denis was thrown into intimacy with one of them because they were both in the infirmary together . . . The house has been getting steadily better all the time D. has been at school . . . I gave him a little sermon on the whole subject . . . I will write to David.[26]

He evidently did so at length, and received a friendly reply. From this time on Denis's school career caused his parents no trouble. Murray by this time probably no longer pressed him to attain academic heights which were clearly beyond his reach, and wrote of him after the last episode as 'so good and nice'.[27] However, it is unlikely that Denis ever shook off entirely the feeling that he had somehow failed his remarkable parents by being just a nice, average boy.

The other children too might be overshadowed by this sort of contrast; and Rosalind—academically the ablest of them—eventually found that the intellectual companionship of her father imposed other strains upon her. But their childhood was not completely over-shadowed by such tensions. Murray delighted in the idiosyncrasies of his children, and they must have enjoyed (if sometimes with a certain puzzlement) his flow of wit and nonsense. To Rosalind for example he wrote in 1905 from 'Naworth Castle, Frogley-in-the-Mud, Chillingham Wetley'.[28] Bertrand Russell recorded similar fantasies. In summer 1903 Murray was looking for a school for Denis, and reported in Russell's hearing that he had found one:

'The Headmaster is the Rev. V. Ermin, of the Creepers, Crawley Down.' At this point Mary exclaimed indignantly 'Oh, Gilbert! He's not Reverend'. The only sub-stratum of fact in the story was that the school was at Crawley.[29]

Rosalind was most often the recipient of his imaginative excursions. The other children may have been equally favoured—it is only Murray's letters to Rosalind that survive in any quantity; but it is likely that she was his best audience and that she got more than an equal share of letters. They form a delightful series of which the following are typical extracts:

14 Oct. 1902. H.R.H. Princess Louise has gone to Newcastle to-day, to open the Bazaar, with the Duke of Argyll, grandfather and grand-mother, mother, a suite and four policemen! The policemen are to see that nobody assassinates anybody else on the way. Or at least, no stranger. Members of the party can assassinate each other as much as they like, because they are all in a saloon together and the police in a separate carriage.

On 29 December 1905 Murray described a visit from Tolstoy's secretary, Tchertkoff, who, as he left after a visit in London, interrogated him:

'What is your religious position? Do you believe in violence, and do you cling to the divinity of Christ?' I felt quite ashamed when I said that I still believed in a little violence, in extreme cases; he sighed kindly, like a stoutish angel, and went off into the night on his bicycle.[30]

Probably the other side of Murray's correspondence with his children gave much delight; little is preserved of it, but one letter from Agnes survives among the many messages of congratulations which Murray received on the announcement of his Oxford professorship:

My own most darling Dad,

Joy, joy, joy.

I used to think it was the Eggregious Professorship. The first thing almost that Enid Wedgwood said was 'Oh, will it stop his translations?' It won't Dadells will it?[31]

There was plenty of fun, as well as plenty of problems, in the Murray family at this period.

3

The problems inevitably centred around Lady Mary, as mother, housekeeper, invalid, and the one who had to bear the brunt of Lady Carlisle's temperament. The copious correspondence between Murray and his wife contains indications that their own relations over the period 1899 to 1908 were subjected to considerable strain. Internal evidence shows that the letters have been weeded to remove evidence on this subject.[32] However, much remains and the biographer has to decide whether the full story is one of much higher tension than can be deduced from the existing documents.

Many marriages are from time to time exposed to strains such as affected the Murrays, but it must have been particularly hard for Lady Mary, brought up to think of a joint campaign of high endeavour in the service of humanity, to realize that her part of the joint career was to lie mainly in looking after the comforts and material needs of her husband. Murray did not adjust his own aims (she would not have had him do so) nor his burden of work. He preserved in his letters the tone of total intimacy and confidence. For example the old endearments remained—they had ranged widely over the animal kingdom, Murray himself figured for long as an opossum, and Lady Mary for a time as a wombat. Husband and wife by the early twentieth century had settled down in this respect to a cat and dog life. Lady Mary figured mainly as 'Puss', Murray himself often lamenting his 'unbecatted' state, and styling himself Mr Dog, Thomas Dog, Dog Tray, or Dog Harris. The old flow of letters continued, when one was away from the other, including full health bulletins, stories about the children, and increasing concern over the children's problems.

Lady Carlisle was another firm family link. Murray at this point faced both ways. He still confided his deepest plans to his mother-in-law, displayed almost extravagant sympathy with her sufferings, and sometimes wrote of Lady Mary as a problem common to the two of them.[33] To Lady Mary he would gaily report on Lady Carlisle's moods, whims, illnesses, and hypochrondria:

Thurs. 14 Oct. 1904;

Your mother arrived . . . and we had an early and somewhat turmoiled and lowering breakfast . . . she does not seem to be angry with you — not in the least; but the atmosphere is dreadfully charged with thunder in general.[34]

May 1905

Your mother is not well, but not, I think, really ill. She eloquently argues that she is really in a desperate condition, and makes a good case, which interests but does not convince the house.[35]

Outside the family, many of the old common interests remained, even if Lady Mary could no longer take such an active part in pursuing them. Husband and wife continued to share, for example, the profound distaste for aestheticism — taste without works — exemplified in Murray's letters from *I Tatti*, and for all organized religion, the Catholic Church most of all. It was a typical letter that Murray wrote in spring 1903 after a day's expedition to Assisi:

I won't attempt to describe the impression made on me by the Monastery, except that in the end I felt that it was, after all, *mad*, and its fruits were the crowding beggars in the streets and monks who had to be suppressed — to say nothing of religious persecution . . . So I went up with a certain feeling of liberation to the old temple of Minerva on the hill — where Propertius probably worshipped, to little purpose, certainly.[36]

Here was a constant background of shared convictions, and above all Lady Mary never faltered in her assurance of the importance of Murray's own career. Her dealings with the Vice-chancellor in spring 1908 about the Professorship of Greek at Oxford show her as a devoted and sensible helpmate at a most crucial point of Murray's career. This is the total context against which their undoubted difficulties, particularly in 1908, should be seen.

The first signs of anything more than minor tiffs and misunderstandings date from the summer of 1900, towards the end of Murray's first year of retirement from Glasgow. From Burgenstock in Switzerland, where he was on holiday with the Verralls, he issued a sort of declaration of independence. It is not clear how the need for this had arisen; but Murray's tone anticipates Shaw's description of Professor Cusins — always courteous, but with set purposes from which he would not be bent;

I am not blinking the difficulties of the situation; as to that I told you all there is to know before coming out. But the chief thing I should ask of you — and do ask — is that in facing any possible future phase of the matter I may be entirely free. I want to act consciously on my own judgment and responsibility and not to feel that you are 'forbidding' things — I think you will agree with me about this; and I do not really think that the matter need give us a moment's uneasiness. My love for you is rooted in the rock.[37]

Whatever was the difficulty between them (and some of their exchanges at this point are missing), it was soon shelved and by the end of June Murray was again at his most tender.

I have been thinking about . . . how ill I have treated you . . . I cannot think what would happen if you were either to die or to get thoroughly indifferent or hostile to me. I imagine both . . . it grieves me so much to think of your getting my disagreeable and hurt letters so long afterwards . . . There should be no biting by correspondence, I am very sorry for mine . . .[38]

Another difficult period was in the second half of 1902, after the birth of Basil in June. Murray confided his difficulties at least partially to Russell:

I have to make her [Lady Mary] rather a first care, without her sensing it, hanging about and taking the children and doing things for visitors . . .

There was some competition in invalidism, too. Murray continued in the same letter:

I am not ill; but I have an amount of physical discomfort, often reaching the dignity of pain, that sometimes astonishes me to think of! I could describe it, pretty accurately, in language which would make it seem as if life was incessant torment to me. Which it isn't . . . Not by no means. But how odd it must be never to be ill![39]

A few months later, Russell was pressing Murray to join him at *I Tatti*. Murray refused at length, and again with some confidential remarks on his family difficulties:

Another [reason] better not mentioned — is that after all Mary's proud words I found her in tears because she did not know how she could manage the children's holidays and the other burdens of life and housekeeping if I went away. The reasons are not really desperate . . . but I am on the verge of an illness, and think it safest to stay at home and work in the woods and hedges as much as I can . . .

I am beset by depression of the most ridiculous tormenting sort. I have sufficient control over them [*sic*] to know that they are all nonsense, thanks to middle age. In youth, I should have been in measurable distance of suicide — at least, so it seems to me, as I look back.[40]

By 1905, Murray had found his way back to Oxford and his career as a scholar was being successfully re-established. To that extent life must have been much easier for him and for Lady Mary than in 1902.

There are few signs of strain in the correspondence between Murray and Lady Mary which survives over the next three years; but Lady Mary's letters particularly for the year 1906 are not numerous in comparison with Murray's own. Her side of the correspondence was probably heavily weeded, and it is not difficult to guess the reasons. She did not much enjoy Oxford life;[41] and these too were the years of Murray's most intense preoccupation with the living theatre, and the living theatre inevitably included leading ladies. 'We did so hurt each other on Sunday', Murray wrote at the end of July 1905;[42] and a few months later he assured Lady Mary, perhaps rather too jauntily, that he 'had had no communication with strange ladies in any way'.[43]

Among the potential *femmes fatales* who crossed Murray's path were Florence Farr, who was in charge of the first London production of Murray's translations, and Mrs Patrick Campbell. Neither seems greatly to have fascinated Murray, but there were other no doubt charming ladies. It was often Murray's task to coach them in the delivery of his lines, and naturally he wanted to get the best out of them dramatically. He was only 40 in 1906, and though the portrait of him at this time by Francis Newberry (of which he himself approved) shows him as a balding, severe, eminently professorial type,[44] that was not the whole truth about him. He had a golden voice, a delightful wit, and a playful charm about his conversation. There is no reason to suppose that he did not enjoy exercising his talents on women. Indeed his correspondence shows that he lapsed into a mildly flirtatious tone with them almost as a matter of course.[45] It would have needed a wife of very easy going temperament not to feel some resentment on occasion, and a woman of mature character to keep her resentment to herself. Lady Mary was never easy going and by 1908 her nerves were in an extremely raw state. Whatever strains there may have been over the previous years then came to a head.

At the beginning of the year, Lady Mary was far advanced in her last pregnancy (the Murray's youngest son, Stephen, was born in February), and had undoubted priority as an invalid over her husband. He wrote from Naworth after receiving bad reports of her health: 'I always feel that every little worsening of your illness is Mr. Dog's fault, though I know it is not so.'[46] The new baby's health gave rise at first to much anxiety and he had to have a foot put into splints. Lady Murray and Murray were much apart that spring. She went to convalesce with the baby at Sidmouth, while Murray looked after the other children as best he could at Oxford and at Rottingdean, where he shared a house with Lady Mary's doctor, Christopher Wheeler and his wife, the actress Penelope Wheeler.

Here lay the main cause of Lady Mary's jealousy. Christopher Wheeler was a leading homeopathic physician of his day, and Penelope, a talented actress, was at this time studying the part of Phaedra for a production of *Hippolytus* at Birmingham. She and her husband were both very friendly with both Murrays, and nothing could have been more respectable and natural in appearance than for Murray to stay with them, with or without his children, when Lady Mary was incapacitated. However Penelope was an attractive woman, who was clearly fascinated by Murray and his work, and had good claims to work intimately with him. And Murray himself? He was pleased by other people's interest in his personality and his writings. He wrote once to Lady Mary of Charles Masterman 'Too anxious to please—rather like myself.' Like other men he particularly enjoyed pleasing attractive women.

In spring 1908, while Lady Mary was still convalescing at Sidmouth and Murray was at Rottingdean with the older children, he made further plans to go off on holiday with Rosalind to the Wheelers in Cornwall early in June for a complete rest (he had for some time been doing more than his share of family supervision). Lady Mary evidently expressed (in a letter no longer extant) her mistrust of people of the theatre and their free manners. Murray, conscious of his virtuous conduct as a father, was somewhat aggrieved, and the rest of the story can be told by quoting his letters:

27 April 1908: That is a very troubled letter from you this morning, and leaves Mr. Dog a little helpless. I mean, as to Puss's mistrust of radicals and playwrights. You know, dear one, you are in the same boat with me. You were as much Ibsenite as I ever was . . . why should you suspect people now? I don't think you would if you were quite well . . . But if you would sooner that I avoided the Wheelers, I will . . . My nerves are all rather overworn . . . I should be quite as disagreeable to Penelope as to anybody else, if she were to call.

4 May 1908: [I have been] wondering why I was always disappointing and hurting you . . . I wonder if it mostly is that we did not make a real imaginative effort to understand each other twenty years ago.

7 May 1908: (Lady Mary): I'm afraid it will take some time before I can get used to Penelope—even, you see, if it was all my fault and not hers.

I can't forget the harm my unhappiness about her did Baby and me: I hope that remembrance will grow less vivid in time, but I don't suppose I should rest well in her company till it had . . .

By 9 June (just after Wilamowitz's visit to Oxford) Murray and Rosalind had joined the Wheelers at Kynance in Cornwall.

12 June: I feel sure that under happier circumstances, you could not but like Penelope. She is really such a frank, kind and young-hearted person.

25 June: I behave all right, but of course I do become charmed by a certain kind of beauty . . . beauty mixed with something else always; and though I feel that I love you now perhaps more than ever in my life, I realise that these rather emotional friendships do come drifting across my heart, and that such things could not happen to you and would seem to you a sort of treason if they did. I don't feel any element of treason in them myself.

27 June: The sort of breath of imaginative love which shoots here and there through my friendship with Penelope or Margaret [probably Mackail] — or, I might even say, if it does not sound odd, for Rosalind, makes me only feel how much deeper and wider my love for my wife is — altogether not to be compared. Does it hurt you, all this? I hope not.[47]

This correspondence, it should be remembered, took place as it were in counterpoint with Murray's confidences to Lady Mary about his fitness for the Oxford professorship, and only a month or two after they had been exchanging news and views about Denis's adolescent problems. Their differences of 1908 were composed, but Lady Mary's feelings were not fully assuaged.

She had the last words preserved in the Murray Papers about this phase of her husband's relationship with Penelope Wheeler. On 19 December 1908 she wrote to him: 'More and more — I can't help saying it, this apotheosis of freedom — the dramatic profession — so entirely at the cost of an excellent husband — seems to me — well, ridiculous.[48]

Murray did not renounce Penelope Wheeler's company, and she was not the only object of Lady Mary's jealousy. He was on the defensive again in summer 1909, when he took the older children on holiday to Aldeburgh and stayed on with them and Jane Harrison after Lady Mary went back to Oxford. He wrote in answer to a letter (not preserved):

Your kind but dreadfully sad letter . . . I have been miserable too about the same thing, I think a large part of the misunderstanding came from this; that I regarded myself as performing a rather difficult duty by being here, and the Puss thought I was deserting her for my pleasure . . . Nothing is further from the poor Dog's desires than to 'keep house' with this or any other strange lady.[49]

And a little later he added: 'I may be so unsatisfactory when I am really with you as I was at Aldeburgh . . . I am a great burden upon you with my health and my "habits". But I do belong to you so much . . . '[50]

All these apologies, and the accusations which presumably occasioned them, must be seen as a result of a deep crisis in Lady Mary's self-confidence, possibly associated with the not uncommon psychological problems of a late pregnancy. This is made plain by a letter of early 1909:

Who knows better than you how being ill has left me with no imagination, no idealism, not much understanding of Art and not much belief in Love (with a big L)—it sounds an odious thing to say; it is a more odious thing to feel. Perhaps I shall emerge some day; at present I feel crushed by Mother's and your personalities, by the extent to which I disagree with you both, by the feeling that—though there is something in my opinion (I have too little faith to dignify any of my opinions with the name of belief)—I'm not really strong enough to make anything of it, etc. etc. . . .

Then, after an exposition of her newly-forming socialist views:

There now, I do mean that, but do you think I could explain myself or get a chance of being accorded any reason—and yet I'm sure I'm right—but what chance has a Puritan Bohemian with no brains . . .

I'll be a good girl when you come home—keep house as well as ever I can—care for Drama more than anything and never, never, never be jealous of anyone.[51]

Murray's own reply has been mutilated, and deals only with the incidental point of suitable reading for Rosalind (then in her nineteenth year)—he found it 'rather painful to read the Tolstoy (A. K.) with her.'[52] A more substantial reaction may be found, strangely enough, in Murray's inaugural address to the University College of Aberystwyth, reprinted in the *Sociological Review*, July 1909. It is a revealing speech in its emphasis on the virtues of temperance and self-denial, but above all as it underlines the need, not only for equal opportunities for women in education and the intellectual world, but also for those changes in social conditions which would enable women to harvest fully the fruits of educational opportunity:

I have been asked by a lady of my acquaintance to add—I should not dare to say such a thing for myself—that this is one of the reasons why the wives of clever men, when they reach middle-age, are so often stupid. They were not stupid to begin with. They meant to share their husband's wider interests. But an anxious and incessant pressure of trivial cares and duties has left them no time to read, no energy to think or use their imagination. There is here a great unconscious oppression, a great wasting of high common life. It is for the coming generation to try to amend it.[53]

Murray worked throughout his life to extend educational chances for women; but he had played some part in the process of 'unconscious oppression'. Lady Mary promised early in their married life to put his career first. She loyally did this, and suffered as a result from considerable nervous strain. The strain was increased by Murray's theatrical preoccupations, and further by his frank explanation of those 'shadows drifting across his heart' (not for him *le courage du mensonge* or even *le courage de se taire*), and by his refusal to give up 'untreasonable friendships' with younger women which were a recurrent feature of his later life. He too suffered from nervous strain caused, as Shaw perceptively noted in *Major Barbara*, not only by his battle with ill health, but also by his determination to preserve in all circumstances his armour of reason and gentle manners. Sufficient causes for tension on both sides, without presupposing any marital infidelities. It was no doubt all perfectly reasonable, but Murray was, perhaps, slowly learning to pay more attention to the reasons of the heart.

CHAPTER XII
Professor at Oxford

1

IN autumn 1908 Murray set about the duties of his new post. His doubts about his ability to perform them were certainly genuine; but he had deeply-rooted ideas of how he could make the best use of the Chair and of what changes should be made in the teaching of Greek. Fourteen years before, he had written to Arthur Sidgwick:

I think a prophet is a good deal wanted in Oxford to teach that there are really life and poetry and things to move one in ancient literature. Bywater, I suppose, knows that this is so, but I doubt if he can make anyone else know it.[1]

However it was not Bywater, the learned but austere scholar, who was the main target of his criticism at that time. He was more concerned with the way in which the quality of Greek literature had been obscured by a cloud of trite phrases about the glories of the classics:

Phrases like 'the perfection of the Greek art', 'the ancient sense of form', etc. . . . are flowing so glibly about in everybody's mouths that most of those who use the words do not either believe or understand them; and I think most pupils in their hearts think it is more than half humbug when we tell them that we enjoy Greek poetry as much as we really do. The bright ones, who care for poetry, generally feel that ancient poetry is altogether on a lower level than Modern.[2]

Something of these sentiments found its way into the text and even more into the preface of Murray's *History of Ancient Greek Literature* ; and in the five years before he became Professor at

Oxford he had tried to reveal Euripides in a new light, partly by his editing of the text, partly by the production of his translations.

In an editorial note of welcome to the new professor, the *Oxford Magazine* spoke of his 're-creation' of Euripides.[3] Murray was always ready to accept the word and the risk that it could be used as an accusation. His aim was indeed to 're-create' not only the Greek dramatists, but also literary scholarship as a whole. He had learned from the Cambridge School of the need to integrate the study of ancient literature with that of ancient religion and other forms of art, and to supplement the findings of literary criticism with those of archaeology and anthropology. Much was expected of him in this sense by some of his Oxford colleagues. L. R. Farnell wrote on his appointment that he could 'expand the whole conception of Greek in our University, and by your all-round sympathies with art, religion and poetry . . . abolish the old view that the Greek chair could only be sat in by a textual-critical book man.'[4] He received some cautions, too. Charles Cookson of Magdalen warned him that: 'There will be indifference, scepticism or even opposition in some quarters, but it wasn't merely the green trees but the "mountain tops that freeze" which followed Orpheus. Put yourself at the head of the Faculty, and we will have a Greek Renaissance yet.'[5] In other words, if Murray gave a lead, not only the young radicals but the old conservatives too would follow. Wilamowitz warned Murray politely not to throw out the baby with the bathwater. New ways were clearly necessary and Murray could introduce them, he thought, but 'The old tradition of the great masters of language who discovered a century ago what pure Attic was must not perish in England — all the less because it is threatened the world over.'[6] Among famous British scholars, Housman was particularly friendly in his congratulations, in spite of differences between his and Murray's conceptions of the duties of the professional scholar. After some typical references to the horrors of a Scottish professorship successfully endured, Housman wrote:

I think you are now well on your way to take that place in the public eye which used to be occupied by Jowett and then by Jebb; and as you are a much better scholar than the one and a much better man of letters than the other, the public will be a gainer without knowing it, and good judges (by which I mean myself) will be less at variance with the public.[7]

All qualified compliments, if carefully read, but the tone was warm.

Murray set out his own credo and programme in his Inaugural Lecture, delivered early in February 1909. It is a document extremely important for his conception of his own duties as a scholar, and as a teacher in the broadest sense of the word. The starting-point of his argument was that 'The best life of Greece represents one of those highest moments in the life of Humanity. The business to which the world has set us as Greek scholars is to see that it does not die.'[8]

The literature and life of Greece could not be recaptured by reading 'with a slack imagination'—here Murray was quoting his friend A. C. Bradley on the proper approach to Shakespeare. He paid tribute to the great work done by the British universities in the past without any conscious effort at popularization; they had made Homer, Sophocles, and Plato living forces that worked upon English thought continuously as a permeating influence. No doubt Gladstone was very much in Murray's mind, with his devotion to Homeric studies, and his conviction that Homer was a sort of secular *preparatio evangelica* for the Gospel message, parallel to the religious preparation in the Old Testament.[9]

However in 1909 it was no longer enough, in Murray's view, for university teachers simply to continue in the tradition of their predecessors. The scope of Greek studies had been enormously extended since Murray had come to Oxford as an undergraduate. The modern writer saw ten things where previous scholars saw one. Modern literary criticism alone had brilliant achievements to its credit—Murray cited some of Verrall's work as a proof, which modern scholars would be unlikely to regard as adequate. Comparative mythology and comparative philology were virtually new subjects; so too was the special study of Greek religion. Murray's implicit conclusion was that to interpret Greek literature successfully to his contemporaries a scholar must have studied all these subjects. He quoted the peroration of one of Wilamowitz's Oxford lectures to emphasize the dedication which was required for this task: 'We all know that ghosts will not speak until they have drunk blood: and we must give them the blood of our hearts.'[10] Murray went on from this to his own peroration about the profound satisfactions of a scholar's career—a passage typical of him not only in its earnestness but also in its self-mocking humour:

It is for this that we are content to become what we are, a somewhat bloodless company, sensitive, low-spirited, lacking in spring; in business ill at ease, in social life thin and embarrassed, objects of solicitude to kind hostesses. We have, more than most people, the joy of having given ourselves up to something greater than ourselves. We stand between the living and the dead. We are mediators through whom the power of great men over their kind may still live after death.

Such was the main argument of a lecture which Murray reckoned to have been the greatest public success he had ever had 'to judge by the praises of . . . especially oldish and conservative people. I begin to suspect that it was really a conservative manifesto.'[11] It attracted some attention in the press, where the more serious articles were often written by men with a good classical education for others who had been similarly trained. *The Times* published a leader on 'the value of Greek Literature', based largely on Murray's Inaugural:

Euripides seems to us the youngest poet in the world, and we owe our understanding of him largely to the brilliant translations of Professor Murray, who in them has proved better than by any argument the value of Greek literature and Greek studies.[12]

The *Nation* was also appreciative and confident: 'Never since it ascended the throne of culture at the Renaissance has Greek thought exercised so wide an influence.'[13]

2

Murray had successfully made his public profession of faith. It was of course a different matter to translate this into practice, and to adapt the form of Greek studies at Oxford to his ideas. In his Inaugural he had not confined himself to broad objectives and had indeed prefaced his more general argument by some specific suggestions. He recognized the importance of specialist seminar work, and stated his belief that there was too sharp a division in Oxford between the first and second parts of the standard classical course (Mods. and Greats), traditionally designed to cover respectively Greek and Latin literature, and then Greek and Roman history, and philosophy (not only that of classical times).

From the time of his return to Oxford in 1905, Murray had been interested in transforming Mods. from a rather mechanical fairly detailed examination over a wide range of classical literature into something which would encourage a deeper study of a few set books, and a wider range of other literature for translation purposes only. In brief he wanted to liberate students from the full tyranny of examinations, and appeal to their artistic and literary enthusiasm. His correspondence on these themes with H. E. Butler, Charles Cookson, R. W. Livingstone, and Alfred Zimmern is of considerable interest to the specialist,[14] and his aims were to a large extent accomplished.

However, in 1909 Murray's principal aim was to widen the scope of Greats on the historical side, and to give students some idea of the many new sources of history. He succeeded in introducing a sort of pre-Greats 'bridging course', entitled 'Preparatory to Greats'. He himself lectured on the study of Greek literature, Greek history, and Ancient philosophy; and he persuaded other experts to talk on excavations, inscriptions, papyri, philology, anthropology, and Greek vases in a series jokingly known in traditionalist Oxford as 'The Seven against Greats'.[15] The 'bridging' lectures did not survive as an institution, but at least by the early 1930s students reading Greek history in 'Greats' were made well aware of the importance of archaeological and artistic evidence,[16] as a supplement or even in contradiction to the histories of Herodotus and Thucydides, and as an aid to interpreting them.[17]

Murray as Professor of Greek was soon up against a tougher problem. Should there be a compulsory Greek test for entrance to Oxford? The test was an established fact; Winston Churchill had been prevented by it from reading history at Oxford as a mature student.[18] It was not abolished until 1920, but early in the twentieth century there was a strong movement against it in Oxford. This was re-launched in 1909, and Murray was inevitably at the centre of controversy. His deepest conviction was against compulsion. Great harm, he felt, was done by unimaginative routine teaching and unwilling routine learning; many good students as a result acquired a hatred of the whole subject. Murray's own first proposal, made in 1909, was that there should be only one compulsory test in a classical language—either Latin or Greek (Latin would of course be the choice of the large majority of students). Teachers and educational authorities were consulted. A number of schoolmasters, including Edward Lyttelton at Eton and A. C. Benson, thought that for many boys compulsory Greek at best took up time which could more usefully be devoted to other subjects, and resulted in no gains which could not be equally well acquired by the study of translations.[19] On the other side was, for example, George Macdonald of the Scottish Education Department, Murray's former assistant at Glasgow, who thought that the abolition of a compulsory Greek test at University entrance stage would inevitably hasten the 'decay of Greek' in schools throughout the country.[20]

Murray tried out a further compromise proposal on compulsion early in 1910. He explained this to Archer:

I go for a normal list of subjects of preliminary examinations, of which Greek is to be one; no subject absolutely compulsory, but before exemption is granted a definite reason must be given, and the candidate must take some other subject at a higher standard.[21]

A later modification was that scientists would be absolutely exempted from a Greek test (this exception was not supported by the Professor of Medicine, William Osler), but that it should be compulsory for students of modern languages, history, and English.

The debate on compulsory Greek was conducted up to its last stages amid considerable publicity, Murray for example writing an article for *The Times* on 4 February 1910, and a letter on 28 February. The whole theme was one of great concern for the British 'establishment' from the Prime Minister downwards (Asquith had been a notable classical scholar in his time). At the end of November 1910, a draft Statute for the abolition of the compulsory Greek test was put to the vote in the Oxford Congregation. Murray tried to secure the second compromise proposal noted above. Opposition to the statute was led by A. D. Godley, a scholar whose wit and command of Greek and Latin rivalled Murray's own. He was in favour of somewhat modifying the existing tests; but he expressed strongly the view that, if once compulsory Greek was abolished, compulsory Latin would follow and the classical element in education would soon be removed.[22] Murray's compromise proposals got little support and the attempt to abolish compulsory Greek at Oxford again failed. The issue was raised again after the war and in March 1920 compulsory Greek was finally abolished. (See Chapter XIX sect. 1.)

In 1910, Murray had also to preside over a committee to discuss the possibility of instituting new final 'schools' to cover part of the Greats ground. The main proponent of innovation was J. A. Smith, the idiosyncratic and combative Waynflete Professor of Philosophy. He argued with Murray for 'Greats without Greek',[23] (i.e., not for a reform of the Greats school, but for the institution of a new Greekless final course for philosophy students). Why should all students wanting to study philosophy have to do so within the classical framework? Plato and Aristotle in good translations should give the aspiring philosopher all that he needed—why should he have to bother with often very difficult language? 'Greats without Greek' would reduce the upper-class flavour of Oxford by opening a respectable philosophy school to students who had not come from the great Greek-teaching public schools. There was heat on either side of the debate, not perhaps greatly reduced by Smith, who wrote to Murray, 'except in opinion, I am sure we do not differ'.[24] Two schemes were discussed for new Schools in which the Greekless students could get a good training in philosophy. One was for a school of philosophy and natural science (which did not attract universal support from scientists); another, for a combination of Philosophy, Politics, and Economics, was warmly championed by Murray's friend Sandy Lindsay, who had just been appointed to a lectureship at Balliol. For ten years, for various reasons, nothing came of the discussions; but after the First World War the second proposal for 'PPE' or 'Modern Greats' was accepted and has proved very successful. [25]

Murray was only connected incidentally with the proposals for the new schools when these were originated. However, he was widely regarded in Oxford as a backslider, who had not defended compulsory Greek whole-heartedly. This was thought inexcusable for one in his professorial position. There was a bitter attack on him in the *Classical Quarterly* on this point, and all he could say to his wife was that he had 'mostly got over it'. [26] Moreover as at Glasgow his politics were held against him, particularly when he actively supported the Liberal candidate for Oxford University in the bitterly fought election of January 1910. His new college, Christ Church, to which his Chair was attached, made its disapproval very obvious. He wrote to Rosalind at the end of January 'I don't go to College—the tutors are sending almost nobody to my lectures on Homer. Only New College, Balliol, and Jesus are coming.' [27]

Murray was never a good 'college man', and became less so after leaving New College. The college system may have made it easier for him informally to cultivate young dons and keen undergraduates, and such opportunities he would savour to the full. But the personal hostility so often evoked in learned societies, the differences of view on points of scholarship, administration, or politics, was very distasteful to one who himself was scrupulous in his courtesy. A letter to Rosalind at the end of 1912 illustrates his deep disillusion:

[J. L.] Stocks brought his young woman [the later Baroness Mary Stocks] last night and there was a great battle. She is very pretty and radical and downright and was led to expressing her mind on the general hennish and prudish quality of Oxford and Cambridge. Stocks and I were led into agreeing that this really is a pretty rotten University—largely through the fault of the residential Colleges. [28]

However, disillusion did not extend to Murray's teaching and writing.

3

Murray was also much preoccupied from 1908 onwards with the study of Greek religion. Early in 1908 he had been invited to give the Gifford Lectures on some religious subject at Glasgow in the following winter. His election to the Oxford professorship forced him to go back on his acceptance, but in the mean time he had devoted much thought to possible subjects.

In the early years of his professorship, Murray had worked very closely with Jane Harrison. He could and did criticize her professional work to her. In 1908 he wrote to Lady Mary that his criticisms of her work were so unsympathetic that they 'nearly made her cry'.[29] He recognized that she sometimes lapsed into amateurism, and is reported once to have told her that she had never done an hour's serious work in her life.[30] Murray could also laugh at her, which involved more risks. He described to his wife an explosion over some criticism of her dress:

Logan [Pearsall Smith] observed calmly that there was something provocative about the present fashions and went away to work, leaving a perfect storm behind him. The word provocative, which I did not originate but defended, upset Miss H. altogether.[31]

Nevertheless Murray had given Jane Harrison important scholarly support after the publication of her *Prolegomena* in 1903. He had also been deeply involved with the draft of the book which she published in 1912, *Themis: A Study of the Social Origins of Greek Religion*. In this she continued her attack on the Olympian religion, as divorced from the deeper springs of human nature. At the same time she 'socialized' her view of the Greek primitive cults, particularly that of Dionysus. Its main importance, she now urged (as the influence of Frazer and Durkheim worked more deeply on her thought), lay in the opportunity it provided for the worshipper to sink his individual self in the worshipping group, and to achieve collective thinking or feeling. Ritual was here all important. From ritual, mythology derived, and the essential myth was that of the Eniautos-daemon or year-spirit. This is the essence of Jane Harrison's doctrine, in so far as it affected Murray.

Jane Harrison induced both her Cambridge colleague, F. M. Cornford, and Murray to write chapters for *Themis*. Murray's chapter, on the origins of Greek tragedy in Dionysiac ritual, was a substantial contribution to the book. Unfortunately for his subsequent reputation as a scholar, he gave his whole-hearted backing not only to the concept of the year-spirit of vegetation and fertility, killed, buried, and born again each year, as the central idea of Greek religion, but also to the thesis that Greek tragedy had its origins in the annual rituals connected with this year-spirit.

Murray's clearest statement of this thesis may be found in his book on *Euripides and his Age*, published in 1913 in the Home University Library. He describes it (perhaps with his tongue in his cheek?) as the 'orthodox view of the origin of tragedy', arguing that Greek tragedy was much more nearly akin to the medieval mystery play than to Shakespearian drama:

Greek tragedy was developed out of a definite ritual . . . tragedy originated in a dance, ritual or magical, intended to represent the death of Vegetation this year and its coming return in triumph next year . . . vegetation . . . to the ancient was a personal being, not 'it', but 'He' . . . The Year Daemon . . . waxes proud and is slain by his enemy, who becomes thereby a murderer and must in turn perish at the hands of the expected avenger, who is at the same time the Wronged One re-risen . . .

. . . Greek tragedy extended its range first to embrace the histories of other Heroes . . . who were essentially like Dionysus: Pentheus . . . Hippolytus . . . and, especially, I should be inclined to add, Orestes . . .

. . . the general temper of tragedy moved strongly away from the monotony of fixed ritual . . . what had begun as almost pure ritual ended by being almost pure drama . . . whole generations have read his [Aeschylus'] plays without even suspecting the ritual form that lies behind them . . .[32]

The last sentence quoted is surely a two-edged weapon.

Murray's argument was put in the simplest possible form for his Home University Library book. It has been further simplified here by the omission of some qualifications and details, but with all allowances made it remains wildly simplistic, and shows the influence of Jane Harrison and Verrall at its most pernicious. Many of Murray's contemporaries felt the same way about it. Wilamowitz, his 'Pope', had not been enthusiastic about Murray's contribution to *Themis*. He expressed himself curious 'about your mystical doctrine of tragedy. The more I think about religion, the less mystic I become, which is something opposed to the taste of our time . . .[33]

Other famous scholars had seen and criticized the chapter at proof stage. An Oxford colleague, A. W. Pickard-Cambridge, objected strongly to Murray's thesis that the fairly constant form of Euripides' plays was due to the original basis of ritual. Pickard-Cambridge concluded a detailed critique: 'I am not sure that I couldn't prove a primitive ritual foundation for the plays of Shakespeare. (I am sure you could—Do try!)[34]

Unfortunately the challenge must have attracted Murray and stayed at the back of his mind. More than two years later he was invited by the British Academy to give their annual Shakespeare Lecture in June 1914. He wrote to Janet Spens, who was herself

working on the role of the *Pharmakos* or scapegoat in ancient ritual.
'I might lecture on your sort of line. I would chiefly run the Orestes–
Hamlet business, and the effect of the Year Ritual on Drama as well
as Religion.'[35]

The lecture was duly delivered, under the title of 'Hamlet and
Orestes'. Its theme was the basic similarity between the two heroes,
as slayers of usurping kings who had slain their predecessors and
married their widows:

There is . . . a common element in all these stories . . . It is the world-wide
ritual story of what we may call the Golden-Bough Kings . . . the fundamental
conception that forms the basis of Greek tragedy . . . It also forms the basis
of the traditional Mummers' Play which . . . is not quite dead yet in the
countries of Northern Europe and lies at the root of so large a part of all
the religions of mankind.[36]

Murray displayed great ingenuity and exhibited wide and various
learning in working out his parallel. It led him to the 'rather terrifying
hypothesis, that the field of tragedy is by nature so limited that these
similarities are inevitable . . . ' In its detailed form Murray's theory of
the origins of tragedy is far too reductionist; it would not be easy for
example to find more than one other tragedy of Shakespeare which
fitted the scheme at all (no doubt research into the primitive sources of
Macbeth would show that Lady Macbeth had originally been married
to Duncan). An appropriate *envoi* to this story is Murray's own naïve
remark about Hamlet as a mythical character: 'I find almost to my
surprise, exactly the evidence I should have liked to find.'[37]

4

It is refreshing to return from the wilder shores of conjecture to
Murray's more soundly based scholarship. In summer and autumn
1911 he received a series of invitations from the USA which led to
the production of one of his best works.

Murray's lectures in 1907 had caused a stir among classical
scholars in the USA. The book which resulted from them, *The Rise
of the Greek Epic*, had been well received there, and even found its
way to the desk of President Roosevelt, who wrote appreciatively
to Murray about it.[38] At the beginning of 1909, Murray received
another invitation from Harvard, asking whether he would accept
a permanent or temporary professorship there, or a lectureship in
the Department of Greek. The timing of this enquiry, coming so soon
after Murray's appointment at Oxford, suggests that the Harvard

Classical Faculty was well insulated; but it was proof of Murray's reputation in the USA. Another illustration of this was a letter from James Loeb of August 1910, asking Murray's opinion about the feasibility of publishing a comprehensive edition of Greek and Latin authors, with an English translation printed opposite the original text. Murray evidently replied positively and was soon associated as a member of the Editorial Board with a scheme which did much to make classical literature available again to former students whose scholarship had grown rusty.[39]

Further invitations to lecture in the USA followed in 1911, from Amherst and Oberlin Colleges, Brown University, and the Lowell Institute in Boston. At Amherst Murray was asked to spend up to six weeks in spring or autumn 1912, lecturing and stimulating interest in classical studies.[40] Finally Nicholas Murray Butler, President of Columbia University, New York, invited Murray to give three lectures there, if possible on the origins of Greek religion, to be published subsequently by the Columbia University Press.[41] Murray accepted the invitations from Amherst, Boston, and Columbia, constructing the rest of his second visit to the USA around these principal engagements.

In replying to President Murray Butler, Murray wrote:

I shall not be starting in the best of health. But I can't resist coming to Columbia, and the subject you propose is just the one that I happen to be full of at the present moment. I would sooner make it 'Greek Religion' than 'The Origins of Greek Religion.'[42]

By late autumn 1911 Murray had completed his contribution to *Themis*, and was able to devote himself mainly to the composition of the lectures for Columbia. He travelled to the USA in mid-March 1912 on board SS *Mauretania*, with Lady Mary. The lectures and classes at Amherst College occupied most of the time that he spent in the USA, and he described his method of work in some detail when accepting the invitation of George Plimpton, President of its Board of Trustees. He proposed:

(a) to give a few popular lectures, and perhaps some readings from Greek plays. This is the fringe of the subject.
(b) to read carefully with a class, large or small, as you like, some one definite piece of classical literature, best perhaps a play by Euripides.
(c) to take a small class in composition and translation, setting them pieces of Greek to turn into English and pieces of English, into Greek.
So far as I have any method of my own of teaching the Classics, it is a method of getting at the spirit and beauty of works of literature, by means of great attention to the exact meaning and connection of words.[43]

Here is an interesting indication of how Murray liked to organize
his personal teaching when given a free hand with a class probably
not very advanced by English standards of the time. As in the case
of his first visit to the USA in 1907 there are few specific indications
of Murray's success. It is therefore worth quoting an article published
in the *Amherst Graduate Quarterly* (June 1912) on 'Dr. Murray in
the Class Room'.

It was an advanced class, for which detailed and comprehensive knowledge
of Greek grammar and syntax was needed, but it was Murray's personality
rather than his learning which impressed the audience. There was an utter
lack of self-consciousness in him, an immaculate courtesy, whimsical humour,
and irony, but without any malice ('Oh dear, Wecklein has been altering
this again!') The voice was low, musical and always under complete control.
The students immediately sensed the 'mild force' of Dr. Murray's personality.
We did not need to be told that he was great; we could feel his greatness.[44]

The lectures given at Columbia on 15, 19 and 22 April developed
into a work very important for Murray's reputation as a classical
scholar. They covered the origins of Greek religion, as requested.
They also dealt with the rise and decline of the Olympian religion.
The titles of the lectures (which were changed for publication in book
form) were *The Raw Material*, *The Attempt at Order*, and *The
Failure of Nerve*.[45] The whole series was originally called *Three
Stages of Greek Religion*. The lectures were enlarged and published
in 1912 by Columbia University Press under the title *Four Stages
of Greek Religion*; in 1925 a further chapter was added, and the
Four Stages became *Five*. The *Five Stages*, as it will henceforth be
called, is the one of Murray's books which, in the opinion of expert
classical scholars, has most successfully stood the test of time.[46]
Murray's own preface to the first edition tells us about the work's
origins, about the influences at work upon him when he wrote the
various chapters, and (as so often with his explanatory writings)
about his own attitude to the current problems of scholarship. He
wrote of his great debt to Jane Harrison:

I cannot adequately describe the advantage I have derived from many years
of frequent discussions and comparison of results with a Hellenist whose
learning and originality of mind are only equalled by her vivid generosity
towards her fellow-workers.[47]

In Murray's first chapter (*Saturnia Regna*), he said, his debt to her
was great and obvious. It was on the theme of the second lecture
or chapter (*The Olympian Conquest*) that he diverged openly from
her. Miss Harrison, he wrote,

has by now made the title of 'Olympian' almost a term of reproach, and thrown down so many a scornful challenge to the canonical gods of Greece, that I have ventured on this attempt to explain their historical origin and plead for their religious value.[48]

Murray would readily admit that the Olympians started as the gods of the tribes who conquered Greece in pre-Homeric times from the north — local gods associated primarily with the northern Mount Olympus. Doubtless they attracted to themselves many of the cults associated with the primitive deities of the conquered peoples. But Murray's argument was (and this is where his thought about Greek religion linked most obviously with his Homeric studies) that the Olympian gods grew up along with the Greeks, and along with Homer, as we know the Homeric epic. The Homeric version of the Olympian religion is a much reformed one — 'a step in the self-realisation of Greece.'[49] The great sculptural relief showing the battles of Olympian gods with Titans and Giants represented symbolically:

the strife, the ultimate victory, of human intelligence, reason and gentleness against what seems at first the overwhelming power of Passion and unguided strength. It is Hellas against the brute World.[50]

To illustrate the partial achievements of the Olympian movement (for Murray regarded it as a 'baffled endeavour' not as a victory), he described the changing function of oracles, which in the primitive religion of the Greeks had transmitted guidance in practical emergencies to the perplexed tribe from their wise ancestor-heroes, now among the dead:

the oracles hated change and strangled the progress of knowledge. Also, like most manifestations of early religion, they throve upon human terror. . . .

The sins of the modern world in dealing with the heretics and witches have perhaps been more gigantic than those of primitive man, but one can hardly rise from the record of these ancient observances without being haunted by the judgment of the Roman poet:

Tantum religio potuit suadere malorum[51]
[so much of evil could religion urge]

and feeling with him that the lightening of this cloud, the taming of this blind dragon, must rank among the very greatest services that Hellenism wrought for mankind.[52]

He could not follow Jane Harrison in her reverence for the dark instincts, and in her feeling that these, and the rituals in which they expressed themselves, were the basic stuff of life, truer to human nature, less artificial, and therefore in some moral sense better than more rational forms of religion. In his obituary notice on Murray, Professor J. A. K. Thomson, who knew him better than most, wrote:

. . . when it came to the point—when he was drawn into the Nietzschean battle between the calm Apollo and the instinctive Dionysus—he had to side with Apollo. The Olympian gods *were* an advance on the romantic but unprogressive monsters of an earlier age . . . The Victorian Liberal, the believer in Progress, had re-asserted himself.[53]

5

To Murray's biographer, *Five Stages* has another important dimension. It illustrates better than any of his published works his own attitude to religion in his intellectual prime. The days of Murray's purely destructive criticism of established religions and churches were long past—if indeed they survived the impact of Charles Gore's personality in his undergraduate days. In 1897 he had told Lady Carlisle of a 'great wish to say something constructive, not merely critical, about Religion.'[54] A little later he was corresponding with J. W. Mackail about the need for a new 'Serious Call' (to parallel a famous book by William Law addressed to Christians) for serious agnostics.[55] No doubt in his Gifford Lectures Murray would have revealed something of his own inmost beliefs.

As none of these projects materialized, it is from the later chapters of *Five Stages* that his attitude towards religion emerges. As he describes the adaptation of the Olympian religion to the evolution of civilized cities, Murray embarks on a passage of clear self-revelation:

As soon as the Stoics had proclaimed the world to be 'one great City of gods and men', the only Gods with which Greeks could satisfactorily people that City were the idealised band of the old Olympians.

They are artistic dreams . . . ideals . . . symbols of something beyond themselves . . . They are gods to whom doubtful philosophers can pray, with all a philosopher's due caution, as to so many radiant and heart-searching hypotheses. They are not gods in whom anyone believes as a hard fact. Does this condemn them? Or is it just the other way? Is it perhaps that one difference between Religion and superstition lies exactly in this, that superstition degrades its worship by turning its belief into so many statements of brute fact, on which it must needs act without question, without any respect for others, or any desire for higher or fuller truth? It is only an accident—though perhaps an invaluable accident—that all the supposed facts are false. In Religion, however precious you may consider the truth you draw from it, you know that it is a truth seen dimly and possibly seen by others better than you. You know that all your creeds and definitions are merely metaphors . . . Your concepts are, by the nature of things, inadequate; the truth is not in you but beyond you, a thing not conquered but still to be pursued. Something like this, I take it, was the character of the Olympian Religion in the higher minds of later Greece.[56]

Murray writes with beautiful clarity and persuasiveness; but his argument, as so often, tells as much about himself and his beliefs as about Greece in the Olympian or Hellenic Age. Indeed the phrase 'I take it' in the last sentence has undertones of self-mockery. He knew that many other scholars would not 'take it'; all that he could communicate to his readers or audience was his own wisdom — unlikely to be complete, but coherent, and based on a considerable foundation of scholarship. He would, 'I take it', have argued that it was better to convey a coherent vision than a number of undoubted facts without a context. In describing a past civilization, to quote Murray's argument again: 'Your concepts are, by the nature of things, inadequate, the truth is not in you, but beyond you, a thing not conquered, but still to be pursued.'

Five Stages of Greek Religion, however much its arguments may have been overtaken by later visions of Hellas and later scholarship, remains a compulsively readable book as a chapter in the history of thought, and as an intellectual self-portrait. Indeed in these respects it is probably better worth reading today than in 1912, when Murray could be heard and known personally, and currents of thought were not so clearly visible. His early dislike of Christianity can be detected at the beginning of Chapter IV, 'The Failure of Nerve':

Anyone who turns from the great writers of Classical Athens . . . to those of the Christian era must be conscious of a great difference in tone . . . The new quality is not specifically Christian; it is just as marked in the Gnostics and Mithras worshippers as in the Gospels and the Apocalypse . . . It is a rise of asceticism, of mysticism, in a sense, of Pessimism; a loss of self-confidence, of hope in this life and of faith in normal human effort: a despair of patient inquiry, a cry for infallible revelation; an indifference to the welfare of the State, a conversion of the soul to God. It is an atmosphere in which the aim of the good man is not so much to live justly, to help the society to which he belongs and enjoy the esteem of his fellow creatures; but rather, by means of a burning faith, by contempt for the world and its standards . . . to be granted pardon for his unspeakable unworthiness, his immeasurable sins. There is . . . a failure of nerve.[57]

Murray's faith in the works of this world and in the possibility of progress (rather than its inevitability) should be seen against the background, not only of his upbringing and devotion to J. S. Mill, but also of the great social achievements of the Liberal Governments between 1908 and 1914. His faith in reason was not unlimited. He was well, if not at this time well enough, aware of its limitations. At the end of the chapter on the 'Failure of Nerve' he admits that he has neither the confidence felt by so many of his friends and most of his fellow-creatures in any divine revelation, nor any absolute faith in reason:

The uncharted surrounds us on every side. . . . As far as knowledge and conscious reason will go we must follow their austere guidance. When they cease, as cease they must, we must use as best we can those fainter powers of apprehension and surmise and sensitiveness . . .[58]

'The Uncharted surrounds us on every side . . . ' Here is the voice of a man rationally aware of the bounds of reason, admitting and sometimes groping beyond the limits of the conscious mind. It was at this period of his life that Murray became interested in the philosophy of Bergson, and increasingly in extra-sensory perception. This had to some extent exercised his mind since he had come to know A. W. Verrall and his family, and Murray's close connection with the Society for Psychical Research is discussed in Chapter XX.

Murray's former pupil, the theologian Edwyn Bevan, wrote to him showing a large measure of sympathy with his cautious and reverent attitude towards the 'Uncharted'. Bevan confessed himself unable to distinguish precisely the ephemeral from the essential in Christianity, and emphasized only his sense of 'getting very hot' when he came into touch with it.[59] There was a gap but not a gulf between theologian and classical scholar.

CHAPTER XIII

Theatrical and Literary Life 1908–1914

1. Further productions of Euripides' plays and Sophocles' *Oedipus Tyrannus*.
2. Problems of music for the production—works with Vaughan Williams.
3. Murray's *Nefrekepta*—member of Academic Committee of English Letters—works towards abolishing censorship—friendship with Galsworthy and Masefield.

1

MURRAY'S output of books and articles on classical subjects, and his activities as Professor of Greek at Oxford, were enough to have filled the life of an ordinary man. And though the invalid or hypochondriac note does not sound so clearly as before in his correspondence of these years, his health was certainly not robust. Nevertheless he was engaged at this time on a bewildering variety of 'outside' or secondary activities.

Chief among these was his work for the theatre which in the previous years had generated its own considerable momentum. The *Hippolytus* in Murray's translation was put on in Oxford early in 1908.[1] In the autumn it was repeated at Birmingham, for the annual meeting of the Classical Association.[2] This latter production was played by Miss Horniman's Manchester company, and was a great success, Murray thought. The production was later transferred to Manchester; during the rehearsals for it, Murray first met Sybil Thorndike, wife of Lewis Casson, who was playing the Messenger.[3] She became a regular correspondent and an ardent enthusiast both for Murray's translations and for his personality (there is no trace of her having inspired any jealousy in Lady Mary). She herself was playing Artemis and wrote nearly fifty years later of the inspiration which she derived from Murray. His first advice to her was to be 'like an opalescent dawn'—enlightening, she found, but difficult to put into practice![4]

In the same autumn there was a disastrous production of the *Bacchae* at the Court Theatre, put on by William Poel of the Elizabethan Stage Society, who had been much interested in Murray's work since 1904. The play is full of problems. The story of Dionysus' revenge, through his intoxicated devotees, on the law-abiding and rigidly respectable King Pentheus who tries to forbid his orgies, is a strange mixture of brutality, comedy, and lyricism. Bertrand Russell, when he first read Murray's translation, found no difficulty in understanding it as an expression of the eternal conflict between inspiration and respectability.[5] Murray himself was less sure of its meaning and recognized the difficulty of interpreting it for a modern audience, although the choruses inspired him to some of his most successful Swinburnian verse—there were lines which achieved the status of holy writ in his family.[6] Poel's cast was strong enough. Lillah McCarthy, Barker's wife, played Dionysus, and Esmé Percy Pentheus; but Poel himself had odd ideas about the play, seeming at times to regard it as a satire against drunkenness,[7] and aiming to contrast the savage story with a setting 'full of repose, dignity, and grace'.[8]

The performance was ruthlessly criticized by A. B. Walkley in *The Times*, and Murray insisted that it should be taken off after only two performances. He gave Lillah McCarthy performing rights in the play till the end of 1909 only on condition that the production should be completely remodelled.[9] This was by far the greatest failure among the productions of Murray's translations.

Between the end of 1908 and the outbreak of World War I in August 1914, there were a number of revivals of the translations already produced. In the UK these were largely due to Penelope Wheeler, who had played Phaedra in the Manchester Company's production of *Hippolytus* in 1908. She formed her own company in 1909 to take Murray's works on tour, and was generous in her help to amateur productions of them.[10] In the USA it was Maurice Browne, of the Little Theatre, Chicago, who launched productions of Murray's translations in 1912–13—as usual with some critical acclaim and limited financial success (Murray received £16 6s. 0d. in royalties).[11]

By 1910 Murray was at work on a new translation—*Iphigenia in Tauris*, a late and comparatively romantic 'adventure story' by Euripides. He corresponded with Barker about the possibility of including it in a repertory season at the Duke of York's Theatre; but plans for this fell through in May 1910[12]; *Iphigenia* was not produced till March 1912, when Barker put it on at the Kingsway Theatre, with Lillah McCarthy in the title role—Murray had not originally been enthusiastic about this bit of casting,[13] but the production turned out well. One of Murray's classical colleagues at Oxford, H. E. Butler, found the staging amirable, the music (by

Granville Bantock) 'just right', and Lillah McCarthy 'much better than usual.'[14]

Meanwhile, Murray had been engaged on a theatrical project quite outside his usual range. In 1910 he had correspondence with Herbert Trench of the Haymarket Theatre about the possibility of producing his translation of Sophocles' *Oedipus Tyrannus*. Early in December 1910, Trench received his licence to perform. Murray understood that there was a project to adapt a spectacular production by Max Reinhardt, then running with great success in Berlin ('in a circus with a vast crowd and performing elephants' as he put it more privately to Barker).[15] A production suitable for the German translation, by Hugo von Hofmannsthal, might not fit his own. He was doubtful particularly if the music used in the Berlin production would be suitable. And he wanted Barker as producer. However, Reinhardt's emissary, Ordynski, visited London in mid-February and told Murray that Reinhardt himself was anxious to put on the *Oedipus* in London, in Murray's translation.[16]

It was about this time that Murray and Shaw exchanged letters about the theme and treatment of the Oedipus story. Shaw was not impressed by Sophocles' stagecraft, and sent Murray an extremely funny résumé of the story, emphasizing the part played in it by the long arm of coincidence.[17] Murray's reply to Shaw illuminates his own view of the inner meaning of the play:

> What strikes me now is the thorough-going blasphemousness and anti-theism of the whole thing. I suspect that Sophocles was not the old ram that we take him for . . . He could steal a horse while they all yelled at Euripides for looking over the hedge . . .[18]

Negotiations with Reinhardt were conducted through Frederick Whelen, and came to a temporary halt in May, when the financier who intended to put up money for a production in the Kingsway Theatre was killed in an accident. However, by the end of July plans had been launched to produce the *Oedipus* at Covent Garden early in 1912. Martin-Harvey (later Sir John) was in Reinhardt's absence the moving spirit of the London production, in which he himself played Oedipus. He urged Murray to help him in setting up a committee of distinguished patrons, and Murray was successful in inducing the Prime Minister, Asquith, to let his name be used.[19] The production was duly launched in January 1912.

It was spectacular, and generally successful. Apart from Martin-Harvey, the principal successes of the cast were Lillah McCarthy (Jocasta) and Franklin Dyall (Messenger). Murray himself worked closely with Martin-Harvey in the months preceding production, helping him to evolve his conception of Oedipus before Reinhardt's arrival in London, early in December 1911. The production as a whole was criticized, by *The Times* particularly, as over-sensational and un-Greek (the notion of the perfectly poised and unemotional Greek died hard). It was thought that some of the details of the Berlin production were transferred too uncritically to London, 'the vast crowd which opened the production pouring in from all sides into the stalls, became involved with late-coming playgoers and caused much embarrassment to everyone concerned.' Murray had explained to Martin-Harvey his view of the play as containing many elements of pre-classical primitive religion, to which Reinhardt's production did full justice; and it was at Martin-Harvey's instance that he developed this view in a letter to *The Times*.[20]

However, he was not entirely out of sympathy with *The Times* criticism, and put his own points in a letter to Martin-Harvey (designed, he told his wife, primarily to discourage him from cutting the Messenger's speech into fragments 'to be screamed by handmaids' with Mrs Harvey as 'the chief screamer').[21] To Martin-Harvey he wrote:

What the play wants is not more screams and distraction and violence, but just the reverse, more calm and beauty, and religious awe. More stress on the sense of the mysterious and less on physical pain. There is a real clash here between Reinhardt and Sophocles.

Murray went on to make specific suggestions about Martin-Harvey's own playing of Oedipus. His entrance, after Oedipus had blinded himself, should be more symbolic and less realistic. The real terror for the crowd should lie in the sight of a man 'self-convicted of unspeakable pollution.' No one will dare to touch him.

Your exit is exactly right. The greatness of the man triumphs over all the sin and misery and suffering. But I want the impression to come earlier. I should like to feel right from your first entrance blinded: 'Here is a man who has been through all suffering and has come out at the other end; who has done judgment upon himself to the uttermost and now stands above all common men.'[22]

Martin-Harvey expressed his agreement with the sense of Murray's letter. In May he went on tour with the *Oedipus*, and for the next year he corresponded with Murray, first on the possibility of also producing *Oedipus at Colonus* (Sophocles' sequel), and then on plans for a more ambitious festival of Greek drama, combining the two parts of *Oedipus* with a new translation by Murray (to be specially made for the purpose) of Aeschylus' *Oresteia*.[23] The outbreak of war in August 1914 put an end to these plans, and when they were later renewed, Martin-Harvey's ambitious and lavish expenditure on production made collaboration difficult.

Murray continued to encourage the drama in general, and not merely the production of his own translations, as and where he could. He played a prominent part in the inauguration of the Oxford Drama Society in 1909[24] (not to be confused with the Oxford University Dramatic Society). He also took an active interest from 1910 onwards in amateur productions of his translations, particularly those organized by Mrs Charlotte King of Stonelands in Surrey—the first of such experiments, and one of the longest-lived.[25] Murray continued for the rest of his life to produce translations of classical plays, and to advise on their production whenever possible. However, 1912 proved to be the peak of his fame as a translator-dramatist.

2

This is an appropriate point at which to consider how Murray tried to tackle one of the main difficulties of performing Greek drama in modern times. How is the chorus to be presented? Some purely musical element was normally considered essential, not least for historical reasons; but Murray's lyrics, with their Swinburnian rhythms, were emphatic in their verbal music. One of his chief worries was lest this (and the literal meaning of the words) should be drowned in an over-heavy musical setting. He had hard things to say about the way of composers with words. He wrote to his daughter Rosalind in 1912:

I am getting clearer and clearer in my mind that musicians are devils. I have been studying a song of Goethe as set by Brahms (Es fürchte die Götter, etc.) who is supposed to be comparatively respectable, and the things he does are incredible—an utter distraction both of rhythm and sense.[26]

However he had to tolerate some music in the production of his Greek tragedies. Its absence would be represented as contrary to Greek practice. And he had to take the best advice available, for he himself was confessedly insensitive to music. He wrote to Isobel Monro (later Henderson):

I love . . . trying to imagine what [music] is like to those who really know it. . . . It is odd, I always feel as if there really was ἐν οὐρανίῳ τόπῳ [in some heavenly place] a music which would send me into ecstasies . . . but at a real concert I just get lost and sometimes want to howl like a dog.[27]

Murray did not exaggerate this particular insensitivity. He once entered his own drawing-room where his wife and son were listening to a record of a Beethoven symphony. 'Extraordinary,' he said, 'What stuff Americans dance to.'[28]

He was therefore very much in the hands of 'experts' when he faced the musical problems of the Greek tragic chorus. The first musical 'expert' to cross his path was an extremely colourful figure, Florence Farr (Mrs Emery). She was a lady of a passionate nature, which she had indulged with Shaw and even with Yeats, and of high-flown artistic ideas. At the end of 1903 she initiated the 'Fellowship of the Dance' with the purpose of fighting 'the High and Powerful Devil, Solemnity, called by some the Master of the World'. Its monthly meetings were to be held in beautiful and simple dresses, and opened by the dancing of the farandola and chanting from Nietzsche.[29] Florence Farr seemed to embody most of those conceptions about the Greeks which Murray most disliked, including the worst features of Leighton's Grecian pictures and Yeats's 'Theatre of Beauty'. However, she was firmly established. She had already publicly chanted, to the accompaniment of her own psaltery, Murray's chorus from the *Bacchae*,

> Will they ever come to me again, the long, long dances,

and had asked him to restore for her the missing parts of the play. She was in charge of the music for the first performance of the Murray / Euripides *Hippolytus* at the Lyric Theatre in Spring 1904, and for the subsequent performances at the Court. Here the stage was small, and elaborate choral movement was out of the question. Florence Farr herself composed the music, and provided the accompaniment on her psaltery. The choruses were sung or chanted by single voices. Murray was dissatisfied with her, but liked the psaltery (or feared something louder); Barker agreed that her harmonies were 'jejune', and for the production of *Electra* early in 1906 the music had to be 'constructed' more or less impromptu by the German conductor, Theodor Stier. Murray described the scene in a letter to Lady Carlisle, whom he thought of calling in as musical adviser:

> I read each lyric; then in various ways we tried to get the same effect helped by the music. No melody. Chords here and there to emphasise important words . . . If Stier understands . . . I think the music will be better than we have ever had—better for my purpose, that is . . .[30]

As the productions of Murray's works reached larger theatres, more elaborate efforts were thought necessary. For the Birmingham production of *Hippolytus* in 1908, Granville Bantock wrote and conducted music for a small orchestra—harps, flutes, horns, double basses (pizzicato), and drums. The music was said to be based on the melody of an old Greek hymn to Apollo; and Bantock wanted to introduce certain leitmotivs to be associated (not only in choral passages) with the principal characters.[31] Later in 1908, Bantock was working on music for the *Bacchae* and was anxious to discuss with Murray new music for the *Electra*.[32]

However Bantock by now had a formidable rival. Herbert Fisher had written to Murray, after seeing *Medea* in November 1907, that his brother-in-law, Ralph Vaughan Williams, would like to hear some 'frankly modern' music provided for it by a big orchestra.[33] In 1909 another Oxford figure, Henry Hadow, again recommended Vaughan Williams as 'a *very* good musician—also keen on poetry and full of understanding'.[34]

In the event Vaughan Williams wrote a good deal of music for Murray's choruses. Most of it is preserved, but little has been published and none of it was performed in the context intended. In fact the closest collaboration between Murray and Vaughan Williams was over an intriguing side-issue, which also came to nothing. In mid-December 1909, Murray received a telegram from Isadora Duncan and her brother Augustin, asking to see him urgently.[35] No meeting took place at the time, but correspondence was resumed in September 1911. Isadora Duncan, signing herself 'your enthusiastic Admirer', was contemplating the production of Greek tragedy in the grand style of Murray's translations. Her brother Augustin was 'an actor of great talent' and wanted to form a small company of people who for one year would 'devote themselves solely under his guardianship to the study of three of your plays, with the object of producing them at the end of the year.' Isadora herself would choose two pupils from her school of dancing and train them for the Chorus, and a composer, not yet found, would work meanwhile on the music.[36]

Murray lunched with Isadora at the Savoy and found that her plan 'became very like the nebular hypothesis as she talked'. But he liked Augustin, and Penelope Wheeler was delighted with him as a teacher.[37] In a subsequent and undated letter of 1911, Augustin wrote that the original plans had been abandoned owing to the ingratitude of the dancer-trainees. However, he hoped that they could produce one of Murray's translations next spring.[38]

At this point in an obscure story, the favoured composer appears. Isadora Duncan had also been in touch with Ralph Vaughan Williams; she had asked for music for one chorus from the *Bacchae*, but disappeared without leaving an address, or any very firm directions. Among the unpublished scores left behind by Vaughan Williams is a setting of a chorus from the *Bacchae* dated in his own hand 17 October 1911.[39] Meanwhile he had got into touch with Murray, to see if the translator had any idea what sort of music was needed. Another telegram from Isadora Duncan to Murray suggests that at the end of October there may have been a meeting between her, the dramatist, and the composer; but Vaughan Williams remained thoroughly puzzled. The Duncans knew no more than anyone else what was required, and 'the problem gets more insoluble the more I work at it'. He had tried chanting without accompaniment and more operatic methods, and needed 'a sort of trial performance of some of the music when it is ready.' In any case he couldn't hope 'to satisfy you *and* Miss Duncan and Augustin (who wants choruses spoken)'.[40] No more can be traced from Murray's or Vaughan Williams's papers about collaboration with the Duncans; but Murray and Vaughan Williams remained in touch and tried to work out together their own common problems—difficult enough without the Duncans. Vaughan Williams wrote that it had greatly distressed him 'to hear the wonderful lines in the Electra and your other plays mauled about by, as it seems to me, quite the wrong kind of musical setting.'[41] He wrote a little later that he had 'done two Electra choruses and was finishing two Bacchae choruses and had notes for several more.'[42]

He and Murray met in November and December. Murray thought the *Bacchae* and *Electra* music 'splendid—for the most part. It completely drowned the words, but it somehow did seem to translate into music the emotion I wanted to convey by the words.'[43] No poet can say fairer than that to any composer. Vaughan Williams continued work on Murray's texts after their meeting and produced sketches of music for *Iphigenia in Tauris* 'for the Liverpool people . . . I have made it *very* simple and tried to get the declamation right.'[44] In the London production of *Iphigenia* in March 1912 Vaughan Williams's music was not used (Bantock's had no doubt been commissioned long before). However, a complete score and parts for a Prelude and four choruses exist. Vaughan Williams's note on the score would have pleased Murray:

These choruses must be sung throughout with due regard to the true declamation of the words and the metre of the poetry. The note values of the voice part are, for the most part, only approximate. The solos may be divided among the members of the chorus according to the compass and nature of their voices.[45]

The author has found no record of Murray's translations being performed to Vaughan Williams's music. The style preferred by Murray himself was probably the minimum of music to mark key points in the drama. This method was used in the OUDS production of *Oedipus* in summer 1932, when Murray directed and Alan Ker (then a classical Fellow of Brasenose College) produced. Ker encouraged the biographer, then an undergraduate member of the chorus, to explain to Murray the possible use of leitmotiv in the music; but it must be admitted that he did not appear interested.

3

By the second decade of the twentieth century Murray had established a position in the literary world as a 'man of letters', based mainly on his translations. Shaw tried to persuade him into extending the range of these by producing a version for the London stage of Edmond Rostand's *Cyrano de Bergerac*. Murray's refusal was unfortunately categoric:

Deaf alike to the alluring call of Avarice and the seductive whisper of Vanity, I am bound to decline the tempting offer made by you on behalf of your friend, Mr. Garrick, that I should translate a well-known French masterpiece for his use at Drury Lane this spring . . .[46]

Slightly later, in spring 1911, Murray was inspired by an old Egyptian story preserved in a recently discovered papyrus, to publish an original work in verse, *Nefrekepta*, submitting it first to the Egyptologist, F. Lloyd-Griffith, for a check on accuracy of detail.[47] This work is something of a curiosity in Murray's output. The story is told in a metre which he did not otherwise use—the 'Omar Khayyam' translation of Edward FitzGerald. The book was a finely printed edition issued by the Clarendon Press, with a frontispiece and a woodcut tailpiece by Florence Kingsford Cockerell,[48] at a price 'which none but the truly Refined can afford to pay.'[49] Masefield and Hardy both wrote enthusiastically about the result. The former suggested dramatizing the story, while Hardy found it 'excellently weird and romantic', and was held by the 'grotesque horror' of the climax.[50]

Murray's position as a 'man of letters' was confirmed by his involvement in the movement (1910) to establish an Academic Committee of English Letters. The title is confusing. The Committee was not intended to have anything to do with academic studies, or universities. It was designed rather to occupy a position in regard to literature analogous to those of the Royal Society in relation to science, the Royal Academy in relation to art, or the British Academy in relation to non-scientific studies. As the classical scholar S. H. Butcher explained to Murray, it should perform some of the functions of the French Academy and should make occasional awards. A joint committee of the Royal Society of Literature and the Society of Authors drew up a list of possible members. Butcher asked Murray to join and could tell him that R. B. Haldane, Thomas Hardy, Henry James, and John Morley among others had already agreed to do so.[51] Murray gave his agreement rather half-heartedly and expressed his doubts to Shaw:

I see that [the idea] emanated partly from the Society of Authors. I agreed to go on it, and think, if well constituted, it may be of some use in many ways. But why are you and Wells not on it? I believe Kipling and Barrie declined, though I don't know.[52]

Murray went ahead, and in fact gave the address—an eloge for Butcher, who had recently died—at the opening meeting of the Committee.[53] However, the Committee did not have a very long or useful life.

Murray used his literary prestige to greater effect on the concrete question of censorship, a moral and political issue of great importance to practising dramatists. It was the prevailing practice to pre-censor plays in the name of the Lord Chamberlain, and to refuse licences if it was thought likely that they would corrupt public morals. Archer had started an active campaign for abolishing censorship early in 1907. Later in the year Edward Garnett was refused a licence for his play *The Breaking Point*. He suggested to John Galsworthy the formation of a society of literary men to protest against censorship. Galsworthy, who had no more than a casual acquaintance with Murray at this time, asked him to join in furthering this idea, and to induce J. M. Barrie to co-operate.[54] The three men constituted a provisional Committee, with Archer and Granville Barker to help them. Early in October the *Nation* published a long article by Murray on the anomalies of censorship. Later in the month Galsworthy, with Barrie and Murray, drafted a letter to *The Times*,[55] which was signed by seventy-one authors in all, including Conrad, Hardy, and Henry James. The Prime Minister, Sir Henry Campbell-Bannerman, promised to receive a deputation of authors on 19 November, but had to put them off. They made their representations, with Murray among their number, on 10 February 1908 to the Home Secretary, Herbert Gladstone.

Thereafter a Joint Committee of both Houses of Parliament was set up, with Herbert Samuel in the chair, and held meetings from 29 July to 2 November 1908. The first non-official witnesses to give evidence were Archer and Shaw; the latter, in trying to prove the stupidity of the censors, was typically over-clever, making the point that the censors had failed to appreciate the full immorality of *Mrs Warren's Profession*; this greatly upset many of his fellow-authors, including Galsworthy. Murray gave evidence to the Committee on 20 August 1908. His main point was that censorship was not based on any published law and was exercised according to no definite criteria; the Censor's decisions were bound to be arbitrary and it was thus impossible to argue logically or to lodge appeals against them. The Joint Committee's conclusions were published in November. They recommended that it should be legal to perform plays without a licence, but plays could still be provisionally submitted if managers and authors wished to guard securely against any risk of prosecution.[56] However, managers on the whole preferred the inconvenient but known devil of pre-censorship to the unknown one of post-censorship, which involved obvious dangers for them, and the system eventually was only abolished by the Theatres Act of 1968.

In 1907 Granville Barker's play *Waste* — a tragedy hinging on the effect of scandal in private life on a political career — was submitted to the Censor and refused a licence, because of a reference to abortion. In order to secure copyright Barker arranged a reading of his play to a select audience at the Savoy Theatre on 28 January 1908. The cast was one of extraordinary distinction, and included Archer, Mr and Mrs H. G. Wells, Shaw, and Murray as 'Lord Charles Cantelupe'; it was his first public appearance on a stage since his schooldays, but his performance did not result in any subsequent theatrical engagement.[57]

A year later Murray was involved in another specific difficulty over censorship, when there was an official threat to the Abbey Theatre, Dublin, that its licence would be withdrawn if the management proceeded with putting on Bernard Shaw's *The Showing-up of Blanco Posnet*. Murray was mobilized by Shaw to intervene on his behalf and wrote to Lord Crewe, Colonial Secretary at the time, presumably under the impression either that Crewe was Lord Chamberlain or that he had some responsibility for Irish affairs. The letter was a powerful one, illustrating Murray's own religious views, and his views on Shaw, as much as Shaw's own intentions:

I do think, first, that the actual theme of the play is both grand and tragic, in spite of its ugly and grotesque setting; and secondly, that this is the play in which Shaw has quite directly and without any subterfuge or nervous laughter expressed his religious faith — or a fragment of it. The point is that there is something in a man's own heart which, at certain crises, compels him to act according to righteousness or some law of love, even if he lose everything by it . . . This internal moral law or impulse or whatever it is, Shaw calls *God* ; it comes over the man 'like a sneak' and has him in his [*sic*] power.[58]

Shaw won his case, and wrote to Murray, assuring him that although Lord Crewe had not been the right man to address, Murray had been a great help.

The main indirect result of Murray's increasing involvement in the problems of censorship was a growing friendship with John Galsworthy, better known at the time as a dramatist with a serious social purpose than as a novelist. Initially Murray was not greatly attracted; he admired *The Man of Property*, the first instalment of what was to develop into *The Forsyte Saga*, but described Galsworthy to Archer as 'A very clever man, but . . . so infernally self-satisfied with his own self-righteous contempt for the self-righteous.'[59] He dined with the Galsworthys soon after the beginning of the anti-censorship campaign in late summer 1907, and wrote again rather coolly to Lady Mary that Galsworthy 'could stand criticism, but revels in praise.' The play *Strife* he read in MS and found it good and thoughtful, but not entertaining or moving.[60] The two men grew much closer to one another, though Galsworthy could never be reckoned as one of Murray's most intimate friends. Murray admired the play *Justice*, and congratulated Galsworthy on his achievement in contributing so much to the reduction of solitary confinement (announced by Winston Churchill, as Home Secretary, with a clear reference to Galsworthy's play). He wrote:

It is a fine thing to have achieved, a really great thing. How much greater it is to have saved a lot of men and women from two months of solitary confinement than to have sent any number of over-fed audiences into raptures.[61]

Henceforward until the outbreak of war, Galsworthy consulted Murray closely on the formative stages of his new works, plays and novels alike. Drafts of *The Patrician* were twice read aloud to Murray, who was asked his opinion on many details of the plot — from what political posts, for example, should the hero be forced to resign as a penalty for running off with someone else's wife? And what would be a good quotation for the title-page? Murray in fact provided that which was finally printed there.[62] These are small details, but Murray did not hesitate to give advice and comment on major themes. Thus typically on the *Patrician* :

I find rather much about the physical disturbance of the men . . . under their emotions of love . . .

I incline to believe that, mostly, the senses can be dealt with, it is the imagination which bowls people over without their knowing. The senses only deliver frontal attacks, so to speak. Or rather, when they do show cunning, they make the imagination do their work for them.[63]

Changes were made, and a few weeks later Murray was able to say that all his previous complaints now fell to the ground.

A year later Murray was criticizing on equally high-minded grounds a draft of Galsworthy's play *The Pigeon* (he wrote to Lady Mary of a 'dreadfully outspoken letter').[64] Why the constant implication that regular social workers are imbeciles and their work all useless? And why

. . . the omnipresence of rum? I can stand Dickens' brandy and water because it belongs to that date, but nowadays the rum seems aggressive . . . I admit I was startled at the Professor . . . accepting rum for tea.[65]

This was a passage which Galsworthy agreed to take out.

By 1913 Murray was ready—a sign of growing friendship—to don his Dickens' mask in writing to Galsworthy, as in the following request for theatre-tickets:

Dear Sir—Knowing your kind heart which once I was a gentleman like yourself but what with [various family affairs] and not a crust in the house indeed Sir, I have seen better days and trowsers is always welcome if it does not fit it can be cut down but most of all I would like it Sir if you would be so kind as give me a ticket for the *Fugitive* say Tuesday Sept. 30 which I shall be at Dr. Wheeler's house where I have temporary got a job and scorning to beg believe me—Yours gratefully Simon Magus[66]

Another of Murray's lasting friendships which dated from this time was that with John Masefield, in later years a resident on Boar's Hill. Masefield wrote to Murray at the end of 1905, asking whether at the end of his 'terrible Cotswold story', the *Tragedy of the Campden Wonder*, he might quote the chorus from the *Bacchae* in Murray's translation—'There be many shapes of mystery'. Here, Masefield wrote, was precisely the thing which he wished to express at this point.[67] However, there was no such constant flow of ideas between Murray and Masefield at this time as there was between Murray and Galsworthy.

Such correspondence between the two men as survives from before 1914 is interesting mainly as showing how highly Masefield regarded Murray as a poetic dramatist. Like Galsworthy, he sent work to Murray for comment—in this case the draft of his poetic drama *Pompey*. This caused Murray some difficulty; he wrote to Lady Mary that he 'hated some parts of it very much'.[68] However, he must have phrased his criticisms tactfully. Masefield thanked him for his knack of putting his finger on the failings of the play, and said that his own 'coloured' prose was modelled on Murray's prose translations from the Greek in the *History of Ancient Greek Literature*.[69]

Murray was engaged in one more theatrical project of national importance before the war. This was an abortive attempt to revive Archer's scheme for a National Theatre, in the form of a national Repertory Company. The chief sponsors of the idea were (apart from Murray), Barker, Barrie, John Masefield, and Shaw—Galsworthy was away in the USA at the time. Lord Howard de Walden, Barrie, and Murray were selected as possible trustees, and Murray drafted an appeal with the object of getting a thousand people to subscribe £25 each. This was circulated with a trust deed to a number of likely subscribers to test their reaction before accepting any money. It proved that support was inadequate and the scheme was dropped.[70]

Murray always retained a strong interest in the theatre and his translations were performed over a number of years after the war. But his theatrical style went out of fashion. Archer died in 1924. Barker's most brilliant days as a producer were over. Shaw and Galsworthy had enjoyed their greatest successes; and Murray himself acquired many other interests outside what might be called his main secondary profession. He would never again be part of any national movement in the theatrical world.

CHAPTER XIV

Politics and Publishing

1. Refuses offers to stand for Parliament—campaigns for Liberals—political journalism dwindles.
2. Views on Empire—correspondence with Leys in Africa and Maynard in India.
3. Work for Women's Suffrage.
4. Sympathy with Socialism—supports Beatrice Webb—contacts with Socialist thinkers.
5. Workers' Educational Association—Simplified Spelling—Home University Library.

1

BY the second decade of the twentieth century Murray could no longer think of a political career. However, it was impossible for him to renounce his political interests. The years of Liberal Government from 1905 to 1914 were exciting and important ones in British political history. At the turn of the century, Murray had been a lonely radical, disgusted with official Liberal policy on the South African war, ready to discuss many of his favourite domestic causes with the Fabians, but finding them too deeply over-committed to Empire. By 1914 and even before the outbreak of war, he could be regarded as essentially an Establishment figure, connected by many ties with the Asquith leadership. This was not merely the result of incipient middle age and preoccupation with his primary and non-political interests. He could reasonably claim that it was the Liberal Party and Government which had changed the direction of their policies.

Various efforts were made in the first decade of the twentieth century to induce him to stand for Parliament. In 1903, he was asked to stand for the College division of Glasgow; in 1910 the Liberal Association of Glasgow University repeated the invitation.[1] At the end of 1909, he was approached as a possible candidate for London University in opposition to Sir West Ridgway, as a candidate committed to the cause of Women's Suffrage.[2] None of these invitations was accepted, but Murray and his family were very active in support of the Liberal candidate for Oxford University during the election campaigns of 1906 (a close-run affair) and 1909–10. On this latter occasion the contest centred on Lloyd George's radical

Budget of 1909, the House of Lords' opposition to it, and Asquith's proposals for limiting their powers. The election was inevitably fought in an atmosphere of the utmost bitterness. Murray's family was mobilized in force for the campaign. He wrote to Rosalind:

The Election is very exciting, and I'm sorry you're out of it. But Denis is in, up to his neck . . . Bertie Russell is speaking all over the place, and is having excellent meetings . . . Mother has been standing at booths with Women's Suffrage petitions . . .[3]

The Liberals were defeated, this time handsomely, by 1,210 votes. Murray wrote sadly to Archer:

The Elections make life here rather unpleasant, I am practising urbanity to its utmost limits whenever I meet people, but I find it better not to go to College. But my temper is improving because I received a quite wantonly insulting letter yesterday from a Christ Church colleague — generally rather a decent sort of man — and the other side having lost their tempers it is easier for me to keep mine.[4]

For two years after his return to Oxford Murray hoped to exercise some indirect influence by his contacts with political journalists. His friend, J. L. Hammond, was editor of the *Speaker*. Here was an intimate friend of Murray, whom he could trust completely on matters of foreign policy (the *Speaker* was at this time very much in favour of the Anglo-French *entente*, and very suspicious of German foreign policy). In 1906 Hammond also began to work as a leader-writer on the new Liberal daily, the *Tribune*, launched by the Lancashire business man, Franklin Thomasson, with Murray's old friend, L. T. Hobhouse, as political editor. However, the life of the *Tribune* was short and unhappy. With Hobhouse, Hammond, and Brailsford all at work writing critical leaders, there were likely to be business difficulties, and these duly materialized. In January 1907 a new editor, S. J. Pryor, was appointed and given complete control of the paper's political line. At the same time there was to be a large infusion of American capital. Hobhouse resigned, Brailsford was restive, and Hammond, thinking that in return for the new capital there was to be no more criticism of German foreign policy, also decided to resign. Murray at first did not understand the situation and suspected Hammond of taking a purist line about foreign capital: 'You will, I suppose, take up a rationalist position and say "Good or bad, they are foreigners, and I will not take foreign money". Now I think that position out-Kiplings Kipling.'

Hammond was deeply hurt by such a comparison 'from the friend whose good opinion I value more than that of anybody else outside this house'. Murray immediately ate his hard words. 'It is a most distressing and indeed disgusting business'; he could not possibly advise Hammond to go against his own conscience.[5] Shortly afterwards Hammond also gave up the editorship of the *Speaker*, and this was transformed in March 1907 into the *Nation*, of which the moving spirits were H. W. Massingham, the editor, Hobhouse, and J. A. Hobson. Murray wrote frequently to and for the *Nation*, but with Hammond's virtual disappearance from the world of journalism, his connections with the political press became less direct.

2

Murray found it easiest to remain a good Radical on questions of foreign policy. The Peace of Vereeniging with the Boers in 1902 had removed one cause of bitterness, and Murray could now discuss Imperial problems with conservative friends. His correspondence with John Buchan about the merits and dangers of the new Imperialism has already been quoted (pp. 76–7).[6]

Another former student of Glasgow University, Norman Leys, kept Murray posted from 1902 to 1914 about one of the darker sides of British imperial policy. Leys had left Britain determined to play a political part in making the subjects of Empire 'stand up to the circumstances of the new Civilisation that I suppose is coming to them'.[7] By 1908 he was working as a medical officer in British East Africa, and had embarked on a long-term campaign of criticizing official policy there — particularly the imposition of a 'hut tax' and the expulsion of Africans from areas originally reserved for them, both with the object of securing cheap native labour. The general pattern was that Colonial Governors started out with good intentions, found themselves forced to give way to the demands of British settlers, and then had to go half-way back to their original policies as the result of humanitarian pressure in the British Parliament.

Murray had kept Leys supplied with books during Leys's early years in Africa, and the latter wrote regularly to him about political problems, particularly from 1908 to 1914. He used Murray as an intermediary with Seely at the Colonial Office, and with Ramsay MacDonald, to press his case in Parliament, particularly on the proposed removal of the Masai tribe from their reserve.[8] While Murray did his best for Leys, he was not an uncritical anti-Imperialist.

In 1907 he refused to sign a protest about the killing of some Egyptian civilians at Denshawi by British officers; he regarded the text as too provocative, and as carrying a clear implication that the British Foreign Secretary approved of violence and injustice.[9] Murray was no 'Trouble Maker' in A. J. P. Taylor's sense of the word.

He made some use of his academic prestige to convey his views on current affairs, as he had done in the preface to his translations published at the end of 1902. This could be effective at a time when so many leading Conservative and Liberal politicians had been educated in the Greek and Latin classics and took some pride in keeping up their reading in Greek and Latin literature. In 1908–9 for example the Earl of Cromer, Britain's great proconsul in Egypt, was President of the Classical Association, and wished in this capacity to give a lecture comparing in detail ancient and modern forms of Imperialism. He consulted Murray about Greek practice, and in doing so referred to many current problems of the British Empire. Were not the ancient Greeks, for example, more successful than ourselves in the fusion of governing and subject races? He heartily agreed with a point made by Murray, that ease of communication with the mother country now stood in the way of successful assimilation in the colonies.[10] In the summer of 1910 Murray addressed a Conference on Nationalities and Subject Races in London on 'Empire and Subject Races' from much the same historical standpoint. On this occasion he drew considerably from the experience of his brother Hubert, by this time a notably sympathetic Governor of Papua, as well as from that of his old friend John Maynard.[11]

It was probably due to Maynard's influence and the information which he provided in his letters that Murray's interest in Imperial affairs now began to concentrate on India. Here was part of the British Empire which had a strong intellectual tradition. For India Murray could see the advantages of independence, while for the African colonies, for example, he did not wish to see more than enlightened and long-sighted British rule.

3

During the years of the Liberal Government's boldest social reforms, Murray and Lady Mary gave more attention to these than to foreign affairs. One of the principal current issues was that of Women's Suffrage, a cause for which he and Lady Mary had fought consistently since their marriage in 1889. Notes are preserved for one of the speeches which Murray made during his election campaign for early 1910. Archer, reviewing the *Rise of the Greek Epic* in 1907, quoted Murray to the effect that, though the ancient Greeks did hold dominion over women, they were also 'the first nation that realized and protested against the subjection of women.' Murray himself never cited Medea as a prototype fighter for women's liberation, though he admitted in 1913 that songs and speeches from his translations of the *Medea* had been chanted at 'suffragist' meetings.[12] Murray regarded more freedom for women as a mark of advancing civilization. He spoke publicly (but with much careful circumlocution) in favour of change in the divorce laws—also for some restraint in the reporting of divorce cases. 'We must accustom ourselves—and we must begin young—to regard women in all respects and in all relations of life as Fellow-citizens and not as property. (I hope this view will be reciprocated).'[13] He also strongly supported the 'suffragist' tactics of making full use of public meetings, the press, and Parliament for rational argument in favour of Women's Suffrage. However he was no uncritical defender of the thesis that women were constantly subject to oppression. In answer to Elizabeth Robins, who sent him in 1909 a pamphlet on the suffragist case, he wrote:

I think I first wrote in favour of the suffrage for women when I was at school 25 years ago . . . I believe that in ordinary circumstances the woman slightly oppresses the man, but that in really hard circumstances or when the man is roused he can generally at a pinch cruelly tyrannise over the woman.[14]

Perhaps there was an echo here of domestic battles, not so long ago.

In August 1910, Murray was able to put his views before a wide and largely conservative audience. *The Times* published a special Women's supplement, and its editor, wanting in Murray's words 'to get some progressive stuff in it', asked Murray to contribute a leader. He obliged with a highly ironical piece, approved by Russell to whom he submitted it in advance, but probably not understood by all its readers. It was called 'The Weaker Sex', and needs no more description in view of its title, Murray's admission of irony, and the male masochist statement already quoted.[15]

Murray strongly disapproved of the 'suffragette' as opposed to the suffragist campaign. He would have nothing to do with the Suffragettes' hunger strike or with the organized protests against forcible feeding of the strikers from 1909 onwards.[16] Writing to Rosalind about his growing conservative tendencies, he appended

some verses in a Swinburnian form very popular among undergraduates at the time as a vehicle for comic verse:

> If I were Mrs. Margo [Asquith]
> And you were Christabel,
>   I'd either educate you,
>   Or else I'd simply hate you
>   And send you with your cargo
> Of suffragettes to . . . well
>
> If I were Mrs. Margo
> You'd catch it, Christabel.[17]

However, the Murray family still had its rebels. Murray's half-
sister 'Ev' Morrison was one of these. There is a contemporary
glimpse of Ev at her subversive work in one of Murray's letters to
Lady Mary, of July 1912: 'I saw Ev carrying a sandwich board in
High Street, Kensington. I was on a motor bus, and started to get
down, but changed my mind. We should not have been
sympathetic—at least perhaps not.'[18]

Kensington seems to have been Ev's beat. There is a further passage
about her in Murray's autobiography:

Inevitably she was at last caught up in the Militant Suffrage movement
. . . she felt obliged to do things that were most repugnant to her, especially
if other women were afraid to do them. She was once ordered to break
somebody's windows—I forget whose—but as she walked in misery towards
the house, a kindly policeman laid his hand on hers and removed the stone
it was carrying. 'No, madam, I think not.' My wife and I have met her
standing in the rain, selling *Votes for Women* outside Barker's in Kensington.
She was stationed in a wet gutter, since to stand on the pavement was held
to be 'obstructing the traffic'. She looked very cold. My wife begged her
to take more care of herself, but in the meantime took her into Barker's
and made her accept a pair of tall woolly boots.[19]

In July 1912 the militants' campaign was intensified, while at the
same time, Asquith's government introduced a democratic Reform
Bill which applied as it stood to men only, but could apparently be
amended to include women. At the end of the year, the government
promised to accept any amendment in this sense that might be passed
by the House of Commons. This seemed to clear the way for a
general reform of suffrage arrangements, which should include
arrangements for Women's Suffrage. Murray stood wholeheartedly
behind the Women's Liberal Federation (of which Lady Carlisle
and Lady Mary were pillars) in resolving to make full use of the
Parliamentary opportunities likely to be available.[20] In fact the

Speaker of the House of Commons quite unexpectedly ruled the amendments to the Reform Bill out of order; and women had to wait for the vote until after the First World War.

Murray continued to fight for their cause. Lloyd George visited Oxford at the end of 1913, and Murray was one of a deputation which called on him at Christ Church on behalf of the National Union of Women's Suffrage Societies. They pressed Lloyd George to leave behind him a 'triple monument to his humanitarian genius' by bringing into effect measures for Women's Suffrage as well as for National Insurance and Land Reform. Murray added that, 'it was impossible to give that support to the Liberal cause that one otherwise would whilst women were denied the vote.'[21]

Within Oxford, Women's Suffrage was by no means a lost cause, particularly for the younger generation. For example, a joint meeting of Balliol's Arnold Society and Somerville's Debating Society in 1912 carried by 86 votes to 26 a motion to the effect that 'in matters of franchise no distinction should be made between men and women'. However there remained plenty of discrimination against women students within the university. They had been allowed to take the university's Honours examination since 1884, but were not admitted to university degrees till 1920. A Statute to allow them full degrees had been defeated in 1896. The Chancellor of the university, Lord Curzon, in his proposals of 1910 for university reform, went no further than to suggest the granting of a titular degree for women, still denying them the rights of full members of the university. It was left to individual colleges (Balliol and Corpus prominent among them) to admit women to college lectures—A. C. Bradley and Arthur Sidgwick were among the first volunteers to take women pupils.

In this atmosphere Murray's main contribution to the cause of equal rights for women lay not in the sphere of national politics so much as in his quiet activity in Oxford, as a member of the Council of Somerville College from 1909 onwards (it did not become self-governing until 1926, and before that its Council consisted largely of distinguished 'outsiders'). His most conspicuous service here was to help in inducing Lady Carlisle to endow in 1912 the Research Fellowship named after her. Her initiative, according to Murray's account at the time, was typically impulsive:

Lady Carlisle suddenly said to me last week: 'Gilbert, if you had a largish sum you wanted to give to a public purpose, what purpose would you select?' I said: 'Found a Fellowship at Somerville.' A pause: then 'What earthly good is a fellowship?' Then a long conversation with no particular end, till yesterday she proposed the gift to me.[22]

Murray was also enthusiastically concerned in 1911 with the college's plan for new buildings—the money (£14,000) was raised by loans from former students, repaid from the income resulting from additional fees.[23] His enthusiasm for women's education involved him in much administrative activity at Somerville; for example he was Chairman of the college's library committee from 1911 almost until his death. He was also a ready lecturer to college societies, and his daughter, Agnes, was a scholar of the college from 1913 to 1915, when she left it to do war work. Murray's connection with Somerville seems in most ways to have been closer and more enjoyable to him than his participation in the affairs of Christ Church, to which he belonged in virtue of his professorship.

4

Murray's political outlook was often represented as simply (in every sense of the word) Liberal. This view needs some qualification, particularly at a time when an active Liberal Government was in process of stealing a good many of the socialists' clothes. Murray and Lady Mary were both thoroughly anti-conservative. They both believed in 'progress', or at least in the importance of trying to ameliorate material conditions for the poorer classes of people. They both believed in the importance of rational argument, and of education—increasing people's ability to argue rationally. Both— and this is highly relevant to their political attitudes—disapproved of luxurious living and practised the simple life. To this extent they tended to be anti-establishment, and anti-government—whatever government. Murray much disliked Hilaire Belloc,[24] but his lines,

> The accursèd power which stands on Privilege
> (And goes with Women, and Champagne and Bridge)
> Broke—and Democracy resumed her reign:
> (Which goes with Bridge, and Women and Champagne).

would have met with his (and even more Lady Mary's) approval; her view of Winston Churchill was strongly coloured by his enjoyment of life's good things. Murray's own feelings were complicated by a certain relish for his position of friend and adviser to at least the classically educated leaders of the Establishment. Lady Mary, the Earl's daughter, was above such minor snobberies, and was correspondingly distrusted for her bluestocking qualities.

At the beginning of 1909, in a letter already quoted, she wrote to Murray about her reasons for becoming a socialist:

I do with all my heart and strength I have left, want to establish as a matter
of course a decent physical standard for everyone, so that then they may
enjoy the radiance of all kinds of love and proceed to the cultivation of the
artistic and intellectual things which differentiate them from beasts. There
now, I do mean that . . . but what chance has a Puritan Bohemian with
no brains?[25]

Murray did not differ very greatly from her. Writing about his
intellectual relations with Rosalind, he found she was reluctant 'to
join him in singing vivant Ruskin et Wesley. As I grow old, I feel
that I care for almost nothing else except Liberalism or Christianity
or something—the sort of religion you get in Tolstoy and, in a sense,
in Ruskin and Wesley.'[26]

Tolstoy and Ruskin clearly cover simple living, and the importance
of education in the highest things of life. Wesley is rather more
puzzling—this is not a name which occurs elsewhere in Murray's
writings or correspondence. The allusion is probably to Wesley's zeal
for the general education of his followers and for improving the
material conditions of their lives.

Against this background it is not surprising that Murray felt himself
able to join Beatrice Webb's campaign, starting in spring 1909,
against destitution—an extension of the line which she had pursued
on the Commission for Reform of the Poor Law (1905–9) and
embodied in her Minority Report. Murray agreed to join her
National Committee for the Break-up of the Poor Law and, by later
extension, for the Prevention of Destitution. His friends, Hobhouse
and Hobson, also joined the Committee. Murray was never an active
member, though he addressed a meeting in the Queen's Hall,
London, in November 1911 on 'The Break-up of the Poor Law', his
main theme being, apparently, our lack of adequate statistics and
thus of the means for complete social self-knowledge.[27] However,
his name, as that of a prominent Liberal, had some weight and
Beatrice Webb expressed warm gratitude simply for his moral
support of her plans to prevent rather than merely to relieve
destitution.[28] The break-up of the Poor Law in fact had to wait
until 1929; but in other respects the Minority Report was more
successful. A National Insurance Bill was introduced in 1910, and
did much to satisfy the more Liberal and less socialist supporters
of the Webbs' campaign; many of them were in any case deeply
suspicious of the co-ordinating part to be played by the Registrar,
'an officer of high status and practical permanence of tenure', under
the Webb scheme. Murray from the start had warned Beatrice Webb
that he would not play an active part in it,[29] and there is no reason

to think that he shared her highly critical point of view about the National Insurance Bill. The most important effect of the whole episode was to reintroduce him to the Webbs and other socialist thinkers.

This was important in a local context. The prolonged strike by Oxford tram-workers in spring 1913 aligned Murray with 'Christian Socialists' (the term is not used precisely), among them H. S. Holland, Dean of Christ Church, and his old friend, Charles Gore, by now Bishop of Oxford. They pressed for a more accommodating line by the employers in this case and emphasized that society as a whole was concerned with industrial disputes (not a difficult point to make, after the great series of strikes, affecting railways, mines, docks, and shipbuilding among other branches of industry, in 1910–12). There is no record of action by Murray on this issue, but he was bound to sympathize with a cause which won the support not only of Charles Gore, but also of such various academic characters as M. L. Jacks, G. N. Clark, and G. D. H. Cole.[30]

The last of these was becoming a familiar figure in the Murray family circles. He had made a great personal impression on Murray's young daughter Agnes, a girl of 19 at the time, evidently both flirtatious and impressionable. She was now 'inclined to syndicalism', Murray wrote to Rosalind.[31] Both Murray and Hammond found Cole a very attractive figure. He appealed to their dormant Radical and romantic instincts which found little delight in the establishments of either the Labour Party or the Fabians. Inveighing against the respectability of the Labour Party, Hammond declared that there were no true Radicals left to fight for the liberties of the poor, except for Bernard Shaw, Wedgwood, Chesterton, Murray, and himself—a strange list.[32] Murray agreed to write a foreword for Cole's book on Labour, published in 1913, which enabled him to shorten his own preface and to feel like 'a little world-movement'.[33] He described Cole to Hammond with amused enthusiasm:

Very clever, handsome, austere, ferocious, and young, and his views are violence personified. His eyes flash fire at the mention of Peace or Prudence or Liberalism or Ramsay MacDonald or the Insurance Act . . . he regards the *Nation* much as we regard the *Church Times*.[34]

It is curious to find Murray, shortly afterwards, offering to introduce him to Ramsay MacDonald.[35]

Murray had a wider range of political and human sympathies than is often credited to him, and he was able—with some help from his daughters—to exercise his charm in unlikely quarters.

5

Murray's most effective public work still lay in the field of education, not merely in the popularization of Greek and the spreading of the Hellenic message, as he understood it, but also in the provision of more educational facilities for all. His views on this wide theme were summarized in the resolution moved by J. R. Clynes, MP, and seconded by Murray himself at a National Demonstration held at Reading in October 1910, in connection with the 7th Annual Meeting of the Workers' Educational Association. The resolution 'expressed confidence in the WEA's unsectarian non-party . . . attempts to stimulate and to satisfy the demand among working men and working women for education.'[36]

Murray's interest in furthering general education had already led him to support Archer in efforts to introduce a system of simplified spelling (curiously enough there is no trace in Murray's correspondence with Shaw that they ever discussed this subject, so dear to Shaw in his later years). In May 1907 Archer wrote to Murray about the need for a Committee to evolve new and reasonable spelling for the English language, and in autumn 1908 Murray wrote that he would be glad to join the Committee of the Simplified Spelling Society.[37] There seem to have been delays; perhaps Murray cooled off after being appointed to his Oxford professorship. However, he wrote again to Archer in summer 1910, admitting that he was 'getting to think the cause of proper spelling more and more important'; and in reply Archer urged him to join the Committee and become Treasurer.[38]

Now things moved faster than either had envisaged. In February 1911 Murray was elected President of the Society. Sir James Murray, the lexicographer, was one of the Vice-presidents and warned his namesake that the cause was almost hopeless—he had been sanguine thirty years before and was by now only wishful.[39] Murray himself did not play a very active part, and wrote to his wife at the end of November 1911 that he would probably retire soon from his Presidential post.[40] He was not always wholly serious about the cause. He would sometimes write to Archer in 'Nuspel': 'Bie Jove I forgot! What the paiper seems to need is sum indicaishon ov the kiend of Boerd or Comiti you contemplait . . . '[41]

By this time Murray was deeply involved in what proved to be his main project for general education. In August he was asked by the publishers, Williams and Norgate, to help in launching a new series of short books (about 50,000 words each), written by experts in simple style to convey the essential facts and context of a wide variety of subjects to a new type of reader. The series was aimed at those who had passed through newly established secondary schools, had acquired a taste for knowledge and had no chance of going to a university. The Home University Library of Modern Knowledge was quickly launched, with Murray as general editor, together with his friend Herbert Fisher, and the scientist Professor J. Arthur Thomson (not to be confused with Professor J. A. K. Thomson, the classical scholar). The first task was to agree a list of subjects and of experts to write about them, and progress was remarkably quick. The normal terms were for a first printing of 20,000, an advance of £50 and authors' royalties of one penny in the shilling (8 per cent). Some authors (D. G. Hogarth, for example, who contributed a volume on *The Ancient East*) [42] found the royalty rate absurdly low, but on the whole there was a quick and good response from the experts.

The general editors all made their own contributions as authors. Fisher wrote a famous little book on Napoleon, and J. A. Thomson was joint author, with P. Geddes, of a book on Evolution. Various subjects were suggested for Murray. He himself contemplated a joint book with Canon R. H. Charles on 'The Coming of Christianity' (the subject was not treated under this title in the Home University Library, though Charles contributed a volume on *Between the Testaments*). Murray was then asked to write on *Ancient Greece*, and started work on this subject; but eventually his contribution to the series was his book on Euripides. It was of course a subject which Murray had at his fingers' ends.

The bulk of Murray's work for the Home University Library initially lay in suggesting possible authors and doing his share of correspondence with those whom it was decided to approach. A good number of his personal friends appeared on the authors' list for the first hundred volumes—Brailsford (*Shelley, Godwin, and their Circle*), Charles Gore (*Jesus of Nazareth*), Hobhouse (*Liberalism*), Hobson (*The Science of Wealth*), Ramsay MacDonald (*The Socialist Movement*), Margoliouth (*Mohammedanism*), John Masefield (*Shakespeare*), J. L. Myres (*The Dawn of History*), and Logan Pearsall Smith (*The English Language*) among others. It is a wide-ranging and impressive list.

The principal 'big fish' who got away from Murray and his colleagues was Bernard Shaw. Murray waited to approach him until he could give some details of progress. At the end of February 1911, he wrote:

Does your conscience never remind you of the existence of this Home University Library? The first ten volumes will burst on the world in April, and Fisher and I hope, before we have done with it, to make it the Vulgarest and most successful thing ever seen in the publishing trade. First edition of 20,000 . . . on sale in all European capitals, as well as U.S.A. . . . We want you to do a book on Music [a subject eventually treated by Sir Henry Hadow].[43]

Shaw never considered the proposition seriously, and told Murray that such plans were fifty years out of date—the smallest paying edition would be 40,000 and Williams and Norgate's distributing machinery would be inadequate.[44]

Murray had to deal with a large variety of problems—Sidney Webb's complaints about being exploited[45], for example, and the accusations of plagiarism by a *T.L.S.* reviewer (who proved to be Robert Bridges) against Logan Pearsall Smith.[46] He was particularly concerned with certain volumes which he had commissioned himself, and two instances may be given of his editorial activities and trials. The first concerns the volume on the Renaissance, ultimately written by Edith Sichel. Murray originally commissioned this from Rachel Annand Taylor, a somewhat exquisite young poetess, who wrote under the pseudonym *Fiammetta*. She had an over-fine Italian hand, and a record of ill health equal to Murray's own in his most delicate years. She had written Murray a fan letter in spring 1910, urging him to continue his work as a playwright, and to pen 'the great romantic drama of flame and darkness we need to shrivel up those grey unreal things they call plays in these fallen times.'[47] Murray was sufficiently pleased and flattered to reply that 'Your letter . . . gave me a delicious moment in which I wished to abandon all this educational nonsense and write plays like a free man.'[48]

Her name was thus in his mind when he came to consider the *Renaissance*. Mrs Taylor proved to be a poor choice. Her work came in late and was too highly coloured. However, Murray took it seriously, and she preserved his letters. Indeed their correspondence continued to the end of his life. It throws an interesting light on his editorial methods with a difficult author, and illustrates both his willingness to suffer certain types of folly too gladly, and a sort of mild intellectual flirtatiousness typical of his later years (though he did not suggest using Christian names with her until the end of 1952).

On 18 October 1911 Murray wrote to her: 'the first seven chapters have rolled in . . . they may be too gorgeous for the H.U.L. series.' They were.

On 27 September 1912 he wrote:

The Publishers say (1) you have 'utterly failed to come up to time'. I fear there is some truth in this. (2) the manuscript is unsuitable to the Home University Library.
(3) nevertheless the volume is interesting and they propose to publish it separately for 7/6d.

[*In Lady Mary's writing, at the end of the letter:*]

Your work was really fine in quality . . . too exotic in expression for one of those rough and cheap little volumes . . . You should have been told this a year ago, and I thought this had been done.[49]

The second instance of Murray's editorial activity concerned a book which did appear in the Home University Library, his friend Bertrand Russell's *Problems of Philosophy*. Russell was one of the first authors approached by Murray, who wanted him to contribute a book on mathematics; philosophy was Murray's second choice.

You have got a message for the shop-assistant about philosophy, if you would only think it out. If you don't want to tell them what Mathematics is, can you not tell them what Philosophy is? You could do it with great detachment from the conventional schools; and you could put all the main problems in their very lowest terms.[50]

Russell produced his volume, which has given a good deal of stimulus to successive generations of undergraduates, if not necessarily to 'shop-assistants'. On receiving the typescript Murray wrote to Russell: 'One impression that the book makes on me is that philosophy is a nice simple subject just fit for treatment in 50,000 words.'[51] This was not the view of the experts to whom the Editorial Board referred the draft: 'the book as a whole is inadequate, and is written with practically no appreciation of the present status of philosophy.' Murray made a list of suggestions to Russell, though it is hard to say how many alterations were made to meet his criticism. What has survived (it is printed in Russell's *Autobiography*[52]) is a letter from Murray in parody of the initial reactions which might be expected from the more literal-minded of the publishers' readers on receipt of Russell's manuscript. Murray's letter refers to the following statements in Russell's book:

(i) It may be true that an earwig is in my room . . . (p. 90).
(ii) I have not the honour to be acquainted with the Emperor of China, but I truly judge that he exists (p. 44, cf. p. 75).
(iii) If not . . . we have no ground whatever for . . . expecting the bread we shall eat at our next meal not to poison us (p. 62, cf. p. 111).

(iv) If I say 'a bald man is a man', 'A plane figure is a figure', 'A bad poet is a poet' I make a purely analytic judgement . . . (p. 82).

Murray wrote as follows, as if from the publishers:

Messrs. Williams and Norgate will be glad to meet Mr. Russell's wishes as far as practicable, but have some difficulty in understanding his point of view. About the earwig for instance, they are ready, if Mr. Russell is inconvenienced by his suspicions of its presence in his room, to pay a rat-catcher (who is also accustomed to earwigs) two shillings an hour to look for it and make sure, provided the total payment does not exceed Ten Shillings (10s). The animal, if caught, shall be regarded as Mr. Russell's property, but in no case shall the capture, or the failure to capture it, be held as exonerating Mr. Russell from his contract with Messrs. W. & N. Mr. Russell's further complaint that he has not the acquaintance of the Emperor of China cannot be regarded by Messrs. W. & N. as due in any way to an oversight or neglect of theirs. Mr. R. should have stipulated for an introduction before signing his contract. As to Mr. Russell's memory of his breakfast and his constantly returning alarm lest his next meal should poison him, Messrs. W. & N. express their fullest sympathy with Mr. R. in his trying situation, but would point out that remonstrances should be addressed not to them but the Head Cook at Trinity College. In the meantime they trust that they do not exceed their duty in reminding Mr. Russell that, in his own words, a philosopher should not always have his mind centred upon such subjects. They would observe further that their senior editor [Murray] is much gratified by Mr. Russell's frank admission that a bald man is, nevertheless, a man, while his next sentence has caused some little trouble among the staff.

All three editors have rather good figures; at least there is no one among them who could be called conspicuously 'plain' in that respect. Perhaps Mr. Russell referred to Mr. Perris? If so, however, we do not quite understand who is meant by the poet. We would almost venture to suggest the omission of these personalities. When gratifying to one individual, they nearly always give pain to others.

This minor academic masterpiece was a pleasant by-product of the Home University Library. Murray's contribution as a joint general editor was a considerable and serious one, and the series proved to be one of the most successful ever launched in the field of general education. Whether it effectively hit its target—the product of the new system of secondary education—may be a subject of doubt, though the large sales of many books in the series suggest that it was successful in this respect. The series certainly provided useful introductory reading for undergraduates and postgraduates interested in arts subjects. The scientific side of it, never so strong, was bound to date quicker and was less successful, though the

early lists contained some books which would still have a considerable interest for the student of the history of science, for example
G. P. Thomson on *The Atom* and A. N. Whitehead's *Introduction
to Mathematics*.

The total sales of Home University Library titles—some 80 in
all—down to 31 October 1913, amounted to 1,017,846 copies,
including 5,733 copies of Murray's own *Euripides* in a very short
time. The sales were on an upward curve at the end of the year—
22,800 in December 1913, as compared with 8,422 only in December
1912.[53] None the less by the end of 1913 the publishers found
themselves in difficulties, with too much of their capital tied up
in a venture which was bringing them little or no profit. Murray
had put in £500 at the outset, when he agreed to become a joint
editor.[54] At the beginning of September 1913 he received 350 guineas
as payment for his services as editor for the first hundred volumes
of the Home University Library, and as an advance on his *Euripides*.
He offered to resign as editor on the issue of the hundredth volume,
but his services were retained—at some net expense to himself. Early
in 1914 Williams and Norgate decided to raise new capital of £6,000
by the issue of debenture shares. Murray offered to take up £500
worth of these, if the whole issue was subscribed. By midsummer
it looked as if this condition was fulfilled, but by mid-November
1914, after the outbreak of war, prospects seemed more doubtful.[55]
Murray wrote to Fisher reminding him of the condition attached to
his original offer to take up shares. If the scheme was not floated,
the publishers would, he thought, go bankrupt; if it was, the
debenture holders would suffer.[56] However, Sir Home Gordon was
able to reassure him that shares had been taken up to the value of
£5,000, and Murray made his further contribution.[57]

Thus Shaw's suspicions about the financial side of the project had
not been far out. However, it was a bold venture which produced
far-reaching results. In June 1914, the Congress of Associated
Booksellers in Edinburgh greeted it as the one live development to
have occurred in the trade in the nine years since their last Congress.
And the series continued until in 1941 it was taken over by the
OUP under the same title, with Murray and Fisher still editors.
Julian Huxley had become science editor. Murray remained an active
editor until his death.

CHAPTER XV

The Classical Scholar: An Assessment

1. By 1914 Murray a recognized public figure and scholar—his treatment of Euripides the measure of his scholarship.
2. The OUP text of Euripides—the translations—criticism of T. S. Eliot—Murray's blindness towards certain poetry.
3. *Euripides and his Age*—criticisms of his treatment of the *Medea*; the *Trojan Women*; the *Ion*—Aristophanes on Euripides—conclusion.

1

IN the summer of 1914 Murray, now 48 years old, was at the height of his main career. He had scholarly achievements to his credit, and had accomplished to a considerable extent his aim of putting before a wide public his conception of the message of Hellenism. His list of academic distinctions was already a long one, including Honorary Doctorates of Law at Glasgow (1901) and St Andrew's (1906), and a Doctorate of Letters at Oxford (1910); he was a Fellow of the British Academy (1910), and a Trustee of the British Museum.

More public recognition had not been lacking. He refused a knighthood at the beginning of 1912 (he was fairly, but not totally, indifferent to such honours).[1] But he was above all a man of influence, and the wide circle of his personal friends included political leaders of both the main parties. Curzon invited him to house parties at Hackwood.[2] He spent a weekend at Stanway, as guest of the Elchos and met among others Arthur Balfour, whom he found 'very friendly and quite easy to talk to—not like Curzon'.[3] He records a political dinner party in London at Lady Burne-Jones's house, when one of the company expressed the view that 'British civilisation depends on the flannel sheet—I mean, the Channel fleet'.[4] He got to know Asquith and his family better than any of these casual contacts; but that was at a later stage.

There is no doubt that Murray thoroughly enjoyed this privileged position. However, it did not distract him unduly from his primary work. The essence of this, as he saw it, was to combine scholarship with imagination. Only thus would he keep the spirit of Hellas alive for young scholars. Only thus could he communicate with the Greekless. By 1914 his most substantial as well as his most popular work in the classical field was done. What then had he achieved? Had he set himself impossible tasks? How much scope should a true scholar allow to his imagination? And is he bound to simplify unduly his own process of thought by trying to express the results of it in widely readable form?

In the search for an answer to these questions, it is best to concentrate upon Murray's treatment of Euripides, the Greek author with whom he was always most closely associated. His work on Euripides covered almost the full range of classical scholarship as he envisaged it. He produced a complete new text for scholars, working on newly found fragments of papyri as well as on existing manuscripts. His lectures to classical students at Oxford were among his most notable.[5] His verse translations of the plays were successfully performed for a time on the stage—here was an almost entirely new form of popularization—and sold very well as paperback books. Finally in 1913 Murray published for the Home University Library a short popular book on *Euripides and his Age*, which remains a brilliant example of its kind.

Murray's original choice of Euripides as his special field of study is a matter of interest. Euripides' reputation had not stood very high in Victorian England. He was generally regarded as much inferior, both as dramatist and poet, to Aeschylus and Sophocles, whose 'rugged grandeur' and 'formal perfection' were among the received ideas of the Victorian Age. Goethe had indeed appreciated and enlarged on Aristotle's verdict that Euripides was the 'most tragic' of the poets.[6] By the end of the century Wilamowitz had presented him to the Germans as a precursor of Ibsen, and Verrall had exercised his full ingenuity in portraying him as a thoroughgoing and atheistical 'rationalist'. However, by and large Euripides had been neglected in Britain. Murray was no doubt conscious of this, and also as an agnostic felt a strong attraction for a dramatist whose work obviously included rationalist elements. In 1895 (before Verrall's work on *Euripides the Rationalist* was published), Murray wrote about his feelings to Archer: 'I feel now about Euripides two things—(1) that he is a very great dramatist and thinker: and (2) that he has some big curious fault, which I cannot exactly lay my fingers on.'[7]

In the same letter Murray aired thoughts about individual plays of Euripides, particularly the *Ion*, which foreshadow much that he said in 1897 in his *History of Ancient Greek Literature* and in 1913

Basil Murray

Denis Murray

Rosalind Murray

Agnes Murray

Stephen Murray

Gilbert Murray, 1937

Gilbert and Lady Mary Murray on their diamond wedding day

in *Euripides and his Age*. The essence of these thoughts was that Euripides was essentially a free-thinker who did what he could to show up, throughout his career, the subhuman behaviour of the Olympian gods; but he had to take account of the danger of prosecution for blasphemy in Athens and thus tended to tack happy endings, with stage appearances of the gods, on to tragedies which artistically required very different conclusions.[8]

Murray's complete revised text of Euripides for the OUP's classical series was not superseded by a new edition until the 1970s; and close on seventy years is a long life for such a text in conditions of modern scholarship. Here is the verdict of Professor Hugh Lloyd-Jones, the present holder of the Oxford Regius Professorship of Greek:

He lacked the sound training which study in Germany would have given him, and in some ways never made up that deficiency; but his wide knowledge and his strong feeling for Greek stood him in good stead. In many places he is right where Wilamowitz and other eminent critics have been wrong . . . He was a subtle and ingenious textual critic; indeed his main fault lies in the excess of these qualities . . .[9]

2

Time and taste have dealt less kindly with Murray's translations than with his texts. A good deal has been said already about the metres which he chose after much deliberation to use — the rhymed ten-syllable couplet for translating the normal line of Greek tragedy (two syllables longer than the ten-syllable line, but less stiff than the French alexandrine verse of twelve syllables), and Swinburnian lyrical metres for the choruses. Murray's own reasons for his choice have already been quoted.[10] He added an important supplementary argument later:

Greek and Latin could do without rhyme because they had such clear metres. Rhyme is needed to mark clearly the end of the line and to provide the ear with fixed resting-places. Without such divisions, the metrical form would become dull and obscure. The hearer would not be sure where one line ended and the other began; he might not even be sure whether he was listening to verse or prose.[11]

Good arguments in themselves, though a critic might assume from the second of them that Murray would translate in the Dryden/Pope type of rhymed couplet, rather than in the much looser 'riding rhyme' of Chaucer and Morris. Murray was also influenced by the need to avoid the traps of literalism, admirably illustrated by

A. E. Housman's *Fragment of a Greek Tragedy*, which he loved to quote:

CHORUS.

> O suitably-attired in leather boots,
> Head of a traveller, wherefore seeking whom,
> Whence, by what way, how purposed art thou come
> To this well-nightingaled vicinity?
> My object in inquiring is to know . . .[12]

And he felt, in the words of Sir Maurice Bowra, that

English, after centuries of hard use, had lost the freshness which survived in Greek . . . he tried to compensate for this by providing an emphasis which the Greek does not possess and does not need.[13]

In avoiding one set of dangers, Murray inevitably ran into others. Jane Harrison was the first to complain to him about these.[14] Apart from any jingling effect, which Murray usually succeeded in evading, the search for rhyme led him too far from the literal sense and (more important) from the mood of the original. A. W. Gomme was one of the first scholars to publish the criticism that Murray's versions disguised the terse and witty nature of Euripides' verse.[15]

Modern feeling was more fully expressed or anticipated in an acid essay by T. S. Eliot, which took the form of a much delayed dramatic criticism of Sybil Thorndike's performance as Medea at the Holborn Empire in 1918.[16] Eliot's criticism has so often been summarized or sloganized that it is worth while to present it rather fully. He discussed the production of *Medea* in relation to 'the drama, the present standing of Greek literature, and the importance of good contemporary translation'. He attributed the success of the performance very largely to Sybil Thorndike. 'Her personality triumphed over . . . Professor Murray's verse . . . '; the lyrics of the chorus were 'happily inaudible'; the rest of the cast 'mumbled unintelligibly'. But again they 'were forced to speak in the language of Professor Gilbert Murray'.

The classics, Eliot continued, had lost their assured and privileged position. We badly needed educated poets to expound and justify the Greek drama to us.

And it must be said that Professor Gilbert Murray is not the man for this. Greek poetry will never have the slightest vitalising effect upon English poetry if it can only appear masquerading as a vulgar debasement of the eminently personal idiom of Swinburne. These are strong words to use against the most popular Hellenist of his time; but we must bear witness of Professor Murray ere we die that these things are not otherwise but thus.

Eliot goes on to criticize in detail and with quotations from the Greek, 'random examples' of Murray's translation of the *Medea*. Here are Eliot's translations of words spoken by Medea (*a*) followed by Murray's versions (*b*).

(*a*) Women of Corinth, I have come out of the house. . . .
(*b*) Women of Corinth, I am come
       To show my face.
(*a*) This thing has fallen on me and has ruined my
       life; I have let go my delight in life and long
       for death.
(*b*) This thing undreamed of sudden from on high
       Hath sapped my soul; I dazzle where I stand
       The cup of life all shattered in my hand.

After ironic mention of Murray's 'gifts' to us, and of the striking phrases which we owe to him, Eliot concludes this section by saying that:

Professor Murray has simply interposed between Euripides and ourselves a barrier more impenetrable than the Greek language. We do not reproach him for preferring apparently Euripides to Aeschylus. But if he does, he should at least appreciate Euripides. And it is inconceivable that anyone with a genuine feeling for the sound of Greek verse should deliberately choose the William Morris couplet, or the Swinburnian lyric, as an equivalent.

As a poet, Mr. Murray is merely a very insignificant follower of the pre-Raphaelite movement. As a Hellenist, he is very much of the present day, and a very important figure in that day.

Eliot hopes that 'we may be grateful to Professor Murray for what he has done' while neutralizing the influence of his translations on Greek literature and the English language. What we need, he concludes, is

an eye which can see the past in its place . . . and yet so lively that it shall be as present to us as the present. This is the creative eye; and it is because Professor Murray has no creative instinct that he leaves Euripides quite dead.

Eliot's condescending sacerdotal style is quite as distasteful as any falsity to the original Greek in Murray's translations. There is no indication that Murray himself, who lived for nearly forty years after Eliot's criticism was written, was unduly worried by it. He had made his choice of means for his translation consciously and after much consideration. He was writing for his own contemporaries, and for some time at least he managed to communicate to them something of his own vision. The success of his private readings, of many of the stage performances, and of the published texts of his translations (nearly half a million of these in all had been sold by the time that an 'omnibus edition' was published in 1954) is all incontrovertible evidence. Eliot's talk of a 'veil more impenetrable than the Greek language' is no more than silly rhetoric. So is his statement that Sybil Thorndike, in the production which he criticized, triumphed in spite of Murray's text. She herself was enthusiastic about it, and regarded it as extremely speakable.[17]

The general verdict of his time, as voiced by (for example) Archer, John Buchan, and Bernard Shaw, was that the speeches and dialogue in Murray's versions were dramatically effective and the poetry of the lyrical choruses beautiful. Among classical scholars Housman agreed at least with the latter part of this verdict.[18]

However, when all is said, Murray's translations are poorly regarded today. It is worth noting that Murray uses the same type of rhymed couplet in translating Euripides, Sophocles, and Aeschylus. His metre consequently has the effect of ironing out the differences between Euripides and Aeschylus; between, say, Medea's venomous but simply-phrased monologue as she plots revenge on Jason, the thunderous (perhaps ironically high-falutin) language of Prometheus' address to Okeanos, and the high heroic narrative of Salamis in the *Persae*. There must be something wrong with a medium which acts to such an extent as a leveller.

Murray's 'message' as well as his 'medium' may at times have interfered with his translations. Cyril Bailey, a good Christian but a friendly critic, found in 1911 that Murray had deliberately heightened the language of his translation of the *Bacchae* in order to hint at a Christ-like passion and transfiguration of Dionysus in the play.[19]

As regards the choruses, Murray's Swinburnian rhythms seem to be a rather better equivalent for Greek lyric metres than his rhymed couplets are for Greek iambics—'seem', because we have little idea of how the combination of words, music, and dancing worked out in the original productions. Swinburne too is out of tune with our age. There is a monotony about his and Murray's echoing rhymes and dactylic rhythms, however subtly varied. Surely, we feel, whatever the Greek tragedians' lyrics were like, they were not so like Swinburne as this. Then too, in his lyrics as well as in his rhymed couplets, Murray adds much to the original. An old Oxford story, quoted by Bowra,[20] and in Aristotelian terms more probable than true, tells of Murray expanding the emotive cries ἒ ἒ, ἆ ἆ, into a resonant phrase 'Death and a cold white thing within the house'.

Even here, he could claim to be preserving the mood of the poem, or emphasizing a dramatic point. At times, however, Murray seems to have blinded himself to the distinction between translation and paraphrase. His most famous lyric is his translation of a chorus in the *Hippolytus* ('Could I take me to some cavern for my hiding'); it reaches a climax in Murray's best-known line, 'The apple-tree, the singing and the gold.'[21] In answer to criticisms about his freedom of translation, Murray would take this as an example and claim that it was a literal translation. Now to simpler minds the Greek means literally 'the shore where apples grow, the shore of the minstrels'; and 'of the minstrels' seems more naturally to mean 'renowned in song' than 'where the minstrels are'; which is what Murray's version most naturally implies.

Another passage from the same chorus illustrates changes of taste. In the first stanza, Murray uses the phrase: 'As a bird among the bird-droves of God'. This is indeed a nearly literal translation, and seems effective; but it worried Bertrand Russell, who was otherwise deeply impressed by hearing Murray reading the passage in Cambridge in 1902, and Murray did his best (luckily in vain) to find something more 'poetic'.[22]

The flaws of Murray's translations are in one sense the counterparts of their virtues. Translation, or the preliminary condition for it, was for him an intense poetic experience. In his book *The Classical Tradition in Poetry* (1927) he described this:

I begin to see differently some poem which I already, in the ordinary sense, know perfectly well, I see it differently, more charged with meaning and beauty. It occupies my whole mind and I feel a sort of union with it. If any one told me I had not myself written it, I think I should for the moment feel hurt and surprised. It seems like a very important truth which I have seen and possess and wish to express. Then bits of it, turns of phrases, fragments of rhythm, begin to sing themselves in my mind in English. And so the poem gets started. I do not think that this experience would be essentially different if I were contemplating something quite unliterary, such as my mistress's eyebrow or the Retreat through Serbia, as the raw material of my poem. I seem to see the inspiration towards poetic creation as caused by something which I contemplate, love and strive somehow to be one with.[23]

Now Murray's poetic vision, though intense, was also limited. Shelley, Tennyson, and Swinburne were his poetic Gods. He read widely, but Shakespeare, Milton, Wordsworth, and Browning, all in the Victorian canon, did not greatly delight him. He mentions in *The Classical Tradition in Poetry* a large number of poets, ancient

and modern, French and German as well as Greek, Latin and
English, but usually without deep sympathy. Few outside the chosen
three appear in the vast bulk of his letters and papers. Moreover
agnosticism could still blind him. He seems never to have read the
religious poets of the seventeenth century and can write that 'in the
sphere of pure imagination, where an enthusiasm for Christian
principles involves no disagreeable practical results whatever,
Christianity has had . . . little effect.'[24]

His ear too had limitations not confined to music in the most literal
sense. In an earlier essay he could say that Milton has 'nothing near
the musical swing' of Homer; and that 'in the matter of lyrical skill
in the Greek sense, Elizabethan song is absolutely rudimentary' (for
him, only Swinburne had a Greek mastery of metre).

Such are the deeper limitations which affected the poetic quality
of Murray's translations. The freedom of them, it now seems, is
seldom justified by any special poetic beauty, and their faults are
accentuated by a sense of poetry which, however intense, is strangely
narrow. But present-day taste is no final arbiter and in their day
Murray's verse translations were justified by great success on the stage
as well as in the library.

3

If Murray's translations are more than others a distorting medium,
reflecting a flaw in his own vision, is the same sort of flaw to be
detected in his expository works about Greek literature? Murray was
one of the greatest communicators of his time, not only to a large
middle-brow readership, but also to students and colleagues and later
in his life to an even wider public by means of his broadcasts.
His successor in the Chair of Greek at Oxford, E. R. Dodds, bore
eloquent witness to the inspirational quality of his lectures to
students.[25] Murray's expository writings, even the most popular of
them, were the work of a scholar, who wanted to communicate his
knowledge widely, rather than of a visionary or propagandist with
some pretence to scholarship. Murray's younger friend, Professor
J. A. K. Thomson, wrote in a not uncritical obituary notice:

The kind of writing in which Murray excelled was always founded on exact
scholarship and represented a consistent body of opinion. It was a genuine
criticism . . . not slap-dash, hit-or-miss pronouncements.[26]

The two most important books which emerged from the main
series of Murray's scholarly lectures — *The Rise of the Greek Epic*

and *Five Stages of Greek Religion*—have already been discussed in Chapters X and XII. His book for the Home University Library, *Euripides and his Age* is intended for a popular audience, and for that reason conveys clearly a general message. It remains the easiest of his books to read, and in many ways the most stimulating. Professor LLoyd-Jones has written concisely of its virtues and vices: 'The work . . . did more than any other to make me want to be a scholar when I read it at the age of fourteen. But I now believe it to be almost totally misguided.'[27]

In *Euripides and his Age*, Murray describes chronologically the plots and general character of Euripides' surviving plays, and also writes of the leading ideas which Euripides was trying to convey to his audience: these in Murray's view often derived from the contemporary political and social situation. This view of Euripides has been the subject of much subsequent criticism. Thus he has been accused of regarding Euripides as a 'committed feminist'[28] because of certain speeches put into the mouth of Medea. Here is a good instance of the need to look carefully at what Murray said. He could indeed be quoted as saying that the subjection of women was diminished in classical Greece; but as regards the *Medea* he is more subtle. Of course when translating or commenting on the *Medea* Murray did not insulate himself from all thought of the political campaign for women's rights in the first decade of the twentieth century AD—a campaign with which he was much concerned personally; but he certainly did not bring any modern 'parallel' specifically into his discussion of the *Medea*, nor can it fairly be held against him that a chorus from it in his version was once chanted by a meeting of suffragettes![29] He may have over-interpreted but not crudely or simplistically.

The *Trojan Women* is another play into which Murray is accused of reading too much message—this time a message from the fifth century BC, not the twentieth century AD. The play is a stark picture of the results of the Trojan War as seen through the eyes of the captured Trojan women and children. Murray puts all this firmly in a Greek political context. He quotes at length from the historian Thucydides' famous 'Melian dialogue'—his account of the cynical savagery of the Athenians' treatment of the tiny and refractory subject island of Melos, and of the subsequent sailing of their disastrous expedition to Sicily (416 and 415 BC). The *Trojan Women* was produced in spring 415. Euripides, Murray writes,

must have been brooding on the crime of Melos during the autumn and winter. In the spring, when the great fleet was getting ready to sail, he produced a strange play, the work of a prophet rather than of a mere artist . . . which set a flame of discord for ever between himself and his people.[30]

The first and last phrases of this are dangerous; 'must have beens' are as illusory as 'might have beens'; but it is also dangerous to accuse Murray on the basis of such phrases of treating the *Trojan Women* simply as a tract for the times, rather than as the exposition in a particular time and setting of a universal theme, that the result of war, whoever wins, is absolutely and universally tragic; it is at least hard to disprove his theory that such a play, written at a crucial point in what was already a major war, was intended to have some contemporary application.

A third and more complicated case is that of another of Euripides' 'middle-period' plays, the *Ion*. For Murray this is one of Euripides' most 'ironical and enigmatic' plays; it is also, of all those that have survived, 'the most definitely blasphemous against the traditional gods'.[31] Here he has been criticized for attributing to Euripides himself the sentiments put into Creusa's mouth.

Conjecture at this point goes well beyond the evidence advanced. Euripides could be voicing for dramatic and rhetorical effect ideas in which he did not necessarily believe. This particular case is certainly one in which Murray's critics are on strong ground.

However, it is a case which it would be wise not to press too hard. Murray no doubt exaggerated in some of his interpretations of Euripides as a committed champion of anti-religious, social, or political causes. However, this is not to say that Euripides was not a man of strong religious and political views. Murray may have interpreted the thoughts and passions of the Athenians too much in terms of his own age. But it would be hard to deny the existence of classical Greek writers who are profoundly committed for or against political ideas—Herodotus for the greatness of Greece and Athens, Thucydides and Plato against the follies and blindness of Athenian democracy. Is it so unlikely that Euripides sometimes thought and wrote in his plays about the political and social problems of his age?

There is unique contemporary evidence of at least one eminent contemporary's view about Euripides. As Murray points out: 'Of the eleven comedies of Aristophanes which have come down to us three are largely devoted to Euripides, and not one has managed altogether to avoid touching him. I know of no parallel . . . in the study of literature.'[32] It seems clear from Aristophanes that Euripides was regarded by his contemporaries as intensely interested in ideas, and in extending the field of tragedy to the themes of everyday life. It is a short step from this (but perhaps one which goes beyond the existing evidence) to suggesting that Euripides intended the ideas which his stage characters aired to have contemporary applications. This is, in slogan terms, to admit the concept of Euripides the Shavian. It is a longer step, again beyond the evidence, to suggest that he was making propaganda in his tragedies for particular social or political causes—or, in similar terms, that he was an Ibsenite. Murray certainly took the penultimate steps, and had reasonable (he thought compelling) grounds for doing so. In so far as he took the last step of all, the weight of evidence is that he was wrong, but the details of his arguments are always worth careful weighing.

Inevitably Murray's views have been overtaken and are not the last word in scholarship. But the *Five Stages* and *Euripides* remain eminently readable today.

CHAPTER XVI

Family and Personal 1908–1914

1. The marriage settles — house move within Oxford — purchase of holiday home at Overstrand.
2. Growing independence of the older children — Denis and aeronautics — Agnes's flirtations — Rosalind's divergence from Murray — her marriage.
3. Mystery of Murray's invalidism in face of his extensive physical and mental activities.
4. Political interests remain, but thoughts of an active political role abandoned.

1

THE crisis of the Murrays' family life in 1908 was successfully overcome. The copious correspondence between husband and wife over the next years is tender on both sides and free from the sometimes hysterical overtones which marked exchanges during that unhappy spring and summer. There was no break in Murray's friendship with the Wheelers, but also no further written sign of jealousy from Lady Mary. In July 1909 for example, Murray was staying with the Wheelers at Hammersmith, and gave £10 to Penelope for immediate financial relief: 'I know we are hard up, but . . .'.[1] In 1910 he went on holiday to Walberswick with the Wheelers and Jane Harrison — a combination which in 1908 would surely have led to tears.

During these years before the First World War, husband and wife were bound by many joint practical worries. Within Oxford the move was accomplished at the end of summer 1909 from 131 Banbury Road to 82 Woodstock Road, a large and unsightly pile, with plenty of room for family, staff, and friends.

The Murrays were also looking at this time for a holiday house by the sea. The new baby's health was for some years a cause of anxiety, and Lady Mary felt that he should have the benefit of sea air. Her own health was also uncertain, and much of the burden of house-hunting, whether for temporary lodgings at the seaside or for a holiday residence, continued to fall on Murray himself, assisted more or less by Rosalind. The search for bracing air had begun as far back as 1906. In a letter to Rosalind that year there is a note of exasperation about the charms of the East Anglian coast, which had been recommended for her health:

[It] is the coldest and ugliest. Also there are more east winds and more sand in the air to make your eyes sore . . . Another advantage . . . is that it is falling into the sea. We already have the offer of a vicarage near Southwold from which the Vicar has fled, because it was slipping over the cliff. It is only five guineas a week, and, if the cliff falls, he buries you free of charge.[2]

In the troubled summer of 1908, Murray and Rosalind were looking for family lodgings at Rottingdean. He wrote to Lady Mary that 'the Earl's granddaughter is less useful as a critic than she might be, because she likes spacious lands and retainers and 200 acres of forest and ravine.'[3]

In 1911 the Murrays finally decided to buy a house, Beckhythe Manor, at Overstrand, near Cromer in Norfolk. Murray wrote to Archer: 'We have bought a Gentleman's Marine Cottage Residence . . . among the Jews at Overstrand. It has dry rot and bad drains. We are waiting until the former is wet and the latter dry.'[4]

'The Jews' refers particularly to Sir Edward Speyer, who had a house in the neighbourhood. This seems to have aroused some uncharacteristic racial instinct, or English aristocratic sentiment in Murray; he expressed it also in writing to Hammond, sending him a sketch-map of Overstrand, full of signs 'to the synagogue'.[5]

They kept the house at Overstrand till they moved to Yatscombe in 1919. Stephen records that on the outbreak of war he, now aged 6, was 'incarcerated' there in his 'golden cage' in the care of his nurse. Lady Mary wrote daily — always to the nurse — with detailed instructions about his diet, medicines, clothing, etc. His father, however, sent him a series of postcards purporting to concern the life of one Rabbit Bland: these Stephen much enjoyed till M.I.5 put a stop to them convinced they must be coded messages. Not until he went to prep school did Stephen receive postcards from his mother, but as they were open cards beginning 'Dear Lambkin' he asked her to discontinue.[6]

The move within Oxford in 1909 coupled with the purchase of the Overstrand house involved the Murrays in some temporary financial difficulties. In summer 1911 Murray for once refused to give financial backing to a good cause — the establishment of Ruskin Hall (later Ruskin College) at Oxford, on the grounds that his finances were in a critical state, and that he could not afford to put down £200 as guarantee money.[7]

Three years later in spring 1914 there was another minor financial alarm, when the publishing firm of George Allen, which had hitherto published Murray's translations and sold many thousand copies of them, went bankrupt. This was the result partly of George Allen's taking over the publishing firm of Sonnenschein in 1911, without taking full account of their liabilities; partly of the attitude of Allen's debenture holders who insisted on the receivers being sent in as soon as they failed to receive interest payment. A debt of £270 to Murray was outstanding. He entrusted his interests to the Society of Authors, and a new settlement was reached without much delay. Murray was to receive immediately a quarter of the debt, the rest to be paid in instalments as soon as the new firm of George Allen & Unwin was fairly launched. In return he undertook that 'as far as he could see at present he would let them go on publishing his works' (they had pressed for a more definite guarantee, but the Society of Authors was strongly against Murray tying his own hands). The arrangement worked for over forty years to the satisfaction of both parties.[8]

2

Meanwhile family life produced more daily worries than the financial situation. A price was paid for Lady Carlisle's generous financial support of her daughter and son-in-law. In a letter to Rosalind dated April 1912 Murray alluded to the strain of living with the Countess:

Grandmother talks all day long to relays of people about all possible subjects. Of course a good many subjects are dangerous: naturally. I have sometimes been in request to turn the conversation away to such safe themes as the Epistle to the Galatians, St. Paul and Hellenistic philosophy, the Homeric question, etc. The strain on Mother and her sisters is about as much as they can bear . . .[9]

Spring 1912 would have been a particularly difficult time. Lord Carlisle had died in 1911 and had left Naworth Castle to their eldest son Charles—now the 10th Earl. Tragically he died of cancer in 1912 and his 16-year-old son became the 11th Earl. Lady Carlisle's move from Naworth to Boothby was fraught with difficulties.

However, the main joint concern of Murray and Lady Mary, after some twenty years of marriage, was the development of their elder children, and their departure from the parental home. Murray had to remind Lady Mary that the two of them had been happy to live for one another, 'before these troublesome creatures appeared', and they could do so again.[10]

The eldest son, Denis, was the source of the most obvious problems. Perhaps in other families this would not have been the case. Denis clearly did not fit the academic world familiar to Murray, though at Winchester he became sufficiently noticeable to be taken on one of the traditional holiday climbing parties by the famous Alpinist, Graham Irving.[11] In Autumn 1910 Denis went to New College, but was again a misfit. The academic hurdle of 'Pass Mods.' was too high for his first attempt in March 1911. In the following summer Warden Spooner had to communicate his second failure to Murray: 'he has worked quite well; he was gated for a fortnight for example's sake.'[12] Evidently the rebellious blood of Murrays and Howards alike ran strongly in his veins.

Meanwhile the Murray parents had taken a sensible decision. Denis had shown already an interest in motor cycles and some aptitude for handling them; he was sent the next autumn to study engineering at the University of Birmingham, with the encouragement of Oliver Lodge, the Vice-chancellor there, who was also a friend of Murray.[13] The new experiment was more successful, even if Denis did not achieve a degree. By 1913 he had joined an aircraft manufacturing company, and had embarked on the training necessary for a pilot's certificate. The company was soon involved in financial difficulties, but Denis seemed to be fairly launched on an interesting and adventurous career—one moreover of unexpected interest to his father.

The Murray daughters had by this time begun to provide more worries for their parents. An exchange of letters with Shaw in 1913 gave Murray the opportunity of generalizing some of his own problems:

I am horrified continually at the rude and overbearing way in which adults treat children, simply because they are too small to retaliate. I agree that they ought to be treated—until a state of war breaks out—with as much courtesy as adults, and rather more because they are sensible . . . children are usually easy and pleasant to manage if you give them your whole attention, they are maddening if you are trying to do something else, and listening to them with half your mind.

In the same letter Murray complained of 'the incapacity of the young to endure boredom or follow argument not immediately interesting. How will they get through life?'[14]

Shaw was quick to detect the particular beneath the general, and indeed at this stage Murray was beginning to be concerned about his second daughter, Agnes, who in 1913 was 19. Murray was probably always more at ease with his daughters than with his sons, and had great hopes that Agnes might turn out to be the scholar and the writer of the new generation. She as well as Rosalind had occasional poems published in the *Nation*,[15] and much later Murray wrote to Isobel Henderson of her real feeling for poetry.[16] She was also very beautiful and, it appears, flirtatious. In April 1913 she was staying with her father and a party of young men from Oxford at the Villa Serbelloni (then a hotel) on Lake Como. Murray found himself: 'Out of touch with the young. It is like a kind of sentence of death. Of course I can talk with one alone, but . . . '[17] His letter to Lady Mary is mutilated at this point. Probably he had said something derogatory about Agnes's behaviour with the young gentlemen of the party (to Rosalind he had written at the same time that she 'threw herself with zest at her natural prey').[18] Lady Mary replied sensibly that 'when your liver and nerves are out of order, you *do* lose elasticity . . . ' She also observed that 'the naughty girl has evidently been turning everyone's head', at which Murray wrote in her defence that he was as much struck by her goodness as by her 'less interesting qualities.'[19]

Agnes remained susceptible, as well as flirtatious. Although she was 19 she had not had time to grow away from her parents, nor had she ever had quite the special relationship with her father that had been enjoyed by her elder sister.

This relationship rendered Murray extremely vulnerable to the natural growth of independence in Rosalind, and by 1909, when she was only 18, Murray began to note signs of rebellion. Not for nothing was she her mother's daughter and her grandmother's granddaughter. Murray wrote to Lady Mary that she was

consciously forming her own opinions and occasionally building them up against yours and mine . . . though this rarely and with scruples . . . You and I are both rather stern to her, too averse to pleasures and the motor-carish sort of life on the one hand, and to sentimental religion on the other. I don't mean real religion, but the joy of Nuns in white hoods, etc.[20]

Rosalind had begun to write copiously, and her first novel, *The Leading Note*, was published in 1910, after being submitted to Galsworthy[21] for an opinion and refused by one or two publishers. Friendships with a strain of romance followed with young men at Oxford, particularly Dick Gleadowe of New College, later art master at Winchester and Slade Professor at Oxford. 'I am very glad', wrote Murray in 1911, 'that you have struck up an intimacy with him'; but the next summer he enjoined Lady Mary 'not to throw Rosalind at Mr. G.'[22]

Shaw had a shrewd eye for Murray's family affairs and wrote to him early in 1911 that he saw in Rosalind a completely mature character, 'condemned to live in tutelage to two much younger children, Gilbert and Lady Mary, to wit.'[23]

The tutelage was now coming to an end and Murray was not without apprehension. On Rosalind's twenty-first birthday (21 Oct. 1911) he wrote:

Dearest little Miss Petkoff [a nickname derived from Shaw's *Arms and the Man*]

It is very strange to think of your being a grown-up woman, though in a way you have been like a companion to me since you were about eleven.[24]

Over the next two years there were phases of estrangement between Rosalind and her parents. Lady Mary's view of her had always been rather cool—the maternal verdict in summer 1913 was that there had been 'very little tender thoughtfulness' towards her parents.[25] But for Murray himself Rosalind's more extreme assertions of independence were bound to be traumatic. Two letters to her of 1912 reveal the depth and bitterness of the wounds. In midsummer 1912 he wrote:

I quite understand your wanting to get away from us and stand on your own feet. It is perfectly natural at your time of life that you should go away, and even make some definite effort to break the bonds of dependence . . . Also in your special case, I understand that we, and especially I, must be a trial to one so clever and full of personal life as you, because we cannot help in a way over-shadowing you. People think of you as my daughter, and you cannot talk quite freely in my presence. I hate being overshadowed myself, so I quite see that you must.

Secondly there is a personal matter between you and me. We used to be rather specially close and intimate and to agree in our interests and ideas. Perhaps I caught you young and over-influenced you. And now you are thinking for yourself in all sorts of ways and differing from me, not so much in views as in your feelings. That is all right. Only the process of breaking asunder is necessarily a painful one; it has been to me and I imagine it probably has to you. And I know that I have sometimes been sarcastic and unkind and sometimes gloomy and depressed about it. And, dear, I am very sorry and won't do it any more. And I am quite sure that you, with your knowledge of human nature—which is much the same in the middle-aged as in the young—will forgive me all right and understand how it happened.[26]

At this point a sheet of the letter has been destroyed (and as usual any replies from Rosalind have not been preserved). For the rest of the year Murray was writing to Rosalind in his familiar vein. Then in mid-December came a major crisis, this time about Rosalind's expressed intention to go hunting. Murray was stirred to a long and intimate letter from Overstrand:

Thanks for your letter. This business, which seems at first sight a trifle, is really of some importance so I will answer you at length and with perfect frankness.

About morality: I dont for a moment say that hunting or shooting is wrong. (At least not in the ordinary sense; there is a sort of ultimate sense in which I should think it so. I cant quite imagine Jesus Christ hunting.) It is conventionally accepted as right and rather praiseworthy, and I have no right to say a word against the people who practise it. Nor do I want to.

So, if you want to stay on this plane, I have not a word to say. Only there is something else which I must try somehow to express.

For some reason, either some special sensitiveness or because I saw so much cruelty to animals as a boy, I do happen to feel very intensely about all the 'sports' in which human beings associate their pleasure with the pain and death of weak animals. Such pursuits seem to me unpleasing in a man and, if you will excuse my saying so, rather loathsome in a woman. I mean, they give me a feeling of physical disgust. Of course I argue with myself and can see that hundreds of things which I dont much mind are far more morally wrong, and as far as outward conduct goes I can be civil and just to sportswomen, and even like them very much on general grounds, as I do Dr. Maude.

I think here of two things. As a boy I was once rather in love with a pretty West-Indian, when it turned up in conversation that she was chaffed at home for her fondness of going to see sheep and goats killed and even holding their necks for the knife. It nearly made me sick and my interest in her vanished. Yet I believe her to be a most respectable and conventionally high-principled person. The other thing was a day at school when Southey was shooting and made me and two other boys collect his birds for him. I thought I should go mad and eventually ran away and lay in a sort of hole I found, crying and crying.

What I mean by all this is that there is no particular moral issue at stake. There is chiefly a personal issue between you and me. You have somehow succeeded in finding the thing of all others in which you can most hurt me without doing anything that the world will call wrong. It is as if I was a Russian exile and you went to court at St. Petersburg, or as if I were a French legitimist noble and you wrote for L'Asino.

All this is meant not as a justification of myself, but as a confession. I can see that my feeling is not, and does not profess to be, purely disinterested. It is a personal bitterness that the person whom, in some ways, I have loved most and been most intimate with, should side against me on the point about which I have the most 'message' or the clearest instinctive feeling. I fully realize that if you gambled or turned up with an illegitimate baby I should not mind nearly so much, though it would be infinitely more serious. . . .

On the whole it looks to me as if the hunting was a flag to wave: a sort of indirect way of telling us that your moral standard in life was different from ours and that you meant to act on it. Is this so? If so, I do wish you would choose another flag. . . . I think, in trying to readjust our relations from parent and child to friend and friend, we have both made a lot of blunders. It is a difficult job and we were sure to do so. But it would be rather humiliating if you and I had not enough brains and sensitiveness to avoid the most ordinary pitfalls of life.

About coming here, I also had my doubts and was thinking of going away when you came. If you feel that you dont want to talk things out or try to reach a better understanding, that you would sooner hunt and not be preached to, I think it would be painful for us all for you to be here. (Or I could go away quite well, if you wanted to come for other reasons.) But of course that would leave one very sad. I would much sooner that you should come and try to get a little nearer to some understanding. . . . I had a lot of stories to tell you about my duchesses.

Your loving
DAD.[27]

Again there was a reconciliation, and on the last day of 1912 Murray wrote again to say how much he had enjoyed talking with her (she had evidently come down to see him at Overstrand). This was the most important of the early family dramas involving her, and a foretaste of later events, more deeply wounding to Murray.

In summer 1913 Rosalind became engaged to Arnold Toynbee and, not without dramatic preludes, the two were married in the following autumn. Her choice was unexpected but welcome to her parents. Toynbee, by 1913 a young Fellow of Balliol, had been a regular visitor for two years at the Murrays' house in Woodstock Road. They had thought of him as a scholar rather than as a suitor. To Archer, Murray described Toynbee as 'only 25, no money, and very middling health; but he really is a man of very fine character and exceptional brains . . . Not particularly her sort, but an extraordinarily good sort.'[28] To Russell he wrote

Not the man we should have guessed, though we like and admire him greatly. Fellow of Balliol, radical and, as far as I can make out, a quite satisfactory free-thinker with no nonsense about the Absolute; tremendous strength of character. He was, for instance, caught by brigands at Phocis, and just argued them down.[29]

There was a typical interchange with Shaw, who had professed to think that the Toynbee in question was the famous social worker of a past generation. Murray replied in kind:

You have, as usual, laid your finger on the one possible flaw in our projected marriage. Arnold is a little old; seventy-seven to be exact. But he shaves clean and his wig is so extraordinarily good that he has no difficulty in passing as his own nephew on the rare occasions when he ventures out of Toynbee Hall.[30]

There were more real difficulties in the way of the marriage. Toynbee's mother wanted a long engagement, Rosalind reacted nervously to all the excitement, and she and her satisfactorily free-thinking fiancé began to wonder whether it would not be best to avoid what they regarded as the hypocrisies of the marriage service and to set up house without ceremony.[31] Lady Mary wrote bitterly to Murray:

I wonder if she's talked freely with you about her cynicism. She really does feel that everything we think good is either mere instinct or only Mumbo Jumbo . . . her friends Rupert [Brooke?] and Dick [Gleadowe?] have had a pretty bad effect on her.[32]

The young couple were over-persuaded, though no papers survive to show how. The next trouble was where to hold the service. The Murray parents rather surprisingly wanted a religious service, and Murray wrote on the subject to Canon Scott Holland of Christ Church. Rosalind had not been baptized and (he said)

from one point of view I should prefer a purely secular service, in order to be free from any taint of pretence. On the other hand, we feel that there is something religious in marriage, and not having any church of our own . . . we seemed to find in the spirit that you stand for—you and some other Christian Socialists—the best religion from our point of view . . . We would have been sincere and reverent, though of course a little allegorical in our interpretations. This sounds patronising, which is the last thing that I feel . . .[33]

As appears from the penultimate sentence, Scott Holland did not feel able to take the wedding for the Murrays in Oxford Cathedral. However it duly and quietly took place in October, followed by a large reception in New College Hall. The troubles between father and daughter were over for a time, and Murray was soon to embark on an outstandingly successful career as a grandfather.

One member of the family does not have happy memories of the wedding. Stephen records that he was made to act as a 'page' in a velvet suit worthy of Little Lord Fauntleroy. The cruelty was compounded as Lady Mary, oblivious of her son's mortification, ordained he should thereafter wear it for his appearances in the drawing room at 5 p.m. to receive 'wet kisses from old ladies'.

Perhaps it is not so surprising that Jane Harrison on one such occasion announced that she 'did not like little boys'.[34] One wonders whether it was a genuine childish slip of the tongue or precocity when Stephen spoke to his mother of Jane Harrison as 'our extinguished guest'—Lady Mary, who was not much enamoured of Jane Harrison, was delighted.

3

G. M. Trevelyan wrote of the great Duke and Duchess of Marlborough: 'She unpacked her heart in words; but her husband hid himself in the cloud of his mighty deeds.[35] Murray expressed himself copiously in deed and word alike, but even the most private of his letters, to his wife and elder daughter, seem to leave a core of himself unrevealed. Perhaps his personality might be better understood through a deep study of his illnesses, hypochondria, and physical activity, but such a study could be undertaken only by a qualified doctor or psychologist. Here are some indications of the sort of material on which he would have to work.

From 1908 to 1914 there are fewer references in Murray's correspondence to specific and recondite ailments, such as 'cramp in the throat', than during his latter years at Glasgow. At the same time he would probably have repudiated sorrowfully any suggestion that his health was good, and have been amazed to learn that he still had nearly fifty years to live. To Lady Mary he continued to record various symptoms, but by now perhaps no more than any husband to any wife. In July 1910, when he was 44, he wrote 'my hair, the hair of my head—went and turned grey last night. It gave me a shock, it did.'[36]

Early in 1911, he wrote that he was very tired and thought of cancelling the coming term's lectures and travelling abroad.[37] At about the same time he wrote a very gloomy description to Hammond of himself and the invalid family: 'Agnes kept back from school with a heart; Rosalind nearly blind in one eye and poorly all round—worse than she has been for a good time; Mary no great shakes and me such as I describe.'[38] Their son Stephen puts it rather differently: Lady Mary, he said, was always looking for an invalid and his father was happy to supply one—a view that certainly has an element of truth in it as far as Lady Mary was concerned.

Of course, as is amply apparent from the preceding chapters, all this talk did not prevent Murray from leading a life which seems to have been often wantonly strenuous, and he could be tempted into even further commitments. In 1911 he was seriously thinking of the long journey to Australia in order to give a series of lectures. He had refused to participate the year before in the fifty-year jubilee celebrations of Sydney University, and this time Lady Mary again discouraged him by severe remarks about family considerations and the physical discomforts which he would have to endure.[39]

More usually he could see plenty of physical difficulties for himself, and even in accepting Nicholas Murray Butler's invitation to lecture at Columbia in spring 1912 he was careful to draw attention to his weak state of health;[40] the least of his troubles would be the disorder of liver and nerves which had made him so impatient with the young generation at Lake Como.

The Murrays were by now confirmed vegetarians, and he found the regime good for his health. He had recorded in 1908 that, during one of the prolonged bouts of dentistry to which he was subject, he took gas very well, and attributed this to his vegetarian diet.[41] At the same time he suggested some relaxation of it for Lady Mary in the same year, in order to strengthen her after the birth of Stephen.[42] Murray would stipulate for vegetarian food on what seemed appropriate occasions. He could also, it seemed, endure the sight of others eating and drinking in proper Edwardian or Georgian style; for example, at a dinner of the New College Essay Society, when he was guest of honour, the undergraduates were served with nine courses with appropriate wines, while Murray no doubt refrained.[43]

Perhaps because of such abstinence, he remained a keen and versatile athlete. In these years he seems to have given up village cricket with Barrie's team, and his golfing days did not last beyond the end of his Glasgow appointment. However, he remained a keen and accomplished tennis player. Much to his own delight he won the local tournament at Overstrand, in 1913.[44] He was pleased also to discover, when his brother Hubert visited England in 1907, that he could still throw the boomerang.[45] And there is an unexpected glimpse of him as an active devotee of Morris dancing. Possibly as a result of his collaboration with Ralph Vaughan Williams, he had met and much liked Cecil Sharp, founder of the English Folk Song and Dance Society. He wrote to Rosalind: 'I went to a Morris the other day and have been surreptitiously practising since. My London teachers gave me quite an ovation at the end of my course.'[46]

In these pre-war years he had also begun his long and quite dangerous career as a motor-cyclist. He bought a new Douglas machine in 1913 and enjoyed visiting his country friends on it (for example John Masefield at Cholsey) not without occasional spills.[47] And Murray was soon giving lessons in motor-cycling at Overstrand to his friend Sandy Lindsay of Balliol. It was Murray's son Denis who had inspired this new interest, and had further successes in the same direction, taking him to Hendon airfield in June 1913. Murray was 'sorely tempted' to go up, and on a second visit, three months later, he gave way to temptation: 'Rising in the air was delightful, and so was the vol-plané, when the engine was turned off and we simply glided to the ground like a big bird.' But steep banking was a frightening experience.[48] Here was a new and promising link between father and son.

There is nothing in Murray's correspondence in these years about the dangerous feats of amateur Alpinism, or the various physical tricks (such as removing his waistcoat without taking off his coat) with which later memoirists credited him.[49] However, there is plenty of evidence that Murray was physically agile and in some ways tough; he continued to delight in games, and had some taste for contemporary machines. All this must be set in the balance against the over-activity of his intellect and his hypochondria.

4

In 1914 Murray was 48, with nearly half of his life ahead of him. He was at the height of his powers as a lecturer and teacher, and there seemed to be no reason why he should not continue to exercise them on classical subjects for many years. However, his most serious original writings in the field of classical scholarship already lay behind him, and perhaps he sensed at some deep level of the mind that this was so. His verse translations from the Greek had also had their hour of maximum popularity, as things turned out. It was perhaps for these reasons that he appeared over-ready at this period of his life to dissipate his energies on work incidental to his main purposes, in a way which was certainly not suitable for one whose state of health was delicate, and which would have induced a nervous breakdown in many of coarser fibre. He devoted time and strength to attacking the censorship of plays, to the Academic Committee for Literature, to the furtherance of simplified spelling, to reading in MS the novels or plays of John Galsworthy and John Masefield. There were no doubt many reasons for such reckless expenditure of spirit, including a Puritan conscience which prompted him to back any cause that might further progress, and a mild vanity, which stimulated him to exercise his notable talents in the public eye, and to enjoy his growing position as a 'man of letters'. However, behind all these motives there probably lurked the deeper feeling that his main work in his main field was already done.

In the political field too Murray's outlook and ambitions had changed. He was getting older: 'Deeds for the young, counsel for the middle-aged, prayers for the old,' said the Greeks. Murray was still very ready to canvass or write for political causes, whether that of the Liberal Party at General Elections, or that of oppressed intellectuals in Russia. However, by 1914 he had put finally behind him the idea, inspired by his mother and cherished by Lady Carlisle, that he himself should play any serious part in British domestic politics. Moreover some of his radical ambitions for furthering the march of progress and lessening human inequalities and miseries were being realized in the years immediately preceding 1914 by a Government which combined Liberalism with a considerable dash of state socialism. It was simpler and more effective for Murray to give counsel according to the Greek formula, and to work politically from the sidelines, as a friendly stimulant to His Majesty's Ministers. This too was a role which he enjoyed, involving friendship with the great and entry into the charmed circle. The Regius Professor was becoming a man of the establishment.

Murray then was no longer the passionate radical with political ambitions beyond the scope of his own health and talents. He was growing out of the figure portrayed by Shaw in *Major Barbara*, so impatient with so many human stupidities that his own health and nerves were seriously affected, and was much more content to work through the political powers that be. However, he remained an idealist committed to educational and political goals, and still ready to commit himself whole-heartedly to some major political cause. What remained unchanged was the good-tempered wit and delicate self-conscious humour always at work on the surface of his personality; and the great will-power and reserves of strength, mental and physical, which still lay concealed beneath the coruscating surface.

CHAPTER XVII
World War 1914–1918

1. Murray radical but not pacifist — convinced by Grey that war is a necessity Aug. 1914 — Murray as governmental propagandist.
2. Continues work as professor and for social causes — principal author of *Foreign Policy of Sir Edward Grey* 1915 — quarrels with Bertrand Russell.
3. Scandinavian lecture tour March 1916 — visits Flanders preparatory to July lecture tour in USA May.
4. The Murrays' mistrust of Lloyd George now (Dec. 1916) Prime Minister — Murray refuses honours 1917 — joins H. A. L. Fisher at Board of Education Jan. 1917.
5. The family in war — Denis shot down, interned in Holland — Murray joins Oxford Volunteers 1914–1917 — lighter moments.
6. Humour — defends freedom of Press in war — conscription Jan. 1916 — Murray defends COs, particularly Russell and Stephen Hobhouse.

1

IN summer 1914 it would have been difficult to forecast Murray's attitude to the outbreak of a war between Britain and Germany; everything would depend on the circumstances in which war broke out. Murray was by this time a favourite intellectual of middle-of-the-road Liberals, particularly of Asquith who had been an eminent classical scholar; and he enjoyed his position as part-time member of the political establishment. On the other hand, the Radical in him was by no means dead; he was still committed to the cause of Votes for Women and progress towards Home Rule for Ireland, including Ulster. He had been associated with the Webbs and the Fabians in their efforts to reform the Poor Law, and with Christian Socialists at Oxford on local social issues, such as the tramway strike in 1912. He was in touch with the Independent Labour Party through Ramsay MacDonald, and with other groups on the left through Douglas Cole.

Murray had not played any active part in the movement within the Liberal Party for less secret diplomacy and more Parliamentary control of foreign policy; but he was on friendly terms with a number of those who in the course of 1914 had been evolving the Union of Democratic Control. He had corresponded with J. A. Hobson on the nature of Imperialism, and had remained close to his old pupil, H. N. Brailsford, who developed Hobson's ideas about the competition for external investment markets as a main source of war. Murray was not persuaded, but his closest friends, Bertrand Russell and even J. L. Hammond tended to think along these lines and thus to be very doubtful about the British cause for going to war in 1914. Even the more orthodox Liberals were divided, and many felt, like Murray's old political mentor, John Morley, that war between Britain and Germany could not be justified. A point of particular difficulty was that the *entente cordiale* with France had led the British Government step by step into international agreements with Russia. Whatever might be said against Kaiser Wilhelm II's regime in Germany, there was no doubt in Liberal minds about the nature of the Tsar's regime in Russia. At home it oppressed all political opponents and intellectuals; and its foreign policy was imperialist in the worst sense. There was particularly strong feeling among British Liberals about the Anglo-Russian Convention of 1907. This included an agreement partitioning Persia into Russian and British spheres of influence with a neutral zone in between; Liberals suspected that this was merely a cover for the gradual spread of the Russian Empire to Persia. Anti-Russian sentiment had been exacerbated at the end of 1911, when Morgan Shuster, the American treasurer-general and financial adviser to the Persian government, was dismissed by the Shah after two Russian ultimatums. With this in mind, many Liberals found it hard to back Asquith and Grey whole-heartedly.

But the manifest sincerity and decency of Grey, as he explained the British position to the House of Commons on 3 August 1914, made an enormous impression on Murray, who was in the Strangers' Gallery. Faced with a choice of evils, war against Germany was a lesser evil than acquiescence, which would allow German militarism to triumph. On 7 September, Murray expressed his feelings to his wife:

I have hours in which I feel as you do, utterly abased and crushed by the misery of the war, feeling that the death and maiming and starving of Germans and Austrians is just as horrible a thing as the same suffering in Englishmen. But mostly I feel strung up and exalted by a feeling of the tremendous issue and the absolute duty that lies upon us to save Europe and humanity. We did not know until the war revealed it what this German system meant. Once it is revealed I do feel that we must strike it down or die.[1]

A number of Murray's personal friends and old political associates thought differently and this was in itself enough to prevent him from adopting a crudely simplistic attitude. But his own view remained that the British Government had been right in deciding to fight. The Government White Paper, published after the outbreak of war, confirmed the impressions made on him by Grey's speech. He wrote to Lady Mary: 'It leaves me convinced that we had no choice'.[2]

It was not long before Murray's enthusiasm and literary talents were mobilized by the government. A meeting of eminent writers was convened on 2 September, to discuss how best to counteract German propaganda among the neutral countries, and Murray was invited to attend. This proved to be an important occasion. The meeting was convened by the Chancellor of the Duchy of Lancaster, C. F. G. Masterman, the Minister responsible for information or propaganda. It was attended on the government side by two Parliamentary Under-secretaries, Sir Francis Dyke Acland for the Foreign Office, and Charles Roberts (husband of Lady Mary Murray's sister, Cecilia) for the India Office. The writers present included, apart from Murray, A. H. Hawkins (the novelist 'Anthony Hope'), Sir Owen Seaman, G. M. Trevelyan, and H. G. Wells. It was unanimously resolved that a Bureau of Information should be set up, with sections devoted to various groups of neutral countries; and that a manifesto should be prepared for signature by the greatest possible number of eminent writers, in support of the war.[3]

This was the beginning of Murray's connection with what he usually called the 'Mendacity Bureau' at Wellington House, Buckingham Gate, and its brisk and energetic official organizer, Sir Claud Schuster, a lawyer who had made his mark as legal member of the National Health Insurance Joint Committee. Murray entered on his propagandist work with a slightly bewildered zeal. There were specific tasks to do, but he suspected that 'they simply want an extra person because Schuster is overworked'.[4]

The Writers' Manifesto appeared in the form of a letter to *The Times* of 18 September 1914. It was signed by (among others), Granville Barker, Barrie, Bridges, Chesterton, Conan Doyle, Galsworthy, Hardy, Kipling, Masefield, Trevelyan, and Wells. Murray was in good company.[5] One who refused to sign was W. B. Yeats on the ground that the war had resulted from secret diplomacy. Shaw too had returned the text of the manifesto, saying that he was willing to sign at the price of a few amendments (which of course changed the whole sense). Murray assured Owen Seaman, Chairman of the drafting committee, that there was no need to trouble GBS again—his own friend 'Gavin Boosey Shaw, a Scotch literary man in reduced circumstances', was willing to sign with his initials only.[6]

Murray was also concerned with the drafting of two other documents. One was an answer to a public statement by a number of German professors, denouncing British policy 'in terms so utterly baseless that we can hardly believe that it expresses their spontaneous and considered opinion.'[7]

The second was a manifesto addressed to Russian intellectuals. Murray went further in a pamphlet, *Thoughts on the War*, published in October, in which he wrote of the presence in Russia, above all nations, of a vast untapped reservoir of spiritual power, of idealism, of striving for a nobler life.[8] No Slavophil could have put it better. However, there were dissentient voices about. Kipling preferred not to sign, probably thinking of the 'Great Game' between Britain and Russia on India's North-West frontier.[9] Walter Raleigh also refused, finding 'something quaint about a chorus of authors saying that they all feel as Keats felt when he felt like Cortez.'[10] But Henry James overcame his inevitable hesitation as 'no very confirmed signer of manifestos', and found Murray's draft 'wise and beautiful, likely to be beneficent.'[11] Ten thousand copies of the manifesto were sent to the Russian Foreign Minister to distribute in his country.[12] Their fate is unknown.

The British government was seriously concerned with the prestige of its Russian ally. On 11 November, there was a further meeting at Wellington House of 'people interested in Russia', including experts on the country as well as representative British writers. Murray urged the desirability of dissociating Russia from the image of Siberian prison camps; and it was agreed that Mackail, with the assistance of various experts, should draft a comprehensive pamphlet about Russia's cultural achievements, and its place among the higher civilizations of the world.[13] This project too seems to have been abortive.

In a more private capacity, Murray wrote articles or pamphlets on broader themes. One, an 'Oxford Pamphlet', *How Can War Ever Be Right?*, was translated into many languages. Here Murray admitted his opposition to war in general, mentioning particularly his own translation of the *Trojan Women*, and stated fully the pacifist case; he proceeded to answer it with a combination of strategic and moral arguments—the need to keep the Germans away from the Channel ports and to make a stand against violation of international law and the rights of nations.[14]

The pamphlet, *Thoughts on the War*, already quoted, was less conventional. Murray caused scandal (to Russell in particular) by admitting his satisfaction at news of German casualties, but dwelt also on the ultimate need for a generous settlement with Germany. Above all, he wrote, we must not allow ourselves to become militarized in feeling, and must preserve the bond of fellowship which now united the nation:

In time past I have sometimes envied the working men who simply hail a stranger as 'mate'; we dons and men of letters seem in ordinary times to have no 'mates' and no gift for getting them.

2

In the early stages of the war, Murray continued many of his normal duties at Oxford. He gave individual guidance to young scholars, including his eventual successor as Regius Professor E. R. Dodds, then in Dublin, warning him of the 'unmanageability' of the neo-Platonists.[15] He was also still deeply engaged himself in the study of Greek religion — in September 1914 he delivered to the editors of the *Biblical Encyclopaedia* a substantial essay on the philosophical background of the New Testament.[16] In November he gave a carefully wrought lecture at Leeds University on the Stoics, substantially repeated in London in March 1915.[17]

At this early stage in the war Murray found time for his old social causes. On 16 December 1914, for example, he spoke at the Queen's Hall in London on Women's Suffrage.[18] In Oxford too he continued the battle against an ancient enemy, supporting a campaign early in 1915 to induce colleges to follow King George V's example, and 'suspend for the period of the war all supply of alcoholic drinks'. The Dean of Christ Church expressed his sympathy with Murray's efforts, but reminded him formally that this was a matter for decision by the Governing Body of the college.[19] Much in fact went on as before, and it would be impossible here to record all the social, academic, and political causes which Murray continued to support, by lecturing or other means, throughout the war. The total load of his work must have been extraordinarily heavy.

Early in 1915 he managed to exchange letters with Wilamowitz, through a Danish intermediary, Professor Bang. Wilamowitz wrote to him:

It is unfortunately true that we shall not meet again in our life time, and that memories such as I cherish of my stay in Oxford . . . will for years

seem to the younger generation like something from a lost Paradise . . .
I don't know if greetings from me will still be welcome to my former friends
at Oxford, but if so please pass them on.[20]

Murray's serious involvement in government propaganda can be
dated from March 1915. By this time the Union of Democratic
Control, which included many dissident Liberals, was campaigning
strongly against secret diplomacy and the commitments resulting
from it and for effective parliamentary control of foreign policy.
Implicit in these aims was a strong condemnation of Sir Edward
Grey's conduct of foreign policy. Among the UDC's most prominent
writers was Murray's old pupil, Brailsford. Murray found his *Origin
of the Great War* very clever but disingenuous.[21] He was evidently
discussing at this time with members of the Information Bureau the
damage done by the UDC arguments, and the need to counter them:

. . . the U.D.C. and I.L.P. are carrying on a quiet and very harmful campaign
of attack — I might almost say of slander — on British policy and on Grey
. . . see pamphlets by Brailsford and Bertie Russell, and especially 'How
the War came', No. 1 of the I.L.P. pamphlets . . . I have been reading
carefully Morel's *Ten Years of Secret Diplomacy* and Price's *Diplomatic
History of the War* and divers pamphlets, and see how to answer most of
them.
    However some weeks ago I told Schuster about this campaign of the
U.D.C. and I.L.P., and said he ought to answer it. He, after some days,
urged me to do it, and the F.O. has agreed to let me see certain papers
. . . Of course I do not know that I shall bless Grey altogether or think him
very adroit; but I am certain that he is not a corrupt schemer, and that he
did not lead Germany into war in order to jump on her back.[22]

Murray agreed to undertake the work, and on 4 April he wrote to
Archer suggesting collaboration on what turned out to be a substantial
pamphlet or small book, *The Foreign Policy of Sir Edward Grey*.[23]
Archer helped Murray in drafting and was allowed to see some
official papers; Arnold Toynbee also contributed some research.
However, the prime responsibility for *The Foreign Policy of Sir
Edward Grey* was Murray's own. He was sensitive to the charge,
made later by Bertrand Russell, that he had allowed himself to be
a spokesman for the Foreign Office. He saw the main despatches,
and his proof was sent to the man chiefly concerned in the FO, who
gave Murray some 'very interesting notes but none at all confidential
or out of the way.' But Murray felt able to assure Russell that the
work had not been inspired by the Foreign Office and that he had
not had access to their internal minutes and memoranda.[24]

The draft was ready for typing by the end of May. Schuster himself found Murray's impartiality excessive. The devil would take his due soon enough, without being given it.[25] In fact Murray laid about the UDC and some of his old friends in surprisingly provocative terms as 'often very clever', but 'not at present in a state of mind which enables them to see or even to seek the truth.' They had become so much immersed in domestic controversy that 'as far as their own combative feelings are concerned, the central enemy of the race is Sir Edward Grey'. The Kaiser had become 'just a romantic unfortunate'.[26]

Murray's main public argument was that Grey—operating in the real world of foreign policy, about which there is 'to the eye of a thorough-going Liberal . . . something sordid and even odious'—[27] knew of German aggressive designs, and had to build up a system of alliances to counter them, without openly denouncing Germany and thereby closing the door to peaceful accommodation with her. At the same time he must do so without deceiving his cabinet colleagues. This involved the settlement of points of dispute between Britain and Russia. Russia, Murray maintained, was not so black as it had been painted: ' . . . anyone who will study the actual bills passed by the Duma (in 1907) in the matters of education, social reform, etc. . . . will, I think, realise that hardly any nation in the world is advancing faster.'[28]

The book appeared at the beginning of July 1915. Murray sent a copy to Grey himself, with a covering letter describing it as an 'act of homage from one of your rather critical supporters'. Grey, in acknowledging Murray's letter, said that 'the terms in which you write are a very real pleasure and encouragement'.[29]

The booklet's circulation was of course promoted by the 'Mendacity Bureau', and Schuster reported in September that it was selling 'like hot cakes', demand being especially strong from Branch Secretaries of the British Federation of Trade Unions.[30] Like many works of controversy, Murray's book strengthened the faith of believers, perhaps did something to turn the waverers, and had no effect on the opponents of official policy. Indeed even some of Murray's warmest supporters were not convinced at all points. Bryce still thought Lloyd George's Mansion House speech of 1911 indefensible (after the German ship *Panther* had been sent to Agadir), and Hammond thought that Murray had shown excessive trust in the Foreign Office documents on Persia.[31] Others among Murray's old friends were much more critical. Shaw accused Murray of such extraordinary sympathy with Grey that he had succeeded in showing him up completely.[32] Ramsay MacDonald wrote a bitter review in the *Labour Leader*, which he admitted in a private letter to have been 'too hot-blooded'.[33] However, it was Bertrand Russell who counter-attacked most strongly. He published a booklet, *The Foreign Policy of the Entente*, specifically sub-titled 'A reply to Professor Murray', and in it he probed Murray's defences with much skill. Why had we not made clear in advance what our attitude would be on the invasion of Belgium (always a strong probability, if Germany went to war)? Why had we not realized that expert staff discussions would inevitably commit us to the French? Why (and here were the stock UDC arguments) should diplomacy be secret? Why should the public, and even the Cabinet, be kept in ignorance of the risks to which the country was being put? Why should not the House of Commons, and through it the public, have better control of foreign policy? Murray had anticipated some of these arguments, but up to this point Russell had a strong if not obviously convincing case. It could be credibly argued that the only way in which diplomacy could be kept on safe paths was by the habit of informing and instructing the people and that Grey had been far too secretive or had even deliberately deceived them. (There was an angry correspondence between Murray and E. D. Morel on this point in 1918–19 each publicly accusing the other of bad faith.)[34] However, Russell typically pushed his own argument much further towards the position of Hobson's *Imperialism*. Grey's policy, he concluded, was merely a part of a long-standing plot by the governing classes of Britain against the people; under the British capitalist system war inevitably resulted from underconsumption at home and the competition to secure outlets for investment abroad.

These arguments were in a sense the lineal descendants of Bright's criticisms of Palmerston, and of criticisms by Murray himself, among others, of Rosebery and Chamberlain. However, in 1915 Murray was more troubled by British dealings with Russia than by the suggestion of a capitalist conspiracy, or even by the effects of secret diplomacy. He wrote a friendly letter to Russell:

I have been trying to think out where it is that the difference between us lies, a comparatively small difference of intellectual judgement leading to an enormous difference of feeling. I think it is this. You always have the habit of judging people in a clear-cut and ruthless way: isolating some motive — often some simple animal motive, or even a bad one — and judging by that. I think of their minds as much more blurred and muddled and struggling. The result is that I am content to judge by a lower standard, accepting (for psychological purposes) customary and conventional standards, whereas you want to apply the standard of a saint or philosopher . . .

According to Murray's standard, the entente powers were like

so many average traders, full no doubt of jealousy and dishonesty, but on the whole keeping mostly within the limits of decency, and one man among them — or one Government — courteously and sincerely if often ineffectually trying to raise the standard by its frankness and unselfishness, while terribly hampered by its fears. And I draw a strong line between that sort of conduct and the deliberate arrangement of an European war — the line between *l'homme moyen sensuel* and the criminal.

Murray concluded by saying that he ached over the general misery of the world and at

the thought that our friendship, which mattered so much to me, was for the time being broken; and at our age, or at least at mine, broken things do not grow again. So I should like, in a Stoic sense, and with all necessary limitations, to say God bless you.[35]

Russell had deeply resented what he regarded as Murray's intellectual treachery, and in November 1914 had written that he was 'ashamed of ever having liked him'.[36] However, he now replied in kind:

I thought it necessary to answer you, just as you thought it necessary to write your pamphlet; but I did not mean that there should be anything offensive in my answer; if there was, I am sorry. I feel our friendship still lives in the eternal world, whatever may happen to it here and now. And I too can say God bless you.[37]

The Foreign Policy of Sir Edward Grey marked a turning point in Murray's political development, and in his career. His sincere defence of official foreign policy parted him for a time from old friends of his radical days, though he was later able to resume friendly relations with Russell and even with Ramsay MacDonald. It confirmed his position as a man of the Liberal establishment. It also introduced him to Edward Grey, who was to help him later at a vital point in the development of the League of Nations idea, and of popular support for it in Britain. More immediately Murray was recognized at Wellington House and by Ministers as a most effective propagandist. His talents were much in request by government during the next year.

3

Towards the end of 1915 Robert Vansittart of the Foreign Office asked Archer to give a series of lectures in Sweden, with the basic if not explicit object of undermining Swedish sympathy for Germany. Archer told Vansittart that Murray was the man for the job, and begged Murray not to turn the idea down out of hand. Murray had some doubts—he knew no Swedish, and was 'no good at conviviality'.[38] However his hesitations soon gave way. By 25 December, Vansittart, whom he much liked, had persuaded him to go. Lady Mary was ready to accompany him, and a highly suitable secretary was soon found, Bertha Philpotts (later Newall). She was the first 'Lady Carlisle Fellow' of Somerville and a specialist in old Norse epic studies; her brother was a Secretary of the Legation at Stockholm, where Sir Esmé Howard, a cousin of Lady Mary, was Minister. It promised to be a party.

Preparations for the lecture tour in March were thorough. Murray tackled the Swedish language with zest; by the end of the year he was able to write 'I find that the Swedish for "joke" is "upptak": can that be the origin of "quick in the uptake"? The noun "uptake" does not seem to occur in any other phrase.'[39] Beatrice Webb provided Murray with a background reading list. Sir Esmé Howard warned him not to touch on any German history later than the Bellum Gallicum . . . and to talk only about England.[40]

The lectures were to be given at Christiana (in Norway), Uppsala, Lund, Göteborg, and Stockholm, on a mixture of classical and contemporary themes. Murray sent an official account of his activities to the Foreign Office in April 1916. It was entitled 'Informal Report of a Lecturing Tour in Scandinavia', and was sent under cover of a personal letter to Sir Edward Grey: 'it was a great inspiration to me to feel that, in however remote a way, I was working . . . under the orders of yourself and the Prime Minister',[41] Murray wrote.

In Norway Murray had no problems; lecturing on 'Currents in Contemporary English Literature', he had his first meeting with Fridtjof Nansen, afterwards his colleague and friend at the League of Nations. Nansen, like many others in Scandinavia, was anxious about British intentions to impose a Carthaginian peace upon Germany; on this point, by temperament at least, Murray was well fitted to reassure him.

While at Christiana Murray received a telegram from Stockholm saying that the Swedish authorities would not allow him to lecture in public on any subject connected with the war; thus even an account of England at war fell under the ban, and Murray had to devote himself entirely to classical subjects, introducing politics only indirectly and in answer to questions. At Göteborg, where he was talking on 'Pagan Religion at the Time of the Coming of Christianity', his hosts had prepared a trap for him:

the president of the Students rather took me aback by suddenly addressing me in Latin from a written paper he held in his hand; so I answered him in Greek, in the new pronunciation. I feel pretty sure that any errors I may have made escaped detection.[42]

It is pleasant to find official confirmation of one of the best established stories about Murray. There was strong anti-Russian feeling in Sweden, a strong reverence for military prowess, and close connections between the Swedish and German courts. At Uppsala, the Chief Pastor suggested to Murray that Britain's best course would be to lay down its arms, and ask the Kaiser to arbitrate, while the Archbishop insisted that we had given the Germans some assurance that we would not intervene if they invaded Belgium. All through Scandinavia Murray found that the Germans had collected and disseminated both the violent anti-German outbursts of British militarists, and the Radical attacks on the British Government's foreign and imperial policy, using the first to make the second credible.

The formal recommendations in Murray's report to the Foreign Office were that our universities should admit more Scandinavian students (at Oxford under the Rhodes fund, if possible) and should encourage the formation of Scandinavian societies; in Stockholm we should set up a distributing centre for our book trade (British books available at the time were mainly frivolous—e.g., the novels of Elinor Glyn).[43] Grey wrote a personal letter of thanks, saying that the work Murray had done was of great value.[44] Perhaps a better idea of his achievement lay in a brief note from Lady Mary to Archer. She had never, she said, seen him 'play up so splendidly'.[45] Meanwhile, in March 1916, Murray had received an invitation from Nicholas Murray Butler of Columbia to visit New York for two or three weeks in July or August. The main object was to participate in a conference on Classical Studies, but Murray Butler mentioned as an incidental advantage that he would be able to enlighten US public opinion.[46] Murray consulted Grey personally on whether the summer of 1916 was likely to be an opportune time for a visit by someone who was known, whatever his eminence as a Greek scholar, to be closely connected with the British Foreign Secretary. Grey's first reaction was to share his doubts, but within two weeks he pronounced that Murray should go but be careful in what he said, since 'the U.S.A. is in a very excitable condition'. This final verdict had been preceded by a long talk with Grey at the Foreign Office.[47]

Murray prepared himself for his American engagements by a visit to France and Flanders early in May 1916. The arrangements seem to have been pleasantly casual. He took his own ticket to Boulogne and from there on was the guest of GHQ. It was a beautiful passage, 'with mine sweepers on each side and a destroyer for chaperone.' At the front he had a 'wonderful and perfectly indescribable day . . . The courage and magnanimity and cheerful discipline of the men quite amazes me.'[48]

He embodied his impressions in three articles for the *Daily News* early in June, dated from 'Somewhere in France'. In the first two of these Murray described vividly an average day at or near the front under medium heavy shelling. There was, he said, a feeling of confidence in long-term victory. Was the Boche confident too? German deserters looked unpleasant, but well-nourished. There was certainly no shortage of German shells. The third article took the reader back to GHQ, where Murray fell among Intelligence Officers, into a sort of Buchan-land, where one might meet hardbitten young heroes, with strange and romantic adventures in the Middle East behind them.[49] It is good, unpretentious, impressionistic journalism; and the reader today must remember with a shudder that it refers to the period of build-up for the great slaughter on the Somme in July.

The Classical Conference took place at Columbia from 14 to 24 July. Murray lectured to it and also, together with Lady Mary, underwent a strenuous programme of dinners and speaking engagements including addresses to the Pilgrims and the Union Club at Boston. In the USA, still deeply divided on the question of entering the war, Murray kept company mainly with those already convinced of the rightness of the Allied cause. His most prestigious engagement was a lunch with Theodore Roosevelt, who found his visit too short and would have liked to talk over with him some aboriginal ghost stories.[50]

His most important success was an agreement with the National Editorial Service to provide them with regular articles for syndication, and to suggest other British authors for similar treatment. They wanted fifteen articles monthly from Murray, including five of two thousand words each for use in Sunday papers. Murray's first article was on 'The Professor in Wartime'; he never accomplished the full quota suggested, but did make occasional contributions, and convinced the 'Mendacity Bureau' that the arrangement was very much in British interests.[51] The British Ambassador in Washington, Sir Cecil Spring-Rice, thanked him generously.[52]

Murray's main business in the USA had been to listen, in order to return to explain to his countrymen the currents of US opinion. He related his impressions in a number of articles during the late summer and autumn of 1916. These were very cautious. There was massive sympathy in the USA, Murray said, for the Allied cause. But there was also an instinctive pride in standing apart from Europe, and much resentment at the restrictions involved in the British blockade of Germany. He emphasized that at the end of the war the USA would be the richest and least exhausted power, with every prospect of being able to exercise world leadership.[53]

Murray developed these themes in a pamphlet on *The US and the War*, which an American historian later described as 'the very best form of propaganda for American readers.'[54] In this he took the line that a decision had already been taken by the two main parties in the USA not to enter the war. But the fervour with which the British case was supported by Americans was significant: 'there might arise some new and unexpected issue which would compel the U.S.A. to change her policy', he concluded.

In one respect Murray was fortunate in the timing of his visit. In the aftermath of the Easter rebellion in Dublin, Sir Roger Casement, who had landed in Ireland on Good Friday from a German submarine, was tried at the Old Bailey for high treason and condemned to death. He was hanged on 3 August, but until the last moment it was thought that the British Government might show clemency. Feeling in the USA was strongly in favour of it, even among pro-Allied circles. Murray's second article for the National Editorial Service, received by 1 August, was on the theme 'Shall Casement hang?'[55] and he telegraphed personally to Sir Edward Grey his view that the execution of Casement would produce the most unfortunate effects in the USA.[56] This proved only too true, and Murray must have been glad to be out of the country by the time the execution took place.

4

By the end of 1916 Murray's relations with the British government were completely changed. On 7 December Asquith was forced to resign as Prime Minister in favour of Lloyd George, and Sir Edward Grey retired as Foreign Secretary. Murray's two Liberal heroes were thus put on the shelf. He wrote publicly and bitterly about Lloyd George's new government as the creation of a press campaign. Were we to be ruled by the War Council or by Lord Northcliffe and the *Morning Post*?[57] He dined privately with Asquith on 17 December, and found him 'rather grave, very simple and kindly',[58] Murray and Lady Mary seemed to overlook the weaknesses of Asquith's character, one of which (his fondness for strong drink) was well known at the time. They were considerably less tolerant of Margot Asquith; in a letter to Murray dated 21 December 1916, she sent him her 'love'. This elicited seven exclamation marks from Lady Mary, to whom Murray wrote: 'Mrs. A's letter surpassed even my expectations. I laughed till I shook, to see it and the Puss's row of shrieks in the margin.'[59] For Lloyd George the Murrays had no time at all. They did not see the war-winning qualities which went with his devious political manœuvres.

So Murray's position as a trusted agent to the government was undermined, and he had no wish to build it up again, even though the new director of the Information Directorate (soon to become a Ministry) was his old friend, John Buchan. Lloyd George made conciliatory gestures. Murray refused in July 1917 the offer of a CH, in recognition of his services. He was at first inclined to accept, but decided finally that, if he did so, he would be considered to have 'other companions besides Honour'.[60] Undeterred, Lloyd George offered him a knighthood at the end of the year. He refused, this time without any hesitation.[61] Meanwhile, rather surprisingly, Murray had become a Civil Servant. At the end of October 1916 he agreed to become educational adviser for the YMCA with the forces in France,[62] a post which naturally brought him into contact with the Army educational authorities. At New Year 1917 Lloyd George persuaded Murray's old friend, H. A. L. Fisher, to become Minister of Education; and Fisher in turn persuaded Murray to work for him on a part-time basis.

'I'm sorry darling,' wrote Lady Mary, 'but I think it's a mistake and puts us in the wrong. However, it can't be helped.'[63] Murray himself was in two minds. He liked the thought of working for Fisher and advising him on educational policy, particularly relating to universities. And he thought that a niche at the Board of Education might spare him further offers of more political work for the Lloyd George government. On the other hand he was bored with organizational work, and might find himself muzzled on political issues. A few days later he decided that he had no choice but to accept

Fisher's offer. The 'Reviewing Committee', chaired by Haldane, would soon be reporting; then a new bill or at least a definite policy would have to be drafted, dealing among other things with the provincial universities,

and with my own special policy, the provision of classical and literary teaching in secondary schools. It is Selby-Bigge, the Permanent-Secretary, who wanted me to come in for this special work, and, curiously enough, I promised Haldane before the war that I would help . . .[64]

Murray was formally appointed as Principal Assistant Secretary to the University Branch of the Board of Education, at a salary of £600 a year.[65] A room was found for him, from which much of his correspondence over the next two years was addressed. His activities at the Board were very various, and the story of them belongs more to a history of the Board than to a biography of Murray. He wrote to Lady Mary that he was busy with a number of proposals from the Workers' Educational Association, and with arranging education courses for prisoners of war.[66] Soon he was drafting a memorandum on the reform 'or creation' of commercial education. In 1918 he worked on Fisher's plans for part-time education up to the age of sixteen in 'continuation schools', chairing a committee which investigated the supply of teachers for them.[67]

Murray was also involved in the educational side of British foreign policy. The Anglo-Russian Commission, still functioning in Petrograd in summer 1917, had decided on the need for closer relations between Russia and England. One of the first objects was to reorganize Russian technical schools on English lines, and Murray was asked to help in establishing a bureau of Educational Information.[68] A month or two later he was following up his own mission to Scandinavia (of 1916) by arranging for the supply of English lecturers to Norway.[69]

Throughout his time at the Board of Education, one of Murray's principal activities lay in the provision of lecturers and books for educational courses for the troops, either at home or in France. He was in close touch with the organizer of Army schools in France and with the Army educational authorities at Aldershot. Above all he acted as a sort of liaison officer between Basil Yeaxlee of the YMCA, the YMCA branches in France, the Army authorities, and the Board of Education.[70] Murray paid at least one more visit to France in connection with YMCA affairs. They afforded him a good deal of trouble, particularly when in spring 1918 GHQ, for reasons quite

understandable at a supreme crisis of the war, required the YMCA
to cease their educational activities throughout France.[71]

Meanwhile the perils of war had come near to the Board of
Education itself. Murray preserved a circular of 21 January 1918:

What was apparently a bomb was this morning discovered in a coal box
in a room at Whitehall. The matter has not yet been fully investigated, but
in the meantime officers should most carefully scrutinise coal before putting
it on their fires. Every effort will be made to see that the coal supplied to
the boxes is carefully looked over first.[72]

5

Since autumn 1914 the Murray family had been to some extent
involved in the primary business of war. Denis, with his aeronaut-
ical training, was most directly concerned. He joined the Royal
Flying Corps, and was the only one of the family to be on active
service. He had 'visited Ostend' by 26 August 1914. He was then
posted first to Calshot and thereafter to Felixstowe, to go through
a course of marine flying. Murray stayed with him there in October
1914 'in a world of destroyers and wire entanglements and forts'.[73]
In mid-February 1915, Denis was shot down near the Dutch coast,
and telegraphed his parents from Flushing: 'Brought down, managed
to reach Holland, am unhurt.' (In fact he had been wounded and
suffered some burns.)[74] Holland was a neutral country, but the
officers were strictly confined at Groningen, since Winston Churchill
would not let them give their parole (an undertaking not to attempt
any escape). This restriction was lifted in January 1916.[75] Denis
did not take well to the boredom of what amounted to captivity.
Lady Mary was able to visit him occasionally, and reported unhap-
pily about him in March 1915, saying ominously that he had 'given
up teetotalism'.[76] By June 1915 he was trying to escape and his
parents were involved in efforts to help him. They managed first to
send him a trench tool suitably concealed in a parcel. Then Murray
consulted a doctor about drugs to make him temporarily ill—it
was thought that the Dutch authorities would connive and release
him.[77] Later there was a more adventurous scheme. Murray was
in touch through the War Office with an enterprising clergyman
who was prepared to visit internees for their spiritual comfort
and to help them to escape.[78] In fact all plans for escape came
to nothing, and Denis was released, suffering from genuine pleurisy,
in February 1917, after two years of captivity;[79] he saw no more
active service.

Murray's other sons, Basil and Stephen, were both too young to fight, and the health of his son-in-law, Arnold Toynbee, confined him to the field of political intelligence. Rosalind had her growing family to look after (her two elder sons, Tony and Philip, were born in 1914 and 1916 respectively). However, Agnes had an adventurous war. She stayed at Somerville long enough to take Third Class Honours in Mods. in spring 1915, somewhat to Murray's disappointment.[80] Thereafter she was working at Bart's, and driving ambulances in London and France.[81]

Lady Mary was tireless in organizing a supply of books for young friends at the front and in visiting and providing comforts for wounded soldiers at the hospitals of Oxford. A touching letter of 1918 illustrates her hectic activity, and her pride in her husband. At the end of a talk with a wounded man, she introduced herself as 'Gilbert Murray's wife'

Then slowly, very slowly, a look of puzzlement, of wonder, of recognition and great pleasure, came into his face . . . I saw you were his friend . . . I never saw anything which gave me more pride for you or made me realise your *endless* friends . . . for it wasn't your fame, it was like a man recognising a friend.[82]

Murray himself from the first was dissatisfied with his indirect role in the war effort. He was deeply impressed by what his younger colleagues were doing and suffering. Few of them survived even the end of 1915. On 23 September 1914, he received a farewell visit from his young colleague, Jack Denniston ('Denny' to his admirers of later generations), in uniform, looking sunburnt and strong: 'He does not like the life, and . . . does not think he will make a good officer . . . He joins the K.O.S.B. at Aldershot next week.' In the same letter he writes of Sandy Lindsay drilling from 7.00 to 8.00 and from 2.00 to 3.00. 'I wonder if I ought to drill,' he pondered, 'I would rather like to.'[83] Memories of days with the volunteers in 1887–8 came back to him. He congratulated Cornford on his appointment as a musketry instructor in October 1914, describing himself as 'a plain Lance-Corporal, who by no gifts but honesty and dogged valour raised himself to that eminence shortly after the Crimean War.'[84]

Soon after this he joined the Oxford Volunteer Training Corps or Reserve, which figures under other names in his correspondence — 'Godley's Roarers' or the 'Noumenal Fusiliers'. The classical scholar, A. D. Godley, was in command, and the philosopher H. W. B. Joseph was adjutant. Private Murray devoted himself to his battalion, and resisted the temptation to join John Masefield, for example, as a medical orderly in the Argonne.[85] He had to seek leave of absence, or even temporarily to resign his duties from time to time, but he was as diligent at drills, or in guarding ammunition at Didcot station, as his other official commitments, his health, or his wife permitted. One of Joseph's circulars about an early parade carries a peremptory message from Lady Mary: 'Don't do this unless the doctor approves.'[86] Murray was promoted Corporal in June 1916, and finally resigned with effect from 18 May 1917, by which time he was working mainly in London. He had genuinely enjoyed, it appears, turning out on the parade ground, and satisfied a tender conscience by imposing on himself some extra physical strain and some of the boredom of military routine, while his young friends were suffering in Flanders. Given all Murray's other commitments, it is hard to think that he served his country best by adding to them the burden of drill, particularly as he suffered his usual quota of illnesses in these years.[87] However, he was careful to avoid false heroics in giving advice to academic friends. To J. A. K. Thomson he wrote early in 1915:

It is right to offer oneself. I shall be delighted to die of a chill on the liver in Flanders if Lord Kitchener wishes it, and will kill as many Germans as I can in the process; but if I were K I don't think I should send me. And I feel something the same about you.[88]

This letter shows that Murray, within his own intimate circle, was not always submerged by care for the Allied cause. His mind could still sparkle on occasion. To Tony Toynbee, on his first birthday in September 1915, he wrote a letter in explanation of a birthday gift from his Uncle Basil — presumably a Russian Matrushka series of dolls:

You will receive from this house in celebration of your first birthday, Moral Gifts, intended to warn you against the errors which you may be tempted to commit in later life . . . Your Uncle Basil is particularly anxious that you should not, however successful in smaller things, attempt to invade Russia. If you do, you will find, as soon as you have destroyed one army of peasants, another starting up behind.[89]

Another charming parergon celebrated the occasion in 1918 when, in spite of rationing restrictions, Agnes produced a genuine apple pie. *The Apple Pie: A Ballad of Sin*, is prefaced by a note: 'Agnes had saved up her butter and sugar and actually got hold of some cream. She invited Beatrice Ross and me to a "real Apple Pie", the sort of thing we had not seen for years.' The verse is among Murray's best in his lighter vein:

> We three, we bold, black, lonely three!
> What reck we now of human laws?
> The door is locked. Take out the key.
> A fig for Rhonda and his claws!
> I know they watch. I saw them run
> With truncheons drawn to take alive
> That Friend who comforted with bun
> An alien enemy aged five.
> That grocer who blasphemed alone,
> Saying that Welshmen sometimes lied,
> They heard him with their microphone
> And food-controlled him till he died.
> Two M.M. agents, chief and sub.,
> Disguised as cooks infest the place,
> And that man in the corner pub
> Has very much Lord Derby's face. . . . [90]

Nor were other occasional relaxations entirely wanting. In September 1915 Murray began lessons in 'motor-driving' starting at the top with his brother-in-law Geoffrey Howard's Rolls.[91] And Christmas 1916 found him overtiring himself at Castle Howard with games of ice-hockey—a dangerous trade—'I would as soon gather samphire any day.'[92]

6

Murray's conversion to support of the wartime government had not been, and could not be, total. There was too much of the rationalist radical, too much humour, and too much compassion in his nature. He both enjoyed and despised the wilder manifestations of spy mania in England, and was subject to some of them at Overstrand:

A wounded Major . . . had discovered for the *Daily Mail* that Winstone [*sic*] on some occasions, when staying here, used Sir Edward Speyer's telephone. Apparently Germans get themselves attached to all political circuits and overhear all that we say; I need hardly mention that Asquith and Haldane know all about it, but are too lazy or frightened to speak.[93]

W. B. Yeats was another who complained to Murray about interference with the liberty of the subject; the authorities had illegally seized, as a wireless receiver, a machine invented by a friend of his, for recording messages from the other world.[94]

..ay also observed quizzically the official habit of relating
..ost unlikely activities to the 'war effort'. Thus a report to
Mary of a meeting of the British Museum trustees early in 1916:

..e chief question was how much of the Natural History Museum should
be kept open. Mammals, birds, yes; mineralogy, no: But what of Fish? 'No
one wants to see stuffed fish . . . ' 'And there is the whale.' 'Everyone likes
to see a whale.' 'And Colonials, having come across the sea, are much
interested in whales.' 'The question is, will seeing the whale help them to
win the war?' . . . For the present, the whale is left ajar.[95]

However, there was much about the 'war effort' to perturb him
deeply. From the first he insisted on the need to remember 'the other
Germany', and on the need for reaching ultimately a generous peace.
He was disgusted with the anti-German riots in London, which
followed the sinking of the *Lusitania* in May 1915. He wrote to
Archer:

Evidently the Bishops and Headmasters who write to the *Times* will soon
be urging a pogrom? Why are Bishops and Headmasters such infernal owls?
It cannot be classical education, because none of them know any classics
to speak of.[96]

This was strong language for Murray, and represented about the
limit of his intolerance. He stood for the maximum freedom of the
press in time of war. In March 1917 for example, C. K. Ogden,
editor of the *Cambridge Magazine*, was publicly attacked by the
'Fight for Right' movement, for printing extracts from the foreign
press alleged to be of a pacifist tendency. Murray drafted a protest
for signature by a number of distinguished authors and academics,
including Arnold Bennett and Thomas Hardy, who protested against
the victimization of the *Cambridge Magazine* for its attempt to
preserve the tradition of independent and original thought. At the
same time Murray wrote privately to Ogden making it clear that their
views on the war were very different.[97]

Above all Murray was deeply perturbed at any sign of encroachment
by government on the field of private judgement and convictions.
Precisely because he differed from many of his old friends about the
necessity for war, it remained for him a debt of honour to see that
they and others should not be forced, in the supposed interests of
the war effort, to act against their deepest convictions. The central
issues for them were those of conscription, conscientious objection,
and the forms of war service which a conscientious objector could
be permitted to refuse.

The question of conscription began to loom large in autumn 1915. It was more than doubtful whether the army could equip and train more men than were already volunteering; but the monthly figures of Volunteers were beginning to decline, and there was strong political pressure within Asquith's Cabinet for conscription. Asquith compromised with it in October 1915 by organizing a scheme, through Lord Derby, under which men of military age 'attested' their readiness to serve when the call came. This could be interpreted as a means of preserving the voluntary system; but he also promised that all unmarried men would be called up before any 'attested' married men, and this was a step towards conscription.

In fact the Derby scheme was soon followed by the first Military Service Act of January 1916, imposing conscription on unmarried men between the ages of 18 and 41. There was no serious political protest from Liberal or Labour MPs. Only Sir John Simon resigned from the Asquith Cabinet. Some comfort had already been provided for Liberal consciences by the establishment of local tribunals to hear the cases of Conscientious Objectors, empowered to grant them conditional or absolute exemption. There was also a central tribunal, which heard appeals against the decisions of the local tribunals. The ground for exemption, stated in a clause of the Bill added after Simon's resignation, was 'a conscientious objection to bearing arms'. The natural interpretation of this clause was that it would cover political as well as religious objections, but that such objections would exempt from military service only, not from non-combatant service. In introducing the Bill on 5 January 1916, Asquith explained that its terms were based on the successful experience of compulsory national service in South Africa and Australia, and that the exemption which objectors should get (and all that they would claim) should be from military combatant duties only.

This proved to be a mistaken estimate. The majority of COs agreed to perform non-combatant service, often in ambulance work, or to work in labour camps; but there remained a number (about 1,500) who for various reasons absolutely refused any form of work which contributed directly or indirectly to the 'war effort'.

Murray's position at Oxford first involved him with 'undergraduates who became COs.' After using his utmost exertions to overcome their scruples he did what little he could to see that they obtained their legal rights.[98] A typical case was that of Raymond Postgate, a classical scholar of St John's, son of Professor J. P. Postgate, and brother of Douglas Cole's future wife, Margaret. He had been allocated to non-combatant duties, and found that these included digging trenches and fixing barbed wire. His appeal was dismissed and he was committed to gaol for failing to turn up for his duties. Owing to Murray's intervention, Postgate was soon released from prison, but this was only the first of many troubles for him and other conscientious objectors, including a high proportion of Quakers, usually men of high principle and extreme obstinacy. In spring 1916 confrontations were inevitable between them and the local tribunals. It was a case, Murray wrote at the time, of 'obstinate mules' against 'rampant griffins'.[99] The 'mules' tended to be most obstinate in refusing to undertake non-combatant duties which they regarded as obviously connected with the fighting needs of the armed services. The 'griffins' displayed little or no patience in trying to distinguish men of real conviction from shirkers, or in finding suitable jobs for tender consciences. 'Mules' who refused to fulfil the civilian non-combatant duties to which they were directed were, like Raymond Postgate, sent to prison, often under squalid and humiliating conditions. Those who were drafted to the Non-combatant Corps were subject to military discipline and courts martial. They feared, as the result of threats made to them, that their units would be sent to France where the result of refusing tasks could be summary execution.

The intellectual who fought most stubbornly for the 'mules' was Bertrand Russell. In April 1916 he was stimulating resistance to the Military Service Act through the 'No Conscription Fellowship'. Murray wrote to him, asking whether he had any positive proposal for modifying the Act, or was out to sabotage it by agitation:

Can you suggest any method by which a Conscientious Objector to military service can (a) prove that his objection is a matter of conscience, and (b) show that he is ready to make some sacrifice approximately comparable to that which his fellows are making?

Russell's reply was uncompromising. An inquiry should be held into the action of the tribunals and meanwhile proceedings should be suspended against all those who claimed to be Conscientious Objectors. He added outrageously that the sacrifices of the COs were immensely greater than those of the men at the front.[100]

Other intellectuals turned more readily to Murray for support. Clive Bell, who had regarded him as 'a sort of ogre', now appealed to him as 'in some sort the public representative of patriotic intellectualism in England.'[101] Many reports of bad decisions by the tribunals, from Brailsford, Cole, Philip Morrell, and others, led Murray to write to the Home Secretary, Herbert Samuel, about 'unnecessary friction and suffering'.[102] On 30 April he lunched with Asquith, who had already discussed the subject with Lady Ottoline Morrell,[103] who could represent Russell's views. Murray put forward evidence derived mainly from the Quaker journal *The Friend*, about the tribunals' unwillingness to interpret 'non-combatant duties' in such a way as to meet genuinely tender consciences. His principal points were that the Non-combatant Corps was ineffective anyhow, and that genuine objectors who had been caught up through it in the machinery of military command and discipline must somehow be rescued.[104]

When the new Military Service Law (extending conscription to all men up to the age of 41) was announced in May 1916, it contained explicit assurances that tribunals were empowered to grant absolute exemption. After talking with Lady Ottoline Morrell and Murray, Asquith thought that the Act should be amended to exclude the possibility of genuine objectors working under the military authorities. Exactly how to do this was a considerable political problem; but at least the theoretical solution of it was hastened by an episode in which Murray was directly concerned.

The first draft of the Non-combatant Corps to contain men resisting or prepared to resist orders arrived in France on 5 May 1916. The depot commanders in the UK had not received orders to exclude such men, and their inclusion in the draft was probably the result of muddle or chance. However, it seemed to bear out the fears of those who thought that there was a military conspiracy to get objectors to France and deal with them there under martial law, possibly shooting them. Murray had himself been visiting the front in France. He returned on 9 or 10 May[105] to find a telegram from the parents of a CO in Cambridge, Rendel Wyatt, and a letter 'from some other source',[106] saying that some of the COs drafted to France were under sentences of death and were likely to be executed in the next few days. He himself thought that they had probably been sent to France for this purpose. He went at once to the House of Commons, and saw his brother-in-law, Geoffrey Howard, the chief Liberal Whip.

He advised me to see Lord Derby, who was Secretary for War [in fact, Under-secretary]. I managed to see him in the lobby. Lord Derby said the men were condemned to be shot, and would be shot, and quite right too. I was not clear from his manner whether he knew about the business and approved, or whether he was merely bluffing.

Murray went back to Geoffrey Howard, who secured for him immediately a short interview with Asquith:

He listened attentively, read the telegram, and muttered the word 'Abominable'. He asked me two or three questions and then wrote a letter rapidly. He then said 'I have written to the C. in C. directly', if my [Murray's] memory is correct, 'that no sentences on C.O.s were to be carried out without the consent of the Cabinet'. The matter was settled in five minutes, I was greatly struck by his rapidity both in decision and action.[107]

The worst fears of Murray and many COs were probably illusory. Men from a draft arriving in France on 5 May were unlikely to have been court-martialled and sentenced by 10 May. However, the fears were rational enough, and the government took official steps to dispel them. On 22 May, Kitchener announced in the House of Lords that government policy was to place genuine Conscientious Objectors under civilian power, and David Davies informed Murray officially of this statement.[108]

Murray was not involved again in any collective action for COs until early 1918. Then a meeting was held at the House of Commons to discuss these continuing grievances on 28 February, with Lord Parmoor in the chair. Those attending included the Bishop of Lincoln, Lord Hugh Cecil, and Arnold Rowntree, and Murray acted as Secretary.[109] Statistics provided mainly by non-conformist Ministers indicated that 4,680 COs had been sent to prison, of whom 1,137 were still there; 184 had been sentenced to 18 months or longer imprisonment; 484 to ten months; no less than 464 had been court-martialled three times, and 60 four times or more. Several deaths had been recorded, and many cases of severe mental hardship, among those who had accepted the Home Office scheme for national work. It was decided to send a deputation to the Prime Minister to discuss means of improving the administration of the law but, not surprisingly given the state of the war in spring and summer 1918, he more than once deferred an interview with them. In August 1918 the delegates (probably not including Murray) were received by Sir George Cave, the Home Secretary; but by this time victory was near. Soon the most useful service to be performed for COs was to secure the speedy release of the 1,500 still in prison when the war was over. Murray was among the signatories (also including Archer, John Buchan, Keynes, Wells, and W. Temple) of a memorandum on this subject addressed to Lloyd George on 1 January 1919.[110] By May 1919 the majority of COs had been released and only 300 remained in prison.[111]

Murray devoted more energy to the relief of individuals suffering under a system which he thought unlikely to be radically changed in wartime. The list of individuals whom he helped from 1916

onwards is long and contains some distinguished 'trouble-makers'—
Raymond Postgate and Clive Bell, as already noted, C. H. Norman
(who wrote later under the name of D. H. Rolph), R. Palme Dutt,
and E. D. Morel (in chronological order). However, the case that
concerned Murray most closely was that of his once and future
intimate friend, Bertrand Russell. The issue of conscription in spring
1916 had widened the gap between them, and regular correspondence
between Murray and Russell did not reopen until early in 1918.
By then Russell had been deprived of his Lectureship at Trinity
and prosecuted for using allegedly insulting language about the
USA and the US army in a small periodical entitled the *Tribunal*
(3 January 1918). On 9 February Russell was sentenced to six
months' imprisonment in the Second Division (where there were no
amenities for intellectual prisoners).

Murray wrote to Russell expressing his contempt for the Lloyd
George government and their renewed persecution of him. Russell
replied warmly and gratefully, signing his letter 'Yours ever-
affectionately.'[112] Murray consulted Asquith, who advised an
immediate appeal and no attempt to influence the Home Office in
the meantime. Notice of appeal was duly given, and it was heard
on 1 May. The sentence was not remitted or commuted, as Murray
had hoped, to a fine, which Russell's friends would have paid.
However, Russell himself had been fairly conciliatory, stating
beforehand that, long before the publication of his offending article
(in fact after the publication of the Lansdowne letter in November
1917), he had determined to give up political propaganda and
devote himself again to philosophy. He now had the opportunity
of doing so in First Division accommodation at Brixton prison and,
as he afterwards acknowledged, Murray's intervention was largely
responsible for the change. He discussed with Murray, who was on
his list of preferred visitors, plans for a study of the relation between
the structure of primitive languages, starting with Chinese and
Japanese, and contemporary philosophic views about the structure
of the universe.[113]

Meanwhile Russell was also interested in finding academic work
on release which would make it possible for him to avoid any
possibility of a call-up, and he submitted himself to Murray's
guidance. The philosopher A. E. Taylor was consulted, and Murray,
as Visitor of Manchester College, Oxford, tried to get Russell
appointed as a lecturer there (his neatest argument being that, if
Russell were denied the possibility of philosophic work, he would
inevitably take up political propaganda again).[114] Murray's efforts

were in vain, but Russell confided to Lady Otteline Morrell that he trusted Murray 'on the whole' in this business. He had good reason to do so, both before his release and afterwards, when Murray organized a subscription by Russell's admirers, which financed the lectures which he gave at the London School of Economics early in 1919.[115]

The other personal case with which Murray was very particularly concerned was that of Stephen Hobhouse, and it was in connection with this that he wrote his considered reflections on the whole story of the Conscientious Objectors' resistance to authority. Stephen Hobhouse belonged to the family which had produced Murray's old Oxford friend, the Liberal philosopher, L. T. Hobhouse (the 'Hobbler' of old days at Castle Howard), and Emily Hobhouse, who in 1900 had exposed the maladministration of the British 'concentration camps' in South Africa. The young Hobhouse, scholar of Eton and Balliol, had before the war renounced his position as heir to the family property and his post at the Board of Education. He joined the Society of Quakers, lived in a worker's flat at Hoxton, and went to the Balkans during the wars of 1912–13 to look after refugees. In 1916, his local tribunal disallowed his conscientious objection to war and sent him into the army. He refused to appeal because many of his Quaker friends were going to prison, and he could not bear to think that they were worse off than himself. A court martial then sentenced him to various penalties, culminating in 112 days' hard labour. When he emerged, he continued to refuse certain tasks, and received another similar sentence. During this sentence he confessed that he had broken the rule of silence in prison, and was sentenced to solitary confinement. A typical 'mule', no doubt, and obviously a man of the highest integrity.[116]

His mother, Margaret (Mrs Henry) Hobhouse, published in 1917 a pamphlet *I Appeal Unto Caesar*, and for this Murray wrote a passionate and revealing preface. In it he told briefly the story of the introduction of conscription, and of the inevitable conscientious opposition to it; he ascribed great importance in this connection to the doctrines of Tolstoy, which had influenced 'almost every young man and woman in Europe, who possessed any free religious life at all'. He described how he himself had become interested in cases of conscientious objection, and defended the record of the Asquith Government, which had in his view faced the difficulties of conscription with tact and prudence. In 1916 'the Government and higher authorities were most prompt in redressing any case of proved injustice that was brought to them.' But at that time and afterwards, the record of the tribunals had been deplorable; their main anxieties had been to please the War Office, to satisfy the more turbulent newspapers, and to display their own patriotism. Murray ended his preface by some of the most bitter words which he ever wrote:

The worst part of the whole miserable business . . . is that the great majority of ordinary decent people who have come into personal contact with the treatment of objectors by the tribunals and the War Office find themselves both angered and alienated. However wrong-headed, conceited, self-centred and self-righteous . . . the objectors may originally have been, the long and pointless persecution of those few hundred men leaves on the coldest observer the impression of sheer moral heroism on the part of the culprits and sheer moral and intellectual vileness on the side of the Government.[117]

Stephen Hobhouse when released in 1918 used his prison experiences as a means of pressing for prison reform. *The Quarterly Review* of July 1918 printed his observations on 'An English Prison from Within', and this was reprinted in 1919, again with a preface by Murray. Here too he expressed the radical, even anarchist, sympathies which had been revived by his dislike of the Lloyd George government:

It seems to show a certain disharmony between our big blundering central machine and the people who are governed by it, that of late years it has become so common for what I call 'good people' to be sent to prison.

To have been in prison no longer carried any kind of stigma:

Passive resisters, militant suffragists, conscientious objectors, Quakers, pacifists, Sinn Feiners, Labour agitators and the like, are often the most perverse beings, and some of them are no doubt morally repulsive as well, but they may also be, when judged by any moderately intellectual and sensitive standard, considerably superior to the magistrates who condemn them and the leaders of the public sentiment which they defy.

Thus Murray, converted into a government propagandist by Grey's foreign policy, had been to a considerable extent re-radicalized by the policy towards Conscientious Objectors pursued under the Lloyd George coalition.

CHAPTER XVIII

Birth of the League of Nations and the League of Nations Union*

1. Murray's involvement in the evolution of the LN — the Bryce Plan — the Fabian Plan — the League of Nations Society (LNS) — the American League to Enforce Peace (LEP).

2. Murray's radical views developed in *The Way Forward* 1917 — meets Smuts — defends the Lansdowne letter — proposal of a mission to USA comes to nothing.

3. 1917–1918 — Labour War Aims considered too pacifist and pro-German — to counteract, the League of Free Nations Association (LFNA) created — but is amalgamated with the LNS under Lord Grey to form the LNU.

4. 1918–1919 — final drafting of the Covenant of the LN — adopted April 1919.

1

THE war proved to be one of unimagined horror. The great majority of Murray's young colleagues at Oxford, as well as of his pupils, joined up as soon as they could and a very high proportion of them, as young officers, were killed. Of Murray's particular friends among the younger scholars of New College, Philip Brown, G. L. Cheesman, Arthur Heath, and Leslie Hunter did not survive the second year of the war.[1] Their photographs stood on the mantelpiece of Murray's study for the rest of his life. Later these were irreverently referred to by the grandchildren as the Morgue. Murray's introduction to the letters of Heath, published in 1917, is an intensely moving tribute to the lost generation — not only the brilliant all-rounders like Raymond Asquith, but also the aimless undergraduates who found a sense of purpose, and the shy scholars who proved themselves as good practical officers. It is an expression of Murray's deepest feelings. The war had to be won; but emotion as well as reason stimulated him to do all that he could to see that war should become obsolete as a means of settling international disputes.

Before 1914 Murray had been interested in movements to promote international understanding. At the end of 1912 he presided at a

*See Notes, p. 410, para. 2

meeting of an 'Oxford Committee to promote International Peace and Fellowship'.[2] And six months later he was in correspondence with Andrew Carnegie about the possibility of establishing Chairs of 'Peace History' in universities which supported Chairs of Military History.[3] However, at this time his political interests centred more on questions of social reform at home, and he played little part in the main 'peace movement' which was growing up at the time.

In an essay published in 1923, Murray listed what he believed to be the most powerful currents of unofficial thought which developed into the idea of the League of Nations. He attached particular importance to the 'great peace tradition' of Cobden and Bright, the idealists of the free trade movement; and this tradition, he said, was brilliantly restated by Norman Angell in his book *The Great Illusion*, published in 1911.[4] The illusion, in Angell's view, was that anyone gained anything by war. Military conquest would not increase national wealth and, conversely, military defeat did not necessarily involve economic and financial disaster. International commerce and the international credit system were so vital to the prosperity of all advanced nations that the Germans, for example, would be most reluctant to bombard the port of Liverpool or loot the Bank of England. Private brigandage had become obsolete; so would international war.

From this argument Angell did not draw the deterministic conclusion that war was impossible between great nations. It was important first to convince the British public that war did not pay, and then at government level to convince the Germans that such was the general understanding in Britain and that they themselves need not feel threatened. From 1912 onwards War and Peace societies spread throughout Britain, and the movement spread to the USA. In Oxford, Murray himself was intermittently involved. In May 1914 he presided at a meeting of the Oxford War and Peace Society, at which E. D. Morel (Secretary of the UDC) spoke on Norman Angell's themes.[5]

Murray himself saw the German militarist system as the main cause of the war; but from the first he recognized the existence of 'another Germany', and warned against the dangers of a Carthaginian peace. He developed his views more systematically in his Oxford pamphlet of October 1914, *Thoughts on the War*. A settlement, he argued, must solve more than Anglo-German problems. War must be extinguished, as leprosy and typhus had been extirpated. There must be a drastic resettlement of all problems, especially territorial ones, which carried the seeds of future war. There should be a permanent

Conference of Europe, and perhaps a permanent Council. A year later he talked of the existence of 'some real basis for a sort of Alliance of Europe—that sort of better concert for which we hope'.[6] Murray has sometimes been regarded as an impractical theorist in international affairs, and it should be emphasized that in 1914 and 1915 he did not publicly advocate a more ambitious programme than winning the war and developing from the wartime alliance an improved version of the nineteenth-century concert of Europe.

Meanwhile various disparate groups had been formed to discuss the shape of the peace. Prominent among these was the 'Bryce Group'.[7] Lord Bryce was a universally respected elder statesman who had been Ambassador in the USA and worked closely with President Taft. His prestige was an important safeguard for the group against charges of defeatism and pacifism. Murray was an old friend of Bryce from his undergraduate days, though not himself a member of the group. In February 1915 he was one of the first to receive a copy of their plan entitled 'Proposals for the Avoidance of War, by Viscount Bryce'. The main proposals were that a union should be formed after the war including at least seven European nations, and if possible the USA. These powers should pledge themselves to refer all disputes either to a Court of Arbitration or to a Council of Conciliation; not to declare war until the Court or the Council had reported; and to bring diplomatic, economic, or 'forcible' pressure to bear on any signatory power that should violate these conditions.

Marginal notes on Murray's copy raise some shrewd questions. Would an international court have been the right organ to determine Serbia's responsibility for the murder of Archduke Franz Ferdinand at Sarajevo? Would an aggressor nation wait while the Court or Council deliberated? What about the revision of obsolete treaties, and a fixed term for treaties made in future? Could a member of the Court or Council commit his government to war? Would proceedings be public?[8]

Meanwhile the Fabians were also concerned with the shape of the peace. In December 1914 Murray was invited by Beatrice Webb to take an active interest in the small Fabian Committee on 'Internationalism'.[9] Murray declined, but Leonard Woolf's study on 'International Government' produced for the Fabians proved to be important for him later, particularly in the stress it laid on 'functional internationalism', using the Universal Postal Union as its principal example.

In the summer of 1915 the League of Nations Society (LNS) was formed and it largely took over the work of the Fabians. Its object was to interest a broad public in the idea of some kind of League after the war. Murray himself became a Vice-president in November 1916, but had little time to devote to it. The LNS included members of the Bryce Group, but those most active in it were the radicals of the Union of Democratic Control; Brailsford and Hobson were on its Executive Committee, together with Lowes Dickinson and Leonard Woolf, and the Society pursued its aim largely through Norman Angell's magazine *War and Peace*, which had taken on a UDC flavour, to the distress of Angell himself.

On the other side of the Atlantic, there was also much interest in the shape of the peace, and in 1915 the American League to Enforce Peace (LEP) published a plan for post-war international organization, based largely on Taft's ideas about arbitration, and with considerable emphasis on sanctions. When Murray visited the USA in 1916, Edward Grey (now Viscount Grey) had asked him to notice carefully what feeling there was in America about the project of a League of Nations.[10] There is, however, no contemporary record of interviews or talks about a League of Nations during the visit; but in the pamphlet which recorded his impressions, *The United States and the War* (autumn 1916), Murray wrote of the prevalent enthusiasm for a League of Powers: ' . . . bound to settle their differences by Conference or arbitration, and equally bound to make joint war on any Power which . . . refuses . . . arbitration.'

Woodrow Wilson, whom Murray already knew personally, had not seen him during his visit to the USA — presumably to avoid the appearance of receiving a British semi-official spokesman at a crucial stage in the evolution of US policy. But by the summer of 1917, the USA was in the war and the President had committed himself repeatedly to the support of a League of Nations after the War. Soon it became clear that a consensus was forming among the allies and within Britain on some of the main features to be embodied in the post-war League. The 'Bryce Plan', eventually published in summer 1917, embodied what might be regarded as a minimum scheme but it did not envisage universal membership of the League (certainly not immediate membership for Germany); and it had no place for the Fabian ideas on technical co-operation between members; but it gave expression in draft Treaty form to a considerable common stock of ideas. To these the League of Nations Society added an important provision for regular 'conferences to consider international matters of a general character.'

Murray had not been directly involved with the Bryce plan, but in 1917 and 1918 he became much more closely concerned with the prospects of a peace settlement and with the evolution of the League idea.

2

1917 was a year of momentous international developments. The USA entered the war in April, but Russia, as it proved, had been effectively knocked out of it in March. In November the newly established Bolshevik regime concluded a separate peace with Germany (Murray at the Board of Education was involved in some dealings with the Kerensky regime and was much impressed by him when the two men eventually met).[11] Meanwhile Lloyd George was still committed to the policy of a 'knock-out blow' against Germany, and a further British offensive at Passchendaele had been halted in autumn 1917 with enormous casualties. Murray thoroughly distrusted the Lloyd George coalition and the policy of the 'knock-out blow'.

In August 1917 Murray published a series of articles in the *Daily News* on the right policies for Britain after the War. They were reissued in November in pamphlet form as *The Way Forward*.[12] These articles marked another step for Murray away from the Lloyd George government and apparently back to his radical past. On the domestic front he advocated much less government interference in private affairs, much more industrial democracy (on this subject he was perhaps influenced by his friendship with Douglas Cole) and, as in the old days at Castle Howard, Local Option to keep the demon drink under control.

In the field of foreign affairs, Murray urged the establishment of a League of Nations, without going into much detail—it could be taken as established Allied policy by now, and Edward Grey emphasized this in the introduction which he wrote for the pamphlet. More interesting and more symptomatic of Murray's state of mind at the time were the paragraphs in which he argued that if good Liberals (unlike Conservatives, revolutionaries, or pacifists) had been willing to fight for the self-determination of nations, they must be willing also to admit the application of these concepts to Ireland and the British Empire. On the future of Empire, Murray wrote of the possibilities of some exchange of colonial territories in Africa with Germany, and of some international control of tropical territories under a League of Nations; he did not make it clear whether the reference was to direct international rule, as favoured at one time by the Webbs, or to a sort of Mandate system, as advocated by the Independent Labour Party (ILP), under which developed 'colonist' nations should be responsible to the League for the administration of particular territories.[13]

The publication of *The Way Forward* had one important result for Murray: it led to his working closely with General Smuts. Later it was at Smuts's invitation that Murray represented South Africa as a delegate to the second and third assemblies of the League of Nations at Geneva in 1921 and 1922.

Smuts, who had come to England to attend a meeting of the Imperial War Cabinet in March 1917, had been invited by Lloyd George to stay on as a member of the British War Cabinet—a unique distinction, as he had no connection with either house of Parliament. He wrote to Murray that he valued *The Way Forward* particularly, because it developed the ideas they had discussed when they met in May 1917 at a lunch given by Reginald McKenna, the Chancellor of the Exchequer.[14]

Smuts and Murray shared many interests. In March 1917 Smuts had taken up the cause of conscientious objectors in the Imperial War Cabinet. Both men wished to explore the possibilities of a negotiated peace to end the carnage in France. Murray could not in fact have known at the time that Smuts in November 1917 was conducting highly secret talks with the Austrian Count Mensdorff about the possibility of negotiating a peace between the powers of Central and West Europe.[15]

The unofficial counterpart, so to speak, of those secret operations was the letter from Lord Lansdowne, a former Viceroy of India and Foreign Secretary, published by the *Daily Telegraph* on 29 November 1917. In this he advocated a plan rejected by the Cabinet a year before, for negotiating a peace with the Central Powers on the basis essentially of the status quo in 1914, with more emphasis on new international machinery.[16] Lansdowne was publicly and bitterly accused of defeatism bordering on treachery, and Murray, who had lunched with Asquith and Lansdowne on the day when the Lansdowne letter was published, wrote a letter (also to the *Daily Telegraph*) in defence of him. It was couched in spirited terms which seemed to presage a *rapprochement* between Murray and the UDC and the ILP:

Lord Lansdowne's critics write as if his policy implied a weakening of the will to fight. Not so. The question is whether we should not fight better if we know what we are fighting for, and have a moderate and just objective . . . It [the Lansdowne letter] will, if allowed to circulate, damp fighting spirits in Germany and Austria. What the enemy Governments want their subjects to believe is the exact opposite of Lord Lansdowne's policy. We do wish to destroy Germany, to strangle her trade, to make of the League of Nations a vast anti-German alliance, to refuse to discuss any international problems, related to sea-power or not.[17]

Murray supported Lansdowne's arguments as a statement of intent rather than as a basis for immediate negotiations. He put the point clearly in a New Year article for the *Daily News*. The time to press for a just peace would be after the impending German offensive had been repulsed. He himself had criticized H. A. L. Fisher to Lady Mary for callousness in making the same calculation, and his own article exposed him to a bitter attack for having said 'the last word in exploitation of vicarious suffering by deliberately prolonging the war . . . In this "war for freedom" Abraham offers up Isaac with untold modern tortures superadded.'[18]

In the summer of 1917, shortly after the USA entered the war, an Anglo-American Committee of intellectuals was formed with the encouragement of Lord Robert Cecil, then Minister of Blockade. Murray played an active part in this, and was involved in discussions about the need for closer links between American and British public men. There were plans for visits to the USA, where there was still room for informal diplomacy under academic cover. It seemed at this time to Murray, and to many others, that the most useful way in which he could work for new post-war institutions would be by acting as a sort of unofficial ambassador to the USA. He was trusted on both sides of the Atlantic partly because he was not himself committed to any particular plan or set of planners.

Before the end of the year a fresh possibility was under discussion. The US League to Enforce Peace (LEP) was to hold a Congress in Chicago in February 1918 about post-war plans, and the organizers consulted Bryce about a suitable British participant. He told the Foreign Secretary, Arthur Balfour, that Murray would be the best man.[19] Balfour agreed and wrote to Murray on 8 January that, while he would not be an official delegate, his presence would be most valuable to the Foreign Office, 'who desire to be fully informed as to the line taken by the best minds in America.'[20] However unofficial his position, he would be well qualified to dispel the fear, widespread in the USA, that Britain was aiming at an imperialist peace.[21] But the Chicago Congress was postponed and at the beginning of March, the Foreign Office changed its mind about sponsoring Murray. He had had a message published in the *New York Times* of 7 February, in which he emphasized the importance of negotiating generous terms with Germany in due course if a durable peace was to be considered. On 6 March the *Globe* described him as 'bleating' about the 'poor dear Germans' and adopting a pacifist attitude.[22] In a pompous official letter, a member of Balfour's staff told Murray that the Foreign Secretary 'profoundly disagreed with what one may call the "tone" of the message and with some of the alleged facts.' Murray must consider Balfour's letter of 8 January as unwritten, and return it: 'this course will, no doubt, make it easier for you to speak the more freely if you decide to attend the Congress in the States.'[23]

Murray replied directly to Balfour:

I fully understand you not wishing to give me anything like a certificate of approval. I have always felt that my differences with the present Government would make my position in America rather awkward, in spite of my general confidence in the F.O. and my personal respect for and, if I may say so, affection for you.

You will, I hope, recognize that my message to the *New York Times* expresses exactly the same political views which I have always put forward in England in my very numerous war-writings. They are those of the average non-ministerial Liberal.[24]

There was a further exchange of friendly letters between Balfour and Murray, the latter saying that, while he trusted Balfour and Lord Robert Cecil, he could not entirely trust Lloyd George, nor 'his chosen interpreters, the Northcliffe and Beaverbrook press'.[25] Meanwhile Murray informed the US Ambassador in London that the FO did not wish him to attend the Congress, and its sponsors might like to withdraw their invitation.[26] In the event Murray did not go to America in 1918 in any capacity.

3

In 1918 Murray became more formally involved in unofficial plans for the development of a League of Nations, and in due course with the shaping of Government policy towards the League. By the summer of 1918 he was almost completely caught up in the work on the future international organization, and Lady Mary was urging him to give up all other work.[27] In July he reported to Lady Mary that John Buchan at the Ministry of Information had sounded him out about a proposal that

Our League of Nations propaganda in Central Europe should be put under a Central Bureau in Zurich. The head of that Bureau should be your old friend Harris [Murray himself] . . . Harris would need an accomplished female secretary (perhaps Ka Cox or Lady Ottiline [*sic*])[28]

Lady Mary replied with some dark cautions. She did not trust Buchan, and 'this Government is under the thumb of those who, not unnaturally, dislike you'. Asquith too advised great prudence and suggested consulting Lord Robert Cecil, who had by then assumed responsibility for the League at the Foreign Office.[29]

Meantime views about the League of Nations were beginning to be polarized along party lines. Arthur Henderson had resigned from the government in August 1917, and began to work closely with MacDonald and the ILP on formulating Labour War Aims. The Labour and Trade Union joint statement, drafted at the end of 1917, was based largely on the Bryce and Fabian plans so far as concerned the League of Nations; but there was also much emphasis on reconciliation with Germany, no economic discrimination against her, and no secret diplomacy. Douglas Cole tried to arrange a meeting between Murray and Arthur Henderson to secure his support for the Labour statement.[30] But Murray was unwilling; probably he thought the statement too redolent of those UDC ideas which he had opposed from 1914 onwards.

All Conservatives and many Liberals felt that the Labour Party War Aims went too far towards reconciliation with Germany, and that the League of Nations Society, in which many of the drafters were prominent, had been infected by a pacifist and defeatist spirit. This feeling was strengthened by the events of March and April 1918, when the long-anticipated German offensive in the West came near to breaking the Allied armies. More than ever it seemed that the first need for the Allies was military victory, and that premature talk about reconciliation with Germany could give the appearance of military weakness. In his summary history, *The Origins of The League of Nations* (1922) Murray wrote:

To clear the LNS from the suspicion of being the creation of pacifist faddists a new society was set up early in 1918 at the initiative of Major David Davies, M.P., the League of Free Nations Association [LFNA]. Germany must be defeated, but a liberalised and democratical Germany would be welcome as a member.[31]

The LFNA was formally established at the end of June 1918. The immediate inspiration behind it had been David Davies, who had money which he wished to spend on the cause of international order, and who was profoundly dissatisfied with the League of Nations Society. On 26 June its Executive Committee was formally appointed with Murray as Chairman and Davies as Vice-chairman.[32] (Murray also held the position of Vice-president in the LNS but had not been active in it.) Murray's most important qualifications for the post were the breadth of his political sympathies and his knowledge of the American scene.

The main justification for the creation of another Society concerned with League plans was the credentials of its sponsors—all established non-pacifists. Also it should be easier to co-ordinate the activities of such a group with those of the American League to Enforce Peace—a point of which Murray was well aware.[33] The major point of difference in policy between the LNS and the LFNA was whether Germany should immediately be represented on the new international organization which would inevitably come into being at the end of the war. It seemed obvious to use the inter-allied wartime machinery (such as the Allied Maritime Transport Commission) to form the basis of the new post-war technical organizations. But that would automatically exclude German participation at the beginning. The UDC/ILP wing of the LNS regarded this gradualist approach as part of a deliberately repressive policy against Germany designed to keep her out of the League and to impose a peace of revenge upon her.

In fact the new League of Free Nations Association had hardly begun separate work before it embarked on negotiations for amalgamation with the LNS. Lady Mary felt that the establishment of the LFNA had been over-hasty, distrusted Davies as a 'Georgite', and reported bitter feeling among old LNS members.[34] Murray disapproved of the dissipation of effort involved in the coexistence of the two Societies, and felt the need to harness the prestige of Edward Grey, who was associated with the LNS. Preliminary negotiations soon began for amalgamation, and by mid-August agreement had been reached.

On 15 August Grey authorized Murray to 'take the plunge' and tell those concerned that, if the two organizations would amalgamate, he would become President of the new united body.[35] For two months thereafter delegates of the two organizations worked out details of the merger. On the crucial issue of Germany, what was essentially the LFNA line prevailed. Grey announced on 10 October that Germany must be a member of the League, but only as a purified and democratic nation; thus Germany was *de facto* excluded for some time to come.

The new amalgamated body formally came into being at a meeting in Caxton Hall, London, held on 9 November, two days before the

Armistice. The 987 members of the LFNA joined the 2,230 members of the LNS in the new League of Nations Union, with the object of promoting 'the formation of a World League of Free Peoples for the securing of international justice, mutual defence and permanent peace.' Asquith, Balfour, and Lloyd George joined Grey as Honorary Presidents, and Murray became the first Chairman of the Executive Committee.

Murray's appointment, taken together with the formula about the admission of Germany to the League, certainly represented a defeat for the UDC and radical members of the LNS. In fact it was a wise choice, which made for conciliation within the ranks of the LNU, and for its considerable potential as a pressure group on any government. From the government point of view, Murray had a respectable record as a semi-official propagandist for the Asquith coalition. This may have been held against him, by for example, Lowes Dickinson and Leonard Woolf from the LNS, but in their eyes he had at least partially redeemed himself by his refusal to work for the Lloyd George coalition, by his defence of the rights of Conscientious Objectors, and by his stand on behalf of Lord Lansdowne in December 1917. No one could question his sincerity and desire for conciliation. Above all he had the advantage of an enormous range of friendly contacts with personalities of every political colour—Asquith, Balfour, Bryce, Grey, and Smuts; John Buchan at the Ministry of Information; the Webbs, Hobson, Woolf, and Douglas Cole on the Left. Murray, if anyone, could make the LNU into an efficient two-way channel for conveying to government the movements of public opinion and for explaining to a wide public the problems and constraints of governments.

4

After the Armistice, events moved quickly. The Armistice was signed on 11 November 1918, the Covenant on 28 April 1919, and the Peace Treaty on 28 June 1919. In the interval many bodies and many individuals were at work on drafts for the Covenant, collating and selecting from the wealth of material prepared during the war in anticipation. Murray was not, as he had hoped he might be, a member of the British Peace Delegation to Versailles. However, Lord Robert Cecil (along with General Smuts) was one of the British delegates to the Peace Conference as special adviser on League questions. Cecil kept closely in touch with Murray throughout. This was the start of a lifelong co-operation between these two men: men of very different background, who shared a high-minded idealism, and without whose leadership the course of the LNU would have run very differently. Cecil, an accepted member of the Tory establishment, was the chief protagonist of the League within the British official machine. Murray, don and scholar, whose quiet courtesy concealed principles held with passion and a sturdy Australian independence, held the LNU together between the wars as a force not to be ignored. The history of the LNU can be seen in one facet as a dialogue between the two men: both men of vision, but in the long-term, it is Murray who proves the more practical politician.

By the end of 1918 the LNU policy statement had emerged from the drafting stage and was sent to the FO for comment. At the same time Murray received from General Smuts an advance copy of his pamphlet on the League which he published in January 1919; and from Zimmern, a copy of the FO draft for comment. When President Wilson came to London in December 1918, Asquith, Grey, and Murray went with Cecil to a dinner for the President at Buckingham Palace.

Early in 1919 Cecil invited Murray to serve on the Phillimore Committee to discuss the FO draft for the Covenant:[36] Murray was able to report to the Executive of the LNU that there was little difference between the LNU scheme and that of the FO.

Early in January 1919 a Conference of Inter-allied League Societies was held in Brussels. At the instigation of the LNU it was decided to institute an International Federation of League of Nations Societies, in the hope that the unanimous resolutions of such a body would carry more weight with the League than resolutions from individual national societies. But unanimity was hard to achieve: delegates tended to look over their shoulders and defer to their home governments. The LNU as the most active and most independent of the societies, and usually better prepared, exercised a disproportionate influence and, on occasion, could carry a resolution of importance: the quality of the UK leaders told, and in particular Murray's skill in holding together a diverse membership. So on this first occasion, the draft programme for the Covenant which the Conference adopted was virtually identical with that of the LNU. A deputation headed by Leon Bourgeois, former Prime Minster of France, presented it to the 'Big Four' at the Paris Peace Conference.

Thus Murray had been involved in all stages of British drafting, whether official or non-official. The Covenant as formally adopted on 28 April 1919 had been shaped almost exclusively by British and

American influence. The programme of the LNU had been largely included and the LNU had every reason to be satisfied. The Covenant certainly was a long way ahead of any previous attempts at the international co-ordination of foreign policies.

CHAPTER XIX
Return to Oxford 1919–1922

1. Fails as Liberal Candidate for Oxford — issue of Compulsory Greek — University Committees.
2. Move to Yatscombe 1919 — Lady Carlisle dies 1921 — Agnes's death 1922.
3. Lloyd George coalition disintegrating 1921 — Murray approaches Grey and Asquith to form new coalition — further attempts to gain university seat.

1

1919 was a year of transition for Murray. He had left the Board of Education: the League of Nations was still only in embryo. It was not yet clear what demands his work for the League would make upon him, but it was clear that such work would have a very high priority.

When he returned to Oxford to resume his duties as Professor, he was induced by the Oxford Liberal Association to stand as their candidate for one of the two university seats in Parliament. His sponsors emphasized that he would not have to give up his professorial Chair were he successful; he would have had to resign it had he been elected to a non-university seat, and for this reason among others, he declined Lady Carlisle's appeal to him to stand for North Cumberland.[1] Oxford at that time was strongly Conservative and there was never any likelihood that he would be elected. He did not campaign at all and despite energetic work by his sponsors, particularly Cyril and Gemma Bailey, he only just saved his deposit — an ILP candidate having split the minority of non-Conservative voters.[2]

The return to Oxford was not an unmixed pleasure. In January 1919 he wrote to his daughter Rosalind: 'Had my first lecture on Thursday last. As I got out at the station I loathed Oxford, the squalor, the damp, the envious and captious atmosphere. Then, as I met individuals, I liked them and I loved my class when I got to it.'[3]

For Murray teaching was always a delight, and now it could be combined with family life; in spring 1919 he was reading Plato with Agnes (now released from war duties) at Overstrand in Norfolk. She was studying Greek under the tuition of Sandy Lindsay and Murray consulted the bible (the old-fashioned *sortes*) on the prospect of success. He was delighted by the reply, 'He that winketh the eye causeth sorrow'.[4]

One of the aspects of university life to which Murray found it hard to reconcile himself was the prevalence of alcohol. During the war he had warned the Vice-Chancellor of the dangers to which it would subject young men back from the fighting. He also revived the question of the legality of the sale of wine and spirits in his own college, Christ Church. The university career of his son Basil must have shown him painfully how little success his efforts had had.

Maurice Bowra in his *Memories* refers to the 'unpredictable streak of puritanism which would break out in Murray from time to time'—not only against the demon drink. Bowra records that Murray told Fisher (now Warden of New College) that undergraduates used motorcars for making love. Fisher took this seriously and tried to get the use of cars forbidden to undergraduates. After some sparring and comedy in the Hebdomadal Council, the matter was eventually dropped when a member pointed out that 'if undergraduates wished to commit fornication, they could do so equally well by train'.[5]

Some of Murray's academic duties were also disagreeable. He had to resume the battle about Greek as a compulsory subject in the preliminary examination (Responsions) which qualified students to take an Honours course. After the war, as before, the issue was hotly debated. A Statute providing that Greek should simply be one of various subjects which could be taken in Responsions was passed in May 1919 by 'Congregation' (the MAs resident in Oxford) and then turned down by 'Convocation' (in which all Oxford MAs, wherever they resided, could vote). Murray, as a Professor of Greek who was against compulsion, incurred his full share of the rancour generated by these debates.

The proponents of change resumed their campaign almost immediately. Murray still favoured the voluntary principle but, partly because of his position as professor, he agreed to amendments providing that for certain Honours schools a preliminary examination in Greek (no longer purely linguistic) should be compulsory. Ernest Barker, against Murray's wishes, modified the proposal to provide that the candidates concerned need not offer more than the subject matter of a Greek book, in English translation. In November 1919, the rejected 'voluntarist' Statute was again put to Convocation and passed. The Murray/Barker amendments were rejected by a narrow majority, but in March 1920 they were adopted and the revised new Statute passed by Convocation.

The verdict of the *Oxford Magazine* was that the so-called 'compromise' was repugnant even to many who had voted for the Statute, and that it would not last for long. Convocation, it said, had dealt what was likely to be a death-blow to classical learning in Oxford. The first prophecy proved more accurate than the second.[6]

In November 1919 a Committee on the teaching of classics and their place in the educational system had been set up, and Murray was inevitably a member: other members included the Marquess of Crewe as chairman, the Revd C. A. Alington, Professor Burnet, Sir Henry Hadow, Professor W. P. Ker, R. W. Livingstone, Cyril Norwood, and Professor A. N. Whitehead. When the Committee's report was drafted, the new Statute on Responsions at Oxford had not yet been adopted, but there was little doubt that Greek would no longer be a compulsory subject for admission to an Honours course, and that emphasis on Greek teaching would henceforth be diminished. Even at the famous public schools Greek was already a minority subject, though perhaps not yet in final decline.

Those who were convinced of the value of Greek studies were more than ever concerned to prove they were worth while and recognized to be so by those who controlled entry into the non-specialist professions. The introduction to part I of the Report was clearly drafted very largely by Murray and is a good statement of the case for classical studies. A knowledge of the Greek and Latin classics, it is argued, gives access to literature which is often thought the noblest in the world and is at the least unique and irreplaceable (translations even of the historical and philosophic works cannot give the full value of the original). Classical literature enables us to study civilizations in which many problems similar to those of our own age appear, but in simpler form and on a smaller scale. And the training for an understanding of the classics exercises many different parts of the mind — memory, imagination, aesthetic appreciation, and scientific method.

The Committee took evidence from a large variety of witnesses, representing professions or giving individual views. Those from the business world were unanimous in regarding premature specialization as a mistake, and the committee were able to argue that the position of classics in education had received serious and sympathetic consideration from many quarters hitherto regarded as hostile.

The Committee's conclusions, not surprisingly, were that strenuous efforts should be made to preserve the study of Latin and Greek as a minority subject in secondary and university education; and that, if this were to be done, more imaginative teaching would be required than had usually prevailed in the days of compulsory classics.

These were arguments that had long been used and put into practice by Murray, who had always preferred an audience 'fit but few' to a large class of reluctant conscripts. The conclusions of the Report were also such as to justify fully his own efforts over two decades to spread more widely knowledge of 'the Greek Spirit' by means of translations and stage performances.

However, public life encroached increasingly on Murray's activities as a scholar, and he was called upon to take a full share in university administration. In his early fifties, he was by now an eminent figure in the educational field as a whole. His experience in the war as a government spokesman, and later as an official in the Board of Education, made him an obvious choice for the new committee through which the Lloyd George government was trying to shape a new educational policy. In May 1919 Murray was invited to serve on the newly constituted University Grants Committee, 'to enquire into the financial needs of University Education in the U.K. and to advise H.M.G. as to the application of any grants that may be made by Parliament towards meeting them.'[7] This led to meetings with the Board of Education about State Scholarships to be granted at Oxford; Murray represented the University along with the Dean of Christ Church, the Master of Balliol, the President of Magdalen, and Ernest Barker, and they had to accept the principle of a general enquiry into the university's finances.[8]

Meanwhile it was not only official business which diverted Murray from his professorial tasks. He was also asked for and provided advice, active help, or the prestige of his name in a bewildering variety of other fields. For example, he was President of the Oxford branch of the English Association, of the Anglo-Norse Society, and (in 1920) of the Geographical Association. The mathematician G. H. Hardy consulted him about how to secure for Indian students educated in England suitable jobs in the Indian Educational Service.[9] H. G. Wells enlisted his active co-operation for the *Outline of World History*, though he came to mistrust Murray's enthusiasm for fifth-century Athens, accusing him of creating a 'city of demigods', glossing over slavery, and generally reading too many modern ideas into ancient times.[10]

2

Lady Mary even more than Murray himself was exhausted by her wartime activities—in the summer of 1918 she weighed under seven stone in her clothes.[11] At the end of the year she had somewhat recovered, but decided that the time had come for a move from central Oxford to more rural surroundings—a move which the Murrays had long contemplated. 82 Woodstock Road was sold early in 1919, and the Murrays bought Yatscombe on Boar's Hill, not far from the Bridges and Masefields. By March they had moved temporarily and were at 2 Fyfield Road, visiting Yatscombe frequently and picnicking there in the summer. The move was completed in July. It involved some academic difficulties. By statute the Regius Professor had to reside within three miles of the centre of Oxford, and Yatscombe was further away by road. However, it was discovered that, as the crow flies, the house was within the limit, and the Vice-chancellor conveniently ruled that 'the statute goes by the crow'.[12] Yatscombe was the Murrays' main base for the rest of their lives—not far short of forty years. Here at least was a constant background of natural beauty where they could find peace.

In July 1921 Lady Carlisle died, just after completing a move from the old family house at 1 Palace Green to 13 Palace Gardens (now the Soviet Embassy). Her husband, who had died in 1911, had broken up the Howard estates under his will, and left the greater part of them away from his eldest son, Charles, Lord Morpeth (who died only a few months after his father). Castle Howard had fallen to Lady Carlisle, and she had debated with many changes of mind what to do with it on her own death. She decided to leave it jointly to her eldest daughter Lady Mary, and to Murray. This and other arrangements under her will were unsatisfactory to the Murrays (who had been named as executors) and to other members of the family, who decided to alter the terms of the will, so far as was legally possible, under a Deed of Family Arrangement.[13]

So far as the Murrays were concerned, the least of their problems was how to dispose of Castle Howard. Lady Mary wanted from the first to make it over to her younger brother, Geoffrey, and Murray had no objection.[14] In return she was to receive parts of the Howard property in Cumberland, near Naworth. The details of this are unimportant, but the correspondence between husband and wife over the next months provides interesting details of their financial situation and customary expenditure. Murray's professorial salary was £1,500, and in addition he earned about £500 per annum. Now, Lady Mary reckoned, they would receive about £10,000 unearned income annually; about half of this would go in taxes, and of the rest £800 would go to the children, £1,000 on charities, and £1,200 on housekeeping. Murray thought that the figures for gifts were excessive; indeed he had to put his foot down firmly once, when Lady Mary proposed to sell all her Cumberland property and give the proceeds to the Society of Friends for the relief of famine in Central Europe.[15] Largely for Lady Mary's sake, he was anxious that they should live rather more comfortably themselves, and Lady Mary herself confessed to some jealousy of the comparatively ample life-style enjoyed by her sisters and brothers-in-law; but their own way of life continued to be austere.[16]

There was also the problem of whether the properties which Lady Mary took over in exchange for Castle Howard should be held in her name alone or jointly. Murray favoured joint holding, in order to avoid death duties if Lady Mary should predecease him. She seems to have felt that this was not quite honest, and quoted Sir George Trevelyan's opinion that Lady Carlisle's gifts to Murray during her lifetime had gone against the spirit of the law. She wanted to keep the property in her own name and then to hand over to Murray an income equivalent to that derived from his professorship, 'if or when you resign' — she probably thought that he might wish or be forced to do so, in favour of his League of Nations work. Another reason for keeping income from the property separate and not in a common account was due to past troubles — 'partly my own mistakes and partly, if you forgive me for saying it — yours.' She had been left to cope with much business for which Murray had had no time, and 'criticism of what I do rankles'. However, her course in the whole affair would be determined largely by her brothers and sisters: 'From the moment *any* of the others take their property in their joint names, I could not properly do otherwise' — to do so would imply distrust of Murray.[17]

The main changes in the Murrays' life resulting from the new arrangements proved to be that Lady Mary regularly stayed in Cumberland during the late summer to look after her new properties (in which Murray took little interest), while he was at Geneva on League of Nations business and then on holiday in Switzerland; and that the Toynbees settled at Ganthorpe on the edge of the Castle Howard estate, there to receive frequent visits from Murray in particular.

There were other family problems at this period. Of the five Murray children, Rosalind Toynbee was well settled, and Stephen was still at school (prep. schools till 1922, then at Shrewsbury).[18] He had been expelled from his first prep. school (Bedales) for teaching Sandy Lindsay's son to say 'damn'. The three remaining children were each the cause of many anxieties. Denis, who returned from internment in 1917, aged 25, had not fully recovered from the strains which it had imposed on him — including a recurrent drink problem. It was hard for him to find a suitable job — thousands of ex-officers had the same difficulty. Murray hoped that one might be available for him in the air section of the League of Nations 'Mixed Commission on Armaments', set up in 1921 — he knew, after all, a lot about aeronautics; but nothing came of this idea.[19] Basil, now aged 18, had good academic talents; he had left Charterhouse and come up to New College with an exhibition in autumn 1920. His career was mixed and colourful; it earned him the reputation of being one of the originals on whom Evelyn Waugh based the character of 'Basil Seal'. He won the Charles Oldham University Essay prize in 1924, but did not achieve more than Third Class Honours in classics; and he incurred considerable debts which his parents had to meet. Lady Mary was intensely distressed and felt a strong sense of guilt; it was not too late, she wrote, for Basil to pull himself up, 'if once . . . he realises how his mind is placed on inferior objects . . . you [Murray] ought to have had such a good clever family. Do you remember you said once it was my brothers coming out in them? Of course I was hurt, but I don't think it's so much my brothers as me, and too much money and insufficient discipline.'[20]

The Murrays' second daughter, Agnes, was much beloved and a source of great pride to them both. It was she, after Rosalind had married and gone her own way in life, who was closest to Murray in intellectual tastes, and to Lady Mary in her practical devotion to good causes. She had gone to Somerville in 1913 and taken a Third Class in Classical Moderations in 1915, but did not complete her Greats course. She wished to take a more active part in war work, and from 1916 to 1918 worked first as a nurse, then as a lorry driver. In 1916 she got engaged to a young officer, Saumarez Main, who was later killed in France. For a short while in 1919 she resumed her Greek studies (privately) and was capable of corresponding with General Smuts about his philosophy of 'holism'.[21] By spring 1920 she was looking again for active work in some relief organization for Europe, still stricken with epidemics and famine. She hoped first to visit Russia as secretary to a Dr Munro. When this plan fell through she accompanied Lady Mary to Vienna in summer 1920 and was active as a local representative of the International Committee for help to the universities of Austria, interviewing candidates for hospitality in Britain. A few weeks later, she applied for a post on the Reparations Commission, but the Foreign Office turned her down.[22]

There was another side to Agnes's character, which her parents had greater difficulty in understanding. Murray had remarked as far back as 1913 on her powers of attracting her 'natural prey' in the shape of young men, and these powers had not diminished (she was only 24 at the end of the war). Lady Mary's letters mention a long succession of suitors and male friends, usually with sighs of dissatisfaction. 'What *is* she about now? . . . I suppose it's all right, but these children are a terror . . . Each time I am brought up afresh against her men and her mode of life I am puzzled and distressed . . . ' Or, apropos of the visit to Yatscombe of a young Greek, 'Why oh why can't we have some ordinary right-thinking straight, unmarried English gentlemen as playfellows?'[23]

It was to end all too soon in tragedy. In July 1922 Agnes was on holiday with the young Greek in the Auvergne. News came separately to Lady Mary and to Murray (then in Geneva) that she was seriously ill. 'For some reason', he wrote, 'I feel quite sick with anxiety about the child—though I generally bear my children's troubles with perfect equanimity.'[24] By the end of the month, Lady Mary had travelled out to be with her daughter, accompanied by Archie MacDonnell; here was a young 'right-thinking and straight' gentleman who was devoted to Agnes, and was invaluable in attending to practical details for Lady Mary. Agnes proved to be suffering from acute peritonitis and the case had been badly mishandled, in Lady Mary's opinion, by the local doctors. It was some time before Murray realized the full gravity of the crisis, and Lady Mary at first did not encourage him to join her. ('Were things practical otherwise, I should care more than anything to have you—As it is, and at present, I feel that worry for you would add to my minor cares.')[25] In fact, Murray set out from Geneva soon after receiving this letter, in time to see Agnes before she died on 21 August. Of all the blows which fell on him in his family life this was the heaviest. To an old friend, the Dante scholar Philip Wicksteed, he wrote:

Agnes went down with her flag flying, loving and brave to the end. And beautiful, too, which would have been a pleasure to her if she had known it.

'Gone like a wild bird, like a blowing flame'—There was a good deal of the wild bird in her, but she was a most loving child to those at home . . .

Our own [bereavement] hurts like a physical wound, especially now that we are home again in places that are saturated with memories of the child.[26]

Stephen Murray wrote:

she was a very scintillating and lovable character, such that in spite of the sort of behaviour of which her parents disapproved, they loved her intensely. Something of the same sort applies to Basil. His intellectual capacity formed a strong link with his father, such that when he died in the first year of the Spanish War . . . it was my father who went to his funeral.[27]

Beyond the circle of her family and close friends Agnes (or Elizabeth as she was sometimes known towards the end of her life) made a most vivid impression. Vera Brittain, her Somerville contemporary, wrote of her in 1933 in terms of which Murray himself approved. She described 'the meteoric radiance which had flashed through my first year at Somerville. Characteristically crowding into a few spectacular years the adventures and experiments and emotions of a lifetime, Agnes Elizabeth Murray, it seemed, had broken beneath the combined over-intensity of work and play . . . if one does a great deal of both, either one's work gives up the ghost, or one gives it up one's self. All honour to Agnes Murray for letting it be herself and not her work if she chose a short life and a gay one.'[28]

For both Lady Mary and Murray, these early 1920s were years of experiment and new beginnings, some of them unexpected. For example, Murray's enthusiastic adaptation to the age of the automobile brought its troubles. There was now a car as well as a motor-cycle, and in November 1920 Murray was involved in his first car accident—evidently not a serious one.[29] There was a more dangerous spill next summer, when he was thrown heavily from his motor-cycle on to his head, and had to rest for some days.[30] However, in general Murray's own health seems to have stood up well to the new strains, at least in comparison with the physical crises that he underwent at the turn of the century.

It was Lady Mary whose general health, physical and psychological, was now in greater danger. In March 1922 she wrote pathetically, after 'divergences of opinion' and 'hard words', that she was too old to begin afresh and to learn lessons of humility and contrition:

I've not had quite an easy life. Your work is so important and so hard. You haven't had time to share in the ordinary cares and responsibilities of the family . . . But if Nursie's kindness and the passage of time restores me to any measure of strength and serenity—I will indeed start afresh and try to keep order and to please you and make you happy.[31]

In many respects indeed their lives were to become more separate in the inter-war period. However, in 1922 Lady Mary was intensely proud of Murray's work for the League of Nations and convinced of its importance; the death of Agnes brought them very close to one another in their sorrow; and Yatscombe was becoming a meeting place for foreign, particularly German and Austrian scholars, and a place of pilgrimage for those whose main interest was in the League of Nations. Fridtjof Nansen, who was entertained by the Murrays in February 1922, confronted them with one unexpected problem when he expressed a strong desire to take part in an English fox-hunt. Murray swallowed his principles in this case, and Basil was able to procure suitable clothes for Nansen from undergraduate friends. George Schuster, who had met the Murray family in Vienna, provided Nansen with a horse, and took him out with the Heythrop hounds, and treasured the memory of him galloping about at top speed with no regard for what the hounds might be doing.[32]

3

The year 1921 witnessed Murray's only serious effort to play a role, at least as an intermediary, in politics. At the end of the war the country was in a violently anti-German mood: in the election of November 1918 the Lloyd George coalition was triumphantly returned with 339 coalition Unionists and the 136 coalition Liberals: Labour increased their seats to 59 but the Independent Liberals only got 26 seats. Liberalism, Murray wrote to Lady Carlisle, is 'apparently doomed'.[33]

But by 1921 it was clear the coalition was falling apart. Cecil, in many respects a rogue Tory, found it increasingly hard, on his return from Geneva in 1920, to acquiesce in the Conservative role in the Lloyd George coalition. When Bonar Law resigned from the coalition in April 1921, Cecil decided that the time had come for a gesture. He ceased to sit on the government side of the House and was deprived of the Conservative Whip. Cecil was more nearly in agreement with the Independent Liberals than with any other political group, and he hoped that a new coalition might be formed after the next election, under Grey but including Asquith, some rebel Conservatives (including of course himself) and some Labour members.[34]

Murray, no longer a safe middle-of-the-road Liberal, was intensely disillusioned by the new parliament and the new Lloyd George coalition. In Ireland ruthless terrorist operations by the IRA were being met with equal ruthlessness by the British. Asquith for the Independent Liberals condemned the British government's policy in the strongest possible terms,[35] and Murray was not far behind. In December 1920 Murray was due to make a speaking tour in the USA to expound the principles of the League; but his hosts had to put off his visit owing to the 'extension of the Irish Civil War to New York City'.[36]

Personal antipathies and loyalties also played their part. Even so rational a man as Murray could not do without political villains: Lloyd George was long cast for this role. Correspondingly he was loyal to his political heroes, above all to Asquith and Grey. He was ready to grasp at any opportunity of broadening the basis of the Liberal party under the old and prestigious leaders.

Murray's increasing familiarity with both Asquith and Grey made him a valued intermediary for those who wished to tempt either or both back into active politics. He was now a regular guest at the Asquith's Thameside home, The Wharf, and had struck up a friendship with his daughter, Violet Bonham Carter. A lively correspondence between the two continued until Murray's death.

In August 1920, Murray was a guest of the Glenconnors (the family of Grey's second wife) at Innerleithen, and reported much political and other talk with Grey, in whose company he delighted. 'I never saw anybody who was so much a moralist, and so far from a prig.'[37] He presented Grey with a letter from a number of political figures urging him to return to public life, but Grey would not commit himself.

Viscount Gladstone, one of the Liberals most interested in luring Grey back as leader of a new coalition, deputed Murray to find out what Asquith's reactions and conditions would be:[38] Murray reported that he had put it to Asquith that the country was on the verge of disaster (the troubles in Ireland were at their worst); the best solution would be a new coalition with Asquith leading the Liberals, Cecil a Conservative group, and Clynes and Henderson representing Labour: Grey was the only possible man under whom such elements would unite; with which, Murray reported, Asquith agreed.

Yet Grey remained hesitant, and Asquith would not serve under any other political leader. Cecil warned Murray in April 1921 that Asquith would not commit himself on difficult issues such as reparations; he, and even more 'the female members of his family', were quite determined he should return to politics only as Prime Minister.[39] Two months later Murray wrote that the situation would be ripe if Grey wanted to strike—'but then he doesn't.'[40] Lady Mary displayed both irritation and clear-sightedness about Murray's 'participation in all these leadership pourparlers'. She did not consider Grey's pre-1914 policies so defensible as did Murray himself. Grey would never lead, even if he was driven. Neither Grey nor Cecil 'played the game', and both she and Murray considered Asquith 'a roué and a tiresome flirt'. Grey and Cecil were more to her taste personally than Asquith and his family, but did not 'lose themselves in the cause, as Asquith does'.[41]

Over the next two years social meetings between Murray and Asquith continued, and general talk about politics; but any prospect of the Liberals' return to power under Grey or Asquith had faded.

In the mean time in March 1919 there had occurred a further vacancy for one of the Oxford University parliamentary seats, when one of the two members was raised to the peerage. Murray stood again—and again without success, though he got a fair number of votes. He stood four more times for Oxford University—in the elections of November 1922, in 1923, 1924, and 1929—in 1924 as an Independent candidate, but otherwise as a Liberal. He came nearest to success in 1923 and it was only the peculiar university voting system which kept him out of the second seat.[42]

He was also twice invited by the Liberals of Glasgow University to stand for the Rectorship. He accepted on both occasions—it was an honour he would have valued: in 1919 he was defeated by Bonar Law, but the margin, 1073 votes to 726 was not overwhelming—Bertrand Russell only got 80 votes.[43] In 1931 he was beaten by Compton Mackenzie, and wrote philosophically that this was 'just one more instance of a world epidemic of Nationalism'.[44]

Liberalism for Murray was a question of principle and of passionate interest, but never a career.

CHAPTER XX
Writings and Psychic Powers

1. *Essays and Addresses* by GM 1921.
2. Psychic gifts—telepathy or hyperaesthesia.

1

THE impression conveyed by the foregoing chapter may be that Murray had lost a sense of the main purpose of his life, that he was dissipating his energies rather wildly. This would be a false impression. At the end of his life he could say that he had never wavered in the pursuit of his main objectives—an understanding of ancient Greece and the achieving of peace between nations. It was because he had a sure sense of purpose, because there was an unmoved spiritual centre, that he was able to take on so many comparatively minor tasks without being overwhelmed by them.

Much of the central core of Murray's mind is illustrated by what is perhaps the most unjustly neglected of his major books, *Essays and Addresses*, published in 1921. This is a collection of articles, speeches, and lectures delivered or written originally between 1901 and 1920. Whatever the title of each piece, the collection has a certain unity and deals with the borderlands between literature—particularly ancient Greek literature—and philosophy, politics, and religion. The treatment of the main themes, and even more some of the incidental arguments, illustrates the essence of Murray's mind; the book is a sort of mental and spiritual autobiography. A complete recapitulation is unnecessary; two of the essays—those on 'National Ideals '(1901) and 'The Bacchae of Euripides' (1902) have been mentioned at some length already, and that on the 'Stoic Philosophy' (1905) develops themes later to be found in *Five Stages of Greek Religion* (1912). Of the others, 'Aristophanes and the War Party' (1919), with its parallels between the Peloponnesian War of the late fifth century BC, and the recently concluded World War, should be allowed, in Murray's own words, 'only to amuse our reflections, not to distort our judgments'.

The final essay on 'Mandates' (1921) concerns Murray's work for the League of Nations. During 1919–20 Murray and the LNU were busy drafting suggestions for inclusion in the mandates eventually

to be issued by the League, not least to the British for the administration of Mesopotamia (Iraq).[1] Murray had been informed by
Arnold Toynbee how the British had bombed Iraq's villages in order
to put down an Arab rebellion. His essay includes some sharp
criticism of British colonial *realpolitik* and this had led him into a
brisk correspondence with Gertrude Bell who strongly defended the
British action.[2] In the same essay he wrote that he looked forward
to the maximum use of the new Mandates Commission, and to the
transformation of Western Imperialism under the auspices of the
League. Murray accepted in 1920, as he had done in 1888, that there
were more or less developed races, that the Western Europeans
belonged to the former category, and that they had at least a
temporary responsibility, involving imperial rule, towards the latter.
The new and hopeful element in the situation, he thought, was that
the mandatory principle had been enunciated, by 'divine inadvertence'
as he put it, and had been accepted by the Assembly of the League
as a whole, when individual member governments would never have
accepted it on their own. 'The world has not yet sounded or measured
the immense power of mere publicity', wrote Murray. It was the only
weapon possessed by the League of Nations, but it could be the most
powerful of all.

There remain four essays, dating from 1917 to 1919, in which
the constant elements of Murray's innermost mind seem to be
revealed. The first and slightest of them is entitled 'Literature as
Revelation'. In it Murray restates his deeply held view that the
ultimate mark of great literature is the moral message which it
conveys. A great poet 'ought to and does save souls'. To a man who
has once read himself into Shelley, 'the world never looks the same
again'. The revelation of literature lies never in the field of fact but
'in directing attention towards a particular part of life, concerned
with the uncharted parts of our voyage.' However, Murray rather
uncomfortably finds a place for that very undidactic poet, Keats,
perhaps with some memory of the Berensons' 'golden Urn'; Keats
'enables a living man to rise above himself . . . and to see beauty
and wonder in places where he had hitherto seen nothing.'

'The Soul As It Is and How to Deal With It' (1918) is the most
directly religious in content of the collection. This is a meditation
based on a text of Bergson, who

has for middle-aged men added a new terror to life. He makes you watch
yourself becoming mechanical; moving in conformity with outside stimulus;
growing more and more dependent on your surroundings—as if the little

soul carrying the corpse had found it too heavy and was letting it lie, or perhaps roll, while the soul itself fell half asleep.[4]

Murray goes on to consider those who have been inspired by their 'souls' to stand against the obvious course of events, the Belgians, Serbs, and Poles during the war, and who knows 'how many followers of Liebknecht in Germany itself . . . ' The great bulk of the argument is devoted to two individual cases. First there is Gandhi (Murray had met him in 1914) and his triumph of 1913 on behalf of the Indians of South Africa, won by passive resistance and by 'simply doing no wrong'. More directly within Murray's personal experience was the case of Stephen Hobhouse, which he rehearsed in detail. He himself thought conscription on balance was right, and recognized that conscientious objection to it could be humbug; but Hobhouse was an eminent example of

the actual working of the soul in shaping a man's life, and sometimes bringing him into conflict, not only with his own apparent interest, but with the general stress of will in the society around him . . . A wise ruler will be circumspect . . . before challenging the lowliest of human souls to battle on the soul's own ground.[5]

And finally, those whose lives have been spared in the war must keep their own spirit from falling into the power of the 'corpus' and ensure that 'the soul within us shall not die.'

'Satanism and the World Order' (1919) expounds the faith behind Murray's efforts to establish a new order of international relations. In it he contrasts the attitude to this world of the persecuted early Christians with that of 'almost all great moral philosophers'. For the author of the book of Revelations, this world is the realm of Satan, where evil and lies reign exclusively; in contrast to this view, Murray states cautiously enough the case for active efforts to improve the world as it is. Some progress has been made, if we take a long enough view, and it is worth striving for more.

Almost every element for success has been put into the hands of those now governing the world, except, as an old Stoic would say, the things we must provide ourselves . . . A resolute will seems lacking; the people blame their rulers for lack of it, and the rulers explain that they dare not offend their peoples.[6]

The exception, even in 1919, seemed very important; but Murray and many others were animated by a sober faith which inspired them to undertake an extraordinary burden of work. Elsewhere in the collection Murray expressed the same faith and sense of duty. At the end of his preface he wrote that the last 'half-desperate' pages of the essay on 'National Ideals' seem almost like a 'conscious argument for the foundation of the League of Nations' and he concluded 'Aristophanes and the War Party' with words which had little to do with the subject of the essay:

Our war has ended right; and we have such an opportunity as no generation of mankind has ever had of building out of those ruins a better international life and concomitantly a better life within each nation . . . by some spirit of sobriety in public and private things, and surely by some self-consecration to the great hope for which those who loved us gave their lives.[7]

What Murray explicitly called a 'Confession of Faith', covering his scholarly as well as his political activities, is contained in his Presidential address to the Classical Association (January 1918), reprinted in *Essays and Addresses* under the title 'Religio Grammatici' (a scholar's religion). He was not sorry to have studied Greek even if in future knowledge of it would probably be regarded as proof of 'either a reactionary or an unusually feckless temper'. The greater part of a man's life was ἐπὶ συμφοραῖς, exposed to and determined by circumstances:

What we call a man's religion is, to a great extent, the thing that offers him a secret and permanent escape from that prison, a breaking of the prison walls which leaves him standing of course in the present, but in a present so enlarged and enfranchised that it becomes not a prison but a free world . . . A scholar secures his freedom by keeping hold always of the past and treasuring up the best out of it.

He can keep the past alive and pass it on to the others, and in so doing attains the most compelling desire of every human being, a work in life which it is worth living for, and which is not cut short by the accident of his own death.

But, it may be asked, has not the thought of the ancients been satisfactorily absorbed into the wisdom of our time? Murray answers that, whereas the use of the telephone gives us no share in the glory of having invented it, the glory of, for example, *Romeo and Juliet* can be recaptured and shared by one who reads it with scholarly attention and imaginative effort; so much of the best early work in so many fields is in Greek, and the imaginative scholar can share in the glory of the original writers by keeping it alive.

All very well, says Murray's imaginary critic; but this is all traditional superstition and will disappear after one or two Greekless generations; to which the answer is *securus judicavit orbis terrarum*. There has been a consensus of sound judgement up till now on the value of Greek studies, and it is unlikely to have been wrong. The importance of the Greek and Latin traditions to Western European literature can hardly be denied. The love and care which has gone into the tradition (in its literal sense of 'passing on') should be preserved. The classical scholar's love of Greek can coexist with all sorts of other loves and traditions—not least that of scientific scholarship. The real clash is not between the classics and science, but between the classics and indifference—slavery to the present and to casual circumstance.

Murray finally sounds a severely ascetic note in writing of the self-discipline required of the dedicated scholar. It would be a fine thing if all men of science and letters were bound, like some medieval monastic order, by a vow of renunciation or poverty. The service of the body blunts or binds the spirit. The enemy is he

who puts always the body before the spirit, the dead before the living, the ἀναγκαῖον before the καλὸν; who makes things only in order to sell them; who has forgotten that there is such a thing as truth.[8]

Another ascetic to whom such doctrine appealed was President Wilson, who found *Essays and Addresses* delightful and 'fragrant throughout with memories of a friendship which I greatly value.'[9]

2

The faith expressed in the essays was the centre of Murray's thinking and practical activity. He had long been proud to call himself a rationalist. However, he was also well aware that one of the prime functions of reason is to discern what are the limits of the rational process. These limits are of two kinds, both well described by Murray himself. There is 'the enormous dominion of those forces in man of which he is normally unconscious . . . the blind powers beneath the threshold';[10] and, not necessarily connected with these, is the 'Uncharted which surrounds us on every side'. In our relation with it, we must follow the guidance of reason, so far as it will go; but when this ceases, we must use our 'fainter powers of apprehension and surmise and sensitiveness.'[11]

Murray possessed some of these 'fainter powers' in marked degree. His use of them was much discussed by those devoted to the study of psychical research, and was of great interest to others who knew him well in his lifetime, including two of his most famous friends, Smuts and Henri Bergson. No attempt to describe the essence of Murray's character can be complete without attention to his extra-ordinary powers of apprehension.

It is impossible to say exactly when or how Murray became seriously concerned with extra-sensory perception, to use a comparatively modern and inclusive term. His interest in Buddhism, which he linked with current forms of spiritualism, probably dates from 1887–9.[12] In 1895, writing to Archer about his second play, *Leaves of the Sibyl*, he mentioned an acquaintance with a lady who used a planchette.[13] Slightly later, while Murray was still at Glasgow, an unidentified correspondent wrote to him of a meeting at which they had 'compared telepathic notes'; and he himself wrote to Lady Mary of his deep interest in such things and 'desire to follow them up more'.[14]

Most probably it was Murray's growing friendship with Arthur Verrall which increased his interest in 'spiritualistic' experiments. The two men became intimate in the last years of the nineteenth century. Margaret Verrall, Arthur's wife, was a deeply committed member of the Society for Psychical Research, which was formed in 1882; it was probably she who induced Murray to join the Society early in the twentieth century. He reported to Lady Mary a session of table-turning with the Verralls at Cambridge in 1903, when strangely accurate messages were transmitted about the movements of the Storr family.[15] While in Glasgow Murray had evolved, for the amusement of his daughter Rosalind, a sort of bedtime game that involved guessing what she was thinking: and this game was later developed into the series of experiments in 'thought-transference' which became famous from 1915 onwards. At an early age Rosalind had found herself protesting, 'But, Dad, how do you *know*?' He was just as surprised as she was!

Murray had not at first been an active member of the Society for Psychical Research, but he knew a number of eminent men who were interested in psychic phenomena, among them Arthur and Gerald (Lord) Balfour, Andrew Lang, and Oliver Lodge, who had all been Presidents of the Society. Some details of his own 'guessing game' experiments had become known within the Society, thanks to William Archer, who also had a strong interest in 'the uncharted'. In 1915 Murray became President, and in his Presidential Address he gave a good account of how his 'game' had grown.

The experiments took place within a small, usually family, circle at Murray's home (82 Woodstock Road, Oxford, at this time):

I go out of the room and of course out of earshot. Someone in the room, usually my eldest daughter, thinks of a scene or an incident or anything she likes, and says it aloud. It is written down, and I am called. I come in, usually taking my daughter's hand and then, if I have luck, describe in detail what she has thought of. The least disturbance of our customary method, change of time or place, presence of stranger, controversy and especially noise, is apt to make things go wrong.

The words 'and especially noise' are important. They suggested to Murray himself, and even more strongly to critics of his own account and analysis of his experiments, that his success at 'guessing' was due to a sort of sub-conscious hyperdevelopment of the sense of hearing, which became abnormally acute when the 'game' was in progress;[16] and that noises other than those of the main group talking to each other, out of his normal earshot, would prevent him from subconsciously hearing them.

In 1916, shortly after Murray's Presidential Address, Helen Verrall, (daughter of Arthur and Margaret), published in the SPR *Proceedings* a detailed analysis of a selection of Murray's experiments. These were very numerous and were recorded from 1910 onwards. The experiments continued with diminishing frequency until 1935, and very occasionally until 1946, when Murray was 80. The whole body of recorded experiments was listed in 1972 by E. H. Dodds, Murray's successor as the Oxford Professor of Greek and a subsequent President of the SPR.[17] A few illustrative examples may here be quoted from this and the previously printed records.[18]

(*a*) 10 September 1916:

W. MELLOR (*agent*): I'm thinking of the operating theatre in the nursing home in which I was operated.

GM: I get an impression of a theatre. No. I can't get it. I'm now guessing — Covent Garden and Oedipus.

(*b*) 14 July 1918:

P. MAIN: Sir Francis Drake drinking the health of Doughty before he was led out to be hanged.

GM: Is this a [?] No. I've a faint feeling of Arabia or desert.

(*c*) 30 May 1920:

ROSALIND: Grandmother (Lady Carlisle) sitting on a merry-go-round that plays on Kew Bridge.

GM: That's very funny — it's something I had almost forgotten. It's you and Denis in fits of laughter — your old joke about Grandmother on the Highway Board. She's on a merry-go-round — can't get the place, should say it's somewhere . . . the Lakes.

(*d*) 30 May 1920:

ROSALIND: Julian Sorel trying to deal with the ladder outside a lady's window.

GM: This is a book and rather pretentious—French book. Oh, I know what it is—a scene you once told me about—a young man stole in through a lady's window and they did not know what to do with the ladder.

(*e*) 31 May 1920:

ROSALIND: The people at the ford giving Dad strong tea when he was lost in the bush.

GM: I should say it was Australian. It's got something to do with the time when I got lost in the Bush at Southey's. Is it the people giving me tea?

(*f*)

ROSALIND: Cleopatra's needle being tugged along across the sea.

GM: Got a sort of splashing feeling—not the Boat-race and not the Bradford ship [an educational ship talked of during the evening]. It's rather like the Bradford ship dragging something long and heavy. I'm not clear about the thing. Oh, didn't a ship bring Cleopatra's needle, dragging it behind?

(*g*) 17 November 1924:

MM: A scene in a book by Aksakoff where the children are taken to their grandparents and the little boy sees and hears his mother kneeling beside the sofa where his father is lying, lamenting at having to leave them.

GM: I should say this was Russian. I think it's a book I haven't read . . . somebody's remembrances of childhood or something and a family travelling, I think the children and father and mother. I should think they were going to cross the Volga. I don't think I can get it more accurately; the children are watching their parents or seeing something about their parents. I should think Aksakoff. They are going to see their grandmother.

On this, the note-taker commented:

This is noteworthy because in the book there is a great deal about the family crossing big rivers on their journey to see the grandparents. Murray himself commented more precisely: 'They did just afterwards have to cross the Volga, and Rosalind said she had been thinking of it, though she did not mention it.')[19]

(*h*) 1 March 1946:

ROSALIND: Well this is two things. It's the Curé d'Ars, first hiding from the army and later being buffeted by the Devil.

GM: It seems rather medieval—a priest. He seems to be hiding somehow. But it's confused: he seems also to be fighting with the Devil.

The experiments, together with Murray's own comments upon them, have given rise to considerable controversy among those concerned with experiments in telepathy or other forms of extra-sensory perception. The main issue is whether Murray's results (which were totally or partially successful in over two-thirds of the cases recorded from 1920 to 1946) depended on hyperaesthesia— abnormally acute hearing in this case—or could be classed as genuine thought transference. Professor Dodds thought that the evidence for the latter was very strong. Dr Eric Dingwall, who criticized Dodds's findings in volume 56 of the *Proceedings of the Society for Psychical Research* (1973) did not regard the case as made. The records cited above have been chosen to illustrate both sides of the controversy, which it is impossible here to cover at all fully.

Murray's own mind was open to both possible explanations— telepathy and hyperaesthesia. He had written appreciatively of the Stoics who believed in the pervading forethought of the divine mind, and in the Συμπάθεια τῶν ὅλων—the Sympathy of all Creation, whereby whatever happens to one part, however remote and insig-nificant, affects all the rest.[20]

He was also acutely aware of the importance of semi-conscious or unconscious perception:

We perceive virtually (δυνάμει) many more things than we perceive actually (ἔργῳ) . . . and the part that our body plays is that of shutting out from the field of our consciousness all that is of no practical interest to us . . . May there not be round our normal perception a fringe of perception, most often unconscious . . . ? Hyperaesthesia [involves] making the most of extremely faint sense-impressions or of sense-impressions too faint to be consciously perceived at all . . . sense perception can occur without reference to the special organs of sense . . . by a curious sense of propinquity. You know you are coming to a wall . . . it may be some strange sense-perception which makes one feel hostility on the other side of the room.[21]

Murray's own first verdict on his own experiments stated in his Presidential Address to the Society for Psychical Research in 1915 was that

the basis of these telepathic impressions is unconscious sense-perception; but we must be prepared for the possibility that this sense-perception is not confined to the canonical five channels of sight, sound, smell, taste, touch.

His own faculty would thus, as he thought at the time, be a form of hyperaesthesia. According to J. J. Thomson, Murray thought that his hearing became so acute while the 'game' was in progress that he heard something of the conversation between the thinkers as they settled on the subject—not the distinct words, but enough to suggest something of the theme.[22] However, another non-professional commentator, Aldous Huxley, who himself participated in a session of March 1915, had no doubt that Murray's powers were telepathic and was impressed by the fact that Murray came very near to guessing a subject chosen by Huxley himself, a comparative stranger (the Master of Balliol listening to an essay on Meredith's *Egoist*, which he had not read).[23] Among the observers who were more professionally interested in psychical research, Helen Verrall and Eleanor Sidgwick did not regard hyperaesthesia as a sufficient explanation of the results achieved by Murray, and they seem to have convinced him that they were right.[24]

If we turn to the selected evidence quoted above, instances (*a*) and (*b*) point to confusion by Murray due to mishearing—in (*b*) for example he could have heard the name 'Doughty' and thought of G. M. Doughty, author of *Arabia Deserta*. This supports the idea that at least at the time of the experiments he had unusually acute hearing. The others are *prima facie* more easily explained (at least to the mind of a layman) on the theory of some kind of telepathic power; this hypothesis seems to apply particularly to instance (*g*), where the subject was taken from a book which Murray had not read, and he guessed an important detail which was not part of Lady Mary's description, though it occurred in the book and was in the thoughts of his daughter Rosalind. Then too Murray's general method of homing in on a subject, distinguishing between scenes from real life, from books, and fantastic subjects, or between for example an Australian or a Russian atmosphere, seems to correspond better with the exercise of some telepathic power than with that of temporarily hyper-acute hearing. This conclusion was certainly favoured by Dodds, a comparatively expert witness, and by Bowra (who was involved at least once in the guessing-game); and Bowra also mentions Murray's 'almost telepathic' power of grasping in normal conversation what was in the mind of his companion.[25] However, the evidence for the telepathic theory was not regarded as conclusive by those who favoured the hyperaesthetic explanation, or indeed by those who wished to apply the highest scientific standards to Murray's experiments.

Murray's attitude to his own experiments was rather ambiguous. With the conscious part of his mind he seemed to be embarrassed. He was 'as sceptical a person as you will find,' and 'found the whole business rather unpleasant.' It was 'a sort of joke that Nature has played upon me . . . I don't like these vague things.' Again, more in jest, 'I am naturally ashamed of [my gift] and keep it hidden as far as possible. A German has already written a little treatise comparing me with Nostradamus . . . a well-known charlatan in the 17th century.' Or as Helen Salter (formerly Verrall) wrote in 1935, 'any suggestion that the faculties of a perfectly respectable Professor of Greek might have a supernormal taint is confessedly repugnant to him.'[26]

Yet for all the 'mild unpleasantness of the experiments to conscious and sub-conscious mind alike', Murray had taken part in no less than 505 of them by the time that Mrs Verrall analysed a selection in 1916. A further selection from 171 experiments between 1916 and 1929 was analysed by Mrs Sidgwick, and in the series extending from 1920 to 1946, 128 more were noted. Obviously they were a popular occupation within the family circle.

Another point calling for explanation was Murray's reluctance to have the experiments conducted by the strictest possible scientific standards, which might have determined the limits of normal or abnormal hearing at Murray's home and elsewhere. There was a good deal of correspondence about Murray's experiments in 1924–5, after Mrs Sidgwick had published her analysis. Henri Bergson found them extremely convincing, and wrote to Murray: 'Jamais on n'avait expérimenté dans cette direction d'une manière aussi méthodique, ni avec tant de sûreté, ni avec des résultats aussi probants.'[27]

Others with something like a professional interest in the subject were less satisfied. W. R. H. Thouless, for example, then a lecturer in Experimental Psychology at Manchester, asked for details of Murray's experiments after reading a summary account of them in the *Manchester Guardian*. In reply Murray expressed his own opinion in favour of hyperaesthesia as against telepathy, and made it clear that his experiments had not been scientifically designed to discriminate between these alternative possibilities. Thouless suggested further experiments with this end in view. 'It might be easy to find out whether increase in the distance between the reader and the subject does or does not cause a rapid increase in the percentage of error.' Murray refused, evidently on the ground of being too busy, and Thouless could only express polite regret that a 'subject with such interesting powers should happen to be a particularly busy man.'[28]

A lively debate continued in the correspondence columns of *The Times* between the proponents of the theory of telepathy (especially Gerald Balfour) and scientific critics of it. Murray absolutely refused to join in. Lady Mary noted her own reply to a request from the

New York *International Magazine* for an interview: 'I'm afraid he [GM] does not wish to take any part in publicity about his thought-transference.'[29]

In the address which Murray gave to the Society for Psychical Research when he became President again in 1952, he made light of the question of 'control'. His experiments, he said, were little more than a parlour game, belonging to the pre-statistical stage of psychical research. In any case he did not see that there could have been 'any significant failure in control . . . however slippery the behaviour of my sub-conscious, too many respectable people would have had to be its accomplices.'

This attitude, even after Murray's death, continued to provoke argument among the members of the SPR. In 1972 Professor Dodds, who knew Murray well, personally speculated that his reluctance to participate in very strictly controlled experiments arose from the sense that they would not confirm the comparatively rationalist theory of hyperaesthesia, and from unwillingness to be more firmly associated with the hypothesis of telepathy.[30] This attitude seems hardly consistent with Murray's generally open-minded attitude to the 'Great Unknown', or with the conclusion of his second Presidential address to the Society for Psychical Research in which he admitted that the theory of 'hyperaesthesia' now seemed to him an inadequate, or at least not the most simple, explanation of the results which he had attained in his 'guessing-game'.

In reply to Dodds, Dr Dingwall in 1973 wrote severely about Murray's statement on controls in his second Presidential address, and argued powerfully for hyperaesthesia as against telepathy. He suggested that Murray had unconscious reasons for refusing to submit his experiments to more severe tests. Many of Murray's friends believed passionately in telepathy, and he may have had some 'deep-seated, perhaps to some extent unconscious, wish to convince himself that telepathy and all that it implied was true.'[31]

Murray may have had more reasons than were cited by Dr Dingwall to hope that the possibilities of extra-sensory communication should not be explained away in rational terms, or to spare the sensibilities of those who did so hope. The appalling casualties of the First World War had led to a widespread interest in the possibility of communicating with the dead through mediums. William Archer's son Tom (whom Murray had coached privately in Greek) had been killed in France in 1917; the Murrays had suffered themselves a grievous blow with the death of their daughter Agnes in 1922. From Murray's correspondence with William Archer it appears that both Archer and

Lady Mary were interested in experiments with 'media' through whom they might communicate with a spirit world, though Archer at least was sceptical.[32] He died at the end of 1924, but there are further suggestions that Lady Mary's interest in this form of spiritualism continued.[33] In these circumstances Murray might perhaps have preferred not to encourage completely rationalist explanations of the 'guessing-game', and so indirectly to shake her belief in the possibilities of communicating with a spiritual world.

This is pure conjecture, and there may be simpler explanations. He was spiritually aloof and probably cared little whether or not other people believed that he had telepathic powers. He also always disliked 'fuss' and there would have been a good deal of fuss involved in becoming the centre of further controversy on a subject which he did not reckon to be of the first importance in his extremely busy life. He seems to have felt that his experiments were already subject to the sort of controls appropriate to their very informal nature. Any attempt to intensify controls might have made it difficult or impossible for him to exercise powers which were clearly at their height in a purely family atmosphere.

And what in the end could strictly scientific investigation prove? Those who pursued it could establish that Murray was not a conscious fraud (and he could be forgiven for thinking this unnecessary). By an examination of the exact distances between Murray and those who set him the subjects to be guessed, and of the acoustic properties of the house, they could determine the limits of normal and of, so to speak, normally hyper-acute hearing in the circumstances. Many members of the Society for Psychical Research would have regarded it as useful to establish more precisely the limits within which Murray exercised his gift, and perhaps to moderate the extreme public claims of those who supported either the hyperaesthetic or the telepathic hypothesis. Perhaps he was something less than a fully conscientious member of the Society for Psychical Research in refusing to submit to more thorough experiments. But could any experiments have determined what, for example, he himself heard subconsciously in circumstances which stimulated his hearing to an unusual degree, or what was the interaction between his unconscious hearing and some telepathic faculty? He may well have persuaded himself that so much 'fuss' would not have been worth while.

Murray talked much in his later years with his granddaughter Ann, Basil's elder girl. It was to her he confided the story of the lady on the steamer in 1877 who held his father's ring and then told him things about his father which 'she couldn't possibly have known'.

Murray said to Ann that he had in the end shied away from further psychic experiments as it was attracting cheap publicity and was damaging his work for Greek and Peace. This has the ring of truth.[34]

Murray's final attitude to the mysteries of telepathy was expressed in his Presidential address of 1952 to the Society for Psychical Research:

Our whole range of sensitivity has been so widely increased by our possession of such tools as hands and language. We cannot see like a hawk or track like a dog or hear like a hunted deer; but we can see a Rembrandt picture and feel the thrill of a Beethoven sonata or a great poem. And surely it is noteworthy that just here our sensitivity passes beyond the reason of mere observation into that of feeling; beyond the facts that you observe there is a sense of other things, not fully known, which have value and importance . . . Our faculty of telepathy, such as it is, seems to operate best in just these spheres where our normal instrument, language, either fails or works with difficulty.

CHAPTER XXI

The League of Nations 1920–1924

1. The LN formally constituted Jan. 1920—first Assembly of the LN Nov. 1920—Cecil delegate for South Africa.

2. Second Assembly 1921—Murray also appointed delegate for South Africa—member of Commission I (Amendments to Covenant) and II (Humanitarian)—first speech on minorities—French obstruction of opium control.

3. Murray on personalities.

4. Murray South African delegate to third Assembly 1922—attends fourth Assembly as rapporteur to Commission V (minorities) 1923—British delegate to fifth Assembly 1924—achieves Greco-Bulgar Agreement but it is repudiated by FO.

5. Madariaga contrasts Murray's skill in Committee with Cecil's 'thrusting intolerance'.

1

THE League of Nations was officially born on 10 January 1920. For some time its importance on the international scene was far from clear. The League Council was mainly occupied with setting up its own machinery or with minor political problems. On more important international disputes it had as yet no *locus standi*. The Allied Supreme Council continued to meet in Paris until 1923 and was at first the only body which could deal effectively with the practical problems of post-war reconstruction. In the humanitarian field there was all too much scope for action in 1920. Hundreds of thousands of prisoners had not yet returned home. A typhus epidemic was raging in Eastern Europe and there was widespread starvation. But for the moment immediate steps to meet these needs had to be taken by the Red Cross, the Quakers, and other voluntary bodies. (In this work the Murray family were very much concerned, as is told elsewhere.[1])

An international Secretariat for the League had been set up in the summer of 1919 under the British diplomat Sir Eric Drummond. The Council of the League met ten times in Paris during 1920, but the first Assembly did not meet till November in Geneva. The British official delegates to the Assembly were H. A. L. Fisher (still President of the Board of Education) and the Labour politician George Barnes; but Balfour, who as Foreign Secretary had represented Britain at the Council meeting preceding the Assembly, played an important part. Cecil attended on the invitation of General Smuts, as second delegate for South Africa, and probably to the displeasure of the British Government.

The achievements of the Assembly did not at first sight appear very striking. Much time was spent in defining the limits of its competence *vis-à-vis* the League Council, and in establishing its own rules of procedure; it set up new organizations to deal with Economics and Finance, Transit and Communications, and problems of World Health; it set up its own Mandates Commission, and it initiated the work of special committees to deal with opium and the white slave traffic. It also determined the final text of the Statute of the Permanent Court of International Justice. A resolution in favour of Arms Limitation was not accepted unanimously; and a South African proposal, inspired by Cecil, for the admission of Germany to the League, was easily stalled by the French, who were far from appreciating the 'lofty vein of Anglo-Saxon idealism' which Cecil exhibited at Geneva.[2]

2

General Smuts had been pleased by the success of Cecil as a delegate of South Africa to the first Assembly of the League in 1920. In 1921 he proposed to have Murray too on the South African delegation as an expert adviser, who would be allowed to sit on Assembly committees. Murray accepted gladly, and the weeks spent at Geneva affected deeply his view of the possibilities of the League. He recorded his impressions informally and vividly in diary letters to his wife. Her own letters show that she fully shared his sense of excitement at being engaged in a new and important international adventure.

The first meeting of the second Assembly was on 5 September 1921, following a meeting of the League Council. The Foreign Secretary, Mr Balfour, had been present at the Council, and he briefed the British delegates (including Australians, Canadians, and 'South Africans') before the Assembly began. Murray described its initial meeting in the first of his diary letters:

Beautiful morning. Walked alone to Salle des Victoires; found it easily. Great crowd in the big room; extraordinarily foreign in appearance; great buzzing and noise . . . We are next to Albania, Chili [*sic*] just behind, but Canada within call. An extraordinary sight to see a mild young Chinaman, Wellington Koo, presiding . . . We appointed a Committee to examine credentials, and adjourned till four.

In the afternoon the Dutchman, Karnebeeck, was duly elected as President of the Assembly, as a result of a bargain previously struck by the Council; but not without some heat:

An old eloquent Columbian, Restrepo, who is said to have been drunk and disorderly last year, waxed generally indignant especially because Mr Balfour had proposed Karnebeeck. The Colombian said this was 'imposing on the Assembly' and contrary to the spirit of the ballot.[3]

Murray found that he had been made a member of two of the Commissions of the Assembly: I (Amendments to the Covenant), and V (Humanitarian, including opium, white slaves, minorities, and questions of intellectual co-operation). 'They are not the most interesting', he wrote, 'but I like both . . . '[4] Early in the proceedings Murray had to speak on minorities with particular reference to Turkish oppression of the Armenians. This was his first major speech to the Assembly.

I moved two resolutions (1) that Council should set up a Permanent Commission with power of Inquiry on the spot, to deal with grievances of minorities. I distinguished between old Ottoman Empire, affected by centuries of internecine war, the old problem, and the new problem of highly educated powerful (German) minorities in succession states. No peace until they were satisfied and felt common patriotism for new fatherland. I knew some of the new governments felt this and were doing their best, but difficult and needed our help. AJB had asked me to be polite to the Governments, and I had already determined to be so. Then, (2) that the question of 'National Home for Armenia' be referred to Comm VI [Political]. Austria, Bulgaria and the British Empire applauded me, and oppressed minorities (including Ukrainians) have been dogging my steps ever since. I was far shorter than anybody with anything like so much matter, probably the shortest speech delivered — about ten minutes . . . Oh, I am glad my speech is over. The poor Bulgarian was trembling with excitement when he spoke to me of it afterwards. His people are suffering horrors from the Serbs in Macedonia.[5]

The Macedonians themselves were among those putting their 'most distressing' case to Murray:

They want, poor people, to be constituted a separate state, as they were under Hilmi Pasha, not divided up among Greeks, Serbs, and Bulgars, each of whom persecute the others, while all persecute the Turks and Vlachs. I explained my views to them in French. Their solution would have been the best, but it is now impossible. All we can do is to try to enforce the Minority Protection clauses. These, they say, are a dead letter.[6]

When Murray had spoken in the Assembly, the Albanian representative, Bishop Fan Noli, expressed the special gratitude of his country, saying

that the age of Chivalry was evidently not dead. A curious black-bearded rather wild figure, speaking with genuine emotions. AJB said that he was aiming at the votes of South Africa, getting at me by his literary allusions and at Lord Robert by quoting the Lord's prayer.[7]

The Assembly eventually withdrew Murray's resolution on minorities, when it was understood that the Council had already devised other machinery for protecting them.[8]

Murray's principal tasks were on his two Commissions. The work on Commission I (Amendments to the Covenant) was bedevilled by the opinion of legal experts, not least the British, that Amendments could not be passed except by unanimous vote. Murray described the eventual solution:

At 9.30 meeting in A.J.B.'s rooms on Amendments. Great bewilderment and despair over the language of Art. 26 [of the Covenant]. It does seem clearly to refer only to ratification, leaving the rule of unanimity apparently in force. Some wanted to get a unanimous vote of the Assembly to change the rule; some to apply to the Supreme Court — both risky proceedings . . . AJB wanted to omit all action in the Assembly, and simply get the majority of the states to ratify — a view which shocked the lawyers. A dog of yours [i.e. Murray himself] seems to have hit on the right solution . . . you could get a Recommendation or Voeue [sic] of the Assembly in favour of a particular amendment by a bare majority; then the Council could act on that Voeue. If it was unanimous, it could send a protocol round to the representatives of the states-members, and there you are! Very funny.[9]

In Commission V (Humanitarian) the discussion of the opium traffic was also fraught with procedural difficulties. The object was to constitute the Committee itself as an effective body for supervising the execution of the Hague Convention of 1912. India was the real 'villain of the piece', since it relied on the export of opium for a substantial part of its revenue; but the Indian representative had allies:

All Tuesday afternoon I fought the French and over-threw them bloodily by 22 to 4 . . . A very simple point about the Opium Commission. The Commission wanted to invite the various states to furnish them with any information about the illicit traffic, etc., which they thought would be useful.

I moved this, and Hennessey, the French representative, took one point after another against it; eventually it was that it would encourage spying and delation![10]

The next move was an attempt to reconcile Indian and Chinese interests. It was clear that much opium was being grown in Southern China, where the Central government had little control. Perhaps the Chinese government should employ British Consular agents to convey their representations to the Provincial Governors.[11] Finally Murray could report that he had squared the Chinese, Indians, and French, and could submit a unanimous report on Commission V to the Assembly.[12]

The attitude of the French throughout the session of the Assembly was a major problem for the British delegation as well as for the honorary South Africans, Cecil, and Murray. They were continuously obstructive on points of procedure. There was an interesting difference about tactics between the amateurs and the professionals. Murray wrote of it to his wife:

Dining with AJB last night. I had a long talk with Sir Cecil Hurst (legal adviser to the F.O.) about France. I urged . . . the need of satisfying all France's reasonable anxieties, and then getting her reasonable. Hurst said that no one in the F.O. would agree with me. The French pressed always for all they could get and success only inspired them to demand more. It is their form of devotion to la patrie. And, if baulked in one place, they make themselves disagreeable everywhere. AJB and Fisher are as pro-French as ever they can make themselves; but the effort is great, even for them. Certainly the difference made by the French attitude is enormous. If they are in good humour, business goes through like lightning, and they are most agreeable.[13]

The French contribution to the final debate in the Assembly was reported by Murray in some detail:

I was bored at the sight of [Noblemaire] after an hour of him in the morning, but he soon rivetted my attention. He would explain frankly the feelings of France. She accepted wholly and without reserve the Committee's recommendations. She longed for peace. A young soldier of his [acquaintance] in the war, dying, had tried to send a message to his mother, and could only get out 'Mon Colonel, dites à ma mère, vive la France!' He knew thousands of young Germans had written to their mothers 'Vive l'Allemagne'. France was already disarmed morally, in spirit. But . . . security! France was the gendarme of the Treaty. Germany, they knew, was torn between Republicans and militarists. Till they knew which would win, how could France disarm? However her motto would be for the future: Si vis pacem para Pacem.

It was all beautifully done, as if by a most accomplished actor. And the man seems sincere. Fisher answered him very graciously . . . Bob said the speech was the event of the Assembly, and got Noblemaire to agree that the 'moral disarmament' of Germany could only be brought about by moral means, not by material. So we broke up in a state of enthusiasm . . . my spirits began to sink. For, after all, what had Noblemaire said which would prevent him proposing to keep an army on the Rhine for ever? . . . Mensdorff . . . said the speech might almost have been delivered at a French regimental dinner.[14]

French eloquence on minor matters was a constant delight. To Rosalind Toynbee he recorded a characteristic French argument in favour of the uniform to be worn by the League Secretariat clerks — 'le charme souriant d'une discrète élégance dans l'habillement féminin . . . I now hear that no uniform had ever been suggested. They had invented it in order to get in that last sentence.'[15]

Murray's personal report to Smuts after the Assembly had dissolved was on the whole positive: 'Some intrigue, some loquacity, a rather high proportion of small dark Latin nations.'[16] But it had been extremely impressive as the expression of the common feeling of forty-eight nations. There was openness and co-operation even between the representatives of nations firmly opposed to each other, for example the Albanians and the Serbs. In a lecture to the LNU in London, shortly after his return from Geneva, Murray gave a wider-ranging survey. He emphasized the effect of world public opinion, as expressed in the Assembly, with slightly veiled references to the French retreat from open opposition to procedural obstruction about the white slave traffic. On this as on the opium traffic some progress had been made in publicizing abuses. Another item on the credit side was the repatriation of some 360,000 prisoners of war, largely as the result of Nansen's mission to Russia. However, there were enormous practical problems awaiting solution, and some failures to record in the field of international politics. Little had been done for the Armenians, or to settle the Polish-Lithuanian dispute. The USA still opposed the issue of mandates from the League to powers in charge of dependent territories. Murray concluded his survey by comparing the idealism of the League enthusiasts with that of the reformers in the mid-nineteenth century, who (apparently against great odds) set out to combat the abuses resulting from the Industrial Revolution, and achieved in time such success.

3

For the historian, Murray's vivid impressions of incidents and personalities are no doubt as interesting as his detailed account of procedural manœuvres and his general conclusions. There are little sketches of secondary personalities, like the Chilean representative, 'a beefy choleric man . . . treating all opposition with contempt. Like a tyrannical speech in Thucydides';[17] the French Viviani, part of whose method 'seems to be to make a calculated misstatement in such a rush of words that it may be overlooked';[18] a cheery heavy colonial [Australian] who has asked Lord Bob to come and tell him 'what the L of N is all about';[19] an Italian who 'cannot get an answer from his Government to say whether he has powers or not. Apparently he has forgotten its address!';[20] and the Haitian black who, when deep in conversation with Murray, was suddenly called on to give a vote: 'He stood up bewildered and said "Mais je ne comprends pas . . . qu'est ce qui se fait?" and I whispered to him "Dites Oui". So he said "Oui" in a hesitating voice. It was the admission of Latvia that he was agreeing to.'[21]

There are also fuller sketches. Nansen was universally loved and admired. 'A fine but very long speech from Nansen about the Russian famine: it made a great impression. Bob kept murmuring "I do like that man!" '[22] Balfour received full treatment. In the opening days

AJB dominates the Assembly, easily and without effort. It is very curious, and has to be seen to be believed. It is partly mere charm and unassuming dignity, partly his great prestige, partly a real diplomatic power of making almost anyone do what he wants. It reminds me of what the auto-suggestion people say, that any conflict or effort defeats itself. He makes no effort and is irresistible.[23]

Three days later:

The Assembly was enlivened by a most brilliant speech by AJB. Really one sat marvelling at his skill and mastery. He answered Branting with great politeness and severity. Absolutely wiped the floor with a Serb who had made a shocking speech — still with the same dignity and urbanity; answered Lord Bob very well, and finished by a really eloquent panegyric on the League, in spite of its difficulties and failures.[24]

And at the end of the session:

AJB makes himself loved by all his staff, and by everyone who has to do with him. They treat him as something frail and precious, eagerly saving him from fatigue and worry. All become sad if he looks ill or if he forgets words, as he sometimes does. Indeed it will be an incalculable loss to the

League if he dies or retires. He and Fisher are its only pillars, as far as I can see, inside the Government, and he carries far more weight than Fisher and has more independence and courage.[25]

'As for Cecil [usually 'Bob' in Murray's letters, but 'only for short, I don't call him so'], 'he has an extraordinary position. People are coming to him all day long, and crowding round him at the Assembly. The French actually objected to Motta (a candidate for the Presidency of the Assembly) on the ground that he was under B's influence — as if B were a nation!'[26] Two days later came Cecil's speech on the Annual Report of the Council:

It was much the best thing we have had yet. A long speech divided into four parts, at the end of which he sat down to rest his voice . . . He has a real big voice which he manages well, no rhetoric, and a curious power — rather like Grey's — suggesting responsibility and statesmanship. He had something of an ovation from this very undemonstrative assembly . . . It was most amusing to see how nervous AJB and Fisher were while Bob was speaking. In the end he let them off very easily . . .[27]

In his official and social life Murray enjoyed one advantage over many professional diplomats. As an amateur he did not need to worry over his personal status, and as a character he was probably incapable of doing so. Lady Mary felt that he was being put upon, and made to act as a factotum. He replied:

I do not agree with you that I ought to be like Bob and only take big meetings. I am not really an important person (tho' I get letters here addressed 'for Excellence Lord Gilbert Murray'), and it would be a great mistake to act as if I was. I am quite useful here, but my being here is half a joke and dependent purely on Smuts. What I shall miss most when I come away will be the coffee and rolls.[28]

Murray had indeed discovered a new indication of the pecking order among delegates:

The mark of a great statesman is to be called on while you are dressing. To hold levées, in fact. Bob constantly gives interviews in pyjamas; so does AJB. Fisher is generally dressed early. Of course I, being small, always am. However yesterday Lucien Wolff came with proposals about minorities while I was dressing for dinner.[29]

The round of diplomatic entertainment became increasingly a burden, and indeed Murray had every excuse for being tired. Returning hospitality was also a nightmare. He 'would sooner stand up and face the Assembly', he said, 'than greet my own guests'.[30]

4

Murray attended the three subsequent Assemblies: in 1922 as a delegate of South Africa, in 1923 as a British rapporteur for the Committee on Minorities, and in 1924 as a delegate of the first Labour Government.

The treatment of minorities had been the first obviously political subject with which Murray had had to concern himself at the Assembly of 1921. It continued to occupy him at Geneva over the next three years, and his heart as well as his head was engaged. During the third Assembly in 1922 he received constant letters from a Bulgarian delegate, Mattheev, on the grievances of the Bulgarian minorities in Greece and Yugoslavia; and the behaviour of Yugoslav delegates at Geneva did nothing in Murray's eyes to lessen the probability of Mattheev's charges against the Serbs being true.[31]

During this Assembly, Murray had to act as rapporteur of the fifth Committee on minority questions, and to present recommendations to the Assembly in plenary session. These provided for checks on the observance of the existing minority treaties, for an extension of the principles of these Treaties to all member States, and for the observance of certain principles by the minorities themselves. They were unanimously adopted by the Assembly, but led to no concrete results.

By 1923 the rights of appeal by minorities had been substantially diminished. The League Secretariat had been flooded by a mass of private petitions, and had no means of telling which of these were more than frivolous; at the instance of the Secretariat, the Council ruled that petitions from members of minorities should preferably be received through the governments concerned. Murray pointed out to the fifth Committee the obvious difficulties involved in this procedure. Later he wrote privately to the Secretary-general of the League, Sir Eric Drummond, suggesting that the door had been closed too tightly against the direct submission of memoranda to the Secretariat by private societies and international associations (he was clearly thinking of the comparatively objective findings of, for example, Quaker missions, rather than of individual complaints by members of the minorities concerned). He asked for any guidance which Drummond could give about the line to be taken on this matter by the LNU — a good instance of his attempt to combine the private contacts of the old diplomacy with recourse to the power of public opinion. Murray got a somewhat evasive and naïve answer from one of Drummond's deputies, pointing out that direct petitions from mandated territories and the Saar were not excluded, and that governments forwarding petitions could always explain that they took no responsibility for the contents.[32]

The Assembly of 1924 was the last attended by Murray. In general he took a less prominent part than hitherto, but this time, as a member of the sixth Committee on political questions, he was again concerned with minority problems, particularly with differences between Greece and Bulgaria. Largely as a result of his personal influence, it was agreed between the Greek and Bulgarian representatives that the Mixed Emigration Commission of the League (which had been constituted in 1922 to supervise voluntary emigration between the Macedonian regions of Greece and Bulgaria) should extend its functions and advise about the protection of the relevant minorities in either country. Murray reported this agreement 'with particular pleasure' to the League Council in public session on 19 September 1924. It took the form of simultaneous proposals from the Bulgarian and Greek governments. He was thanked by the Greek delegate as one 'whose generous heart and spirit makes him the protector of all good and just causes'.[33]

Wilson Harris, Geneva correspondent of the *Daily News*, emphasized that this was a great personal success for Murray.[34] The Foreign Office was less enthusiastic when it was realized what had been done. This was essentially a Macedonian problem involving Yugoslavia (Serbia) as well as Bulgaria and Greece. Murray had forgotten this; he had also, it was said, failed to consult Lord Parmoor, the chief British delegate at Geneva, and to inform the Foreign Office. The Greek and Bulgarian delegates had not informed the Yugoslav delegates at Geneva, and the news of the agreement was greeted 'by a storm of indignation at Belgrade'; the essence of the Yugoslav objection was that the Greeks had implicitly recognized their Macedonian minority as being of Bulgarian race, and that this would enable the Bulgarians to claim as fellow-countrymen the Macedonians in Yugoslavia. The news of the Graeco-Bulgarian agreement reached Belgrade shortly before the fall of one government, and its successor immediately denounced the Serbo-Greek Treaty of Alliance. The Greek government itself was the less amused by this in that the Greek delegate at Geneva had failed to inform them of what he had done.

Austen Chamberlain, the new Conservative Foreign Secretary, was presented at his own request with this information, admirably set out in a memorandum by Harold Nicolson, before receiving Murray and others on an LNU deputation early in 1925. Chamberlain accepted the recommendation by Nicolson's seniors that the Graeco-Bulgarian agreement be allowed to die quietly owing to official Greek opposition (the Greek government was informed that Murray had been acting on his own initiative). It is not clear whether he said anything to enforce Sir Eyre Crowe's concluding recommendation that 'in future British delegates are not allowed to act on their own impulsive initiative in this way'.[35] In any case it was a sad ending to Murray's essay in personal diplomacy; the arrangement which he had sponsored was in fact replaced in 1926 by a more official agreement between Greece and Bulgaria.

5

It was easy to highlight and exaggerate the naïvety of high-minded Liberals (or Conservatives) thrust on to the international stage. Salvador de Madariaga wrote a shrewd and amusing sketch of Cecil and Murray, the two incurably high-minded 'civic monks' of the Anglo-Saxon world, feeling their way with some distaste among all the surprisingly foreign foreigners whom they encountered abroad— those over-numerous and eloquent 'small dark people'. Cecil was 'gaunt, powerful, thrusting and intolerant'. He was indeed apt to remark that all foreigners were mad, but Madariaga hardly grasped the self-conscious humour of such very British judgements. Murray by contrast impressed Madariaga by 'a quiet, smiling indrawn strength. His spare figure could seldom be seen moving about . . . and when in motion it would be at a leisurely pace, with an air almost of resignation, and willingness to go through it since it had to be gone through.'[36]

Madariaga implied that both Cecil and Murray were quite unprepared for the foreigners' persistent pursuit of national ends under cover of torrential eloquence about international ideals. This is something of a caricature. In fact Murray, whatever his initial innocence, was not slow to master procedural finesse or to appreciate foreign subtleties. He developed quickly into an effective member or chairman of Committees, not least because of the great trouble he took in mastering the papers, and of the constant courtesy which he showed in discussion. His work on humanitarian matters in the League left him with few illusions about the chances of the international cause when faced by the lively remnants of the national spirit and the old diplomacy. Nor had he many illusions about the part likely to be played by a British Conservative government in relation to the League, much though he admired Balfour. He can more legitimately be charged with over-sanguine expectations about the emergence of an 'Assembly spirit' which could make headway against the separate national interests of governments, and about the power of public opinion within and outside the Assembly to shame governments into modifying their national policies. Here was more faith than reason. However, without some faith it is hard for statesmen and diplomats to keep at their task; Murray was well able to combine instinctive faith with more pessimistic rational calculations, and probably shared to a great extent the sentiment of Cecil, that 'apart from some instinctive optimism, he saw no reason to think we should avoid utter catastrophe.'[37]

CHAPTER XXII

The League of Nations Union 1920–1931: Murray and Cecil

1. Cecil and Murray's views on the role of the LNU — differences of approach.

2. 1920–1922 — Murray's political writings — warnings on reparations — hesitations over the more activist policy urged on the LNU by Cecil.

3. 1922–1923 — the French occupation of the Ruhr played down by Cecil to secure French agreement on disarmament — but Murray supports LNU's pro-German line.

4. 1923 — Murray chairman of LNU — persuades Oxford that his LNU position is compatible with his professorship.

5. 1924 — LNU hopes of first Labour government — Murray's doubts — MacDonald at LN Assembly supports Geneva Protocol and Optional Clause, but Government falls Nov. 1924.

6. Nov. 1924–1929 — Baldwin's Conservative government rejects Geneva Protocol — LNU supports Locarno Pact — Cecil resigns from government in order to push preparations for Disarmament Conference of 1932 — Murray sees campaign will antagonize government and could split LNU — exchange of letters with Austen Chamberlain.

7. 1929–1931 — Second Labour government signs Optional Clause — economic crisis takes over — Murray sees it as priority number one, Cecil eventually concurs.

1

BOTH Cecil and Murray profoundly believed in the important part which the League of Nations Union could play in educating public opinion towards an international outlook. If enough people in Britain wanted an effective League of Nations, such a League would be created. The moment was favourable: the generation which had experienced the war with all its miseries and horrors, would see the need for a new international organization as their sons and grandsons might not. Further there would be no more secret diplomacy: in the post-war era, foreign policy should and would be openly debated — certainly in the League of Nations; hence politicians would have to pay more attention to public opinion, and public opinion must be educated.

It is easy to see with hindsight that Murray and Cecil overestimated the importance of public opinion in the making of foreign policy. Nor did they envisage clearly some of the troubles which the LNU would encounter in its task of attracting wide public interest. Murray talked early in 1920 about the difficulties of inculcating the international outlook in an interesting way;[1] 'Kings and battles' were more colourful than the struggles of good citizens and good peacemakers towards their goals. However, this was a comparatively superficial obstacle. It had been assumed without discussion, when the LNU was set up, that it should be an all-party organization and above inter-party battles. In 1919 it had become clear that it was easier to recruit independent Liberal or Labour supporters for the LNU than Conservatives; and equally clear that the country, like parliament, was in an essentially conservative mood. If the LNU was to retain its Conservative supporters, it had to be cautious in its criticism of the government and take care not to appear to subordinate the interests of the nation to those of an international organization.

But the LNU had little means of bringing its influence to bear. As a non-party or an all-party organization it did not stand for any large bloc of votes, and found it hard to define any but the vaguest policies which appealed to all its members. Governments could make soothing noises, in public and private, about the great importance of the principles of the League and still be very cautious about the measures necessary to implement them. This applied particularly but not only to Conservative governments: Labour governments too did not want to have their detailed policies dictated by the LNU Executive. The practical difficulties arising from those contradictions lay for the most part in the more distant future; but the contradictions were there from the start.

Until 1931 the main concern of the LNU was to secure the peace; its themes — disarmament, collective security, and arbitration. The League of Nations must be the cornerstone on which a lasting peace was to be built — not regional pacts and the old pre-war power policies. But the old Adam survived in nations as in individuals. For the French no disarming without military security: for the Dominions, the British Navy must give priority to its imperial commitments: and the British Service chiefs were mistrustful and cautious. Again and again the same obstacles recur.

Cecil, the visionary, could go bald-headed for his goals: ready to disregard the government of the day in his first enthusiasm: ready—illogically—to ignore public opinion as represented by the LNU: Murray's ear was always nearer the ground: he weighed and counter-weighed, conscious that the LNU could only be effective if held together. This pattern too repeats itself throughout the twenties.

2

It was not easy in 1920 to keep up the morale and add to the membership of the LNU: the League of Nations was only feeling its way and had no significant status as yet: in January the US had rejected the Peace Treaty and refused to join the League. To many men of liberal outlook the prospects for sustained international co-operation seemed very gloomy, especially after the publication in May 1919 of the terms of the Peace Treaty with Germany. Murray was among a group of forty scholars and men of letters who signed a letter, published in the *Daily News* on 24 May, protesting against it.

The terms of the Peace Treaty confirmed the Council of the LNU, particularly David Davies, in their opinion that the main function of the Union would be first to shape public opinion in favour of an effective League of Nations, and then to bring its pressure to bear on a government all too ready to lapse into the traditional errors of pre-war diplomacy.

Thus, if the LNU was to be effective, it must be a mass organization; a strong centre was needed, and flourishing local branches, which would need a steady supply of speakers and printed material. At the beginning of 1919 this was very far from being a reality. The LNU was in fact still a very small organization, having increased its members from 3,217 (the figure at the time of the amalgamation of the LNS with the LFNA) to 3,841. If a transformation was to be effected, a lot of money was required. Davies, who had provided the LNU with its office in Grosvenor Crescent, was willing to put up considerable sums himself, if these were matched by sums collected from other donors or from regular income. In April 1919 he under-took to guarantee an expenditure of £10,000 to cover the expense of a 'whirlwind campaign' to raise £1,000,000 for the LNU.

A special series of matinées of the *Trojan Women* was put on at the Old Vic in October 1919. Sybil Thorndike played Hecuba and the proceeds were devoted to the LNU. It was a prestigious occasion.

The King and Queen consented to be patrons, and members of the royal family attended the opening performance. Sybil Thorndike wrote long afterwards that it 'caught the public mood'.[2] Murray in his 70th birthday speech described how it was interpreted as anti-war and pro-League propaganda. The production was afterwards repeated with success at the Holborn Empire; immediately it raised about £250 for the funds of the LNU (not quite a tenth of the organization's overdraft at the beginning of November 1919).[3]

But fund-raising was not merely a matter of staging Euripides. Cecil, who had taken over the Chairmanship from Murray on his return from Paris in 1919, deputed Murray (now Vice-chairman) to ask Rowntree, Cadbury, and Hugh Bell to guarantee support for the LNU on the same terms as had been agreed by Lord Cowdray — £10,000 a year for five years. At the same time the LNU publicity section was reorganized and the size and price of its monthly journal, *Headway*, were reduced to increase its popular appeal. But essentially, for these early months, the LNU was largely concerned with organizational and financial problems, and was cautious in putting forward its own policies.

Murray's personal contribution to LNU propaganda was considerable. His short book *Problems of Foreign Policy* was published early in 1921, as a general statement in favour of arbitration, conciliation, and disarmament. In it he bitterly attacked Lloyd George for not pursuing a more active pro-League policy after the war and for wasting the great opportunity to exercise for the common international good the power that was his. The *Times Literary Supplement* found that Murray had unfairly ignored not only the practical limitations to which Lloyd George, as a Liberal leader of a largely Conservative coalition, was subject, but also the highly conservative nature of public opinion in the UK at the end of the war: democracies were not always open to reason.[4]

He also published a significant article in the UDC's monthly *Foreign Affairs* in March 1921 warning the government of the dangers likely to ensue when the London Conference on Reparations broke down. Above all the government must avoid giving the impression to the French that we would support any use of force by them to enforce claims which we thought unreasonable. Here is an interesting example of Murray's political foresight, which has to be set against his over-optimistic and idealistic pronouncements in some of his public speeches. Had his warning been heeded, the French might have thought twice about sending troops into the Ruhr in 1923.

In spring 1922 Cecil was also dissatisfied with the Lloyd George coalition and its neglect of the League. He urged that the LNU should no longer wait upon government initiatives, but should define its own policy and put forward some specific objectives. Murray was at first doubtful: it was one thing to express criticisms in his personal writings, another for the LNU to be openly critical of the government of the day. But Cecil, who saw that there would shortly be an election and could look forward to office under a Conservative or a new coalition government, did not mind if the LNU in putting forward its own 'constructive policy' was charged with departing from its role as a non-political pressure group. Cecil had his way and in pamphlet No. 76 the LNU notably broadened its demands. The government, it was said, should formally instruct its representatives that the League was the keystone of its Foreign Policy: it should aim at including Germany, the USSR and the USA in the League. The Prime Minister or Foreign Secretary should attend important meetings of the League Council; and a Minister for League Affairs should be appointed with Cabinet status.

3

The first meeting of the Assembly in November 1920 marked an upward turn in the fortunes of the League and provided the LNU with some material for a pro-League policy. In 1921 the one field in which the LNU took some initiative was on the issue of disarmament. Internationally no progress had been made on a very limited proposal for a reduction of armaments. The subject was one of the utmost importance to Liberal and Labour supporters of the League in the UK. In February 1921 the LNU established its own Arms Limitation Committee: and at the end of 1922, as part of the activist policy instigated by Cecil, the LNU launched a vigorous publicity campaign on disarmament. This led indirectly to a typical crisis within the LNU and to much trouble for Murray.

Cecil, as the principal British representative on the League's Committee dealing with disarmament (the Temporary Mixed Commission or the TMC), was at the centre of negotiations. At the end of 1922 he thought that his emphasis on the provisions for security in parallel with the progress of disarmament was beginning to overcome French objections and allay their fears, and that an agreement was in sight. The Lloyd George coalition had fallen in October and a Conservative government under Bonar Law taken over and hopes were high.

In January 1923 the French sent a large body of troops (mainly Senegalese) into the Ruhr, in order to have in their hands a guarantee for the payment of reparations by Germany. This was a step which outraged many LNU supporters, particularly those in the Liberal and Labour parties. However, Cecil gave priority to his disarmament negotiations. With Murray's reluctant backing, he ensured that the first reaction of the LNU Executive was muted. There was strong opposition to this line. The German sub-committee of the LNU urged from the first that the Council of the League should take official cognizance of French action in the Ruhr, and that the International Court should examine its legality (Cecil professed to think the French case legally arguable, but Murray doubted this). Cecil's guidance prevailed for a time, and the Executive Committee warned LNU branches and speakers of the dangers involved (even for the future of the Ruhr) in antagonizing the French unduly.

Murray, though still only Vice-chairman of the LNU, was more fully occupied with it than Cecil, and saw more clearly the difficulties which this policy was causing for the left-wing members. They were very sensitive to the charge that the League of Nations was nothing but a tool of the victorious powers, and was lending itself to the wicked devices of the old diplomacy. Murray expressed his fears to Cecil early in February 1923. If the LNU continued to be so prudent, it would apear to be engaged in some sort of conspiracy to smother the indignation felt by so many members. Murray cited branch meetings held recently in Dulwich, Ealing, and Oxford. He suggested various means of relieving pressure: at the very least the LNU should put up a strong resolution at a meeting and give the appearance of supporting the deeply held opinion of so many members.[5] However, a crisis within the LNU was not averted. In March 1923 the German sub-committee resigned *en masse* with scathing comment about the Executive's rejection of their plans for a more active policy in favour of Germany.[6]

This action forced a change of line on the Executive Committee — perhaps made easier by Cecil's absence in the USA for the whole of April 1923 — and the Executive produced its own plan early in May. Britain should refer the crisis to the League Council, German territory should be evacuated, and an international commission including American experts should be established to determine the sum of reparations to be paid. Germany should be admitted to the League as a member of the Council, and France and Germany should be guaranteed security under an inclusive treaty for mutual defence.

The substance of the LNU's aims in relation to the Ruhr was largely realized in the next three years but through the Dawes plan, not through the League. However, the episode well illustrates the sort of difficulties which Murray's work at the LNU involved. Some realistic role had to be found for it as a pressure group. It had to tread a delicate course in stimulating or criticizing the government of the day without obviously indulging in party politics. And within the LNU a number of different political outlooks had somehow to be brought into harmony.

4

In May 1923 Bonar Law resigned because of ill health and Baldwin became Prime Minister. Cecil joined the government as Lord Privy Seal, with nominal responsibility for League of Nations questions, but no clear understanding with the Foreign Secretary, Lord Curzon. The immediate result for Murray was a change in his formal position in the LNU. Cecil as a Minister of the Crown could not continue as Chairman of the Executive Committee, and Murray succeeded him as Chairman. This added little to his responsibilities, but had one important result. It brought to a head the question how far he could combine his university with his political activities.

In June 1923, the Vice-chancellor of Oxford, L. R. Farnell, asked him, 'as the very last person who would like to be drawn into a false position', how far his new work at the LNU would be compatible with the position of Regius Professor in Oxford. Would he still be able to exercise his full influence on 'the intellectual life and the practical administration of the cause of learning and the furtherance of Research?' There would be some feeling that, if he accepted the Chairmanship of the LNU, he would be 'finally drifting away'. Murray replied firmly:

I have for four years been Vice-Chairman of the Executive of the L.N.U.; and for various periods have acted as Chairman. This has involved my going to London every Thursday: all the rest of the week, except for alternate Saturdays at the British Museum, I have been teaching at Oxford [this can only refer to 'full term', about half the calendar year].

He cited an impressive list of lectures, pupils, and publications, and one resignation (from the Council of Somerville):

It seems now to be almost necessary for me to take on the Chairmanship of the Union, at any rate for a transitional period, and this will involve certainly some extra responsibility and some slight additional call upon my time . . .

I care more for teaching Greek than for any other pursuit in life, and I mean to go on teaching Greek. Also I am inclined to think that the cause of Greek throughout the country would suffer rather than gain by my resignation.

At the same time Murray recognized implicitly that there was a case for criticism. He proposed that up to half his annual stipend should be docked over the next five years, to enable the university to appoint an additional Reader in Greek, and thus make up for his own absences from Oxford. Farnell professed himself much moved, and very glad that Murray felt he could combine his public duties with his professorship. Murray's financial offer was welcomed as a generous and appropriate gesture and partially accepted; it resulted in the appointment of a brilliant young scholar, Edgar Lobel, to a new readership.

Murray clearly acted in perfectly good faith, and, given his powers of work and acute sense of public duty, it may well be argued that any other decision would have been out of character. As he himself hinted, his prestige as a scholar was an asset to the university and to the cause of Greek scholarship. This was his first and continuing love. His most lasting classical work had indeed been done by 1914, but down to his resignation as Professor in 1936, he continued to produce copiously his own kind of writings on Greek literature — probably he could not in any circumstances have written anything of a different kind, more intensely scholarly and less broadly literary. Murray's influence as a teacher is harder to assess, but there is much evidence that it remained considerable. None the less one may remain doubtful about the wisdom of his decision to combine so much work for the League of Nations with his activities as Professor. He drove himself hard in order to do so, and was far from shirking any obvious duty in either sphere; but even his well-organized and capacious mind could hardly have the breathing-space for the sort of subconscious meditation on his subjects which for most people is essential for the production of their best work.

5

In January 1924 the first Labour government in Britain took office under Ramsay MacDonald. The LNU had good reason to hope that it would give favourable consideration to the cause of disarmament. However, Murray had personal reasons for doubting whether co-operation with Ramsay MacDonald would be easy. Soon after becoming Chairman of the LNU Executive, he had asked MacDonald as leader of the Labour Party to be one of the Honorary Presidents of the LNU — a purely decorative post, to balance the Honorary Presidentships held by the other Parties. MacDonald had refused in a peevish letter.

The invitation was renewed after MacDonald had become Prime Minister, but again refused through his private secretary, who quoted his chief as saying that the action of the LNU had constituted a 'gross personal insult'. Murray replied firmly and with dignity, claiming that he had no idea what the insult might have been:

I cannot refrain from adding that I should have thought that a friendship of nearly thirty years would have given me a claim to some frank and definite statement from Mr. MacDonald as to how I or a Society for whose actions I was largely responsible had given cause for complaint . . . I need not add, of course, I continue to support the government's foreign policy, and that I deeply regret this personal misunderstanding with its leader.

Murray probably underestimated the lasting effect on MacDonald of the difference which had arisen between them on the outbreak of war in 1914, and the bitterness felt by MacDonald about the persecutions which he had then suffered. Lady Mary felt mortified by MacDonald's attitude, and Murray regarded it as certain that he himself would not be among the British official representatives to the fifth Assembly of the League in August 1924.[7] However, he was appointed, though he had to attend mainly to the affairs of the Committee for Intellectual Co-operation. He found the Prime Minister's behaviour towards him 'civil but not exactly friendly'.

By this time there were more substantial reasons for disillusion within the LNU about the Labour government's attitude to the League. In summer 1924 they turned down the draft Treaty of Military Assistance proposed by the League's Disarmament Committee (the TMC). Lord Parmoor, speaking in the House of Lords, stated that the Dominions were reluctant to accept the obligations for collective defence in which the Treaty might involve them and that its emphasis on the possible use of force would lessen the possibility of the USA joining the League; an argument readily accepted by Conservatives and Liberals. Murray wrote an article for the weekly *Westminster*, referring to the legal firm of Spenlow and Jorkins in Dickens's *David Copperfield*. For Murray the USA had become the 'Great Jorkins of the West', who forbade the British government to do anything which it disliked itself. Here, he suggested, was a fine example of the 'unconscious mythopoeic faculty of the libido (our clumsy forefathers merely used to say that "the wish is father to the thought").'

Murray was one of those who signed a letter to the Prime Minister pointing out that Britain's rejection of the Treaty might be regarded as opposition to the principle of linking security arrangements with disarmament and as an attempt to lessen the responsibilities of the League.

MacDonald rendered his best service to the League by attending the fifth Assembly in August 1924, the first British Foreign Minister and the only Prime Minister to do so. There he supported the Geneva Protocol, which pledged member states to accept arbitration in international disputes and to disarm. In the event of unprovoked aggression, the signatories were to come to the aid of the injured party and be prepared to use sanctions. But in the end a number of governments, including the British, would not accept such a sweeping proposal without modification, and it was agreed that the Permanent Court of International Justice at the Hague should only adjudicate between States which had accepted a further special clause empowering it to do so. This was the 'Optional Clause' which was rejected by the Conservatives in 1925 but eventually signed by the Labour government in 1929. The objections of the British rested essentially on a dislike of absolute commitments which might cause successor governments embarrassment. Murray caricatured this attitude in the suggestion that British governments welcomed arbitration with stronger powers when they were sure of the validity of their case, but if their case was doubtful and related to a weaker power, it would be provident to reserve the right to go to war.

Cecil agreed with the Conservative view that the Protocol laid far too much stress on arbitration, but the LNU welcomed it as 'a great advance towards permanent peace', and it urged the government to form a special committee representing all sections of British and Dominion opinion to examine and endorse the Protocol proposal.

Murray as usual wrote copiously to the press, emphasizing that British obligations under the Protocol were no greater than under Article 16 of the Covenant.[8] He had good reason to dwell on this point. As a member of the British delegation to Geneva, he had been present at meetings of the British Empire delegates, and had heard the fears expressed by the New Zealand representatives in particular about the possibility that the Royal Navy might be diverted from its role as protector of the British Empire into helping to protect the *status quo* in Europe. It was the Conservatives who were most alive to such considerations, but the LNU was an all-party body, and within it there were growing doubts about many aspects of the Protocol. It was a foregone conclusion that the new Conservative government which took office at the end of 1924 would reject the Protocol. It duly did so in March 1925, when the new Foreign Secretary, Austen Chamberlain, criticized its emphasis on sanctions.[9]

The Labour government's brief spell in office had failed to realize the hopes of the LNU. Murray in 1924 could only write that 'a few faint beginnings had been made towards establishing the rule of law; the greatest service of the League hitherto had been to organize the forces of *Aidos* (the shame a man feels for himself) and *Nemesis* (the hostile feelings of others towards him as the natural result of his bad actions).'

6

Chamberlain's rejection of the Protocol was not simply a negative gesture. It was combined with proposals, made in the light of German approaches, for mutual guarantees of security between France and Germany with Britain and Italy as guarantors (proposals which eventually took shape in the Locarno Pact of 1925). This looked like by-passing the League, abandoning the concept of collective defence (and with it the coercive clauses of the Covenant), and returning to something like the nineteenth-century concert of Great Powers.

Murray as Chairman of the LNU Executive had a difficult course to steer. Cecil was again a Minister, he had at least to make the best of Chamberlain's ideas, and did not much like the Protocol in any case. On the other hand the Labour rank and file of the LNU still regarded arrangements for compulsory arbitration as a first priority. Thus as a matter of internal LNU politics, Murray had to keep up some pressure on the government for amending the Protocol. On the other hand it would be absurd in practice to deny the virtue of the Locarno proposals which would reconcile France and Germany and result in the admission of Germany to the League, and the limited arrangements proposed by Chamberlain could be regarded as a first step. So the LNU Executive was able officially to welcome the conclusion of the Locarno Pact, and particularly the statement that once the treaties were in force, disarmament could proceed under the Covenant. Murray himself took the same line to the press.[10] Harmony was preserved on the surface between the Conservative government (including Cecil) and the LNU; but this surface hardly concealed tensions within the government, within the LNU, and between the government and the LNU.

Germany was admitted to the League of Nations in September 1926, the Locarno Pact entered into force and it could still be regarded as the springboard for further achievements. Reparations were proceeding smoothly under the Dawes plan. The most urgent problems of the post-war period seemed to have been solved. There was widespread euphoria. 'As far as human foresight can divine', there would never again be war between France and Germany, Murray said in a speech in Boston before leaving the USA in December 1926. The League was no longer an alliance, but a new way of life. An important symbol of this was the development of the Hague Court of Justice into the Permanent Court of International Justice. Murray was careful to emphasize that its decisions were not enforceable by war.[11] But on 6 September Murray had given Rosalind his private view of the pact:

The Pact is excellent between France and Germany, but a miserable thing as a piece of British policy. We make no agreement for peace whatever, but merely bind ourselves to fight — if France and Germany ever do. The silliest way out of the difficulty that one could devise.

By 1926 the LNU numbered over 600,000 members, and Cecil, its most influential spokesman, was still in the government: but not for long. The League set up a preparatory commission for the future Disarmament Conference. Cecil was appointed to it, but he found it an ineffective body when faced with objections by the French government and the British Service advisers. He resigned from Baldwin's government on 9 August 1927, saying that he now felt bound to see whether he could do more outside the government than in it for the cause of disarmament.[12] He 'felt that most Conservative politicians . . . not only rejected in their hearts the League of Nations, but they did not propose to take any step for getting rid of war.'[13] He refused Murray's offer to resign the Chairmanship of the LNU, and threw himself into an all-out campaign for disarmament, with Murray's whole-hearted support.

This soon began to cause difficulties among the Conservative supporters of the LNU, not least within the Headquarters staff. Murray was acutely aware of these developments and soon realized that the campaign would split the LNU before it had much effect on the government. Cecil was temporarily undeterred. He wrote to Murray at the end of October and pronounced it (with marked understatement) 'not at all unlikely that we shall have to take up a more or less hostile attitude to the Government.' He argued further that, whatever the results for the LNU of pursuing the campaign, the effect of dropping it would be worse. By the end of 1927 the LNU was, in spite of Murray's efforts to neutralize the situation, open to the charge that it was becoming an instrument of the Liberal party. At the LNU General Council in December, Cecil had to retreat and declare that he had never intended to harm the government by the Disarmament campaign.[14]

Murray in the mean time was engaged in an exchange of letters with Austen Chamberlain, who wrote to him on 31 December 1927 accusing the LNU Executive of party bias against the Conservatives. The ensuing interchange of arguments is important. Murray first assured Chamberlain of his own unceasing efforts on the Executive 'to prevent the Union taking sides in party politics'. He had tried his best, and this, he said, would be confirmed by Conservative members of the Executive—Lady Selborne, Major J. W. Hills, and Duff Cooper among others. More important was the duty of the LNU as a whole under its Royal Charter of 1925 to induce people to understand and support the League. 'Our object is education, not propaganda' but an educational body must have the right to criticize a government from which it differed. 'Is there not a very distinct line between criticism and attack? In fact, if we are not to criticize, what good are we? We should be confined to support the government of the day, whatever it was, and however much we disagreed with it.' That Liberals greatly outnumbered Conservatives within the LNU was a fact that Murray regretted as much as Chamberlain; but it was due to another undoubted fact, that at branch level it was Liberals who were much more interested than Conservatives in League affairs. In reply Chamberlain renewed his charges of bias, against *Headway* in particular, and proceeded to expound his own ideas of what should be the limits to the LNU's activity. Surely the LNU ought to be satisfied if the government based its whole foreign policy upon the League without trying to prescribe a particular scheme such as the Protocol.

Without backing down completely on such issues as disarmament the LNU came to exercise great care. *Headway*, however, proclaimed its independent position. How long would it have taken to abolish slavery if Wilberforce and Clarkson had thrown up the sponge because the government was against them?[15] But, Cecil wrote later, constant vigilance was exercised to prevent the LNU becoming an electoral ally of the opposition, and to mitigate the suspicions of the Conservative Central Office; he professed himself 'amazed at our moderation'.[16] And the result was that in 1928 the LNU's great campaign for disarmament, started in autumn 1927, petered out, though it flickered back into life towards the end of the year and a further campaign was launched in 1930–1.

Meanwhile in 1927, the French Foreign Minister, Briand, had proposed a treaty between France and the USA outlawing war; and in spring 1928 the so-called Kellogg Pact (named after the US Secretary of State) was put forward for signature by all countries. Signatories were to denounce war as an instrument of international policy and to undertake to settle their differences only by pacific means. No sanctions were proposed for breaches of undertakings under the pact, and the task of 'harmonization' with the Covenant was left to one side. Thus the Kellogg Pact did not in itself seem to be of much substance. However, it was very important as linking the USA with the question of security in Europe. And the attempts of the British and French governments to attach conditions appeared to be niggling. Here, therefore, was an opportunity for the LNU to fight for a cause which involved some movement forward without being obviously likely to split their membership. They therefore supported the Kellogg proposals, and the Pact was eventually signed by all countries in August 1928.

Though Murray openly criticized the government for their hesitation over the proposals, he was also much concerned with the tendency of British newspapers and their readers to rely for security on the 'outlawing' of war. He continued to write frequently to the Press, arguing that the Pact represented an extension not a contradiction of our obligations to the League and did not remove the necessity of other steps to promote the aims of arbitration, security, and disarmament. He strongly defended the LNU's revived advocacy of the Optional Clause on arbitration.[17]

His private criticism of Chamberlain for his caution with regard to the Pact, and for his attempts in summer 1928 to reach a bilateral naval agreement with the French, was more trenchant; he was 'furious' about government reservations, and thought that it was 'mad' to curry favour with the French.[18]

7

When the second Labour government under MacDonald took office in June 1929, the LNU looked forward to a change of British policy towards the League. At the tenth Assembly of the League that year, MacDonald announced that Britain would sign the 'Optional Clause' committing Britain to accept the arbitration of the Permanent Court of International Justice. Henderson, the new Foreign Secretary, who was very much his own man, held him to his commitment against some pressure from the Dominions. Henderson took seriously the problems of Disarmament. In January 1930 a Five Power Conference (UK, USA, France, Italy, and Japan) met in London and a new tripartite naval agreement was in fact reached between the UK, the USA, and Japan limiting their cruisers, destroyers, and submarines to the old Washington ratio of 1921 (5:5:3). The LNU professed disappointment at this result—they had hoped for the abolition of submarines and a ban (rather than a 'holiday') on the construction of ships over 10,000 tons.[19]

But MacDonald himself and others on the government side realized there was a new dimension to the disarmament problem. Too much zeal on the British side could too easily be interpreted by now as a sign of Britain's growing economic weakness.[20] The world economic recession was beginning to bite. In these circumstances Murray wanted to make international economic co-operation the main aim of LNU activity, rather than launch another campaign for disarmament. In the *Nation* (12 May 1930), he dwelt on the dangers of an isolationist policy. This was in the context of Briand's proposals for a European Federal Union. Murray and the LNU were generally mistrustful of these—the French, he thought, were aiming at an organization parallel to and independent of the League, and it was important that the British government should reply to them through the Assembly of the League.[21] But the French proposals might be used to further economic co-operation. Arthur Salter wrote to Murray emphasizing the importance to the UK of being associated early with any new European organization, if this were not to become 'inward-turned'.[22] His words fell upon willing ears. Murray was a stout Liberal on matters of trade. Even campaigns to 'Buy British' mildly irritated him. He wrote to the *Manchester Guardian* in September 1925:

Whenever I write to a friend abroad, the Postmaster General gets hold of the envelope and stamps on it the statement 'British Goods are best'. This remark is in the first place gratuitous, irrelevant, and often untrue, and in the second place is calculated to irritate any foreign correspondents. I cannot remember who the Postmaster General is, and I can believe that he is a dangerously eccentric and tyrannical person whom his colleagues will hesitate to interfere with; but surely there must be some legal method of restraining him from this sort of meddling with private correspondence . . .[23]

In 1930 he was more seriously concerned with the movement towards Empire Free Trade, which bore fruit later in the Ottawa

Agreements. He congratulated Baldwin on speaking out against
attempted dictation by the 'newspaper lords' on the 'coming controversy about tariffs' and supplied an apposite reminiscence:

> I was sitting with Mr. Asquith in his study, when a message came from
> Lord Beaverbrook offering the support of all his newspapers on certain
> conditions. Mr. Asquith refused to see the emissary, but when pressed for
> an answer, said curtly 'Tell him I will give him half-a-crown for the lot',
> and resumed a discussion of Jane Austen.

Murray proceeded to reiterate the LNU's adherence to the principles
of the World Economic Conference of May 1927 — support for
lower, more stable, and more uniform tariff barriers, rather than
absolute free trade — and to warn Baldwin that the LNU would
be bound to fight on the Free Trade side if it came to a political
choice.[24]

To Cecil he pressed the case for new priorities in the LNU's
publicity work, and for a big LNU campaign on international
economic co-operation. 'I cannot help feeling more and more the
message of all others which we ought to preach at present is that
an Isolationist policy in economics is anti-League and suicidal.'[25]
But Cecil, though himself a champion of Free Trade, was acutely
aware as a Conservative of the dangers of making propaganda for
a 'League of Nations economic policy'. Besides, with his usual
optimism, he had 'great hopes of a draft Disarmament Treaty by
Christmas.'[26] So Cecil decided that disarmament should remain
target number one for the LNU.

The LNU campaigned for disarmament until the opening of the
World Disarmament Conference in February 1932. However, at
the end of summer 1931, before the final preparations for the
Conference, the British public was interested almost exclusively
in the economic crisis, the formation of the National Government
under MacDonald, the new national economy campaign and the
abandonment of the gold standard. Murray had been justified in
thinking that the international economic crisis was of more importance
than disarmament to the world, and even Cecil was now ready to
recognize this. But there was little that the LNU could do about it,
given that, in Cecil's probably not much exaggerated view, the
National Government 'has not the faintest inkling that the crisis is
an international one.'[27] Seen with the hindsight of over fifty years
on, the crisis of autumn of 1931 was the herald of an 'iron age'.
Neither Murray nor the professional statesmen of the time could
foresee the rapidity of its onset.

CHAPTER XXIII

The Oxford Professorship 1923–1936

1. Writings on classical subjects—Harvard lectures of 1926 published as *The Classical Tradition in Poetry* (1927)—last exchanges with Wilamowitz.
2. Publication of *Aristophanes* 1933—correspondence with scholars—possibility of becoming Warden of New College—Murray's later views on Oxford.
3. Murray co-operates with Fraenkel on new Aeschylus text—text coolly received.
4. Drama—translations and performances.
5. Retires as Professor 1936—embarrassments over the successor—seventieth birthday.

1

MURRAY'S international work was not entirely unrelated to his activities as Regius Professor of Greek at Oxford. His contacts at Geneva probably enabled him to renew relations earlier than would otherwise have been possible with German and Austrian classical scholars; Ludwig Radermacher, for example, was introduced to him as the result of Lady Mary's and Agnes's activities in Vienna.[1] Some of his personal work at the CIC related directly to classical subjects. In 1925 he was able to prepare for an international conference at Oxford suggestions for the organization of the bibliography of classical Antiquity,[2] and for over a year he was engaged in fruitless committee discussions at the CIC about the possibility of dividing bibliographical work by subject between those countries with the most active traditions of classical scholarship.[3] However, these were exceptional occasions. By and large his classical and his international work were strictly separate.

Murray's output in the field of classical scholarship down to the time of his retirement from his Chair (1936) was to a considerable extent a revision of his former books, or an obvious extension of these. In 1926 the original publishers of the *History of Ancient Greek Literature*, Heinemann—stimulated by enquiries from the Oxford University Press—suggested a revised edition of Murray's first book. Murray replied that he would prefer to write a new book, 'Second Thoughts on Greek Literature', but he did not find time either for revision or for reworking until much later in life.[4]

The Rise of the Greek Epic continued to be in demand among scholars; Maurice Bowra was among those who acknowledged a great debt to Murray's work on Homer.[5] The third edition issued in 1924 cost Murray a good deal of work. At a considerable distance of time he could look at the book with some objectivity, and recognized that it suffered from being 'partly extreme specialism and partly belles lettres.'[6]

More radical revision was needed for the transformation of *Four Stages of Greek Religion* to its final form of *Five Stages* (by the addition of what is now Chapter III on 'The Great Schools'). This work was also undertaken in 1924. 'It strikes me as a good book', Murray wrote to Rosalind Toynbee,[7] 'but the addition won't be up to sample.' It was the occasion of some correspondence with E. R. Dodds, who supplied some detailed comments at Murray's request. His general verdict remained favourable, and he was impressed by Murray's 'power of imaginative understanding and putting real life into the dry bones of documents'.[8]

An extension of the *Five Stages* was Murray's work for a symposium, *The History of Christianity in the Light of Modern Knowledge*, published by Blackie and Co. in 1929. For this Murray contributed a chapter on Greek philosophy and thought, in which he stressed the continuity of Christian thought and worship with various Greek traditions, and the social and political setting which favoured the rise of Christianity. His standard agnostic thesis involved him in an interesting correspondence with E. R. Bevan, who had also contributed a chapter (on Mystery Religions) to the Blackie symposium; he argued against Murray's derivation of the Christian Communion service by continuous descent from a primitive rite of ὠμοφαγία (eating the raw flesh of a sacrificial victim), and for the unique nature of the Christian story of God's coming down among men.[9]

A comparatively new work was published in 1927. This resulted from an invitation to Murray from A. L. Lowell, President of Harvard, to be the holder of a Chair of Poetry founded in memory of Charles Eliot Norton, Professor of Poetry at Harvard. Murray was first invited in May 1925 to deliver the lectures in the following autumn, but he asked whether in view of his existing engagements the date could be postponed for a year.[10] Agreement was reached on the autumn of 1926; in April 1926 the title of the series had been announced as *The Classical Tradition in Poetry*. There were to be eight lectures, on Tradition, the Molpê (or chant), Metre, Poetic

Diction, Architecture (this title was later changed to Unity and Organic Construction), the Heroic Age, Hamlet and Orestes (a repetition, with minor revisions, of Murray's address to the British Academy in 1914), and Conclusion.[11]

The lectures were published under the same general title in 1927. In his introductory words to the series, Murray spoke of Norton in terms which could easily be applied to himself:

Distinguished, critical, courteous and a little aloof, breathing an atmosphere of serenity and depth of thought, he possessed to an exquisite degree the taste that is rightly called classic; that is, his interest lay, not in the things that attract attention or exercise charm at a particular place and moment, but in those that outlive the changes of taste and fashion.

In the end the subject of Murray's lecture and book was not Greek poetry but poetry 'as it has manifested itself . . . in the long line of tradition which begins with some nameless predecessor of Homer . . . and reaches to the verses in to-day's newspaper.'[12]

The Classical Tradition in Poetry is not an easy book to classify. There is much in it, of course, about Greek poetry, but little that was new. When writing on poetry generally Murray admitted himself to be an amateur and it is improbable that experts on English literature would turn later to Murray's lectures, though Helen Gardner remembered listening to them, when first delivered in England, with devoted attention.

The lectures as delivered by Murray were no doubt brilliant and compelling. The book is less than this. It illustrates not only the range of Murray's mind, and the intensity of his sympathies, but also what seem to a later generation the strange limitations of both. He mentions and quotes a large number of poets, ancient and modern, French and German as well as Greek, Latin, and English, but few outside his chosen three, Shelley, Tennyson, and Swinburne, are quoted with deep sympathy. Shakespeare was less than a favourite with him, Chaucer was at the least a seldom-opened book. Moreover the old agnosticism could still blind him. As has earlier been noted, he seems never to have read the religious poets of the seventeenth century and can write that 'in the sphere of pure imagination, where an enthusiasm for Christian principles involves no disagreeable practical results whatever, Christianity has had . . . little effect.'[13]

None the less, the argument of *The Classical Tradition in Poetry*, however wide open to criticism by specialists either in the Greek and Latin classics or in English literature, must be grasped as illustrating an important and permanent part of Murray's thinking; his convictions that a good scholar had to have the sympathies of a poet and that the great poets had been, if not preachers of the good, at least concerned with the great and eternal issues of life. It remains not so much a contribution to scholarship as the expression of a highly personal view of the place of poetry and scholarship in the world, an extension of the arguments of Murray's Oxford Inaugural Lecture and of his later *Religio Grammatici* (1918).

Predictably, critical reaction to the *Classical Tradition* was at best lukewarm. There were sharp comments in the *Times Literary Supplement* and the *Classical Review* to which Murray was with difficulty restrained from replying.[14] Indeed in an age of increasing scholarly specialization, Murray's published work as a whole had a waning influence among his learned colleagues. He did not let himself be diverted from his own conception of his duty as a teacher, and there were still kindred spirits. To J. T. Sheppard at Cambridge he wrote in 1927:

. . . it gives me a very real and permanent pleasure to see how you are carrying on the tradition of teaching the classics as live literature. It seems to me that as the Classics are disappearing from general education, they are also losing their character as an element in general culture, and becoming more and more a specialist's study. I can only hope that if we row hard against the stream for a generation or two the current may change.[15]

Rather later he wrote even more explicitly to Sheppard: 'You and I belong to the same main current in Greek scholarship, working not so much to make new discoveries in obscure places, as to keep the great things really alive.'[16]

The death of Wilamowitz in 1929 may be taken as marking the end of an era in classical scholarship—the era to which Murray as a scholar belonged. Wilamowitz was from the first Murray's hero; a greater master than Murray of many technical details of scholarship, he also believed in the need to preserve Hellenic values, to make Greek literature available to a wide public, and to exercise poetic imagination in doing so. He would have approved of the terms in which T. R. Glover, Orator of Cambridge University, described Murray, when presenting him for an Honorary Doctorate at Cambridge in summer 1927:

You are aware of what this man's name means to all in this country and to all who speak our tongue throughout the world, of how he teaches us to live and feel humanely and to serve the common republic of all men and all nations. I present to you Gilbert Murray, poet.[17]

It was a matter of satisfaction to Murray that his last contacts with Wilamowitz were friendly. Murray made contact with him through A. C. Clark of Oxford, in 1923, and offered to send some books;[18] but Wilamowitz, in his *Memoirs* published early in 1929, wrote that Murray had displayed some coolness to him after the war. There was then a final exchange of letters, of which only Wilamowitz's survive. He wrote first to thank Murray for his contribution to a subscription to secure the publication of his collected works. The approach of death, he said, made him ponder on the immortality of knowledge, and nothing could be more pleasant than to know that, in meeting some demand of the day, he had been able to transmit his knowledge beyond the limits of his own life. The last letter was more personal. Murray had written to *The Times* on reading Wilamowitz's *Memoirs* that there had never been any intentional coolness on his side. He probably wrote in the same sense personally to Wilamowitz, who replied:

My wife said that your letter was 'the best reward that your Memoirs could bring you'. It is now of only secondary importance if the short time remaining to me passes without any further contact between us. I know you have not turned away from me, that you continue to work with a noble purpose, and my loyal friendship will be with you everywhere.[19]

In one respect Wilamowitz was lucky to die when he did. As Murray remarked to one of his faithful correspondents on the staff of Winchester, the great scholar did not live to see his dream of a renewed and powerful Germany realized as the nightmare of Nazism.

2

Murray continued to produce a considerable quantity of lectures and articles, and to refuse requests for many more. Meanwhile he found it hard to settle down to work on any major project. This is hardly surprising in the light of his preoccupation with the LNU, the CIC and the normal details of a Professorial job. In 1930 he was still wondering what book to undertake next—Homer, in a popular series on Greek Poets; 'Second Thoughts on Greek Literature'; a new text of Aeschylus 'just crying out to be done'; or a commentary on the *Agamemnon*?[20]

Murray's next classical book was his study of Aristophanes, published in 1933. It is not a major work of scholarship (the preface opens, 'There is little or no research in the book'); again, like the *Classical Tradition in Poetry* it may be regarded as more important for the intellectual biography of Murray than for the scholarly study of Aristophanes. The contemporary poetical context of Murray's book is made clear by the dedication to Shaw, 'lover of ideas and hater of cruelty, who has filled many lands with laughter and whose courage has never failed' (alas, Shaw's sense of realities was about to fail in face of the Stalinist and Nazi regimes), and above all by the preface. Murray confesses that he has been moved to write his study by the inadequacy of accepted accounts of Aristophanes, 'and notably with the chapter upon him in my own *Ancient Greek Literature* . . . It is only late in life that I have learnt to care for Aristophanes and, I hope, to understand him.'

Murray's preface merits further quotation, which may serve as a description of the book in the context of his own life. He is concerned to efface three current impressions of Aristophanes, a figure so vividly alive in his works that he attracts current catchwords. He is no 'Tory journalist'. If he 'disliked the ascendancy of the mob as heartily as the *Morning Post*, he hated militarism and cruelty as much as the *Manchester Guardian*.' Then those who are offended (or, the Author might have added, delighted) by the 'frequent indecency' of his language have failed to take account of the ritual conventions of Greek comedy. Aristophanes is no 'loud fellow in a public bar, who may be funny but has no manners.' Again many critics, perhaps interpreting Aristophanes as the originator of the European tradition of cruel political satire, credit him 'with a grim and conscientious hatred of all the things he laughs at—notably such objects as Euripides, Socrates, and women. My own view is that we must distinguish, and that the distinction is not difficult, for when Aristophanes does hate a thing, he takes some pains to let us know it.'

Murray proceeds to give his own general impression of his subject. 'I see him devoted to three great subjects, Peace, Poetry and philosophic criticism of life. He laughs, and cannot help laughing, about all of them, except indeed sometimes about the first; for the loss of Peace means ultimately the subjection of all life to the reign of brute force and that, even to the Prince of Comedy, is too ghastly a thing for laughter.' From this the general reader can form an adequate idea of Murray's Aristophanes, a character which certainly does not command complete credibility, though it would be facile to dismiss it as a disguised self-portrait.

In the early thirties Murray's most useful work in the classical field was probably his correspondence with other scholars. Dodds, Pickard-Cambridge, and Sheppard have already been mentioned. He continued to help A. S. Hunt, as before 1914, in establishing the text of newly-discovered papyrus fragments.[21] Bowra, writing about his *Tradition and Design in the Iliad*, could say that, in spite of their differences, 'it is from your books and lectures that I begin and end.'[22] More striking than these are the exchanges with the brilliant young Denys Page, who was setting out in 1930 for a year of research in Vienna, and wrote at length to Murray about the relations between Euripides' *Iphigenia in Aulis* and the new comedy of Menander. Murray replied also in detail, reminding Page that our text of Euripides has to be treated with care in this context, representing in all probability the play as it was acted or read in Alexandrian times, and not as it was performed originally in Athens.[23] He was always ready too to comment on classical literature outside his own particular field, as when he gave John Sparrow his views about the half-lines of Vergil;[24] or outside professional academic circles, as in an interesting answer to Edward Lyttelton's enquiry whether the Greeks considered humility a virtue (in Murray's view, yes).[25]

This was for Murray far the most rewarding side of academic life. He still missed the contact with undergraduate pupils which he had enjoyed some twenty years before at New College, before he became Professor; and, so far as he was a 'college man' at all, he belonged as much to New College or Balliol as to Christ Church. Indeed one of the few mentions of Christ Church in his correspondence is a resolve, noted in a letter to Lady Mary, to dine in college on Fridays, when he could invite as guests undergraduates from other colleges.[26]

If it had not been for his League of Nations work, Murray might at this stage have preferred being Head of a College to being a Professor; he would have had, no doubt, as much administrative work, but more of the human contacts at which he excelled. The opportunity arose in 1924—the year in which his friend Sandy Lindsay was appointed Master of Balliol after a good deal of internal controversy.[27] Warden Spooner of New College was due to retire in May 1924; and Julian Huxley sounded Murray about the possibility of his standing for the vacancy, meeting with a provisional refusal. Murray reported this to Lady Mary, adding details which suggested that Fisher was the established candidate, and that it now was financially possible for Fisher to take the post. Lady Mary was tempted—'we would make nice Wardens and work well with Sandie at Balliol'—and Huxley pressed his case in a letter; Murray, he wrote, had said that his refusal was not necessarily final, and that he might be giving up his League of Nations work. This time the reply was definite, and Lady Mary could only say with regret that she would have liked him at a previous stage to have the Wardenship, but that now it was clearly out of the question.[28]

Murray's attitude was rather ambiguous towards Oxford in the last years of his career there. For teaching and research, he would probably have echoed throughout his life his own judgement of 1893 that it was 'the only place'; but he found the prevailing tone of classical scholarship unimaginative. There was an interesting exchange between him and A. S. L. Farquharson, who tried to interest him in getting the University to honour Jane Harrison on her retirement from Cambridge in 1927. Murray replied in resigned terms. He had made an effort long ago, but 'came up against a solid body of prejudice . . . I doubt if there is much to be done now.'[29]

The later years of Murray's professorship were not darkened by any controversy such as that which had raged about the abolition of compulsory Greek. Oxford in his eyes remained too conservative, not only in its political ways. However, he had learnt to be more understanding. His own college, Christ Church, he described as 'not half so bad . . . as people make out. It is so safe in its conservative and aristocratic and clerical tradition that it can afford to be surprisingly open-minded and tolerant.'[30] He gave a balanced verdict in a letter to Isobel Henderson, who consulted him in 1930 about whether to put in for a fellowship at Somerville:

I see your difficulty. Oxford is narrow, provincial, stick-in-the-mud. Also a woman as gifted as you ought to have the society of a lot of interesting men, with wide outlook and experience. Undergraduates are too young and silly, and dons wither fast—or fatten, which is worse. On the other hand, Oxford only suffers in this way because the wide-minded people leave it—Stocks, Toynbee, Zimmern, Barker, etc. . . . Then there is this—that to a keenly intellectual person most ordinary life, away from a University and from some special literary or artistic group, is certainly dull; the daily round is more brainless than one realises beforehand. And, further, Oxford people are conscientious and honourable, and seldom really beastly.[31]

There is much of Murray here—the exaltation of the 'wide mind' over the intensely concentrated one; a certain limitation in his conception of what intellectuals can enjoy; an ascetic sense of duty applied not only to 'fattening' dons but also quite as severely to himself; and a realistic sense that choice is not between good and bad, but between not so good and not so bad.

3

Classical scholarship at Oxford was in fact shortly to receive a stimulus which did much to revive it. In the preface to his *Aristophanes*, Murray viewed his subject against the political background of 1933:

In times like these one often longs for the return to earth of one of the great laughing philosophers of the past. In the War one longed for a breath of Voltaire to show the madness of men and the unhealthy superstitions in which they were nursed, or for Erasmus to induce them for a space to be gentle and honest with one another, and to think for a moment or two before they struck or lied. But for many years I have wished quite particularly for Aristophanes, and wondered whether, like the great men who rise from the dead in two of his own comedies, he could bring us later generations some help. Could he fight against our European war fevers and nationalism as he fought against those of his own country, facing unpopularity — facing death, if it must be — yet always ready with his gallant laughter and never collapsing into spitefulness or mere self-pity? He might do it, if only the Fascists and Nazis and Ogpus could refrain from forbidding him to land in England.

The influx of the refugee scholars had begun by spring 1933 and was to assume dimensions which were of great importance to the general intellectual development of Britain, not merely to classical scholarship. Murray played a major part both individually and more formally in finding places for German scholars in Britain. One of the first Germans to appeal to him personally was Thomas Mann whom he had met in the course of his work for the CIC. In April 1933, Mann sought his advice about finding some opportunities for his son (Klaus) to teach and study in England.[32] Shortly afterwards Murray received a more general request from Dr Leo Szilard to discuss the situation of German inventors and scholars under the Nazi regime.[33] He agreed to do what he could to co-ordinate international action through the CIC, particularly in drawing up a list of scholars who should be helped; though the problem of intellectual refugees was not held to be directly within the CIC's terms of reference (see Ch. XXV, Sect. 4). Murray wrote immediately to obtain information from his old friend, Stephen Duggan, in the USA about the American Emergency Committee, the primary aim of which was to make grants to help exiled German scholars to stay in Europe at universities of their own choice.[34] More important was Murray's first contact with William Beveridge at the London School of Economics. Beveridge had proposed a cut of salaries at the School, in order to contribute to an international fund for the relief of scholars in distress. As an indirect result of Szilard's initiative, Beveridge joined forces with Murray in setting up (and acting as secretary for) what became the Academic Assistance Committee in Britain. To this Committee (renamed in 1934 the Society for the Protection of Science and Learning) Murray could refer a number of the requests for help made to him either directly by German scholars or indirectly through his contacts at the League of Nations (particularly Gustav Kullmann of the LN Secretariat).

As a sort of 'member for Oxford' on the Committee, Murray did his best to ensure that funds were available to it from scholarly institutions in the UK—he had learned from experience at the CIC that there was little hope of financial support from the government. The University of Oxford collectively was no more generous, but Murray explored with Fisher, then Vice-Chancellor, the possibility of colleges at least encouraging contributions to the Academic Assistance Committee's funds, and as late as 1939 he was trying to interest colleges in establishing travelling lectureships for refugee scholars.[35]

The story of Murray's individual efforts at Oxford for German scholars of all kinds and of his hospitality to them at Yatscombe belongs to the next chapters. However, one particular case must be mentioned in this context, that of the classical scholar, Eduard Fraenkel, then a young man who had not yet established an international reputation. Murray did not know his work, but after consulting the Provost of Oriel, W. D. Ross, he was able to secure for him a grant from the Academic Assistance Committee provided that a place was found for him. Oxford was the obvious place, and in the summer term of 1934 Christ Church provided rooms for him. Thereafter it seemed likely that, on Housman's advice, he would become a Fellow of Trinity College, Cambridge. However, in spring 1935 the Chair of Latin at Oxford became vacant, and Fraenkel was elected to it, taking up residence at Corpus Christi College, Oxford.

This appointment proved to be of great importance, not only to the course of classical scholarship, but also to Murray personally. He was by now engaged on an edition of Aeschylus, for the series of *Oxford Classical Texts*, and Fraenkel played an important part in helping him. The first letter from Fraenkel to Murray must be quoted in the original. It starts with business:

Noli in male pertinacium hominum numero me habere, vir venerandissime, quod ad Cassandrae canticum (Ag. 1137) recurro . . .

[Most honoured Sir, do not count me among the tiresomely stubborn, if I come back to that line of Cassandra (Ag. 1137) . . .]

After some scholarly discussion, Fraenkel put into stately Latin what must have been the feeling of many immigrant scholars:

Verbis exprimere nequeo, quantopere tua coniugisque tuae incomparabili hospitalitate atque humanitate delectus sim. Iniquitatis temporum prorsus obliviscitur cuicumque amicitia vestra frui licet, neque quisquam cogitare potest praeter illud Menandri:

ὡς χαριέν ἐστ᾿ ἄνθρωπος ὅταν ανθρωπος ᾖ

Valete, pulcherrimae domus domine dominaque,

ζεῦγος φιλανθρωπότατον

[I cannot express in words, how much I have been delighted by your wife's and your own incomparable hospitality and humanity. Whoever is privileged to enjoy your friendship will put out of his mind completely the evil nature of our times, and can think of nothing but what Menander said: 'What a gracious thing is man when he acts as a man'. Farewell, master and mistress of that beautiful house, the most philanthropic of pairs.]

Fraenkel became in fact one of Murray's main correspondents on detailed points in the new text of Aeschylus, which reached proof stage in summer 1936. Others on whom he relied for criticism were Ludwig Radermacher of Vienna and D. S. Robertson of Cambridge. To the latter he wrote: 'Please do not hesitate in your comments. I am prepared to bear "putide" and "proh! pudor" '[36] ("rottenly" and "for shame!" in the sort of language which classical critics reserved for their colleagues). There was much detailed exchange of views on the proofs until late autumn 1936, and Murray began to discover that Fraenkel, a great scholar, was not a very comfortable colleague: 'Dear Murray, dear maestro,' he wrote, 'some of my Latin notes sound much too peremptory.'[37] They certainly did so to Murray who complained to Isobel Henderson: 'I am plodding on with the proofs of Aeschylus. Fraenkel treats me with much severity, whereas Radermacher says "Schön" or εὖ γε [excellent] to my emendations. But I fear Fraenkel puts far more work into it.' He was not always so tolerant, and later criticized severely Fraenkel's own book on Aeschylus. 'He has so little taste. Echtdeutsch [*sic*] for all his knowledge'.[38]

The text of Aeschylus was published early in 1937. It was reckoned to be far from successful, and inferior to Murray's work on Euripides. Nor was there much financial compensation for him. He received £250 for his work, and even Murray, the least grasping of men, compared this unfavourably with his own lecture fees.[39] Between

1936 and the outbreak of war, Murray undertook no other considerable work in the classical field—the League of Nations and international politics kept him busy enough. In these years he prepared, largely from essays already written, a book on Aeschylus which was published in 1940, roughly parallel in style to his work on Aristophanes. Aeschylus was another author whom he felt he had misunderstood as a young scholar. Indeed he wrote that, at the time of his *History of Ancient Greek Literature*, he had no conception of the meaning of the *Eumenides*. He came to question a number of the conceptions on which he had been brought up. Prometheus remained for him the 'eternal under-dog', the voice of rational humanity oppressed by an irrational ruler; but Prometheus is not always mocking the gods or demi-gods. 'About the scene with Ὠκεανός I feel pretty strongly that it was a mistake to interpret it as ironical or mocking. When I was at school I was taught to translate σῶζε τὸν παρόντα νοῦν as "preserve the remains of your intelligence", whereas of course it must mean "Keep to your present plan".'[40] At the same time he developed for Miss M. R. Glover a thought which was to become the essence of his later book on Aeschylus. Zeus the new tyrant of the gods, as seen through the eyes of Prometheus, represented only one phase of the growth of the divine figure: 'I think Zeus, as the inventor of the power of learning by suffering, himself shared the power and learnt. Only thus can one explain his freeing of the Titans and his redemption of Io.' (Io herself representing one particular type of oppression—that of women.)[41]

This thought in particular was developed in the preface to Murray's translation of the *Eumenides*, the third play of Aeschylus' trilogy which began with the *Agamemnon*. In the first part, Agamemnon is killed by his wife, in the second, their son, Orestes, kills his mother. He is pursued by the avenging Furies. In the third play the Eumenides (the 'Kindly ones' as the Greeks euphemistically called the Furies) are finally appeased by the ruling of Athena and Zeus, and the terrible cycle of murder, revenge, and inevitable punishment is ended. Murray saw in Aeschylus' treatment of the fate overhanging the house of Atreus an illustration of how the concept of the Olympian gods humanized the non-human welter of primitive taboos and terrors of primitive religion. The Olympian system 'sought to make religion humane at the expense of making it anthropomorphic.'

Murray continued, in a passage which illustrates how far he let himself be carried from a rational starting-point by the powerful wings of his own thoughts and has afforded ample reason for criticizing his imaginative treatment of classical themes:

The Aeschylean doctrine is in essence an early and less elaborate stage of the theological system which we associate with St. Paul;[42] the suppression of the Law by a personal relation to a divine person, and a consequent disregard for the crude coarse test of a man's 'works' or 'deeds' in comparison with the one unfailing test of the spirit, its 'faith' or 'faithfulness' towards God. Aeschylus would have understood Paul's exhortation to escape beyond the 'beggarly elements' to him who made them, beyond the Creation to the Creator; and Paul would have understood Aeschylus' insistence on the forgiveness of the supplicant, that is, of him who believes and repents and prays. It is noteworthy, indeed, that Paul made one great concession to primitive thought which Aeschylus had entirely rejected. When Orestes is pardoned by the will of Zeus, the Furies yield; the Law is deemed to be satisfied; there is no talk of its demanding to be paid off with another victim. But in Paul, when man is to be forgiven, the sin still claims its punishment, the blood will still have blood; and the only way to appease it is for the Divine King, himself or his son, to 'die for the people'. Thus the pollution is cleansed and sin duly paid with blood, though it happens to be the blood of the innocent. Aeschylus, as a poet, was familiar with that conception . . . But for him such practices belonged to that primitive and barbaric world which Hellenic Zeus had swept away, so he hoped, for ever.

A modern reader is more likely to ask why, if Orestes only fulfilled the command of Zeus, he should be punished at all, why is there any talk of suffering, and forgiveness? The answer is quite straightforward. He has after all broken the Law; he has offended against Themis and Moira, and he must suffer. In modern language, a man who kills his mother, even if he is amply justified in doing so, is bound to suffer acute grief and distress; if he did not, he would really deserve to be punished. It is only in the end that Zeus can overrule and make good, just as he did with Io and with Prometheus. It is in the end, after suffering and struggle, after cleansing and supplication, that union is achieved between the Law which acts like blind fate and the Father who understands.

Thus at last the offender who deserves pardon can be pardoned. But that is not all. The Law that can pardon and understand can itself be understood and loved. Its ministers are no longer alien and hostile beings . . . their Law [is] recognised as an inward aspiration, a standard of right living which men consciously need and seek. The 'Furies' have become 'Eumenides'.

Here is a parallel which suggests the brilliant undergraduate with an undeveloped historical sense rather than the ripe scholar; it seems almost calculated to offend Christian believers and classical experts alike. However, without the parallel in the first paragraph quoted, there is a substantial argument in the other two. No doubt it is also open to many counter-arguments, but it is on this that Murray's study of Aeschylus must primarily be judged.[43]

He had no time for other substantial work on the classics. He rejected an invitation from Harvard to give another course of lectures on Ancient Greek Literature, which would no doubt have resulted in a revised version of the *History* of 1897,[44] and refused to consider other suggestions leading in the same direction. With the higher ends of international co-operation in mind, Murray undertook to write for Professor Baldensperger of the Sorbonne a chapter on Greek literature for a volume designed to provide a conspectus of the great literatures of the world. He repented bitterly of his weakness in agreeing to do so. He wrote to Lady Mary in 1934 that 'Baldensperger has become a nightmare',[46] and let himself go further in a letter to Isobel Henderson:

You remember the lines in Milton:

> Him, Baldensperger, o'er the foul Sorbonne
> In sin supreme and monstrous evil throned,
> Hurled from the sunlight . . .

He stole me in my cups and extorted a promise to write for him the Greek part of a large Comparative Literature which he is editing. A bas Hitler! A bas Musso! A bas Stalin! A bas le Saint Père! A bas Baldensperger! In fact, in general terms, écrasez l'infâme. But love to Isobel.[47]

The task was completed shortly afterwards, but Murray did not consider it suitable for separate publication, and the papers for Baldensperger's complete project were lost during the war.[48]

Murray's double life between the wars left him little time for what he regarded as his relaxation—translating the Greek dramatists. Nevertheless he found time to translate seven of Aeschylus' plays between 1920 and 1939: *Agamemnon* (1920); *Choephoroe* (1923); *Eumenides* (1925)—published together as the *Oresteia* in 1928— *Suppliant Women* (1930); *Prometheus* (1931); *Seven Against Thebes* (1935); the *Persae* (1939). However, it seemed to many then and now that Murray's 'riding rhyme' couplets formed an inappropriate medium for Aeschylus' heroic verse. He himself was far from satisfied with the *Eumenides*.[49] But the *Suppliants* drew warm praise from his old friend and opponent, Pickard-Cambridge, who found that it preserved the beauty of the original language 'without over-refining the stiffness . . . of the ideas'.[50] The *Persae* had a special appeal for Murray: he liked to contrast the attitude of the Athenians to the conquered Persians, the absence of gloating over defeat, with the less magnanimous manners of his own time; nor could he refrain from pointing out to his daughter Rosalind (who by then had turned

Catholic) how much in this respect the Christian had deteriorated from the 'good pagan'.[51]

Between the wars there were few prestigious performances of the plays, though a number were put on in provincial theatres: more often they were performed by amateur companies and in schools. In the USA Murray had warm supporters at the University of California, Los Angeles, who presented *Hippolytus* in 1928 and *Iphigenia in Tauris* in 1930, with a number of other productions to follow. Oxford was less willing to take its Professor seriously as a translator-dramatist. The Balliol Players performed his version of *Oedipus Tyrannus* in 1935, and Murray himself acted as director of the *Oedipus* in the original Greek in 1932—a production notable for William Devlin's remarkably mature performance as the hero, and also for its financial success, though Murray was far from satisfied with the performance of the chorus.[52]

The occasions to which Murray devoted most personal attention were the annual performances organized by Mrs Charlotte King, at her house in Stonelands, near West Hoathly in Sussex, with casts drawn from the local villages. The series started in 1910 and, after interruption by the First World War, continued with few breaks till 1939. Murray sometimes attended himself and his letters to Mrs King illustrate the care which he devoted to the productions. 'I myself always say "Alsestis". I do not mind "Alkestis", but I rather hate "Alkeestis" . . . The best plan [for the chorus] is to have the words simply recited by the leader alone . . . or occasionally by two persons speaking together. Then have full music for one or two choruses.' Murray was most appreciative of the results:

You have kindly made these plays a possession for all kinds of people who would otherwise never have known that there were such things, or at least would have known them as odd little books which no sensible person would read.

Meanwhile a new medium for performance was open to Murray in the form of broadcasting. From the mid-thirties onwards Murray became a familiar figure at the BBC, first as a translator-dramatist and then increasingly as something of a star solo broadcaster. In October 1936 the *Hippolytus* was given, with a personal introduction by Murray (it was on this occasion that he remarked on his own 'dreadful Oxford accent').[53] He described the play as the 'first love tragedy in the history of drama'; the performance was notable for Robert Speaight's playing of the Messenger. This broadcast was followed by others in 1937 and 1939 of the *Trojan Women* and the newly translated *Persians*. Murray was not easy to satisfy. He complained tactfully to the BBC about 'weak spots' in the *Trojan Women*. Many of the cast he thought over-dramatic and insufficiently lyrical: 'It would be an exaggeration to say that they ought to speak their lines as if they were reciting Milton, but something like that is what is really wanted.' Privately he was delighted when his sister-in-law, Dorothy Henley, described the performance to him as murder. 'Do you remember', he wrote to her, 'an old Punch picture where a refined lady, who has just missed her train, turns to thank a choleric old gentelman, who has burst into a stream of oaths about it? I feel rather like that refined lady.'[54]

5

Murray's time as Regius Professor of Greek at Oxford was up at the end of the academic year 1935–6, and from the beginning of 1936 the question of finding a successor to him began to be discussed. His own part in the search was a matter of much controversy. The tradition in such cases is that the incumbent Professor has no say, or at least only the most discreet say, in the choice of the new one. The authorized version of what happened in this case is given by Bowra. According to him Baldwin, who as Prime Minister in effect had the disposal of the Professorship as a Crown appointment, simply gave an unwilling Murray *carte blanche* to make a recommendation.[55] This is a reasonably accurate account of a complicated transaction, which caused much scandal in Oxford. The first move in fact came from Murray himself, and was probably less than wise, given Baldwin's reputation for indolence. Murray wrote to him in January 1936, asking whether he himself could be of any use 'in either making enquiries or expressing my own opinion about the various possible candidates for the Chair of Greek.'[56] Baldwin in reply said that he would be grateful for any information and suggested a talk. Murray soon afterwards wrote to E. R. Dodds, then Professor at Birmingham, in a letter no longer extant; he evidently revived a suggestion which he had already made in Michaelmas term 1935, and in terms which produced in Dodds 'a complex mixture of alarm and gratification'. If Murray who knew the field at Oxford and elsewhere, considered him a serious candidate, he could hardly refuse to stand.[57] At about the same time Murray consulted the American scholar, A. D. Nock, about the level of scholarship shown in Dodds's edition of Proclus, evidently with a view to reporting to the Prime Minister on the standing of Dodds and other candidates.

An important point in Dodds's favour proved in fact to be Nock's enthusiasm for his work.[58]

There is no trace of further activity by Murray until late in April, when he wrote consulting scholarly friends at Oxford (Cyril Bailey and A. B. Poynton) about the comparative merits of various Oxford candidates, including Bowra and Denniston, and mentioning the names of others from outside Oxford, including Dodds. Poynton put Dodds at the head of his short list (though, if Lobel would stand, he would have been Poynton's choice); but after talking with Bailey, Murray wrote to him 'though nothing was settled definitely we agreed that the choice was between Bowra and Denniston, unless evidence was forthcoming about Dodds which made it necessary to reconsider him.' Bailey himself evidently had doubts about Dodds's personality and record from 1915 onwards. There were no doubt many in Oxford who remembered with some bitterness Dodds's record in the First World War, when he opposed British participation, and would later describe himself as a 'moderate Sinn Feiner'. It may well also have been known that Murray had over the years supported Dodds's applications for various academic posts.[59] Bailey wrote to Murray with his usual tact that what was now needed in Oxford was someone who knew the local ropes rather than a 'rebel', excellent as Dodds's testimonials were. Meanwhile, Theodore Wade-Gery, who persuaded Bowra to stand, had written a powerful testimonial in his favour, and something parallel was needed for Denniston— in many ways the obvious candidate in virtue of his age, character, and published works of scholarship. Murray wrote to C. R. M. F. Cruttwell, the Principal of Denniston's College, Hertford, for an estimate of Denniston's worth as a teacher and a lecturer, and as an influence on younger scholars. Cruttwell, no classical scholar himself, damned with rather faint praise. The young men of Hertford, he said, were mostly unpromising material; Denniston was very good with them in tutorials, but saw nothing of them outside. He was much trusted by younger teachers, and was a good but not inspiring lecturer, who did not rise to heights of eloquence.[60]

It was on the basis of this material, and the excellent testimonials received for Dodds, that Murray finally wrote to Baldwin on 2 June 1936, assessing the relative merits of Bowra, Denniston, and Dodds. In Bowra's scholarship he found 'a certain lack of quality, precision and reality'. Denniston was a great friend, universally liked and respected. 'In actual knowledge of the Greek language I doubt if he has his equal in Oxford and Cambridge'; but he was only a 'moderately attractive' lecturer, and his book on Greek particles, 'though very exact and capable, has not much illumination in it'. It would hardly 'kindle any general enthusiasm for Greek'. As against him, the case for Dodds seemed irresistibly strong—both Murray himself and Fraenkel had found his lecture 'Hellenism in Philosophy' quite masterly.[61]

The Vice-chancellor went to see the Prime Minister on 16 June and Dodds was duly appointed. Murray had to face some outraged feeling in Oxford. He wrote briefly to Bowra and fully to Denniston about the Prime Minister's choice, saying 'how difficult the decision has been and how unhappy I have felt about it . . . I did my best to put before Baldwin the case for each . . . I do not know Dodds nearly so well as I know you and Bowra. Meanwhile it is difficult to me to say how much I owe to you both as a scholar and a friend.' Denniston replied brusquely, mainly it seems to take the chance to deny any connection with some of the very unfavourable comment which had appeared in the local Oxford papers. Denys Page expressed to Murray rather naïvely his feelings on the appointment: 'When Basil [Murray] was convicted [in connection with Oswald Mosley's meeting—described in the next chapter], I thought, and when Dodds was appointed, I knew that there is no more justice in the world. φησί τις εἶναι δῆτ' ἐν οὐρανῷ θεούς; οὐκ εἰσίν, οὐδὲ εἷς.' [And does one say that there are gods in heaven? No, there are none!] Murray replied grimly: 'If you'd seen the evidence in favour of Dodds, you would not revert so suddenly to atheism.'[62]

A few months later, after Dodds's inaugural, Murray could tell Baldwin that their 'bold choice' had been amply justified. 'After a first slight explosion of surprise, I have heard nothing but fair opinions.'[63] He cannot have had his ear very close to the ground. Dodds himself found for some time that his appointment was much resented—not least by Bowra and his young supporters. Bowra was consoled soon enough by becoming Warden of his College, Wadham. For Denniston the disappointment must have been great, but he was not the man to make a fuss or cause difficulties for Dodds; and Dodds proved before long to be an excellent choice, as Bowra admitted in his *Memories*.[64]

Murray may be faulted in this affair on a number of counts. He would probably have done better in the first place not to offer his services to Baldwin, though he would no doubt have found it hard completely to resist all pressure to give advice and opinion, at least indirectly. On a point of detail, it seems extraordinary not to have gone further than Cruttwell, who was well past the peak of his powers, for an opinion on Denniston's lecturing and general tutorial work; lastly it seems strange to have insisted that the main qualifications for the Professorship should be the ability to take broad views and 'kindle general enthusiasm'. Denniston was in fact a man of wide and passionate interests, which he could certainly communicate to the young,[65] and there was surely a strong case for electing to the Professorship a man whose qualifications were quite different from Murray's.

It was unfortunate that Murray's last weeks as Regius Professor were marred by this controversy. But all turned out well in the end. Five years later, when Murray was awarded an OM, Denniston wrote to him with a typically generous and full appreciation of his contribution to Greek studies:

I am sure that we are at the beginning of a new era of classical scholarship, in which people will lose themselves neither in linguistic pedantry nor in pseudo-philosophy and Quellengeschichte [history of sources], but will look at the great works of Greek literature as Bradley looked at Hamlet and Othello. And I am sure that, when the reckoning is cast up, you will be recognised as the pioneer in this new and better Greek scholarship.[66]

A dinner for Murray's 70th birthday was given in Christ Church Hall on 13 February 1936, when the Festschrift printed as *Essays in Honour of Gilbert Murray* was formally presented to him; it had to be paralleled (surely a unique honour) by another volume of essays by experts in the field of Greek literature (*Greek Poetry and Life*), including contributions by Mackail, Pickard-Cambridge, Wade-Gery, and Cyril Bailey, as well as by the protagonists in the drama of the successorship, Bowra, Denniston, and Dodds. Murray made a moving and eloquent reply on the presentation.[67] An old man's memory, he said, takes long leaps:

Mine goes back to a little boy in the Australian bush, whom I knew — or rather was — $\epsilon i' \pi o \tau' \, \check{\epsilon} \eta \nu \, \gamma \acute{\epsilon}$ [if it was really me] . . . rather a ragged little boy, with buttons not always sufficient to keep his clothes together; who had fallen in love with Greek.

He talked of the friendships commemorated by the Essays — with Sybil Thorndike and Granville Barker, 'reminding me of our glorious days in the Theatre, convincing people that Greek plays were really plays'; and with Mrs Salter (Verrall's daughter) 'unveiling the most disreputable of my titles to fame, as a psychical medium.'

Now he had given up all but two sides of the life represented in the Essays — Greek and Peace:

I could not give up Greek; but for the rest I seemed to have no choice. I saw what War was; I saw many of my best friends and pupils killed in the flower of youth; I saw the cruelties, the lapse into barbarism, and the ultimate poisoning of all human relations that followed from the Great War. I had to give what powers I possessed to the movement for making secure some peaceful life for mankind, not merely avoiding war, but preventing war by the formation of a Society of Nations.

In looking back, Murray did not know whether to be more struck by the changes in his life, or by the strong unity which pervaded it: 'Fortune changes, but ἦθος ἀνθρώπῳ δαίμων: temperament is destiny.'

Private Life 1923–1939

1

NOT all his other preoccupations could prevent Murray from continuing to interest himself whenever possible in Liberal politics and Liberal policies. He was consulted by a wide variety of reformers. In September 1925 for instance, shortly before the Locarno Treaty was signed, Mrs K. M. Swanick, an indefatigable proponent of equal rights for Germany, asked for his advice and co-operation on a draft manifesto in favour of abrogating Articles 227–30 of the Treaty of Versailles (subjecting Germans to the judgement of Allied Courts for war crimes). Murray preferred less formal abrogation, by means of government statements, such as had been used to discontinue the confiscation of German property abroad.[1] A month later, R. H. Tawney pressed him to sign a letter condemning anti-communist action by the Baldwin government, as an infringement of the right of free speech; Murray was cautious and wanted to be clear first on what the communists had actually done.[2] In 1925 too he wrote an introduction to Norman Leys's book on Kenya, which was extremely critical of the white settlers' policy, and little less so of successive colonial secretaries.[3] In 1928, Winifred Holtby, then campaigning on behalf of the coloured workers of the South African Industrial and Commercial Workers Union, informed him fully of her work and asked him to guarantee her respectability.[4]

More important was Murray's attitude to the General Strike in May 1926. He was deeply disturbed like many others by the possibility of a polarization between hard right and militant left. Murray was one of the main speakers who moved a resolution on 6 May in Oxford Town Hall, 'that this meeting earnestly hopes, for the future peace and unity of this country, that nothing will be allowed to stand in the way of an attempt to resume negotiations' (between government and trade union representatives). A week later, after the main dispute had been settled, Murray gave a broadcast, dwelling on the solidity of the social organization which had not been impaired by the strike, the strength of the general wish for industrial peace and reconciliation, and the moderation of the trade union leaders, who had been brave enough to admit that they had made a mistake. There was one indignant protest about the Oxford meeting; it had been advertised as a religious one, with Gore in the chair, but the socialist Master of Balliol, Sandy Lindsay, as well as Murray, had spoken at it. The broadcast naturally evoked a wider reaction, mostly unfavourable from people who objected to the description of the trade union leaders as 'men of honour'.[5]

Meanwhile disagreements between husband and wife on politics seem to have been accepted with total toleration on both sides and in no way to have disturbed the marriage. Stephen records that during the General Strike of 1926 his father allowed him (at the age of 18) to take the family car and drive a party of Oxford students to Hull to work in the Docks as strike breakers—'ignorant young pup that I was', added Stephen, who later joined the Communist Party. Lady Mary, however, out of loyalty to the strikers, would not use the buses in Oxford which were being driven by students. Now 60 years of age she walked the long two to three miles up Boar's Hill laden with shopping. Once a car stopped to offer her a lift; she resolved not to yield to temptation until she saw that the driver was the manager of the Co-operative in Oxford, which made it quite all right to accept. This must have been about the time when Stephen declares he heard his mother in one breath describe herself as 'a respectable working woman', and a new neighbour on Boar's Hill as 'hardly a lady'.

Murray was always ready to co-operate with Sandy Lindsay on

university and town issues in Oxford, and Lady Mary had transferred her own allegiance from the Liberal Party to the Labour Party in 1924. Murray was not prepared to follow her. Among his papers of this period are preserved some stencilled notes 'Why I joined the Labour Party' (probably not by Lady Mary), with some brief and significant marginal comments by Murray himself. Against the statement that Liberals approved of private enterprise as fair to individual producers and advantageous to the community, Murray pencilled an emphatic 'yes'; against the statement that the organization of workers in trade unions has secured free play for the enterprise of industrial workers, he wrote: 'No, it destroys it.'[6]

In fact Murray moved a certain way towards the Labour Party, but still stood as a Liberal at the General Election of 1929. Lindsay assured him of Labour support if he stood openly as an Independent (as he had done in 1924), and not 'nominally as a Lloyd George Liberal';[7] and shortly afterwards Murray defined his attitude in answer to questions by the Oxford Labour Club by repeating what he had said in 1925: 'I should like best to see a Liberal Government with a Labour wing, next to that a Labour Government a little better-tempered than the last, and ready to accept some Liberal support and listen to some Liberal criticism.'[8] This was at least enough to attract high Conservative wrath. The historian J. E. Neale circulated a statement saying that he looked on Murray as a 'full-blooded and rabid Communist and internationalist', who voiced extremist and anti-British slogans.[9] The result of the election for Oxford University was as usual. In the count for first place Murray came second to the senior Conservative candidate, Lord Hugh Cecil; on the count for the second seat, he was outvoted by supporters of the other Conservative, Sir Charles Oman.[10] This was his last attempt to stand for parliament. His failure was immortalized by A. D. Godley who thus apostrophized Oxford:

> Still a brace of arrant Tories
> You on Parliament bestow.
> Where (o tempora, o mores
> As we read in Cicero)
> O Magistri et Doctores
> *Where* do you expect to go?[11]

In 1930 and 1931 Murray was deeply concerned with the rising tide of protectionism. This was a political issue on which he could make common cause with Lloyd George, who had not given up all hope of making a political come-back. For Murray the restoration of international free trade was the key to recovery from the world economic depression, and Lloyd George thanked him warmly for his support against a trade policy 'which would wreck every chance of applying Liberal principles to the solution of the economic situation at home and of the peace problem of the world.'[12]

As recounted in Chapter XXII (sect. 7), in 1930 Murray did his best to persuade the LNU to campaign actively for international economic co-operation and free trade, but he was over-ruled by Cecil. This did not stop Murray from expressing his own views in print. In the *Manchester Guardian* of 20 October 1930 he asked for some clarification of Conservative policy. Was it, as he understood it (1) to tax food and raw materials 'in order to restrain the appetites of the poor; (2) to have an experimental general tariff to be first put on and then taken off, in order to determine which course did more harm; (3) to start a tariff war for reasons unstated, but generally because other nations sold good stuff at low prices, in order to see how long our densely-populated island could hold out against countries self-sufficient in food and raw materials; (4) to build a naval base at Singapore in order to show the Japanese how we understood the Kellogg Pact and, in case of war, to give the enemy a fair chance by dividing our battle-fleet into two parts?'[13] In another and private letter Murray referred to his 'little tract' on Protection (a pamphlet issued in Autumn 1930), and his conviction that the establishment of protective tariffs throughout the world would bring ruin to Britain rather quicker than a free trade policy—hardly a sanguine prophecy.[14] The main enemy in this context was of course the Conservative party, but the Labour government could not be relied upon to stand for free trade during a depression.

By the time of the formation of the National Government in autumn 1931, Murray's interest in politics was effective only in the field of foreign affairs. There was no question any longer of his playing any role behind the scenes of British domestic politics. In 1929, however, he came near to being removed altogether from academic studies and activity at the League of Nations. By July 1929, after MacDonald's second Labour government had assumed office, there were rumours that Murray would be sent as Ambassador to Washington, probably to mark some kind of break with the 'old diplomacy', and to interest the US Administration as far as possible in the work of the League. Talk about the appointment was certainly widespread. Margaret Cole, among Murray's younger friends, wrote of the 'larger hope' [MacDonald] sending him 'to the Yanks', and at a reception he was introduced to some Americans by a tactless lady as 'the future Ambassador'.[15]

I have found no record of what was actually said or written to Murray on the subject, but it was enough to make him take it very seriously for some weeks. He got so far as to write to Lady Mary about possible secretaries. Miss Stafford, she thought, would not do — 'too grande dame'.[16] Murray was confident enough of his ability to carry the new load of work: 'it is after all a one-man job, and . . . most of the elderly diplomats who occupy embassies are not such hard workers as to make it difficult for me to keep up with them.'[17] In early August the prospect of appointment was still real and disagreeable: 'I woke up frightened and disgusted at the thought of going to Washington.' Soon afterwards Murray began to feel convinced that MacDonald intended to tackle the main problems of Anglo-American relations himself, and would be best served by an 'inconspicuous professional' on the spot. Lady Mary was not convinced, but glad that Murray did not want the job too much.[18] The appointment was not finally settled till October. Murray wrote to Isobel Henderson;

The F.O. which formerly thought the new Ambassador ought to be non-diplomat, now think that Ramsay's successful visit has so changed the situation that a diplomat can carry on all right and would be better than a layman . . . On the whole I am relieved: I have so much enjoyed lecturing on Homer and Greek Lyric Metres — and I should never be allowed to do either in Washington.[19]

Cecil — an interested party, who would greatly have missed Murray at the LNU — thought that he was well out of it and he himself seems to have had no regrets.

2

Before the First World War Murray gained some reputation as a 'man of letters', an author himself, a friend of authors, and a champion of their rights. After 1919 his other occupations were more demanding. Moreover a new school of writers, with whom he had little sympathy, was taking the place of those whom he had known before 1914. Between the two World Wars there are few works from his pen unconnected with either classical studies or the League of Nations. Of the more purely literary tasks which he undertook the most interesting is a series of lectures for the University of Liverpool in 1938, on *Themes and Forms of Drama*. Unfortunately these have not survived in printed or even draft shape; but the secretary who worked for him at the time remembers her amazement at the scope of his acquaintance with English and French drama, and her delight in Murray's humorous treatment of, for example, the *Italian Straw Hat*. A minor work of some biographical interest is Murray's preface to Tolstoy's *Essays and Letters* in Aylmer Maude's centenary edition; his essay is a tribute to the enormous influence which Tolstoy exercised on his younger British contemporaries.[20]

Murray took on one further commitment as a sort of literary elder statesman in 1926, when he became Vice-president of the English Verse-speaking Association (he turned down the Presidency at the time but accepted it in due course).[21] With his friend and neighbour on Boar's Hill, John Masefield, he helped to arrange and judge verse-speaking contests in Oxford from 1923 to 1934. Masefield came to feel that the contests (or 'Oxford recitals', as they were known) approximated too closely to formal examinations and after 1930, when Masefield became Poet Laureate, they were replaced by the award (with which Murray was also associated) of King's Poetry Medals for first or second volumes of verse published by poets under 35. Murray's correspondence with Masefield on this subject contains a number of his judgements on contemporary poetry, which in the main represented for him many regrettable deviations from the 'classical tradition'.[22]

As a public figure he remained ready to support the cause of freedom of expression against any form of censorship. Thus he was, rather improbably, involved in the argument which developed around the trial (1929) of Radclyffe Hall, for corrupting public morals by her novel *The Well of Loneliness*, a study of lesbianism, and the effective suppression of another novel, *Sleeveless Errand*, by Norah James. Murray argued privately with the Home Office, which claimed that no administrative action had been taken in the latter case—sales were simply suspended until the case was heard.[23] In taking up such a matter Murray acted on a stern sense of principle, since the subject-matter of the books was most distasteful to him. He made this clear in a letter to the *Nation* of 23 March on 'Obscenity in Literature', which won the applause of Murray's Home Office correspondent among others:

Why do fashionable critics talk such hypocrisy? Writers who talk so much about excretion, sweating and procreation don't do so out of love of truth . . . but simply out of love of dirt. Juvenal pretends to excoriate vices but enjoys writing about them . . . and finds sexual stimulation in doing so . . .

Why is the great imaginative literature of the world free from obscenity? This has the power of destroying higher imaginative values in its neighbourhood. The great Victorian novelists conquered the world *because* they entirely abstained from the lure of obscenity.

This drew sharp rejoinders from Leonard Woolf and Lytton Strachey, who reminded Murray of a large number of classical writers, not least Catullus and Aristophanes, who were great, imaginative, and obscene. Strachey's most telling argument was from Acts III and IV of *King Lear*, where the obscenities certainly do not keep down the 'higher imaginative values'.

Murray and 'Bloomsbury'—a group noun which he used in an unfavourable sense—were never likely to see eye to eye. He was always concerned with the moral content of literature and the positive side of the Classical Tradition, while Strachey and others were concerned with the sort of hypocrisies and conventional processes of mind which the moralist approach encouraged. Murray and Strachey could have found common ground in teasing dogmatic pillars of the Church, and Murray rather reluctantly appreciated Virginia Woolf's brilliant skill as a novelist in depicting impressionistically the impact of successive moments on the mind.[24] Leonard Woolf had considerable respect for Murray's work on behalf of the League, but to Virginia and her friends he seemed to be irrevocably part of a literary 'establishment' which they despised. Murray must be seen briefly from their angle, if his portrait is to be complete, and it can best be illustrated by one of a number of unappreciative references in Virginia Woolf's *Diary*. On 28 October 1918 she had tea with the Murrays in London, and noted his 'unmeasured' niceness and simplicity. But was not the simplicity consciously maintained in the face of 'years of worship and adulation'? The proper thing to say was clearly, 'How wonderfully simple dear Gilbert Murray is!' The worst of it all for her was not the 'absence of intellect' but the prevalent respectability, and an atmosphere which reminded her of 'certain dun-coloured misty days in autumn'. She talked to Gilbert about their love of sweets, about the Greek love of wine, about his standing with the government. His cleanliness was most remarkable to her: 'a great nurse must rub him smooth with pumice stone every morning; he is so discreet, so sensitive, so low in tone and immaculate in taste, that you hardly understand how he has the boldness to beget children.'[25] 'Malicious enough', as the diarist herself remarked on her judgements here. Even so perceptive an observer could not penetrate beneath Murray's 'establishment' mask to the radical and idealist fires which in 1918 burned within him.

It is not surprising that this should be so. Whatever his political views, the author of *The Classical Tradition in Poetry* was separated by a wide gulf from the literary prophets and fashions of the inter-war years. Many landmarks of British literary life which he had known were fading or being removed. Shaw had passed his best and politically was becoming more and more eccentric or frivolous. Galsworthy died in 1933; and Kipling early in 1936, when Murray wrote to his cousin, Stanley Baldwin, that, however, much he had differed from Kipling on 'most subjects', he had always felt a 'great attraction for him personally'.[26]

A loss which affected him more deeply was the death of A. E. Housman in the same year. Housman's poetry and the classical art with which he made every word and syllable tell, had always evoked Murray's warmest admiration, a feeling which outweighed any resentment he may have felt towards Housman's at best reserved attitude towards his own scholarly and poetic gifts.[27]

One landmark remained, an author whose books were for Murray much desired holiday companions. This was P. G. Wodehouse, whose nomination as a Doctor of Letters at Oxford Murray warmly supported. 'Your many learned admirers here', he wrote, 'have at last had their way, and routed the insignificant rabble of unlettered Philistines, who did not see why you should take your due place among the Oxford Doctors, with Wilamowitz and Mark Twain.'[28]

Murray accepted that he himself as a literary figure was out of fashion. Indeed he would on occasion share a laugh at his own addiction to Gilbertian or Swinburnian metres:

> 'Deafer than a newt to the sound of the lute,
>   Deafer than a stone to the sea,
> Deafer than a heifer to the sighing of the zephyr,
>   Are your deaf ears to me.

This is the sort of poetry which appeals to me.'[29]

There was more than self-mockery here. He could not accept the negation of those 'classical traditions' of metre and diction which he defended. T. S. Eliot seemed to him to be the high priest of the new school. He never appeared publicly to resent Eliot's criticism of his translations, but it was impossible for him to appreciate Eliot's poetry, and still less the 'message' of Eliot's poetry and criticism:

I find two things [in him]; first a tiresome mixture of criticism with poetic creation. They don't go together; one spoils the other, except in direct satire. Second, the criticism is not based on a profound or fruitful view of the world, but largely on a sort of reactionary fretfulness. . . . he has now discovered that neither Milton nor Shelley are good poets![30]

3

The years from 1923 to 1931 were not a happy time in the Murray's family life. The eldest son, Denis, was more and more clearly a war casualty. His health and powers of concentration had been permanently affected by his period of captivity, and his bouts of drinking grew upon him. But he was happily married, and various jobs were found for him on the Cumberland estates of Lady Mary and her sister and brother-in-law, Cecilia and Charles Roberts. When he died suddenly and unexpectedly in 1930, Murray wrote to Isobel Henderson: 'I did not see Denis often and had not many interests in common with him, though we got on well and did not quarrel. But it is curious how the death of a child affects one like a wound.'[31]

The other Murray sons provided their parents with some of the usual problems of the 'generation-gap', perhaps in intensified form. Basil never found his feet securely in a profession after leaving Oxford, acting as secretary to his father on League of Nations business, as a journalist for the Beaverbrook Press, as a parliamentary candidate in northern Scotland during the 1929 election, and as an official in the LNU publicity department.

Stephen reacted to his parents' example in a different way. Basil, with an elder brother's lofty penetration, diagnosed a 'complete lack of repression' and an 'anti-virtue complex'.[32] Lady Mary was upset; Murray—who felt himself able to meet his son happily in the workshop or on the tennis court—much less so. He reflected wisely that it was as hard for children to have intellectual parents as it notoriously is for them to have stupid ones.[33] In 1927 Stephen went to Balliol, to be under the avuncular eye of Sandy Lindsay. His temporary attachment to the Oxford Group movement caused difficulties with his mother; but he settled to a profession—the law— more quickly than his brothers. In 1931 he married Margaret Gillett, who came of a well known Oxford Quaker family, and his parents hoped his marriage would have a stabilizing influence.

Lady Mary had to contend not only with family worries, but with her new duties on the Cumberland estates, and with ill health. She was near to a breakdown in 1924, and took refuge in a Quaker nursing home—'I simply funk life'. Early in 1925 she had to have an operation, and the strain of leading a life so largely separated in interest from Murray probably told on her. The note of pride in his work at Geneva faded from her letters. She felt increasingly that he had taken on too much, and that he should confine himself more strictly to what he could do best. In July 1925 she wrote to him, analysing shrewdly the value of his various talents. She started by quoting Asquith to the effect that having Murray in parliament would be like taking a razor to cut a block. This, she said, bore out what she knew—'You are *very* great as a writer, very able and wise in guiding people, adequate (but not so great) at the organization of offices and the like—and so at 59½ I want you to take breath and *write*!'[34]

Good advice, but of no use to Murray at the time, who had no major work in his mind and was deeply committed to the League of Nations. Lady Mary too was drawing away from him in her own interests. She had become deeply involved in the affairs of the Quakers, and they worked her hard; and she had joined the Labour Party late in 1924.[35] The sense that the two of them were growing apart was strong upon Murray. He urged Lady Mary particularly to come to the USA with him in the autumn of 1926. 'If you stay behind, the separation that there now is will be greater. We shall both be more unhappy, and we shall neither of us do our work as we should.'[36]

Lady Mary duly accompanied Murray to Harvard, but the pattern of their life continued to include long periods when each went his or her own way. To the periods spent on League business at Geneva, Murray began to add weeks of relaxation in the Swiss Alps with chosen friends. The first of these holidays was with Stephen and Maxwell Garnett (General Secretary of the LNU) at the Riffelalp in August 1923. It did not exclude work, but Murray wrote to Lady Mary of the 'waste of life; you just walk and eat, and compare your burns and stiffnesses'; but he much enjoyed mountain walking and the renewed experience of climbing on a rope. He found that he climbed 'quite as well as 25 years ago', and Lady Mary had to remind him with much concern and some exaggeration that he had never climbed 'since the Dolomites with Gore' (1886).[37] The summer pattern of work and holiday in Switzerland became a regular one for Murray. In 1925 he paid the first of what became regular visits to Riederfurka near the Aletsch glacier, which he delighted to cross by improvised routes: 'I hate to hear of your last walk on the glacier', wrote Lady Mary; less anxious companions were impressed by his athletic skill and frightened by the risks which he appeared to take.[38] Murray's spirits rose among the mountains. He confessed

to long-forgotten impulses—'It is a *very* odd thing, but I have
been having a longing for wine after my days in the open here: a
real longing'; and he indulged in light verse for the amusement of
Roy Harrod and his other companions:

> A certain lady made it seem
> That I would forfeit her esteem
> Unless I went at once to fetch her,
> From near the Ober-Aletsch Gletscher,
> Between the Sparrhorn and the screes,
> A bunch of pale anemones . . .[39]

Another part of Murray's new pattern of life was the springtime
'Lunn', or holiday cruise to Greece. The first of these took place in
March 1930—it was in fact his first visit to Greece since 1894, and
he was powerfully impressed. After a day on the Acropolis he wrote:
'I keep feeling how infinitely that century of Athens has mattered
in the world—how little most of the time since . . . I go about
murmuring Aeschylus and Homer beneath my breath.'[40]

4

But in the decade before the Second World War Murray and his
wife were jointly and increasingly concerned with common family
problems and troubles. These were years in which the growth of
totalitarianism abroad and the apparent inability of the Conservative
and Liberal 'establishment' in Britain to cope either with this or
with unemployment at home opened up an increasing gap between
Murray's generation and that which succeeded it. The ideals of
Liberalism had begun to seem both ineffective and irrelevant. Murray
was well aware that this was so. In July 1939 he wrote to Lady Mary
about the children of his Cambridge colleague, Francis Cornford,
who had joined the Communist Party and regarded their parents as
'of no contemporary significance. Do you think we are like that?'[41]
Undoubtedly many of their own children's contemporaries would
have said so.

Murray had plenty of friends among the young, even among the
rebellious young, and could understand their need for some political
short-cuts to a better world. There is unfortunately no record of
what he replied to Naomi Mitchison when in 1932 she described
enthusiastically a visit to Soviet Russia, and said that she now realized
what fifth-century Athens must have been like.[42] At the beginning

of the War, he wrote to Cornford with much sympathy about the political revolt of the young:

I think the main thing underlying this Communist attitude in the young is discontent, first with their own prospects and secondly with the civilization which gave them such black prospects. Christopher thinks it ridiculous to expect the world to be reformed by high-minded Liberal intellectuals, but this is to underrate the slow indirect influence of thinkers, and to ignore the lesson of history that you cannot obtain justice by merely killing the people you think unjust. However, these are only truisms. The Bolshevik frame of mind is a symptom of the failure of civilization. It is not yet dominant in the world, but the World War gave it a chance, and the present war may in the end strengthen it. I think it will be accompanied by a great recrudescence of superstition. However, I am twaddling.

I was reading last night Kipling's 'William the Conqueror' and feeling (a) the magnificent sense of devotion and duty expected from Englishmen; (b) the disastrous contempt for Indians in the mass which R.K. represented.

Within Murray's own family, reaction against the high-minded Liberalism of the parents took various shapes. Stephen had reacted by joining the Communist party together with his wife. Lady Mary accepted that the *Daily Worker* could be taken at Yatscombe 'as long as the servants didn't see it.' Stephen could not resist taking a rise out of his mother, not always kindly. Kathleen Haynes called it 'tormenting' her. It was never 'well I must be off now', but 'I must be off to the pub.' Basil developed political views but his reaction, as a young man no less than as an undergraduate, was to find any fixed job unattractive and to get into what Murray later called a series of 'terrible scrapes'. Early in 1932 he had to give up work for the publicity department of the LNU, and was soon involved in both a matrimonial and a financial crisis. The latter was mitigated by some journalistic work, but was the occasion if not the sole cause of his parents' discussing some drastic economies in their way of life. In September 1932, Murray was talking of selling Yatscombe, resigning his professorship (he was, he said, 'beginning to feel mental decay') and moving to London. He and Lady Mary would have to make drastic economies. They could live in Yatscombe cottage rather than in the main house. He could dispense with a secretary. The gardener, Edgington—a most faithful family servant—could be asked to accept a reduced wage. They might do without a car, but while they stayed on Boar's Hill one was indispensable. Perhaps such speculations were part of a recurring pattern of worry rather than the signs of an immediate crisis.

Three years later in 1935, Murray had further thoughts of moving to the cottage or of selling Yatscombe and buying a smaller house nearer Oxford.[43] By this time Basil was launched in journalism, and towards the end of 1936 Murray could conscientiously recommend him to Leonard Woolf as a possible author of an article for the *Political Quarterly* on the 'United Front'—he had, Murray said, 'good precise ideas about it.' Basil had meanwhile become more directly involved in politics. At the General Election of November 1935 he stood as an anti-government Liberal for Argyll, and 'made a good run', in Murray's words, his election address being 'pure League'.[44] On 25 May 1936 Basil was involved in what became a notorious incident when he attended a meeting of the British Union of Fascists, addressed by Oswald Mosley, at the Carfax Assembly Rooms (following one at the Oxford Town Hall). There was a considerable group within the audience who regarded the British Fascists' behaviour as generally provocative, and interrupted the speeches sometimes by shouting the words 'Red Front'. At one point Oswald Mosley challenged them to say the words again. Basil Murray did so, and was physically attacked, along with Frank Pakenham, Philip Toynbee, and others, by the Fascist stewards. Frank Pakenham was quite seriously hurt. The BUF proceeded to take out a summons against Basil Murray and Bernard Floud for 'acting in a disorderly way at a public meeting and inciting other persons to do so.' Murray himself wrote to Sir John Simon, then Home Secretary, asking him to receive Patrick Gordon-Walker and Frank Pakenham to give an account of the meeting; but Simon declined to hear them until the result of the summons was known. The case was heard on 25 June. It was alleged that Basil Murray had distributed newspapers at the meeting, and signalled to hecklers to interrupt by 'organized opening and shutting' of these papers, to stand in gangways in opposition to the stewards, and to make loud comments. He admitted some interruptions (including the words 'Red Front'), and was fined £2 on each count and £33 costs. It was thought that the black beard which he sported at the time told against him with the magistrates.[45] Murray consulted Professor Brierly at New College about what he regarded as a 'grave miscarriage of justice', but was unable to take the case any further. Basil in any case had emerged well from the whole affair.

Within a year he was dead. Early in 1937 he decided to work in Spain for the anti-Fascist cause, as a correspondent. He travelled out at the end of January and died of pneumonia within three months on the journey back from Malaga . . . 'The experience there seems to have been very terrible and, I think, weakened his power of resistance'. The loss hurt Murray deeply. Basil, with all his 'scrapes', was a vivid and sympathetic character — 'always good-tempered and gay', his father wrote, 'and generous in his outlook in the face of great trials — a great friend and companion to me.'[46]

Murray's grandson, Philip Toynbee, was a more thorough-going rebel than Basil both in political and in sexual affairs according to the portrait of him presented by Jessica Mitford.[47] Perhaps he had more to rebel against. In 1934 Murray described him drily to his mother as having 'too many views and not enough knowledge'.[48] Three years later Murray wrote to Lady Mary about Philip's first novel (*Savage Days*) in words which suggested that he found the moral rebellion of the young generation more distasteful than their political stance: 'If the young Communists are like that, they are indescribably loathsome . . . I thought that there were signs of madness in the disconnected, senseless chain of violent emotions. If he does not go mad, I think he will turn Catholic'.[49]

5

These last words reflected some of the distress and sense of failure which Murray had experienced when his daughter Rosalind Toynbee had been converted to Catholicism in 1933. Her conversion was indeed not a sudden affair, and had been preceded by a long process of mental estrangement from her father. Murray's original anti-clericalism had indeed long been mitigated by a reverent awareness of the unseen and unknown surrounding the existence of man on earth, and a sense that this awareness was often shared by clergymen. However, with his intimates he dropped easily into anti-ecclesiastical banter. He was delighted, for instance, to read of an early African bishop, Synexius:

When they wanted him to be a Bishop, he said he would not, because he would not leave his wife; so they waived the wife. Then he said that he did not really believe the Creed — e.g. the resurrection of the body. So they waived the Creed. Then he made a very good Bishop.[50]

The atmosphere of the Toynbee's home at Ganthorpe, where Murray often stayed, was not conducive to much rationalist frivolity. In 1928 he reported to Lady Mary Rosalind's conviction that she had experienced 'definite religious conviction and support by divine strength.' Of course she was 'very sensible' about it, and admitted the possibilities of psychological explanations. Her book,

Hard Liberty, published in 1929, he found to be a queer complex of prejudices, 'which makes her attribute all the evil of the world to those people and things which she thinks she has been pressed to admire.' A few months later he found her 'rather markedly religious, though, I think, more Quakerish than Catholic, at any rate below the surface.'[51] He was clearly not yet prepared for the full shock of Rosalind's conversion to Catholicism, but wrote in 1930 of the way in which nearly all his friends and relatives were becoming Catholics or Anglo-Catholics 'or else Christian Scientists or Neo-Buddhists or Seventh-Day Asphyxiasts. I become quite oppressed from time to time and long for the sight of a good old-fashioned anti-clerical.'[52]

For a time it may have seemed to Murray that Arnold Toynbee, quite as much as his wife, was in danger of backsliding from rationalism. In 1932 Murray had his first taste of Toynbee's 'Nonsense Book' (the *Study of History*)—1,400 foolscap pages—and found it most brilliant: 'The large "planetary" view is so striking; the variety and vividness of the illustration; and the imaginative background, full of quotations from the Bible and the classics. There is no one else who could have written it.'[53] From the first, however, Murray felt that Toynbee had 'let himself go in places in rather a fanciful way' and that his key concept of civilizations meeting challenges with responses was a sort of metaphor from psychoanalysis—'really a Crichton-Miller idea; the neurotic people are always funking "challenges" instead of meeting them.'[54]

In 1940 he wrote to Barbara Hammond about Toynbee's Burge lecture:

I too was a good deal shocked. I think he holds contradictory opinions at the same time . . . As Catholicism under Rosalind's influence grew upon him, he was worried by its obvious inconsistency with his theory of civilization, and he has found a most ingenious way of solving that inconsistency. The various religions are all a 'preparatio Evangelica' not exactly for the C of E or the present Catholic Church but for the True Religion that is to come: then with an amazing collapse of common sense, he finds the essence of the True Religion in the Catholic Hierarchy and the Mass. This, I confess, I find deplorable . . . I think he became alienated from Modern Civilization at the Abyssinian crisis and after, he felt that all statesmen were pursuing gross worldly and material aims and neglecting higher considerations. He was in a state of great emotion about this, and I suspect that R somehow got him to identify the 'higher things' with the Catholic Christianity. He was alienated again from the Catholics by their behaviour in Spain. Another element in the whole curious business is that both R and A are in their hearts always 'Protestant Dissenters'. They are against their surroundings . . . As Geoffrey Howard says 'R is never pro—she is always anti'. And paradoxically the neatest way to be in opposition in ordinary intellectual circles, is to become a devout Catholic!

The Toynbees' marriage broke up in the 1940s, but Arnold Toynbee remained on close terms with the Murrays and was a frequent visitor at Yatscombe; and on the death of Isobel Henderson, he became Murray's literary executor.

There was no kind of break between father and daughter after Rosalind joined the Roman Catholic Church in 1933. As Murray wrote to Vera Brittain about Agnes, he was always 'on terms of frank argument, if not of agreement,' with his daughters. He could tease Rosalind by saying he was 'fighting the battles of her Church' in the CIC, or about the confusion caused in human affairs by the annual celebration of the 'birthday of Mithras' (Christmas Day). He could criticize freely one of her novels as reflecting too faithfully through its heroine the author's own disillusion—and contrasted with it the inspiration and enthusiasm which he had observed twenty years earlier among both young officers fighting for the Allied Cause and conscientious objectors.

In fact, as was to be expected, Murray behaved in a thoroughly rational and civilized way. However, to his most intimate friends he did not conceal his feelings about the depth of the difference which had now opened up within his family. To Hammond, for example, he wrote of the parallel which he saw between Stoic and Catholic arguments: 'We behave better than others, therefore our beliefs must be truer.'[55]

It was Rosalind Toynbee rather than Murray himself who publicly advertized the differences between them by publishing early in 1939 *The Good Pagan's Failure*, a sort of anti-rationalist manifesto, in which Murray himself figured very obviously as the 'Good Pagan'— over-confident in the powers of man to improve his own environment, through social legislation or the League of Nations, remote from the 'barbarous' crowd and élitist in his way of life, forgetful of his own sins and inadequacies, of the essential problem of evil and of his need for divine help.

The most interesting passages of the book, for the purpose of this biography, are personal. Rosalind Toynbee confessed that it was the outlook, standards, and values of 'enlightened Pagans' by which she was first educated, and that she retained 'a deep regard, a very real respect for the good Pagans' whom she now felt bound to oppose. As a child she had heard frequent references of a satirical nature to the 'Old Man' up in the sky who sent people to Hell. How could intelligent rational beings accept a morality based on such barbarous conceptions? From an enlightened rationalist viewpoint, religion stood for illusion, refusal to face the truth, shirking of human responsibility, flight from reality. This was the essence of the conception which she had found inadequate as a guide for her own life, and a principal cause of the reversion to barbarism in the world which had been so largely controlled by 'Good Pagans' since the Renaissance.

There is one further very revealing passage, which suggests a sort of 'dialogue of the deaf' about religion between father and daughter. The good Pagan is represented as covertly envious of the 'secret way of happiness' found by the Christian, asking to be allowed to share the secret, and offering in return 'a share of goods which he himself possesses, freedom of thought and action, an open mind, an independent judgement'. But this is merely a source of fresh misunderstanding, since the good Christian wants none of these. The good Pagan thus finds that the good Christian denies him an equal footing—Catholicism is totalitarianism, the author specifically says. 'This wounds his self-respect and irritates him; he feels himself and his world depreciated.'[56] It is not clear whether this represents any particular exchange between Murray and Rosalind, or a summary of arguments used on either side over a long period. The Murray papers, as preserved, contain no exchanges between them on the book as published (Murray had probably seen the draft beforehand).[57] Possibly some relevant letters have been destroyed.

Lady Mary may have been even more deeply hurt than Murray himself by *The Good Pagan's Failure*. He, the 'Good Pagan' himself, was treated with some respect. She is not mentioned by name, but is characterized unkindly in a paragraph which clearly refers to her, as one of those 'so deeply Pagan in their heart, so essentially rebellious and self-assertive, so abnormally sensitive to the slightest yoke, that greater knowledge would but further alienate them . . . Such people . . . are as a rule misfits in whatever circles they move, inharmonious, nonconformist, and discordant; these rebels would be only more rebellious . . . the more they understood of real religion.'[58]

6

In the address given at a dinner held in Christ Church to celebrate his 70th birthday and forthcoming retirement from his professorship, Murray spoke movingly of Lady Mary's part in their joint life: 'No one coming to her for friendship or sympathy has ever been sent empty away, and I have the negative merit of not having interfered.'[59] More privately he assured Lady Mary a little later that all that was wrong with her was 'a sort of irresistible generosity' which always made him proud of her.[60] Such genuine admiration did not prevent occasional explosions on one side, as when Lady Mary accused Murray in summer 1936 of indifference to the sale of arms to the Italian government, which would use them 'for wholesale murder in breach of all its treaties'.[61] The first impressions of a number of memoirists were that the two made a very disparate pair, and that it needed all Murray's finesse and humour to mitigate the effect of Lady Mary's lack of tact and sensitivity.[62] Those who knew them better could see further into their relationship. Douglas Cole wrote to Murray in summer 1936, when Lady Mary was seriously ill with an internal ulcer, of how he had for long liked and respected her, as being always 'on the side of the angels'.[63] Murray himself could always turn to her with a deep sense of shared experience, often tragic, and of common ideals, held now in opposition to prevalent trends: 'I just sit and think of dear Ba [Basil] and beloved Agnes and you — and incidentally of Isobel [Henderson] and other young people threatened with death. One wants to weep and weep.'[64]

But neither husband nor wife let themselves be overwhelmed by these personal sorrows. They were jointly involved from 1933 onwards in very personal care for intellectual refugees from Nazi Germany, and Yatscombe became a home for a few of these, and a place of comfort and practical help for many more.

The principal recipient of the Murrays' hospitality was Rudolf Olden, formerly political correspondent of the *Berliner Tageblatt*, who had done his active and courageous best to counter the influence of the Nazis and had no possibility of staying in Germany under Hitler's government. He and his family were settled in the Yatscombe cottage by mid-1935. Many German and (from 1938) Austrian refugees visited them there, and, as Murray wrote, 'the whole wound' was kept open under their eyes, to remind him constantly of the 'incredible brutality of Governments and nations' — and to his constant surprise, of the contrast between this and 'the abundant goodwill and kindliness which I find in individuals'. Yatscombe itself was a place of refreshment for many more temporary German guests. Among the names that occur among Murray's letters are those of Adam von Trott, and Heinz Koeppler, an enthusiastic correspondent, after the war the director of Wilton Park — an institution of which Murray surely approved whole-heartedly. By means of such contacts and friendship, Murray did much for scholarship in Britain. He and

Lady Mary also did something more, and of equal importance, something touchingly described in the words of some Austrian guests: 'You may not have saved our lives but you saved our faith, our hope and our love—and that is more. So we do not say anything more to-day than—thank you, we thank you—for you.'[65]

Murray increasingly armed himself against the blows of fate and age by viewing the world, his colleagues, and himself with a humorous detachment—a form of protection not available to Lady Mary's ardent temperament. For many years from the early 1920s he kept a scrap-book of cuttings and illustrations which caught his fancy as he read on train journeys. These were connected by suitably inappropriate titles and passages of narrative referring to his own household, their neighbours on Boar's Hill, and people working for the LNU, the whole forming a sort of picaresque novel called 'Broken Lives'.[66] A rather similar scrap-book was also kept, full of limericks composed by Murray himself, with similarly inappropriate illustrations cut from newspapers.

Such exercises were regarded by Lady Mary as frivolous and a waste of a great scholar's time. She could not understand that Murray's favourite spare-time reading should be either detective stories or the works of P. G. Wodehouse. To a former secretary, Audrey Richards, Murray described his domestic routine during a bout of eye-trouble:

Lady Mary reads detective novels to me with an expression of outspoken contempt and occasional ejaculations such as 'What is the good of this sort of book?' 'No character study at all!' 'A drinking book!' Then Lucy [Mair, his secretary at the time] comes and reads Sophocles or the Times. Then I go and dig up roots in the garden.[67]

As he grew older the circle of his intimate friends enlarged, and he kept up a large correspondence, much of which is preserved. The letters show him at his most endearing; particularly those to Isobel Henderson, Audrey Richards, and, later, to Rose Macaulay. Isobel Henderson had been elected Craven Fellow of Oxford University in 1929: shortly afterwards Murray wrote to her:

The Regius Professor presents his compliments to the Craven Fellow. He walks about the bamboos and azaleas in company with the Chairman of the L.N.U. and the President of the C.I.C. and other dignitaries, but finds their company entirely unsatisfying—as to say the truth, they seem to find his. So he writes to you: But what is he to write about? A description of the garden: how the pneumonias are in full bloom, and the creeping arthritis gracefully coiling itself over the espaliers, and the side of the pond all ablaze with pink neurasthenia . . .

Describing an LNU subscription dinner he wrote:

It is raising money by a dinner at the Guildhall to which it refuses to invite the wives of meritorious men but does invite (a few) meritorious women—consequently the non-meritorious wives want the blood of a human victim.[68]

Another more active relaxation was the writing of short humorous pieces for his friends. This was an occasional temptation which Murray found it hard to resist. When Audrey Richards asked him for a testimonial, she received the following (no doubt as well as a more serious document):

I am happy to state that Miss Richards as a secretary is a fair treat. She speaks bettern I do myself; and after all what does it matter, since her appearance is such as cheers but not inebriates, at least not always . . . I write as a plain business man, the same as won the war. And as for papers, she will hide them so as no inspector could find them, not in a month, and when he has gone she will have them out again in two jiffs.[69]

A further example, is a mock-official letter supposedly addressed in 1933 to the Prime Minister, Ramsay MacDonald. It refers to Archie Macdonell's novel *England, Their England*, which Murray had much enjoyed (though he confessed to Macdonell that he 'had never happened to strike on that heavy-drinking literary set in London' which the author had caricatured).[70] Murray wrote in the character of one who had been consulted on the propriety of awarding a high honour to the author.

Strictly Unconfidential. My dear Prime Minister, Order of the Garter to Mr. Archie Macdonell. No doubt, as you may say, he is now one of the most eminent literary figures in Europe, second perhaps only to Wilhelmina Stitch; also, you are certainly right in supposing that your generous offer would be enough to make him instantly change his party and support the National Government with all the zeal and eloquence which he now devotes to Liberalism. But, my dear Prime Minister, what is genius without character? The man simply cannot be relied on. He promised me, in the presence of witnesses and in the most categorical manner, that he would send me a copy of 'England their England' with his name written in it, so that I could if necessary sell it at a large profit, but do you suppose that he has done so? No, he is one of those Celts whose promises are piecrust.

Yours obediently, G.M.

There may have been some private joke between Murray and the Prime Minister—it is not impossible; but more probably the letter was sent to Macdonell to remind him he had not received his copy of the novel.[71]

On the subject of the League of Nations and the LNU, Murray led a sort of double life. There was the public and devoted worker for great international causes. There was also, yoked to him, an observer, sometimes dispassionate, sometimes sharply satirical, of governments, officials, enthusiasts, and their typically strange ways. The latter personality expressed itself in a number of letters from Geneva already quoted—also, much more often than can be assessed, in Murray's conversation (he was a brilliant mimic), and in some dramatic skits on League of Nations affairs, which are preserved. However, the best in this kind are Murray's anonymous prognostications, published in three successive Decembers by the *New Statesman* as 'Old Moore's Almanack' for the coming year (examples are quoted for 1933 and 1934 in Chapter XXVI).

There was a good deal of satirical passion behind this jesting but in general Murray was prepared to view with relaxed good humour his chances of success in various good causes, without giving up his efforts to realize them. Early in 1933 he refused to associate himself with an appeal for some cause affecting London:

There must be some cause which I leave in peace . . . I am already protesting against the Government, the Japanese, the League, the male sex in relation to the female, predatory animals in relation to other animals . . . the Almighty on all counts . . . I might have added Ramsay and Sir John Simon to the above list.[72]

And a year later he wrote for the *Spectator* a delightfully relaxed 'Defence of Old Age' and the joys of not caring so much about so much: 'I suffered greatly from fear in my 'teens and twenties; fear that people in power in the world would take offence at my views or behaviour or manner of dress and consequently hate me.' Such fears had faded as old age grew upon him; at the same time his conscience was, he confessed, 'nothing like what it was in my prime, when, unless memory deceives me, its beak and wings were rather a terror of the neighbourhood'.[73]

This was not entirely banter; but no one who knew Murray could doubt that neither his fears as a young man, nor comparative relaxation in old age, would deter him from striving for the causes that he thought most important.

CHAPTER XXV

Committee for Intellectual Co-operation

1. CIC constituted May 1922—Murray first British delegate—first CIC meeting deals mainly with organization Aug. 1922—teething troubles.

2. French offer Institute of International Intellectual Co-operation with financial support 1924—French dominance feared, but Institute established 1925—Britain refuses financial contribution—Murray becomes Chairman of CIC 1928.

3. Organizational developments 1925–1931—problems with the Institute—reports and plans—reorganization of CIC adopted 1930.

4. Work of reformed CIC 1931–1939—Convention on Broadcasting 1935—Committee for Literature and Arts—Conferences on International Relations—CIC unable to help intellectual victims of Nazis directly.

5. Murray's difficulties over HMG's lack of support.

6. Assessment of CIC—Murray sees humorous side—his loyalty to distinguished colleagues—his view of positive factors.

1

IN the course of the second Assembly of the League in 1921, Murray began to be associated with what was known as 'intellectual co-operation' between member states. He was an obvious choice for such work. None the less he felt initially that he was being side-tracked towards subjects of secondary interest. Writing to Lady Mary from Geneva during the second Assembly, Murray complained: 'I see they will put me on to the organization of Intellectual Work, a subject that bores me stiff.' Two days later there was a four-hour discussion, 'devastating and drivelling' on 'that beastly Intellectual Travail'. After a fortnight he had to report on it to the Assembly—the subject was 'almost a joke'. He had to make a long speech, to a 'tired and inattentive' audience, but 'I find that I am getting interested in the wretched business, from having to explain and defend it!' The interest was still by no means enthusiastic, and in reporting to Smuts on the Assembly, Murray wrote of the organization of Intellectual Work as 'a somewhat hazy and obscure subject, on which nobody but a few cranks seem to have any clear views'.[1]

The Committee for Intellectual Co-operation was formally constituted in May 1922. The early months of its life witnessed a number of bureaucratic comedies, played out by people of the highest intellectual distinction. The League Secretariat had difficulty in agreeing on countries which should be represented on the Committee, and in obtaining from their Governments suitable nominees. The Secretariat informed the Council that it would be indispensable for the British government to nominate Murray, and he made no difficulty.[2] Other governments and nominees were more troublesome. The French delayed, but finally appointed very eminent delegates: the philosopher Henri Bergson, who became the Committee's first chairman, and Madame Curie, the famous physicist. Germany was not yet a member of the League, and so could not be a member of the CIC. However, it was felt that Germany should be represented and Albert Einstein was approached. He at first agreed, but soon had second thoughts: he could not represent German intellectuals because of his 'international attitude', his Swiss citizenship, and his Jewish origin. Murray was called upon to persuade him and succeeded temporarily, but the events of January 1923 produced another and more determined resignation.[3] Einstein felt that the French occupation of the Ruhr proved the League to have 'neither the power, nor the good will to fulfil its great mission'. Murray was again charged with the task of reconciliation. As one who had much sympathy with Einstein's point of view, he wrote to the League Secretariat that it would be better for the CIC not to meet until the Ruhr issue had been referred to arbitration, or at least until after the 1923 meeting of the Assembly. At the same time he told Einstein that there was plenty of good will in the CIC and that his resignation was unfortunate. Einstein remained unrepentant for some months, but a year later felt able to write to Murray that his disillusion with the League had been only temporary—a letter which could be deemed by the French member of the League Council to constitute an apology. He was duly re-elected to the CIC in June 1924.[4]

Very different difficulties arose over the representative of India, Bannerjea. He had been appointed on the understanding that he was a professor at Calcutta University. It proved he had never held a teaching post at any Indian University. The government of India urged Murray to press for his resignation to avoid the unpleasantness

of having him publicly rejected: but there was considerable delay
before he understood the message which was being diplomatically
conveyed to him.[5]

The intellectuals, more and less eminent, assembled at the first
meeting of the CIC in August 1922 were faced by some oddly
assorted questions and by a number of administrative tasks. The
Foreign Relations Secretary of the Royal Society, for example, Sir
Arthur Schuster, wanted to talk with Murray about the relations
between the League and existing international scientific societies; and
the League's Commission on Armaments wanted the Committee to
make recommendations on whether the discoveries of scientists about
gases that might be used in warfare should be published compulsorily.
It was decided that member countries should be asked to appoint
National Committees (for the CIC).

The more routine duties of the Committee were well defined in
a paper prepared, probably by Murray, for the British Delegation
to the League Council in December 1923, under the title 'The League
of Nations and Intellectual Co-operation'. The CIC was to provide
assistance to those countries whose intellectual life was threatened
with something like extinction as the result of the war, principally
by the provision of books and scientific periodicals, and by the
building up of libraries. A Universities Information Bureau had been
established at Geneva, to collect data on the needs of recipient
countries, and a number of useful memoranda on their educational
systems had been published. Attempts were being made to promote
international conventions for the protection of intellectual property
(authors' rights, etc.), and arrangements were in hand for the
publication of bibliographical material.

This line of approach, emphasizing the practical down-to-earth
nature of the CIC's activities was clearly designed to appeal to the
pragmatic inclinations of the British government, which had so
far conspicuously failed to show any interest in the CIC. British
educational authorities did not immediately recognize that it was
worth any serious attention. One principal reason for this failure
was a most unfortunately-conceived project dating from the first
months of the Committee's existence. The CIC passed a resolution
at the end of its first meeting in August 1922, requesting the League
Council 'to constitute an enquiry into the conditions of intellectual
work in various countries, the evils from which intellectual life is
suffering and the remedies suggested.' This was bad enough, but the
CIC (and the Council of the League) decided that the enquiry should
be conducted by means of a comprehensive questionnaire addressed

in identical terms to a large variety of countries. Murray's contact at the Board of Education warned him immediately that this was a hopeless means of collecting information, and it was soon clear to him that Oxford University for one would not reply. Murray's distaste for such a procedure was shared by Cecil.[6] Cecil could just tolerate the general idea of intellectual co-operation, as 'the sort of crazy thing foreigners do',· but the questionnaire was too much for him—'What lunatics foreigners are!'[7] Murray put the arguments against the questionnaire to the CIC and was immediately asked to redraft it himself.[8] Thenceforward he found it simplest to act on his instructions, and on getting the expected unfavourable answers, be able to say 'I told you so' to the CIC.[9] In the end, Murray's old friend from Merchant Taylors' and St John's, F. S. Marvin, produced a memorandum on intellectual life in Britain which was deemed an adequate answer;[10] and it was agreed that the Universities Bureau of the Board of Education should act as the British National Committee.[11]

2

By the end of 1924 the CIC's initial crises seemed to be over. But a major organizational problem remained which was to cause Murray many headaches. In theory the CIC was to think out projects, then pass their resolutions to the League Council for approval: it was then for the League Secretariat to implement them. Needless to say the League Secretariat was very reluctant to take on this extra work: and, in any case, it was clear the CIC needed some permanent base and some sort of secretariat of its own.

In the summer of 1924, the French government offered a site in Paris and financial support for the establishment of an International Institute of Intellectual Co-operation to serve as a permanent executive organ of the CIC. Here was an offer difficult to refuse, but not altogether easy to accept in the international context of the time. In 1924 Franco-German relations were not so tense as they had been, but still difficult. Murray hoped to secure official German co-operation in the work of the CIC. Was this the time to accept an invitation which might result in French dominance over the CIC's work? A manuscript draft memorandum by Murray shows that he shared the official fears about the motives of the French. His advice was to accept their offer but with the declared intention of establishing similar technical institutes in other Allied capitals—a practice which was followed on a larger scale after 1945.[12]

The Institute was duly established in 1925, with a Governing Body consisting mainly of CIC members, a Director-general, inevitably French, and sections to correspond with the various fields of work and sub-committees of the CIC—General, University Relations, Legal, and Information. The problems arising were predictable. The Institute provided posts for a number of academics who combined great talents with an underdeveloped sense of co-operation. The appointment of senior officers was usually a matter for some kind of international bargaining. It was difficult exactly to demarcate the limits of activity between the Institute, the CIC itself, and the League Secretariat. It also became painfully obvious that, if the Institute were not to become effectively a French body, other governments would have to contribute to its expenses; and equally obvious that the British government, having paid a general subscription to the League, was unwilling to pay anything to the CIC itself, and much less to its subordinate institutions.

However, 1925 saw a development which was only good for the CIC. A formula was found to enable the US, though not a member of the League itself, to send a representative to the CIC. This meant for Murray one colleague who spoke the same language and who was able to draw on the interest and good will of many high-minded Americans, and who also had access to the richly endowed American Foundations: and, in the event, perhaps most important of all, America provided a home and generous support for many members of the CIC and the Institute during the Second World War.

At the end of summer 1925, Bergson's health made it impossible for him to continue as Chairman of the CIC. Murray was the obvious successor, particularly as Bergson felt very warmly towards him— 'aucun de mes liens n'était plus fort que ma sympathie pour vous.'[13] However, the distinguished Dutch scientist, A. H. A. Lorentz, became Chairman until 1928 when Murray took over. The work involved annual visits to Geneva in the late summer to report to the Assembly— usually combined with mountain holidays in Switzerland—and quite frequent visits to Paris during the rest of the year.

3

From 1928 to 1931 Murray's work for the CIC broadly speaking can be seen as developing on three main lines. Firstly, he was involved in chairing not only the CIC itself, but also many of its sub-committees. Secondly, he was much exercised over relations between the CIC and the Institute in Paris. Thirdly, he was continuously engaged in providing progress reports, and evolving a sensible programme for the CIC and in allocating responsibilities.

First the committee work: Murray's practised eye quickly distinguished between the more 'airy' topics, and those which could be translated into useful action. A sub-committee had been set up in 1926 on the instruction of youth on the existence and aims of the League of Nations. Although the education of youth was a subject close to Murray's heart, he did not hesitate to point out at the sub-committee's opening meeting in August 1926[14] that for better or worse—and he himself thought for worse—it had been decided that educational work was the responsibility of national governments and the CIC could only try to co-ordinate and advise on the efforts made in various countries. The following year this sub-committee dissolved itself,[15] though it was revived as an Advisory Committee in 1934.

On the other hand, the work of two other sub-committees chaired by Murray—on Intellectual Rights and on Arts and Letters—led to permanent and useful results. The former recommended further study of the rights of wage-earning inventors, and of the terms of engagement of opera singers, and of stage and cinema actors. The latter recommended the establishment of a uniform international copyright of fifty years after an author's death, and the setting up of national groups of translators, to be followed in due course by an International Translators' Office.[16]

The second field of Murray's activity—relations with the Paris Institute—remained a thorny problem until the end. In November 1925 Alfred Zimmern had been appointed Deputy to Jules Luchaire, the French Director of the Institute. At first all had gone well, but early in 1927 Murray was informed that Luchaire needed a deputy less full of ideas and with more administrative talent than Zimmern.[17] The main trouble was that Zimmern had too many irons in the fire, and was apt to involve the Institute in his own personal interests. For example, he had done much to launch, under the auspices of the League, an Institute of International Policy at Geneva and a summer school associated with this. In connection with it, he had interested the Oxford University Press in publishing a book on *The New Germany* and had tried to get Murray to write a preface for it. Murray had refused, on diplomatic grounds; he was as keen as anyone to get Germany involved in an exchange of ideas about international affairs but a preface by him would hardly be dissociated from the CIC and might alienate the French from its work and from the Geneva Institute. Zimmern's reaction was to write the preface himself. Murray regarded this as 'undesirable and indiscreet in every way', and wrote sternly on the subject to Zimmern. The sense of the preface, he said, was that the Geneva summer school was an integral part of the Paris Institute's work; but both the CIC and the Institute were pledged to take no direct part in educational activity. If Zimmern's introduction was not changed, the CIC would probably move that the work of the school be discontinued. It is typical of Murray that this severe letter was followed by detailed correspondence with Zimmern about a possible new scheme for financing the summer school.[18]

Murray's private thoughts about the Institute were bitter: nevertheless the Institute was there and the CIC had to make the best of it. Murray recognized that the Institute could easily lose its intellectual character and become involved in politics, and come under French dominance. There were also problems of competence: what was the relationship between the National Committees working for the CIC and the governmental delegates accredited to the Institute? Should the Secretary of the Institute take his orders from the CIC or from the League Secretariat? In frank memorandums to the Foreign Office in January and December 1928, Murray made no attempt to defend the Institute, though he tried to dissociate the CIC itself from the ill-repute increasingly attached to the Institute.[19] He was ready enough at this stage to concede that Britain should not subscribe to it, if only some official contribution were made to the CIC.[20] But the British government displayed little interest either in the merits of the CIC or in the defects of the Institute; Murray never succeeded in extracting from them any kind of monetary contribution to either body.

The third part of Murray's activity—reporting and planning—makes repetitious reading. In a report of the first five years of the CIC which he wrote for the British government in 1927, he could be frank. It was not over-complacent. It listed a variety of conferences held under its auspices over the past year—for example, of International Students' Associations, museum representatives, library experts, and experts on the bibliography of biology and the social and economic sciences. The CIC, he wrote, was a co-ordinating body not concerned with the execution of agreed plans. The horrendous experience of organizing a 'Congress of the Popular Arts' (foreshadowing some of the more bizarre activities of Unesco) should deter the CIC from ever undertaking such a task again. It should, for example, be relieved of the responsibilities for any kind of international library service. It was useful to have discussed the quality of inks and papers to be used in documents of historical value, but any practical action on this should be taken by the International

Association of Historical Studies. On the other hand, the CIC, as an organization of the League, was particularly well qualified to secure support for the International Committee of Annual Tables and Constants in mathematical quantities for chemistry and physics. The Institute too was discussed as described above.

From 1928 to 1930 Murray was heavily engaged in discussion about the reorganization of the CIC and the reallocation of duties between it, the Paris Institute, and the League Secretariat.

In April 1929 Murray asked all members of the CIC to contribute ideas about the future work of the Committee. Murray's own suggestions included efforts to raise the standard of teaching in modern languages and the writing of history from a more international point of view. (In 1937 he actually approached Maisky, the Soviet Ambassador in London, about the possibility of securing 'better treatment' of Britain in Soviet school texts and vice versa.)[21] He also advocated regular institutional exchanges in the field of higher education. The US representative on the CIC, Raymond Millikan, had constantly emphasized the need for student and teacher exchanges, which could attract financial support from the great American foundations.[22]

As a result of these discussions, in July 1929 Murray was asked by the League Secretariat to chair a Committee of Inquiry to examine the work the CIC had done, and intended to do, and the relation of the CIC to the Paris Institute.[23] The report was warmly welcomed by the Secretariat and formally adopted by the League Council in autumn 1930.

In 1930 Luchaire resigned as Director of the Paris Institute after a furious row with Zimmern, who that summer was appointed to the new chair of International Relations at Oxford.[24] This greatly eased Murray's dealings with the Institute as he found Henri Bonnet, the new Director, a good colleague.[25]

4

After the adoption of the report of the Committee of Inquiry in late 1930, the work of the CIC and the Institute assumed a form which lasted until the outbreak of war. At the end of 1938 Murray described it to Smuts:

The actual scope of our work has increased greatly; we have regular meetings of Museums, libraries, directors of education and the like from all countries. We have had considerable success over matters of copyright and inventors' rights.

By 1934 the Institute had published *The Co-ordination of Documents Centres*, an *Index of Bibliographies*, and an *Index of Major Translations*. The work of some of its committees, particularly that on Literature and the Arts, was carried out in part by famous figures. The composer, Bartók, for example, urged the need for help in publishing authentic editions of the musical classics and making them available to the public.[26]

Murray himself was now concerned mainly with the policy committees which had to survey the detailed work undertaken in the various fields; and the annual CIC conferences in Paris meant a punishing three weeks for him in late June and early July.[27]

Murray himself was much concerned with the potential effects of broadcasting, and in 1931 the twelfth Assembly of the League, stimulated by the British LNU, resolved that the Institute should continue the study of broadcasting and extend it to cover educational films. The study produced some results and a Convention on the use of broadcasting was drafted in 1932 and finally adopted in 1935.[28]

The CIC's Committee for Literature and the Arts held a distinguished meeting in summer 1931 with Murray in the Chair, and Béla Bartók, Karel Capek, Thomas Mann, John Masefield, and Paul Valéry in attendance. Murray opened proceedings with a lofty speech on the contribution of artists to the good life, and the way in which that contribution could be improved by a heightened awareness in each nation of what was achieved by others. 'If only Victor Hugo and Tennyson had known each other, we would have been spared the ridiculously narrow patriotism of each.' Masefield spoke of the importance of poetry readings in original languages — a point developed by Murray and at some length by Valéry. Mann said little on literature but dwelt more on the potential influence of music and films; Murray later said that though Mann had come to the conference as a sceptic, he had been converted by what he heard. Bartók spoke of the possibilities of international record centres, and Valéry suggested that this idea should be extended to films. The full official record of this extraordinary gathering of stars is of considerable interest.[29]

The same Committee developed a series of 'Conventions' (*Entretiens* or seminars). Perhaps the most successful of these was that held at Frankfurt in May 1932 to celebrate the bicentenary of Goethe's birth. This was an occasion of much symbolic significance — the first meeting of a major League of Nations Committee in Germany to pay tribute to a German figure of major European importance.

Murray spoke twice: on Goethe as a Hellenist, and on Goethe in relation to the Anglo-Saxon world.[30]

The 'Conventions' which succeeded this one do not seem to have been of much value and both they, and more generally the meetings of the CIC's Letters and Arts Committee, suggest increasingly Arthur Koestler's vision of the intellectual 'Call Girls' of the world, travelling from conference to conference in regular and fruitless discussion of lofty themes.

From 1932 onwards the CIC was active in encouraging regular Conferences of Institutes of International Relations. An important international conference of 'Chatham House' type institutes, held in London in the summer of 1935, was occupied with a detailed and extremely interesting study of the concept of 'Collective Security', which included excellent papers on the possibilities of international military action, and the probable limitations of economic sanctions. The studies could not have been more timely, in relation to the Abyssinian Crisis, but the lessons to be drawn from them did not penetrate to the minds of the politicians concerned.[31]

The CIC took no direct part in exposing the ideology and activity of the 'Axis' powers. Germany had withdrawn from the League in 1933 and the CIC felt unable to tackle the Nazi persecution of Jewish and other intellectuals on a political plane. In 1935 Dr Leo Szilard, lately of Berlin University, appealed to Murray to set up an international committee under the aegis of the CIC to help refugee scholars. By this time action on a national level was being taken by various other countries (though in Britain's case admission was restricted) and Murray took the line that nothing could be done by the CIC in a corporate capacity.[32]

Similarly when the CIC was asked to finance the publication of the works of non-Aryan scholars, Murray felt that, apart from political difficulties, such action would not be proper for the CIC with its limited budget and general policy of not taking part in any educational activity. However, he was typically active in exploring alternative means of publication; and personally, both in his academic capacity and privately, he was ceaselessly active in helping intellectual refugees (*see* Ch. XXIII sect. 2, XXIV sect. 5, and XXV sect. 5).

5

Murray's work at the CIC involved him in considerable political problems: the most embarrassing were those caused by his own government. There was a brief period of hope when Arthur Henderson was Foreign Secretary (1929–31), when it seemed that the CIC might be used to stimulate a public feeling for disarmament or political co-operation ('moral disarmament') in Europe.[34] But British Foreign Secretaries in general displayed little or no interest in intellectual co-operation. The international conventions on broadcasting and the teaching of history, Murray claimed, were neglected because of the indifference of the 'League's major power'.[35] However, his greatest difficulty arose from successive governments' unwillingness to subscribe a penny to the CIC. A typical CIC budget (for 1935) showed that the French contributed 2,000,000 francs out of a total of 2.5 million; Italy 15,000 fr., Brazil 75,000 fr., and Mexico 60,000 fr.[36] The British contributed nothing but the argument that they paid a substantial general contribution to the League of Nations and it was for them to divide it as seemed best among its subordinate organs.

Murray wrote to successive Prime Ministers and Foreign Secretaries about this situation. To MacDonald he complained of the personal embarrassment caused to him: not least when it proved to be impossible to hold a meeting of the Committee on Letters and the Arts in Oxford. With Simon, he tried flattery — the British Foreign Secretary could give a lead at the League. With Cranborne, Halifax, and R. A. Butler, he patiently rehearsed the arguments for a special British contribution.[37] He also attempted to build a small lobby in the House of Commons, by means of a committee with John Buchan, Philip Noel-Baker, and Herbert Samuel as members, to keep the government up to the mark.[38] But it was all to no avail.

After the Conservative victory in the Election of November 1935, and the initiation of a programme of rearmament (which Murray on the whole supported), he realized there was likely to be very little official interest in cultural affairs. Nevertheless he was very bitter about the establishment of the British Council (in 1937) with government funds used, as he thought, for national and propagandist rather than international and educational purposes. His resentment against the government increased when, under the heading 'Obstacles to International Intellectual Co-operation', the Austrian delegation to the CIC insisted on adding to the Institute's report for 1938 an Annex complaining of Britain's restrictive policy on the admission of refugee musicians and scientific workers.[39]

6

In the whole context of Hitler's rise to power, the aggressive policy of Nazis and Fascists, their obvious inaccessibility to reasoned argument, and indeed their exalting of national instinct over reason, the efforts of the CIC to lay an educational and intellectual foundation for the future co-operation of European nations, and on a wider scale between Europe and the East, seem with hindsight futile. At best Murray and his colleagues were engaged in a process the results of which could only be seen in the very long term, and would inevitably be overwhelmed in the mean time by the dark forces of unreason. Murray himself was officially over-sanguine about the value of the CIC's work. As late as mid-July 1939 he could tell the annual meeting of the CIC in Geneva that more and more use was being made of the committee, and that the work to which they devoted their energies was indestructible.[40]

Such an estimate may be partially discounted as the sort of pep talk in which the President of an international committee is bound to indulge. What were Murray's private sentiments about the work of the CIC as Europe slid rapidly towards the abyss — a process of which, as Chairman of the LNU, he was more acutely aware than most? Of course he saw the absurd side of applying the machinery of international committees to intellectual and educational work. Conversation with the Soviet delegate on intellectual unemployment was a *dialogue des sourds* ; so was discussion of textbooks with the Japanese: 'In Japan the textbooks are by nature faultless, being approved by the Emperor, who is a divine being.'[41] Murray enjoyed indulging his friends with affectionately humorous descriptions of the CIC's proceedings. To Rosalind Haywood he wrote (July 1931):

I wish you could have been present at 11.30 p.m. Kruse (Head of the Berlin Library) looking obstinate and a tiny bit — only tiny — drunk; Painlevé leaping in the air like an india-rubber ball and screaming when he got to the highest point of each jump; Madame Curie biting her lips and looking like a martyr; me in the Chair soothing them as best I could. And it was all about methods of bibliography.[42]

Arts and Letters produced even more striking results, which Murray enjoyed relating to Isobel Henderson:

Yesterday a really interesting discussion . . . Old Destrée [the Belgian delegate] thought he ought to make an original speech. Looking like a bloated crocodile, with eyes half shut, he held forth on . . . 'le spectacle de la jeunesse moderne dévouée aux jouissances matérielles' — just as Margaret Wilson, my secretary, looking very Quakerly and clean, came in . . . Destrée's secretary had been explaining to her with admiration what a dog Destrée was, how 'il aime toutes les bonnes choses, les vins, les femmes, les bonnes viandes' . . . It was rather like a Shaw play.[43]

At a later meeting of the governing body of the Institute:

Mme. Curie, à propos of nothing and entirely out of order, said that M. Paderewsky ought to be a member of the Cttee. of Lettres. I said she was out of order . . . But De Reynold, who had been looking at a new translation of the Kalevala [the Finnish epic] . . . told Mme. Curie that he thought M. Kalevala would be even better than M. Paderewsky. She, nice woman that she is, said she did not know M. Kalevala . . . Whereupon De Reynold invented a wonderful Cursus Vitae for him. I hope she will never find out. It was a shame.[44]

In 1921 Murray would have made comments of this kind in a fairly cynical spirit. At that time he was bored with the idea of being edged out of the political activities of the League, and landed with responsibility for the 'intellectual travail'. However, the work had grown on him, and after the reorganization of the Institute in 1931, he came to feel that the Committee had the opportunity of making a really useful long-term contribution to the peace of the world.

Moreover, Murray developed a strong personal loyalty to the remarkable company which he kept in the CIC. Einstein was the most eminent of the original group, and Murray had played a major part in getting him to withdraw his resignation. Broadcasting many years later about the CIC's original team, Murray said that he felt in them a 'purity of heart'; and in Einstein particularly, but also in Madame Curie, Lorentz, and the Japanese Count Nitobe (the original secretary), immense intellectual power combined with good will and simplicity.[45] Murray fitted well into such a company, and would not give up his work on the CIC while they continued to participate in it.

In autumn 1933, while it was still possible not to appreciate the full menace of Nazi Germany, Murray wrote a special article for *The Times* on the work of the CIC, describing the vision which inspired him. Had an average man been able to attend the whole series of CIC meetings that year, and to keep awake, he wrote, 'he would at least have realised that he was listening to a record—fragmentary indeed and imperfect—of the unseen process which creates and maintains human progress; a process which seldom gets into the front page of any popular newspaper, because it does not consist of explosions or spectacular triumphs; only of the steady growth, and amid much discouragement, of the activity that will save civilisation, if civilisation is to be saved.'[45]

In July 1935, Murray addressed the annual conference of the CIC with a 'measured optimism', partly official but partly also reflecting his deep inner convictions about the state of the world. He spoke openly of the anarchy in inter-governmental relations, of the increased repression of the innocent, of the growing misery of refugees. Against this, he could put into the balance the great advance of mass education. He remarked too among the student generation as a whole more seriousness of purpose than in the years before 1914, more public spirit, a greater sense of international brotherhood.[47] On the corresponding occasion a year later Murray added another positive factor. 'I cannot but be impressed by the goodness of individual men and women and the immense amount of kindly will, of public spirit, of activity in good causes which I see around me.'[48] In 1936, as in 1935, he compared the state of the modern world to that of the Hellenistic world after the death of Alexander the Great. There is no excessive spirit of optimism implicit in these remarks. But they do imply that in Murray's view there was still a foundation on which to base attempts to create a new international order, and that he would have considered it a betrayal of the younger generation's seriousness of purpose and of the kindly goodness of so many individuals to give up such attempts, however likely it was that they would be frustrated by the 'anarchy in inter-governmental relations'. It should be remembered that at the same time Murray was doing what he could to organize political resistance to Hitler and Mussolini on an international basis; he may still have overestimated the power of public opinion and the importance of educating it, but he was far from relying on that alone to stop the advance of the Nazis and Fascists.

Curiously enough it was Bernard Shaw who, in his play *Geneva* (1938), expressed what were perhaps Murray's unspoken and final ambitions for the work of the CIC. Writing to Bonnet, the Secretary of the Institute, Murray remarked that it was by no means one of Shaw's best plays, but it did show the CIC in the centre of the picture, and the complete neglect of it by the British government. 'He makes the C.I.C. summon the Dictators before the International Court', and they comply with the summons in order to gain the good opinion of the world. In the *Spectator* Murray wrote that Shaw's moral was correct. World public opinion was still important, though as a tribunal it was 'weak and slow and helpless and confused, and would not always test the evidence before it.'[49] Here too was something intangible which might be fostered and must not be betrayed.

CHAPTER XXVI

The League of Nations 1931–1939: Disillusion

1

IN February 1931 Murray concluded an article in *Headway* with the sentence, 'No war at present is in the faintest degree probable'; and as late as 10 September 1931 Cecil told the League Assembly: 'there has scarcely been a period in the world's history when war seemed less likely than it does at present.'

Eleven days later on 21 September the Chinese delegate informed the League Council that Japanese troops had occupied Mukden, capital of the Chinese province of Manchuria, and requested action under Article XI of the Covenant to safeguard the peace.

The Japanese had hitherto been regarded as a force for peace, unfailingly loyal to the League. Most League members were reluctant to believe that Japan was now instigating a major international crisis. Japan, they were told, had no territorial ambitions, and would withdraw troops as soon as the safety of its citizens in Manchuria was assured: hostile action by the Chinese had given rise to the trouble. The Council of the League passed an anodyne resolution urging both parties to refrain from violence and to withdraw troops from each other's territory.

It was not yet clear that this was a major crisis rather than a transitory incident. In Britain the National Government, which had just been formed in August 1931 as a result of the economic crisis, was particularly anxious to regard it as the latter; they wished to focus all their attention on financial and economic affairs.

Murray's first public utterance on the Manchurian crisis was a letter to *The Times* of 14 October 1931 in which he described the

Eastern situation as a 'complicated tangle', strongly implying that a firm attitude by the League, if backed by the USA, would be enough to secure a Japanese withdrawal: the peace party in Japan was strong, as was the Japanese League of Nations Society. The LNU Executive on 15 October described the Manchurian crisis as crucial for the League, but went no further than asking the government to do everything possible to uphold the League's authority.

There was no widespread sympathy for China. Cecil's brother, Lord Hugh, suggested to Murray that the Japanese had been quite right in intervening to restore order.[1] A new National Government had been returned at the election of 27 October and at an LNU lunch in honour of the new Foreign Secretary, Simon, Murray himself had admitted that in the opinion of jurists it was not clear that Japan had contravened any particular article of the Covenant. This may well have been one of the occasions Cecil had in mind when he later wrote to his wife that 'Gilbert makes me nervous when he speaks. He always seems on the point of giving the whole case away and sometimes does.' The Liberal press did not fail to exploit Murray's speech on this occasion.

But by the end of November Murray was getting restive and wanted a special meeting of the League Assembly summoned to condemn Japan for violating the Covenant. Cecil was more cautious and preferred the idea of sending a mission to the spot and exercising quiet pressure on the Japanese[2] and he was supported by the LNU Executive. On 10 December the Council of the League agreed that a commission of representatives of Britain, France, Germany, Italy, and the USA should visit Manchuria. The Earl of Lytton (a Conservative member of the LNU Executive) was appointed to represent Britain and as Chairman of the Commission.

Although Cecil had advocated the sending of the mission, he later wrote that he privately regarded it as inadequate to restrain the Japanese military party, which was now unquestionably in a dominant position.[3] This indeed was the opinion of the more fiery spirits within the LNU. The meeting of the LNU Council was stormy and to many of those present Cecil's public defence of the League Council seemed to imply an undue confidence in Japanese good faith.

There was also public criticism of the LNU: the *Manchester Guardian* was particularly bitter in commenting on the complacency and feebleness of the LNU Executive and General Council, which could do no more than 'deplore the initiation of hostilities in Manchuria before application to the League'. Murray himself was personally criticized for the doubts he had expressed about the illegality of Japanese actions.

Although Murray had hoped for stronger action by the League, he wrote to the *Manchester Guardian* on 16 December in reply to those criticisms, loyally defending the LNU and the League. 'As for the [League] Council itself, I can only say that when men like M. Briand, Senor Madariaga, and Lord Cecil have worked . . . in a desperately difficult situation and eventually come to us with a unanimous settlement, partly good, partly faulty, telling us they have done their best, for my part I believe them and simply cannot understand the mentality of those professed friends of the League cause who greet them with derision because their victory was not complete.' The *Manchester Guardian* printed a leader in connection with this letter, emphasizing that in fact everything of importance had been given to the Japanese.[4]

The *Manchester Guardian* was not a lone voice, but it spoke for a very small minority. The LNU's greatest trouble in connection with Manchuria was that for some months after the first Chinese complaint the British public, and therefore to a great extent the British government, was quite uninterested in it. Public opinion, so long thought to be the ultimate threat, seemed to have failed entirely in this case. Murray wrote in *Headway* (January 1932) that from the British press the Japanese would conclude that the League did not matter and that they could break treaties with impunity.

At the beginning of the new year there were two new developments. On 7 January 1932, Stimson, the US Secretary of State, addressed a note to the governments of China and Japan calling for the preservation of the integrity of China and the maintenance of the 'Open Door' for trade there, and asked for diplomatic support. Murray sent a telegram to Simon, expressing the hope that the UK would associate itself with the US in pressing on Japan the sanctity of Treaties;[5] but the government professed itself content with the assurances already given by the Japanese about freedom of trade, and gave no diplomatic support to Stimson's initiative.

More important were events in Shanghai towards the end of January. A Chinese boycott of Japanese ships had led indirectly to the bombardment by Japanese warships of the suburb of Chapei, and to a situation which seemed to involve a threat to the international settlements there. British warships were immediately sent to the area; the Japanese were convinced that the Western powers were seriously concerned, and they stopped their military action in Shanghai. Here was an issue directly affecting British commercial interests over which British public opinion was roused easily enough; and prompt action and a Japanese withdrawal had resulted. For some weeks Murray hoped that the lesson could be learnt and public opinion could be stimulated to put pressure on the British government over the wider problems of Japanese aggression.

At this stage the LNU Executive began openly to demand a more active policy by the government and the League itself against Japan. Murray led a delegation to Simon on 16 February 1932, and left him with some suggestions for action, emphasizing that Japan could not resist joint pressure from Britain, France, and the USA. In any case there must be no diplomatic recognition of Japan's illegal territorial gains.[6] Finally a special Assembly of the League met on 11 March 1932 and adopted a resolution to bring about a solution under Article XV of the Covenant. An armistice was by then expected in Shanghai, the League Commission was on its way to the Far East, and it was widely thought that this was the beginning of the end of the crisis in Manchuria. Murray wrote to Drummond in a spirit of surprising optimism: 'One breathes again after the resolution of the Assembly. Unless something goes very wrong in the next few weeks, I think we shall have had a real triumph for the Assembly . . . It seems to me clearer than ever that public opinion is the real weapon of the League of Nations, and that boycotts and blockades, even if they have to be used, will always be a mark of failure.' To Simon, Murray repeated much the same sentiments, and added his warmest congratulations. Even Noel-Baker assumed that the Assembly had achieved a triumph, and that the LNU had played some part in this behind the scenes.[7] This optimism rested on the assumptions that the Lytton Commission would find against the Japanese and that the Japanese would accept their findings. The second assumption was much bolder than the first. Murray was content to make it, partly because, like Cecil, he was anxious for the LNU to devote the maximum of attention to the issues of disarmament. When he spoke to the LNU General Council at the end of June, he could assure them that on the Manchurian issue public opinion had by then taken the right line, and leave it at that.

The policy of 'waiting for Lytton' came to an end in October 1932, by which time a Japanese puppet state (Manchukuo) had been established in Manchuria. The Lytton Report was completed in August, presented to the League Council in September, and published in October. It clearly established Japanese responsibility for initiating armed action, and the unpopularity of the Japanese regime with the local population, and proposed a settlement which would safeguard the integrity of China and the Treaty rights of Japan. The Report was warmly welcomed by Murray and the LNU but its conclusions were not regarded as necessitating the immediate application of sanctions to Japan. Lytton himself was strong on this point. He persuaded Murray that the main problem was now to make it possible for the Japanese government to accept the conclusions of the Report, and both seemed to think the problem soluble.[8] Lytton himself argued that the most pressing need was for caution, in order to preserve unanimity in the League—which had not yet formally accepted his Report—and to secure American co-operation; a *Headway* editorial duly emphasized that talk of boycott and blockade was premature.[9]

However, the period of unanimity was soon to end in the face of Japan's determination to hang on to its conquests, and the British government's apparent willingness to acquiesce. Murray was subject to continuous letters from disappointed supporters of the League. Freda White, a member of the LNU staff, wrote to him in disgust about Simon's statement to the League Assembly of 6 December 1932,[10] and this seemed even to Cecil to be pro-Japanese. Murray felt bound to warn Simon that LNU opinion was getting 'worked up'; the fact was that Simon 'was going too far in the direction of conciliation . . . and that any failure to stand firm for the Lytton Report . . . will result in a betrayal of the League.'[11]

Murray's own mind was hardening against the government's attitude. LNU policy, he wrote to one correspondent, must remain that the Assembly should condemn Japan formally, and then proceed to steps up to and including those envisaged under Article XVI of the Covenant (i.e., using sanctions).[12] His plans, he wrote, were based on the assumption (comparatively new and realistic) that China would accept and Japan reject the conclusions of the Lytton Report.[13]

As a mediator, Murray was kept busy at this time. Simon wrote to him in mid-January 1933, complaining of the injustice of accusations in the *Manchester Guardian* that he [Simon] did not back the conclusions of the Lytton Report. Murray replied softly, but urged him to work for an international agreement on the non-recognition of Manchukuo.[14] On 31 January the two met and Murray explained to Simon the strong feeling within the LNU in favour of an embargo on arms exports to Japan. Simon was reluctant; an embargo by Britain alone would be useless, and how could we ensure that it would be universal?[15]

The League Assembly on 24 February 1933 accepted a resolution substantially based on the Lytton Report and urging reconciliation between China and Japan; the US administration endorsed the Assembly's action. The Japanese reply was to give notice that Japan would leave the League, and to sit tight in Manchukuo. As a result of these developments, the British government took some action on 27 February, suspending the export of arms to both China and Japan, while 'international discussions' on Manchuria were in progress. Murray and Cecil accepted this as a step in the right direction: to denounce it as totally inadequate would have infuriated the right wing of the LNU including two important members of the Executive, Lytton himself, who publicly damped down hopes of effective action by the League, and Austen Chamberlain, who had always regarded the LNU's role as merely declaratory—a mobilizer or non-mobilizer of world public opinion. Murray and Cecil might still correspond about the need for firmer action against Japan, and about the government's 'vacillatory and insincere' policy, but by now there was no hope of effective international action against Japan.

The 'Manchurian crisis' was over. Its full importance as an illustration of the League of Nations' limitations might not yet be as obvious as they were to later historians, or to protagonists such as Cecil later in their lives; but at best the Japanese victory was a severe setback for those who had placed high hopes in the force of world public opinion.

Murray's private views of the situation were probably best expressed by one of the parerga in which at this period he would anonymously relieve his frustrations. This was 'Old Moore's League Almanack' for 1933, published in the *New Statesman* at the beginning of the year (he typically sent a copy of this to Lady Cecil, referring to his 'old and valued teacher, Mr. Moore, from whom I have learned all the astrology that I know').[16] The situation envisaged is that the Eskimo air force has bombed Stockholm, and the Swedes have referred the matter to the League Council. The Eskimos dispute their right to do so: can a country without a capital be considered as a nation? Sir John Simon suggests reference of this point to a Committee of Jurists. M. Benes proposes a fund of a million francs for the relief of Swedish refugees. Simon approves and limits the British contribution to five dollars. Señor da Madariaga proposed the expulsion of the Eskimos from the League; Simon urges extreme circumspection; the Eskimo air force is very powerful, and it is doubtful whether force has been used to settle a dispute between nations, since there has been no dispute. In a conciliatory speech, M. Paul Boncour observes that France is the soldier of humanity and continues to march, head erect towards the ideal.

2

The problems of the Far East had not been the exclusive or even the main preoccupation of the League of Nations or the LNU in the period between September 1931 and March 1933. The governments of Europe at the beginning of this period were mainly concerned with retrenchment and recovery in the face of the general economic depression, and Murray had wanted the LNU to exercise its full influence in urging an international solution for world economic problems. But disarmament, widely held to be an economic necessity, was high on the agenda of the League. A general Disarmament Conference was due to take place at Geneva in February 1932. Preparations for it were in hand, and Murray as well as Cecil had to concern himself with these in some detail.

Murray based his own attitude on an assumption later made famous by Stanley Baldwin and more appropriate to the nuclear than to the high explosive age. If bombers were not prohibited, he argued, 'every capital in case of war would be destroyed by air attack in the course of a few hours.'[17] At heart, then, he was more in sympathy with the pacifists and abolitionists over matters of disarmament than with those who wished to see peace secured by the creation of an international force. In theory the obvious method of reaching agreement on disarmament was a reduction in the forces of the other main European powers to the levels agreed for Germany under the Treaty of Versailles, levels to which the Germans had duly reduced their forces according to the official conviction of Allied Commissioners (though the French government privately and correctly disagreed with them). But to satisfy the French desire for security against possible German rearmament there would have to be international guarantees which depended for their effectiveness on something less than total and immediate reductions by the Allied governments; the Germans would not easily agree to anything less, and Britain, with world-wide imperial commitments in mind, would not easily agree to so much. This was the essence of the difficulties on which a Disarmament Conference, even in more favourable circumstances than those of 1932–3, was likely to founder.

The Conference opened in February 1932 unpropitiously: the Japanese had just bombarded Chapei and British warships were on their way to protect Shanghai. First was presented a French plan, which included the establishment of an armed international force and new commitments to collective action involving the retention of such 'offensive weapons' as bombers, battleships, and heavy artillery. The British government was most reluctant to undertake further commitments. The idea of any kind of international force was equally repellent to Austen Chamberlain and the LNU Conservatives and to the pacifist wing of the LNU. Only David Davies and his supporters were pleased. Murray reluctantly concluded that the paramount need was to secure French co-operation and that some concessions must be made to meet their demands, if there was to be any progress.[18] But when it came to defending their own interest, France, Japan, and Britain were equally intransigent.

Simon was among those statesmen who gave some support to the idea of abolishing some offensive weapons, and here was a vague enough general theme on which LNU leaders could unite. An impressive group of them including Murray, Cecil, Austen Chamberlain, Lord Parmoor, and Norman Angell voiced their whole-hearted support of Simon in a letter to *The Times* (3 June). But in Geneva the issue was soon bogged down in the details of technical definition.

Hopes revived for a short time when President Hoover presented new proposals for arms limitation on 22 June 1932: as usual the LNU warmly welcomed the US initiative, while the difficulties of arriving at a concrete agreement remained the same.

Towards the end of July, the Disarmament Conference adjourned after issuing a resolution in the form of a statement recording progress on a number of points—the repudiation of bombing, the prohibition of chemical warfare, the principal of budgetary limitations on armament expenditure, and of supervision by a permanent disarmament commission. The Germans voted against this resolution, as denying them equal rights, and stated their intention not to return to the Conference. Little cause it seemed was there for joy, and Murray until the last days of the Conference had been pessimistic about results. However, he returned to London in an apparently sanguine mood. It is not easy to account for this, but perhaps Cecil provided the right perspective when he said later that in the summer of 1932 the international position appeared very favourable; the Japanese had withdrawn from Shanghai; the Nazis seemed weak, the French government of the time was comparatively conciliatory, and the Americans had made some definite proposals. For these or other reasons Murray was encouraged to interpret very optimistically the Conference's resolution on adjournment.

To the press he wrote:

I return from Geneva inspirited, almost elated. The Disarmament Conference has not been a failure. It is a first step, which has perhaps not taken us very far in itself, but has left us on a springboard.[19]

The 'criminal classes', as he unkindly called the government's professional advisers, had this time been defeated.[20] This was not simply a tactical display of optimism for the benefit of the LNU. To Herbert Samuel he wrote privately that on the whole he was much pleased; the resolution was hollow in itself, but all countries except Japan wanted to go further, and the strength of 'peace feeling' in Europe was now revealed. Murray's euphoria even extended to Sir John Simon. He had explained to Noel-Baker that Simon needed to be handled by flattery, and now wrote to him privately in terms of warm congratulations: Simon was not to be caught so easily, and asked Murray in reply whether a few public words of praise would not be possible.[21] Within the LNU, however, Murray's attitude was subject to criticism. One critic wrote of the LNU, led by its chairman towards its grave, with 'exquisite Japanese politeness, deferential and obsequious to the Government'.[22]

By mid-September Murray's optimism was seen to be misplaced. Cecil wrote in *Headway* that the LNU had lost its faith in some of the delegations at Geneva—'notably, alas, in that of Britain'. The Cabinet agreed at the end of the month to a meeting with LNU delegates and others to discuss how to bring Germany back to the Disarmament Conference (they did not want to alienate the pacifist wing of the LNU);[23] but when the deputation, led by Murray, was received on 20 October, it could do little more than urge on the government more decisive intervention in the Conference discussions.[24]

3

At the beginning of 1933, when Hitler seized power in Germany, a new dimension was added to all international problems, and from the first the prospects of effective collaboration with Germany in Europe seemed very slender.

Germany did not withdraw immediately from the League of Nations, and indeed a German representative was again attending the Disarmament Conference, though Noel-Baker wrote from Geneva about the 'wrecking tactics' he there employed.[25]

Murray, although privately much involved with Jewish and other academic refugees from Nazi oppression, had no part in the foundation at Geneva of the High Commission for Jewish Refugees from Germany. This was deliberately separated from the League in order to facilitate co-operation with Germany (which was of course never forthcoming), but Cecil was appointed Chairman of its governing body.[26] Murray drafted himself a powerful letter to the German League of Nations Society (*Deutsche Liga für das Völkerbund*), asking how 'men of good will' in the light of what had been done to the Jews in Germany, could be expected to trust Hitler.[27]

As chairman of the LNU Murray's main concern was with the British government's willingness to revert to Great Power diplomacy rather than using the machinery of the League, in order to do business with Nazi Germany. For the time being the policy of Hitler was not a problem for the LNU, or for the British government. Even when Germany withdrew from the League in October 1933, this was not thought to be an irrevocable step. Murray regarded it as serious but not tragic. Hitler, it was supposed, was acting mainly to satisfy opinion in Germany rather than from the desire to pursue an aggressive foreign policy unhampered. The collective forces for peace seemed still very powerful.[28] Nevertheless Murray was in favour of sending a warning letter from the LNU to Hitler, and was disappointed when his 'love-letter' was not approved by the Executive.[29]

In talks with Foreign Office officials and Ministers on disarmament, the question of Hitler's intentions loomed large. Murray renewed relations with Vansittart, now promoted to the doubtfully important post of 'Diplomatic Adviser' to the government. Murray found him alarmed by Nazi penetration of London high society, and pondering the question of a special Anglo-German treaty. At about the same time he lunched with MacDonald at Chequers; the Prime Minster was much concerned by the extent of German rearmament but Murray was unable to have any serious conversation with him.[30] To Kathleen Courtney he reported his 'horror' at a broadcast by MacDonald, and (a significant link) at isolationist remarks by Lord Londonderry in the House of Lords. His 'Old Moore' prophecies for 1934 were almost rancorous in their treatment of the Prime Minister, who is made to call it 'a foul lie that the National Government has either done or not done anything which it should not have done or done or vice versa.' He was then to be translated as 'Lord Diddums of Blessumsthen'.[31]

In March 1934 Murray had detailed consultations with Simon and Eden—newly appointed to look after League of Nations affairs at the Foreign Office—about the Working Plan through which Simon hoped to salvage something from the Disarmament Conference. Murray's impression was that it represented too great concessions to the German point of view and aimed at agreement at a level of armament which the LNU found too high. Simon replied that it was still insufficient for the Germans; the 'concessions' which Hitler was prepared to make, they said, depended on the French being ready to disarm substantially after five years. Murray expressed scepticism about German desire for an agreement. Eden disagreed with him — the Germans wanted an agreement because they could not rearm up to the French level. However, on another essential point it was Simon and Eden who were more realistic. Simon asked how we were to give guarantees of collective enforcement if we had not the armaments for it. What did the LNU say to this? Murray replied that they would be against it, reckoning that for sanctions it would be enough to use our great strength in the economic and financial fields.[32] Simon did not dispute this but remarked on the danger of air bombardment in response to economic sanctions. He later confirmed to Murray that the British government's aim amounted to allowing and approving of a gradual and partial rearmament of Germany; it would be of no practical use to try to insist on budgetary limitations. The official policy of the government evoked bitter opposition from the centre and left wing of the LNU; and within the LNU Austen Chamberlain and the Conservatives bitterly criticized the attitude of the left wing. But German policy *per se* was not yet the centre of debate.

Within the LNU, as elsewhere in Britain, there were many who were prepared, if not to condone the excesses of Nazism, at least to forget or look away from them or to argue that embarrassing manifestations of nationalism must be expected from a country which had been humiliated as deeply as Germany in the years immediately following the war. Hitler or no Hitler, it was argued, Germany still had national grievances which could be met. So far as Murray was inclined to adopt such attitudes a personal interview with Ribbentrop, the German Ambassador in London at the time, went far to dispel them. Ribbentrop called on him at Oxford on Armistice Day, 11 November 1934. Murray opened the conversation with a reminder of the stand which he had taken after the war in favour of more equitable treatment of Germany by the Allied Powers. He went on to say that he had been forced reluctantly to an unhappy conclusion: Germany had abandoned the path of international co-operation and was following that of *revanche*. Ribbentrop replied by accusing Murray of furthering Marxist principles (Murray's gloss was that this apparently meant the 'Fourteen Points', the League of Nations, and international co-operation in general). These had brought Germany to ruin, and it was due to Hitler that Eastern Europe as a whole had not been overwhelmed by Communism. As it was, the Führer, who loved peace, had effected a moral revolution in Germany. Murray insisted that the British did not want any exclusive alliance; they had tried the path of reconciliation, and had been firmly rejected by Germany. Murray dealt with the subject which most concerned him personally, emphasizing the ingrained abhorrence of the British people to persecution. Ribbentrop replied that there had in fact been very little bloodshed in the German revolution, and Murray had the last word (at least the last recorded word) saying that torture in concentration camps was worse than death in battle.[33]

Meanwhile Murray had been making contact with 'the Bolshevik danger' in the person of the Soviet Ambassador, Ivan Maisky, whom he found a good deal more persuasive than Ribbentrop when they lunched together in March 1934. Maisky dwelt on the danger constituted by Germany and Japan and on the need for Britain, France, the USA, and the Soviet Union to face it together. He commented shrewdly that Simon wanted to keep the peace without making commitments, which made the problem insoluble. Murray asked him about the revolutionary activities of the Soviet Union. Maisky gave a smiling reply: 'At the beginning, we were all excited. We thought your capitalist system of society would be overthrown in a few months. You thought that our government would not last even that long—we have both learned that we must put up with each other, and see which system lasts best.'[34]

4

By the beginning of 1934 the LNU had every reason to feel discouraged. Japan was sitting pretty in Manchukuo and had left the League. The Disarmament Conference had come to nothing and Germany too had left the League.

Yet Cecil and Murray still believed in the power of public opinion. What could be done to rally the LNU members and prove to the government that there would be whole-hearted popular support for a strong pro-League policy? The idea hit upon was to hold a national poll—officially called The National Declaration on the League of Nations and Armaments, popularly known as the Peace Ballot. Such an exercise had been carried out very successfully, on a local scale, by the Ilford Branch of the LNU and Cecil took up the idea with his usual flamboyance. Murray was far from enthusiastic: he foresaw that the organization of such a Ballot on a national scale would be a crippling expense for the LNU. It is improbable that he did not also foresee there would be party divisions, but there is no record of this: probably nobody foresaw just how disastrous such splits would be this time for the LNU.

Every elector was to receive a questionnaire comprising six short questions, essentially asking whether they supported the League and Disarmament.[35] The government and the Conservatives were wholly opposed to the idea from the start. They objected that the questions were too involved to be answered by a simple 'yes'. The more clear-headed Conservatives, and the service chiefs, saw that the failure of the Disarmament Conference could be summed up in the syllogism:

No Disarmament without Collective Security.

No Collective Security without armaments.

Thus from 1934 onwards—reluctantly, and only on a small scale and as far as possible without publicity—the government was beginning to rearm. It did not therefore want 'overwhelming support' for Disarmament, when it could be seen to be rearming; nor for collective security which it had no intention of providing single-handed and indeed had not the means to provide. It therefore wanted to keep a low profile on these subjects, while for public purposes sheltering behind Baldwin's bland assurance that 'the League is the keystone of Britain's foreign policy'.

The idea of the Peace Ballot was conceived in January 1934, but results were only announced in June 1935. Trouble with the Conservatives came to a head in November 1934, when Austen Chamberlain wrote to *The Times* complaining that a tendentious leaflet was being distributed with the ballot papers. He also wrote personally to Murray deploring the 'lop-sided expression of public feeling'.[36] Other prominent Conservatives voiced strong disagreement. Baldwin in a speech in Glasgow in November openly said that Collective Security was impracticable as long as the US, Germany, and Italy were outside the League. Duff Cooper later told Murray that the Ballot had been exploited by Labour and done the LNU much harm. Murray wrote to *The Times*, defending himself and his colleagues:

The action of the L.N.U. was meant to be—and in my judgment has been—scrupulously non-party. But when eminent politicians implore people not to think at all about these questions but to tear their ballot papers up at sight, when Mr. Duff Cooper talks about 'poisonous propaganda' and Mr. Amery about 'political gangsters', I fear I cannot, though I try my hardest, prevent their political opponents from making capital out of such remarks.

It is they, not we, who are importing party politics into the business.[37]

Despite the fact that Conservatives were advised not to participate in the Ballot, over eleven million people (about one third of the electors) filled in the forms. The only question which received less than an 82 per cent affirmative answer was the question asking if, in the last resort, military measures should be taken against an aggressor, and even then 56 per cent answered 'yes'.

Cecil, announcing the results in June 1935, regarded it as a magnificent response. But the LNU was financially crippled for the rest of its existence and lost many of its Conservative (and richest) members.

5

Meantime, in parallel with the Peace Ballot, events were marching on. On 4 March 1935 the service chiefs and the FO issued a White Paper on defence, announcing that the British government had ceased to rely on collective security, and were going to rely on armed force. Hitler's response was to proclaim conscription in Germany. In April Ramsay MacDonald, already ill, met Laval, the French Premier, and Mussolini and the three set up the 'Stresa front' against breaches of international order: it was tantamount to saying they were going to go back to relying on Pacts and ignore the League. In June 1935 Baldwin took over as Prime Minister. Almost his first act was to conclude an agreement with Germany over the limitation of naval armaments—an open repudiation of disarmament by international agreement.[38]

All this made the Peace Ballot look like pie in the sky, as Cecil drove on enthusiastically to its triumphant conclusion. How far was Murray aware of the parallel events? Once LNU policy was decided upon, Murray always defended it in public. But quite often there are private letters revealing his own misgivings, as for example his views on the Locarno Pact (Chapter XXII). Unfortunately there is no record of his private opinions in early 1935.

In December 1934 a cloud had appeared on the horizon: there was a skirmish between Italian and Abyssinian troops at Wal-Wal in the Somali Desert over an ill-defined boundary. The red light was showing as it became clear in 1935 that Italy was building up large military forces in Africa preparatory to an attack on Abyssinia. At this point, however, neither the British nor the French were prepared to talk firmly to the Italians. Neither wished to offend their 'prized partner' of the Stresa front and drive Italy into the arms of Germany,[39] if she could be kept sweet with a bit of Abyssinian territory. Three times Abyssinia appealed to the League Council: in January and March, and only at the third attempt in May was the question considered. Throughout the summer various conciliatory proposals were made, usually accepted by Abyssinia, but always rejected by Italy.

The LNU from the start, led by Murray and Cecil, urged the government to take a strong line with Italy, but in vain. In June, Murray saw Sir Samuel Hoare, newly appointed Foreign Secretary when Baldwin took over as Premier. In July he went to Paris to try to put backbone into his French colleagues at the CIC, but reported to Cecil that 'French opinion could not be changed in time to help resolve the crisis'. He wrote to Cecil that 'the chief need of British policy was to convince Mussolini that we mean business'. In August the LNU Executive again urged the government to tell the League Council that, as the Peace Ballot showed, the British nation was ready to bear its part in any action that might prove necessary.

The LNU's pressure did convince the government that it was necessary 'to play out the League hand'.[40] On 11 September Hoare announced to the Assembly in Geneva Britain's whole-hearted support for Collective Security, provided the other members of the League also played their part. Hoare intended both parts of his speech to carry equal emphasis: in practice the League enthusiasts concentrated on the first part, the Italians with French support on the second. Murray wrote to Hoare congratulating him on his 'magnificent speech'. He seems to have overlooked the warning that Britain would only do as much as others were prepared to do.

On 3 October Mussolini's troops crossed the Abyssinian frontier. On 11 October the League Council declared that Italy had resorted to war in defiance of the Covenant. An overwhelming majority of League members agreed to put a limited number of sanctions into force. Everything seemed to be working out as it should and Baldwin took advantage of the lull to have a General Election and again talked of the League as being the 'keystone of Britain's foreign policy'. The National Government were returned with a reduced but still substantial majority (largely Conservative) and Murray wrote 'we are absolutely in the hands of the Tories for a long time ahead . . . if the enlightened minority can really carry the day . . . the worst disasters may yet be averted.' In the election Murray used his residential vote for the Liberal and voted for the Labour candidate for Oxford University (the Liberal having stood down).

In fact the application of sanctions against Italy was half-hearted: diplomatic relations with Italy were not broken and the most telling sanction—the oil sanction—was not imposed, though the LNU pressed strongly for it, and for blocking the Suez Canal.[41] The Service chiefs objected that such measures could provoke Italy to bomb our Mediterranean fleet—Britain alone would carry the can.

They were the less ready to take risks in the Mediterranean when the British fleet was pledged to defend the Far Eastern Dominions against Japanese aggression, the threat of which, though little publicized, was nevertheless taken very seriously by the cabinet at that time.

Further, it was objected, what good would oil sanctions do if the US did not co-operate? They might even step up their oil exports to Italy. Murray conferred with an American industrialist, James Shotwell, on this point and in November Washington announced that it would keep its oil and other exports to Italy at their normal level, which disposed of that objection. But still no oil sanctions were imposed.

In October Murray wrote to Rosalind, 'I would like to see 'naval' sanctions, i.e. the severance of communication between Italy and her African armies, as soon as possible.'[42] At the end of October the LNU organized a mass meeting in the Albert Hall to prove the strength of public support: it was to be addressed by a three-party line-up: Austen Chamberlain, Violet Bonham-Carter, and Herbert Morrison. But in order to get such notables, care had still to be exercised not to offend Italy. Murray cautiously advised Cecil that 'the meeting should make its subject Collective Security in the full sense rather than an indignation meeting against Italy; [though] personally I am bursting with rage and indignation about Italy.'

Then on 7 December came the leak from Paris of the Hoare–Laval plan to buy off Italy by giving her the fertile plains of Abyssinia. There was a public outcry from *The Times* and Conservative back-benchers as well as from the LNU. On 13 December Murray was a member of the LNU delegation to protest to the Prime Minister. He reported 'We did not say much. We merely listened to depressing and unconvincing statements by him'. On 18 December Hoare resigned and Eden, the new Foreign Secretary, announced that the proposals had been dropped. On 29 February 1936, Murray wrote, 'Baldwin had to give way to an outburst of National feeling over the Hoare–Laval proposals, but those proposals are the real policy of the government and they are clinging to this idiotic hope of conciliating Mussolini. I think it is terribly serious, perhaps fatal'.[43]

On 7 March 1936 Hitler occupied the demilitarized parts of the Rhineland, thereby knocking the bottom out of the Locarno Treaties.

The French government failed to take military action, partly because the British government made clear its reluctance to support any such action. As Germany was no longer a member of the League and had not invaded anybody else's territory, it was hard to charge her with having violated the Covenant. What had been difficult enough before became quite impossible afterwards. The Sanctions Committee which on 2 March had decided to do nothing until its next meeting, never met again.

In January Murray had protested in *The Times* against the theory which was being put about that nothing need be done about further sanctions because time, the rains, and the mountains would combine to give the Abyssinians the victory. Three months later Eden was warning his colleagues that the Abyssinian situation was desperate, and on 2 May the Emperor had to leave his country. On 8 May ten thousand people attended an LNU meeting on the theme of 'Stop the War in Abyssinia and prevent war elsewhere' (Murray was absent, probably ill). But the war was stopping anyhow and all that remained was a pathetic wrangle as to whether sanctions should be maintained.

On 10 June 1936 Neville Chamberlain made his 'calculated indiscretion', publicly denouncing the continuation of sanctions as 'the very mid-summer of madness'. On 17 June the British proposed at Geneva that sanctions be ended. On 4 July the League Assembly accepted the proposal by 44 votes to 1 (that of Abyssinia herself).

The government had fallen between two stools, alienating Mussolini without overthrowing him. Its solicitude for French susceptibilities had little effect on French policy. So far from avoiding having to fight Hitler, Britain had to do so in the end single-handed. The LNU itself lost heavily: its non-party status was impaired for good: Austen Chamberlain resigned from the Executive and many of its remaining Conservatives, including many of its most generous subscribers, left it.

On 14 June Murray wrote:

Neville Chamberlain's 'calculated indiscretion' has thrown some light into the darkness of British policy. My own reading is 'Sanctions will be dropped and Italy conciliated.' This with a view to the reconstruction of the Stresa front. At the same time Germany must also be placated. Article 16 of the Covenant must be eliminated. This spurious form of collective security having been done away with, a policy of rearmament becomes the only alternative. We shall be back at the old system of the Balance of Power. Gone is the dream of world peace and the Covenant as the keystone of British policy . . . What can poor Geneva do but register the death sentence which is being prepared in the great capitals? . . . It is undoubtedly a time of the most profound discouragement and disappointment. My own course is in the deep shadows. I shall stand by the League to the end but that will not mean anything against the forces ranged against it. Did we try too much? Was our faith in humanity too great? Is another long march through the night ahead of us? It almost looks like it. I feel dejected beyond words. And yet. And yet. I hear those brave words which Paul repeated 'My strength is made perfect in your weakness.' Can such great faith be practised in human affairs or does it belong merely to the ideal religious sphere?[44]

Certainly very many people would agree with Murray's summing-up of the Abyssinian question: 'The League of Nations was right, the League's policy was right. All that failed was the resolution of the statesmen.'[45]

6

The approach and the outbreak of the Spanish Civil War in the summer of 1936 provoked passionate anti-Fascist feelings in France and other continental countries. One manifestation of this was the foundation of the International Peace Campaign (*Ralliement universel pour la Paix*) designed as a coalition of the various associations, cultural as well as political, which might be prepared to join in a Popular Front against the aggressive threats of Hitler and Mussolini. The organizations represented in the IPC claimed 400 m members.

Cecil, looking round for a way to revivify the League and the LNU after the Abyssinian humiliation, was much attracted by the IPC and accepted the Chairmanship. A paper presented to the LNU Executive in October 1936 said that:

If the collective will for peace of the peoples of the world can be organised, there will be more likelihood of Governments adhering to their pledges. At a moment when national governments have conspicuously failed to show a collective will, the will of the peoples has found expression in an almost explosive demand for collective action. That spontaneous outburst has led to the IPC. It is the continental counterpart of the Peace Ballot and is wholly and absolutely welcome. The question is how to encourage it.[46]

Although Murray put his name to this paper (along with Cecil and Lytton) he had misgivings from the start, as did a number of LNU officials and members.

How the LNU should be related to the IPC became a matter of controversy. At first Cecil and Murray took the line that to have two organizations working for much the same ends would waste resources and that therefore the LNU should act as the British arm of the IPC. But Murray was nervous lest the experience of the Peace Ballot be repeated, with an uncontrollable IPC involving the LNU in big and expensive campaigns which would offend its remaining Conservative supporters and prove the last straw for its already shaky finances. It was therefore decided that the two organizations should work side by side, with the LNU being represented in the British section of the IPC on the same footing as other societies. But this solution led to the absurdity which had been foreseen. Each organization sent out appeals for money signed by the same man (Cecil) to much the same people for much the same purposes.

Relationships between the IPC and the LNU were bad from the start. Already in October 1936 Murray was writing to Rosalind 'The Devil's own imbroglio is going on at the Union about our relations with the I.P.C.'[47] Matters eventually came to a head at the LNU Christmas staff party in 1937. Murray wrote to Rosalind 'Eppstein has put his foot in it again. I am having a hard struggle to defend him. He wrote the staff party play this year, very amusing, but largely a skit on the I.P.C. and with one scene at the end rather offensive towards Lord Robert, so the I.P.C. people want his blood.'[48] Cecil demanded Eppstein's dismissal; Murray objected that to sack Eppstein would destroy the LNU as there would be many resignations among the staff.

Throughout January 1938 the storm raged at Grosvenor Crescent. 'You'd be surprised', wrote Murray to Rosalind, 'at the energy with which I am fighting the battles of your Church [Eppstein was a Catholic]. . . . Rum, I can keep the Executive in a good temper and fairly united on all large questions of policy, but when it gets to personal questions, they become quite human in the worst sense of the word. I think it is partly the exasperation of mind caused by continual defeats in world affairs that makes them so.'[49]

Cecil was on the rampage; he was intent also on removing Maxwell Garnett from being General Secretary on the grounds that the low morale of the staff was his responsibility. He further wished Murray to give up the chairmanship and be co-President with himself: the new Chairman should live in London and have more time to supervise the staff than Murray had had. Murray tried to dissuade him, arguing that the matter could be dealt with by appointing a Vice-chairman to supervise the staff, adding that his giving up the Chairmanship would lead people to suppose that there was a major split in the LNU. 'If Eppstein were to go and the Dame [Adelaide Livingstone] were put to death, and an effective vice-chairman appointed, I believe we could make things go,'[50] he concluded in lighter vein. Cecil was not assuaged, although in the end he accepted an apology from Eppstein. After some argument Murray, typically and without rancour, accepted Cecil's proposals and resigned as Chairman. He wrote to Lady Mary that he was 'glad to be rid of it'. It seems a very unworthy end to all that Murray had done to hold the LNU together during his chairmanship. When Austen Chamberlain resigned in 1936 he had written to Murray, 'I think you and I might have continued to run in double harness though at times we should have jolted one another, but I cannot keep pace with Cecil's raging propaganda.'[51]

In fact, as we shall see, as co-President of the LNU, Murray was as much in demand as ever to fulfil the role of mediator and conciliator. There can be little doubt that without Murray's tactful and skilful guidance from the Chair, the LNU would have fallen apart much earlier and would not have enjoyed the standing it did in government circles between the two wars. It is notable that the LNU was the only member of the Federation of League of Nations' Societies which had any serious influence with its home government, and the credit for this must largely be given to Murray.

There is little record of Murray's thoughts at this time, but it is not hard to imagine his anguish and disillusion as he watched the inexorable march of events towards the outbreak of war—a war without (at least for the British) the appalling trench slaughter of 1914–18, but in which civilians too shared the discomfort and danger. But, distressed as Murray must have been, he did not spare himself, for all his 73 years, in shouldering his part in the 'war work', and subsequently in building for peace.

The Last Years

1

ON 1 January 1941 Murray received the Order of Merit in the New Year Honours. Congratulations poured in from all manner of men: from Lloyd George, politicians, friends, family, and from numerous societies. These ranged from Liberal Associations, LNU Branches, Chatham House, and the PEN Club, to the Czech Journalist Relief Committee, the Committee for Spanish Relief, the Jewish Agency for Palestine, and even to the Incorporated Association of Rating and Valuation Officers, and the Pit Ponies Protection Society, to take a random selection.

The telegram from Lloyd George is interesting, as Kenneth Rose in his book on King George V writes that:

in 1921 at the suggestion of Balfour and after thorough enquiries the King proposed that Gilbert Murray . . . should be admitted to the Order.

Before the appointment was gazetted, the King followed his usual practice of informing Lloyd George as a matter of courtesy. To his astonishment, the Prime Minister replied that Murray's name must be withdrawn. He alleged that during the war Murray had been a pacifist and 'almost pro-German', adding that 'it would cause much annoyance to the Unionist Party, who were already in a mood which required to be placated rather than irritated'. The King replied that politics did not enter into the matter and that the Prime Minister had no say in disposing of the Order of Merit. Lloyd George however, insisted and the King abandoned the proposal rather than risk a constitutional conflict.

The only occasion on record when Murray met King George V was in 1918 when, together with Cecil, he attended a dinner at Buckingham Palace in honour of President Wilson.

Lloyd George's objections seem very strange when he had himself offered Murray first a CH and then a Knighthood in 1917 (both of which Murray refused). Presumably it was Murray's defence of the Lansdowne letter at the end of 1917, and of Conscientious Objectors in 1918, his criticism of the Treaty of Versailles, and of Lloyd George himself in his book of early 1921 *Problems of Foreign Policy* (see p. 298) which had offended the Prime Minister. There is no indication that the Murrays had any inkling of the proposal of 1921. We read later of Murray and Lloyd George collaborating well in 1930 and 1931 against the imposition of tariffs.

It might have been expected that this accolade heralded Murray's gradual withdrawal from the public scene into the shadows of retirement. But his last years saw little decrease in the volume of his work and correspondence. He remained President first of the LNU and then of the United Nations Association, Chairman of the Council for Education in World Citizenship (CEWC), and sole literary editor of the Home University Library (HUL) until his death. He was a British Museum Trustee until 1948, President of the Liberal International Association from 1947 to 1949, President of the Hellenic Society from 1944 to 1947; he was President of the Society for Psychical Research in 1952 and of the Classical Association in 1954, in both cases for the second time—a rare honour. These were no honorary positions; they all involved much correspondence and, in war, commuting in the black-out in unheated trains.

Though Murray was no longer Chairman of the LNU, he played a very active part first as President of the LNU and then of the United Nations Association (UNA), and until his last two or three years he seldom missed a Council meeting or an Executive Committee. In 1942 he wrote to Lady Mary that he was considering retiring as President of the LNU as 'I'm out of sympathy with Judd's flock. I believe in the U.N., they believe in Left politics with all the appropriate prejudices'.[1] However, he remained President until he died.

The voluminous correspondence on LNU affairs shows how Murray was till the end looked to for his opinion and counsel, as a mediator and speaker, to soothe and explain, to redraft the more controversial resolutions, to lead delegations to Whitehall, to put over appeals for funds. The Executive Committee of the LNU met regularly during the war, busy with plans to reconstitute the League on a broader basis. When the United Nations Charter was finally drawn up at San Francisco in 1945, Murray was able to report that the LNU had submitted 33 minor amendments, all of which had been accepted. In July 1945 he wrote to Lady Mary 'The L.N.U.-U.N.A. news is good . . . The F.O. want a Society like the L.N.U. and are delighted with what we've done.'[2] When the United Nations Association was formally constituted, Cecil became Honorary Life President and Murray and the Earl of Lytton co-Presidents.

The UNA, no less than the LNU before the war, had to deal with members who held widely differing opinions, and some of the officers, particularly left-wing sympathizers, were over-ready to formalize and publish their opinions as representing the views of the UNA as a whole. Murray's experience and skill as a mediator continued to be much in demand when things got out of hand.

During Kathleen Courtney's chairmanship of the UNA (1948–51) there is a constant stream of long handwritten letters from her to Murray asking for his advice and active help. She felt that the then Secretary of UNA, W. C. Judd, was 'too indulgent to the Left' and over-hasty. For example in 1949 Judd had written a letter to *The Times* accusing the Greek government of committing atrocities against the communist rebels. Left-wing members of the UNA were pressing the Executive Committee to pass a resolution condemning the Greek government in strong terms. This, however, the Executive Committee were reluctant to do, knowing that HMG did not want to see Greece go communist and therefore did not wish to highlight the crimes of the Greek government whom they were officially supporting. It is Murray who writes to an angry branch officer:

As to Greece itself, my general feeling is 1) that Greece is a Balkan country, so when there is civil strife, there are atrocities on both sides; also there is habitual corruption and oppression of the poor.
2) that it is a very wicked thing for foreign countries to stir up and encourage civil strife in a country in order to get it into their power, as Italy and Germany did in Spain and Yugoslavia and Albania are doing in Greece, presumably under Russian influence.[3]

Murray's tactics seem to have been effective, for Kathleen Courtney writes to him in June 1949 thanking him for 'your wonderful contributions to the Council Meeting. Thanks to your intervention, the Atlantic Pact resolution and the resolution on Greece were both passed.'[4]

On a later occasion in 1952 the UNA Secretariat had been previous in circulating to the branches copies of a resolution which the Political Committee had sent to the Foreign Secretary, Selwyn Lloyd, disagreeing with government policy over Seretse Khama.[5] Murray was then 86 and had told Cecil that he had 'harangued against it [the resolution] in the Executive which makes me so tired'.[6] But, 86 or not, it is still Murray who drafts the corrective manifesto to be sent to the branches.

In August 1953 Murray signed a letter to Selwyn Lloyd giving the views of the UNA on the Korean Settlement, and in October he was asked to approach the BBC over an appeal for the UN Fund for Korean refugees. In April 1954 he made the speech of thanks on behalf of UNA to Jebb on his retirement from being permanent UK delegate to the UN. In July of the same year, he was asked if, in his capacity as Chairman of the Council for Education in World Citizenship, he could 'do something' about an article in the *Times Educational Supplement* in which the CEWC were said to have indulged in Soviet propaganda. In November 1955 the Press Officer of UNA sent to Murray (now close on 90) at his own request eleven special reports to read. It seems strange that Murray should have complained to Rosalind in 1949 that he

felt out of things with United Europe and the U.N. etc. because I no longer have an official position — for Bob [Cecil] it's not quite the same thing as he, at least, is in the House of Lords and can speak when called upon.[7]

Murray's work as President of the Committee for Intellectual Co-operation did not totally lapse during the war. He was involved in a considerable correspondence with Bonnet (ex-Director of the Paris Institute) who had reached America, along with others of his staff. They, with generous American support, succeeded in maintaining skeletal activities at various centres in the US. Meantime in London under the auspices of the LNU and the CEWC meetings were being held under Murray's Chairmanship, attended by ministers of education or people of university experience from all the allied countries except Russia, together with leading representatives of the CEWC. They were engaged in drawing up reports on the re-education of Germany, on the re-establishment of education in enemy occupied territories, and a report on the ideals of education for a United Europe, or for the UN as a whole after the war.[8] A history of the CIC was commissioned from Raestad, a Norwegian ex-member of the CIC in Geneva, but there was some difficulty in getting this printed. A. L. P. Norrington, when asked if the Oxford University Press would take it as one of their Pamphlets on World Affairs, replied that the history of Intellectual Co-operation was of too limited interest to be included in a series from a University Press.[9]

At the end of the war, the work of the CIC was absorbed by Unesco and it formally ceased to exist in 1951. In 1956 Murray in a broadcast: 'Intellectual Co-operation—the Idea' was able to record that after the war, 'the re-building was swift; the U.N. in place of the League, and U.N.E.S.C.O. with many times the funds and a much broader programme to carry out on a much larger and more effective scale the enterprises for which we had fought our best and had at least made a beginning.'

Murray has been accused of being a dreamy idealist in League matters. Salvador de Madariaga saw further than that.[10] He wrote of the British 'Civic Monks' who began at Geneva with 'all too vague and limited notions of what a permanent peace required'. Cecil, he said, could be drawn into serious errors of judgement, but Murray never lacked empirical common sense; he understood that government was the art of the possible. In 1954 he could write to E. R. Dodds, 'In [19]23 and 24 quite reasonable people thought we were on the verge of Coll[ective] Security—not only Lord Robert [Cecil] and Benes, but Grey and even Austen Chamberlain.'

However optimistically Murray may have started working for the League, by the end of the thirties he had no illusions. He was totally unpompous about his own work. In January 1943 he wrote to J. A. K. Thomson:

I have been terribly busy with unimportant things, committees, L.N.U. things, Education Conferences, L.I.A. [Liberal International Association]. On the one hand it is obvious that all one's work will have little or no result, on the other I cannot suddenly resign my various chairmanships, etc. without making the impression I have lost my belief in L. of N. policy, etc. The same with Liberalism. These things are more needed than ever, and we must go on talking about them.[11]

This was Murray's contribution to his generation: seeing the worst, he never lost sight of the best. In the darkest days of the war in England he could still find causes for optimism, writing in 1942:

As a student of history, there are certain facts which stay in my mind: the extraordinary humanity of our Social Services, the noble spirit of the Atlantic Charter, and the political pronouncements of our leading statesmen; the high generosity of our recent proposals to India; the steady unvindictive courage of the great mass of the people; I may add the unpretentious self-sacrifice with which my friends and neighbours go about their private and public acts of service and the intense interest with which an almost absurd number of unofficial societies devote themselves to plans for the reeducation and welfare both of ourselves and our enemies. I cannot easily find in history any parallel to the humanity and the unconscious idealism of this generation which we have inherited from the efforts of our forefathers. It is a splendid thing and does not deserve to die.[12]

and in 1956 he could write:

For the making of world peace there are great gains to record. There is all the great non-political work of the United Nations, bringing relief to suffering human beings all over the world, help to refugees, help to children, help to the underfed, to the sick or plague-stricken, to the nations that are held down by low standards or lack of knowledge. And this work . . . is now accepted as a normal official duty by the governments of the civilized world. That is a new thing in history.[13]

2

In June 1949 Murray wrote to J. A. K. Thomson that he had been attending a Liberal Summer School at Oxford: 'Rum how right they [the Liberals] are and how extinct'.[14] It was already clear that the Liberals had no chance of forming a government—indeed they only got nine seats in the 1950 election, reduced to six in the elections of 1951 and 1955. So it is no surprise when he records that in February 1950 he had voted Conservative for the first time in his life.[15] He later told Cecil that he considered the best way to promote Liberalism was to vote Conservative.[16] After the 1955 election he wrote to Rosalind in May, 'I am pleased with the election result. Nearly all the educated people I meet are Liberal, but vote Conservative.' Through his work in the League, he said, he had 'grown out of Party spirit in politics, as it could not survive the friendships he had formed in his work.'[17] Just as in his student days he ceased to be anti-clerical thanks to his friendship with Bishop Gore.[18]

Murray's liberalism was at bottom that of the Victorian Paternalist. He was a radical in the cause of the oppressed—the Boers, Conscientious Objectors, Refugees—but essentially he was a Platonist, believing, as de Madariaga wrote, 'in Paternal aristocratic government both for the Governed Britons and internationally for the "small dark" nations.' Some of Murray's private letters illustrate well what de Madariaga had in mind:

The Trade Unions were alright as long as they were the underdogs . . . but
are intolerable as governors, being consciously activated by class interest
and . . . committed to intolerance . . . yet individually such decent, honest
people though with limited horizons.[19]

And:

We lie at the mercy of a mass of little barbarous nations, intoxicated with
their own nationality who constitute a great majority of the Assembly.[20]

Or again:

Did you listen to Arnold [Toynbee]'s Reith lectures? Wonderfully
interesting, but the last one rather shocked me. He wilfully ignored the fact
that our Western or Christian civilization is better than that of Asia or
Africa.[21]

The most controversial act of Murray's life was his support of Eden
in the Suez crisis of 1956. In no sense could this be regarded as
'promoting Liberalism'. His Liberal friends were dismayed: many
regarded it as the act of a 'hypergerontic' who had swung entirely
to the Conservatives.

But Murray was lucid till the last: for him Suez was not a question
of domestic politics: it concerned World Order and was a matter
of logic. In the post-war years he had remained acutely conscious
that the League had failed in the thirties when it came to stopping
aggression by sanctions, and that nothing short of military intervention would stop aggression by a major power. He acknowledged
that he and Cecil had put too much faith in public opinion and the
whole idea of collective security. He realized that neither the League
nor the United Nations had any teeth, and were too cumbrous for
the prompt action called for in order to be effective in the face of
armed aggression. During the post-war period there began to be a
divergence of opinion between Murray and Cecil over foreign policy.
Murray was actively in favour of the various regional alliances. Cecil
still felt that if the UN was to work nations must be taught to
use it and rely on it; regional (military) pacts meant a return to
Balance of Power policies. In April 1948 Murray had written that
he had been

trying to persuade Winston that the British-American entente plus Benelux
and the Marshal Nations are really the U.N. force for preventing aggression,
a short cut for getting round the veto and really a natural result of Russian
sabotage.[22]

Murray in fact had clearly given up hope that the UN would be able to deploy armed force promptly in an emergency and was looking for it elsewhere. Thus his pro-Eden stand over Suez can be seen as an extension of this line of thought. It is a measure of his disillusion with his high hopes of the League in the thirties. On 10 November 1956 he sent a letter to the editor of *Time and Tide* supporting Eden, in which he argued:

First it is a question of International Law. The U.N. was intended to have a means of enforcing the law. It has no such means. Egypt and Israel have been breaking the law for 9 years without correction.

Secondly, the Nasser danger is much more serious than a local friction. The real danger is we should be faced by a coalition of Arab, Muslim and anti-Western states, led nominally by Egypt but really by Russia . . . Such a danger, the Prime Minister saw, must be stopped, however irregularly, by those nations who can act at once . . . The next step of course is the creation of a police force for the U.N.[23]

Lady Violet Bonham-Carter did not spare Murray when she heard of his action:

I simply cannot believe it—that *you* should support an act of aggression which has dishonoured us in the eyes of the whole world—U.S.A., the Commonwealth, Asia—and sowed seeds of hatred and mistrust between ourselves and all the Arab peoples—is to me quite incredible . . . So far from paving the way for the entry of the U.N. Force we voted against the summoning of the Assembly which alone could create it [the Force]. We cast our first veto (a weapon we've always denounced) against America's resolution in the Security Council to settle the dispute by peaceful means.[24]

Murray replied:

As one of the architects of the L.N. and the U.N. I have always been aware of its two terrible weaknesses—the Council paralysed by the veto, the Assembly with no powers of action—weakness remedied by giving the Assembly power to sanction action by a two-thirds majority—it seemed alright . . . but . . . the original 50 members have been increased to 79, nearly all of them uncivilized, Asiatic, Arabic, or South American nations with a violent anti-west prejudice or anti-civilization majority. Why the U.S.A. should join all the anti Wests I think is because of their obsession with Colonialism.[25]

Lady Violet returned to the attack, but Murray avoided further argument, though he did not yield ground.

Kathleen Courtney wrote more kindly to Murray:

I don't think I differ from you as much as you suppose, though I have not
objected to the resolutions of U.N.A. [anti-Eden] as in general I agree with
them . . . I think Eden and Selwyn Lloyd acted from the best motives, i.e.
they thought that by taking the action they did, they would prevent greater
evil . . . However, they have not done so. Nasser's position so far from being
undermined has been consolidated, the whole Arab world united against
us, the Soviet Government given a handle which it does not fail to use. In
the meantime the Suez Canal is blocked and our oil supply is endangered.[26]

How ironical that the first and probably only occasion when world
public opinion might be said to have stopped aggression should have
found Murray aligned with the aggressors.

Whatever view is taken of Suez, it seems a very sad moment for
Murray, as he reached his 91st birthday, having just lost Lady Mary,
to find himself differing so widely from nearly all his closest friends
and collaborators over so many years, and to stand accused of
deserting his lifelong principles. He clearly felt touchy, or he would
not have thought (as evidently he did) that the words of a draft
message to the UNA branches (proposed by Judd) were meant to
include himself among those 'who rejoiced in our armed intervention
in Egypt and who dreamt of a return to gun-boat policy.'[27] But
Murray, boy or man, never lacked moral courage; he still commands
our respect if not our agreement. He was 'genial yet at the same
time detached', wrote Toynbee. 'At any moment he could stand
alone. He was not psychologically dependent on the human relations
that meant so much to him.'[28] J. A. K. Thomson, perhaps the man
who knew Murray best, wrote that he was 'one of the friendliest
but one of the remotest of men. He had the central serenity and
self-sufficiency ($\alpha\dot{\upsilon}\tau\acute{\alpha}\varrho\varkappa\epsilon\iota\alpha$) of the ancient philosophers, the self-
sufficiency of the good man, he saw two sides of a question: he was
a champion, but not a partisan.'[29]

3

Murray continued with his classical work till the end of his life. In
1941 he was revising the *Oresteia* and his text of Euripides; and
when he died he had not quite completed the revision of his text of
Aeschylus with the help of another distinguished refugee, Paul Maas,
ex-Professor of Classics at Königsberg. The revised text is not
regarded as a substantial improvement. During his last years Murray
translated seven more plays.[30] He liked always to have on hand a

Greek play to translate. This he regarded as relaxation. He also kept up a steady exchange of letters with his friend, J. A. K. Thomson, Professor of Greek at King's College, discussing minutiae of classical scholarship.

Although his translations of plays were now seldom performed in live theatre, they began to reach a wider public through the BBC. Eleven of his plays were broadcast between 1941 and 1956,[31] and many of them were repeated—the *Electra* five times, *The Frogs* four times, despite the difficulty of 'making it intelligible to the Greekless'. His two completed Menander fragments were evidently very successful and were also repeated: a BBC file carries the note that '*The Arbitration* is extremely amusing and playable . . . the translation is hardly recognisable as Gilbert Murray—far above standard.'[32] A mixed compliment; but the surprising thing is not so much the implied criticism as that his plays were put on so often by a not unsceptical BBC.

The plays usually lasted one-and-a-half hours, the fee was 25 guineas. Murray took great pains to help and encourage the producer, Val Gielgud, and his successor. He would write (and usually himself deliver) a five-minute introductory talk; he liked to attend the first reading and the last rehearsal; if unable to come himself he would send notes on the pronunciation of Greek names, and hints on producing. He always listened himself and afterwards would send an appreciative letter, giving both praise and criticism, and telling of the reactions that had come his way—how 'our nice parlour maid had listened with shining eyes' (to the *Electra*).[33]

Murray remained President of the Simplified Spelling Society until 1949, but his correspondence in that connection must have strained his courtesy to the limit. Not surprisingly the society was a hotbed for cranks: but one admires Murray's mild reply to a screed from one particularly trying member: 'Thanks for your redraft of Proes and Konz; does not the introduction of the y in 'yuezij' rather confuse matters?'[34] Perhaps this was the sort of thing J. A. K. Thomson had in mind when he wrote in his obituary of Murray that 'he suffered fools a little too gladly'.[35]

Murray's work for the Home University Library is striking evidence of his continuing capacity for work, his lucidity of mind and the wide range of his interests and imagination during these last eighteen years. The HUL, now taken over by the Oxford University Press, still had only three editors: for Literature, for History, and for Science; Murray remained the sole Literary editor until his death. This involved thinking up subjects for books or considering suggestions from other people; selecting suitable authors, approving the synopses of what they proposed to write, and reading and criticizing the completed MSS. In March 1942 Murray acknowledges a cheque for £37. 10s. for half a year's work: and in 1943 Sir Humphrey Milford, head of the OUP, writes to him 'Please don't think of resigning — you are fully earning your salary'[36]

In 1941 Murray was commissioning books on Village Life, Prisons, Latin Literature, Greek Civilization, Trade Unions, the Industrial Revolution, and a book on the fourth Gospel. In 1946 he suggests seven new titles and elaborates the themes: a new book on China, books on Modern War, Anthropology, and Psychology; on the Dissemination of Truth, the New Instruments of Education (wireless and cinema), and a book on the problem of writing involving 'a reformed European alphabet; also the problem of dealing with the Chinese who have no alphabet, and the problems of the Japanese and Indian languages' — some book.[37] His list in 1950 comprised some seventeen titles including books on Thomas Aquinas, Descartes, Hobbes, Locke, Bacon; and on Shakespeare, 'though we can't offend Masefield, the Poet Laureate, while he is still alive'[38] (Masefield had already written on Shakespeare for the HUL). His offer to write a book himself on the 'Pursuit of Security' was accepted, though it was never written.[39]

A letter to him from the OUP dated 27 February 1957 (within six weeks of his fatal illness) thanks him for returning Geoffrey Warnock's typescript on 'English Philosophy Since 1900', saying that the MS 'is being sent to Professor Austin with your two points about Ethics and Existentialism'.[40]

4

In his later years Murray was increasingly in demand as a speaker. Until his late eighties he seldom turned down a request to speak, whether from students, schools, teachers, branches of the UNA, or from the BBC. He delivered a number of prestigious lectures; the last was the Lord Davies Memorial Lecture in 1955 on 'Memories of the Peace Movement'. Most remarkable of all was his emergence as a star speaker for the BBC. There cannot be many men who achieve fame as a broadcaster in their seventies and eighties. Between 1939 and his death Murray gave some eighty talks to the BBC, ranging over a wide variety of themes — classical, religious, philosophic; he talked about people — Julian Huxley, Asquith, Jane Harrison; on Socrates; on his brother Sir Hubert Murray; on Cornford's translation of Plato's Republic—this to Australia and the Dominions: 'I don't suppose they will like it', he commented. 'One can only hope it will be good for them'.[41] Some of his most engaging talks were his reminiscences. He spoke on the Home, European, Overseas, and Hindustani Services; to Germany, Sweden, Norway, Greece, and Australia. He was also a great favourite on the Brains Trust—'So different from Joad and Campbell'.[42] One still meets people from all walks of life who glow with warmth as they tell how they 'never missed a Gilbert Murray broadcast'.

On classical subjects and the United Nations Murray spoke as a man with a mission: one of his schools scripts in the BBC files is annotated: 'This reads more like a sermon than a schools talk, but he does not seem to respond to suggestion'; and the Schools Editor writes to him: 'Few of your audience would think of "opening their hearts"—better to say "talk freely" about books and poetry'.[43] None the less Murray himself records that he had talked for an hour in Leicester to a school of five hundred boys and 'there followed over an hour of vigorous and friendly questioning'.[44] Isobel Henderson remarks that 'most of Murray's books grew out of his lectures; his prose is written with the speaking voice in his ear',[45] which in part explains his success as a speaker; but it must also have been in great measure due to his personal magnetism and to the spell of his beautiful voice. In 1922 he wrote to Rosalind:

I had a nice experience yesterday. I was lecturing, not very well, on the Cassandra scene, when I realized the room was extraordinarily quiet. I looked up and saw that the men were all, as it were, holding their breath under the spell of the scene.[46]

Murray himself said that missing the whole world of music had perhaps given him a finer ear for the music of words. 'Whether talking or writing I listen to the music of words.'[47] Henry Fairlie described how Murray was due to address the Oxford University Liberal Club on VE Day. The students turned up out of respect for Murray, though in no mood for speeches. 'Yet from the moment he stood on his feet, and the high-pitched cultivated voice began to utter its words of sanity, they sat enraptured.'[48]

The published work of Murray's later years consists mainly of reproductions and adaptations of his earlier works. In March 1946 he writes to J. A. K. Thomson: 'I am going through a lot of lectures and essays . . . with a view to publication and republication, rather a tiresome business, partly because I have, naturally enough, repeated the same thing so often in different forms.'[49] The only substantial book of this period is *Stoic, Christian, and Humanist* (1940), which consists of two earlier lectures and two essays already published. The most interesting part of the book is perhaps the preface, where he traces his own spiritual development:

These essays are merely by-products of a long life in which I have had almost constantly at the back of my mind, as a half conscious pre-occupation, the aspirations, problems and moral compulsions which form part at least of the substance of religion.

  My reaction towards the traditional religion of the society in which I was born, began early as a moral rebellion in early childhood. Oddly enough it was the miracle of the Gadarene Swine which first shocked me . . . I began in my teens to be uneasy about other elements in the New Testament, the unreasonable cursing of the fig tree, the doctrine of eternal damnation, and the whole conception of vicarious atonement. It seems to me looking back I was a very innocent and priggish boy, crudely humanitarian and idealist.

  The intellectual reasons for disbelief came to me much later. Here I was influenced not so much by the obviously unscientific character of the account of the creation and other stories in the Old Testament as by the discovery that different nations had different religions and by a comparative study of religion and anthropology . . .

  The World War and events in post-war Europe have revealed a vast and awful gulf between the fundamental faiths of different kinds of man . . . it is not in any strict sense a clash between Christianity and Scepticism . . . the worst abominations have not been due to Scepticism but to various forms of fanaticism . . . In the more civilized communities there has always been a minority who have felt convinced that the traditional frame of dogmas . . . did not represent the exhaustive truth, the probable truth, or even any exact truth about the ultimate mysteries.

  From passages such as this, and from the broadcast reminiscences, emerges the picture of Murray the man in the round. For instance in September 1943 he gave a broadcast talk on poetry, entitled 'Escape'. In it he tells how a small granddaughter recited to him most of Macaulay's *Horatius* :

She loved it and I loved it; I at any rate had tears in my eyes. I remembered how as a boy my feelings had been hurt by some prig of a critic who said that there was no excuse for anyone who liked really bad poetry, such as Macaulay's lays. I was mostly a good obedient little boy, but at that I rebelled, and I am sure I was right to rebel. I loved Macaulay's lays and it is altogether wrong to snub any child's genuine love of poetry. . . . The new critics get fiercer than the old ones; they now condemn some of the best poetry for being Escapist, as if it is not one of the greatest achievements of art, particularly of poetry and music, that it enables one to escape from the prison of the material present.

In another talk he chooses as his four greatest books the sixth book of the *Iliad*, the first Epistle to the Corinthians, *Hamlet*, and *War and Peace* : an interesting choice for an agnostic.

So we return full circle to the small boy born into the freedom of the Australian bush and into the security of a loving and upright family. In the boy who hated cruelty and loved Greek, who was unafraid to stand up to prigs or critics, or to reject a God who could damn one or other of his parents, it is not hard to discern the courtly old gentleman who was the best of grandfathers, who could not bear to hurt, yet who could 'view with a steady clarity the stupidity and wickedness of men's treatment of each other, and who would give the Devil not only his due, but understanding and courtesy too.'[50]

'Gilbert Murray will be mourned by three generations,' wrote Henry Fairlie, 'by his contemporaries, by the fortunate ones whom he taught and by those who came to know him only in his later years. All of them knew the same man, because the man never changed.'[51] In his own 90th birthday broadcast, 'Unfinished Battle', Murray said:

Of course I cannot work as I did. Still, there has never been a day, I suppose, when I have failed to give thought to the work for peace and for Hellenism. The one is a matter of life and death for all of us; the other of maintaining amid all the dust of modern industrial life our love and appreciation of eternal values.

The Times on 1 January 1956 wrote:

His two main themes, Hellenic Scholarship and International Co-operation, may seem a little detached, but there is a link. He might not wholly have satisfied the Scholar, but he awoke the imagination of the playgoer. In the same way, his labours in the service of International Co-operation may have had no important direct impact on the course of affairs, but through his work for the L.N.U. he brought to thousands of people a sense of the human values and the moral issues implicit in what was then apt to seem to many people an almost tedious rigmarole of international bickering and bargaining. In both fields, literature and politics, the spirit quickeneth; and he has always been a champion of the spirit of man, like the poets whose interpreter he became.

5

On 25 May 1940 came the order to intern all male enemy aliens under the age of 60 who had been classed as unreliable by the tribunals. On 25 June this order was extended to unemployed males from Category C (reliable). Naturally this caused great resentment and distress. Unfortunately very inadequate provision had been made for this contingency and camps were overcrowded with the result that 'reliable' and 'unreliable' aliens were interned together in cramped quarters with poor facilities.

Murray was immediately bombarded with pathetic letters from wives, relations, and friends of internees, and he was prominent among those who laboured to obtain release and work for the deserving. Typical of his prompt action is the case of Rudolph Olden[52] who had been interned on 25 June: on the 26th Murray cabled on his behalf to his friend Duggan of the Board of International Education in New York.[53] Within two weeks a cable came back saying Olden had been given a two-year appointment as Assistant Professor of History in the College of Social Science in New York; but the story has a tragic ending as Olden and his wife were drowned in August when the ship on which they were travelling to New York was torpedoed.

On 8 July 1940 *The Times* printed a letter from Murray protesting strongly about the conditions of internment and the lack of discrimination. Next day a huge post arrived at Yatscombe—touching letters of gratitude from refugee families, and also letters from many Englishmen in support of his stand. As a result of the agitation a new Advisory Committee was appointed to hear appeals with Cyril Asquith as Chairman, backed by a large Advisory Council chaired by Lord Lytton. A new wave of indignation swept the country when it became known that some of the internees were being deported to Canada and Australia against their will. Murray again took up the cudgels and on 8 August he received a letter from Lord Lytton assuring him that no more internees would be sent abroad without their consent or unaccompanied by any relations who might wish to join them.[54]

Meantime at Yatscombe there was a constant stream of guests— refugees, the bombed, grandchildren. The strain began to tell on Lady Mary's health, especially as it became harder and harder to find servants. On 7 January 1940 Murray wrote:

We have the house packed to the ceiling with Germans, Czechs, Stephen's family and the latter's pets, one guinea pig, one dog, two cats and fifteen hens. Two Germans and a Czech went ill on us . . . and now we are without housemaid or parlourmaid. Mary is actually for the first time in her life refusing to give beds to chance callers.[55]

On 5 July 1946 he wrote, 'Our nice Germans in our cottage are moving to London and we are looking for other Destitute Aliens— the most destitute are not always the most attractive.'[56] The scale of the refugee problem was of course much reduced after the war, but it did not go away, as refugees began to come in from other parts of the world. The Murrays' hospitality was perforce limited, but Murray still gave much help in finding work for exiles, especially the more intellectual. As late as July 1954 Murray wrote to Rosalind, 'We had ten German children to tea and games—refugees from the East, they come from camps and barracks, and are spending three months (here) with private hosts. How kind people are!'[57]

But not always, and not everybody. Rose Macaulay wrote to Murray in April 1944: 'The resentment against us among our refugee guests is terrific . . . they are met [in Britain] by blocks of ice, faces of wood. I wish that there were more houses like Yatscombe, who will throw open their doors to Mitteleuropa.'[58] Murray replied, 'It is sad about the Central Europeans. The truth is . . . we do not much like them and that is what they cannot forgive.'[59] But at Yatscombe, 'Mary really did care, and they felt that.'[60] Marianne Grafe, a refugee, summed up the expressions of gratitude: 'Lady Mary's interest for all kinds of human beings is simply a sacred miracle.'[61] Bowra used to complain that Lady Mary brought the grandchildren to see not him but his cook, who was a refugee.

Whatever may have been their troubles as parents, the Murrays' role as grandparents was entirely happy. After the death of Denis, his widow and their only child, a daughter, Pamela, occupied the cottage in the garden of Yatscombe for six months or more. All the daughters-in-law were devoted to Lady Mary: and Pam, as the first granddaughter, held a very special place in the hearts of both grandparents. After Basil's death, Yatscombe became a second home for his two girls, Ann and Venetia, and often too for their half-brother Oliver. There were no nursery meals at Yatscombe: all sat together round the family table and joined equally in the ever lively and wide-ranging talk. To Sunday lunches came students on their bicycles, dons, visiting dignitaries refugees and their families. Ann and Venetia's nurse who sat with them, could never have believed such talk was possible and she was amazed at how Lady Mary sitting at the head of the table chatted fluently in Italian on one side, then turned to the other in equally fluent German.

Murray did not like to see a child too solemn. He kept a clockwork mouse which would tip up the sugar to make a two-year-old great grandson laugh—and, one suspects, so as to hear Lady Mary say 'Oh, Gilbert!'. There was a special white woolly mouse kept to be popped into the sugar and offered to Lady Mary. 'Your grandfather was irresistible with children', wrote Arnold Toynbee to Ann. 'People like your grandparents are immortal. The effects on other people of their quite extraordinary lovingness and goodness will go on continuing.'[62]

The household was run for grandfather: his mornings upstairs in his study must be totally undisturbed. But after lunch every day he set off for a walk with a grandchild and a pair of secateurs to cut the brambles and nettles from the woodland paths. It was talk all the way; and talk between equals; no subjects were barred. Ann heard how he had had eggs thrown at him in the Boer War; how he had listened in the Strangers Gallery to Gladstone: 'a small old man with an unimpressive voice started to speak, and, as he spoke he grew bigger and bigger and the voice stronger and stronger, till after 4 hours it died away and there was the little old man again.' After an operation Ann missed six weeks' school and her grandfather gave her lessons: she had to learn some Latin verse every day — word perfect: 'if a thing is worth doing, it is worth doing well', he said.

One imagines the arrival of Stephen's children caused more stir, with their pets, not to mention the *Daily Worker* ('Golly, what a paper', wrote Murray). They seem to have loved all the grandchildren impartially: Sandy (Stephen's second son) had an accident on his bicycle in 1940 and Murray sent him a delightful version of the accident composed of cuttings and captions to cheer him up in hospital. Ann describes how, after the last exam in her Schools, she cycled up to Yatscombe and how the two old people stood at the gate waving goodbye to her as she left, their eyes full of tears.

Life was not easy for octogenarians after the war. Reliable service was hard to come by, though in some ways the Murrays were fortunate. Their old gardener Edgington, who could drive the car, was with them till the end; and, more important, for her last years Lady Mary was looked after by a faithful and devoted young nurse, Kathleen Haynes. Murray too had a secretary, or rather a succession of secretaries as one after the other they got married; cooks seldom lasted long, and it was not uncommon for the secretarial work to be done in the kitchen to 'help out'. Murray also wrote many letters in his own hand or on his antiquated and moody typewriter which accompanied him on holiday. He wrote loving and tender letters to Lady Mary daily if he was away, as long as she could read or follow them: and kept up a lively and humorous correspondence with many friends.

In November 1949 the Murrays celebrated their diamond wedding and it is touching to read the letters from all the grandchildren and grandnieces and nephews. The Australian descendants still wrote to 'Dear Uncle George'. But by 1951 Lady Mary's memory was beginning to fail. Murray wrote to Rosalind in July 1953:

Thanks for your birthday letter [to Lady M.]. Moth[63] cannot read letters now, nor quite understand them when I read them to her, but she is pleased to have them and particularly pleased with yours. She carries it about with her. I cannot make out how she is. She eats and sleeps quite well, except that she rather waits for me to insist on her eating what she has on her plate.[64]

Murray found it very distressing to watch his wife's increasing helplessness. He himself on more than one occasion had to spend two or three weeks in the Acland Nursing Home: in 1944–5 he was there over the New Year with a skin infection; in October 1953 he was there again, it would seem suffering mainly from exhaustion, or, as he put it, from 'cold, gloom, catarrh and other plagues such as are reserved for the righteous.'[65] But on the whole he kept remarkably fit, playing crafty tennis even in his eighties and walking every day. Arnold Toynbee used to say 'I'm off for a game on the Murrays' eighteen-hole tennis court'. Murray still took 3 or 4 weeks' holiday every summer; in the fifties his regular companions were Barbara Hammond (now a widow), J. A. K. Thomson, and the current secretary. But his holidays seldom passed without calls upon him as a speaker, and he usually had some writing or translating on hand. In 1948 the holiday was in Wales at Ogmore-on-Sea. He was translating *The Birds* ('my chief comfort'), writing for the BBC, and preparing three speeches for a Council meeting of UNA at Cardiff where he stopped off on his way home. He had also addressed a group of teachers on a classical subject.[66] On these occasions Lady Mary used to go to her family in Cumberland while she was still fit to travel, but latterly she went to a nearby nursing home in order to give Kathleen Haynes a holiday.

The flavour of Murray's day-to-day life over this period and his unfailing humour cannot be better illustrated than by quoting his own letters. The excerpts are mainly from letters to Barbara Hammond, Rose Macaulay, J. A. K. Thomson, and to Lady Mary and Rosalind.

9 Feb. 1940, GM to Wilson Harris:

I think it might be a good thing to intern, perhaps decapitate, a few of the Young Fellows of All Souls and certain other colleagues. What do you feel?

22 April 1940, GM to Isobel Henderson:

I am rather depressed by the way my friends are dying on me, Buchan, Margoliouth, Fisher, and many of my pupils are over 70. And even my grandchildren repent of their Communism and marry rich wives — a frightfully middle-aged proceeding.

24 Sept. 1942, GM to MM:

My letter about the American attitude to negroes has fallen into the midst of a great controversy. Our war office, to please the Americans, has given orders to military canteens not to serve our own black troops, and what is worse, to do so by various pretences, and not by a direct refusal. The Colonial office is protesting to the Cabinet.

30 June 1943, GM to J. A. K. Thomson:

I seem always busy and with business that might just as well not be done; except that this term I've been lecturing on the Bacchae; I greatly enjoyed it. Otherwise I seem to be always making speeches for Poles, Greeks, Czechs, Amalekites, etc. and attending to the re-education of Germans — God help them!

15 May 1944, GM to MM:

I went to church yesterday to hear Bob read the lesson and was much shocked to hear them start the service with God Save the King. Really they should leave God's House to God.

24 June 1944, GM to RM:

Stephen responded to an enquiry [about how he fared with the doodle-bugs] by ordering us to take in two unknown women who deserved well of the State of Spain but cannot stand bombs at night. (They come to-day).

1 Oct. 1944, GM to Venetia Murray [Basil's younger daughter]:

My dear Animalcule . . . I am going up to a Brains Trust to-morrow. Lord Vansittart will be there, who is rampageously anti-German, so probably we shall fight, or at least I shall make fun of him. I don't much believe anything that people at war say about their enemies; for instance Nelson said: 'I cannot breathe while a single Frenchman remains alive.' . . . Ever so much love from Grandfather.

16 May 1948, GM to RM:

I am reading bits of the *Birds* to an international Classical Society at the North London Collegiate . . . The school seems to be near Vladivostok, but a little to the North.

4 June 1948, GM to RM:

I rang you up 4 times yesterday—but either I was hopelessly incompetent or you were away . . . (Neither Asquith nor Balfour could use a telephone, so perhaps I am going to be P.M.).

7 June 1948, GM to Violet Bonham-Carter [commenting on her broadcast on Women's Suffrage]:

It looks now as though intellectual women were going to be exterminated. Don't kill your wife with dusting, do it with a Hoover! At any rate, prevent her reading and studying by taking away nurses and servants.

29 June 1948, GM to RM:

The U.N.A. Council [at Cardiff] was exhausting . . . though we had satisfactory majorities over Fellow Travellers and Turbulent Youth and they buttered Cecil and me to a degree really almost equal to our merits . . . I have a broadcast on the Olympic Games and an address on Agnosticism.

16 August 1948, GM to RM:

Our disagreeable servants have gone, after which Lady Mary became exultant in the garden and broke her leg—she is now in the Acland which she hates . . . Cooks continue to appear on the horizon and vanish.

18 August 1949, GM to BH:

We've had 4 grandchildren staying—and sometimes giving extra trouble to the cook. A complaint from the cook makes one tremble, like the threat of a third world war.

8 April 1950, GM to BH:

Curious those one misses and those—even dear friends—who just pass away. I miss Agnes and Basil a great deal—the naughtiest and most affectionate of our children.

13 May 1950, GM to RM:

I am overworked and miserable—Mary ill and hating to be left alone, the cook [German] doing the usual vanishing trick; the Liberal party dissolving and the poor Liberal International living and perhaps dying beyond its means.

29 December 1952, GM to BH:

I have been thinking how funny and how priggish Mary and I were when young, and half think of writing a reminiscence—in the 3rd person—of 'A Victorian Prig'. We were really nice young people, but so unlike the nice young people of to-day . . .

14 October 1953, GM to BH [from the Acland Nursing Home]:

There's nothing much wrong with me—just fatigue and worry. But I had a lot of engagements ahead, and feel wonderfully refreshed by having to put them off—failing them one by one was soul destroying work . . . Rum about British Guiana. What can you expect if you tell these negroid-Indian South Americans that they are everybody's equals and have a right to self-government and then give them universal suffrage. How many countries in the world can stand universal suffrage?

21 October 1953, GM to BH:

Have you heard of the Sisyphus complex? Evidently that is what I had or have. As soon as I was in the Acland and all my engagements for the U.N. week were definitely put off, my temperature, which had been dancing from 94–101, went normal and my cold ceased. The remedy for the sisyphus complex is to let the blooming stone roll where it bally well likes.

20 January 1954, GM to BH:

I missed Bertie Russell's account of Lytton Strachey, of whom I really had and have a horror. He has had a sort of permanent bad influence.

21 August 1954, GM to RT:

I am dispirited . . . partly the depression caused by Moth's continual and increasing helplessness . . . and I don't think I can leave her. My company from time to time seems to be one of the very few things she is really conscious of and cares for.

22 March 1955, GM to BH [about plans for a holiday at Hassocks— a new venue]:

I propose to go ahead and engage the rooms. (I think it will be possible to disengage them if you or J. A. K. find you have a hereditary enemy there, or it is the scene of an ancient crime which you wish to forget.)

11 and 29 May 1955, GM to RT:

Moth is in a very poor state though fortunately not in pain and never cross. I don't go out to dinners at all nor to meetings in London . . . The Azaleas and bluebells are a real delight. They make me laugh aloud. I hate the thought of leaving them.

14 July 1955, GM to JAKT:

The new cook is a complete success . . . She has not even complained about the frightful heat, at least not in such a way as to attribute it entirely to our fault. [The cook lasted 5 days.]

29 March 1956, GM to RM:

I'm full of misfortune: 1) fatigue after London, 2) a blister on my heel, 3) bruised ribs—not as you expect, from challenging that negro champion boxer, but from falling over against the side of the bath. The Bishop who uplifted our hearts this morning said it was all the Wages of Sin which

I thought rather hard. However, he admitted later that it might be his sins and not mine that were to blame.

14 July 1956, GM to JAKT:

Lorna [Chubb, secretary] is proving a most excellent nurse though it is a wonder how she combines that not only with Greek but with a more or less perpetual state of ecstasy over a world which contains such objects as John and a marvellous wedding dress and a perfectly dazzling future. The ecstasy more or less illuminates the house.

6

On Murray's 90th birthday, 2 January 1956, four sacks of mail were delivered at Yatscombe and 131 telegrams. The first three telegrams opened came from the British Prime Minister (Eden), the Australian Prime Minister, and P. G. Wodehouse; and there was one from Philip and Elizabeth R. Again there are loving letters from his grandchildren; and from the Australian side to 'Dear Uncle George'. Lady Mary had had her 90th birthday in September 1955. She lingered on, fragile, but 'happily she doesn't suffer and is just as kind and generous as ever—never cross'.[67] Murray wrote to Rosalind 'at 90 one is lonely, having no wife to consult and talk things over with'.[68] But Kathleen Haynes records that, even though Lady Mary was no longer able 'to talk over everything' as before, Murray always wanted her with him—going out for lunch, or for a drive, she must always come too. She was still a dearly loved companion.

Eight months later she died and Murray wrote to Barbara Hammond and Lady Cecil describing how beautiful she had looked in death. Gilbert and Mary—theirs was an undemonstrative partnership, but Honor Balfour remembers how Lady Mary 'would so proudly and so fondly bid you farewell as you went off for a walk or a game of tennis'. Roy Harrod, a friend of Basil's, wrote, 'I was always so completely overwhelmed by a sense of her fineness, warmth and goodness that I was never able to talk sensibly to her, (as she often told me)'.

Murray survived her by eight months. In October—the time of Suez—he wrote to J. A. K. Thomson 'I am not getting on very well; The loss of a life-long companion is somehow surprisingly heavy in its effect'. Kathleen Haynes stayed on to the end.

Murray's grandson Philip Toynbee described how his 'grandfather, suddenly and deathly old since his wife died last September, was usually stretched on a sofa talking in a frail relic of his beautiful and gentle voice.'[69] The last photographs of Murray clearly show this marked change, and tell, more movingly than any words can, what these two wonderful old people meant to each other. But Murray's mind remained alert to the last; he chaired a meeting of the Somerville College Library Committee in February 1957. His neighbour on Boar's Hill, Sir Arthur Curvengen, a regular companion on his walks, described how in March 1957 he found him lying on his couch reading an article on Existentialism: and how, only a few days before he fell ill in April, Murray said to him he was thinking of translating the *Lysistrata* — 'it's nice to have something you can pick up in your spare moments'.[70]

Dr Gilbert George Aimé Murray, OM, died on 20 May 1957. His ashes were buried in Westminster Abbey at the request of the United Nations Association. The concluding words of Murray's moving address at the Memorial Service of his friend Lawrence Hammond in 1949, seem wholly appropriate for Murray himself:

If we apply a higher test, and think of him in connexion with those words of St. Paul in the wonderful chapter that was read to us today, it is fair to say that he had the quality translated Faith, the Roman Fides, Faithfulness; through good and evil fortunes he kept Faith; he never failed a friend, never failed the great causes for which he worked; he had the gift of Hope and the courage that goes with it. He never lost heart . . . never in the worst days despaired of our free Christian civilization; and assuredly possessed that Charity which is 'the greatest of these'.[71]

When he broadcast to Poland in 1942 about German atrocities, Murray ended by quoting 'He hath shown thee, O Man, what is good, and what doth the Lord require of thee but to do justly, to love Mercy and to walk humbly with thy God'. So walked Gilbert Murray throughout his life.

The story came out after Murray's death that during his last illness he was visited by a Roman Catholic priest who blessed him and administered extreme unction, and it was claimed by some (though not officially by any Catholic authority) that he had died a Catholic. The visit of the priest is an undisputed fact: there is room for doubt about the conversion, as it is impossible to prove how much Murray had been aware of what was going on: he was certainly very ill. His grandson, Philip Toynbee, had asked him, only two months before his death, 'Whether his present state . . . had at all affected his convictions about the finality of death. He said that it had not.'[72] The non-Catholic members of his family were in no doubt he had died as he had lived, an agnostic; but it remains an open question.

In a broadcast, 'On Myself When Young', made in August 1949, Murray concluded:

I have learned a great deal . . . I realize more and more that fundamental sympathy between friends . . . depends on something much deeper than mere agreement in opinion about politics and economics or religious dogma. I am more conscious than ever of the uncertainty of political decisions and forecasts; more conscious in the sphere of religion of the impenetrable mystery that surrounds our little island of knowledge. But while I am in the strict sense of the word agnostic, some of my dearest friends have been ardent Christians.

In *Stoic, Christian, and Humanist*, Murray had written, 'To be cocksure is to be without religion. The essence of religion is the consciousness of a vast unknown.' In this sense Murray was deeply religious. The most moving profession of his faith (the word seems more appropriate than 'of his agnosticism') is to be found in the *Five Stages of Greek Religion* :[73]

The Uncharted surrounds us on every side and we must needs have some relation towards it, a relation which will depend on the general discipline of a man's mind and the bias of his whole character. As far as knowledge and conscious reason go, we should follow resolutely their austere guidance. When they cease, as cease they must, we must use as best we can these fainter powers of apprehension, surmise and sensitiveness by which, after all, most high truth has been reached, as well as most high art and poetry; careful always to seek for truth and not for our emotional satisfaction, careful not to neglect the real needs of men and women through basing our life on dreams; and remembering above all to walk gently in a world where lights are dim and the very stars wander.

NOTES

The main sources for this biography are the Gilbert Murray papers, given to the Bodleian by Murray's children and literary executors in 1958. A detailed catalogue of these papers (referenced MSS Gilbert Murray 1–568), and of similar papers given by the executors at subsequent dates (referenced MSS Gilbert Murray *Adds* 1–14), was completed in 1980. Throughout this work reference has been made to these papers as, for example [MS Gilbert Murray] 476 [folio] 5 and [MS Gilbert Murray] *Adds* 5 [folio] 7.

A much fuller version of the LN, LNU, and CIC chapters is given in Duncan Wilson's uncut MS now with the other Murray papers in the Bodleian Library.

Abbreviations of GM's major titles (in chronological order)

HAGL   *History of Ancient Greek Literature* (1897).
RGE   *Rise of the Greek Epic* (1907).
Five Stages   *Five Stages of Greek Religion* (*Four Stages* (1912)); *Five Stages* (1925)).
Euripides   *Euripides and his Age* (1913).
E and A   *Essays and Addresses* (1921).
CTP   *The Classical Tradition in Poetry* (1927).
SCH   *Stoic, Christian, and Humanist* (1940).

Chapter I

The chief source for this chapter is Murray's own *An Unfinished Autobiography* [*UA*], ed. J. Smith and A. Toynbee (George Allen & Unwin, 1960). This consists of some eighty pages covering his life to 1899, followed by essays by some of his friends on various aspects of his work and character. Further and not always quite consistent autobiographical material is contained in various later speeches and broadcasts by Murray, and in occasional family letters, cited in the detailed notes.

On Murray's family background in Australia, see Francis West, *The Australian Expatriates* (Oxford, 1968) and *Hubert Murray* (Oxford, 1968), and Gwendolen Wilson, *Murray of Yarralumla* (Oxford, 1968).

[1] *485* 28, broadcast 'Myself When Young', 14 Aug. 1949.
[2] Ib.
[3] Francis West, *The Australian Expatriates*, p. 58.
[4] *120* 161, GM/Lady Violet Bonham-Carter, 1 Apr. 1933.
[5] GM's phrase, quoted in Francis West, *Biography as History* (Annual Lecture to the Australian Academy of Humanities, 15 May 1973), p. 12 and n. 13; see also C. M. Bowra, *Memories* (Weidenfeld & Nicolson, 1966), p. 233.
[6] Francis West, *Hubert Murray*, p. 18.
[7] Ib.
[8] Speech at 70th Birthday dinner, Christ Church, Oxford; *Oxford Magazine*, 20 Feb. 1936.
[9] Francis West, *Hubert Murray*, p. 24.
[10] *449* 120, 173, GM/MM, 6 and 23 Dec. 1892.
[11] Letter to Lady Carlisle, 27 Nov. 1889, cited in Gwendolen Wilson, op. cit., p. 310.

[12] *453* 176, 7 Sept. 1898.
[13] *UA, p. 24.*
[14] *Adds* 8 24, GM/Bertrand Russell, 12 June 1951.
[15] *UA*, p. 40 n. 1.
[16] Ib., p. 26.
[17] GM, *Stoic, Christian, and Humanist* (1940), p. 7.
[18] Ib.
[19] *UA*, p. 56.
[20] Ib., p. 58.
[21] *485* 5, broadcast 'As I See It', 14 Dec. 1937.
[22] MS in the possession of Stephen Murray.
[23] *UA*, p. 65.
[24] Ib.
[25] Speech cited at n. 8.
[26] *UA*, p. 150 (Thorndike).
[27] Bowra, op. cit., p. 215.
[28] Letter to author 8 Mar. 1981. Much the same point is made by my Oxford contemporary Sir Archibald Ross (letter to author 1982).
[29] *449* 53, 18 Nov. 1892.
[30] Ib. 142, 14 Dec. 1892.

Chapter II

Main sources are the *Unfinished Autobiography* and occasional broadcasts delivered by Murray in his old age.

For his schooldays, the Merchant Taylors' school magazine, the *Taylorian*, provides some valuable detail, and I have also had access to the school's *Exercise Book*, for Murray's early translations into Greek and Latin.

For his university days, there are various details in the Oxford Union Society's records and in the *Oxford Magazine*.

Further incidental information about Murray's Oxford life is contained in the series of his letters to Mrs Howard, afterwards Countess of Carlisle, 1887–9. The originals are in the Castle Howard archives, J 23–7, 23–8.

[1] *UA*, pp. 72–3; another account mentions whisky rather than port (Lucy Mair, letter to author 8 Mar. 1981).
[2] Told to Lady Wilson by Ann Paludan (née Murray) in Nov. 1984.
[3] *UA*, p. 73.
[4] Ib., p. 84.
[5] *Taylorian*, 4, p. 79.
[6] Ib., 6, p. 206.
[7] *33* 21, Harold Bøgbie/GM, 28 Dec. 1916.
[8] *Taylorian*, 4, p. 60.
[9] Ib., 4, pp. 118, 164.
[10] Castle Howard archives, J 23–7, no. 10; GM/Mrs Howard, 22 Sept. 1887.
[11] *Taylorian*, 6, p. 169.
[12] Isobel Henderson, obituary notice of GM in *Journal of Hellenic Studies*, lxxvii, ii, 1957.
[13] Broadcast, 25 Feb. 1954, *485* 33.
[14] The Murray papers include one box (*160*) of letters from Marvin 1889 onwards; and Marvin's own papers, also in the Bodleian Library, contain a

number of letters from Murray. Letters from Maynard (much more interesting) are to be found in Murray's general correspondence *1*, and see catalogue.

[15] GM corresponded later with E. H. Carr (*469* 144-5) on the embarrassment caused to the Edwards's household by the facts that Bakunin had only one shirt and it could not be washed as he slept in it. The story is repeated in E. H. Carr's *Bakunin* (1975), p. 248. GM, in *Essays and Addresses* (1921), p. 210, claims himself to have met Bakunin: this is chronologically impossible.

[16] *Bowra, Memories*, p. 216.

[17] *UA*, pp. 78-9.

[18] *479* 1, Warren/Lady Murray, 1 June 1882.

[19] *Adds* 2 198, 4 July 1902.

[20] *485* 30, broadcast 'Myself When Young', 14 Aug. 1949; the poem is printed in the *Taylorian*.

[21] *UA*, p. 83. It was at this time Murray first saw and heard Frederic Harrison preaching in his chapel at Newton Hall (*501* 83).

[22] Broadcast 'Myself When Young' (n. 20).

[23] *483* 92, Lady Murray/GM, 5 June 1889.

[24] Broadcast 'Myself When Young' (n. 20).

[25] By J. Connington and D. S. Margoliouth.

[26] Castle Howard archives, J 23-7, n. 23, GM/Mrs Howard, 23 Jan. 1888.

[27] *Bowra*, op. cit., pp. 219-20.

[28] Personal Communication to the author, Apr. 1981.

[29] *Taylorian* 9, p. 165; see also various letters to Mrs Howard in the Castle Howard archives, J 23-7, especially no. 18, 12 Oct. 1887, in which GM says his eyes 'have broken down emphatically'.

[30] *UA*, p. 86; the *Oxford Magazine* Apr.-May 1885 reports two Freshmen's Matches, in neither of which Murray played.

[31] Castle Howard archives, J 23-7, nos. 1, 2, 22, 32, GM/Mrs Howard, June 1887-Jan. 1888.

[32] *144* 88 GM/I. Henderson, 28 Feb. 1937.

[33] *UA*, p. 88.

[34] Ib., pp. 89-90.

[35] *Classical Quarterly* (1912), 286; GM obituary of R. Ellis.

[36] *UA*, pp. 90-1.

[37] *Proceedings of the Britiah Academy* XXVI (1940); GM obituary of Margoliouth (also at *502*, 9).

[38] *UA*, pp. 87-8.

[39] *Oxford Magazine*, 16 June 1886, quoted in C. Harvie, *Lights of Liberalism* (1976), pp. 219-20.

[40] *Echoes from the Oxford Magazine* (1900), 4; cf. *168* 11, Sidgwick/GM, 14 Feb. 1892.

[41] Oxford Union Society, *Debates* (1887-8), 94-5; *Oxford Magazine*, 29 Feb. and Mar. 1888.

[42] *1* 158, 5 Sept. 1889.

[43] Oxford Union Society, *Debates* (1887-8), 87, 89, 115.

[44] *UA*, p. 92.

[45] Ib.

[46] Castle Howard archives, J 23-4, nos. 10, 12, 50, Sept. 1887 and June 1888.

[47] F. H. Bradley, *Ethical Studies* (1876), esp. pp. 85, 116-26.

[48] *UA*, p. 83.

[49] *568* 63 GM/RT, 7 Jan. 1922.

[50] *UA*, pp. 88–9.

[51] *1* 1, Gore/GM, 14 Aug. 1886; printed in C. P. Prestige, *Life of Charles Gore* (1935), p. 75.

[52] Castle Howard archives, J 23–7 no. 26, GM/Mrs Howard, 5 Nov. 1887.

[53] Broadcast 'As I See It', 14 Dec. 1937; *485* 5.

[54] Ib.

[55] *2* 90 Gerald Bradshaw/GM, 29 Oct. 1889.

[56] *168* 19 Sidgwick/GM, Mar. 1895.

Chapter III

The Castle Howard archives, J 23–7, 23–8, contain a detailed account of Murray's courtship, mainly through correspondence with Mrs Howard, afterwards (April 1889) Countess of Carlisle.

The main single printed source continues to be *Unfinished Autobiography*. On Lady Carlisle, her daughter Dorothy Henley's *Rosalind Howard, Countess of Carlisle* (Hogarth Press, 1958), is essential, and contains in an Appendix extracts from letters from GM to Lord Henley. There is also much useful detail in *The Radical Countess* (Steel Bros (Carlisle) Ltd., 1962) by Charles Roberts, husband of another Carlisle daughter, Cecilia. Brian Harrison, *Drink and the Victorians* (1971) gives a valuable survey of the Temperance movement, one of Lady Carlisle's favourite causes.

[1] *485* 86, broadcast 'Unfinished Battle', 1 June 1956.

[2] *UA*, p. 87.

[3] *167* 77, GM/BR, 24 Aug. 1903.

[4] *UA*, p. 101.

[5] *448* 186, MM/GM, 28 Oct. 1892.

[6] Castle Howard archives, J 23–7, no. 3, GM/RH, 13 Aug. 1887.

[7] Ib., no. 4, Aug. 1887; the character 'Dolores' had been sketched in at the end of *Gobi*, before Murray had met Lady Mary.

[8] Ib., no. 10, 22 Sept. 1887.

[9] Ib., no. 4, Aug. 1887.

[10] Ib., no. 8, 12 Sept. 1887.

[11] Ib., no. 9, 15 Sept. 1887.

[12] Ib., J 23–8, no. 2, RH/GM, Sept. 1887.

[13] Ib., J 23–7, no. 10, GM/RH, 22 Sept. 1887.

[14] *446* 1, 22 Sept. 1887.

[15] Castle Howard archives, J 23–7, no. 16, 3 Oct. 1887.

[16] Ib., no. 17, 3 Oct. 1887.

[17] Ib., J 23–8, no. 8, RH/GM, 28 Oct. 1887.

[18] Ib., J 23–7, no. 24, 30 Oct. 1887.

[19] Ib., no. 25, 1 Nov. 1887.

[20] His pledge card as a member of the 'Blue Ribbon Army' is preserved among the papers of Stephen Murray; it is dated 26 July 1887.

[21] Castle Howard archives, J 23–7, no. 5, 20 Aug; no. 7, 5 Sept. 1887.

[22] Ib., J 23–8, no. 5, RH/GM, 2 Oct. 1887.

[23] Ib., J 23–7, no. 22, 25 Oct. 1887.

[24] Ib., no. 32, 23 Jan. 1888.

[25] Ib.

[26] Ib. no. 29, 17 Nov. 1887; no. 33, 20 Feb. 1888.

[27] Ib., nos. 44–5, 10 and 16 May 1888.

[28] Ib., no. 42, 24 Apr. 1888.

[29] Ib., J 23–8, no. 18, RH/GM, 8 Apr. 1888.

[30] Ib., J 23–7, no. 52, 1 July 1888.

[31] Ib., no. 53, 5 July 1888.

[32] Ib., no. 55, 14 Aug. 1888.

[33] Ib., no. 56, 1 Sept. 1888.

[34] Ib., nos. 55 and 56, 57 (30 Nov. 1888), and 59 (15 Jan. 1889).

[35] Ib., no. 61, 17 Apr. 1889; Bryce, GM recalled much later, had been 'kind to him as an undergraduate' (*A Conversation with Bryce*, Bryce Memorial Lecture, 1943).

[36] Ib., nos. 62 and 63, 6 and 13 June 1889; see also *1* 44, John S. Thomas/ GM, 12 May 1889.

[37] Ib., J 23–8, no. 32, RC/GM, 27 June 1889.

[38] *483* 60, 76, 85, 97, 100, 107, 110, Lady Murray/GM, Mar. to July 1889.

[39] Castle Howard archives, J 23–8, no. 27, RC/GM, 10 Apr. 1889.

[40] Copies of the testimonials are at *1*, 56–66; originals are held by Stephen Murray.

[41] Castle Howard archives, J 23–7, no. 67, GM/RC, 12 July 1889.

[42] *476* 1, GM/Lord Carlisle, 18 July 1889.

[43] Castle Howard archives, J 23–7, no. 68, GM/RC, 22 July 1889.

[44] *169* 5, T. C. Snow/GM, 5 Aug. 1889.

[45] Castle Howard archives, J 23–7, nos. 69 and 71, 8 and 12 Aug. 1889.

[46] *483* 110, Lady Murray/GM, 16 July 1889.

[47] Castle Howard archives, J 23–8, nos. 35, 36, 38; RC/GM, 18 and 29 Aug., 27 Sept. 1889.

[48] Ib., No. 39, RC/GM, 7 Oct. 1889.

[49] *446* 10, GM/MH, 8 Oct. 1889.

[50] *483* 140, Lady Murray/MH, 22 Oct. 1889.

[51] *446* 18.

[52] *476* 6, 21 Oct. 1889.

[53] Ib., 8, 5 Nov. 1889.

[54] *483* 187, Lady Murray/MH, 27 Nov. 1889.

[55] *568* 5, GM/RT, 14 Apr. 1914, where he says that Lady Mary 'was in the habit of calling me "Tony" as long as I can remember.'

[56] *446* 18

[57] *483* 110, Lady Murray/GM, 16 July 1889.

[58] Ib., 194, letter of Nov.–Dec. 1889.

[59] *2* 104a, D. H. Secker/GM, 3 Nov. 1889.

[60] *125* 1, J. Bryce/GM, 25 Oct. 1889.

[61] *2* 22, 18 Oct. 1889.

[62] GM/MH, 4 Nov. 1889; printed *UA*, pp. 104–5 (Smith).

[63] MH/GM, 4 Nov. 1889; ib. p. 105.

[64] *Carlisle Journal*, 3 Dec. 1889, from which the further details are also taken.

[65] *446* 55, 3 Nov. 1889.

[66] Dorothy Henley, op. cit., p. 40.

[67] Ib., pp. 145–6 (for all three quotations).

Chapter IV

Unfinished Autobiography, and the two great series of general correspondence and of correspondence with Lady Mary Murray, which begins in 1889, are the main sources; but from his appointment to Glasgow onwards Murray's name begins to appear in the memoirs — autobiographical and biographical — of other more or less well-known figures. For the Glasgow, years, Janet Adam Smith, *John Buchan* (1964) (and her short illustrated biography of 1979), and M. A. Hamilton, *Remembering My Good Friends* (1944), provide most information.

[1] *UA*, p. 7 (Toynbee).

[2] *UA*, p. 94.

[3] Ib.

[4] 476 8, GM/RC, 5 Nov. 1889.

[5] *UA*, p. 95.

[6] 446 128, GM/MM, 7 Nov. 1889; *UA*, p. 130 (Henderson).

[7] Ib., 41, GM/MM, 12 Nov. 1889; *UA*, p. 131 (Henderson).

[8] *UA*, p. 131 (Henderson).

[9] 446 101, GM/MM, 4 Nov. 1889; *UA*, p. 131 (Henderson).

[10] Told to Lady Wilson by Ann Paludan, Nov. 1984.

[11] 440 1 for complete text.

[12] 2 162; *UA*, p. 130 (Henderson).

[13] *Hellenica*, ed. E. Abbott (1880), p. 241; essay by A. C. Bradley on 'Aristotle's Conception of the State' cited by F. M. Turner in *The Greeks and the Victorian Heritage* (1981), p. 365.

[14] 446 142, MM/GM, 10 Nov. 1889.

[15] Ib. 101, GM/MM, 4 Nov. 1889.

[16] e.g. 477 38, MM/GM, 27 July 1890; the last reference to Lady Mary's determination to learn Greek is in a letter of 1915.

[17] 454 100, GM/MM, Apr. 1899, and 455 51, GM/MM, 16 Apr. 1898. In a diary in the possession of Stephen Murray which GM kept on his voyage back from Australia in Jan. 1893, a number of entries on 'besetting vices of Australia' are made in Latin; such as that in one mixed school in Sydney there was hardly a virgin among 400 girls over 12.

[18] 447 2, MM/GM, 21 Apr. 1890.

[19] Ib. 46, GM/MM, 31 July 1890.

[20] Ib. 77, MM/GM, 9 Aug. 1890.

[21] M. A. Hamilton, op. cit., 22.

[22] 479 21, GM/Lady Murray, 30 Jan. 1891.

[23] 489 1–3, notes for speech, misdated Feb. 1886.

[24] 479 33, GM/Lady Murray, 16 Feb. 1891 (GM's last letter to her before her death).

[25] *UA*, p. 101.

[26] Janet Adam Smith, op. cit. p. 64, citing A. McCallum Scott, who placed Janie Malloch first in his Glasgow glamour list, with GM second, and Buchan third.

[27] 476 72, GM/RC, 20 July 1894.

[28] *UA*, p. 101.

[29] Janet Adam Smith, op. cit., p. 32.

[30] 124 5, Brailsford/GM, 25 Mar. 1895.

[31] 454 59, GM/MM, 27 Jan. 1899.

[32] 148 1, Leys/GM, 20 Apr. 1899.

[33] Ib. 31, Leys/GM, 24 Feb. 1903.

[34] *3* 13, letter of 11 May 1892.

[35] *5* 29, 52; correspondence of Oct. 1897; the original of Murray's letter of 7 Oct. is in the National Library of Scotland, MS *4664*, 72. Murray's synopsis is at *440*, item 3.

[36] M. A. Hamilton, op. cit., p. 20.

[37] *479* 29, 30 Jan. 1891; *UA*, p. 132 (Henderson).

[38] *UA*, pp. 132–3 (Henderson); quotes extracts from letter from Constance Tannahill to Janet Spens, 30 Oct. 1957.

[39] Drusilla Scott, *A. D. Lindsay* (1971), pp. 347–8.

[40] *476* 25, 58; GM/RC, 26 Mar. and 30 May 1892.

[41] *476* 159, GM/RC, 5 Oct. 1897.

[42] Ib. 52, GM/RC, 26 Jan. 1894.

[43] Ib. 93, GM/RC, 3 Feb. 1896.

[44] *Adds* 1 147, GM/WA, 17 Jan. 1897.

Chapter V

[1] *1* 65; cited in *Unfinished Autobiography*, p. 129 (Henderson).

[2] Ib.

[3] *446* 125, 1 Nov. 1889; *UA*, p. 129.

[4] *476* 16, GM/RC, 8 Sept. 1890; *118* 37, W. Ashburner/GM, 23 Nov. 1891; *3* 20, R. Ellis/GM, 14 Aug. 1894.

[5] *450* 126, 137, and 144, GM/MM, 22, 24, and 25 Apr. 1894, give full details; ib., 114, GM/MM, 16 Apr. 1894, shows that they had previously made a joint journey together to Greece (perhaps in spring 1890).

[6] *147* 18 is a good example. Andrew Lang wrote to Gosse, 15 Mar. 1897, that GM believed in Wilamowitz-Moellendorff, who was according to J. G. Frazer 'a towering example of German false hypotheses and carelessness of evidence'.

[7] *Antike und Abendland IV* (1954); cited in *UA*, p. 129 (Henderson).

[8] The myth is in Bowra, *Memories*, p. 216; the truth in GM's obituary notice of Wilamowitz, *Classical Review*, Oct. 1931.

[9] *Antike und Abendland IV* ; Murray's letter is not preserved.

[10] *3* 216, letter of 12 Oct. 1894.

[11] Trans. mainly by H. Lloyd-Jones, *Jane Harrison Memorial Lecture* on GM, 1980; repr. in his *Blood for the Ghosts* (1982).

[12] *3* 84.

[13] *Antike und Abendland IV* ; *UA*, p. 129 (Henderson).

[14] Reactions from classical scholars are in *3* 90–173; those cited here are at 111 (Baker) and 115 (Hardie).

[15] *4* 22, letter of 10 Mar. 1895.

[16] *450* 196, GM/MM, 13 May 1894; he hoped that she would be able to help him on this, and estimated that two summers' work would be necessary.

[17] *476* 52, GM/RC, 26 Jan. 1894.

[18] *4* 80, C. Cannan/GM, 7 June 1896.

[19] *4* 178, 185, 197, for proposal by H. F. Fox, 2 Apr. 1897, and subsequent correspondence GM/Edmund Gosse; see also *454* 194, GM/MM, 29 June 1899, for proposal by Professor Warr.

[20] *4* 18–20, memorandum by GM, Mar. 1895.

[21] Ib., 32, 40.

[22] *147* 15, 18, A. Lang/GM, A. Lang/E. Gosse, 15 Mar. 1897; Lang's letter to Gosse of the same date, already cited at n. 6, was typically sent on by Gosse to Murray, who commented 'Frailty, thy name is not woman, but Gosse'.
[23] *4* 190, F. Harrison/GM, Apr. 1897.
[24] *147* 18, Lang/Gosse, 15 Mar. 1897.
[25] *4* 139, letter of 12 Mar. 1897.
[26] Ib., 181, W. H. Secker/GM, 4 Apr. 1897.
[27] *452* 21, MM/GM, 15 Mar. 1897.
[28] In *History of Ancient Greek Literature.*
[29] *452* 29, GM/MM, 16 Mar. 1897.
[30] *4* 164, letter of 23 Mar. 1897.
[31] Ib., 93, GM/E. Gosse, 1 Oct. 1896.
[32] *489* 5–25.
[33] *1* 17, 27, Maynard/GM, 5 Aug. and 31 Oct. 1887.
[34] *5* 43, 57, letters from V. Nash 13 Oct. and E. Caird, 23 Oct. 1897.
[35] Ib., 64, GM/F. Harrison, 24 Oct. 1897.
[36] John Morley, *Recollections* (1917), II. p. 63.
[37] *Adds* 1, 229, GM/WA, 26 Aug. 1897.
[38] *454* 22, GM/MM, 20 Jan. 1899.
[39] *133* 8, GM/H. A. L. Fisher, 17 Mar. 1897; and *452* 35, GM/MM, 18 Mar. 1897.
[40] *UA*, p. 97.
[41] *Adds* 1 164, GM/WA, 5 Mar. 1897.

Chapter VI

For the political background of this chapter, I have made much use of the following: Peter Clark, *Liberals and Social Democrats* (1978); R. C. K. Ensor, *England 1870–1914* (1936); Stephen Koss, *The Pro-Boers* (1973); Norman and Jeanne Mackenzie, *The First Fabians* (1977); H. C. G. Matthew, *The Liberal Imperialists* (1973); Thomas Pakenham, *The Boer War* (1980).

[1] *479* 29, 30 Jan. 1891.
[2] *448* 53, GM/MM, 24 Sept. 1891.
[3] The diary is in the possession of Stephen Murray (see Chap. I, n. 22).
[4] *450* 212, 221; GM/MM, 5 Oct., and MM/GM, 7 Oct. 1894.
[5] *4* 180, GM/H. F. Fox, 3 Apr. 1897.
[6] *452, 453 passim*, for correspondence between GM and MM on his illness. I am indebted to Dr H. M. Adam of Edinburgh for information on medical fashions of this period.
[7] *452* 181, GM/MM, 27 Mar. 1898.
[8] Ib., 183, GM/MM, 27 Mar. 1898.
[9] *453* 24, GM/MM, 27 Mar. 1898.
[10] *Adds* 2 39, GM/WA, May 1898.
[11] *453* 107, 230, GM/MM, 15 May and 5 Nov. 1898.
[12] Ib. 3, MM/GM, 5 Apr. 1898, on Bradley's 'melancholy and nerves'.
[13] *450* 39, GM/MM, 11 Feb. 1893.
[14] Ib. 144, GM/MM, 25 Apr. 1894.
[15] *Adds* 1 52, GM/WA, 12 Sept. 1895.
[16] *2* 140, Alport Robinson/GM, 11 Nov. 1890.
[17] *449* 33, GM/MM, Nov. 1892. He writes of an over-realistic portrait of R. L. Nettleship; the novel also contained what was usually thought to be an

over-faithful portrait of T. H. Green. See William S. Peterson, *Victorian Heretic: Mrs Humphrey Ward's Robert Elsmere* (1971), pp. 133-4.

[18] *3* 178, GM/R. Ellis, 9 Mar. 1894 (marked by MM 'Not sent').

[19] *6* 88, 22 May 1899; it is probable, but not quite certain that this letter was sent.

[20] This story has been pieced together from incomplete documents, *6* 89, 117, 120, 144; *122* 95, Bradley/GM, 5 June 1899; and a letter from Alan E. Clapperton, Secretary to the Glasgow Court, to GM, 6 June 1899 (in the archives of Glasgow University), making it clear that GM had withdrawn his application. Isobel Henderson states categorically (*Unfinished Autobiography*, p. 134) that GM retir~d on pension from Glasgow, and her evidence is important — it often reflected GM's conversations — but on this point there is no support for it.

[21] *453* 153, GM/MM, 1 June 1898.

[22] *Adds 2* 56, 6 Oct. 1898 (the Russian word is nearer 'chort').

[23] *453* 208, MM/GM, 25 Oct; *476* 149, 162, GM/RC, 31 Aug. and 30 Oct. 1898; *453* 169, builder's estimate.

[24] *476* 188.

[25] *140* 13, Hammond/GM, 7 June 1899.

[26] *454* 200, GM/MM, 15 July 1900.

[27] *476* 180, GM/RC, 18 July 1899.

[28] Signed, or otherwise certainly identifiable, contributions by GM to the *Speaker* down to 1903 include reviews of classical books (21 Oct. 1899, 28 Aug. 1900, 2 Mar. 1901, 7 Dec. 1901) and of Bernard Shaw's *Three Plays for Puritans*, 9 Feb. 1900. A letter to Lady Carlisle (*477* 22, 2 Dec. 1901) shows that 'Two or three articles' by GM had been published in the preceding weeks (perhaps articles on Temperance, 19 Oct. and 2 Nov.) In 1902 a regular column signed *M*. under the heading 'Personal Talk' may include some contributions by GM; possible candidates are the columns for 15, 22, and 29 Mar.; probables are 10 May (on Arthur Sidgwick), 17 May ('A visit to the Antipodes some years ago'), and 7 June ('an early experiment in fiction'). Massingham is likely to have written the majority.

[29] *453* 206, GM/MM, 23 Oct. 1898.

[30] *476* 182, GM/RC, 10 Sept. 1899.

[31] Ib., 185, 17 Sept. 1899.

[32] Ib. 220, GM/RC, 20 Oct. 1899.

[33] *118* 117, Ashburner/GM, 10 Nov. 1899; *122* 117, 120, Bradley/GM, 20 Oct. and 21 Dec. 1899.

[34] *476* 197, GM/RC, 8 Feb. 1900; see also *449* 123, GM/MM, 6 Dec. 1892.

[35] *476* 188, 1 Dec. 1899.

[36] *454* 234, 238, GM/MM, 26 and 28 Nov. 1899.

[37] GM's knowledge of birds was theoretical only; he required A. C. Bradley's tuition to recognize a chaffinch (*476 103, GM/RC, 11 Apr. 1896*).

[38] *440* 5, for text.

[39] *455* 10, GM/MM, 25 May 1900.

[40] Stephen Koss, *The Pro-Boers* (1973), pp. 81-5.

[41] *8* 229, Botha/GM, 3 Nov. 1902.

[42] *477* 58, GM/RC, 30 Nov. 1902.

[43] *8* 185-7, June 1902.

[44] *454* 210, GM/MM, 18 July, 1899.

[45] *489*, 67–111.

[46] *153* 1, MacDonald/GM, 2 Jan. 1900.

[47] *477* 33, GM/RC, 9 Apr. 1902.

[48] Ib., 48, 26 Sept. 1902.

[49] *8* 203, Hobson/GM, 17 Aug. 1902.

[50] Ib., 193, 7 Aug. 1902.

[51] *126* 51, 65, Buchan/GM, 30 Jan., and GM/Buchan, 25 Apr. 1903.

[52] See n. 45.

Chapter VII

[1] *476* 191–4, GM/RC, 31 Jan. 1900.

[2] Ib., 195, copy of letter from Morley to GM (30 Jan. 1900) which GM enclosed in his letter of 31 Jan. to Lady Carlisle.

[3] M. A. Hamilton, *Remembering My Good Friends* (1944), p. 22.

[4] Memorandum to author, 7 Apr. 1981.

[5] *448* 1, MM/GM, 5 Jan. 1891.

[6] *476* 120, GM/RC, 29 Dec. 1896 and 22 Mar. 1897.

[7] *Essays in Honour of Gilbert Murray* (1936), p. 31 (C. Archer).

[8] *Adds* 1 3, GM/WA, 12 Apr. 1894; Archer had himself suggested a joint play in 1886 to the then unknown Shaw (Norman and Jeanne Mackenzie, *The First Fabians* (1977), pp. 166–7).

[9] *5* 86, GM/E. Robins, 6 Dec.; and *Adds* 1 283, GM/WA, 2 Dec. 1897.

[10] *Adds* 2 3, 17, 6 Jan., and 7 Mar. 1898.

[11] *6* 37, Mrs Campbell/GM, 2 Mar. 1899.

[12] *454* 175, MM/GM, 2 May 1899.

[13] Ib., 192, GM/MM, 10 May 1899.

[14] *Adds* 2 102, 21 June 1899.

[15] *Unfinished Autobiography*, p. 151 (Thorndike). The remark is quoted as referring to performance rather than rehearsal, but all witnesses agreed that Mrs Campbell acted superbly 'on the night'.

[16] *567* 45, 46, letters of 5 and 12 June 1899.

[17] *Adds* 2 102, 21 Jan. 1899.

[18] *4* 50, letter of 10 July 1895.

[19] *The Times* 20 June 1899; cf. *567* 48, GM/RM, 20 June 1899.

[20] Ib., and *Adds* 2 102, GM/WA, 21 June 1899.

[21] *Manchester Guardian*, 20 June, and *6* 97, WA/GM, 19 June 1899.

[22] *6* 187, Barrie/GM, 21 June 1899.

[23] *Adds* 2 102, GM/WA, 21 June 1899.

[24] *Adds* 1 63, WA/GM, 11 Nov. 1895 ('Duke of Africa'); *Adds* 2 143, GM/WA, 13 Feb. 1900 and *477* 1, GM/RC, 1 Jan. 1901 ('Rousseau-esque comedy').

[25] *Adds* 1 28, 40 GM/WA, 16 June and 1 July 1895; the text of the play is at *439* 79–151.

[26] *7* 164, 167; Mrs Campbell/GM, Sept. 1900.

[27] Text at *439* 153–240.

[28] *Adds* 1 118, WA/GM, 7 Nov. 1896.

[29] Ib., 122, 12 Nov. 1896.

[30] Ib., 233, 9 Sept. 1897.

[31] Ib., 246, 27 Sept. 1897.

[32] Ib., 251, 30 Sept. 1897.

[33] Ib., 261, 16 Oct. 1897.

[34] Ib., 291, 9 Dec. 1897.

[35] *Adds* 2 168, GM/WA, 23 Jan. 1901.

[36] 7 198, Mrs Campbell/GM, 15 Nov. 1900.

[37] *Adds* 2 171, GM/WA, Feb. 1901.

[38] 7 68, Housman/GM, 23 Apr. 1901.

[39] *167 28*, GBS/GM, 24 Feb. 1901.

[40] *Adds* 2 176, 5 Mar. 1901.

[41] *485 1*, GM speech at 70th birthday celebrations, 13 Feb. 1936; printed in *Oxford Magazine*, 20 Feb. 1936.

[42] Particularly of a tragedy, along the lines of *Andromache*, about the Aeschylean heroine, Stheneboea.

[43] BL Add MS 50542 9, GM/GBS, 16 Mar. 1901.

[44] *Adds* 2 162, Oct. 1900.

[45] *144 1*, GM/I. Monro (Henderson), 18 Sept. 1929.

[46] *Adds* 1, 233, GM/WA, 9 Sept. 1897.

[47] 'What English Poetry May Still Learn From Greek', in *Essays and Studies by Members of the English Association* (1912).

[48] *Euripides and his Age* (1913) pp. 202–3.

[49] *477 58*, GM/RC, 30 Nov. 1902.

[50] *456 58*, MM/GM, 25 Nov. 1902; 'Gipsland' is a reference to a type of opossum, one of MM's animal endearments for GM.

[51] *400 30*, G. Allen/GM, 22 Dec. 1902.

[52] 29 Nov. 1902; this and other reviews are in *506*, 40 ff.

[53] *143 10*, 19 Dec. 1902.

[54] *133 11*, 26 Nov. 1902.

[55] *126 51*, 30 Jan. 1903.

[56] *8 245*, J. H. Baddeley/GM, 28 Nov. 1902.

[57] *9 56*, Maynard/GM, 27 June 1903.

Chapter VIII

For Shaw, BL Add MS 50542 contains the originals of his correspondence with Murray; photostat copies of many but not all Murray's letters are in Box 167 of the Murray papers. The references given are in the Murray papers, where possible. A number of letters on both sides are published in *Bernard Shaw: Collected Letters*, Vol. I, 1874–97 (1965); Vol. II, 1898–1910 (1972).

Some brief reminiscences of Shaw by Murray were published in the Shaw Memorial issue of *Drama*, spring 1951.

Occasional letters from Kipling to Shaw are in the 'General Correspondence' boxes of the Murray papers. Murray's letters to Kipling are not preserved in the Kipling archive at Sussex University, and there is no mention of Murray in Kipling's brief and very selective autobiography *Something of Myself* (1937).

The originals of Russell's extensive correspondence with Murray are in the Russell Archives at McMaster University, Hamilton, Ontario, Canada. Photostat copies are in Boxes *165*, *166*, and *Adds* 8 of the Murray papers. A number of letters on both sides are printed in Russell's *Autobiography*, Vol. I.

For Murray's visit to *I Tatti* in spring 1903, the Pearsall Smith papers contain the letters quoted from Mary Berenson. These are in the possession of Mrs Barbara Strachey-Halpern, who kindly allowed me to see them. They are partly printed in her *Remarkable Relations* (1980).

[1] *477* 115, GM/RC, 16 Apr. 1904.

[2] *Drama*, spring 1951, 7–9.

[3] *167*, letter of 1 Sept. 1898; *Bernard Shaw: Collected Letters*, II. pp. 62–3.

[4] *Adds* 2 165, GM/WA n.d. [1900].

[5] BL Add MS 50542 1, 30 July 1900.

[6] *167* 22, 28 July 1900.

[7] Ib., 26, C. Shaw/GM, 12 Feb. 1901.

[8] BL Add. MS 50542 14, 30 Sept. 1903.

[9] Ib., 21, 18 June 1905.

[10] *509* 33, cutting from unidentified local newspaper n.d.; *456* 23, GM/MM, 20 Mar. 1902 refers to similar remarks by Shaw, probably on this occasion.

[11] *167* 35, 23 Feb. 1902; the criticism is developed in Samuel Butler, *Erewhon*.

[12] *167* 184, GBS/GM, 14 Mar. 1911 (original); and BL Add MS 50542 28, GM/GBS, 19 Mar. 1911.

[13] BL Add MS 50542 41, GM/GBS, 13 Sept. 1913.

[14] Ib. 84, 1 May 1949.

[15] *Letters*, II. 884. Shaw's letter was an attempt to secure Pinero's backing for the election of Murray to the National Drama Club.

[16] *449* 36, 9 Nov. 1892.

[17] *Adds* 2 202, 204, GM/WA, 21 and 29 Aug. 1902.

[18] *8* 201, RK/GM, 13 Aug. 1902; Parnesius was finally put in charge of the 7th cohort of the XXXth legion, *Ulpia Victrix*, and given a Numidian nurse; Kipling, *Puck of Pook's Hill* (1907), and *Something of Myself* (1937), p. 188.

[19] *11* 100, 124, RK/GM, 27 Aug. and 14 Nov. 1905; the 'Hymn to Mithras', *Puck of Pook's Hill*, probably owes something to Murray's advice.

[20] *9* 54, RK/GM, 18 June 1903. The reference is probably to Euripides, *Electra*, pp. 842–3.

[21] *165*, BR/GM, 21 June 1900.

[22] BL Add MS 50542 5, GM/GBS, 25 Jan. 1901.

[23] *165* 3, BR/GM, 26 Feb. 1901; Russell, *Autobiography*, 1.156.

[24] Russell, op. cit., I. 156, Mar. 1901.

[25] *477* 76, 13 June 1903.

[26] This contrasts with Murray's own much later account of their conversations in *Unfinished Autobiography*, p. 208, where he suggests a comparison with W. S. Gilbert's two curates in the *Bab Ballads*, each determined to be 'the mildest curate going', with GM well in the lead over BR.

[27] *165* 8, 24 Mar. 1901.

[28] Ib., 13, 7 May 1901.

[29] *Adds* 8 1, 4 Dec. 1902.

[30] Russell, op. cit., I. 162, 12 Dec. 1902.

[31] Ib., p. 161. Russell had written: 'The river shines like burnished bronze, and the barges float dimly through the brightness like dream-memories of childhood.'

[32] *165* 57, 20 Dec. 1902.

[33] References are as follows: GM (i) *456* 108, (iii) ib. 110, (iv) ib. 112, (v) ib. 114, (vi) *Adds* 3 8, (ix) *456* 139, (xi) ib. 144–5, (xii) *477* 72: Mrs Berenson (ii) Strachey-Halpern op. cit., p. 207, (vi) Pearsall Smith papers (not printed), (vii) Strachey-Halpern op. cit., pp. 207–8, (x) ib., p. 208.

[34] Jessie Stewart, *Jane Harrison: A Portrait from Letters* (1959), p. 58; she is quoted as saying 'The fops! The miserable fops!'

Chapter IX

On Murray's career in and around the theatre, the main printed sources are *Bernard Shaw: Collected Letters*, Vol. II (1972) and *Major Barbara* ; also C. B. Purdom, *Harley Granville-Barker* (1955). The latter quotes a number of letters from GM which are not otherwise available. For the importance of the Barker–Vedrenne partnership in British theatrical life, see G. R. Rowell, *The Victorian Theatre* (1914).

Sidney P. Albert, 'In More Ways Than One' a monograph on Shaw's debt to Murray in *Major Barbara*, is in the *Educational Theatre Quarterly* (1968) (rev. vers.). It is invaluable, and contains the text of three letters from Murray to Shaw, now in the Academic Center Library of the University of Texas. Richard Jenkyns, *The Victorians and the Greeks* (1980) has provided many useful leads on painting and the theatre at the turn of the century.

[1] Cited in W. M. Gaunt, *Victorian Olympus* (1952), p. 144.
[2] *456 165*, GM/MM, 30 Mar. 1903.
[3] *13 180*, GM/Yeats, 17 July 1903 (misplaced among papers for 1908).
[4] July 1903, Pearsall Smith papers.
[5] *9 80*, Yeats/GM, 14 Aug. 1903.
[6] C. B. Purdom, op. cit., pp. 20–30.
[7] *Unfinished Autobiography*, p. 153 (Thorndike).
[8] *485 86*, broadcast, 'Unfinished Battle', 1 Jan. 1956.
[9] *10 137*, Housman/GM, 25 Oct. 1904; printed in A. E. Housman, *Letters* (1971), 5.
[10] JH/GM, May 1904, Harrison papers, Newnham College Library, Box 2.
[11] *167 40*, GBS/GM, 6 Jan. 1905.
[12] *457 43*, GM/MM, 5 Nov. 1904.
[13] *UA*, p. 158 (Thorndike).
[14] *477 125*, GM/RC, 1 May 1905; Lady Carlisle had offered to make up the losses, and GM told her not to — they were due, he said, entirely to a muddle about dates between Vedrenne and Barker.
[15] *11 68*, Hobhouse/GM, 5 May 1905.
[16] Purdom, op. cit., pp. 41–3.
[17] *Essays in Honour of Gilbert Murray* (1936), p. 247.
[18] Purdom, op. cit., pp. 44–5.
[19] *135 70*, 84, Barker/GM, 27 Sept. and 4 Nov. 1905; *457 190*, GM/MM, 12 Oct. 1905.
[20] *167 183*, GBS/GM, 16 Jan. 1906 (original); quoted in *UA*, p. 154 (Thorndike).
[21] *567 126* (i), 17 Jan. 1906. There is some duplication of numbering among these papers; there are two f. 126, among others (see n. 24).
[22] Ib.
[23] *Adds 3 83*, GM/WA, 5 Feb. 1906; the reference is to an article in the *Speaker*, 27 Jan. 1906.
[24] *567 126* (ii), 15 May 1906; the chorus is *Medea* 1081–115.
[25] Purdom, op. cit., p. 70.
[26] *12 127–8*, 139, letters to GM, July 1907; Purdom op. cit., p. 75.
[27] From 1904–8, Murray received £183. 5s. 2s. for performances of his translations in London (the list is not quite complete): *Hippolytus* (spring 1904) £30; *Trojan Women* (1905) £22. 18s. 6d.; *Electra* (Jan. 1906) £44; *Electra* and

Hippolytus (Mar. 1906) £42. 5s. 0d.; *Medea* (Oct. 1907) £44. 1s. 8d. — under £200 in all for the figures here recorded. Purdom, op. cit., p. 70.

[28] *485* 54, broadcast, 'Looking Back III',, 28 Mar. 1954.

[29] *457* 144, 160, GM/MM, 1 and 3 Oct. 1905.

[30] GM in *Drama* (Shaw memorial number), spring 1951.

[31] GM/GBS, 2 Oct. 1905; original in Academic Center Library, University of Texas, printed in Sidney P. Albert, op. cit., p. 126.

[32] *457* 156, 160, 1 and 3 Oct. 1905.

[33] *167* 48, GBS/GM, 7 Oct. 1905; printed in *UA*, p. 155, and in *Letters*, I. 565.

[34] *458* 3, GM/MM, 3 Jan. 1906.

[35] Letter of 5 Oct. 1905; original in papers of the Passfield Trust, cited by Albert, op. cit., p. 125.

[36] Lillah McCarthy, *Myself and My Friends* (1933), p. 166; cited in Albert, op. cit., p. 125.

[37] *Major Barbara* (1928 edn.), p. 290.

[38] Ib., p. 277; GM in *New Statesman*, 16 Aug. 1947;

[39] *457* 160, 3 Oct. 1905.

[40] GM/GBS, 5 Dec. 1905; original in University of Texas (cf. n. 31), cited in Albert, op. cit., p. 139.

[41] *457* 160, GM/MM, 3 Oct. 1905.

[42] GM/GBS, 7 Oct. 1905; original in University of Texas, cited in Albert, op. cit., p. 128.

[43] *457* 160, 3 Oct. 1905.

[44] *165* 50, GBS/GM, 29 Nov. 1905; printed in *Letters*, II. 588.

[45] *458* 2, GM/MM, 1 Jan. 1906.

[46] *567* 122, 7 Dec. 1905.

[47] *165* 48, GBS/GM, 7 Oct. 1905; printed in *Letters* II. 565.

[48] *Major Barbara* p. 200.

[49] There is a perceptive reference to Shaw's description by E. R. Dodds, obituary of GM, *Gnomon* 29 (1957) (copy in *Adds* 11, 1); cf. *UA*, p. 18.

Chapter X

I have made much use of F. M. Turner, *The Greek Heritage in Victorian Britain* (1980), which contains copious references to other secondary sources. Wilamowitz's *History of Classical Scholarship* is also useful in a more general way; it has recently been translated and published here, with an introductory essay by Hugh Lloyd-Jones (1982).

R. P. Graves, *A. E. Housman* (1979), quotes the Housman/Murray correspondence with comment; the full text of Housman's letters is printed in *A. E. Housman: Letters* (1971).

Jessie Stewart, *Jane Harrison: A Portrait from Letters* (1959) is based on the large collection of typewritten copies of Jane Harrison's letters (the originals of her correspondence were burnt) in the library of Newnham College, Cambridge. Further copies of most of her letters to GM are in Box *143* of the Murray papers.

Jane Harrison's brief and colourful *Reminiscences of a Student's Life* (1925) is also cited in Stewart's book.

The 'Homeric Question' has a vast bibliography of its own, which I cannot claim to have mastered. The history of the 'question' is covered in Hugh Lloyd-Jones's

'Remarks on the Homeric Question' in *Essays for Lord Dacre* (1981); from this essay the reader may collect a large reading-list ancient and modern (it is significant that there is no mention in it of Murray's work). My own *Life and Times of Vuk Stefanović Karadzić* (1970) looks at the problems of collecting oral poetry from a Serb angle.

[1] *476* 201, GM/RC, 19 Mar. 1900; Peter Sutcliffe, *The Oxford University Press* (1978), p. 92.

[2] C. Archer, in *Essays in Honour of Gilbert Murray* (1936), p. 36.

[3] *8* 72, Wilamowitz/GM, 2 June 1901; some proofs with Wilamowitz's comments are among the Murray papers, e.g., *8* 98, 101–2, 106.

[4] *Adds* 2 180, 29 June 1901.

[5] *Euripidis Fabulae* I (1901), p. xi.

[6] Ib.

[7] *456* 164, GM/MM, 27 Feb. 1903.

[8] *Rise of the Greek epic*, 4th edn. (1934), p. 250.

[9] *126* 65, 25 Apr. 1903.

[10] *456* 174, 3 Apr. 1903.

[11] *476* 153, GM/RC, 5 Sept. 1898; on her son Hubert Howard's death at Omdurman, he said that he was haunted by Housman's line, 'And the few who will carry their strength and their truth to the grave.' 'Strength' is a misquotation for 'looks'.

[12] *15* 43, 50, correspondence with A. W. Mair, Nov. 1908.

[13] *10* 153, Housman/GM, 4 Nov. 1904; *Letters of A. E. Housman* (1971), p. 76.

[14] *9* 98, *10* 124, 137, Housman/GM, Sept. 1903 and Oct. 1904; *Letters* (1971) pp. 68, 75, 99.

[15] *456* 1, GM/MM, 8 Feb. 1902.

[16] In the *Oxford Magazine*, 24 Oct. 1912, GM's obituary notice of Verrall referred to the 'dangerous delights of his work' for many generations of young scholars.

[17] *Adds* 2 181, GM/WA, 2 July 1901.

[18] F. M. Turner, op. cit., p. 117 and n. 63.

[19] Ib., p. 118; cf. *147* 182, Lang/GM, 26 Oct. [1910?] where Lang describes how he read an essay on Jowett as an undergraduate and introduced him to Red Indian songs.

[20] Macaulay, *Lays of Ancient Rome*, 'The Battle of Lake Regillus', p. 10.

[21] J. G. Frazer, *Spirits of the Corn and the Wild* (1912), I. 34; cited by Turner, op. cit., p. 120.

[22] J. E. Harrison, op. cit., pp. 82–3.

[23] *450* 249, GM/MM, 27 Dec. 1894.

[24] *455* 86, 9 July 1900.

[25] Jessie Stewart, op. cit., p. 38.

[26] *143* 10, 24 Dec. 1902.

[27] *477* 48, GM/RC, 4 May 1903.

[28] GM's version is in his Appendix to Jane Harrison's *Prolegomena* 660–74. His help is enthusiastically acknowledged in the Introduction, p. xv.

[29] Pearsall Smith papers; Mary Berenson/Alys Russell, 15 Mar. 1903.

[30] *477* 73, GM/RC, 4 May 1903.

[31] *456* 163, GM/MM, 29 Mar. 1903.

[32] Ib. 157, GM/MM, 26 Mar. 1903.

[33] *Adds* 2 171, GM/WA, Feb. 1901.

[34] 9 67, R. L. A. du Pontet/GM, 17 July 1903.

[35] *10* 145, 30 Oct. 1904.

[36] Ib. 157, 163.

[37] *Adds* 3 60, GM/WA, 5 Nov. 1904.

[38] *457* 56, GM/MM, 5 Nov. 1904.

[39] 477 93, 102, 115; GM/RC, 28 Oct. and 1 Dec. 1903, 16 Apr. 1904.

[40] *456* 275, 247, GM/MM, 15 and 17 Sept. 1903; Hampstead and Wimbledon were also considered.

[41] *11* 30, 48, 74; Macan/GM, 21 Mar., and Bridges/GM, 24 Apr. and 15 May 1905.

[42] Barford was not finally sold till 1907, when the Murrays received £5,800 net for it (*458* 121, GM/MM, 15 Oct. 1907).

[43] *457* 199, GM/MM, 16 Oct. 1905.

[44] *12* 56, H. E. Butler/GM [prob. Dec.] 1906.

[45] *Adds* 3 92, GM/WA, 4 June 1906; cf. *13* 83, A. S. Hunt/GM, 23 Feb. 1907.

[46] In 1906, the OUP asked GM to edit Sophocles in their series of classical texts (*397* 61, C. Cannan/GM, 18 June 1906).

[47] *11* 12, Evans/GM, 26 Jan. 1905.

[48] Ib. 25, 5 Mar. 1905.

[49] *12* 38, 22 Nov. 1906.

[50] Cited by C. H. Roberts *The Periodical*, autumn 1957; cutting in *Adds* 11.

[51] *Adds* 8 18, 27 July 1906.

[52] *165* 110, 17 May 1907.

[53] Ib. 147, 12 Jan. 1914.

[54] *Harvard Crimson* 3, 4, 7, 9, and 11 May 1907.

[55] J. A. K. Thomson, Obituary, 'Gilbert Murray 1866–1957', *Proceedings of British Academy* XLIII (1957), pp. 245–70.

[56] *RGE*, p. 154.

[57] Ib., p. 144.

[58] Ib.

[59] Ib., p. 26.

[60] F. M. Turner, op. cit., p. 151.

[61] Ib.

[62] *RGE*, pp. 237, 238, 327.

[63] *Albany Review*, Jan. 1908.

[64] *12* 186, Wilamowitz/GM, 10 Nov. 1907 (trans. by author).

[65] *13* 3, 14, letters of 4 and 7 Dec. 1907.

[66] *TLS*, 26 Mar. 1908. The review was probably by T. W. Allen (cf. *13* 108, letter of 30 Mar. 1908); *RGE*, preface to 2nd edn.; *Athenaeum*, 16 May and *Westminster Gazette*, 11 July 1908.

[67] *Nation*, 14 Dec. 1907.

[68] 12 Dec. 1907.

[69] Files of OUP under Murray.

[70] Ib.

[71] *Adds* 11 90, GM/Charles Cannan n.d. [1911] quoted by C. H. Roberts in *The Periodical* (1957).

[72] *459* 31, GM/MM, 17 Apr. 1908.

[73] Ib. 12, 3 Apr. 1908.

[74] *13* 133, Wilamowitz/GM, 21 May 1908 (trans. by author).

[75] BL, 'Memories of Wilamowitz', *Antike und Abendland iv* (1954) p. 9; cf. Wilamowitz, *Erinnerungen 1848–1914* (1929), p. 310.

[76] *459* 97.

[77] Ib. 101. 21 June 1908, GM/MM.

[78] Ib. 102. 22 June 1908 GM/MM.

[79] Ib. 106, 25 June 1908 *Unfinished Autobiography*, p. 148. (Henderson).

[80] *479* 74, RC/GM, 18 Oct. 1908.

[81] *14* 115, M. Verrall/GM, 17 Oct. 1908.

Chapter XI

[1] *456* 8, MM/GM, 14 Mar. 1902.

[2] Information from Stephen Murray to Lady Wilson 1984.

[3] *455* 145, MM/GM, 18 Dec. 1900, and *456* 73, GM/MM, 28 Jan. 1903.

[4] *459* GM/MM, 1908. This letter is quoted in F. West, *Gilbert Murray: A Life*, p. 51.

[5] *449* 193, 450, MM/GM, 21 Dec. 1892 and 3 Jan. 1893.

[6] *567* 41, GM/RM, 1 Apr. 1899.

[7] *454* 160, GM/MM, 30 Apr. 1899.

[8] *567* 69, GM/RM, 15 Oct. 1901; Euripides was certainly not thinking of the first line, which is pure GM (Bacchae pp. 897–901).

[9] *Adds* 2 175, GM/WA, 12 Apr. 1901.

[10] Ib. 179, GM/WA, 12 Apr. 1901.

[11] *455* 207, 23 July 1900.

[12] *457* 146, GM/MM, 30 Sept. 1905.

[13] Ib., 242, 29 Oct. 1905.

[14] *Adds* 3 80, GM/WA, 14 Sept. 1906.

[15] *567* 132, GM/RM, 9 Nov. 1906.

[16] *450* 274, MM/GM, 30 Dec. 1894.

[17] *451* 74, GM/MM, 19 May 1896.

[18] *452* 25, GM/MM, 15 Mar. 1897.

[19] Ib., 29, GM/MM, 16 Mar. 1897.

[20] Ib., 32, GM/MM, 17 Mar. 1897.

[21] *476* 199, GM/RC, 7 Mar. 1900.

[22] *457* 5, Mar. 1904.

[23] *456* 218, GM/MM, 24 Aug. 1903.

[24] *567* 114, GM/RM, 22 Sept. 1905; other versions (to Lady Carlisle and Archer) are at *477* 131, and *Adds* 3 81.

[25] *458* 106, GM/Revd F. P. David, 10 Aug. 1907.

[26] *459* 30, GM/MM, 16 Apr. 1908.

[27] Ib., 46, GM/MM, 29 Apr. 1908.

[28] *567* 105, GM/MM, 7 Aug. 1905.

[29] *Unfinished Autobiography*, 207 (Russell).

[30] *567* 75, 14 Oct. 1902, and 125, 29 Dec. 1905.

[31] *478* 62, 14 Oct. 1908.

[32] Mr Jan Nasmyth, son of the Murrays' Oxford doctor and Gilbert Murray's executor, told the author (July 1981) of a conversation with Rosalind Toynbee, after her father's death; she told him that she had destroyed letters illustrating the major disagreements between her parents.

[33] e.g. *477* 82, GM/RC, 11 Aug. 1903, in which he analysed his own behaviour to Lady Mary, 'if she is mostly wrong on the surface, I may be selfish towards her underneath.'

[34] *457* 46.

[35] Ib., 77.

[36] *456* 144, 21 Mar. 1903.

[37] *455* 21, 18 June 1900.

[38] Ib., 44, 25 June 1900.

[39] *165* 35, GM/BR, 16 Sept. 1902.

[40] Ib., 50, Dec. 1902; 100, 3 Feb. 1905, contains further interesting but mysterious family confidences.

[41] *477* 158, GM/RC, 18 June 1908.

[42] *457* 118, 31 July 1905.

[43] *458* 11, 13 Jan. 1906.

[44] *Adds* 3 98, GM/WA, 1 Sept. 1906: ' . . . it took a fearful time, but is, I think, a good picture'. It hangs now in Murray's old class-room at Glasgow University, on loan from Christ Church, Oxford.

[45] His letters to the poetess, Rachel Annand Taylor, are a good example; they are preserved in the National Library of Scotland, Acc. 4116.

[46] *459* 9, 11 Jan. 1908.

[47] Ib.,44, 56, 61, 89, 107, 149; Murray also wrote to Lady Carlisle in June 1908 (*477* 158), saying that he had hesitated about staying with the Wheelers at Kynance, because he 'might hate them at close quarters', which suggests that he may have been a deep diplomat in this affair.

[48] Ib., 149, 19 Dec. 1908.

[49] *460* 52, 12 July 1909.

[50] Ib., 60, 21 July 1909.

[51] Ib., 1, 5 Jan. 1909.

[52] Ib., 6 [Jan. 1909].

[53] *441* item 2.

Chapter XII

[1] *168* 15, 27 Jan. 1894.

[2] Ib.

[3] 22 Oct. 1908.

[4] *14* 53, 16 Oct. 1908.

[5] Ib., 26, 14 Oct. 1908.

[6] Ib., 60, 16 Oct. 1908.

[7] Ib., 90, 17 Oct. 1908; printed in Housman, *Letters* (1971) p. 99. The letter foreshadowed a famous after-dinner speech in Trinity College, Cambridge: 'This hall has seen Porson sober and Wordsworth drunk; here I stand, a better poet than Porson and a greater scholar than Wordsworth, somewhere betwixt and between.'

[8] Text in *441*.

[9] See F. M. Turner, *The Greek Heritage*, p. 166.

[10] A reference to the Homeric story of Odysseus' conversation, after due sacrifice, with the ghosts of famous men. The text of Wilamowitz's lectures is in *441*.

[11] *567* 139 GM/RM, 4 Feb. 1909.

[12] *The Times*, 30 Jan. 1909.

[13] *Nation*, 30 Jan. 1909.

[14] e.g. *11* 94, *9* 104, 115, 146, 161, 167.
[15] *460* 14, GM/MM, 7 Nov. 1910; *24* 2, W. Flinders Petrie/GM, 3 Mar. 1914.
[16] GM, preface to *Greek Studies* (1946).
[17] Author's personal experience, 1932–4.
[18] Churchill, conversation with Bowra, cited in Bowra, *Memories*, p. 331.
[19] *416* 42, E. Lyttleton/GM, Feb. 1910; ib. 168, A. C. Benson/GM, 28 Apr. 1913; *18* 109, A. C. Benson/GM, 15 May 1911.
[20] *416* 8, Aug. 1909.
[21] *Adds* 4 18, 13 Mar. 1910.
[22] *416* 24, A. D. Godley/GM, Feb. 1910.
[23] *460* 121, GM/MM, 18 May 1910.
[24] *18* 129, 137, J. A. Smith/GM, 12 and 13 June 1911.
[25] Drusilla Scott, *A. D. Lindsay* (1971), pp. 49–50.
[26] *460* 148, GM/MM, 4 Nov. 1910.
[27] *567* 153, 28 Jan. 1910.
[28] Ib., 193, 2 Dec. 1912.
[29] *459* 35, GM/MM, 21 Apr. 1908.
[30] Jane Harrison, *Reminiscence of a Student's Life* (1925), p. 64.
[31] *461* 202, GM/MM, 20 Dec. 1913.
[32] *Euripides and his Age*, pp. 61–7.
[33] *19* 75, 12 Dec. 1911.
[34] Ib., 15, 18 Oct. 1911.
[35] *170* 15, 29 Mar. 1914.
[36] 'Hamlet and Orestes', repr. GM, *CTP*, pp. 22–240.
[37] Ib., p. 233.
[38] *15* 14, 11 Nov. 1908.
[39] *17* 90, 124, J. Loeb/GM, 30 Aug. 1910; S. Reinach/GM, 4 Nov. 1910.
[40] *18* 127, George Plimpton/GM, 9 June 1911.
[41] Ib. 238, N. Murray Butler/GM, 27 Sept. 1911; the other invitations are at *15* 80 and 18, and *18* 127, 146, 200, 208, and 209.
[42] Letter of 9th Oct. 1911, Columbia University Library.
[43] *18* 146, 23 June 1911.
[44] *506* 109, Columbia University, Notice of Lectures, 1911–12.
[45] The first two lectures, when printed in book form, were rechristened *Saturnia Regna* and *The Olympian Conquest*. These were originally written for Columbia. The third, 'The Failure of Nerve', had been substantially printed in the *Hibbert Journal* (Jan. 1910). The fourth, 'The Last Protest' (not delivered at Columbia) was developed from an article in the *English Review* (1908). The fifth, added for the 1925 edition, was entitled 'The Great Schools' (Cynics, Stoics, Epicureans, and Peripatetics); it bridged the gap in historical time between the second and third Columbia lectures. The Appendix, a translation of Sallustius on 'The Gods and the World' (mentioned in Murray's inaugural), was prepared in 1907 for a small class at Oxford.
[46] H. Lloyd-Jones, J. E. Harrison Memorial Lecture 1980, on GM, printed in *Blood for the Ghosts* (1982), pp. 195–214.
[47] *Five Stages* (1935 edn.) p. xii.
[48] Ib., p. xiii.
[49] Ib., p. 60.
[50] Ib., p. 61.
[51] Lucretius *De Rerum Natura* I. 101.

[52] *Five Stages*, p. 38.
[53] J. A. K. Thomson in *Proceedings of the British Academy* XLIII, p. 265.
[54] *476* 123, 19 Jan. 1897.
[55] *154* 32, 8 Mar. 1900.
[56] *Five Stages*, pp. 76–7
[57] Ib., p. 123.
[58] *Five Stages*, p. 171.
[59] *21* 66–9, 4 and 9 Nov. 1912.

Chapter XIII

[1] *13* 77, E. A. Sonnenschein/GM, 17 Feb. 1908.
[2] *14* 9, 7 Oct. 1908 (programme).
[3] *459* 143, GM/MM, 7 Oct. 1908, described Casson as rather less 'swift and springy' but 'firmer and more elastic' than Barker in the part.
[4] *Unfinished Autobiography* p. 158 (Thorndike).
[5] *165* 44, BR/GM, 27 Nov. 1902; printed in Russell *Autobiography*, I. 160.
[6] UA, p. 175 (Thorndike); the line cited from the *Bacchae* is 'To stand from fear set free, to breathe and wait'.
[7] *137* 3, Lillah McCarthy/GM, 20 Sept. 1908.
[8] *14* 212, Poel/GM, 25 Oct. 1908.
[9] *137* 7, GM/Lillah McCarthy, 26 Nov. 1908.
[10] GM/Charlotte King, 30 May 1915, refers to previous visits by Penelope Wheeler to help Mrs King's productions; papers in possession of Mr Jasper Ridley.
[11] See *20* 141; *21* 25, 164; *22* 27, 113 (1912–13).
[12] Purdom, *Harley Granville-Barker*, p. 108.
[13] *567* 146, GM/RM, 27 Dec. 1909.
[14] *20* 33, H. E. Butler/GM, 27 Mar. 1912.
[15] Purdom, op. cit., p. 116, GM/Barker, 9 Dec. 1910.
[16] *18* 35, 41; GM correspondence with Ordynski, 13 and 17 Feb. 1911.
[17] *167* 184–93, GBS/GM (original), 14 Mar. 1911.
[18] BL Add. MS 50542 28, GM/GBS, 17 Mar. 1911.
[19] *159* 5 and *18* 198, Martin Harvey/GM, 17 and 28 July 1911.
[20] Ib., 22, Martin Harvey/GM, 19 Jan. 1912; GM's letter in answer to *The Times* critic was published in *The Times* of 23 Jan. 1912.
[21] *461* 95, GM/MM, 14 Feb. 1912.
[22] *159* 31, GM/Martin Harvey, 14 Feb. 1912; the second extract is printed in UA, p. 162 (Thorndike).
[23] Ib., 34, 44, 48, 54, 59; Martin Harvey/GM, Feb. 1912–Aug. 1913.
[24] *Oxford Magazine*, 4 Feb. 1909.
[25] See n. 10 above.
[26] *567* 194, GM/RM, 4 Mar. 1912.
[27] *144* 6, GM/I. Monro, 3 Nov. 1929; part printed in UA, p. 136 (Henderson).
[28] Told to author by Stephen Murray, Sept. 1981.
[29] *9* 171, leaflet, Dec. 1903; UA p. 109 (Smith), p. 154 (Thorndike).
[30] *477* 139, 26 Dec. 1905; Purdom, *Harley Granville-Barker*, pp. 50–2.
[31] *127* 7, Casson/GM, 24 Aug. 1908.
[32] *13* 120, Bantock/GM, 7 May 1908.
[33] *133* 28, Fisher/GM, 5 Nov. 1907.
[34] *460* 139, GM/MM, 2 Oct. 1909.

[35] *16* 129.

[36] *18* 212, I. Duncan/GM, 4 Sept. 1911.

[37] *461* 69, 71, GM/MM, 6 and 19 Oct. 1911.

[38] *18* 245, A. Duncan/GM n.d. [1911]

[39] Michael Kennedy, *The Works of Ralph Vaughan Williams* (1964) p. 452.

[40] *19* 43, Vaughan Williams/GM, 6 Nov. 1911.

[41] Ib., 39, Vaughan Williams/GM n.d. [Oct. or Nov. 1911]

[42] Ib., 43.

[43] *567* 173, GM/RM, 6 Dec. 1911.

[44] *19* 97, Vaughan Williams/GM, 4 Jan. 1912.

[45] Kennedy, op. cit., p. 453.

[46] *167* 79, GBS/GM, 3 Dec. 1909; BL Add MS 50542, 39, GM/GBS, 5 Dec. 1909.

[47] *17* 114, F. Lloyd-Griffith/GM, 12 Oct. 1910; *567* 112, GM/RM, 10 Nov. 1910.

[48] *17* 156, S. Cockerell/GM, 21 Nov. 1910.

[49] BL Add MS 50592, 25, GM/GBS, 6 Mar. 1911.

[50] *161* 29, Masefield/GM, 15 Mar. 1911; *18* 60, Hardy/GM, 17 Mar. 1911.

[51] *17* 21, Butcher/GM, 26 Mar. 1910.

[52] BL Add MS 50542, 23, GM/GBS, 20 Feb. 1910.

[53] *18* 86, E. Gosse/GM, 18 Apr. 1911.

[54] Murray's acquaintance with Barrie was partly due to his prowess at cricket; he appeared occasionally for a team which he called the Allahakbarries.

[55] Oct. 1907; text *12* 169.

[56] The story is pieced together from Purdom, op. cit., and from items of correspondence in *12* and *13*.

[57] Purdom, op. cit. p. 75.

[58] *167* 71, 77, GM/Crewe, 17 Aug. 1909; GBS/GM, 22 May 1909.

[59] *Adds 3* 95, GM/WA, 12 June 1906.

[60] *458* 127, GM/MM, 17 Oct. 1907.

[61] H. V. Marrot, *Life of John Galsworthy*, p. 266, GM/Galsworthy, 20 July 1910; *134* 40, Galsworthy/GM, 23 July 1910.

[62] Ib. 53, Galsworthy/GM, 6 Jan. 1911; the motto is Heraclitus' phrase $\mathring{\eta}\theta o s$ $\overset{\prime}{\alpha}\nu\delta\rho\iota\ \delta\alpha\iota\mu\omega\nu$ (a man's character is his fate).

[63] Marrot, op. cit., p. 278, GM/Galsworthy, 21 Jan. 1910.

[64] *461* 73, GM/MM, 9 Oct. 1911.

[65] Marrot, op. cit. p. 326, GM/Galsworthy, 8 Oct. 1911.

[66] Ib. p. 373, GM/Galsworthy, 20 Sept. 1913.

[67] *165* 1, 26 Dec. 1905.

[68] *459* 126, 30 Sept. 1908.

[69] *165* 11, 26 Jan. 1909.

[70] Purdom, op. cit. p. 136.

Chapter XIV

For Murray's principal political associates among the radicals, see P. Clarke, *Liberals and Social Democrats* (1978) and A. J. P. Taylor, *The Trouble Makers* (1959); on Norman Leys, see the author's *Leonard Woolf: A Political Biography* (1978); on H. N. Brailsford, Professor F. M. Leventhal of Boston University has kindly allowed me to see the relevant part of a still unpublished study.

On Murray's connection with Somerville College, I have been able to consult the minutes of the Council, a file of the college Magazine, and other papers in the college archives. There is an essay by Margery Fry in *Essays in Honour of Gilbert Murray* (1936).

Murray's letters to Rachel Annand Taylor are held in the National Library of Scotland, Acc. 4116; hers to him are in the Murray papers *403* and *404*.

[1] *9* 96, *17* 151.
[2] *140* 97, Hammond/GM, forwarding letter from L. Garrett Anderson, 21 Dec. 1909.
[3] *567* 148, 6 Jan. 1910.
[4] *Adds* 4 16, 23 Jan. 1910.
[5] Hammond papers (Bodleian Library) *30* 28, and 32, GM/Hammond, 29 and 31 Jan. 1907; and *140* 57, Hammond/GM, 30 Jan. 1907.
[6] *126* 65, GM/Buchan, 25 Apr. 1903.
[7] *148* 4, Leys/GM, 13 Jan. 1900.
[8] Ib., 90, 99, Leys/GM, 30 Apr. 1910 and 12 Apr. 1911; see also *153* 2, 5, MacDonald/GM, 18 May 1911 and 6 June 1912.
[9] *458* 110, GM/MM, 27 Sept. 1907.
[10] *15* 145 and *16* 150, Cromer/GM, 2 Mar. 1909 and 13 Jan. 1910.
[11] *441* 6; address of 28 June 1910, printed in *Sociological Review*, July 1910.
[12] *Essays and Addresses*, p. 32.
[13] *441* 2, Inaugural address at University College, Aberystwyth, July 1909.
[14] *16* 54, letter of 9th Sept. 1909.
[15] *165* 17, GM/BR, 26 July 1910, and *17* 87, Harold Child/GM, 9 Aug. 1910.
[16] *22* 16, *23* 14, M. A. Broadhurst/GM, 13 Mar. and 23 Oct. 1913.
[17] *567* 139, GM/RM, 4 Feb. 1909.
[18] *461* 104, GM/MM, 3 July 1912.
[19] *Unfinished Autobiography*, 28.
[20] *21* 174, resolution of Women's Liberal Federation, cited in *Manchester Guardian*, 31 Jan. 1913.
[21] *23* 65, cutting from *Oxford Mail*, 20 Nov. 1913.
[22] GM/Miss Penrose, 13 Oct. 1912; archives of Somerville College, Oxford.
[23] *461* 74, GM/MM, 10 Oct. 1911.
[24] *Adds* 4 55, GM/WA, 24 May 1911.
[25] *460* 3, MM/GM, 5 Jan. 1909; quoted ch. XI, p. 145.
[26] Ib., 8, GM/MM, 7 Jan. 1919.
[27] *Adds* 4 62, GM/WA, 9 Oct. 1911.
[28] *16* 16, B. Webb/GM, 26 May 1909.
[29] Ib., 22, B. Webb/GM, 27 May 1909.
[30] *22* 57, 65, 81, correspondence of Apr. to Aug. 1913.
[31] *567* 237, GM/RM, 16 Sept. 1913.
[32] *140* 127, Hammond/GM, 21 Nov. 1913.
[33] *22* 197, Cole/GM, 5 Sept. 1913.
[34] Hammond papers *30* 55, GM/Hammond, 2 Jan. 1914; quoted in P. Clarke, op. cit., pp. 152–3.
[35] *153* 6, MacDonald/GM, 11 Feb. 1914.
[36] *506* 110.
[37] *Adds* 3 118, 218, WA/GM, 25 May 1907, GM/WA, 25 Sept. 1908.

38 *Adds* 4 24–7, GM/WA and WA/GM, 23 and 25 July 1910.
39 *18* 14, Sir James Murray/GM, 19 Jan. 1911.
40 *461* 71, GM/MM, 19 Oct. 1911.
41 *Adds* 4 62, 77, GM/WA, 9 Oct. 1911.
42 *403* 107, Hogarth/GM, 9 Nov. 1910.
43 BL Add MS 50542 24, GM/GBS, 28 Feb. 1911.
44 *167* 81, GBS/GM, 4 Mar. 1911.
45 *405* 11, 15, letters from G. Perris and S. Webb, May 1912.
46 Ib., 24, 30, 40, letters from L. Pearsall Smith and R. Bridges, May–June 1912.
47 *17* 24, 31 Mar. 1910.
48 Letter of Apr. 1910, National Library of Scotland, Acc. 4116.
49 Ib.
50 *165* 123, GM/BR, 19 Sept. 1910.
51 Ib., 120, GM/BR, 12 Sept. 1910.
52 GM/BR, 10 Aug. 1911; Russell, *Autobiography* I. 216–7.
53 *405* 106, 182, 5 Jan. 1914 and n.d.
54 *406* 30, GM/Sir Home Gordon, 11 June 1914.
55 Ib., 4, 10, 30, 42, Jan.–July 1914.
56 Ib., 63, GM/Fisher, 17 Nov. 1914.
57 Ib., 70, Gordon/GM, 21 Nov. 1914.

Chapter XV

Apart from the principal sources already quoted on Murray as a classical scholar and teacher, E. R. Dodds, *Missing Persons* (1977) and his introduction to Euripides' *Bacchae* (1943) are important. The later lectures of 1926 published as *The Classical Tradition in Poetry* (1927) are also referred to.

1 In a letter to Norman Angell Murray expressed doubts about his wisdom in refusing, and advised Angell to accept a Knighthood. His granddaughter told Lady Wilson (Nov. 1984) that Murray felt he had made a mistake in refusing, as a title would have given him more influence in League of Nations Union affairs.
2 *18* 113, Curzon/GM, 21 May 1911.
3 *567* 195, GM/RM, 8 Dec. 1912.
4 Adds 3 193, GM/WA, June 1906.
5 E. R. Dodds, in *Missing Persons*, pp. 28–9 and his introduction to Euripides' *Bacchae*, record the deep impression made on him by Murray's lectures in 1913.
6 Humphrey Trevelyan, *Geothe and the Greeks* (1981 edn.), p. 268.
7 *Adds* 1 10, 13 Oct. 1895.
8 Ib. and *History of Ancient Greek Literature*.
9 Lloyd-Jones, *J. E. Harrison Memorial Lecture 1980*, printed in *Blood for the Ghosts* (1982).
10 See Ch. VII, p. 89, and n. 48.
11 *Classical Tradition in Poetry*, p. 195.
12 Printed first in *The Bromsgrovian* (1893), and often thereafter: e.g. Dwight Macdonald, *Parodies* (1960), p. 315 misquoted in *Unfinished Autobiography*, p. 137 (Henderson).
13 Bowra, *Memories*, p. 218.
14 See Ch. VII, p. 90, and n. 53.

[15] *Westminster Gazette*, 13 May 1910.
[16] Eliot, *Selected Essays 1917–1932*, pp. 60–1.
[17] *UA*, p. 153 (Thorndike).
[18] 9, 107, Housman/GM, 13 Oct. 1903.
[19] *Classical Review*, XXVI (1911).
[20] Bowra, op. cit.
[21] *Hippolytus*, trans. GM, pp. 742–3.
[22] Ib., pp. 734–5; *165* 3, GM/BR, 26 Feb. 1901; printed in Russell, *Autobiography* I. 156.
[23] *CTP*, p. 248.
[24] Essays and studies by members of the English Association (1912), p. 195.
[25] See n. 5.
[26] Thomson, *Proceedings of the British Academy* XLIII (1957).
[27] Lloyd-Jones, op. cit.
[28] Ib.
[29] Ib.
[30] *Euripides and his Age*, p. 130.
[31] Ib., pp. 120–1.
[32] Ib., p. 30.

Chapter XVI

[1] *460* 62, GM/MM, 22 July 1909.
[2] *567* 127, GM/RM, 15 Mar. 1906.
[3] *459* 74, 10 May 1908.
[4] *Adds* 4 59, 26 Nov. 1911.
[5] Hammond papers 30, 46, 5 Jan. 1913.
[6] Recounted to Lady Wilson by Stephen Murray, Nov. 1984.
[7] *461* 46, GM/MM, 19 July 1911.
[8] *400* 89–189, correspondence GM/George Allen & Unwin, 1914; BL Add MS 56761, 31–49, papers of Society of Authors, 1914.
[9] *567* 174, 23 Apr. 1912.
[10] *461* 106, 4 July 1912.
[11] *460* 109, MM/GM, 30 Mar. 1910.
[12] *18* 192, 20 June 1911.
[13] Ib., 176, Lodge/GM, 10 July 1911.
[14] BL Add MS 50542 41, GM/GBS, 13 Sept. 1913.
[15] *Nation*, 4 Jan. 1913.
[16] *144* 15, 28 Mar. 1930.
[17] *461* 128–44, correspondence GM/MM, Mar.–Apr.1913.
[18] *567* 222, 22 Apr. 1913.
[19] See n. 17.
[20] *460* 11, 13, GM/MM, 12 and 14 Feb. 1909.
[21] *134* 44, Galsworthy/GM, 24 Aug. 1910.
[22] *567* 170, GM/RM, 4 Nov. 1911; *461* 106, GM/MM, 4 July 1912.
[23] *167* 81, GBS/GM, 4 Mar. 1911.
[24] *567* 165, 16 Oct. 1911.
[25] *461* 104, MM/GM, 24 Jan. 1913.
[26] *567* 179, 19 June 1912.
[27] Ib., 197, 14 Dec. 1912.
[28] *Adds* 4 139, GM/WA, 11 June 1913.

[29] *165* 137, GM/BR, 29 July 1913.

[30] BL Add MS 50542 39, GM/GBS, 9 July 1913.

[31] Letter from RM to her parents, Aug. 1913, in the possession of Stephen Murray.

[32] *461* 184, MM/GM, 29 June 1913.

[33] *22* 132–3, correspondence H. Scott Holland/GM, June 1913.

[34] *461* 130, MM/GM Mar. 1913: and information from Stephen Murray to author.

[35] *Blenheim* (Fontana edn. 1965) p. 188.

[36] *460* 133, GM/MM, 12 July 1910.

[37] *461* 3, GM/MM, 3 Jan. 1911.

[38] Hammond MS 30, 41, 21 Jan. 1911.

[39] *461* 41, 10 June 1911.

[40] See Ch. XII, sect. 4.

[41] *459* 15, GM/MM, 7 Apr. 1908.

[42] Ib., 46, GM/MM, 29 Apr. 1908.

[43] Menu at *17* 1, 5 Mar. 1910.

[44] *567* 240, GM/RM, 26 Sept. 1913.

[45] Ib., 130 (2), GM/RM, 14 Apr. 1907 (there are two folios marked 130 in this box).

[46] Ib., 189, 193, 29 Nov. and 2 Dec. 1912.

[47] *165* 42, Masefield/GM, 2 May 1913; *Adds* 4 21, GM/WA, 21 May 1914 (misdated 1910).

[48] *461* 194, GM/MM, Sept. 1913; cf. ib., 83, 147, 160, 161, 192.

[49] e.g., Bowra, op. cit., p. 215.

Chapter XVII

For the general context of British propaganda in the First World War, see: Lucy Masterman, *C. F. G. Masterman* (1935); M. L. Sanders and P. M. Taylor, *British Propaganda During the First World War 1914–1918 (1983)*; M. L. Sanders, 'Wellington House and British Propaganda During the First World War', *Historical Journal* 18 (1975), pp. 119–46. J. D. Squires *British Propaganda at Home and in the USA 1914–1917* (1935); P. M. Taylor, 'The Foreign Office and British Propaganda During the First World War', *Historical Journal* 23 (1980), pp. 875–98. On Conscientious Objectors and pacifists, see: Martin Ceadel, *Pacifism in Britain 1914–1945,* (1980); Ronald Clark, *Bertrand Russell* (1972); John Rae, *Conscience and Politics* (1970); Keith Robbins, *The Abolition of War: The Peace Movement in Britain 1914–1919* (1973).

[1] *462* 74, 7 Sept. 1914.

[2] Ib., 41, 13 Aug. 1914; the White Paper is Cd. 7467 (1914) No. 85.

[3] Ib., 65, GM/MM, 1 Sept. 1914; *25* 11, minutes of meetings, 2 Sept.; Lucy Masterman, op. cit. pp. 262, 272.

[4] Ib., 66, 67, GM/MM, 4 and 9 Sept. 1914.

[5] Ib., 89, GM/MM, 19 Sept. 1914.

[6] Ib., 79, GM/MM, 18 Sept. 1914.

[7] *25* 45, proof, 22 Sept. 1914.

[8] Text at *391* 2.

[9] *25* 147, Kipling/GM, 2 Nov. 1914.

[10] Ib., 131, Raleigh/GM, 30 Oct. 1914.

[11] Ib., 138, James/GM, 31 Oct. 1914.
[12] Ib., 137, Schuster/GM, 9 Mar. 1915.
[13] Ib., 174, minutes of meeting, 11 Nov. 1914.
[14] *26 5*, Schuster/GM, 2 Dec. 1914. The *Trojan Women* proved to be a slight embarrassment in the USA. It was performed in Chicago with pacifist intent in spring 1915, and Murray had to explain that it bore no relation to the current war. *27 22*, Mar. 1915; see also Sutcliffe, *The Oxford University Press*, p. 173.
[15] *26 52*, Dodds/GM, 1 Jan. 1915.
[16] *25 43*, A. S. Peake/GM, 26 Sept. 1914.
[17] In London it was delivered as the Moncure Conway memorial lecture, and afterwards published separately, first as a pamphlet, *The Stoic Philosophy*, with an introduction by William Archer (1915), and then as part of *Stoic, Christian and Humanist* (1940).
[18] *26 37*, Philippa Strachey/GM, 23 Dec. 1914.
[19] *27 82*, Apr. 1915.
[20] Ib., 41, 22 Mar. 1915 (trans. by the author); ib. 9 shows that Prof. J. P. Bang of Copenhagen acted as intermediary.
[21] Hammond Papers *30 58*, GM/Hammond, 18 Mar. 1915.
[22] *Adds 5 6*, GM/WA, 4 Apr. 1915.
[23] Ib., and *27 43*, J. V. Headlam/GM, 22 Mar. 1915.
[24] *Adds 8 27*, GM/BR, 25 Dec. 1915.
[25] *27 191*, Schuster/GM, 14 June 1915.
[26] *The Foreign Policy of Sir Edward Grey*, p. 9.
[27] Ib., p. 41.
[28] Ib., p. 82.
[29] *462 180*, GM/MM, 8 July 1915 and *138 1*, Grey/GM, 14 July 1915.
[30] *28 103*, W. A. Appleton/Schuster, 15 Sept. 1915.
[31] *125 16*, Bryce/GM, 19 Sept. 1915; *140 152*, Hammond/GM, 21 June 1915.
[32] *167 144*, GBS/GM, 14 July 1915.
[33] *153 15*, MacDonald/GM, 13 Sept. 1915.
[34] FPEG, pp. 5, 35, 39, 124. Murray continued to take seriously the charges made against Grey's conduct of foreign policy. *138 33–4* contains records of conversations with Grey in January 1918, about secret agreements before and during the war, and the extent of their secrecy.
On the question of Cabinet consultation by Grey, see Hammond papers *30 58* (GM/Hammond, 18 Mar. 1915), and Haldane papers (National Library of Scotland) *5914 120* (GM/Haldane, 18 Jan. 1920) from which it appears that Grey had specifically reassured GM on this point. See also part of an angry exchange with E. D. Morel 1918–19 (GM and Morel each accusing the other of bad faith), *39 174* and *40 5* and 21.
[35] *Adds 8 27*, GM/BR, 25 Dec. 1915.
[36] Ronald Clark, op. cit., p. 248.
[37] *165 149*, BR/GM, 28 Dec. 1915.
[38] *Adds 5 114*, 116, WA/GM 22 Dec. and GM/WA, 23 Dec. 1915.
[39] *171 180*, 31 Dec. 1915.
[40] *30 16*, 11 Feb. and *29 202*, 26 Jan. 1916.
[41] Ib., 142, 10 Apr.
[42] Ib.
[43] Ib., 112, 114, 116, (GM's 'Impressions of Scandinavia' in *Westminster Gazette*, 19, 25, and 26 Apr.).

[44] *138* 3, 13 Apr.

[45] *Adds* 5 129, 9 Mar.

[46] *30* 51, 2 Mar.

[47] *138* 5 and 6, 6 and 17 June; see also *139*, 97 GM notes for G. M. Trevelyan's biography of Grey, 30 Aug. 1935.

[48] *463* 27, 32, GM/MM, 3 and 5 May 1916.

[49] *509* 122–7, 5, 6, and 8 June.

[50] *31* 119, T. Roosevelt/GM, 6 Aug.

[51] Ib., 107, W. H. Hamilton/GM [Aug. 1916].

[52] Ib., 170, Sir G. Parker/GM, 8 Sept.

[53] *509* 129, 131, 132, articles by GM [Oct. 1916].

[54] J. D. Squires, op. cit., p. 72.

[55] *31* 154, 3 Aug. 1916.

[56] *138* 7, 1 Aug. 1916.

[57] *509* 137; *Westminster Gazette*, 12 Dec. 1916.

[58] *463* 54, GM/MM, 17 Dec. 1916 (on 10 Downing Street notepaper).

[59] *119* 4, and *463* 60, GM/MM, 24 Dec.

[60] Hammond Papers *30* 72, GM/Hammond, 2 July; and *568* 42, GM/RT, 6 July 1917.

[61] *35* 102, GM/Lloyd George, 28 Dec. 1917.

[62] *Adds* 5 160, MM/WA, 23 Oct. 1916.

[63] *463* 89, MM/GM, 28 Jan. 1917.

[64] *477* 173, GM/RC, 12 and 16 Jan. 1917.

[65] *33* 93 and 112, 20 Jan. and 27 Feb.

[66] *463* 86 and 93, 31 Jan. and 7 Feb.

[67] Ib. 131, GM/MM, 9 May.

[68] *37* 128, copy of printed report, [Sept. 1918].

[69] *34* 185, 8 Aug. 1917; cf. *36* 132, on the establishment of an Anglo-Swedish Travel Association, Apr. 1918.

[70] *36* 163, Yeaxley/GM, 9 May 1918.

[71] *34* 191; permission was given for a visit in Sept. 1917.

[72] *35* 156

[73] *461* 61, 67, GM/MM, MM/GM, 26 Aug. and 9 Sept. 1914.

[74] *463* 112, MM/GM, 22 Mar. 1917.

[75] *29* 164, Vernon Harcourt/GM, 9 Jan. 1916.

[76] *462* 118, MM/GM, 20 Mar. 1915; MM also visited Denis in Feb. 1916 (*463* 10, 13).

[77] Ib., 171, 172, 175, GM/MM, 16 June, 2 July, and 24 July 1915.

[78] *Adds* 5 85, 87, GM/WA, 10 and 18 Aug. 1915.

[79] *463* 106, GM/MM, 2 Mar. 1917.

[80] *462* 128, GM/MM, 21 Mar. 1915.

[81] *463* 71, MM/GM, 29 Dec. 1916; obituary notice of Agnes Murray in the Annual Report of Somerville Students Association, Nov. 1922.

[82] *464* 34, MM/GM, 23 Sept. 1918.

[83] *462* 102, GM/MM, 23 Sept. 1914.

[84] BL Add MSS 58427 (Cornford papers), GM/Cornford, 17 Oct. 1914.

[85] *Adds* 5 67, MM/WA, 16 June 1915.

[86] *32* 78, 1 Nov. 1916.

[87] *Adds* 5 22, 69, in which GM gives typical instances to WA—a boil on the bottom in April and heart trouble in June 1915.

[88] *171* 133, 10 Jan. 1915.

[89] *568* 21, GM/RT, 1 Sept. 1915.

[90] *438* 1; the apple pie was consumed before 22 Feb. 1918 (*464* 38).

[91] *Adds 5* 99, GM/WA, 23 Sept. 1915.

[92] Ib. 192, 28 Dec. 1916 (the reference is to *King Lear*, IV. vi.

[93] *568* 23, GM/RT, 2 Sept. 1915; later Murray was able to strike an important blow against spy mania, when he convinced his brother Hubert, Governor of Papua, that Bronislaw Malinowski was not an enemy agent, and should be allowed to continue his study of the habits of the Trobriand Islanders (*35* 177 and 200, J. G. Frazer/GM and G. Wallas/GM, 6 and 11 Feb. 1918).

[94] *33* 150, Yeats/GM, 22 Feb. 1917.

[95] *463* 15, 13 Feb. 1916.

[96] *Adds 5* 59, GM/WA, 29 May 1915.

[97] *33* 165, 171.

[98] GM, preface to M. Hobhouse, *I Appeal Unto Caesar* (1917).

[99] *375* 11, GM/H. Samuel, 9 Apr. 1916, quoted in John Rae, op. cit., p. 134.

[100] *165* 150-2, GM/BR, 15-16 Apr., and BR/GM, 17 Apr. 1916.

[101] *375* 67, May 1916; there are many other undated letters of this period from Clive Bell, at the end of *367*.

[102] See n. 99.

[103] *375* 40, P. Morrell/GM, 28 Apr. 1916.

[104] Ib. 41, Morrell/GM, 2 May.

[105] *376* 128, GM/J. W. Graham, 28 Dec. 1920; printed in Rae, op. cit. p. 152.

[106] Probably Rendel Harris, letter of 4 May 1916, *375* 48.

[107] See GM's preface to *I Appeal Unto Caesar* (n. 117): 'I have notes of conversations with two military authorities, one in a high position . . . who had the definite intention of shooting the objectors.' It is clear that he talked to both personally.

[108] *376* 160 (misplaced), 22 May 1916; Rae, op. cit., p. 158.

[109] *376* 25 contains GM's notes of the meeting.

[110] Text at *377* 97.

[111] *376* 117, Gladys Rinder/GM, 1 May 1919.

[112] *116* 1-2, GM/BR, 10 Feb. and BR/GM, 18 Feb. 1918.

[113] *376* 67, BR/GM, 2 Sept. 1918.

[114] Ib. 60-81, letters of Aug.-Sept. 1918.

[115] R. W. Clark op. cit., p. 355 ff.

[116] *377* 43, article by GM, 'The Soul As It Is', first published in *The Hibbert Journal* (Jan. 1918), and reprinted in GM, *Essays and Addresses* (1921).

[117] Ib., 156-211, text of *I Appeal Unto Caesar* ; *376* 173-216 contains much undated correspondence between GM and Mrs Hobhouse, and *377* 60-96 more undated papers about the maltreatment of COs.

Chapter XVIII

The following are the main secondary sources for this chapter: Donald S. Birn, *The League of Nations Union, 1918-1945.* (1980); Viscount Cecil, *A Great Experiment* (1941); G. M. Trevelyan, *Grey of Fallodon* (1937); Sir Alfred Zimmern, *The League of Nations and the Rule of Law* (1936); Duncan Wilson, *Leonard Woolf: A Political Biography* (1978).

¹ Hammond papers *30* 68, GM/Hammond, 17 Nov. 1915.

² *Oxford Magazine*, 7 Dec. 1912.

³ *22* 124, A. Carnegie/GM, 9 June 1913; *178* 4, J. Estlin Carpenter/GM, 29 May 1913.

⁴ Not 1909 as stated by GM.

⁵ *Oxford Magazine* 14 May 1914: an interesting summary of the War and Peace movement down to 1914, by Angell himself, is at *44* 69, Angell/GM, 2 Jan. 1922.

⁶ *Ethical Problems of the War* : lecture of 27 Oct 1915 to the triennial meeting of the National Conference of Unitarian, Liberal Christian, Presbyterian, and other non-subscribing and kindred organizations.

⁷ *Les Origines et l'œuvre de la Société des Nations*, ed. P. Munch, Vol. I (1923). Among the papers of Willoughby Dickinson in the Bodleian Library there are notes (MS Eng. hist. c. 406, 99 ff.) written, it appears, for Murray's use in 1938, about the 'Bryce Group' which originally met to discuss a paper by Aneurin Williams and produced revised proposals about a possible League of Nations on 15 Feb. 1915. The most prominent members were Clifford Allen (afterwards Lord Allen of Hurtwood), Willoughby Dickinson, Graham Wallas, and Aneurin Williams. G. Lowes Dickinson acted as secretary.

⁸ *246* 35 dated 24 Feb. 1915. Many of GM's pencil notes are cryptic.

⁹ *26*, B. Webb/GM, Dec. 1914.

¹⁰ Trevelyan, op. cit.; *138* 6, Grey/GM, 17 June 1916.

¹¹ *464* 154, GM/MM, 3 Sept. 1918.

¹² Text at *391*, 11.

¹³ *35* 67; L. Woolf, *Beginning Again* (1964), pp. 130–1; D. Wilson op. cit., p. 109; Murray himself set an example in 1917 of contesting the effects of arbitrary rule in a British Colony. D. B. Jayatilleka, later Prime Minister of Ceylon, mobilized his services to press for an impartial inquiry into the repressive action taken by the Governor after riots in Kandy in 1915. Leonard Woolf, himself a former Ceylon Civil Servant, was the chief adviser to a Ceylonese delegation, and spoke for them to the Colonial Office early in 1918, on a deputation in which Murray also participated. See *35* 67; L. Woolf, *Beginning Again* (1964), pp. 130–1; Wilson op. cit., pp. 110–12.

¹⁴ *34* 2, 97, Smuts/GM, 5 May and McKenna/GM, 22 May 1917; W. K. Hancock, *Smuts: The Sanguine Years* (1962), pp. 213, 217.

¹⁵ A. J. P. Taylor, *England 1914-45* (1965), pp. 111–20.

¹⁶ Ib., pp. 65, 94, 116.

¹⁷ *Daily Telegraph*, 3 Dec. 1917; *509* 147.

¹⁸ *464* 26 GM/MM, 25 Jan., 1918; *35* 121, Edith Gulland/GM, 1 Jan. 1918.

¹⁹ *34* 47 Bryce/GM, 21 Dec. 1917.

²⁰ *35* 135, 8 Jan. 1918.

²¹ Ib. 205, S. K. Ratcliffe (New York)/GM, 15 Feb. 1918.

²² *66* 24, with covering letter from E. Drummond, 11 Mar. 1918.

²³ Ib. 41, I. Malcolm/GM, 23 Mar. 1918.

²⁴ Ib. 50, GM/Balfour, 25 Mar. 1918.

²⁵ Ib. 65, GM/Balfour, 29 Mar. 1918.

²⁶ Ib. 51, GM/W. H. Page, 25 Mar. 1918.

²⁷ *464* 75, 18 June 1918; for typical details of GM's activities, ib. 77, 84, GM/MM, 18 and 21 June 1918.

²⁸ Ib. 88, GM/MM, 25 June 1918. The references are to ladies with rather sultry reputations. Katherine Cox had been a flame of Rupert Brooke; Lady Ottoline Morrell was at the time Bertrand Russell's inamorata.

²⁹ Ib., 90, 93, GM/MM, 25 and 26 June 1918.

³⁰ *35* 123, Cole/GM, 2 Jan. 1918.

³¹ *241* 13; Murray's much later broadcast on 'Peace Movements' (2 Oct. 1955), contains further material about the suspicions attached to 'faddists'. A recording is preserved in the BBC Sound Archives.

³² *178* 105.

³³ *464* 130, GM/MM, 23 July; *178* 141–5 memorandum by S. K. Ratcliffe, 6 Aug. 1918.

³⁴ *464* 122, MM/GM, 10 July 1918; *179* 244.

³⁵ *138* 60, Grey/GM, 15 Aug. 1918.

³⁶ *180* 23, meeting of 13 Jan. 1919; see also *183* 49, 53, 59, 67, and 91 for undated LNU papers (all but the first by Willoughby Dickinson on these subjects).

Chapter XIX

The chief sources for this chapter are for section 1 (compulsory Greek): the records of the Congregation and Convocation in the Oxford University Archives and the file of the *Oxford Magazine*, 1918–20; for section 2: Dorothy Henley, *Rosalind Howard* (Hogarth Press, 1959): for section 3: A. J. P. Taylor, *English History 1914–1945* (OUP), and (Viscount) R. T. Cecil, *A Great Experiment* (Jonathan Cape, 1941).

¹ *38* 28, L. R. Phelps/GM, 23 Nov. and *477* 183, GM/RC (Rosalind Carlisle) 22 Nov. 1918.

² *38* 78, 83, H. E. D. Blakeston and L. R. Phelps/GM, 17 and 18 Dec. 1918.

³ *568* 46, GM/RT, 26 Jan.

⁴ *464* 109, 212, GM/MM, 10 and 23 Apr. 1919.

⁵ C. M. Bowra *Memories* (1966) p. 153.

⁶ *Oxford Magazine*, 5 Mar. 1920.

⁷ *39* 112, Austen Chamberlain/GM, 13 May 1919.

⁸ Ib. 185–6, June and July 1919.

⁹ *40* 25, 153, 180, Mar.–June.

¹⁰ Ib. 139; *43* 36–62 n.d.

¹¹ *464* 79, MM/GM, 19 June 1918.

¹² Ib. 178, MM/GM, 2 Mar. 1919; *568* 48, GM/RT, 21 June 1919.

¹³ Information from Mr Stanley Walton, formerly assistant secretary to Lady Carlisle.

¹⁴ *465* 15, GM/MM, 20 July 1921; cf. D. H. Henley op. cit., pp. 140–1.

¹⁵ Information from Mr Stanley Walton.

¹⁶ *465* 165, 210, GM/MM, 2 Aug. and MM/GM, 12 Sept. 1921; *467* 16, MM/GM, 21 Aug. 1923.

¹⁷ *466* 22, GM/MM, 12 Mar. and 24, MM/GM, 13 Mar. 1922.

¹⁸ *464* 57, GM/MM, 10 May 1918, and *466* 132, GM/MM, 4 May 1922.

¹⁹ *466* 31, GM/MM, 19 Mar. 1922.

²⁰ Ib. 78, 11 Apr. 1922.

²¹ *50* 73, Smuts/GM, 20 May 1925.

²² *465* 1, 12, 29, 56, Apr.–Aug. 1920.

²³ *466* 78, 98, 138, Apr.–May 1922.
²⁴ Ib., 146, 17 July 1922.
²⁵ Ib., 159, 5 Aug. 1922.
²⁶ *45* 167, 188, 30 Aug. and 10 Oct. 1922.
²⁷ Letter from Stephen Murray to Lady Wilson, 1984. He also told her that GM, strangely, did *not* attend Agnes's funeral.
²⁸ *Testament of Youth* (1980 edn.) p. 558.
²⁹ *42* 206, A. D. Hunt/GM, 23 Nov. 1920.
³⁰ *Adds* 46476, MM/Lord Gladstone, 3 June 1921.
³¹ *466* 14, MM/GM, 6 Mar. 1922.
³² *189* 41, Nansen/GM, 6 Feb. 1922; George Schuster, *Private Work and Public Causes* (1979), p. 37.
³³ *477* 186, GM/Rosalind Carlisle, 18 Feb. 1919.
³⁴ R. Cecil, op. cit., p. 115; *45* 45, Gladstone/GM, 20 Apr. 1921.
³⁵ A. J. P. Taylor, op. cit., p. 155.
³⁶ *43* 4, James E. MacDonald/GM, 3 Dec. 1920.
³⁷ *465* 64, GM/MM, 16 Aug. 1920.
³⁸ *43* 149, Gladstone/GM, 22 Apr. 1921.
³⁹ *187* 205, 207, R. Cecil/GM, 9 and 11 Apr. 1921.
⁴⁰ *Adds* 46476 18, GM/Gladstone, 29 June 1921.
⁴¹ *466* 86, 89, 135, MM/GM, 13 and 14 Apr. and 6 May 1922.
⁴² *47* 213, 13 Dec. 1923; *48* 16, A. W. Pickard-Cambridge/GM, 5 Nov. 1924.
⁴³ *40* 65, 67, 85.
⁴⁴ *58* 115, 128; *59* 159, GM/T. R. M. Naughton correspondence, Apr.–Oct. 1931.

Chapter XX

The chief sources for this chapter are for section 1: GM's *Essays and Addresses* (1921); for section 2: volumes of the Proceedings of the Society for Psychical Research : Vol. XXIX, GM's Presidential Address in 1915 and Mrs Verrall's analysis of select experiments in which GM was involved down to 1916; Vol. XXXIV, Mrs Henry Sidgwick's account (1925) of further experiments down to 1924; Vol. XLIX, GM's second Presidential Address in 1952; (new numerations of proceedings) 55, E. R. Dodds's analysis (1972) of experiments 1920–46 based on the notes preserved in the Murray papers, *488* 95–196); 56, E. J. Dingwall's critique (1973) of Dodds's analysis (this article also refers to an unpublished account by the neurologist and psychotherapist, Dr J. A. Hadfield, of experiments carried out with GM in 1919). There is a good account of Murray's own evidence in Rosalind Heywood, *Sixth Sense* (1959), pp. 132–40.

¹ *183* 130, 148; *184* 4, 17, 21; undated LNU drafts.
² *41* 70, 191, G. Bell/GM 28 Apr. and 17 July 1921.
³ Essays and Addresses, p. 127. For 'Golden Urn' see Ch. VIII, sect. 4.
⁴ Ib., p. 147; the phrase 'The little soul carrying the corpse' is translated from Marcus Aurelius.
⁵ Ib., p. 158.
⁶ Ib., p. 221.
⁷ Ib., p. 54.
⁸ Ib., p. 30.

[9] *44 54*, Woodrow Wilson/GM, 6 Dec. 1921.

[10] *568 46*, GM/RT, 25 Jan. 1919.

[11] *Five Stages of Greek Religion* (1935), p. 171.

[12] *568 63*, GM/RT, 7 Jan. 1922.

[13] *Adds 1* 40, GM/WA, 16 June and 1 July 1895.

[14] *4* 83, J. E. Gary [?]/GM, 11 July 1896; *453* 20, GM/MM, 4 Apr. 1898.

[15] *456* 239, GM/MM, 10 Sept. 1903.

[16] Dingwall, op. cit., p. 24, argues that GM's hearing was abnormally acute at any time, and that he was 'able to hear a fly crawl over a piece of crisp paper, but thought that anyone would have heard it'. I have not been able to identify the source of the statement.

[17] Dodds, op. cit., p. 396.

[18] The first two instances are quoted by Dingwall, op. cit., from Mrs Sidgwick's account of experiments 1916–24. *Proceedings* XXXIV (1925).

[19] GM's comment occurs in his second Presidential address to the SPR.

[20] *The Stoic Philosophy* (1915), pp. 28–9.

[21] GM, first Presidential Address to SPR.

[22] J. J. Thomson, *Recollections and Reflections* (1936), p. 156.

[23] A. Huxley, *Letters* (1969), p. 196.

[24] Dodds, op. cit., p. 398.

[25] C. M. Bowra, *Memories* (1966) pp. 214–15.

[26] The sources of these quotations are (1) and (3) *Journal of American Society of Psychical Research* XXIII (1929); (2) GM, Presidential Address to SPR (1915); (4) *487* 189, GM/Miss Wace (BBC) 21 Oct. 1933; (5) Mrs W. H. Salter in *Essays in Honour of Gilbert Murray* (1936), p. 266.

[27] *267 6*, Bergson/GM, 19 July 1925.

[28] *487* 77, R. H. Thouless/GM, 28 Dec. 1924; and letter to the author, 10 May 1983.

[29] Ib., 74, a letter of 1 Jan. 1925.

[30] Dodds, op. cit.

[31] Dingwall, op. cit., p. 37.

[32] *Adds 6* 43, 44, 46, 47, 60, 61, 74 correspondence mainly WA/GM, Mar.–Sept. 1919; *16* 104–5, 107 n.d. [1919].

[33] *468* 180, 12 July 1928, ref. seance MM/Mr Brittain; also papers in the possession of Stephen Murray. Mainly undated, and referring to the years immediately following the death of Agnes Murray (1922).

[34] Told to Lady Wilson in Nov. 1984 by Ann Paludan (née Murray).

Chapter XXI

[1] *186 92*.

[2] *Essays in Honour of Gilbert Murray* (1936), pp. 27–9 (H. A. L. Fisher).

[3] *465* 191, GM/MM, 5 Sept. 1921.

[4] Ib., 198, 6 Sept. 1921.

[5] Ib., 214, 12 Sept. 1921.

[6] Ib., 207, 9 Sept. 1921.

[7] Ib., 224, 16 Sept. 1921.

[8] *188 65*, GM/Smuts, 8 Oct. 1921.

[9] *465* 231, 18 Sept. 1921.

[10] Ib., 219, 15 Sept. 1921.

[11] Ib., 224, 16 Sept. 1921.
[12] Ib., 244, 22 Sept. 1921.
[13] Ib., 219, 15 Sept. 1921.
[14] Ib., 263, 2 Oct. 1921.
[15] *568* 62, GM/RT, 2 Oct. 1921.
[16] *188* 65, GM/Smuts, 8 Oct. 1921.
[17] *465* 202, 7 Sept. 1921.
[18] Ib., 207, 9 Sept. 1921.
[19] Ib., 191, 5 Sept. 1921.
[20] Ib., 231, 18 Sept. 1921.
[21] Ib., 244, 22 Sept. 1921.
[22] Ib., 207, 9 Sept. 1921.
[23] Ib., 198, 6 Sept. 1921.
[24] Ib., 207, 9 Sept. 1921.
[25] Ib., 263, 2 Oct. 1921.
[26] Ib., 191, 5 Sept. 1921.
[27] Ib., 202, 7 Sept. 1921.
[28] Ib., 244, 22 Sept. 1921.
[29] Ib., 231, 18 Sept. 1921.
[30] Ib.
[31] Relevant correspondence is at *44* 183 ff., Mar. 1922, and *45* 3, (M. E. Durham/GM), 4 Apr. 1922; from Mattheev Murray learned a favourite story of the Byzantine Emperor, Basil the Bulgar-slayer. After a battle he blinded all his Bulgarian prisoners except one, who was left with the use of one eye, to guide his fellow prisoners home.
[32] *192* 107, GM/E. Drummond, 18 Oct. 1923; and 110, F. P. Walters GM, 23 Oct. 1923.
[33] *194* 196, 29 Sept. 1924.
[34] *Daily News*, 6 Oct. 1924, (*512* 120).
[35] PRO, FO 800/237 (Austen Chamberlain); memorandum by Central Department and other minutes 3–6 Jan. 1925.
[36] *UA*, pp. 178–9 (de Madariaga).
[37] *465* 214, GM/MM, 12 Sept. 1921.

Chapter XXII

The chief sources for this chapter are: D. S. Birn, *The League of Nations Union, 1918–1945* (1980); R. Cecil, *A Great Experiment* (1941); F. P. Walters, *A History of the League of Nations* (1982). Articles of the Covenant of the League of Nations referred to in the text are briefly summarized at Appendix I.

[1] *512* 57, GM, Lecture to LNU Conference, *Oxford Chronicle*, 9 Jan. 1920.
[2] *Essays in Honour of GM* p. 73 (Thorndike).
[3] *182* 25, 186; also 53, 11 Nov. 1919.
[4] GM, *Problems of Foreign Policy* (1921); and review in *TLS*, 28 Apr. 1921 (*512* 66).
[5] BL Add MS 51132, GM/RC, 7 Feb. 1923: see also *196* 17, *192* 178, notes by GM and RC n.d. [1923].
[6] The sub-committee also referred bitterly to the rejection of their similar representations about the administration of the Saar territory, and the partition, under League auspices, of Upper Silesia between Germany and Poland.

[7] *468* 61, GM/MM, 25 June 1924.
[8] *Manchester Guardian*, 17 Oct., *The Times*, 19 Oct. and 15 Nov. 1924.
[9] *468* 164, MM/GM, 13 Mar. 1925.
[10] e.g. *The Times*, 12 Sept. 1925.
[11] *Harvard Crimson*, 18 Dec. 1926.
[12] Cecil op. cit., p. 358.
[13] Ib., p. 189.
[14] *Headway*, Jan. 1928.
[15] *Headway*, May 1928.
[16] Cecil op. cit., pp. 192-3.
[17] *The Times*, 27 Feb. and 10 Apr.; *Manchester Guardian*, 5 Mar., and *Morning Post* 24 Apr. 1928.
[18] *469* 178, GM/MM, 10 July 1928.
[19] *The Times*, 29 May 1929; *207* 199 GM/RC, 30 Jan. 1930.
[20] Birn, op. cit., p. 89.
[21] FO 800/284 (Henderson Papers), GM/Henderson, 20 June 1930.
[22] *208* 109, J. A. Salter/GM, 17 June 1930.
[23] *Manchester Guardian*, 26 Sept. 1925.
[24] *208* 117, GM/Baldwin, 29 June 1930.
[25] Ib., *153*, GM/RC, 27 Aug. 1930.
[26] Adds *51132* 117, RC/GM, 15 Nov. 1930.
[27] *210* 160, RC/GM, 19 Sept. 1931.

Chapter XXIII

[1] *48* 188, L. Radermacher/GM, 28 Dec. 1924.
[2] *267* 105, Oct. 1925.
[3] *268* 181-206, correspondence with D. S. Robertson, Jan.-Feb. 1927.
[4] *50* 204-6, 208, correspondence with D. S. Evans (Heinemann) Feb. 1926; (see also *52* 44, *397* 181-3).
[5] *57* 29, Bowra/GM, 13 May 1930.
[6] *468* 158, GM/MM, 10 Mar. 1925.
[7] *568* 67, GM/RT, 17 Aug. 1924.
[8] *48* 129, E. R. Dodds/GM, 25 July 1924.
[9] *54* 25, E. R. Bevan/GM, 5 May, 1928.
[10] *49* 123, 179, A. L. Lowell/GM, May–June 1925.
[11] *51* 38, *Harvard Gazette*, May 1926; in the book as printed an additional essay on Drama appeared, and some of the titles of the others were slightly changed.
[12] *The Classical Tradition in Poetry*, p. xi.
[13] Ib., p. 195.
[14] *53* 130, C. Bailey/GM, 22 Dec. 1927; 169, F. W. Pember/GM, 17 Jan. 1928.
[15] Sheppard papers, King's College, Cambridge, GM/Sheppard, 14 Feb. 1927.
[16] Ib., GM/Sheppard, 31 Mar. 1936.
[17] *53* 4, 4 June 1927; trans. from Latin by the author.
[18] *46* 159, 179, 19 Feb. and 14 Mar. 1923.
[19] *55* 42, 188, Jan. 1929; the letter (here trans. from German by the author) is quoted in the original by GM in an article on Wilamowitz, *Antike und Abendland* (1954).

[20] *144* 10, GM/I. Henderson, 3 Feb. 1930.

[21] *50* 55, 111, A. S. Hunt/GM, Oct.–Nov. 1925.

[22] *51* 29, Bowra/GM, 13 May 1930.

[23] *58* 6–17, 39 ff., correspondence with D. L. Page, June 1930 and Jan. 1931.

[24] *59* 81, 7 Sept. 1931.

[25] *56* 177, 6 Jan. 1930.

[26] *468* 232, 17 July 1925.

[27] *467* 162, 30 Apr. 1924; Lady Mary reported strong feelings in favour of F. F. Urquhart as Master.

[28] *48* 96, J. Huxley/GM, 13 June 1924; *467* 164, 168, *468* 30, GM/MM correspondence, May–June 1924. (The Murrays always spelt Lindsay's name 'Sandie' in writing to each other.)

[29] *52* 146, 148, correspondence, 10–14 Mar. 1927.

[30] *468* 103, GM/MM, 3 Jan. 1925.

[31] *144* 13, 2 Mar. 1930.

[32] *63* 198, TM/GM, 19 May 1933, 69, 34, 39, GM/S. H. Wood, Board of Education.

[33] *64* 25 LSz/GM, 7 May 1933.

[34] Ib., 1 115, SD/GM, 6 June 1933.

[35] *133* 66, GM/H. A. L. Fisher, 24 May 1934; *86* 227, GM/A. S. L. Farquharson, 22 May 1939.

[36] *76* 210, 25 Apr. 1936.

[37] Ib., 67, 17 Mar. 1936.

[38] *144* 71 GM/Isobel Henderson, 16 Apr. 1936; *174* 147, GM/J. A. K. Thomson, 3 Aug. 1943.

[39] *473* 209, GM/MM, 3 Aug. 1937.

[40] Ib., 1 193, GM/E. R. Garnsey, 27 July 1932.

[41] Ib., 43, 4 Feb. 1932.

[42] *Christian Commonwealth*, 26 Nov. 1913, St Paul 'next to Greek poets is almost my favourite author'.

[43] H. Ll-Jones, *Justice of Zeus*, p. 204.

[44] *73* 232, C. N. Jackson, Harvard, 31 Oct. 1935.

[45] Ib., 154, 167, EHB/GM, 15 Oct. 1935, and Murray's reply, 18 Oct.

[46] *472* 204, GM/MM, 2 Aug. 1934.

[47] *144* 60, 25 Aug. 1934.

[48] There are two references to this in GM's correspondence.

[49] *468* 103, GM/MM, 3 Jan. 1925.

[50] *57* 19, Pickard-Cambridge/GM, 3 May 1930.

[51] *568* 128–9 GM/RT, 26 Dec. 1938.

[52] The author took part in this production in the chorus.

[53] *79* 174, GM/Herbert Worsley, 19 Oct. 1936.

[54] *81* 187, GM/Barbara Burnham, 27 Apr. 1937; *81* 189, GM/DH, 28 Apr. 1937.

[55] C. M. Bowra, *Memories*, p. 268.

[56] *75* 74, GM/SB, 17 Jan. 1936.

[57] Ib., 138, Dodds/GM, 29 Jan. 1936.

[58] Ib., 145, 204, GM/A. D. Nock, 31 Jan. 1936, and Nock's reply, 17 Feb. 1936; *473* 75, draft, GM/Theodore Wade-Gery, 19 June 1936.

[59] See especially letters from Dodds and GM, *38* 142, 157, 168, Jan., Feb. 1919.

[60] *76* 202, 209, 235, 245, 248; *77* 1, 8, 15, 36, correspondence, 24 Apr.– 5 May 1936.

[61] *77* 138–40.

[62] Ib., 218, 219, 220, 241, correspondence, 24–25 June 1936.

[63] *80* 104, 28 Nov. 1936.

[64] Bowra, op. cit. pp. 269–70.

[65] The author's personal knowledge.

[66] *89* 151, 1 Jan. 1941.

[67] Text in *Oxford Magazine*, 20 Feb. 1936.

Chapter XXIV

[1] *50* 23, 24, correspondence with Mrs Swanwick, 3–10 Sept. 1925.

[2] Ib., 86, 90, correspondence with R. H. Tawney, 29–31 Oct. 1925.

[3] Ib., 158, 4 Jan. 1926.

[4] *54* 123, 135, 25 and 27 Sept. 1928.

[5] *51* 57, 60 (notes of Town Hall meeting), 76 (text of broadcast).

[6] *57* 215 n.d. [1930].

[7] *55* 151, A. D. Lindsay/GM, 3 May 1929.

[8] Ib., 167, 14 May.

[9] Ib., 181, 23 May.

[10] Ib., 204.

[11] *56* 2, *Oxford Magazine*, June 1929.

[12] *59* 1 Ll-G/GM, 3 July 1931.

[13] *Manchester Guardian*, 20 Oct. 1930.

[14] *57* 220, GM/Ida Storr n.d. [1930].

[15] *56* 20, 23 July; *470* 37, 24 July 1929.

[16] *470* 127, *129* 37, 24 July 1929.

[17] GM was then 63; FO officials retire at 60!

[18] *470* 127, 129, 19–21 July 1929.

[19] *144* 3, 25 Oct. 1929.

[20] *53* 127, *54* 34, 1927–8.

[21] *50* 189, 201, Jan.–Feb. 1926.

[22] *161* 138, 152, 156–7, correspondence with John Masefield, 1935.

[23] *55* 81, S. W. Harris/GM, 26 Feb. 1929.

[24] Comment by GM on reading Woolf's novel *Mrs Dalloway* (1925).

[25] *The Diary of Virginia Woolf* Vol. I, (ed. Anne Bell), p. 210 (London, 1977), 28 Oct. 1918.

[26] *75* 79, 17 Jan. 1936.

[27] *77* 6, GM/C. Grant Robertson, 2 May 1936.

[28] *86* 242, 30 May 1939.

[29] *Unfinished Autobiography*, p. 136. Isobel Henderson says it was taken from a letter GM wrote to a pupil in 1936.

[30] *85* 59, GM/Chakravarty, 12 June 1938.

[31] *144* 15, GM/IH, 28 Mar. 1930.

[32] *467* 87, 129, GM/MM, Aug.–Sept. 1923.

[33] Ib., 35, Apr. 1923; *468* 213, July 1925.

[34] *468* 193, 3 July 1925.
[35] Ib., 105, *170* 185, *471* 57, GM/MM, 4 Jan. 1925, 17 July 1927, 19 July 1930.
[36] Ib., 163, 12 Mar. 1926.
[37] *467* 48–53, correspondence, 16–18 Aug. 1923.
[38] *468* 267, MM/GM, 23 July 1925; J. A. K. Thomson, Obituary of GM, *Proceedings of the British Academy* (1957).
[39] *468* 240, 250, GM/MM, 15 and 17 July 1925.
[40] *144* 15, GM/IH, 28 Mar. 1930.
[41] *474* 53, 18 July 1939.
[42] *61* 158, 2 July 1932.
[43] *472* 89, 104–110, 123, 139, GM/MM correspondence, Apr.–Sept. 1932; *473* 10, GM/MM, July 1935.
[44] *74* 69, 10 Nov. 1935.
[45] *Oxford Mail* 26 and 29 May 1936; *77* 116, GM/Simon, 29 May 1936, Frank Pakenham (Longford) talked with author (DW).
[46] GM/Norman Angell, 12 Apr. 1937, Balliol Society Papers (1937).
[47] Jessica Mitford, *Hons and Rebels*.
[48] *508* 108, GM/RT, June 1934.
[49] *473* 141, 12 Mar. 1937. The prophecy was not so far out: in his later years Philip was closely associated with a high Anglican order and on a journey in France two years before his death, he several times attended Catholic Mass and took communion.
[50] *467* 180, GM/MM, 18 May 1924.
[51] Ib., 176, 188; *470* 93, GM/MM, 8–18 July 1928, 20 Mar. 1929.
[52] *144* 16, GM/IH, 27 Feb. 1930.
[53] *472* 119, 13 Apr. 1932.
[54] Ib., 84–7, 7 and 8 Apr. 1932.
[55] *141* GM/J. L. Hammond, 21 Sept. 1936.
[56] Rosalind Toynbee, *The Good Pagan's Failure*, pp. 4–5, 10, 96–7.
[57] *568* 128–9, GM/RT, 26 Dec. 1938. Letter contains reference to 'Good Pagan', which was only published in 1939.
[58] *The Good Pagan's Failure*, p. 88.
[59] Speech of 13 Feb. 1936, printed in *Oxford Magazine*, 20 Feb.
[60] *473* 12, 12 July 1936.
[61] Ib., 104, 111, 14 and 29 July 1936.
[62] C. M. Bowra, *Memories*, pp. 221–3.
[63] *78* 148, 25 Aug. 1936.
[64] *473* 146, 1 Apr. 1937. Isobel Henderson had TB at the time.
[65] *85* 208, Albert Erika Ehrenzweig, 17 Nov. 1938.
[66] Told to author by Audrey Richards.
[67] *164* 60, 25 Mar. 1927.
[68] *144* 12, 1929.
[69] *164* 16, 1924.
[70] *63* 124, 10 Mar. 1933.
[71] *153* 72, 25 Feb. 1933.
[72] *63* GM/A. G. Macdonell, 4 Jan. 1933.
[73] 'Defence of Old Age', *Spectator*; *518*, 19 Jan. 1934.

Chapter XXV

[1] *188* 65, GM/Smuts, 8 Oct. 1921.

[2] *265* 22, 23 Mar. 1922; League of Nations files Geneva *13* 14297, correspondence of 17 and 22 May 1922.

[3] *265* 29, 33–5, LN Files Geneva 13 14297, correspondence of July 1922; *265* 118, 124–5, Mar.–Apr. 1923.

[4] *266* 36–42, 45, May–June 1924; *467* 215 GM/MM, 30 May 1924.

[5] *265* 26, Apr. 1922, and 150, 5 Nov. 1923; *266* 1–7 GM/Bannerjea, Jan.–Feb. 1924.

[6] *189* 91, A. N. Whitehead/GM, 9 June; and 219, RC/GM, 27 July 1922.

[7] *192* 98 and *190* 47, RC/GM, 9 Oct. 1923 and 31 Oct. 1922.

[8] *265* 53, 59, GM/Halecki, Oct. 1922; LN files Geneva 13 24056.

[9] Anthony Trollope's favourite method with Sir Rowland Hill was 'to do instantly as I was bid, and then prove that what I was doing was fatuous, dishonest, expensive and impracticable.' (*Autobiography*).

[10] *265* 102 (1923) and *267* 57 (1925).

[11] For a time Murray explored the possibility of the Committee of Vice-chancellors taking over; *268* 28, 165 (1924); *271* 92, GM/A. Cadogan (FO) 20 May 1927.

[12] *266* 51, memorandum on French offer, July 1924.

[13] *267* 59, letter of 24 Aug. 1925.

[14] Ib., 160, speech of 3 Aug. 1926.

[15] *270* 51, 5 July 1927; for revival see *315* 3, G. Kullmann/GM, 17 Mar. 1934.

[16] *271* 26, 47, 160, July 1927.

[17] *269* 1, A. Dufour (LN Secretariat)/GM, 1 Mar. 1927.

[18] *268* 186, GM/Zimmern, 4 Feb. 1927; *269* 12–15, GM/H. Milford and GM/Zimmern, Mar. 1927.

[19] *273* 117, 1928.

[20] *268* 154, GM/J. W. Hendon-Morley, 21 Jan. 1928.

[21] *331* 77, GM/I. Maisky, 29 Dec. 1937.

[22] *278* 11, Millikan/GM, 20 June 1930.

[23] *275* 132, Dufour/E. Drummond, 27 July 1929.

[24] *276* 2, 16, 23; *277*, 128, 1929–30.

[25] *278* 138, letter of 15 Aug. 1930.

[26] *291* 64, memorandum of 7 Mar. 1932.

[27] *473* 151, J. Wilkinson/MM, 7 July 1937 gives GM's programme for annual conference 1937.

[28] *326* Report of Paris Institute for 1935.

[29] *285* 35, 6 July 1931.

[30] *293* 49, 159.

[31] *307* 69; *309* 76; *323* 89; *330*.

[32] *307* G. Kullmann/GM, 9 May; 59 GM/H. Bonnet, 12 May 1933.

[33] *329* 7, 13, 18, 22, 31, 98, 100; various correspondence, especially GM/. Samuel, Sept.–Nov. 1936.

[34] *289* 60, memorandum by GM, 1931; *308* 34, minutes of British National Committee (of CIC) 9 May 1933; *312* 134, CIC paper n.d. [1933].

[35] *313* 85, GM memorandum n.d. [1934?]

[36] *326* 109, CIC memorandum n.d. [1935].

[37] *315* 46 GM/MacDonald, 18 Apr. 1934; *316* 43 and *317* 131, GM/Simon Aug. and Oct. 1934; *328* 182; *329* 2, 4, GM/Cranborne, Aug.–Sept. 1936; *333* 164, GM/Bonnet, Nov. 1938 (account of interviews with Halifax and Butler).

[38] *144* 32, GM/I. Henderson, 1 Mar. 1931; *336* 37, Bonnet/GM, 14 Jan. 1939.

[39] *334* GM/Montenach, 12 Dec. 1938.

[40] *337* 43, meeting of CIC, 17–27 July 1939.

[41] *333* 168, note by GM n.d. [1937?].

[42] *285* 199.

[43] *144* 43, letter of 7 Mar. 1931 (printed in *Unfinished Autobiography*, p. 191).

[44] Ib. . . . , letter of 19 July 1931 (printed ib.).

[45] *UA* p. 200, quoting from broadcast of 1956.

[46] 2 Sept. 1933.

[47] *323* 119, speech of 15 July 1935.

[48] *328* 108, speech of 13 July 1936.

[49] *332* 161, GM/Bonnet, 16 Aug.; *518* 23, *Spectator* 28 Aug. 1938.

Chapter XXVI

[1] *210* 87, 21 Oct. 1931.

[2] FO 800/235 PRO, note by Cecil, 17 Nov. 1931.

[3] Cecil, *Great Experiment*, p. 227.

[4] *Manchester Guardian*, 16 Dec. 1931.

[5] *211* 175, GM/A. Zimmern, text of telegram, 9 Jan. 1932.

[6] FO 800/286, 16 Feb. 1932.

[7] *291* 88 PN-B/GM, 17 Mar. 1932.

[8] *62* 76–8, GM/Lytton correspondence, 14–16 Oct. 1932.

[9] *Headway*, Nov. 1932.

[10] *62* 151, 7 Dec. 1932.

[11] Birn, *The League of Nations Union, 1918–1945*, p. 102; FO 800/287, TS note of interview, 14 Dec. 1932.

[12] *216* 26, GM/K. Courtney, 14 Jan. 1933.

[13] *63* 9 and 28, GM/LW Carruthers, 12 and 28 Jan. 1933.

[14] *216* 82 and 98, 15 and 21 Jan. 1933.

[15] Birn, op. cit. p. 105.

[16] *128* 20, GM/EC, 14 Jan. 1933.

[17] *211* 98, GM/S. Duggan, 23 Dec. 1931.

[18] *212* 160, GM/RC, 14 Apr. 1932; *51132* RC, GM/RC, 24 May 1932; *472* 104, GM/MM, 28 Apr. 1932.

[19] *Manchester Guardian*, 3 Aug. 1932; *Time and Tide*, 6 Aug. 1932.

[20] *516* 93.

[21] *213* 14, GM/PN-B, 2 July 1932, and 176, GM/JS, 3 July 1932.

[22] *214* 48, 53, L. W. Carruthers/GM, 12 and 13 Aug. 1932.

[23] Birn, op. cit., p. 113, and p. 242 n. 22.

[24] *215* 42.

[25] *217* 3, 6 Mar. 1933.

[26] Cecil, op. cit., pp. 252–4.

[27] *217* 79, 25 Apr. 1933.

[28] GM in *Oxford Mail*, 16 Oct., and *Weekend Review*, 28 Oct. 1933.

[29] *218* 105, GM/RC, 20 Oct. 1933.

[30] Ib., 196, GM/RC, *51132* RC, 182, 5 Dec. 1933.

[31] *518* 10, *New Statesman* and *Nation*, 2 Dec. 1933.

[65] *151* GM/R. Macaulay, Oct. 1953.
[66] *475* 104.
[67] Hammond Papers 31, GM/BH, 20 Sept. 1953.
[68] *568* 202.
[69] *Observer*, May 1957.
[70] *Contemporary Review*, Dec. 1957.
[71] Hammond Papers 31.
[72] *Observer. See* n. 69.
[73] *Five Stages* (1935 edn.) p. 171.

APPENDIX I

The Covenant of the League of Nations

The following are the chief passages in the Covenant which have a bearing on the life and views of Gilbert Murray. In one or two places, the text has been slightly abbreviated.

ARTICLE X. The Members of the League undertake to respect and preserve as against external aggression the territorial integrity and existing political independence of all Members. In case of any such aggression or threat or danger of such aggression, the Council shall advise upon the means by which this obligation shall be fulfilled.

ARTICLE XI. Any war or threat of war, whether immediately affecting any Member or not, is hereby declared a matter of concern to the whole League and the League shall take any action which may be deemed wise and effectual to safeguard the peace of nations.

ARTICLE XII. The Members of the League agree that if there should arise between them any dispute likely to lead to a rupture they will submit the matter either to arbitration or to inquiry by the Council and in no case resort to war until three months after the award by the arbitrators or the report by the Council.

ARTICLE XV. Any dispute likely to lead to a rupture which is not submitted to arbitration will be submitted to the Council.

If the Council is successful in resolving the dispute, an explanatory statement will be issued. If the Council is unsuccessful the Council may, either unanimously or by majority vote, make and publish a statement of facts and recommendations.

If the Council is unanimous (except for the parties to the dispute), Members agree not to go to war with any party which complies with the recommendations.

If the Council is not unanimous, Members reserve to themselves the right to take such action as they shall consider necessary.

If the dispute is found by the Council to arise out of a matter which is solely within the domestic jurisdiction of either party, it shall so report and make no recommendation.

ARTICLE XVI. Should any Member resort to war in disregard of its covenants under Articles XII, XIII, or XV, it shall *ipso facto* be deemed to have committed an act of war against all other Members who hereby undertake immediately to subject it to the severance of all trade or financial relations, the prohibition of all intercourse between their nationals and the nationals of the covenant-breaking state and the prevention of all financial, commercial, or personal intercourse between the nationals of the covenant-breaking state and nationals of any other states, whether Members or not.

It shall be the duty of the Council to recommend to the several Governments concerned what effective military, naval, and air force the Members shall severally contribute to the armed forces to be used to protect the covenants of the League.

The 1924 PROTOCOL added four steps to the conciliation procedure laid down in Article XV and provided machinery for determining in every case and as far as possible automatically which party was the aggressor.

The 'OPTIONAL CLAUSE' required those states which signed it to recognize as compulsory the jurisdiction of the Permanent Court of Justice in all justiciable disputes (as defined in Article XIII of the Covenant) in relation to any other Member or state accepting the same obligation.

The British Government signed the Optional Clause in 1929.

APPENDIX II

1939–1957 Greek Plays Translated

Sophocles: *Trachineae* (or *The Wife of Heracles*), 1943.
                     Oedipus Coloneus, 1947.
Aristophanes: *The Birds*, 1948.
                     The Knights, 1955.
Euripides: *Ion*, 1954.
Menander: *Rape of the Locks*, 1942.
                     The Arbitration (*Epitrepontes*), 1945.

Broadcast Performances

Once only: *Persae*, 16 April 1939.
                     Alcestis, 30 March 1941.
                     Trojan Women, 4 March 1946 (starring John Gielgud).
                     Seven Against Thebes, 27 April 1947.
                     Antigone, 3 May 1947.
                     Medea, 26 September 1949.
Twice: *Hippolytus*, 1 October 1945, 13 October 1946.
                     The Arbitration, 3 August 1952, 11 July 1956.
Three times: *Rape of the Locks*, 28 February 1942, 21 June 1942, 13 July 1956.
Four times: *The Frogs*, 3 February 1947, 27 April 1947, 3 December 1950, 9 December 1951.
Five times: *Electra*, 9 February 1948, 12 February 1948, 24 October 1948, 13 April 1953, 1 November 1953.

THE FAMILY OF GILBERT MURRAY

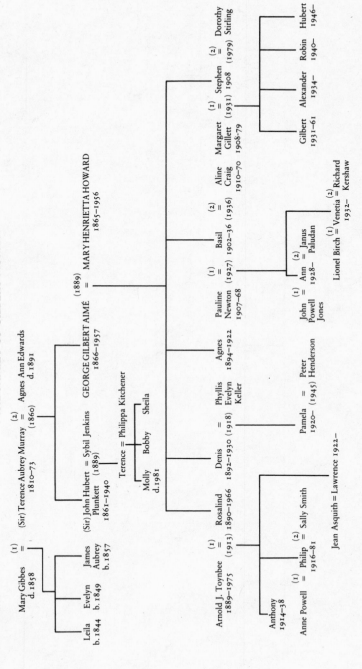

THE FAMILY OF LADY MARY MURRAY

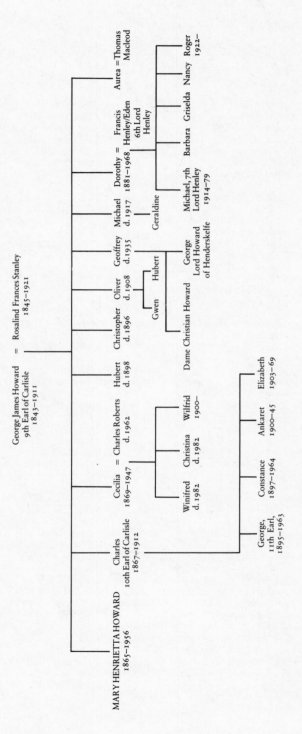

INDEX

Abbey Theatre, Dublin, 173
Aberystwyth: University College, 145
Abyssinian war, 379–80, 382–3
Academic Assistance Committee (*later* Society for the Protection of Science and Learning), 320
Academic Committee of English Letters, 171–2, 215
Achurch, Janet (Mrs Charles Carrington), 79–80
Acland, Sir Francis Dyke, 219
Adamson, Professor Robert, 49
Aeschylus: esteem for, 194; GM translates, 198, 324; GM edits, 320–1, 394; GM's book on, 322–3; *Agamemnon*, 322, 324; *Choephoroe*, 324; *Eumenides*, 322, 324; *Oresteia*, 167, 322–4, 394; *Persae*, 198, 324, 326; *Prometheus*, 324; *Seven Against Thebes*, 324; *Suppliant Women*, 324
Agadir crisis, 1911, 223
Ainley, Henry, 106
alien internment, 399–400
Alington, C.A., 259
Allen, George, 206
Allen and Unwin (publishers), 79, 88–9, 97, 206
Allen, T.W., 129–30
Allied Maritime Transport Commission, 253
Allied Supreme Council, 283
American Emergency Committee, 319
Amery, L.S., 378
Amherst College (USA), 157
Amherst Graduate Quarterly, 158
Angell, Norman, 373; *The Great Illusion*, 245
Anglo-Russian Commission, 231
Anglo-Russian Convention, 1907, 218
anthropology: development of, 118
Aphrodite, 120
archaeology: development of, 118
Archer, Charles (brother of William), 80
Archer, Tom (son of William), 280
Archer, William: friendship with GM, 16, 51, 60, 62, 67, 80–1, 93, 104, 174; and GM in Barford, 69; champions Ibsen, 79; and GM's plays, 80, 82–8; and GM's verse translations, 89–90, 198; and Shaw, 92–3; and GM

at I Tatti, 100; and production of *Hippolytus*, 105; and GM's editing work, 114; and GM's New College fellowship, 122; letters undated, 131; and GM's children, 135; opposes censorship, 172–3; National Theatre plan, 176; death, 176; and GM's political activities, 178; on GM and women's equality, 181; and spelling reform, 187; and GM's wartime lectures in Sweden, 226; and GM on anti-German riots, 236; and conscientious objectors, 240; and GM's interest in the psychic, 274; and spirit world, 280–1
Aristophanes, 79, 202, 315–16; *The Birds*, 403; *Clouds*, 56; *The Frogs*, 88–9, 395
Aristotle, 85; *Ethics*, 57
Ashburner, Walter, 20, 25, 32
Asquith, Cyril, 400
Asquith, Margaret, Countess of Oxford and Asquith (Margot), 182, 230
Asquith, Herbert Henry, 1st Earl of Oxford and Asquith: GM venerates, 15, 267; and Oxford chair of Greek, 129–30; and compulsory Greek controversy, 152; as patron of *Oedipus* production, 165; political leadership, 177; and women's suffrage, 182; acquaintance with GM, 193, 217, 230; foreign policy, 218; resigns as Prime Minister, 229; and wartime conscription, 237, 239; and conscientious objectors, 239–40; and Russell's imprisonment, 241; and peace plans, 249, 252; Hon. President of League of Nations Union, 254; meets Woodrow Wilson, 255; and post-war coalition, 266–8; and Irish policy, 266–7; snubs Beaverbrook on tariffs, 310; on GM as MP, 340
Asquith, Raymond, 122, 244
Athenaeum, The (journal), 90

Bailey, Cyril, 198, 257, 327, 329
Bailey, Gemma, 257
Baker, William, 56
Bakunin, Mikhail, 15
Baldensperger, Fernand, 324

457